PROBLEMS IN LEXICOGRAPHY

WELL HOUSE BOOKS

PROBLEMS IN LEXICOGRAPHY

*Edited by Fred W. Householder
and Sol Saporta*

A Critical / Historical Edition

By Michael Adams

INDIANA UNIVERSITY PRESS

This book is a publication of

Indiana University Press
Office of Scholarly Publishing
Herman B Wells Library 350
1320 East 10th Street
Bloomington, Indiana 47405 USA

iupress.org

© 1967 The Trustees of Indiana University
New Edition © 2022 – The Trustees of Indiana University

All rights reserved
No part of this book may be reproduced or utilized in any form or by any means, electronic or mechanical, including photocopying and recording, or by any information storage and retrieval system, without permission in writing from the publisher. The paper used in this publication meets the minimum requirements of the American National Standard for Information Sciences—Permanence of Paper for Printed Library Materials, ANSI Z39.48–1992.

Manufactured in the United States of America

First printing 2022

Cataloging information is available from the Library of Congress.

ISBN 978-0-253-06327-4 (hardback)
ISBN 978-0-253-06328-1 (paperback)
ISBN 978-0-253-06329-8 (ebook)

CONTENTS

Preface   ix

Part One: Introduction

1   A Conference, a Book, and Their Context   *3*

2   Contents   *41*

3   Reception   *63*

4   Text   *79*

5   Contributors and Contributions   *88*

Notes   118

Part Two: Problems in Lexicography

Foreword   127

I   The Preparation of Dictionaries I: Theoretical Considerations

A Typological Classification of Dictionaries on the Basis of Distinctive Features   *133*
Yakov Malkiel

Lexicographical Definition in Descriptive Semantics   *155*
Uriel Weinreich

What Belongs in a Bilingual Dictionary? 174
Mary R. Haas

Some Notes on Bilingual Lexicography 180
Richard S. Harrell, with an Appendix by Ann M. Driscoll

Recommendations on the Selection of Entries for a Bilingual Dictionary 191
Donald C. Swanson

Comments 203
Dean Stoddard Worth

II Structural Linguistics and the Preparation of Dictionaries

The Relation of Lexicon and Grammar 209
H. A. Gleason, Jr.

Lexicography and Grammar 227
Henry M. Hoenigswald

Structural Linguistics and Bilingual Dictionaries 235
Kemp Malone

Lexicographical Treatment of Folk Taxonomies 243
Harold C. Conklin

Comments 260
James Sledd

III The Preparation of Dictionaries II: Practical Considerations

Selection and Presentation of Ready Equivalents in a Translation Dictionary 271
Samuel E. Martin

Problems in Editing Commercial Monolingual Dictionaries 278
C. L. Barnhart

Use and Preparation of Specialized Glossaries   298
Meredith F. Burrill and Edwin Bonsack, Jr.

Meaning Discrimination in Bilingual Dictionaries   313
James E. Iannucci

The Labeling of National and Regional Variation in Popular Dictionaries   326
Allen Walker Read

Comments   335
William Gedney

IV **Lexicographical Problems in Specific Languages**

Lexicographical Problems in Pashto   343
O. L. Chavarría-Aguilar and Herbert Penzl

Problems in Modern Greek Lexicography   353
Henry and Renée Kahane

Problems of Turkish Lexicography   368
Andreas Tietze

Comments   378
William S. Cornyn

V **Appendices**

Summary Report   383
F. W. Householder

Program of the Conference   387

Participants in the Conference   389

References   391

Index   425

PREFACE

A COMPLEX OF MOTIVES UNDERLIES THIS CRITICAL/HISTORICAL edition of the classic *Problems in Lexicography*. While planning the 22nd Biennial Meeting of the Dictionary Society of North America, held at Indiana University, in Bloomington, on May 8–11, 2019, I wondered how I could celebrate IU's long history of lexicographical achievement during the run-up to the university's bicentennial in 2020. By accident, while looking for something else, my eyes passed over the spine of my tattered copy of *Problems in Lexicography*, the proceedings of a conference on dictionaries held on the Bloomington campus in 1960 and a foundational work last reprinted in 1975. The university was, at the time, providing substantial grants for bicentennial projects, so I applied for one to produce a new edition that put the old book into historical context, as well as to celebrate the original conference and book at the DSNA conference. In the first instance, then, my motive is to make *Problems in Lexicography* available again in the twenty-first century, published in a consistent format and style—not the case originally and in subsequent printings—with the sort of apparatus we expect of university press books today (references, index, etc.) but lacking in earlier printings.

As I demonstrate at various points in this edition and in various ways, *Problems in Lexicography* was and is an important book, a touchstone for lexicographers and linguists since its publication. Arguably, one could write a brief foreword announcing its republication and leave it at that. As for its substance, the book speaks eloquently for itself. Yet few realize now that a conference preceded the book, which serves as its proceedings, and that conference, one of the first in the world dedicated to lexicography, was the first conference of its kind in North America. Lexicography emerges as a profession after the Bloomington conference and in part because of that conference. The origins and nature of the conference, as well as its influence, warrant some extended discussion, then, and thus I arrived at the idea of preparing a critical/historical edition rather than merely a new and improved printing.

Writing a historical introduction to a text poses a problem of scope. In settling on the scope of this one, I saw yet another opportunity: I would write about the conference and the book, also the personnel that made them, as participating in broader conversations across the language sciences. As I pored over letters and memoranda in the archives, read reviews of the book, itemized and epitomized the careers of those who spoke at the conference and contributed to the book, my imagination rearranged the data into a series of photographs, each of them doubtless worth a thousand words. But my pictures of what went on and why, what from the conference succeeded most and why, how their contributions represented the participants and their various commitments, were all in my head, so it has taken thousands of words to explain what one can see in them. As with photos taken at any conference, they are snapshots of the profession as well, specific not only to the place but to the time, and so the introduction expanded some from the conference and book per se into their place in the larger world of ideas about dictionaries, languages, and the people to whom they matter.

Still, however, the introduction concerns a conference and a book, of which I've written a joint microhistory. Someday, someone will write a fantastic book about the culture of academic conferences; another will write about university publishing ventures like those behind *Problems in Lexicography*. Those histories will be composed of broad strokes and strategically selected facts. Microhistories are useful preliminaries to such works, but they also remind us that history occurs at different scales and is written at different scales—they correct and supplement what we lose in aggregation and generalization. Those who know me will not be surprised that I've taken such an approach; I've done so on other related occasions (Adams 2014, 2017, 2019a, 2021b), also in my own lexicography (Adams 2003), and have argued for its value (Adams 2018b and 2021a). At that microhistorical scale, this introduction reaches into book history, the history of book reviewing, the history of academic networks, and the interweaving of scholarship and life, but it also captures, at a larger scale, shifts in the terms of scholarly work and production that reflect both language and professional ideologies. Having decided to produce this edition, I have tried to make the most of it.

Any errors of fact, judgment, and perspective herein are mine, but success has depended on help from others. In general, I've relied on the Indiana University libraries—professors at major midwestern state universities know how lucky they are to have such great libraries at hand—but as I attempted to confirm references and check facts after the onset of the COVID-19 pandemic, I found myself increasingly indebted to HathiTrust, which generously opened its collection to scholars when print materials were off limits. I must thank the librarians, archivists, and assistants at the IU archives who endured my frequent visits, especially Mary Mellon, who for some reason had to put up with me more than the rest did. Emily Alford, the IU librarian most expert in tracking down government information, sought the US Office of Education's original request that Fred Householder organize a conference on bilingual lexicography, to no avail, but not for lack of trying.

This book was made possible by a generous grant from Indiana University's Office of the Bicentennial, directed by Kelly Kish, with Jeremy Hackerd as project manager and my immediate point of contact, the whole bicentennial program established and patronized by Michael McRobbie, president of the university, and the Indiana University Board of Trustees. I have greatly enjoyed celebrating the bicentennial in a lexicographical manner and am most grateful for the chance to bring the university's lexicographical heritage into the present. Peggy Solic acquired the book for Indiana University Press and worked with me on it until she left us for another publisher. On her departure, Gary Dunham, director of IU Press, took responsibility for the unfinished book. Later, it became Darja Malcolm-Clarke's responsibility, and the book benefited from the hands of many others at the press. Allison Gudenau provided excellent copyediting via Amnet, supervised by the ever-friendly and helpful Pete Feely. I am indeed lucky in my editors and so very grateful for their advice, support, and commitment to this new edition of *Problems in Lexicography*.

More personally, I benefitted for a long time from the late Richard W. Bailey's information about lexicographers, linguists, and the interconnected histories of their disciplines. Connie Eble has provided me with materials over the years that found their way into this account, and I'm even more grateful for her generous encouragement. While writing the introduction, I realized how significant it was that Penelope Eckert hired me to be an assistant in the Mischa Titiev Anthropology Library at the University of Michigan. My orientation then was philosophy of language, but I learned new ways of thinking about language from sitting at the circulation desk during the Thursday afternoon anthropology colloquium, and I have an interest and sympathy with some pieces in *Problems in Lexicography* as a result. I owe similar debts to the Department of Philosophy at the University of Michigan and, much later, the Department of English at North Carolina State University, where I had the good fortune to work with Walt

Wolfram and learned something of descriptive linguistics in the Gleason tradition. Ed Finegan read the introduction and gave me good advice, as he always does. John Considine, my generous and outrageously learned friend, found some errors, helped me identify several references beyond my limited capacities, and also contributed to the book indirectly—clever fellow, he'll figure out where. Gary Johnson, of the Library of Congress, helped with cryptic references, too, as did Stephen Turton, of Gonville and Caius College, University of Cambridge, and Paul Kierstein, of Revs Institute, Inc. My wife, Jennifer, who is herself a scholar, writer, and editor while practicing law, has caught errors and infelicities the author would never have seen without her help. Well, that's the pattern of our life together. It's not a debt that can be repaid, but one among innumerable reasons to love.

PROBLEMS IN LEXICOGRAPHY

PART ONE: INTRODUCTION

1

A CONFERENCE, A BOOK, AND THEIR CONTEXT

*P*ROBLEMS IN *LEXICOGRAPHY* (1962; HENCEFORTH, *PiL*), THE proceedings of the Indiana University Conference on Lexicography, held on November 11–12, 1960, is a classic work of both practical lexicography and metalexicography. The expanding universe of lexicography started somewhere, perhaps not in an event, not in a Big Bang, but in a series of events including the conference and its proceedings. Of the conference, Kemp Malone concluded, "Our time is limited, but our topic is as wide as the world" (242).* Few conferences persist in a discipline's practice sixty years on; few books figure in a field's literature for three generations; but *PiL* is an exception. The conference set a standard: it addressed unanticipated topics; the speakers were brilliant; those attending were proven or promising linguists and lexicographers. Their contributions to the conference and *PiL* often figured significantly in their own scholarly careers, and many have been durably influential. This edition extends the life of *PiL* into the future because its contents still deserve attention—though old, it's a current book. It's also a book of historical significance, and this edition explains how the past was prologue to lexicography's present. Its influence, however, depends on accidents, facts on the ground, the who, what, where, when, why, and how of the matter. Perhaps, in this case, it's best to start with the who.

In a memoir, Fred W. Householder, research professor of classics and linguistics at Indiana University, started at the beginning, and, in the beginning, there was the word, there were dictionaries. "Somewhere in there while I was in high school, I got interested in looking at dictionaries. . . . I used to go to the library and read dictionaries, just browse through them.

---

* Unsourced page numbers refer to this volume.

I found them fascinating. I didn't know what a linguist was, but I think that's what I wanted to be, right from the beginning" (1980, 193).¹ To be precise, he started as a philologist, wrote a dissertation on the Assyrian poet Lucian, who wrote in Greek (1941), and migrated into linguistics as the field developed. He still wrote about Ancient Greek and Latin late in his career—witness *The Syntax of Apollonius Dyscolus* (1981). In the meantime, he produced a grammar of Demotic Greek (1964), a textbook on Azerbaijani (1965), and the idiosyncratic classic *Linguistic Speculations* (1971), among other works. Dictionaries never lost their fascination for Householder, though they gathered dust on the bookcases in the back of his mind.

At one point, however, dictionaries were his daily work. Thinking of "beating the draft" at the beginning of World War II, Householder "went down and applied for a job at 165 Broadway" in Manhattan (1980, 197). There, Major Henry Lee "Haxie" Smith led a team of linguists who produced language guides and phrasebooks of languages somehow implicated in the war. Smith was America's celebrity linguist, host of the radio show *Where Are You From?* on which he determined contestants' origins by the way they spoke. After the war, Smith was founding director of the State Department's School of Language and Linguistics. He ended up at Buffalo University, pre-eminently the Smith of Trager–Smith, authors of *An Outline of English Structure* (1951).[2] Householder joined the team as a civilian: "By some quirk I got the job. That was my first contact with lexicography" (1980, 197)—the process of making dictionaries rather than reading them, that is. Householder was an accidental lexicographer, and he recalled his war work and dictionary work together more than once (see note 1).

He started with the easy stuff. "What we were supposed to be doing—what they put me to work on first—was preparing illustrative English sentences for bilingual dictionaries. We would sit down and think up sentences to illustrate every possible use of a word" (1980, 197).[3] As he settled in, he met colleagues who realized his talent with lexicography: "We had got through about letter '*d*' when a guy named Socrates Eliopoulos discovered that I knew a little bit of Modern Greek, so he dragooned me down onto the Modern Greek desk. There we worked on another sort of dictionary: a military dictionary of Modern Greek" (1980, 197), for which they "were trying to find Greek equivalents for all the technical terms in the American military manuals" (1983, 1). Importantly, and well beyond his boyhood romance with them, dictionaries mattered—the defeat of world fascism depended on them—and that was plain enough to Householder once the war was over and won.

In 1959 or 1960, the US Office of Education sought someone to organize a conference focused on bilingual lexicography. They approached Householder, first, because they knew he had firsthand experience compiling bilingual dictionaries through his employment during the war, but also because he was a tried-and-true linguistic contractor, because he investigated distributions within and among word-classes for the United States Air Force—an issue related to cryptography—and also taught, along with others at Indiana University, "a large variety of languages to Air Force officers (and later on to enlisted men, too)" (Householder 1980, 199; Bender 1997, 563). Householder rolled up his sleeves, dusted off the dictionaries he had on the shelves in the back of his mind, and got to work.

"The conference," Householder wrote, "was organized at the contractual instigation (Contract no. SAE 8965) of the US Office of Education"—not his idea, but a good one—"as a possible help to the various teams of scholars then (and now) at work on bilingual dictionaries under contract with them (in accordance with Title VI, Sec. 602 of the National Defense Education Act)" (xx). What grew from the contract was not quite what the US Office of Education expected, as we shall see. The conference was conceived and organized on the fly, not from the immediate interests or commitments of Householder and Sol Saporta, his young colleague and co-organizer, but prompted by an agency outside the university. However haphazardly organized, the conference's program was groundbreaking and influential. Linguistics, lexicography, and anthropology benefited immensely from the Office of Education's request. One hopes the national defense benefited some, too.

On the Program

Obviously, the conference program was key to the conference's success. Householder and Saporta invited senior linguists and lexicographers, as well as high-flying newcomers, those whose contributions to the conference and its published proceedings would draw an audience to lexicography, a largely unexamined subject in North America, and indeed around the world, in 1960. The program had to raise, answer, and balance certain questions about lexical meaning, its relationship to syntax, translation, practical concerns regarding the making of dictionaries, and dictionaries' social roles. Building the program was a recursive process: the organizers prompted contributions on certain topics, striving for thematic coherence, at least among groups of papers; program participants offered papers that grew out of their research and experience, which may or may not have satisfied the organizers' goals; then, the goals were revised, assuring topical breadth across the papers and structural coherence to the extent the papers on offer allowed.

The US Office of Education proposed a conference on bilingual lexicography, with a special focus on "critical languages," those important to the nation's diplomacy and defense but, for the most part, overlooked in American higher education. The conference's structure, therefore, comes as a bit of a surprise. By no means irrelevant to the conference's stated purpose, it approached that purpose somewhat obliquely. (For an overview, see not only the table of contents but also the appended program, pages 387–88.) The first session was devoted to "The Preparation of Dictionaries I: Theoretical Considerations," and three of its five papers did indeed focus on bilingual lexicography (those by Mary Haas, Richard S. Harrell, and Donald C. Swanson), following two papers of more general theoretical interest (those by Yakov Malkiel and Uriel Weinreich). Dean Stoddard Worth provided a response.† Similarly, the second session, "Structural Linguistics and the Preparation of Dictionaries," included general papers by H. A. Gleason and Henry Hoenigswald, and two more, by Kemp Malone and Harold C. Conklin, on bilingual dictionaries, with closing comments by James Sledd. The thematic integrity of the conference slipped some in the third session, "The Preparation of Dictionaries II: Practical Considerations," for while papers by Clarence Barnhart, Meredith F. Burrill and Edwin Bonsack, and Allen Walker Read were practical enough, they had little to do with bilingual lexicography, leaving the thematic responsibility to Samuel E. Martin and James E. Iannucci and, in summation, William Gedney. The final session, "Lexicographical Problems in Specific Languages," embraced lexicography of critical languages, but the papers—by O. L. Chavarría-Aguilar and Herbert Penzl (Pashto), Henry and Renée Kahane (Modern Greek), and Andreas Tietze (Turkish), with comments by William Cornyn—said little about the theoretical or practical problems attending bilingual lexicography.

PiL's table of contents may focus less on bilingual lexicography than the US Office of Education had hoped, but it includes prominent lexicographers

---

† Chapter 5 comprises biographical sketches of those presenting papers or responding to them.

and linguists of the day, a group that only someone with Householder's professional network and reputation could assemble in such short order. As Malkiel (1962, 268/b) observed when reviewing the proceedings of another Indiana University conference of the same period, "the final product," conference or book, "hinges to a large extent on the judicious selection of participants." By 1960, Householder was well established. He had been a professor of classics at Indiana University since 1956 and chair of the Linguistics Committee—there was no department then—since 1959 (Al-Ani 1984, 29). To that point, he had published mostly in classics and was pre-Bloomfieldian (Householder 1980, 193–96), indeed, a philologist of the kind Bloomfield proscribed (Bloomfield 1984 [1933], 512), but he always kept up-to-date with linguistic theory and was a sort of structuralist by the time he organized the 1960 conference.

Householder did not depend on his general reputation for access to those who eventually ended up on the conference program. A few of those who participated were fellow Classicists (Hoenigswald) or had the sorts of interests in Classical Greek (the Kahanes) or Latin (Malkiel, Malone, Sledd), or both (Swanson) that made Householder a well-known—if not quite household—name. Instead, he drew rather heavily on those who had helped to defeat fascism with linguistics during World War II, notably at 165 Broadway, the epicenter of the Language Section of the US Army's Information and Education Division, in which Barnhart, Householder, Gedney, Penzl, Read, and Swanson had all worked, some of them in uniform, some of them not. Thomas Sebeok, the semiotician who ran the publishing program in which *PiL* appeared, also worked there for a while. One might say that the core of the conference—a bit more than 25 percent of the participants—were Householder's wartime linguist colleagues.[4]

Throughout the war, Householder taught Greek and Latin part-time at Columbia University—he was always academically active. Unsurprisingly, then, he attended the Linguistic Society of America (LSA) meeting at the Biltmore Hotel in New York City, on December 29–30, 1944 (Joos 1986, 128–29). Barnhart, Cornyn, Gedney, Hoenigswald, both Kahanes, Malone, Penzl, and Swanson also participated (Joos 1986, 129–31), comprising 40 percent of those who spoke at the 1960 conference. One sees immediately how the list of LSA conferees overlaps with the 165 Broadway roster. Martin Joos (1986, 132) counts ninety-six linguists at the LSA conference: "The 1944 congregation in the Biltmore was almost all composed of 'civilian soldiers' . . . 80 of the 96 give or take two, were being paid by the Government or by the ACLS [American Council of Learned Societies] for militarily crucial work." Sebeok and anthropologist C. F. Voegelin, who edited the series in which *PiL* appeared and who, like Sebeok, was already at Indiana University, were also among the Biltmore linguists.

On a tight schedule to organize the Bloomington conference, Householder turned to his wartime friends. He had reason to believe they would accept his invitation. The Michael Curtiz film *White Christmas* (1954) illustrates the camaraderie I have in mind: In the film, when the entertainers Bob Wallace and Phil Davis discover that Major General Thomas F. Waverly—under whom they served during the war—is about to lose the Vermont inn into which he's sunk his life savings, Wallace phones another former soldier, Ed Harrison, who advertises a fundraising event at the inn during his television show. The entire 151st Division arrives in Vermont, in uniform, to support their commander, at the behest of their comrades. If Wallace and Davis can count on the camaraderie of a whole division, it's hardly a surprise that Householder could count on linguists he knew who had served during the same war. Those who worked at 165 Broadway and the 1944 LSA conferees shared a wartime bond, perhaps sentimental but which, for that very reason, proved strong and influenced the organization of post-war American society, including its academic conferences.

Obviously, however, 60 percent of those who spoke at the 1960 conference had *not* served at 165 Broadway or otherwise during the war, for reasons of age in either direction, gender, refugee status, and the like. I am astonished at those whom Householder convinced to participate. Rarely has such a small conference attracted such outsized figures. Of course, they weren't all giants in the 1950s, but six of them (Hoenigswald, Householder, Henry Kahane, Malkiel, Penzl, and Read)—a quarter of the speakers—were eventually asked to participate in *First Person Singular*, a series of memoirs of the most significant post-war American linguists collected in three volumes and published by John Benjamins (Davis and O'Cain 1980; Koerner 1991 and 1998). Three of them (Conklin, Haas, and Hoenigswald) were elected members of the National Academy of Sciences. Five were members of the American Academy of Arts and Sciences (Conklin, Haas, Hoenigswald, Householder, and Henry Kahane). One of them (Hoenigswald) was elected to the American Philosophical Society and the British Academy, while another was elected to the Austrian Academy of Sciences (Penzl). Six received honorary degrees (Haas, Hoenigswald, Henry Kahane, Renée Kahane, Malone, and Read). Four of them received national medals of honor (both Kahanes, Malone, and Martin), and one was twice knighted (Malone). At least ten served as presidents of learned societies (Barnhart, Burrill, Gedney, Haas, Hoenigswald, Householder, Henry Kahane, Malkiel, Malone, and Read). Thirteen were honored with at least one festschrift, special journal issue, or memorial honor (Gedney, Gleason, Haas, Harrell, the Kahanes, Malone, Martin, Penzl, Read, Saporta, Tietze, and Worth). That Householder could attract such figures to the conference—despite the rushed timeline—suggests his acute awareness of developments in the language sciences, his own well-developed network, and his notable powers of persuasion (see Al-Ani 1984, 18–28).

Householder did not organize the conference on his own, however, and his colleagues probably also shaped the program and its participants somewhat. For instance, Householder (1980, 199) later regretted that he never "had an opportunity to master an American Indian language"—Amerindian languages were outside the scope of his research and teaching. Yet he probably knew of Mary Haas, who devoted part of her research to Amerindian languages, even if he'd never had any previous contact with her. She had participated in wartime language instruction (K. Pike 1999, 3–4; Malkiel 1980b, 92–93), especially in Thai, and thus belonged to the wartime network of linguists. Haas had embarked on what would become the *Thai–English Student's Dictionary* (1964), which made her perspective and experience immediately relevant to the Bloomington conference. Householder may not have known of that forthcoming dictionary, but quite possibly Voegelin did—he and Haas belonged to another network important to the history of American linguistics, that of Edward Sapir's students (Koerner 2002, 29, 43, 78).

As Victoria Fromkin (1984, 26) reports, Householder had "a deep appreciation for the work of both seasoned and young scholars, whatever their particular interest," a view amply supported by the long list of dissertations he supervised in some measure—ninety of them, as of 1984—on a dizzying array of subjects (Al-Ani 1984, 11–17). His students and younger colleagues, like Sol Saporta—co-organizer of the conference—kept him well informed about new theories, obscure languages, and up-and-coming linguists. This may help to explain how relatively young scholars, like Conklin, Harrell, Weinreich, and Worth, ended up on the program alongside relatively senior, well-established figures like Barnhart, Hoenigswald, Malkiel, and Read.

Weinreich, especially, is an interesting case. Born in 1926, he was too young for Householder's wartime network. To put things in perspective, Householder published his first article in 1936, and had Weinreich not been such a prodigy, he could not have risen to a similar reputation by the time he died at 40, in 1967. He was, however, well known in linguistic circles because his father, Max Weinreich, also an eminent Yiddishist, began teaching at City University of New York in 1940 and was a full member of the refugee community of linguists—which included Hoenigswald, the Kahanes, Malkiel, Penzl, Sebeok, Morris Halle, Roman Jakobson, and, somewhat later, André Martinet—especially those involved in the Linguistic Circle of New York, founded in 1943, publisher of the journal *Word*, which brought American linguistics into contact with European linguistic traditions (see Koerner 2002, 212; Malkiel 1968b, 128). In the 1950s, Weinreich and Martinet edited *Word*. Weinreich studied with Jakobson and Martinet. Once he had published *Languages in Contact* (1953), his "rise to prominence, in the mid-Fifties, was truly meteoric" (Malkiel 1968b, 132), and Householder undoubtedly knew his work in advance of the conference, even if they had not yet met.

Weinreich also appealed to young scholars like Saporta, not much older than they but more accomplished at the time. Had Householder, on inviting Malkiel or Hoenigswald, requested advice on whom else to invite—"Do you know anyone else who could address 'theoretical considerations' in lexicography?"—both would have suggested Weinreich. Networks spun within networks, and the refugee network, while perhaps not as foundational to the conference as Householder's wartime network, was nonetheless significant. Malkiel was especially attentive to Weinreich's legacy, writing not one but two memorial articles (Malkiel and Herzog 1967 and Malkiel 1968b). Like Haas, Weinreich had begun writing a dictionary, in his case, a *Modern English-Yiddish Yiddish-English Dictionary* (1968), published posthumously.

We should not underestimate the significance of indirect influence on the developing roster of speakers. For instance, Paul L. Garvin (1991, 127), who served on the executive committee of the Linguistic Circle of New York in the 1950s, was a refugee and had also worked among Householder and the others in the Army Language Section before (129), of all things, a doctoral sojourn at Indiana University, where Voegelin supervised his dissertation (127). After a brief stint at the University of Oklahoma, he moved to Georgetown University's Institute of Language and Linguistics (130–31), where he undoubtedly knew Harrell, thus connecting Harrell to Garvin's professional network. Harrell, however, already had a connection to Indiana University—he had attended the Linguistic Society of America's

Summer Linguistic Institute there in 1952 (Stuart 1967b, ix), so he already knew Voegelin and Householder when they deliberated over who might best serve the interests of the 1960 conference's program. "And so the story goes on," Householder (1971, 1) wrote later, "with a succession of coincidences and marginal motivations."[5]

The choice of respondents for the conference's four sessions shows that selection of participants had been somewhat ad hoc. On one hand, Gleason remarks that he had been "charged" with discussing the relation between the lexicon and grammar (209), which suggests the organizers' vision of and control over the program. On the other hand, however, some spoke squarely in their own domains without regard for the conference's topic, which suggests organizational flexibility. Some of the respondents nearly lacked credentials. Worth, who responded to the first session, "The Preparation of Dictionaries I: Theoretical Considerations," had only started his teaching career at UCLA in 1957, making him the most junior participant, though Harrell, who took his PhD from Harvard just one year earlier (Stuart 1967b, x), and Conklin, who started teaching at Columbia in 1954, weren't far ahead. Conklin, who took his PhD from Yale, may have been recommended by Cornyn, Householder's wartime colleague, who taught there. Worth's presence, let alone his evaluative role, is harder to explain.

James Sledd, who responded to the second session, "Structural Linguistics and the Preparation of Dictionaries," was well-credentialed as an historian of lexicography (see, for instance, Sledd 1947b; Sledd and Kolb 1955), but had little practical lexicographical experience and littler interest in language contact or bilingual dictionaries. If Weinreich was an obvious candidate for the conference, Sledd was not, despite being a name in lexicography at the time. His *Short Introduction to English Grammar* (1959), though drowned in the new wave of transformational grammar, nonetheless qualified him as a critical representative of structural linguistics, and the controversy over his book doubtless caught Householder's attention.[6] By way of contrast, Gedney, who responded to the third session, "The Preparation of Dictionaries II: Theoretical Considerations,", had worked alongside Householder at 165 Broadway, and Cornyn, the fourth respondent, had similarly been one of Joos's "civilian soldiers," all of them practical lexicographers before they had the chance to be anything else.

Thus, personnel for Bloomington's 1960 Conference on Lexicography were selected by the intersection of various networks—those of wartime linguists, refugees, contact linguists, and lexicographers. Alas, no concentrated cache of correspondence allows us to tease out their respective influences, and Householder (1980, 199) avoids details of the matter in his autobiographical sketch: "I think this is a good place to stop," he concludes, "without going on to the Style Conference, the Lexicography Conference, the Michigan Institute (of 1958?), my year at Cornell or my Guggenheim to London, all of which influenced me in various ways." Back then, just five years after *PiL*'s third printing, Householder would not have guessed that the book would be edited yet again and republished sixty years after the conference, nor that an audience so far removed from the original event would want a fuller account of it.

Off the Program

However they ended up on the program, speakers comprised less than half of conference participants, and those "merely" participating must have contributed significantly to the conference's success. Voegelin, introducing *PiL* (129), remarked that it was published "regrettably without benefit of discussant emphasis which remains unpublished and largely unreflected in this volume, though all authors had opportunity to reorganize their papers in light of the discussion." Naturally, we wonder about those discussions, but we're left to imagine them, partly on the basis of personnel, the nonpresenting participants, what we know of their careers and their various lexicographical commitments, and how those might have shaped conversations among all participants, not only during the formal sessions but also during lunches and after hours. What follows, then, accounts for the majority of those attending the conference.

Some of them were predictably interested in bilingual lexicography, especially the small contingent of those already or eventually attached to the Summer Institute of Linguistics (SIL): Bruce R. Moore, Viola Waterhouse, and Loraine I. Bridgeman. Moore (1961a) completed his MA at Indiana University in 1961, and Bridgeman (1966) took her doctorate from Indiana University in 1966, so both attended the conference as students. Moore and Bridgeman both published articles in the *International Journal of American Linguistics* in 1961, which suggests that Householder had seen them in the pipeline. And although Householder did not direct her dissertation, Bridgeman collaborated with him on several works about word classes sponsored by the US Air Force under the rubric "Automation of General Semantics" (e.g., Householder et al. 1964 and 1965). Waterhouse

(1962) took her PhD from the University of Michigan, under the direction of Kenneth L. Pike; her dissertation appeared both as a supplement to *IJAL* and in the same series as *PiL*, in the same year.

As one of its earliest adherents would write, "The desire to help provide ethnic groups with the Scriptures is, of course, what gives SIL its driving force. Therefore it is years after work has begun in a language group before the goal is achieved. By now, however, some of the results can be tallied. By the end of 1973, thirty-five New Testaments had been published, and many more were in various stages of completion" (E. V. Pike 1977, 11). Moore (1961, final unnumbered page), for instance, worked among the Tsachi people of Ecuador for decades—he began that mission before Bloomington—eventually to translate the New Testament and an abridged Old Testament into their language (Staley 2013). Moore (1977, 147) explained that "Part of SIL's *raison d'etre* is the practical application of the knowledge of minority group languages gained through linguistic studies, and a large part of this application involves translation of materials into these languages. Because of this, SIL has become involved in the development of translation theory and techniques." As budding theorists, as well as descriptive linguists, the SIL contingent at the conference fit well with its overarching goal and appreciated the unexpectedly theoretical papers presented there. Dictionaries were essential to understanding minority languages, to developing literacy programs for speakers of those languages (also central to SIL's mission; see Gudschinsky 1977), and to producing the religious texts newly literate speakers would read.[7]

Besides Moore and Bridgeman, other Indiana University students attending the conference included Heles Contreras, eventually of the University of Washington, who completed his dissertation under Householder in September 1961 (Al-Ani 1984, 12) and assisted with the conference (127). Gerd Fraenkel also defended his dissertation, a generative grammar of Azerbaijani, with Householder in November 1961 (Al-Ani 1984, 12), and Oral Carl Brown, defended his dissertation, on Haitian Voodoo, at last in 1972, with Householder on his committee (Brown 1972, ii). Franciszek Lyra—F. Lyra in the participant list (390)—was a Fulbright scholar at Indiana University at the time of the conference, indeed, the very first Fulbright scholar from Poland to visit the United States (Socha and Lyra 2019). He completed his dissertation, "English and Polish in Contact," under Householder in June 1962 (Al-Ani 1984, 12). Presumably, the participant listed as Kim Be (389) also belonged to this group.

Other Indiana University figures present included the participant listed as José Roca (390), that is, Josep Roca-Pons, an eminent Catalan linguist who taught on the Indiana University faculty from 1958–1983 (see Rasico 2000), and John Lyons (1977), who would become the world's preeminent theoretical semanticist, and had arrived the previous summer to work on the "Automation of General Semantics" project that also involved Bridgeman (see Bender 1997, 565–66 and C450, Box 7).* Albert Valdman (2019) had arrived on campus as an assistant professor of French in the fall term of 1960, just in time to attend Householder and Saporta's conference. Apparently, it had little effect on him at the time. His interest in lexicography developed somewhat later, first culminating in the *Haitian Creole-English-French Dictionary* (Valdman et al. 1981). One naturally wonders whether vestiges of the conference figured in Valdman's subsequent career, which has been the most persistently lexicographical of the academic participants (for instance, Valdman et al. 1996, 1998, 2009, 2017, and forthcoming).

Indiana University contributed roughly 22 percent of the conference's total participants, including Householder and the Voegelins, as well as the students and other colleagues listed here. Minus Householder, who delivered the conference's "Summary Report," that group was composed of 38 percent of participants who weren't on the program. One organizes conferences partly to bring one's local colleagues, perhaps especially students, into contact with significant scholars from elsewhere. Many of the Indiana University participants—from those associated with SIL to Valdman—were committed to study of language contact, bilingualism, translation, and other subjects implicated in bilingual lexicography, so were a natural audience for the conference's program. The conference had—in scholarly time—an almost immediate impact: In her dissertation, Bridgeman (1966, 119–121), for example, cited Conklin's and Gleason's articles in *PiL*, as well as one of Lyons's early articles. But it had been organized too quickly to build a bigger on-site audience. Besides, the topic was so new, so unexpected in the disciplinary context of the time, that there was no established audience for such a conference—the 1960 conference founded lexicography as a subdiscipline of applied linguistics. Without the Indiana participants, there would barely

---

* I refer to various collections in the Indiana University Archives, most frequently to the Householder Papers, or "C450." Here and henceforth, in order to keep parenthetical citations as short as possible, I refer to the Householder Papers simply as "C450." This includes correspondence folders, because they are arranged alphabetically by correspondent surname and easily located in the archive. Other, less frequently cited collections are identified more expansively.

have been a conference beyond the program participants. Although it may be no surprise, given the circumstances, the audience seems somewhat manufactured for the occasion.

That observation is doubly true if we add the Georgetown University contingent to their Indiana University counterparts. Harrell brought several colleagues and students along—he had funds to do so as head of the Arabic Division of the Institute of Languages and Linguistics at Georgetown, as well as the Arabic Research Program, which had been established under the National Defense Education Act in June 1960, "largely through Harrell's initiative and efforts" (Stuart 1967b, x). Five colleagues accompanied Harrell to Bloomington, roughly 17 percent of the nonpresenting participants. The two groups constituted 55 percent of those attending but not presenting.

Aside from such audience-packing, however, the Georgetown scholars were well suited to the conference. Moukhtar Ani (Ani Moukhtar in the list of participants, page 389), among the Institute of Languages and Linguistic's associate faculty (Institute 1958, 12) under Harrell's direction, would publish, with Karl Stowasser (1964), *A Dictionary of Syrian Arabic: English–Arabic*, in the series of Arabic studies Harrell founded and which, after his untimely death at the age of 35 in that same year (Stuart 1967b, ix), was named after him. Mark W. Cowell (1964), another researcher at the Institute attending the conference, would publish *A Reference Grammar of Syrian Arabic*, acknowledging his debt to Ani (ix), while Stowasser and Ani (1964, xi) wrote that they were "deeply indebted to a colleague and friend, Mark W. Cowell, who, through fruitful discussion, constructive criticism and knowledgeable advice, rendered invaluable help in clarifying many a difficult point of procedure and substance." In other words, both Ani and Cowell had much to contribute besides mere interest to a conference on bilingual lexicography.

Some others who sailed to Bloomington under the Georgetown flag had less at stake in the conference's subject. Alan W. McAninch (Mcanninch in the list of participants, page 389) took his BA at Georgetown in 1961 and went on to work in the US Defense Language Institute (Kreidler 1965, 208). John Moyne, a pioneer in computational linguistics and expert in early Persian poetry, completed his MA at Georgetown in 1960. These two were a bit green for the Bloomington conference, and its influence is invisible in their subsequent careers. One participant listed as belonging to Georgetown poses a problem of identification. The T. B. Irving listed (xx) may be Thomas Ballantine Irving (also known as Al Haji Ta'linn 'Ali Abu Nasr), the eminent Canadian Qu'ranist, yet I can find no evidence that he was at Georgetown in any capacity in 1960. He had taken his PhD from Princeton in 1940 and accepted a professorship at the University of Minnesota in 1957—either a different T. B. Irving attended the conference, or the participant list misreports his affiliation, or he was somehow affiliated with Georgetown at the time, in addition to his Minnesota appointment.[8]

That some participants were intensely interested in lexicography and others had only peripheral interests cut across nearly all groups in attendance. Two researchers from the Library of Congress, Alexander Rosenberg and Edward Wolski—probably alerted to the conference by the US Office of Education—well illustrate the pattern. Rosenberg, an experienced bilingual lexicographer, had compiled *Russian Abbreviations: A Selective List* (1957) and a *Russian–English Glossary of Guided Missile, Rocket, and Satellite Terms* (1958), both works obviously prompted by the Cold War, before attending the conference. The *Glossary* is extensive—352 double-column pages—but rudimentary, and it would be interesting to know what Rosenberg thought about the various theoretical positions those speaking on the program staked out. By way of contrast, Wolski was no lexicographer; rather, he worked in the Slavic Language Section of the library's Descriptive Cataloguing Division (Cannon 2013, 27), which isn't to say, of course, that the conference held no interest for him whatsoever. Bruce Gaarder, representing the US Office of Education, instigator of the conference, wasn't focused on lexicography per se but on bilingualism, and was a pioneer in bilingual education policy (see Crawford 1992, 325–29).

Two other participants focused precisely on bilingual dictionaries. Andras Balint (1967), a doctoral student at Columbia University, wrote a dissertation titled "A Critique of English–Hungarian and Hungarian–English General Lexicography." He took a position at the University of Papua New Guinea and eventually studied Pacific pidgins (see Balint 1969 and 1973); thus, he may have been invited to the conference via Conklin.[9] Don C. Bailey, listed as at the University of Arizona, must have accepted a position there while at the University of Michigan as a lecturer in Japanese in 1960–1961 (*Proceedings* 1960, 18). He took his doctorate from Michigan in 1960, with a dissertation published as *A Glossary of Japanese Neologisms* (1962). One review began, "For a dictionary, Dr. Bailey's work makes fascinating reading" (Yamagiwa 1963, 485/b).[10] In other words, although they didn't add luster to the event comparable to that brought by the professionally prominent speakers, the student linguists attending weren't lightweights, even if it would take the future to prove it.

Finally, there were the commercial lexicographers, whose commitment to lexicography was undoubted, though none of them worried much about bilingual dictionaries. Laurence Urdang, later a prolific independent lexicographer, had worked with Barnhart on later editions of the *American College Dictionary* (1947) and, at the time of the conference, was managing editor of the *Random House Dictionary of the English Language* (1966). Philip B. Gove, chief editor of *Webster's Third New International Dictionary of the English Language* (1961), though less experienced than Barnhart, rivaled his star power—who could question the importance of a conference that included the two of them? Publication of *Webster's Third*, in September 1961, was less than a year away in November 1960, but the lexicographical work was already completed. One imagines Gove taking a break, listening to people talk about dictionary-making rather than making one himself. As history tells, without knowing it, he was enjoying the calm before the storm of controversy he would weather once journalists caught wind of *Webster's Third* and cast it away as mad, bad, and dangerous to consult (for more on which, see Sledd and Ebbitt 1962; Morton 1994; and David Skinner 2012). Few realized that lexicography had become an academic subject in North America just before dictionaries took hold of the public imagination.

Off Off Program

Timeo Danaos et dona ferentes

Demetrius J. Georgacas, an eminent lexicographer of Greek, had begun preparing a bilingual English and Modern Greek dictionary in the 1950s, dividing his time between the University of North Dakota, at which he had settled, and academic centers in Greece (for more on Georgacas and his accomplishments, see Zgusta 1990). He had hoped to attend the Bloomington conference, but in the end could not manage it: "I asked the Office of Education to find a way for paying for my plane transportation [from Athens, Greece] but it proved impossible," he wrote to Householder on November 4, 1960 (C450, Box 10), just a few days before the conference. He asked that Householder send him "a copy of any report written on it." Yet he participated in the conference minimally and indirectly: "I hope that the enclosed announcement interests you, so I am sending you twenty-five copies, also for the participants in the conference." The subject of the enclosure remains a mystery.

Georgacas appears to have read the Kahanes' paper in advance of the conference. There is considerable evidence that papers or drafts of papers presented at the conference were precirculated.[11] "One feels after reading Barnhart's paper that Barnhart has given away all his professional secrets," Gedney reflected in "Comments" to the third session, but it makes sense that respondents would receive papers in advance of responding. Sledd, who commented on the second session, however, reveals another possibility: "Since I can contribute nothing original to this discussion, and since you hardly need summaries of papers which are already in your hands, I can define my function only as provocative misunderstanding; and even that definition may be optimistic: *provoking* might be a better word" (260). Is it possible that papers were precirculated to all presenters? To all attending? Or were they made available on the site? The answer comes in later "Comments." Speaking of Burrill and Bonsack's paper, Gedney writes, "I realize after hearing their oral presentation that their work in the main is interesting and useful and sensibly conducted; it is clear that in their written paper they overemphasized the difficulties" (338). This helps to explain the variation in lengths among the papers, some of which are conference paper sized and some of which are not—presentations at the conference were all the same length (see the conference schedule, pp. 387–88), but authors otherwise enjoyed considerable freedom to revise and expand their papers or not. In any event, by the time of the conference, the proceedings were already begun, and the written papers circulating.

Thus, in the same letter, Georgacas expressed strong opinions about Henry and Renée Kahane's "Problems in Modern Greek Lexicography," which focused on his editorial principles: "It seems to me that Kahane's [sic] paper on the Modern Greek Dictionary in preparation is a very hastily written one in the absence of any other topic, and the authors did not even bother to ask me for more information about it, as if we had not thought of the few things they discuss. My final proposal to the Office of Education includes details which Professor and Mrs. Kahane have not seen; they thought that we have not done any thinking about these matters. Anyway, I wish that a fruitful discussion will develop following their paper." What Georgacas read naturally alarmed him, as the Kahanes were consultants on his dictionary project—the Kahanes indicate as much in the first sentence of their paper—and his funding through the US Office of Education was pending at the time of the conference.

Householder corresponded with Georgacas frequently, for he was interested in Modern Greek—recall the time he spent working with Socrates Eliopoulos at 165 Broadway, and his grammar of Demotic Greek was already in the making—so he was supportive of Georgacas's dictionary project. He responded reassuringly on November 29, 1960 (C450, Box 10): "I think you are unduly sensitive about the Kahane paper; it was, as you say, fairly hasty, but I do not think they really intended to cast doubts on your methods or your abilities. On one point the opinion of the conference was strongly against him [sic]: his wish to group together all etymologically related words under one heading.[12] Nearly everyone else argued convincingly for the importance to a student of being able to find the word he is looking for as quickly as possible." Given the conference's timeline, the Kahanes' haste was understandable, but it strikes one as odd and not quite fair that they would criticize the project, without complete information, in public, without Georgacas present to answer their criticisms.

Pop a cork for lexicography!

One cannot expect conferees to sit and talk and listen without some social time. Social events are essential components of any conference. Those attending had to eat, and leisurely lunches awaited them in State Room West of the Indiana Memorial Union, enabling conversation (see pages 387–88). The dean of the graduate school, John W. Ashton, went a step further and hosted a reception at his home, 1115 Brooks Drive, at 5:00 on the first day of the dictionary conference (Graduate Dean's Records C212, Box 12, folder titled "Conference on Lexicography 1960–1961"). "Dean Ashton," we're told, "gave strong support to interdisciplinary programs and emerging disciplines such as linguistics, comparative literature, East European Studies, folklore . . . and Uralic and Altaic Studies" (Indiana University 2013). Most of these disciplines contributed to the conference, either explicitly in papers or in the affiliations and varied interests of its participants and publishers. For Ashton, the conference was as much about establishing such disciplines at Indiana University as it was about bilingual lexicography per se: it declared the university's intentions.

Notes scribbled into the same archives indicate that however many participants attended Ashton's reception, some local figures did too.

Householder and Voegelin were there; I would say, "of course," except that Saporta and Sebeok are not on the list. Albert Valdman, a newcomer to campus, also signed up, as a first-term assistant professor probably should. Felix J. Oinas, a folklorist in Slavic and Baltic studies joined the conclave, as did William Riley Parker, biographer of John Milton, former executive secretary of the Modern Language Association and editor of *PMLA*, and, at the time, professor of English Language and Literature. Of the fifteen locals invited, ten responded affirmatively, a good result, as anyone who has organized such a gathering knows well.

Bruce Gaarder of the US Office of Education wrote gratefully to Householder (Graduate Dean's Records C212, Box 12, folder titled "Conference on Lexicography 1960–61"), "We would like to thank you and Professor Saporta for allowing us to attend the conference on lexicography at Bloomington and acquaint ourselves more closely with the complex problems of dictionary production. We profited greatly and judge from the high scholarly level of the work papers that the conferees did too." Such a note may have been ritually polite, of course, and not the last word on the conference's success. In his letter of November 29, however, Householder replied to Georgacas's wishes that the conference would go well: "The conference was, I think, a great and unqualified success." What happened after the conference suggests that he was right.

From Conference to Book

Procedures and prevarications

Publication plans were well advanced soon after the conference; of course, complete and presumably publishable papers were circulated beforehand. Lucky for Householder and Saporta, then, that the conference was "a great and unqualified success." Conklin asked about publication specifically as early as May 12, 1961, in a letter to Householder (C450, Box 10): "Just a note to inquire about the status of our lexicography papers: (1) What publication series will it appear in? (2) What number or issue of that series? (3) When can I expect to receive proof on my paper?" Householder responded immediately, on May 15: "(1) As of present expectations, the Lexicography Conference papers will appear as a publication of the Research Center and a Supplement to IJAL. (2) I do not know yet what number or issue. (3) At the earliest you would not read proof before August, probably later than that." Still, as often happens in proceedings publication, quick work.

Householder explained the publishing process a bit more fully to Swanson, in a letter dated December 8, 1961 (C450, Box 11): "The Research Center is mainly Tommy Sebeok's publishing house. He scouts around for manuscripts, digs up subventions, and brings out offset-printed paper-back books in a variety of fields. Many (like this one) appear as supplements to IJAL. The main series are IUPAL (this one), the Ural–Altaic Series (about nine titles so far), and the East European Series (I don't know how many titles). Tommy himself edits the Ural–Altaic series and used to edit the E.E. series; Voegelin edits the IUPAL series." The local publishing options fit the conference's needs perfectly, allowing Householder and Saporta to move quickly but at their own pace, with unusual control within the process and over the book that would eventually appear.

In 1960, universities and centers within them published considerably more than they do today. Nowadays, in North America, such series are few and far between. The search for an Anglo-American university press willing to publish proceedings of the *PiL* kind would be futile, though such a book might fit into series published by commercial European academic presses like John Benjamins or De Gruyter, notably, in the latter case, "Lexicographica series maior." Some of those series supplement journals—as did the initial issue of *PiL*—but few journals publish book-sized special issues. When university presses avoided proceedings as too miscellaneous in content and unlikely to sell, firms dedicated to publishing proceedings emerged. All these options require planning and time, including time for negative responses and redirected proposals. Arranging publication through *IJAL* and the Research Center in Anthropology, Folklore, and Linguistics series ensured relatively untroubled publication.

As it turned out, the authors received proofs in late November, more or less as Householder had predicted. Weinreich acknowledged receipt in a letter dated November 30, 1961 (C450, Box 11). Saporta probably had little to do with assembling speakers for the program, for reasons already outlined, but he seems to have supervised preparing a text on which participants would register their changes and corrections—the term "proofs" is thus a bit misleading, as what Saporta produced was still a working document. He had the text in hand in September of the same year, for Householder wrote to him on September 22 (C450, Box 11), "Many thanks for the galley sheets. At worst I can get photo-copies if any are urgently needed. I think we are finally going to get going on editing the Lexicography MSS; I hope that fund you mentioned is still available. Elsie Dosch says it will take about $100." Publishing in this mode on this schedule was a shoestring operation, but somebody had to pay for the shoestring.

In response to Householder, Saporta summarized the editorial situation fully on December 13, 1961 (C450, Box 11):

> I haven't made any changes in your report, but thought perhaps a brief paragraph of introduction ought to be included. I assume that we need 25 copies of this report plus about 6 or 7 sets of papers to be sent to the Office of Education. Heles [Contreras] has these sets and will send them out, if you could make sure he has the right address. I assume that will comply with our formal obligations to the Office of Education.
>
> Heles tells me the funds are running low, but we are obliged to pay $100 to each of the discussants since I promised them that and in writing. I'm sorry if that was an unexpected expense, but I had assumed we had agreed on that. I don't think I over-committed ourselves. The first people I would "cut out" would be expenses for the Geography people [Bonsack and Burrill] (and perhaps honorarium, but I think that would be unfair). Could you please let me know how much is left, and what bills are still due?
>
> Carl [Voegelin] has accepted the papers for publication, but I have to write to Tom [Sebeok] about funds. Now, obviously, there are none in the grant for that purpose. I think probably you and I should be co-editors.

Saporta's letter is a linchpin in our understanding of the conference and publication of the proceedings, well beyond an unjustified lack of regard for the geographers that anticipates the relatively weak reception of their contribution subsequent to the conference (see chaps. 3 and 5).

Saporta seems to have introduced changes to some of the contributions, as indicated by his *not* recommending or imposing changes on Householder's summary report. Clearly, he managed matters like providing the Office of Education with the copies of the papers and report they required. The comment on finances, however, suggests that Householder and Saporta had not planned the conference carefully nor communicated with each other effectively about support for those on the program. Saporta appears to have taken charge of post-conference details, however, such as paying the bills. The division of labor between Householder and Saporta, one suspects, reflects differences in professional status, with Householder the delegator and Saporta the delegatee. We learn, too, that Voegelin, who had probably received a set of the galleys when they were sent to authors, had evaluated and accepted the volume in less than a month, which simultaneously illustrates the value of local publication but also a lack of care—we have no evidence that Voegelin suggested revision of any of the contributions. He certainly did not impose a uniform style on the contributions or insist on an index or any such thing.

Two items rise to the top of our interest. Most twenty-first-century readers will be surprised to find no general introduction to the volume, no summary of its contents, and very little context in which to understand the contents. The frontmatter instead includes Householder's "foreword"—apparently the "brief introductory paragraph" Saporta had in mind, though it took two paragraphs in the end—and Voegelin's strangely bracketed note on the reverse of that page. Thus, the editors missed the opportunity to situate lexicography as an emerging discipline in North America. "Lazy" seems like strong language for their approach, yet the archives bear it out. Saporta would write to Householder on June 15, 1961, (C450, Box 11): "About your note regarding an introduction to the lexicography monograph, I had sort of assumed that your comments would serve that purpose. In any case I don't think that I can contribute anything that would not be trivial. I think Carl should either accept or reject the manuscript as is. As a matter of fact, I had sort of assumed that he had already accepted it. In any case I don't think that I can write an introduction. I am sorry not to be able to be more helpful."

One might question why Saporta assumes so much, or why he would be editor of a volume to which he could add nothing that wasn't trivial. Even his style sort of assumes an utter lack of responsibility. Householder was no better when he replied on June 21, 1961 (C450, Box 11): "Since I haven't got time to write an introduction either, I guess that settles it." But his suggestion that Saporta write one suggests awareness of the lapse.

Householder and Saporta aren't the only culprits. Voegelin did not insist on a full-scale introduction, either, and whatever their enthusiasm for dictionaries, the conference, or its proceedings, it's possible that none of them realized what the conference and its proceedings would set in motion. The present edition attempts to supply much of what the volume originally lacked: an introduction, notes on contributors, an index, and, given our historical perspective, much more than anyone could have expected of the original. In any event, Householder and Saporta had embarked on publishing *PiL* without committing to a full editorial apparatus.

Also, and perhaps more surprising, Saporta proposed himself as co-editor more than a year after the conference, a dignity his work on the volume warrants, but which, apparently, he and Householder had not discussed until then. It had taken a year to start on the editing. "I think we are finally going to get going on editing the Lexicography MSS," Householder had written, but whose fault was that? Despite his love of dictionaries, Householder seems not to have focused sufficiently on either the conference or its proceedings. Even given the rush to organize the conference, both the meeting and publication seem semiplanned, extra and unexpected projects supervised by a busy person who relied on junior colleagues to bring them off and underestimated the work they would do and the credit they deserved. On May 15, 1961 (C450, Box 10), he apologized to Conklin: "Sorry I've been such a dilatory editor. I'll try to do better." Conklin probably appreciated his candor then, and, in retrospect, so do we.

Contributors, however, were anxious to publish their papers. The archival record of the book's progress is thin, but correspondence between Householder and two of his colleagues reveals the sorts of revisions effected once contributors had seen the proofs. For instance, Read remarked, on December 22, 1961 (C450, Box 11): "I was beginning to wonder whether the lexicography papers had been forgotten, and I am very happy now to have been sent the enclosed proof. I have marked a few little things throughout, principally some forgotten underlinings and only two bad misprints—the arg- in agricultural, p. 220, and an in for an is, p. 224." Both corrections were made, and he had others in mind: "A possible change that I ought to make, a thing that worries me, is in footnote 23, page 227. I say 'probably written by Dr. Yakov Malkiel,' but he got up in the meeting and pointed out reasons why I should not have thought that he wrote it. I was impressed by the fact that he never actually said that he didn't write it, and I'm inclined to let it go. Would you advise cutting out those words? You can do with it whatever you think best." Householder advised on December 26, 1961 (C450, Box 11), "I should let the reference to Malkiel stand," but it's difficult to know whether this reflected editorial principle or convenience. From a dilatory editor's point of view, even one with his heart in the right place, fewer changes were better, and Read's approach to revision was less than ambitious.

Apparently, Conklin took a somewhat more rigorous approach with his paper, reporting to Householder, on December 16, 1961 (C450, Box 10):

> Here is the proofread and corrected photocopy of my article "Lexicographical Treatment of Folk Taxonomies." I have used blue pencil in proofreading. If questions remain, please let me know. I will answer by return mail. I was out of town when this material arrived or you would have had it back much earlier.

> I am impressed with the quality of the typing on the masters—especially inasmuch as I fully recognize how "demanding" my MS was. I do hope the typist will be able to make all the corrections I have indicated. I will gladly defray whatever extra expenses may be involved, should retyping of my section be necessitated.

Certainly, Conklin's was the longest contribution, and it included three large figures and five pages of references, the only paper founded so extensively on secondary literature. Setting all of it out correctly would indeed have challenged Saporta's typist. In many respects, as Householder noted in his reply, dated December 26, 1961, Conklin was an exemplary contributor: "I guess you're easy to please," he wrote. "The typist made more mistakes with your article than with any other so far. She clearly doesn't know how to divide at line-ends." Yet, Conklin referred to a mass of corrections that, one assumes, went beyond line-ends.

Of course, not all articles should be the same length. Haas's desiderata for bilingual dictionaries, for instance, was not an involved, theoretical argument, and her article's value endures partly because it makes its case briskly, economically—students and nonspecialists can read it with much less strain than that occasioned by Weinreich's piece, for instance. Thoughtful editors would resist insisting that all pegs fit the same-sized hole. Indeed, they might expect articles of various lengths and types to draw a wider variety of readers than a more strictly focused and standardized work would—in editing a book, diversity can be a strategy. It can also be accidental, as evidence suggests the variety of approaches in *PiL* was accidental, driven not by editorial principles but by the authors' individual commitments and ambitions. Certainly the editors could have pushed authors to include more examples or to draw more on the scholarly literature of linguistics and lexicography, but they did not. As a result, reviewers criticized the book for "not going deep enough on some issues" or lacking connection to relevant published work (see chap. 3), lapses that stronger editorial hands might have avoided.

Photocopies and offprints

Having heard of the conference, scholars sought the proceedings immediately and persistently. A year later, on November 15, 1961—well before anyone could reasonably expect a post-conference publication—the Germanist J. Alan Pfeffer asked Householder (C450, Box 11), "Could you send me a copy of your report on Lexicography for Modern Foreign Language Study: Report of a Conference at Indiana University Nov. 11–12, 1960." He and Householder were wartime friends: "1944–45 seems only a short while back." Householder would reply, on November 22 (C450, Box 11), "I will send you a copy of my report on the Lexicography conference. The publication, complete with all the papers, should appear next spring. I still see people from 165 Broadway all the time. Quite a place." Indeed, he had seen several of them at the conference.

Einar Haugen, who would later review *PiL* for *American Anthropologist* (1963a) (see chap. 3), requested copies of all the papers. His request is not extant, but Householder replied on October 6, 1961 (C450, Box 10): "If Sol told you I might have extra copies of the Lexicography papers, I am baffled. There were none left, but I supposed that Contreras had mailed them to Sol, since they're not in his old office. I don't have a complete set myself. The Office of Education has 25 sets; you might persuade Bruce Gaarder to send you one. I'll have to start some sleuthing to find out what became of the leftover copies. I can and will send you a copy of my summary report, but that's the best I can manage now." Householder and Saporta had dallied a bit in producing the book, and, like Pfeffer, Haugen was moved to request a preview—he was that interested. His review's acidity may express disappointment at the delay.

Once *PiL* appeared in print, it should have absorbed demand rather quickly. No one had expected the conference or the book, so the book—partly on the conference's reputation—generated the demand, which soon surpassed the *IJAL* and original Research Center in Anthropology, Folklore, and Linguistics/Mouton & Co. printings published in 1962, leading to subsequent reprintings—with minor changes and corrections—in 1967 and 1975 (see chap. 4). Twenty-first-century readers may assume that the bound volumes constituted the whole of publication, but scholars in 1962 relied on another form of publication and distribution to spread their influence, namely, the offprint, the isolated article or chapter, which they could easily mail to colleagues. Items from *PiL* circulated among professors at colleges and universities that didn't subscribe to *IJAL* or buy volumes of research center series. Those at major universities likely to own both imprints might not read everything their libraries held. Offprints put their colleagues' research directly under their noses, obligating recipients to read it, though many an offprint went straight from the envelope into a file, vertical or circular, overlooked.

Thus, Conklin wrote to Householder on December 16, 1961 (C450, Box 10):

> As confirmed in conversations and correspondence last May, I assume that you or someone in Tom's office will be getting in touch with us soon about the number of reprints we may want to purchase. Since no order form was sent to me with the proof, could you make the appropriate arrangements then so that I will receive 400 reprints of my paper? Whether or not a certain number will be furnished authors gratis, I agree to pay for whatever number is necessary to make 400. Do such reprints come both with and without covers?

Read wrote similarly soon after, on December 22, 1961 (C450, Box 11): "I wish I could order two hundred offprints. Is that possible? Usually at this point the arrangement is made, but no mention was made of it. I would be prepared to pay the cost."

The numbers are shocking to the uninitiated. How many twenty-first-century scholars distribute hundreds of their articles via preprints and postpublication PDF files? Yet, in that earlier age, scholars liberally availed themselves of offprints. Read was well known for sending offprints to friends, but also to introduce his work to those who, he felt, might be interested in it (Adams 2017, 8n7)—two hundred copies would not be too many for someone with Read's habits of scholarly communication. Conklin's request for four hundred offprints may seem overly ambitious, then, yet perhaps his network, consisting of anthropologists as well as linguists, extended further than Read's. Read and Conklin wanted stockpiles of offprints so that they could provide their work to others throughout their careers, not only upon publication, and they were willing to pay for the means to do so; beyond the editors, they bear some responsibility for *PiL*'s success.[13]

Without any antecedent and without much warning, *PiL* instantiated a subfield of applied linguistics, not just because the Indiana University conference was the first North American conference on lexicography but because its proceedings raised issues beyond the history of lexicography, and because publication reiterated lexicography's debut in the academy over four impressions, while offprints of its contents extended lexicography more subtly into professional awareness. *IJAL* and various printings of the book rested on library and private bookshelves, but offprints were gifts of knowledge to friends and colleagues who, perhaps, only learned about the book because they had received one. Covers, Conklin knew, made a better impression. Every offprint received and noted raised the book's reputation slightly, and if contributors sent hundreds of offprints each, they achieved awareness of the book that any university press marketing department—even in the age of social media—would envy.

Ante-1960

When the US Office of Education asked Householder to organize the 1960 Conference on Lexicography, it addressed an urgent need in the interests of national defense, and Householder responded to the call because he was a linguist and a patriot, not because he intended to start a new academic discipline. Yet the call came just when the prospects for academic lexicography and study of lexicography were ripening. No one expected it, but the conference had outsized influence on lexicography and linguistics, bringing the two disciplines into dialogue. In 1959, there had been next to nothing about dictionaries on the minds of universities; the conference made lexicography unavoidable and unforgettable after 1962. Both conference and book suggested—almost promised—other conferences, other books. It wasn't long until other linguists and lexicographers seized the opportunity.

Mind you, there had been plenty of lexicography leading into the 1960s. The first edition of the *Oxford English Dictionary* (*OED*) had only been completed in 1933, yet already Robert W. Burchfield had started work on his four-volume *Supplement* (1972–1986) on July 1, 1957 (Gilliver 2016, 451). America brought out its own historical dictionary, *The Century Dictionary* (1889–1891), edited by William Dwight Whitney of Yale University, and it organized and supported several of the period dictionaries William A. Craigie had proposed to the Philological Society in 1919 (Gilliver 2016, 339), including those Craigie edited in part while at the University of Chicago, the *Dictionary of American English* (1936–1944) and the *Dictionary of the Older Scottish Tongue* (1931–2002), but also the *Middle English Dictionary* (1952–2001), led by Hans Kurath, and the never-completed *Early Modern English Dictionary*, led in the 1930s by Charles C. Fries and in the late 1960s and early 1970s by Richard W. Bailey, both projects of the University of Michigan. Mitford M. Mathews compiled *A Dictionary of Americanisms* (1951), and F. G. Cassidy, at the University of Wisconsin, was developing the plan and material for what would eventually be the *Dictionary of American Regional English* (1985–2013). American universities had never been so committed to historical lexicography before, nor, once these works were completed, were they ever after.[14]

American lexicographical activity rose in languages other than English during the same period. Some of these were also historical, for instance, the *Chicago Assyrian Dictionary* (1956–2011; see Reiner 2002). Others, compiled from field notes, helped to codify Amerindian languages, as Sapir's influence spread across America with his students, like Haas. SIL, founded in 1933, was busily documenting Central and South American languages with missionary zeal (E. Pike 1977, 1–14), and dictionaries figured in that documentation (Rensch 1977, 98–99). Military personnel in World War II relied on phrase books and language guides produced by the Army's Language Section—suddenly, bilingual lexicography was in the hands of average people, and those phrase books preserved in many a box of war memorabilia. But, as already noted, the 1960s saw publication of many bilingual dictionaries begun in the 1950s, including those targeting Thai, Moroccan Arabic, and Yiddish. In 1957, the Canadian Linguistic Association set up a committee to coordinate Canadian dictionary projects (Scargill 1967, vii). As lexicography flourished, the academy exercised some control over it, preparing the ground and planting, weeding and pruning, and enjoying the fruits of their labor when the dictionaries were finally published to fanfares of triumph, not to mention relief.

Commercial lexicography, too, thrived before 1960. Merriam-Webster dominated the big-dictionary landscape with its *Webster's International Dictionary of the English Language* (1890), *Webster's New International Dictionary* (1909), and the second edition of the *Webster's New International Dictionary* (1934). Yet Merriam-Webster wasn't alone: Funk & Wagnalls produced its competitive *Standard Dictionary of the English Language* (1893–95) and the *New Standard Dictionary* (1913). Both Merriam-Webster and Funk & Wagnalls fielded dictionaries for the college crowd, but Barnhart's *American College Dictionary* (*ACD*; Barnhart et al. 1947) took that market by storm. Usually, publishers draw college, school, and desk dictionaries from their big dictionaries, but Random House, which published *ACD*, decided to build a big dictionary on the college one. While the *Random House Dictionary of the English Language* appeared in 1966, preparations began in the 1950s, with Urdang as its managing editor. World Publishing of Cleveland, Ohio, added the well-respected *Webster's New World Dictionary of the English Language* (1951) to the mix, quickly followed by a college edition (Guralnik and Friend 1953). After publication of A. S. Hornby's *A Learner's Dictionary of Current English* (1948)—now famous as the *Oxford Advanced Learner's Dictionary* (1952; see Cowie 1999, 1–54 and 82–105)—publishers awoke to the commercial value of lexicography for nonnative speakers, including bilingual dictionaries. Increasingly, not just soldiers, sailors, and diplomats, but students, businesspeople, and folks walking the world's streets wanted access to them.

As American lexicography entered a golden age, research into dictionaries lagged in a leaden age, though occasionally one finds brassy items in and among layers of historical detritus. Richard Chenevix Trench founded the *OED* as we know it in *On Some Deficiencies in Our English Dictionaries* (1860), lectures delivered to the Philological Society in 1857, an unusually rigorous early example of dictionary criticism in English. Emile Littré's autobiographical *Comment j'ai fait mon dictionnaire de la langue française* (1880) provided an account of making his big dictionary (1863–72). Newspapers and journals reviewed dictionaries as they appeared, and while we lack a bibliography of such articles, the list of reviews of the *OED* compiled by Richard W. Bailey (2000) serves as proof of the concept. Then, James A. H. Murray (1993, 120), principal editor of the *OED*, delivered his Romanes Lecture, *The Evolution of English Lexicography*, in 1900, which concluded on a rather teleological note: "At any rate, it can be maintained that in the Oxford Dictionary, permeated as it is through and through with the scientific method of the century, Lexicography has for the present reached its supreme development." Murray's present is our past, and, in lexicographical terms, it's been a long one, but with less research on dictionaries than one might expect, given their abundance.

The first half of the twentieth century seemed to accept Murray's verdict, however. All questions having been settled, about what else but the *OED* would a scholar of dictionaries write? Mitford M. Mathews (1933) wrote a compact *Survey of English Dictionaries* while working as an assistant editor on the *Dictionary of American English* (*DAE*). J. R. Hulbert (1955), one of the *DAE*'s principal editors, produced the similarly brief *Dictionaries British and American*. Mathews's (1933, 76–85) book includes a ten-page "Review of Lexicographic Methods", and Hulbert (1955, 45–85) dwelled on "making a dictionary" at somewhat greater length, but, at the time, only Trench's work bothered with technicalities extensively. More specifically, Robert Keith Leavitt (1947) wrote his delightful *Noah's Ark, New England Yankees, and the Endless Quest* to celebrate the hundredth anniversary of Merriam-Webster dictionaries, history of a sort, but hardly disinterested, scientific research. When all is said and done, dictionary criticism and research did not keep up with the accumulating dictionaries available for either.

Before World War II, Read—also, for a while, an assistant editor of the *DAE*—had planned to write a history of early English lexicography, from the beginnings to Johnson. He submitted three articles—"Forerunners of Dr. Johnson in the Use of Illustrative Quotations," "The Beginnings of English Lexicography," and "The Development of the Historical Outlook in English Lexicography"—to leading journals, the first and third to *Modern Philology*, the middle one to *PMLA*, but withdrew them, probably to preserve them as chapters of the book he had in mind (see Adams and Bailey 2017, 383–84, items 1932b, 1934c, and 1935d). Soon after the war, however, De Witt Starnes and Gertrude E. Noyes's (1946) *The English Dictionary from Cawdrey to Johnson 1604–1755* burst that bubble, only to have it burst again by James Sledd and Gwin J. Kolb's (1955) *Dr. Johnson's Dictionary: Essays in the Biography of a Book* (see Adams 2018a). Thus, Read had turned to other projects by 1960, although, clearly from his contribution to Householder's conference, lexicography was still in play.

"One of the strangest features of lexicography," Ladislav Zgusta (1971, 10) would write in his *Manual of Lexicography*, "is the fact that lexicographers have only rarely exchanged methodical experience," and "coherent discussions of lexicographical theory and practice are also very rare." Zgusta then notes twenty works of "broader theoretical interest" (10–12), fifteen of which were published before 1960. *PiL* is one of the twenty. In his comprehensive annotated bibliography, *Lexicography Today* (1988, vi), earlier bits of scholarship were deliberately overlooked—"The present Bibliography does not repeat all items from earlier lists"—including those cited in the *Manual*, with this result: just fifty-six of the entries describe pre-1960 works. The bibliography comprises 285 full pages. Counting from the beginning, one reaches the fifty-sixth entry on page seven, which means that pre-1960 material accounts for just 2.5 percent of the whole, which, put another way, implies that over 97 percent of dictionary research followed or appeared concurrently with *PiL*. But the contents of *PiL* all appear in *Lexicography Today*.

Zgusta points to J. Edward Gates's (1973) much less comprehensive bibliography as containing earlier material, as indeed it does. One can find there some 103 pre-1960 items, plus reference to Mitford Mathews's column "Of Matters Lexicographical," published in thirty-four installments in the journal *American Speech*, from May 1951 to May 1960, and oddly missing from Zgusta's bibliography. That looks like nearly 140 items, but some are rather loosely connected to lexicography per se and others overlap with

Zgusta's, so the pre-1960 total is instead closer to one hundred, roughly twice as many as in Zgusta and equal to about 5 percent of Zgusta's overall total. Whichever items from Gates one counts, however, overwhelmingly more happened lexicographically after the Bloomington conference than before it.

Of course, this is not an argument of cause and effect in the broad sweep of events, though, at a different scale, which we'll consider subsequently, the Bloomington conference and *PiL* did affect the development of academic lexicography, not only in America but across the world. At the very least, however, the conference was momentous, an original marker on the road ultimately taken. If we look back at Zgusta's bibliography and count the significant lexicographical works published from 1960 to 1962, we find approximately twenty items, or roughly half the number of works preceding 1960 in total; that is, in the short period of the conference and publication of its proceedings, lexicographical activity had ticked up.

In an international context, lexicographical activity had been rising for nearly a decade before the Bloomington conference. German scholars had met to share ideas about lexicography early in the 1950s; the results of the conference were published as *Begriffssystem als Grundlage für die Lexikographie* (Hallig and von Wartburg 1952; second ed., 1963). Czechoslovakian lexicographers met in 1952, and proceedings of that meeting were published as *Lexikografický sborník* (Havránek et al. 1953). The French lexicographers followed closely on the heels of their European colleagues, holding a conference in November of 1957 and publishing their proceedings, somewhat belatedly, among the lexicographical works that appeared between the Bloomington conference and *PiL* (Imbs 1961; see also Országh 1963, 399/b for a slightly different list of originary works). So the Bloomington conference wasn't the first of its kind, but it was the first North American conference on lexicography, and it both participated in and promoted a rising tide of interest in lexicography as an academic subject on its own.

Yet another significant conference took place just after the one in Bloomington, organized on a similar, if somewhat more deliberate, impulse:

> In 1960, the United Nations Education, Science and Culture Organization (UNESCO) offered a contract to the International Council for Philosophy and Humanistic Sciences (document 866717) to inquire into the situation in the domain of lexicography; the latter body offered the contract, in its turn, to the Union Académique Internationale. The Inquiry was undertaken and the final report was written by Professor C. C. Berg (Leiden). Acting on the recommendation of the report, UNESCO and CIPSH (Conseil International

de la philosophie et des sciences humaines) partly co-sponsored, in 1962, a special international colloquium, organized by the Oriental Institute of the Czechoslovak Academy of Sciences, to discuss the problems of lexicography, mainly in the field of the languages of Africa and Asia. The final resolution of this colloquium mentioned also the desire that a Manual of Lexicography be prepared. (Zgusta 1971, 9)

That manual, Zgusta's (1971) *Manual of Lexicography*, first codified a theory of lexicography, underscoring the progress made in the field since the Bloomington conference. Although the participants in the Czechoslovakian conference met "to discuss the problems of lexicography," the title *Problems in Lexicography* was already taken.

Post-1960

Zgusta's *Manual* influenced American thinking about lexicography profoundly. Georgacas (1976, 359–400) contributed a review essay, titled "The Present State of Lexicography and Zgusta's *Manual of Lexicography*," to *Orbis: Bulletin international de Documentation linguistique*, so extensive that it warranted its own index. *Orbis* is a Belgian journal, it's true, but Georgacas taught at the University of North Dakota and worked within the American network of lexicographers, as well as networks abroad. Although reviews of the *Manual* overall were mixed, Georgacas hails it as "A Landmark" (373), because "in the present state of affairs in the science of language, aids such as the lexicon of any language are focal points in the study of language, and good dictionaries are of primary significance for research work of solid value" (359), not to mention their value for language learning, which is why the US Office of Education proposed a conference on lexicography in the first place.

Not all reviews were so positive. Urdang (1975, 220) found the book inadequate in nearly every way. "Nothing would have given me more pleasure," he wrote, "than to have found in Zgusta's book a work that I could assign as required reading for both fledgling and journeyman dictionary editors. Alas! This is not it. Even the most rudimentary style manual prepared for a dictionary contains more information, certainly in a better organized fashion . . . I cannot recommend it as an introduction for the beginner, nor do I consider it of sufficient scope and high caliber for the professional." Urdang (1975, 220) was a notably cranky reviewer, however, and doubted the value of lexicographical theory to the practicing lexicographer: "Lexicography is a form of applied linguistics, and only certain segments of it can be conceived us as purely theoretical; virtually all lexicographic theory is linguistic theory, so it can be expected that a book on lexicography would treat the interface between linguistic theory and the making of dictionaries." But Urdang rarely found treatment of that interface persuasive—consider his review of *PiL* (1963; see chap. 3). Not all commercial lexicographers agreed, however; Barnhart (1978, 129–31)—Urdang's close colleague—found much of value in the *Manual* and generally approved it.

Conklin (1975, 242–43), who straddled the interface quite successfully in his contribution to *PiL*—an estimate with which Urdang (1963, 592) concurred—agreed that the *Manual* suffered from many of the problems Urdang identified, but came to a sharply different conclusion: "Although one would thus hesitate to consider this an ideal reference work, it does provide a wealth of material not otherwise available in English. Some publications especially familiar to North American readers have escaped notice, but any student of lexicographic problems will find this survey thought-provoking and useful in several ways. It should be of most interest to those concerned with dictionary compilation or with the study and analysis of translation problems, language performance, and semantic relations. The rich array of topics, sources, and illustrative material remains impressive." As he made clear in his review of *PiL*, Urdang (1963) did not count academic lexicographers like Zgusta and Conklin as "real" lexicographers. He measured the success of anything lexicographical on its value to the commercial production of general purpose dictionaries.

Others also disagreed with Urdang about whether fledglings had anything to learn from the *Manual*. Several prominent linguists/lexicographers used it as a classroom text, as lexicography entered university curricula. Adam Makkai, who taught at the University of Illinois in Chicago, assigned the *Manual* in his courses on lexicography, as, apparently, did Gates at Indiana State University (Georgacas 1976, 397) and Roger Steiner at the University of Delaware (Gates 1979, 120–21). Pedagogical uses of the book were not uncritical. As Gates (1977, 27/a) wrote in his extensive review, "An American linguist is likely to read Zgusta's *Manual* with mixed feelings," yet, undoubtedly, "Despite its shortcomings, the *Manual* makes a significant contribution to lexicography. It provides the first full systematic treatment of lexicology and lexicography in English; it acquaints English-speaking readers with the European literature in the field and forms a classified index to it; and it incorporates in a coherent whole theoretical discussions of lexicography with examples of problems and practices of dictionaries in numerous languages" (32/c). Zgusta taught lexicography at the University of Illinois in Urbana, and it comes as no surprise that he put the *Manual* to work there. He also assigned some chapters of *PiL* (Gates 1979, 118).

I consider Zgusta's *Manual* at length because it participates interactively with *PiL* and some other works in establishing lexicography as an academic discipline. Perhaps as important, lexicographers with various commitments—practical, theoretical, historical, pedagogical—were aware of that historical development. For instance, Gates (1979, 123) writes, "Lexicography, then, while not a common subject for courses of study, is nevertheless *becoming* established as an academic discipline" (emphasis added). Zgusta's *Manual* added momentum to lexicography's progress in America, but *PiL* served as point of origin and, as Zgusta and Georgacas made clear, was already a touchstone of the emerging discipline in the 1970s.

Many seemingly disconnected pieces of that discipline formed into a coherent picture of post-Bloomington. Paul Bogaards (2013, 19) summarized the historical situation:

> Although dictionary criticism is almost as old as dictionaries themselves . . . and even if we can find more theoretical reflections on dictionaries from the sixteenth century on . . ., a more focused scientific study of lexicographical works dates from the middle of the twentieth century only. In 1959 the French journal *Cahiers de lexicologie* was launched and one year later a centre for the development of a new national dictionary was created in Nancy (France). In November 1960 a first conference on "Problems in Lexicography" was held in Bloomington, Indiana.[15]
>
> Ten years later, again in the United States and France, the first handbooks on lexicography appeared. Ladislav Zgusta published his *Manual of Lexicography* in 1971, and in the same year Jean and Claude Dubois' *Introduction à la lexicographie* and Josette Rey-Debove's *Étude linguistique et sémiotique des dictionnaires français contemporains* came out. A year before, an issue of the journal *Langages* had also been devoted to lexicography (Rey-Debove 1970). A few years later, in 1975, the Dictionary Society of North America (DSNA) was founded [see Adams 2014] and their journal *Dictionaries* appeared for the first time in 1979.

Bogaards does not suggest that one event in his list caused or even informed the others, but in America, the Bloomington conference served as proof of concept, proof that a conference on lexicography could be significant, proof that proceedings of such a conference had an audience and would influence other major events, like Zgusta's *Manual* and the teaching of lexicography and would do so immediately and durably.

In hindsight, we can describe the American lexicographical landscape at a finer scale, one that better positions the Bloomington conference and its significance. Besides publication of Zgusta's *Manual* in 1971, lexicographers and linguists of various kinds organized the International Conference on English Lexicography, held at the New York Academy of Sciences on June 5–7, 1972, proceedings of which, edited by Raven I. McDavid and Audrey R. Duckert (1973), were published by the Academy as *Lexicography in English*. One might view the conference as how the lexicographers struck back and took control of lexicography and all its problems from the linguists—never mind that most of those were also lexicographers in some measure—who spoke at the Bloomington conference.

Urdang, who found the Bloomington conference too theoretical, too detached from the exigencies of "real" lexicography (see chap. 3), contributed significantly to conception and organization of the New York conference, as McDavid (1973, 7) explained in his "Opening Remarks" to the conference and subsequently published proceedings: "The committee then coopted Mr. Laurence Urdang, a professional lexicographer," who had "been particularly helpful with practical suggestions, and in getting financial support from publishers." The publishers in question were the G. & C. Merriam Company; Holt, Rinehart and Winston of Canada; Laurence Urdang Inc.; the Longman Group; Scott, Foresman and Company; Wm. Collins Sons & Co.—in other words, all publishers of actual dictionaries—plus the Center for Applied Linguistics. In this sense, the New York conference responded to the one held in Bloomington a decade earlier.

McDavid (1973, 5) identified other origins for the New York conference. Publication of *Webster's Third* in 1961 incited public commentary on dictionaries; lexicographers felt the need to explain them and to discuss among themselves the best principles and practices involved in their making. "The proximate point of origin," he wrote, "was a brilliant paper by one of our participants, James Sledd, at the Present-Day English Section of the Modern Language Association in 1968. . . . At the close of this paper, Sledd asked the section to go on record as favoring the appointment of a committee on lexicography, with two specific charges," the first of which was "the calling of an international conference on lexicography in English" (6).

Yet one cannot overlook the fact that Sledd had participated in the Bloomington conference; the New York conference was not his first lexicographical rodeo. The New York conference included a roster of forty-nine speakers in various roles, and the overlap with the Bloomington conference was minimal—just Barnhart, Gleason, Read, Sledd, and Urdang participated in both. But because they did, the Bloomington conference was present in New York. That Bloomington came first was a matter of historical contingency, of course, but one cannot reverse history. Even if distant from later developments, the Bloomington conference and its proceedings had been the prime mover in American lexicography.

In fact, the relationship between the two conferences was rather more concrete than the official record suggests. First, Frederic G. Cassidy, who was on the program committee, invited Householder, who was not primarily a lexicographer, to speak at the New York conference, in a letter dated September 8, 1971:

> You may have heard by grapevine that an International Conference on Lexicography in English is being planned by MLA Group 13. It is now shaping up ... and you are hereby invited to participate in the first session, the general subject of which is "Lexicon and Grammar: Theory and Practice." Preceding you, Al Gleason is to speak on "Grammatical Prerequisites" and his discussant will be Ken Pike or Joe Grimes. We would ask you to frame your own title under the general heading of "Grammatical Problems." Your discussant would be M. H. Scargill of the University of Victoria. (C450, Box 10)

Householder declined. A handwritten draft of his response, in the same archival folder, acknowledges receipt of the invitation and explains that "Ever since it came I've been (a) trying to decide whether to accept, and (b) trying to figure out if I could go or not. Finally my wife settled the issue for me: if the meeting were a few days later, it would be O.K., but June 5–7 is definitely out." Even then, Householder (1975, 28/c) may have suspected the event would not be a fit for him, as he later concluded in his review of the New York proceedings, "On the whole, this book is probably of more interest to the professional lexicographer than to the linguist, even though interesting linguistic points turn up here and there." The invitation is more important than the refusal: Householder was invited because he organized the Bloomington conference; the invitation reiterated that conference's foundational role.

Householder may not have reflected on his conference or its significance, but we read its impact between the lines or in the footnotes of other commentators. Malkiel (1975, 29/b), reviewing Rey-Debove's handbook, summarized recent interest in lexicography that certified the importance of that book and Zgusta's simultaneously published *Manual*: "Another important event was the Bloomington Conference on Lexicography, whose novelty was sharply felt by the participants (including this reviewer) and whose transactions were subsequently published through the efforts of F. Householder and S. Saporta. Quite recently, a more pragmatically oriented (and by its explicit scope, more sharply focused) conference on English lexicography, organized under the auspices of the New York Academy of Sciences, consolidated the earlier gain."

In the main text of the review, then, Malkiel argued that the Bloomington conference had done the heavy lifting, to great effect, and that the influence of the New York conference was historically secondary, a consolidation of what had already been accomplished in Bloomington, which announced that lexicography is a subject worthy of academic study and research.

Malkiel (1975, 32/a) went further in sorting out the relative importance of the two conferences. New York, he insisted, "offered fewer breathtaking flights of the imagination, but was diversified in its appeal, including a number of papers by scholars whose work transcends the domain of English." Bloomington, however, was the ground on which later work would be built; put another way, it started a focused, academic conversation about lexicography: "Even in its original form (1962), as a Supplement to *IJAL*, two years after the conference, the report, titled *Problems in Lexicography*, promptly ignited a good deal of discussion, including reactions from scholars stationed at a midpoint between literary and linguistic studies, such as K. D. Uitti [see chap. 3]. The effect was reinforced when the book was reissued as a separate venture, with a few addenda (1967) [not quite correct; see chap. 4], giving rise to new analyses; cf. the assessment by F. de Tollenaere (1969) [see chap. 3]" (32/a).

Of course, not everyone agreed with Malkiel's assessment, Urdang (1963) and Barnhart (1978, 132–33) among them. But the critics and detractors were not, like Malkiel, thinking historically. The Bloomington conference took the first step into an emerging field much bigger than itself, exerting there an outsized influence until 1975, when *PiL* was published yet again, the same year in which Gates and others founded the Dictionary Society of North America.

Gates counted as one of Urdang's "real" lexicographers. He worked as an assistant editor at the G. & C. Merriam Company for six years, on both *Webster's Third* (1961) and *Webster's Seventh New Collegiate Dictionary* (1963). He taught lexicography at Hartford Seminary Foundation in 1966 while a doctoral student there, the same year in which he and Maxine T. Boatner published the first edition of their *Dictionary of Idioms for the Deaf* (Boatner and Gates 1966). He finished his dissertation under Gleason's direction in 1968, and it was later published as *An Analysis of the Lexicographic Resources Used by American Biblical Scholars Today* (Gates 1972). Though seemingly narrow, it had broader than Biblical ramifications and met with a warm reception (see, for instance, Barnhart 1978, 131). Through Gleason, he had a genealogical relationship to the Bloomington conference. Although he doesn't list *PiL* among his references in that book, he must have been aware of it, if only because he saw a copy in Gleason's office—perhaps Gleason gifted him an offprint of his contribution. He certainly consulted it while preparing "A Bibliography on General and English Lexicography" (Gates 1973) for *Lexicography in English*.

When Gates arrived at Indiana State University (ISU) in 1970, its library had just accepted a gift of rare English dictionaries from one of its notable alumni, Warren N. Cordell, known familiarly in the profession as the Cordell Collection (for more on which, see Vancil 2010). The Cordell Collection sparked Gates's energy. In order to publicize the collection, ISU hosted a series of conferences about the history of English dictionaries. Gates had attempted to organize the conference Sledd proposed in 1968 but lost the bid to Cassidy, McDavid, and their associates. Yet, McDavid (1973, 7) reported,

> At the opening of the Cordell Collection of dictionaries last year, at Indiana State University, the [New York conference] committee not only drew up the program for this conference, essentially as it stands, but reached an understanding with the faculty of Indiana State University, who had themselves been working toward a conference on lexicography. It was agreed that the international conference should be held in New York, with Mr. Gates of Indiana State University serving as conference bibliographer, and that Indiana State should inaugurate a series of conferences on lexicography and teaching, the first of which will take place this year.

"Bibliographer" was thus a consolation prize for an aspiring young professor who had no chance of outmaneuvering some of the most accomplished players of the academic game.

In fact, the first ISU conference, called—like the Bloomington conference—Conference on Lexicography, had taken place already, on April 16, 1971, and focused more on the history of English lexicography than anything else. Read and McDavid gave papers, and Sledd spoke on a panel about "Collecting and Collections of Rare and Out-of-Print Dictionaries." The next ISU conference, held in 1975 and titled "Colloquium on Historical Research on English Dictionaries," ended in organization of the Dictionary Society of North America (DSNA) (see Adams 2014). It was followed by a "Conference on the History and Making of Dictionaries," which took place June 9–11, 1977. Read was the only participant in that conference, the first biennial meeting of DSNA, who also delivered a paper at the 1960 conference. Harold B. Allen was the only participant on the 1977 schedule who, along with Read, had spoken at the New York conference. Iannucci, Read, and Urdang were the only participants in the Bloomington conference to become charter members of DSNA (see Adams 2019a, 54).

On the surface, then, we see little evidence of the Bloomington conference's influence on those held in Terre Haute or in the progress of DSNA. Gates organized his conferences to celebrate the Cordell Collection and to promote study of the history of English lexicography, neither of which had anything to do with the Bloomington conference or *PiL*. Yet Gates's 1971 conference consisted of just five papers and two panel discussions; the 1977 conference slated fourteen papers; neither could have built the momentum of an emerging profession, which is not, of course, to criticize either their motivations or the quality of the conferences. The little conferences that led to DSNA and its journal, *Dictionaries*, succeeded in the draft of the New York conference, which in turn benefited from the draft of the Bloomington conference. They, DSNA, and *Dictionaries* were swept along in the wake of the two alpha conferences.

One might quibble with Robert Ilson's declaration in the title of his important collection of essays about the subject that lexicography was an emerging international profession in 1986, more than a quarter of a century after the Bloomington conference. Looked at one way, Ilson pronounced the emergence rather late in the game. After all, Voegelin insisted that, with the 1960 conference and the publication of *PiL*, lexicography had left one epoch behind and entered another. But let's not quibble. How long, after all, does it take a discipline to emerge? So, let's concede that it was still emerging in 1979, when the first issue of *Dictionaries* appeared, still emerging when R. R. K. Hartmann hosted the first EURALEX conference at the University of Exeter in 1983, still emerging when Ilson published his book. Participants in the Bloomington conference were instrumental in the emerging profession, it's true, but in 1960, it wasn't about emerging. Malkiel, Weinreich, Haas, Harrell, Swanson, Worth, Gleason, Hoenigswald, Malone, Conklin, Sledd, Martin, Barnhart, Burrill, Bonsack, Iannucci, Read, Gedney, Chavarria-Aguilar, Penzl, the Kahanes, Tietze, Cornyn, Householder, Saporta, and the others who attended the Bloomington conference were present at the creation.

2

CONTENTS

Householder and Saporta resisted spending any more editorial time or trouble on *PiL* than necessary. Among other things, they didn't bother to introduce the contents in a comprehensive introduction, opting, instead, for the shortest of forewords—readers would have to take the various chapters as they found them. To be fair, the now well-established convention that editors summarize a collection's contents in an introduction was less observed in 1960, and anyway, these specific editors might have argued, *PiL* was a volume of conference proceedings, not a thematically coherent collection of the kind that needs an introduction. As a result, however, they neglected to make a case for the book as the start of something new, though, again to be fair, they barely registered the significance of the volume in their hands. Here, we can remedy the editors' omission with additional benefits of hindsight.

Most lexicographers and linguists today will no doubt consider much of what they find in the volume dated, if not outdated. For instance, Weinreich and Gleason operate within semantic theory of a bygone era, of which they are now considered part, not the vanguard of new thinking, as they were in 1962. They rely on—and implicitly criticize—works like Richard Robinson's *Definition* (1954), whereas nowadays, lexicographers, at least, will turn to Patrick Hanks' quite different approach in *Lexical Analysis* (2013), one grounded in decades of work as a lexicographer rather than in philosophical logic. Still, it's worth noting that Robinson's influence and the semantics of the 1950s and 1960s are still active among young scholars today—see, for instance, Krista Williams's (2016) new typology of color terms, a subject both Gleason and Conklin address in their contributions to *PiL*.

At a time when lexicography was a protodiscipline, contributors to *PiL* summoned up their knowledge of, experience with, and insight into dictionaries and their making, consolidated all of that and shared it in a public demonstration of lexicography's intellectual and cultural significance, and attempted to bridge the still yawning divide between lexicography and linguistics. Although too lightly edited, *PiL* is still informative and stimulating and—in its historical moment—foundational and ambitious. Besides its place in the broad canvas of the history of the language sciences (see chap. 1), it proved historically important at miniature scales, as well. Each contribution figured in the professional development and reputation of each author; for most contributions, one can connect dots across the professional literature through the generations (see chap. 5). Here follows a preliminary, critical account of those contributions.

Theoretical Considerations

PiL devotes its first section to "The Preparation of Dictionaries: Theoretical Considerations," including chapters by Malkiel, Weinreich, Haas, Harrell, and Swanson, with comments by Worth. Section headings in *PiL* are slightly misleading. Some chapters in later sections, notably Gleason's and Conklin's, are no less theoretical than those of the first section, and one can find little difference in theoretical level, if any, between Swanson's "The Selection of Entries for a Bilingual Dictionary" and Martin's "Selection and Presentation of Ready Equivalents in a Translation Dictionary." But Malkiel's contribution is all theory and draws on one of his career-long fascinations (see chap. 5). He proposes that we can construct "a pervasive classification by lexicographic genres" (133) more subtle than one that merely separates "sharply delineated varieties" (133) of dictionaries. He approaches dictionaries by analogy to speech sounds, devising "distinctive features" that aid in classification.

Malkiel settles on three fundamental categories of features: range, perspective, and presentation. These divide into subcategories. *Range* covers the degree to which a dictionary represents a given vocabulary, the number of languages included—putting aside etymological information—and the amount of lexical data relative to other kinds in entries or in the dictionary's structure. *Perspective* similarly subdivides into three features: the dictionary's chronological approach, synchronic or diachronic; whether entries within the dictionary are arranged alphabetically, semantically, or arbitrarily; and the dictionary's tone, which may be scientifically descriptive, normatively prescriptive, or in some way facetious. The four types of *presentation* are definition, documentation, graphic illustration, and "special features," like pronunciations and restrictive labeling. As Malkiel explains, "perspective concerns the lexicographer's logistics and strategy, while presentation involves his tactics" (135–36).

In his review of *PiL*, Uitti (1963, 418) suggests that "what matters even more than [the] preliminary establishment of distinctive features is the eventual depiction of 'their subtle interplay,' their dynamics. So far the technique has been brought to bear on too few subjects to be empirically conclusive" (see also Urdang 1963, 587). In fact, the final section of Malkiel's contribution, on the "interaction of distinctive features," is far too short, less than a page, and the typology fails to account for dictionaries that cross typological lines—that is, a lot of them. Earlier attempts at dictionary typology had faltered on this point: "As is frequently the case with classification, the core of the difficulty seemed to lie in the overlapping of the categories hastily established on the basis of first impressions" (133–34), yet Malkiel underestimates categorical overlapping in his own typology. Still, his framework allows us to evaluate the interactions among his distinctive features, sets terms on which later theorists would typologize dictionaries, and, to the extent they attend to such typologies, the terms on which lexicographers conceive dictionaries, for a typology, Malkiel argues, "is apt to disclose noteworthy gaps, identifying combinations of features not yet tried out, and may thus open up avenues of approach not only to all sorts of impracticable oddities, but also to rewarding possibilities so far overlooked" (136–37).

Malkiel's contribution to *PiL* not only addresses typologies but is a lexicographical tour de force. It's a somewhat breezy but exact account of the challenges lexicographers face and how they think through them, rather surprising, since Malkiel was not, himself, a lexicographer; but he was an eminently astute user of dictionaries and clearly had learned through them to think like the people who made them. Late in the piece, he writes, "Agriculture has been another longstanding purveyor of specialized dictionaries. A matter of heightened concern to our own guild is the dictionary of linguistic or grammatical terms" (153). Agriculture converges with Conklin's taxonomic concerns, and Gleason had planned a dictionary of linguistic terminology—are these comments prescient, or do they respond to papers presented and conversations had at the Bloomington conference? Regardless, no chapter could have opened the book more felicitously, as several reviewers agreed (see chap. 3).

Whereas Malkiel's contribution engages the broadest theoretical question—what, after all, is a dictionary?—Weinreich's "Lexicographic

Definition in Descriptive Semantics" focuses intensively on problems of definition. Arguably, it's the most theoretical chapter of the book—"mathematically formula-happy," as one reviewer put it (Országh 1963, 400/a; see also Uitti 1963, 420). More an essay in philosophical semantics than lexicography, it brings the two disciplines into productive contact. Weinreich hopes to "explain and criticize what lexicographers do when they define words" (159), having noted that, before 1960, anyway, "lexicographers have been surprisingly silent" (157) about the semantic issues underlying definition, but semantics is really only one aspect of a larger problem: "The indifference which lexicography displays toward its own methodology," he writes, "is astonishing" (156). The Bloomington conference and its proceedings attempted to correct that indifference, so Weinreich's stance, if rather grating to lexicographers, comes as no surprise.

Weinreich argues that lexicographers should identify lexical meaning at the boundaries of synonymic relations and should be "held to the assumption that the terms of a language are, on the whole, complementary" (160), by which he means something close to componential analysis, a legacy—through Jakobson's influence, one suspects—of the Prague School. His advice goes in the opposite direction of much modern semantic theory, in which context is everything (see, for instance, Hanks 2013). He explicitly rejects that "the meaning of a term is its use in the language" (159), because "it would require us to renounce dictionaries and to be satisfied, at most, with concordances" (159). He doesn't anticipate corpus lexicography, nor does he accept the underlying assumptions of historical lexicography. His starting point, then and now, seems wrong-headed to many a practicing lexicographer. Indeed, one reviewer noted these omissions (see Tollenaere 1969, 256–57). Still, finer points of the argument command our attention.

Weinreich focuses on the specificity of definitions, pointing out that the more conditions embedded in a definition, the more specific it becomes, and the editorial task is to ensure that definitions don't become over-specific but include all "criterial" conditions. A condition "may be considered criterial if, were it unfulfilled, our informants would refuse to apply the term in question" (163). While admitting that any language's semantics will prove discontinuous at points, he proposes that it's largely continuous, which may cause problems for unilingual dictionaries: in them, the language of defining is coextensive with the language being defined. Just as good definers achieve semantic economy by minding the Ps of specificity and the Qs of criteriality, they should also, Weinreich believes, develop a defining metalanguage "less rich, rather than as rich as, or richer than, the object language" (167), one in which words are defined with other words of greater frequency than the word being defined. "Another, less rigorous but perhaps more workable limitation, would be to see, by trial and error, how extensively the metalanguage can be economized by agreeing to use as few different words in definitions as possible, but to use each as often as possible" (167). Yes, Weinreich did compile a dictionary, but one can see, in the phrase "trial and error," why those committed wholly to editing dictionaries—and editing them for profit—thought his advice impractical (see chap. 3).

After Malkiel's historical subtleties and Weinreich's logical complications, Mary Haas's "What Belongs in the Bilingual Dictionary?" enters *PiL* like a breath of fresh air and, just as important, orients the book more directly toward the Office of Education's expectations for the 1960 conference, as primarily about bilingual lexicography. At just six pages, it's the shortest contribution to the volume; it briskly moves through twelve desiderata for bilingual dictionaries, from correct and relevant translation of items, to provision of idioms, inflections and derivations, usage levels, personal names, technical and professional terminology, spellings, and pronunciation. Looking forward, Haas recommends that the ideal bilingual dictionary "ought to be as well-adapted to purposes of machine translation as it is to human translation" (174), but the principal demand is that "it should be compact" (174), roughly the size of a college dictionary.

In his review of *PiL*, Karl Uitti (1963, 421) summarized Haas's contribution: "A brief, straightforward listing of a dozen desiderata which, if fulfilled, would provide acceptable bilingual dictionaries. Unfortunately, some of these (compactness ~ completeness of entries) are incompatible. Lexicographers, bearing these in mind, should do their best." Compactness and completeness, however, are competitive, not incompatible, and negotiating the best balance of desiderata is exactly what Haas has in mind. Uitti's view corroborates lexicographers who've ventured an opinion about the article in my hearing over the decades, yet it's the only chapter of the book, as far as I know, regularly assigned to students in lexicography, translation studies, and second-language studies. Other reviews largely overlook Haas's piece, perhaps because, in its brevity and forthrightness, it seems less ambitious than others, but perhaps also because they missed the point: competitive desiderata demand lexicographical decisions.

Harrell challenges Haas's desiderata. Had we a recording of the conference (see chap. 1), we might hear Haas's response to Harrell's principal point, that "It is clearly impossible to pay equal attention to both X-speakers and Y-speakers in one and the same work" (180), directly opposed to Haas's ninth desideratum, that the bilingual dictionary "ought to be equally oriented to speakers of both languages" (174). Harrell also objects to the assumption "that the user of a bilingual dictionary is primarily concerned with understanding a foreign language and scarcely at all with expressing himself in a foreign language" (183), a distinction which surely went to the heart of the Office of Education's expectations for the conference and its proceedings. Haas wants translations "needed for the passage in hand" (174), which corresponds truly to the expectations of bilingual dictionaries constructed before Title VI of the National Defense Education Act. A productive argument, it's just as relevant today as it was in 1960.

Others at the time saw its value, though they tended to side with Harrell. Reviewing *PiL*, Einar Haugen (1963a, 755) agreed that "a dictionary can only be made for one group of users at a time." Also, mildly criticizing Haas, "The American who looks up the Arab word may not be doing so merely to find what it means in a given context"—Haas's "passage at hand"—rather, "he may be a student of Arabic who wants to learn how to use the given word in all its contexts," and so, the "bilingual dictionary becomes not merely a mechanical translator"—not, one notes, what Haas said—"but also an instrument for teaching," which indeed it can be. One might insist that a dictionary can only serve one function at a time, translational or pedagogical, but I don't believe that any more than I think it unreasonable to imagine a bilingual dictionary that serves more than one audience—imagination and practicality forever challenge each other.

Although it's barely a glimmer, Harrell's account of the Georgetown Arabic Research Program—which would produce several dictionaries—is quite welcome. Principles and practices of dictionary programs across the United States are often hidden in grant proposals and proprietary operating documents—lexicographical problems attending one or another project aren't usually public, so generalizations from specific experiences are unlikely outside of lexicographical coteries. Nowadays, in books and articles about dictionaries and their making, such things are more available, but it must have been exciting to hear about them in the context of a singular conference in 1960 or read about them in 1962. Especially interesting in this regard, Harrell appends a memorandum about the "Methodology for [the] Arabic Dictionaries Project," by Ann M. Driscoll, of Merriam-Webster, who had been called in as a consultant. She receives no credit in the original table of contents but does in this edition. Note that the memo was submitted on August 30, 1960, barely in time for the conference, which underscores, I think, the rush in which the conference was organized and the state of the constituent research.

Swanson's contribution, "The Selection of Entries for a Bilingual Dictionary," focuses on issues of word formation and derivation, the intersection of grammatical and syntactic categories with a bilingual dictionary's word list and treatment of words in entry structure. The chapter belongs in the following section, but Householder and Saporta, who balanced sessions on the conference schedule, carelessly retained the conference structure for the book. They appended the conference schedule, so could have rearranged the contents while preserving the conference as history.

Compounds and less transparent derivations, Swanson argues, complicate the bilingual lexicographer's task—what should the dictionary include, and how do entries present, organize, and analyze important linguistic facts given the word-driven structure of modern dictionaries? Further, how consistently and comprehensively can such facts be integrated into the dictionary text? Though languages may have similar structures—Swanson limits his discussion to bilingual dictionaries of Indo-European languages—they are almost always different enough that gaps between their respective word-formative processes pose problems of inclusion and treatment. These are important matters, for unilingual as well as bilingual lexicographers. Uitti (1963, 421) complained that "the premises of [Swanson's] essay are vague, so are some conclusions," yet Swanson raises lexicographical problems unapproached in other contributions.

Anyone who has attended an academic conference knows that the quality of responses to sessions varies widely. Householder and Saporta deserve credit for inviting reliable and insightful respondents for all the sessions. Worth's response to the opening session mediates differences of opinion among the speakers masterfully. He concedes, accommodating Harrell, that "one's first reaction" to Haas's paper might be "that such wishes are a trifle unrealistic" (204), but he goes on to support much of what Haas proposes. Like many subsequent reviewers, Worth questions Weinreich's argument, which "raises a whole series of theoretical issues too thorny to be seized very firmly here" (206) and perhaps at the conference altogether. It might have helped, he suggests, had those issues "been explained in more detail, or perhaps illustrated by more actual words and fewer algebraic symbols" (206). Worth also doubts the value of Malkiel's paper. Although he was one of its junior participants, Worth's forthright criticism and synthetic approach protects the integrity of both the conference and the book and warrants the organizers' confidence in him.

Dictionaries and Structural Linguistics

The conference's second session opened with H. A. Gleason's paper on "The Relation of Lexicon and Grammar," which carefully and methodically articulates the virtues of lexicography that descriptive linguists often overlook, not just then but today. Sometimes, in fact, their attitude exceeds mere neglect: "Descriptive linguists," Gleason writes, "have been immensely critical of dictionaries and dictionary-makers. Commonly the principles on which they have based their criticism have been of very little relevance to dictionaries" (212). Indeed, as several of those who reviewed *PiL* noted, such criticism intruded into the conference and the book. Gleason's position is much more thoughtful and generous than those of some of his colleagues.

Nevertheless, one cannot accomplish "the total descriptive task" (212), as Gleason puts it, without accounting for a language's lexicon, and he sees dictionaries as useful in such an account. When he itemizes several possible functions of dictionaries, he speaks as a descriptive linguist and, to lexicographers and dictionary lovers, he no doubt sounds reductive. For instance, he urges lexicographers to better integrate dictionaries with grammars by making grammatical information explicit and transparent, necessary to dictionaries were they to support the learning of critical languages supported by the National Defense Education Act.

The critical issue for the lexicon, says Gleason, is content, a "loose" systematic structure of meaning integrated with grammar at word-formative points that exhibits "at least three types of interrelations" (222): contrastive relationships, substitution relationships, and collocational relationships. He illustrates the interrelations brilliantly with sets of English color terms. The content system justifies lexicon as an essential component of linguistic description, if not quite on the same footing as syntax and phonology, and dictionaries succeed when they capture and communicate the content system of a language. Thus, Gleason concludes, "Dictionaries and grammatical statements can profitably be designed as parts of a unified program of language description" (225). Overall, however, as Uitti (1963, 422) observed in his review, Gleason's "commentary shed more light on the limits of descriptivism than on the mystery of the lexicon (and the dictionary's role)." Still, it's a theoretically astute and nuanced argument written in a clear and engaging style, more appealing than Weinreich's, perhaps, if no smarter.

Of all the contributions, Henry M. Hoenigswald's "Lexicography and Grammar" is perhaps the most elegant, written with verve and humor—Uitti (1963, 423) notes its "finesse." Hoenigswald focuses more intensively on morphology and morphophonemics than other contributors. Like Gleason, he sympathizes with lexicographers and values their work, but rather than put forward theoretical principles for the relations of lexicon and grammar, he considers in practical terms the types of grammatical information that dictionaries include—labeled grammatical categories, like gender and part of speech, treatment of function words, matters of construction and government, and the like—as well as the sorts of things he believes dictionaries could do better, such as indicating irregularities (a topic also raised by Gleason) rather than implying, by omission, regular paradigms; treatments of case; and, in bilingual dictionaries, the loss of grammatical information in translation. He accomplishes a great deal in small compass, given the article's length, more or less what the Bloomington audience heard on Friday afternoon.

Kemp Malone's "Structural Linguistics and Bilingual Dictionaries" brings the discussion to the point, which is not the theoretical relation of lexicon and grammar—or, at least, not only or primarily—but the interactions of linguistic structures and the lexicons of bilingual dictionaries. His piece is less penetrating than Hoenigswald's, as signaled by its leading question and answer: "What have the structural linguists to say about the bilingual dictionaries as I have described them? In this paper I speak only for myself" (236). After a discussion of morphemes focused on *asparagus* and *likemindedness*, and the recommendation that bilingual dictionaries demonstrate structural principles by entering morphemes rather than words and phrases, he moves to the problems of representing speech sounds in dictionary structure.

The discussion of phonology and phonetics suggests Malone's view of what bilingual dictionaries are and how they work. While it's all true enough, the work that follows his prescription would prove hard for many dictionary users to, well, use. For one thing, he invests a lot in front matter—recall that he had contributed front matter for the *American College Dictionary*—which would be a lesson in phonology and morphology: "One ought to begin by explaining what phonemes are and making clear the standard method of isolating them, the setting up of minimal pairs.

Next allophones should be explained, and after them the syllable" (240). A bilingual dictionary on this model would include a very concise introductory linguistics textbook and achieve a level of detail unknown even in the textbooks: vibrants and surds, straits and broads, "length, stress, pitch, and boundary phenomena."

Nevertheless, he insists, "it is unwise to impose any preexisting system of phonemic or phonetic transcription on your bilingual dictionary. The needs of such a book are best determined after a thorough study of the two languages with which it deals" (240), and which probably goes without saying. Yet he imagines the lexicographer will resort to phonemic transcription, unless the user would thereby "go seriously wrong" without help from a phonetic transcription. "And naturally the two systems should be sharply distinguished in the usual way, phonetic transcriptions being set off by square brackets, phonemic ones by diagonal lines" (241), subtlety likely lost on many a user. While Haas often takes heat for her aspirational list of bilingual dictionary features, Malone's preferences seem far less practical, in some respects, than hers.

Posterity suggests that Harold C. Conklin's "Lexicographical Treatment of Folk Taxonomies" impressed linguists and anthropologists more than any other contribution to *PiL*. While his colleagues tried to work out the relationship of lexicon and grammar, implicitly to justify the linguistic status of both lexicons and dictionaries, Conklin struck out independently, identifying what may seem a peripheral challenge for bilingual dictionaries but one actually critical to their value, the ways in which they deal with folk taxonomies. Vocabularies often contain many folk alternants for the same botanical item, for instance. How do lexicographers parse their meanings or distribute their use over geographical and cultural domains?

Conklin lays out the nature of folk taxonomy and how to classify folk taxa, which he distributes among the categories "unitary simple," "unitary complex," and "composite." The result of this sorting shows that lexicographers compiling bilingual dictionaries cannot expect to define folk botanical terms, for instance, with simple equivalents—an important point, because recourse to synonymic defining is typical of bilingual dictionaries and intuitively the method lexicographers employ. This points not just to the relevance and acuity of the argument but to Conklin's wise refusal to separate lexicon from culture, which is what one does when one assumes that other people with another language organize their folk taxonomies parallel to one's own. Conklin thus implicitly disputes Weinreich's semantics.

The key to determining folk taxonomic meaning, according to Conklin, is semantic contrast and especially hierarchical contrasts. "Folk categories within the same domain," he writes, "may be related in two fundamentally different ways: by *inclusion*, which implies separate levels of contrast, and by *exclusion*, which here applies only within single-level contrastive sets. There may also be subcategoric, or componential, *intersection*" (257). This approach was fresh at the time of the conference, and its innovativeness resonates even today, well after the relevant disciplines had absorbed Conklin's work on Hanunóo language and culture. He further complicates the technique by considering various dimensions of contrast, especially hierarchic contrasts that articulate superordinate, hypernymic, and hyponymic relationships. He concludes by correctly suggesting, for the time, anyway, that dictionaries had never really addressed the problems he describes, let alone worked them out in strategic and tactical detail, which made Conklin's contribution to *PiL* foundational.

In his review of the book, Einar Haugen (1963a, 65) noted that "Conklin's illustrations from the languages of the Philippines are particularly striking, showing how one can analyze hierarchically and systematically the meanings of terms in botany, kinship, and pronominal reference." On reflection, the illustrations are striking because, unlike the contributions discussed so far, Conklin's is replete with them, anchored also in a broader and deeper secondary literature than its companion pieces. Urdang (1963, 592), too, in a largely grouchy review, was impressed by Conklin's paper: "What is interesting and valuable in Conklin's study is that he has interpreted the logical structure of thought as reflected in language in terms of the language itself, and thus has used the language to classify the culture," an ambitious task for a single article, but surprisingly achieved. Urdang further observes that while Conklin addresses bilingual dictionaries, his contrastive method serves monolingual lexicography just as well, perhaps thus making it the most important piece in the collection.

Conklin's article, along with Weinreich's, received some sympathetic criticism from Uitti that applies to Gleason's, as well. All of them build systems, and, Uitti (1963, 424) points out, "A system always exacts its price; complexity and richness tend to yield to systematic coherence. It remains to be seen whether the sacrifices demanded by C. and W. are temporary or implicit in their very techniques." The observation recognizes obliquely a tension within the construction of both conference and book. Some pieces are "observational," with Haas proposing desiderata and Malone considering a set of discrete representational problems, and so forth. Could the volume succeed on the basis of such pieces alone? Shouldn't some contributors ask and attempt to answer some of the bigger, theoretically grounded and productive questions? Of course they should, and they do, with the same mixed results as the more modest pieces, but a mixed bag of lexicographical fruits—apples, oranges, rambutans, and mangosteens.

James Sledd delivered his comments on this session/section, as Országh (1963, 401/a) put it in his review, "in a rather wry vein," which might better be described as "waspish." Ever the skeptic, Sledd tests the contents of his session against the rising decibels of Chomsky's transformational grammar and finds echoes of new theory in the papers under his scrutiny but also some disagreements, rendering, at the same time—in a disingenuously self-effacing style—his own critique of the transformationists' view of grammaticality. To Hoenigswald's observation that verb classification is poorly handled in bilingual dictionaries, Sledd counters with the *Oxford Advanced Learner's Dictionary* (1948), which proposed a robust model of such classification. Malone's views, too, were outdated, since he "seems to make a number of assumptions which the transformationists would reject" (263). While he finds Chomsky confusing—by which he really means "confused"—he notes that "Other theories than Chomsky's can, of course, be baffling, too," and, he regrets, "I have to confess almost complete failure to understand Mr. Gleason" (264), after which he understands him pretty well in a couple of paragraphs. While pedagogues and lexicographers "cannot be indifferent to theory," Sledd acknowledges, they also "cannot shift with every wind that flutters the leaves of *Word*" (264), the journal of which, one recalls, Weinreich was editor at the time. A master of eloquent dissent, Sledd was at once the best and the worst respondent for his assigned session.

The Preparation of Dictionaries II: Practical Considerations

Samuel E. Martin's "Selection and Presentation of Ready Equivalents in a Translation Dictionary" leads the book's third section. Urdang (1963, 589), immediately following a profoundly negative assessment of the whole book, wrote in his review that Martin's is "a very practical discussion of bilingual dictionary problems that have a direct bearing on monolingual dictionaries as well." Focusing on problems of Japanese–Korean–English lexicography, Martin begins by disagreeing with Haas, though his "you" is any lexicographer: "You want to make a dictionary that will be concise but exhaustive; exact while not exacting; linguistically adequate for both languages yet uncluttered with trivial details. Sooner or later you have to concentrate on certain goals and forget others. Each dictionary represents some unique compromise" (271), which, while true enough, dampens lexicographical ambition. Bilingual dictionaries should be made for harried students, not scholars, he insists, and the best bilingual dictionaries would enable machine translation, though that would require rather more syntactic information than is usually embedded in them. "A machine can then be defined," he supposes, "as a very fast but dumb student, with a literal mind and a nagging insistence on explicit directions and forced choices," a view with which Urdang, who knew some things about automating the lexicon, likely agreed (see chap. 3). Haas's desiderata, on this view, would exceed the machine's capacity and very probably the student's as well.

Martin takes the session title seriously, briskly outlining "certain kinds of small improvements"—fourteen of them—without so much as a conclusion to rationalize their places in the same argument. Some suggestions seem obvious enough, for instance, that dictionaries shouldn't "shun" eye-dialect forms, exclamations and interjections, connectives, nonfluencies, and the like, for even if they might seem out of place in monolingual dictionaries, they undoubtedly vex learners of a language and so belong in bilingual dictionaries. Then, he advises, eschew quoted examples to illustrate usage, but contrive them editorially to deliberately expose what's hard or problematic about the word in question. Align the grammatical categories of the two languages in play. All of these are arguable, but they make good sense, and, as Martin points out, preferred treatment of any two languages will differ from that preferred for any two others, so his suggestions are practical, not universal, and later metalexicographers have reproposed them.

But what of his dictum that "We want to boil our material down to essentials," which also seems sensible? When students look up a word in language X, he points out, they want *the* equivalent in language Y, and supplying multiple synonyms or equivalents will only confuse them. While his intuitions about users are probably sound, those listening to his paper at the Bloomington conference would not have forgotten Conklin's arresting exposé of the inadequacies of simple equivalence in treating folk taxonomies. Simply put, the two positions are mutually exclusive, and, with all due respect to Martin, Conklin's paper has left a much larger and deeper footprint in the linguistic, anthropological, and lexicographical literature.

Clarence L. Barnhart's contribution, "Problems in Editing Commercial Monolingual Dictionaries," falls rather far from the tree of bilingual lexicography, to which Martin much more precisely applies his experience and talents. Householder and Saporta no doubt recognized an angle of legitimacy that only he could provide the conference, so they allowed—or perhaps encouraged—him to present what he knew best and probably better than anyone else in America, the challenges that confront commercial lexicographers, whether for the monolingual or bilingual audience. It's a valuable counterweight to the contributions drawn from experience of academic lexicography, since much of the market for bilingual dictionaries—especially for more prominent languages—is commercial and pedagogical, the two lexicographical domains in which Barnhart, as a single figure, uniquely excelled.

Naturally, then, Barnhart denominates the audience of a dictionary as "the buyer" and weighs the importance of various features of dictionary entries—spelling, pronunciation, definition, etymology, and so forth—from the buyer's perspective. We are tempted, in the jargon of our own time, to think of this as a "user perspective" (see chap. 5), but "buyer" hones a distinctive edge, probably American, to that user identity. He spends much time on dictionary scope and on how to develop evidence that warrants editorial decisions. He advocates for trained staffs to support an editor's enterprise—this might seem obvious to university-based editors, who have access to trained personnel on the cheap, but to a commercial lexicographer, trained staff is an expense that has to be justified commercially. He also explains the importance of an editorial advisory committee to sound decisions on policies but also limitations to the "advisory" role—ultimately, editors, not committees, are dictionary authors and make authorial decisions.

Barnhart's account proves that commercial lexicographers live by arithmetic and lists. At a distance, through *PiL*, we can view the work of planning a commercial dictionary over the shoulder of an expert commercial lexicographer. That remains the value of Barnhart's chapter to this day, for, while academic lexicographers write a great deal about their plans and methods and the intersections of the theoretical and practical problems they face, project by project, commercial lexicography is proprietary, methods can be trade secrets, and thus we rarely read about the brass tacks of day-to-day commercial dictionary work.

As Urdang (1963, 590) guessed in his review, Barnhart may have been "unwilling (or unable) to reveal—possibly because he was tipping his hand—some of his really knotty problems and their solutions" (but see Gedney's "Comments," page 337). Although the chapter has little explicit relevance to bilingual lexicography, it is invaluable, even if academic and commercial concerns occasionally rubbed each other the wrong way, as we glean from Urdang's review (see chap. 3). Haugen (1963a, 753) decided that Barnhart "pondered" his subject "somewhat gloomily," and, if he was right, we might attribute that to the continual and stressful challenge of making a living word by word. Uitti (1963, 425) remarked that "Barnhart supplies a charming account of procedures followed in commercial publishing." One wonders whether they read the same chapter and suspects that these opposed evaluations say more about the reviewers than the tenor of Barnhart's approach—readers will have to decide for themselves whether the commercial lexicographer's lot is or is not a happy one.

"Use and Preparation of Specialized Glossaries," by Meredith F. Burrill and Edwin Bonsack, promises something more general than it can deliver. I suggested earlier that Burrill and Bonsack's contribution to the volume never earned the respect afforded some of the others because the authors operated in government circles, rather than academic ones—they took their paper out of network, so to speak, though they were both estimable scholars, and Burrill was especially prominent. However, their subject is toponymy, not really the business of either bilingual or monolingual, commercial or academic dictionaries, and the onomastic emphasis seems out of place in the volume. Those who turn to *PiL* are unlikely to care about place names, and those interested in place names are unlikely to turn to *PiL*.

Problems of finding an audience aside, the chapter is excellent and instructive, both about the relationship between toponymic and generic senses of geographic words—*branch, creek, water, swamp, meadow, glade,* and so forth—and about "a specialized activity—geographic name standardization" (298), in which the authors were engaged, a practice as unfamiliar to most readers as commercial lexicography, in Barnhart's account, and thus similarly absorbing. For example, meanings of common place names or elements of names vary by place, which means that toponymic works must take dialectal variation into account and history, too—those factors intersect, as time and space inevitably do. Some place names are highly metaphorical, and some of those are metaphorical beyond any clear connection with the local features they name. Burrill and Bonsack provide an informative appendix—albeit underanalyzed—of dictionary definitions of *glade* that illustrates all points in the argument. Obliquely, problems of translating place name elements bear on problems of translation in bilingual lexicography, as well as suggest, along with Conklin, that in such taxonomic situations, easy equivalents are insufficient to guide both native and nonnative speakers through the thickets of a language.

Burrill and Bonsack's chapter reckons with the relationships among words—especially generic words that become specific in their toponymic applications—names and things, that is, the geographical facts that underlie but do not necessarily correspond to the semantics of a word like *glade*. Thus, questions about them can't be answered without reference to the "content system" Gleason introduced into the discussion. In the case of toponomy, anyway, content is not purely linguistic in orientation. Caught in a stereotype, one doesn't expect theory from bureaucrats, but while Burrill and Bonsack aren't theorists or system-builders along the lines of Malkiel, Weinreich, Gleason, and Conklin, they introduce from their experience of the relevant semantics the category TOPOCOMPLEX—"the combination of geographic and linguistic phenomena" (301)—which, again, their compendium of *glade* definitions well represents.

James E. Iannucci explores the problem of "Meaning Discrimination in Bilingual Dictionaries," primarily via a collection of seventy-five specimen entries from thirty-seven dictionaries. He identifies one danger of defining with equivalents, a topic of previous papers: different senses of a word in one language correspond to different senses of words in another, and bilingual dictionaries of the time too often simply lumped all of the equivalents together, without discriminating among senses in either language. This proves especially confusing to dictionary users who consult one with a word meaning in mind, while reading a book, for instance, only to discover that the word means many things, but without guidance as to which equivalent or synonym best approximates the expected meaning. Some bilingual dictionaries discriminate meanings on one side—the language more familiar to the user—some on both sides, but also some on neither.

Iannucci closes by recommending that senses of words entered in bilingual dictionaries be keyed to sense discriminations in what we might call monolingual dictionaries of record, so that sense discrimination in ideal bilingual dictionaries would be systematic and consistent. Reviewing the volume, Haugen (1963a, 754) called it "a counsel of despair." Indeed, William Gedney, responding to the section, doubted that such a scheme would succeed, for three reasons: (1) which monolingual dictionary? (2) if we couldn't agree on just one dictionary, students would need to buy either very large bilingual dictionaries or a large number of monolingual partners for dictionaries of the "other" languages; and (3) too many languages—even today, let alone in 1960—lack a good enough monolingual dictionary to serve the purpose.

Thus, we might agree with Gedney (338) that, "The first part of [Iannucci's] paper, in which he studied analytically the organization and arrangement of definitions in a large number of dictionaries, is a priceless piece of work which each of us ought to study and restudy and keep handy for later reference. It seems to me to be one of the most valuable pieces of paper I shall carry away from this conference. I am sorry to say, however, that the recommendation which Iannucci proposes as a result of this fine analysis seems to me unworkable." To the trained eye, the collection of specimens reveals the problems and inconsistencies of bilingual dictionaries of the time, and, to a lesser extent, those of the present day. We can appreciate the specimens without accepting the overarching recommendation. Among the reviewers, Haugen (1963a, 754) and Urdang (1963, 590) came down on Gedney's side.

The extent to which Allen Walker Read's contribution, "The Labeling of National and Regional Variation in Popular Dictionaries," belonged at the conference or in *PiL* is unsure. On one hand, it deals with a practical problem, discerning to whom a word or expression "belongs" and how a dictionary's entry structure records ownership. On the other, the value of regional labeling in bilingual dictionaries, especially those directed at students, seems minimal. Following Barnhart, exactly how much space and labor can a monolingual, let alone a bilingual, desk-sized dictionary devote to discriminations of provenance as well as discriminations of meaning? How many fewer terms or meanings would be entered in such a dictionary to accommodate the labeling and any commentary about regionality that might accompany them?

One must, however, give credit to Read for doing simply what Read always did. From a set of very specifically selected—and, one must admit, out of the way—citations, he built a set of problems: "I feel," he writes, "that the central practical procedure of lexicography will always be the gathering of documented evidence on all aspects of usage" (326), and the procedure applies regardless of the type of dictionary in question. Collecting evidence may be "donkey work," to borrow Read's phrase, but it's paradoxically also a kind of metapractice. Read uses his exemplary citations to show how difficult it is to distinguish Briticisms and Americanisms. He then generalizes the point to labeling of other Anglophone varieties—Scotticisms, Canadianisms, provincialisms, Northern American, Southern American, and so forth—and ends by resisting the term *dialect* and several potential labels, such as *patois* or *vernacular*. In this last section, he responds to an article by André Martinet and admits that "the suggestions of his that [Read thus] attacked seem to [him] the most reprehensible" (332). These are strong words, interestingly aimed against one of Weinreich's mentors and his close associate when they were co-editors of *Word* (see Malkiel and Herzog 1967, 605; Malkiel 1968b, 128). As already noted, Read's wasn't the first barb launched in that direction—recall Sledd's quip about *Word*—and one wonders about ideological crosscurrents of the conference.

Gedney's "Comments" closes this third section of *PiL* affably, with a relatively uncritical nod to Martin, in whose presentation he finds strands of argument initiated in earlier papers, especially about the primary importance of determining the audience of a dictionary, something that seems so obvious today but wasn't then, when lexicographers accounted for vocabulary before considering users' needs. In any event, he writes, "It is high time that our bilingual dictionaries should begin to lean over backwards in the direction of giving quick and easy access to the desired information instead of posing time-wasting puzzles to be solved" (336), which might be taken as criticism of the conference's theorists (Malkiel, Weinreich, Gleason, and Conklin), whose papers complicated rather than streamlined problems of lexicography. We can discover what users want out of certain types of dictionaries, but isolating "the desired information" isn't a simple process. As Barnhart points out (280), etymology isn't a prime interest of college dictionary users; yet, when they want etymologies, they expect to find them, and the same might be said of folk taxonomic meanings, regional labels, and more.

Gedney recognizes Barnhart's paper as "a privileged inside view of how commercial dictionaries are produced" (337) and reflects briefly on the differences between academic and commercial lexicography, concluding that Barnhart can guide even those who produce dictionaries for "a captive audience and market" (337). Whereas he views "Barnhart's work as the art of the possible," he has "the impression that Burrill and Bonsack are trying to do the impossible" (338), codifying words in the topocomplex. His assessment of their work leads to an interesting aside about the tendency in America "today" to privilege short term, large scale research that lacks a sufficient basis in data over the long term drudgery—like Read's—that goes into building up data, potentially for any number of projects.

Lexicographical Problems in Specific Languages

Although contributors to the first three-quarters or more of *PiL* turned frequently to examples from languages that illustrated or fortified arguments about theory or lexicographical procedures, contributions to the last section focused on problems posed by the sorts of languages—Pashto, Modern Greek, and Turkish—the US Office of Education had in mind when commissioning the Bloomington conference in the first place, languages critical to US security interests, languages diplomats and military personnel would have to learn, and for which they would need state of the art bilingual dictionaries. Putting aside theory and Anglophone practice—represented by Barnhart and Read—we learn about the difficulties, both linguistic and cultural, that such languages pose to lexicographers.

O. L. Chavarría-Aguilar and Herbert Penzl consider some "Lexicographical Problems in Pashto," an Indo-Iranian language of Afghanistan and Pakistan spoken in several inadequately described dialects with limited historical textual corpora. Dictionaries of Pashto, especially those available to and usable by Westerners, were very few and outdated, even in 1960. The critical issues in Pashto lexicography are not, it turns out, matters of syntax or grammar that occupied the attention of several contributors in earlier sections of the book, nor even of morphological variation, which the authors suggest, contrary to several co-contributors, "are not the concern of the dictionary, but rather that of the descriptive and reference grammars of the language" (348).

Complications arise, however, over phonology, as the dialects vary considerably. Phonemes distinct in one dialect coalesce in another, and allophonic differences are yet more striking. Distribution of sibilants among the dialects also varies, which, combined with the challenges of transcription and transliteration—Pashto, written in Arabic, is not accessible to many who would need a Pashto–Choose-your-language dictionary—leads the authors to conclude that "the selection of a 'standard' for the transcribed (or transliterated) entries will have to be determined by the phonemic distribution in the main dialectal types of Pashto" (351). Without establishing a "standard" variety for dictionary purposes, lexicographers would find it difficult to compile a word list, and users to locate words when looking them up.

As Henry and Renée Kahane explain in the following chapter, "Problems in Modern Greek Lexicography," a bilingual dictionary of Modern

Greek also suffers from problems of transcription and transliteration. Like Pashto, Modern Greek exhibits allophonic variation among dialects worth noting, even in a bilingual dictionary for general use. As a matter of national pride, Modern Greek is still written with Classical Greek characters, which most dictionary users around the world cannot read. Some problems attending Modern Greek differ significantly from those affecting lexicographical treatment of Pashto; at the time, they seemed pressing, because a *Modern Greek–English Dictionary* was in progress, under the direction of Georgacas, with the Kahanes serving as consultants.

The Kahanes spend considerable time describing the differences between Demotic Greek—the people's Greek—and *katharevusa*, a learned and aesthetically regulated variety of Greek, which leads, details of phonology and morphology aside, to the foundational question for a dictionary: "Whose Greek?" But the details matter, too. Too complete an account of allophonic variation would prove cumbersome in a bilingual dictionary, and morphology follows suit: "Dictionaries often tear apart what should be kept together" (361), which complicates the word list for unsuspecting learners, yet history demands explanation of homonymous morphemes, blends, and distantly related cognates. Finally, the Kahanes examine different ways of analyzing meaning, from the purely semantic to syntheses of lexical and compositional analysis, each of which implies an entry structure competitive with the others.

As Andreas Tietze emphasizes, both in his title and at the outset of his article, "Turkish Is a Language with Problems" that beset the well-intentioned lexicographer. Again, problems posed by Turkish mirror problems posed by Modern Greek and other languages, but one thread that connects all three chapters in this section is their insistence that making a bilingual dictionary is not merely a linguistic problem but a cultural one. Even the most theoretical of contributors to *PiL* might admit culture's role, but only in Conklin's treatment of Hanunóo folk taxonomies, indirectly, and the three chapters of this ultimate section do we confront the matter squarely. Language users have language attitudes and ideologies; at times, the attitudes and ideologies exclude one another; the substance and structure of a dictionary will need to choose—in some measure varying language by language—which cultural assumptions to follow.

In the case of Turkish, such assumptions affect even the name of the language printed on the dictionary's spine; the historical relationship of Turkish to other languages, as well as the treatment of borrowings; decisions regarding the dictionary's historical depth, as well as the inclusion of lexical innovations; and the space the dictionary provides for inclusion of slang, regionalisms, and other nonstandard language. Add to these problems of coverage transliteration from Arabic into Latin characters (especially borrowings, which adds an extra layer of problem), and the translatability of meaning in definitions. Tietze's special contribution is to emphasize the cultural aspects, which occupy seven of nine and a half pages in the original text. None of these problems, cultural or more typically lexicographic, is unique to Turkish, so Tietze and the others contributing to this section articulated issues of common interest that hadn't been straightforwardly addressed by the previous sections.

Given the optimism of papers earlier in *PiL*, these treatments of specific languages have a somewhat deflating effect. As Haugen (1963a, 755) put it, "While the bilingual dictionary should thus ideally be a totally matching description of two distinct languages, it becomes in practice far less. Much of the concern of those discussing such dictionaries was to decide how much less they could settle for." Urdang (1963, 591) correctly observed that the three chapters on specific languages belonged thematically with those by Haas, Harrell, and Swanson, and they bring "little of general interest" to the discussion "not expressed by others," while the language-specific issues they raise are of interest only to those concerned with those languages, not a very charitable view and one reflecting, one suspects, Urdang's Anglophone preoccupations.

William S. Cornyn's "Comments" on the session/section are brief in the extreme and agree with Urdang, with the exception that the papers on specific languages emphasize the roles of background and audience in bilingual lexicography more intently than the other papers, an estimate perhaps more accurate about the former than the latter issue. He ends on an important point that, unfortunately, neither the conference nor the book pursued: "there seems not to have been enough attention paid to the problem of sources," noting that in the languages on which he was focused, Jinghpaw and Burmese, "there is a tremendous difference in source potentialities" (379). One can imagine a whole volume on the subject, written and edited by other hands.

PiL closes with a section of three appendices, two of purely historical interest: the conference schedule and a list of participants. The section's feature is Householder's "Summary Report," which lists "points on which the conferees expressed unanimity or very general agreement" (383), followed by mild disagreements, then issues brought up just once, and concludes that, "in general, nearly all important topics were covered more or less thoroughly during the conference" (386). This last claim seems at least overly optimistic and perhaps also self-congratulatory—reviewers of the book did not agree in general, nor did they agree on what had been left out or might have been treated better, as one can read in chapter 3, though Zgusta's thorough use of *PiL* in his *Manual* better supports the claim (see chap. 1 and note 16).

With hindsight, one can see even more to improve. Most of the volume advances one or the other of two types of criticism: either a contribution takes lexicography to task for not doing semantics or grammar well enough or it shows how a specific language challenges those preparing bilingual dictionaries. These are, of course, legitimate lines of argument, given the Bloomington conference's purpose. One might, however, have expected more. At least in some instances, we should have heard not just what was wrong in bilingual dictionaries or challenging to lexicographers but demonstrations (besides Haas's desiderata) of how to do bilingual lexicography well, given all those constraints. Indeed, it would have been helpful had more of the participants provided sample entries in their papers. Most were engaged in making dictionaries at the time—surely, were a sample entry not at hand, it was time to write one, and the conference could have served as the occasion for doing so. In that case, *PiL* would have gone beyond complaint and set a good example for future lexicographers.

3

RECEPTION

In a sense, *PiL* succeeded from the outset and for more than a decade following its initial publication. After all, it went through four printings—often referred to as "editions," the small amount of correction among them doesn't warrant the designation—first, simultaneous publication as a supplement to the *International Journal of American Linguistics* and as a freestanding volume, as volume 21 of publications of the Indiana University Research Center in Anthropology, Folklore, and Linguistics in 1962; second, a corrected printing of the series volume in 1967; and, third, another reprint in 1975, with minor changes to Householder's foreword (for further information about these various impressions of the book, see chap. 4). Unsuccessful books don't appear in four printings in thirteen years. For its time, it was indispensable as well as foundational.

Vital Statistics

PiL encountered a mixed reception, but its vital statistics were and are relatively strong. As of July 5, 2019, WorldCat tallies just 140 copies of the 1962 edition in libraries worldwide, with an additional eighty-seven copies of the 1967 edition and a mere one copy of the 1975 printing, or 228 copies, total. These totals do not reflect deaccession over a fairly long period, some fifty-seven years, so the original library sales may have been slightly larger than current records reflect. Also, as of the same date, 457 libraries held the *International Journal of American Linguistics* in print—there is no digital edition. Thus, access to *PiL* has been broad and, especially in the journal, more or less permanent, even though libraries subscribing to the journal never agreed explicitly to the book's importance. Sales beyond the journal suggest that major libraries felt they needed it in their collections. Some universities hold the book in both the journal and independent formats.

These modest numbers look somewhat better in context with other dictionary- and lexicography-related titles published from 1960 to 1990. Raven McDavid and Audrey Duckert's *Lexicography in English* (1973) graces the shelves of a similar number of libraries, at 245. W. Pijnenburg and F. de Tollenaere's (1980) more specialized volume on historical lexicography, *Proceedings of the Second International Round Table Conference on Historical Lexicography,* falls short of these numbers, at just 163 copies. Two other conference-based volumes, *New Aspects of Lexicography* (1972)—edited by Howard D. Weinbrot, from papers presented at the (University of California) Riverside Conference on Lexicography in 1969—and *Dictionaries of English* (1987)—papers from the fifth biennial meeting of the Dictionary Society of North America, edited by Richard W. Bailey, in 1985—occupy more shelf space in university libraries, at 463 and 430 copies, respectively, but unlike the others, they were published and distributed by established university presses. *PiL*, though hardly a breakaway hit, nonetheless found its audience. Arguably, its very publication initiated an audience for more successful subsequent publications

That audience was steady in the twentieth century and persists into the twenty-first century. *PiL* and the items it anthologized have been cited continuously, often, and prominently. One gains only a vague outline of its value from notoriously unreliable Google Scholar citation counts, but, with a pinch of skepticism, they are worth considering briefly. The book may have generated as many as 260 citations, again as of July 5, 2019, though some of those records probably overlap. Still, taking seriously the 197 citations Google Scholar reports for the book as a whole seems reasonable—roughly 200 citations, one guesses. Various individual contributions have equally or more impressive citation counts: Weinreich's contribution logs 167 citations; Malkiel's—perhaps surprisingly, given its narrow focus on dictionary typology—has been cited approximately 130 times; Barnhart's has also proved influential at 113 citations; both Malkiel's and Barnhart's were reprinted in Hartmann (2003), and Barnhart's also in Allen (1964); despite criticism within the conference (see chap. 2) and relative neglect from the reviewers (see this chap.), Haas's contribution has been cited frequently, approximately eighty-four times. Conklin's article has been cited well over five hundred times, but not always in its original form—Joshua Fishman reprinted it in *Readings in the Sociology of Language* (1968), and it's cited most frequently by far from that source. Still, its popularity certifies the importance of the conference and its proceedings.

While continual citation certainly measures the importance of a work like *PiL*, the book's earliest influence can hardly be overstated. Zgusta's enthusiasm for the volume in his field-defining *Manual of Lexicography* (1971) is evident, citing it 138 times in 360 pages, roughly at a rate of once per three pages, although the citations cluster at points rather than distribute evenly. Zgusta refers to nineteen of the *PiL*'s twenty-two contributions, excluding only Worth, Burrill and Bonsack, and Read. Significantly, he cites Sledd's, Gedney's, and Cornyn's brief responses, as well as Householder's summary report, each more than once, so they had an impact on the profession of lexicography. Even if they are less cited than other papers overall, they were nonetheless embedded in the field's burgeoning literature. Some of the papers figured more prominently in Zgusta's analysis than others, with pieces by Malkiel, Weinreich, and Martin rising considerably above those of their colleagues.[16]

Zgusta cited items in *PiL* out of necessity—few other works at the time had explored so many relevant issues in lexicography. The same was true a decade or so later, when Jennifer Robinson (1983) compiled a glossary of English lexicographical terminology. Her sources also include most of *PiL*, including Worth, Burrill and Bonsack, and Read, but excluding the entire last section, presumably because their subjects weren't English, though that says nothing about the terminology they employed. She valued the volume differently than Zgusta, but she valued it comprehensively. Citation of *PiL* slowed because the field developed and diversified so much after 1960. When Dolezal and McCreary (1999) published their critical bibliography of pedagogical lexicography—the 96th volume of Lexicographica Series Maior—they included entries only for those works that best met the subject, in their view—Barnhart, Iannucci, Martin, and the whole volume itself, of which they wrote, "This is the seminal work on lexicography as understood within the context of structural linguistics of the 1950s" (57), a compliment that nonetheless indicates obsolescence. Their assessment is typical. For Hartmann (2007, 7), the conference was "famous," and whatever else the conference was, Franjié (2009, 34) somewhat mistakenly asserts, it was "La première conference exclusivement consacrée aux problèmes lexicografiques," a notable event in the genesis of an unexpected discipline.[17]

Mixed Reviews

Reviews of *PiL* anticipated its effects on the discipline—immediate and long term—and recognized its strengths as well as its weaknesses, both as a whole book and paper by paper. When I say the reviews are mixed, I mean two things: (1) they are mixed among themselves, some more affirming, some more critical; and (2) they are mixed within themselves—none offered unalloyed praise, yet the most critical manage one or two favorable comments, and the others are mildly critical while generally favorable. The significant reviews include László Országh's in *Acta Linguistica Academiae Scientiarum Hungaricae* (1963); Einar Haugen's in *American Anthropologist* (1963a); Laurence Urdang's in *Language* (1963); Karl Uitti's in *Romance Philology* (1963); Karl J. Franklin's in *Linguistics: An International Review* (1965); and Félicien de Tollenaere's in *Lingua* (1969).[18]

Top scholars reviewed *PiL* in top journals, so it had an international reputation from the outset. Its interest transcended languages in favor of general lexicographical principles, or it would not have appealed so much to Zgusta, and editors of the journals variously turned to philologists (Uitti), sociolinguists (Haugen), theorists (Országh), historical lexicographers (Tollenaere), and "practical" lexicographers, in this case commercial (Urdang) or missionary (Franklin). It was also covered extensively: Haugen's review is about three pages long, and so is Országh's—three and a half columns in a double-column text—while Tollenaere's exceeds four pages, and Franklin's a bit more than five pages; but Urdang's runs to eight pages, and Uitti's to an astonishing thirteen pages. Books of little account tend to garner little reviews. Even if the reviews of *PiL* are critical, the attention spent on it signals success.

The reviewers grasped the book's significance, even though they also found matters to dispute and criticize. Franklin (1965, 76) captures the reviewers' generally favorable response: "This is a very important monograph for three types of readers: those interested in semantics, those involved in dictionary making, and those engaged in learning previously unanalyzed languages." But Haugen (1963a, 753) caught one of the book's deficiencies, playing a bit on its title: "What one misses is quite simply a reasoned, point-by-point discussion from A to Z of the problems of lexicography." The somewhat impromptu origins of the conference account, partly, for why the papers weren't devised to cover the subject systematically. In various guises, other reviewers agreed as much with Haugen's estimate as with Franklin's.

Sometimes, a reviewer would explain such deficiencies sympathetically. Országh (1963, 400/a) noted that *PiL* "suffers from the teething-troubles of all pioneering efforts: too many aspects of the newly discovered field have been chosen as topics of discussion." The important issue is the volume's foundational role—foundational texts are rarely perfect but start conversations that tend toward more complete, integrated, and systematic research. Tollenaere (1969, 253) likewise observed, "As a result of the different starting points of the participants the content of *P. i. L.* is rather disparate." Haugen (1963a, 752), too, accepted the challenge Householder, Saporta, and the conferees faced: "The papers," he notes, "are uneven and often conflicting or overlapping, since it is impossible to delimit the topic accurately in advance," or, at least, the tempo of the conference, from instigation to completion, made such delimitation unlikely. Haugen suspected loose organization: "The topic is diffuse, the papers likewise. The result is like the description of the elephant by the seven blind men. Each one appears to be talking about something different" (753).[19] No doubt, greater editorial intervention would have mitigated the extent of incoherence, even if it couldn't tie up all loose ends. However, disagreement among reviewers leads one to wonder which elephant each thought he was reviewing.

Haugen (1963a, 753) reassures us that incoherence "does not prevent the papers individually from being interesting and even fruitful, each in its own way. Anyone who contemplates the making of a dictionary can hardly avoid learning a great deal from some of the comments here made." Yet, on this point, not all reviewers agree. Urdang (1963, 589) is especially acerbic: "It is rather sad to report that the uniformity of the papers dealing with bilingual lexicography, with one or two exceptions, hardly makes them worth commenting on. On the whole, they provide little of interest save to those who may be contemplating the preparation of a bilingual dictionary; and even for them, the problems would be of significance only if the source and target languages were the same." The last clause seems insupportable: surely, research on bilingual lexicography of specific languages can speak to broader lexicographical problems, processes, and products—lexicographers are capable of generalizing from other lexicographers' experience, regardless of the languages under consideration. The preceding clause seems obtuse and even a bit churlish. As the only reviewer who attended the conference, he knew its origins, so, yes, the papers on bilingual lexicography would serve "those who may be contemplating the preparation of a bilingual dictionary" —that was the point of the conference. Yet Householder and Saporta invited papers from those with more general linguistic and lexicographical interests, and the book's title reflects that movement away from the conference's original motive.

Again, editorial direction and a sufficient apparatus might have answered some of the reviewers' concerns. Uitti (1963, 417) reiterates less vividly Haugen's sense that the conference program comprised twenty-two blind lexicographers and lexicologists: "One notes disagreement among the participants and considerable incomprehension of one another's aims." That was inevitable, he thought, since "Only one paper deals exclusively with lexicography"—he means Malkiel's—but "the gamut runs from the practical concerns of businessmen producing and selling a useful product to sophisticated theoretical elucubrations."

Could this potpourri of topics be brought into mutually informative contact? Voegelin and others thought discussion of the papers at the conference did some of this work, and Voeglin remarked that publishing *PiL* was a "pleasure ... tinged with regret," because the printed papers were "regrettably without benefit of discussant emphasis which remains unpublished and largely unreflected" in the book, "though all authors had opportunity to reorganize their papers in light of the discussion, and some took advantage of this opportunity" (128). Haugen (1963a, 753) demurred: "Prepared comments on each session were presented by Worth, Sledd, Gedney, and Cornyn; a summary report on the whole conference by Householder concludes the volume. While there is said to have been 'lively discussion,' none of it is printed. The reviewer does not share Voegelin's regret about this, since it is doubtful that much more could have emerged from the discussion than is already in the papers."

Yet more could have emerged, and had discussion been recorded and reproduced in the volume as grist for Householder's "Summary Report," some of the gaps among papers might have narrowed, some connections mutually constructed in dialogue. Uitti (1963, 416) compares *PiL* to another book in Voegelin's series: "Unlike *Style in Language*, the new volume offers no sampling of actual discussion except for the unspontaneous 'Comments' appended to each main division, and Householder's short, informative 'Summary Report.'" *Style in Language*, edited by Sebeok (1960) as the proceedings of an even more ambitious and interdisciplinary conference held at Indiana University in the spring of 1958, was roundly castigated in thorough reviews. The experience may have led Householder and Saporta to exclude discussion, but, conversely, they might have worked a little harder to prove Haugen wrong.[20]

Franklin (1965, 76) believed that "All three groups" he identified—"those interested in semantics, those involved in dictionary making, and those engaged in learning previously unanalyzed languages"—"will find the volume of both theoretical and practical value in assessing previous efforts in the field, in producing studies of semantic systems, and in compiling or reorganizing dictionaries." Urdang (1963, 591) disagreed. Finding little of practical value, he viewed the theorizing of several contributors skeptically. For instance, Gleason argues that "the dictionary should provide an integrated linguistic description of the lexicon of the language. His implications are strongly to the effect that dictionaries do not provide this sort of description and are therefore inadequate. There can be no quarreling with Gleason's point, but is any dictionary or grammar completely adequate or satisfactory?" In other words, linguistic theory ignores the exigencies of practical and especially commercial lexicography, which is an art of the possible—Gedney's description of Barnhart's contribution, you'll recall—rather than one of desiderata.

Urdang (1963, 593) saw practical lexicography elbowed by theory into the volume's corners, which he attributed to the lack of "real" lexicographers on the conference program: "Since only one participant in the symposium (Barnhart) was a professional lexicographer, a word in defense of that small, maligned group seems to be in order, since, by implication at least, some of the papers take rather a superior view of them." Urdang, himself one of the maligned, represented others who attended, like Philip Gove, who worked in the commercial world, while his sense of "professional lexicographer" excluded others, like Read, who had worked on the *Dictionary of American English* in the 1930s and for the rest of his life was engaged in an uncompleted dictionary of Briticisms (Read 1938b and Read 1987), a project eventually transferred to John Algeo (Algeo 1987) and still unfinished at Algeo's death in 2019. Read served as a consultant on Barnhart's *American College Dictionary* for "Usage Levels and Dialect Distribution" and contributed a brief essay to that dictionary on "British and American English" (Read 1947). At the time of the conference, he was on the editorial advisory board (1956–1961) of the *Funk & Wagnalls Standard Dictionary, International Edition* (1961), to which he also contributed front matter. All of this informed his paper for the Indiana conference. Read was no lexicographical pretender.

Urdang's need to subordinate academics in his argument about practical lexicography verged on the pathological—certainly, it was so inaccurate as to be disingenuous. Conklin, Gleason, Hoenigswald, and Penzl all served as outside consultants to *Webster's Third New International Dictionary* (1961). Malone had served on the Editorial Advisory Board of the *American College Dictionary*, as well as chief etymologist on the *Random House*

Dictionary of the English Language (1966). Iannucci (1986b, 328) reported himself a consultant on several bilingual dictionary projects. Gleason, at the time of the conference, was laying plans for a dictionary of linguistic terminology (Adams 2019a, 24). And Sledd helped Mitford M. Mathews (1966) prepare *Americanisms: A Dictionary of Selected Americanisms on Historical Principles*, a shorter, revised version of *A Dictionary of Americanisms* (Mathews 1951) before, during, and after the Bloomington conference (Mathews 1956, 127).

Those participants carry the *weakest* lexicographical credentials. Gedney, besides his work on the *Dictionary of United States Army Terms* (Barnhart et al. 1944), also worked for a while as an associate editor of his Army boss's *American College Dictionary* (Barnhart et al. 1947), and wrote glossaries of several Thai languages published later in a series of his field notes. By the time of the conference, Conklin (1953) had produced a *Hanunóo-English Vocabulary*, Cornyn and Musgrave (1958) had published a *Burmese Glossary* and embarked on an eventually unfinished bilingual English–Burmese dictionary, while Swanson (1959) had edited a bilingual *Vocabulary of Modern Spoken Greek*. Haas had published a Thai dictionary (1945d), a *Tunica Dictionary* (1953a), and a *Thai Vocabulary* (1955), and had been working on her *Thai–English Student's Dictionary* (1964, vi) for several years. Similarly, Weinreich (1968, viii) was preparing his posthumously published *Modern English–Yiddish Yiddish–English Dictionary*, begun in 1948, and Harrell *A Dictionary of Moroccan Arabic: English–Moroccan* (Sobelman and Harrell 1963; see Stowasser and Ani 1964, viii), followed by the reverse volume (Harrell 1966). Martin had initiated *A Korean–English Dictionary* as early as 1953 (Martin, Lee, and Chang 1967, vi). Worth's (1969, 4) Western Kamchadal and English bilingual dictionary appeared in 1969, but he had begun work on it a decade earlier; he also collaborated on a Russian derivational dictionary published in 1970. Tietze and the Kahanes published an etymological dictionary of Turkish seafaring terms borrowed from Latin and Italian (Kahane, Kahane, and Tietze 1958), but even before that, Tietze had led the team that revised Sir James Redhouse's Turkish–English dictionary (Tietze et al. 1968). Roughly four-fifths of those who delivered papers at the conference had some dictionary experience prior to the conference, and more than half of the whole roster had had or were earning considerable practical experience in compiling dictionaries by then.

With a chip on his shoulder, Urdang minimized the role of experienced lexicographers in the conference and book. For him, "professional" lexicographers drew a paycheck for working on dictionaries alone; those who drew university or government salaries but who also compiled dictionaries may have been professionals at something, but, alas, not lexicography. Nonetheless, one takes Urdang's (1963, 594) conclusive point: "Lexicography, in practice, is a form of applied linguistics and, although more theoreticians would be a welcome addition to the field, they must remember that their theories should be interpretable above all in terms of practicability." One might expect subsequent work to do some of the translation of theory into practice; it's perhaps too much to expect a single conference—especially a first conference—to balance and integrate theoretical and practical matters perfectly. But to rest the observation on a spurious distinction between professors and lexicographers misrepresents both the conference and lexicography.

In fairness to Urdang, he was not the only reviewer to notice the imbalance or the tone of superiority sometimes adopted by the theorists. Tollenaere (1969, 253–54), himself an accomplished historical lexicographer—so not professional enough for Urdang but nothing if not practical—observed, "Among the linguists some give the impression of looking down on Samuel Johnson's 'poor drudges.' Some contributions filled with the 'abstrusities of theoretical controversy' (p. 299) are not among the most lucid and are of little help to the practical lexicographer." Interestingly, though, he disagrees directly with Urdang about which theoretical papers could contribute to dictionary-making. "A paper, such as was presented by H. A. Gleason Jr., on 'The Relation of Lexicon and Grammar,'" he averred, "is of a very high quality; indeed it is the most stimulating contribution that I have seen on the subject" (254). One suspects that, having decided to fight tone with tone, Urdang's broad-brush opinion obscured the value of some contributions. Tolleneare had Weinreich's, not Gleason's, abstrusities in his sights (255).

Uitti (1963, 426), too, predicted an argument between the practical lexicographers and their linguist counterparts: "One theoretical problem pervades the entire volume: the relationship between the classificatory system and the material to be classified. Advocates of traditional lexicographic practice . . . defend it on grounds of pragmatic usefulness or commercial expediency. Others, urging sweeping reforms, tend to reinterpret lexicography in terms of values borrowed from other linguistic disciplines."

Extending that observation, Országh (1963, 400/a) argued that the division of sensibilities led to weakness of analysis across the contributions, which "was, in a way, inevitable, because the time available for discussion was severely limited and also because not a few of the contributors had no previous practical experience of dictionary editing. Needless to say, without such experience any attempt at valid theorizing on lexicography is built on insecure foundations. No wonder that those papers of the present volume are the most helpful that are free from a priori theorizing and instead are solidly based on experience acquired in the actual fieldwork of dictionary editing, as the contributions of Barnhart, S. E. Martin, Conklin, A. W. Reed [sic], etc." In contrast to Urdang, Országh opens the "professional lexicographer" category to include Conklin, Martin, and even Read, so implicitly the other practical but academic lexicographers in the book's table of contents.

While Urdang exercises his various grudges, Haugen voices concerns not much considered by the other reviewers and also not grounded in the difference between professional lexicographers and others. As a renowned linguist who was also a bilingual lexicographer—his *Norwegian-English Dictionary: A Pronouncing and Translating Dictionary of Modern Norwegian [Bokmål and Nynorsk]: with a Historical and Grammatical Introduction* (1965) appeared just after his review of *PiL*—he transcends those arguments and sees them for what they are, valid but not, perhaps, the dominating issues others make them out to be. Eminence—real, as in Haugen's case, or self-imagined—can interfere with sound reviewing.

Haugen's (1963a, 753) concerns focus not on who, but on what was missing from the book. "There is also virtually no bibliography," he writes, "and no reference to previous discussions of similar topics. Thus, for instance, no awareness is shown by any of the contributors that the question of monolingual definitions was the topic of a whole section at the Eighth International Congress of Linguists in Oslo in 1957, published in its proceedings pages 92–115." Indeed, most of the contributors—Conklin is the notable exception—avoid secondary references, and this is problematic because a foundational text should demonstrate *how* it's foundational, in part by reviewing the relevant literature. Haugen was right in principle, but he exaggerated the omission: the proceedings in question comprise 885 pages, and the "whole section" but a single report (Knudsen and Sommerfeldt 1958) running just over six pages, followed by—irony of ironies—eighteen pages of transcribed post-paper discussion. Conklin doesn't cite the report Haugen had in mind but does cite another item (Wells 1958) in the Oslo proceedings.

Fixation on the conflict between theory and practice obscures still other issues that any A to Z guide to the problems of lexicography must include. Haugen (1963a, 753) reasonably complains that "There is no consideration of the history of dictionary making, except for a passing allusion by Malkiel; and no thought was given to the topic of the social uses of dictionaries." These would, of course, enter A to Z accounts of lexicography in the future, notably in Zgusta's *Manual* (1971) and subsequent works (for instance, Zgusta 2006) and Sidney I. Landau's *Dictionaries: The Art and Craft of Lexicography* (2001), and their absence from the conference, at least, is explained partly by the US Office of Education's interest in bilingual lexicography, but, given the conference personnel, they were certainly unnecessary: Sledd and Read were fully credentialed historians of lexicography, and Read also wrote prolifically on the various social "uses" of dictionaries. Haugen thus correctly identifies missed opportunities.

This all points away from the value of individual contributions to the volume toward the editors and their fashioning of the conference and volume, which was minimal, to say the least, and one justification for the present edition. If it would prove difficult to delimit the conference's topic, the editors, it must be said, did not rise to the challenge, regardless of the generosity with which their role is framed by various reviewers. Franklin (1976, 76), for instance, notes that "There is much reduplication of material in this volume. This was unavoidable, although the editors could have culled out some of the more obvious." Rather than repeat one another, the contributors might have been prodded to do more with their material. As Országh (1963) observed, "There is a noticeable tendency to oversimplification" (400/b) and "the individual contributions could not dig deep enough. Now and then they only lightly touch and skim the manifold and intricate problems of this almost unexplored field and content themselves with mere pronouncements or counsels of perfection instead of solid analysis" (400/a). The editors might have asked for more, especially any more that would allow the editors to shape contributions into a thematically coherent whole.

Tollenaere (1969, 256) identifies an interesting problem of Americans or those strongly influenced by the recent structuralist turn in American linguistics: "In several papers one perceives the American linguist's uneasiness and pessimism about the phenomenon of meaning. He stands in a Bloomfield tradition that considered meaning as a sort of irregularity." The linguists who contributed to *PiL* may have felt superior to lexicographers, but they may also have simply distrusted lexicography—very much a meaning discipline—on linguistic grounds, which, despite the conference's emphasis on bilingual lexicography made the American conference seem, from across the Atlantic, professionally parochial.

Tollenaere (1969, 257) pointed to another supposed deficiency in the organizers' imaginations: "The matter of automation in lexicography was not raised in 1960 at the Indiana conference. At that time the participants were not aware of possibilities in this field," and so, "As regards a recent development in lexicography, however, viz. automation, *P. i. L.* is simply out of date." The latter statement is true to some extent. By 1969, when Tollenaere reviewed the second printing of *PiL*, computer applications in lexicography were more visible than they had been in 1960.[21] In his thorough account of articles on the subject, however, Zgusta (1988, 253, 310–12) lists only four articles of the 1960s, two of them by Tollenaere himself (1962 and 1965) and another a response to Tollenaere's second article (Bahr 1966), all of them subsequent to the 1960 conference and the first edition of the book. In other words, *PiL* wasn't so out of date when it was first published, but by the 1967 printing the ground had shifted.

In fact, several participants had embraced automation in lexicography or related research by the time of the conference. Householder—along with Lyons—was already dabbling in computational linguistics, under the aegis of the Rome Air Development Center, and had been since the beginning of 1960. Worth had begun working on computer-based machine translation— very early in the game—for the RAND Corporation in the 1950s (see, for instance, Worth 1959 and his contribution to the volume, page 204). Urdang—who was present but not presenting—had initiated use of computers at Random House by 1960 (see Urdang 1984). Malkiel, Haas, Martin, and Burrill and Bonsack refer directly to dictionaries and machine translation. Voegelin mentions "the use of computers in lexical work" in his brief prefatory note. And, as mentioned earlier, another attendee, Moyne, became a leading computational linguist. Even Read "welcome[d] the time when we can give the order, 'Switch on the lexicography machine'" (326). Like Urdang and Haugen, Tollenaere had not read the book carefully enough, nor did he know the conference personnel well enough, for his criticism to withstand criticism.

Of all the reviewers, Uitti (1963, 428) proves most insightful about the book's character and most prescient about its influence: "Though it can hardly claim any degree of finality, *PiL* gives a remarkably accurate picture of present-day American research—thought and actual practice—in a widely misunderstood, yet essential, subdivision of language. Lexicography turns out to be not only far less stagnant, but much richer in applications than expected." *PiL* is historically important partly because it's a snapshot of American lexicography in the early 1960s. Franklin (1965, 76) predicted what I have argued interstitially here, that the Indiana University conference was only the beginning and had to be judged as such: "The theoretical contributions that have been mentioned will be better illustrated as these and other authors produce more studies relating to lexicography." As Uitti (1963, 428n23) puts it, "As matters stand, *PiL* is more valuable for its implications than for its accomplishments." Scholars have been trading on those implications now for decades (see chap. 5, in section C of most notes).

Looking Forward

If we consider the influence of *PiL* once it had been firmly established by 1975, we see it gain traction in the late 1970s, first in a little known publication, *Studies in Lexicography as a Science and as an Art* (Glanze 1978), the proceedings of a special session of the Modern Language Association in December of the same year. Gladys E. Saunders (1978, 1) contributed an article titled "Experimental Lexicography in France: Theoretical and Practical Considerations," "The chief purpose" of which was "To acquaint lexicographers in other languages with various techniques most recently used by lexicographers in France, as best exemplified in the pioneer work, *Dictionnaire du français contemporain* (Larousse, 1967) and in its sequel, *Lexis: Larousse de la langue française* (1975)," not a work we expect to cite *PiL*, perhaps, but it did tangentially, and marked the volume's significance in North American lexicography.

As Saunders (1978, 1) explained, "Almost a decade after the publication of the *Dictionnaire du français contemporain* (hereafter DFC), which marked a date in the history of modern French lexicography, appeared another 'innovative' French dictionary: the *Lexis*. Under the skillful direction of Jean Dubois (like its forerunner) and his team of competent lexicographers, the *Lexis* espoused certain of the techniques employed for the first time in its predecessor of nine years, but it altered or dismissed certain others. Unfortunately, little or no account of this experimental lexicography is to be found in American publications." We must take "little or no account" as idiomatic, for while Saunders did not cite Householder and Saporta explicitly, it nonetheless appears among her references, the "little" she has in mind. Saunders (1978, 14) does cite Urdang, however, in a note:

"Urdang (1963) and Zgusta (1971), among others, have noted the need for more exchange among scholars of lexicographic methods and procedures," which certainly takes the edge off Urdang's review of *PiL*. Those references show that *PiL*, among other works, had begun to guide lexicographical inquiry, and, though she seems dismissive of the book, it seems worth noting that none of her other references predate it. It was, at the time, whether considered centrally or peripherally, an indispensable voice in the developing international conversation about dictionaries and their making.

PiL would not remain marginal for long. Zgusta relied on it heavily in his *Manual*, as described above (see also chap. 1). He opened his massive and comprehensive bibliography of lexicographical theory with praise, positioning it at the forefront of disciplinary literature: "The present Bibliography," he wrote, "does not repeat all the items from earlier lists. Speaking in broad terms, the references in the *Manual of Lexicography* are not repeated here, with the exception of the superb Householder/Saporta volume (1962, 3rd ed. 1975), which is exhaustively itemized" (1988, vi). Zgusta thus asserted that *PiL* was the single early work so important that it could not be excluded from a definitive bibliography of the developing field. If its reputation had been simmering for the first decade or so after publication, Zgusta brought it to a boil.

Sidney I. Landau (1984) also relied on *PiL* as a foundational text in his superb textbook, *Dictionaries: The Art and Craft of Lexicography*, which, in North America, codified the discipline and proved influential overseas, too. *PiL* figured most significantly in the first chapter, titled "What Is a Dictionary?" in which Landau calls it "a valuable collection of lexicographic papers" (312n1). Unsurprisingly, he introduces Malkiel's article on dictionary typology (6–7), arguing that, despite criticism, it treated its subject as well as any work on the subject (312n2). But he also cites the pieces by Haas and Harrell, both twice. Malkiel appears briefly again in chapter 3, "Key Elements of Dictionaries and Other Language References," where Martin's contribution to *PiL* appears newly a couple of times. Barnhart's contribution is discussed in chapter 4, on "Definition" (153) and cited three times in chapter 6, "Dictionary Making." When Landau published a second edition of his book in 2001, he brought along all the references to *PiL*. We might put that down to authorial convenience, but also, if it ain't broke, don't fix it, and for all the specific uses to which Landau put it, *PiL* still worked. Landau's second edition projected the value of *PiL* and the underlying conference into the twenty-first century.

In this century, however, *PiL* has lost some of its earlier status, although it maintains a place at a much larger table. A quick look at a few recent handbooks of lexicography fairly represents the situation. For instance, in his magisterial *A Handbook of Lexicography: The Theory and Practice of Dictionary-Making* (2009; published originally in Swedish, 1987), Bo Svensén includes Barnhart's and Malkiel's contributions, as well as Householder and Saporta among his secondary references, but among 508 references overall. Nowadays, even more than Zgusta, the leading theorists include Atkins, Béjoint, Bergenholtz, Bogaards, Cowie, Fontenelle, Hanks, Hartmann, Hausmann, Heid, Herbst, Moon, Rundell, Sinclair, and Wiegand, among other accomplished lexicographers and theorists, too many to list here, rather than the several contributors to *PiL*. While lexicography is lively in North America, undoubtedly, Europe and Asia now dominate its theory and practice, especially that of bilingual and learners' dictionaries.

Other handbooks conform to the recent pattern. Items in Philip Durkin's *Oxford Handbook of Lexicography* (2016) cite Malkiel's omnipresent article, as well as Weinreich's, again, just two bricks in a massive wall of references. But in Howard Jackson's (2013) *Bloomsbury Companion to Lexicography*, only the chapter by Paul Bogaards (2013), "A History of Research in Lexicography," as quoted earlier, cites Householder and Saporta, which frames its value as historical, not currently substantive. Jackson (2013, 407–17) himself compiled the *Companion*'s annotated bibliography, which omits any mention of *PiL*. Other twenty-first-century works suggest that Householder and Saporta's book is far from merely historical, yet it hasn't the presence or prestige that it once had (see chap. 5, in section C of most notes).

In a sense, however, its diminished role in the lexicographical literature reflects its success. Like a foundation stone, we take it for granted and pay more attention to the lexicographical edifice we've built atop it. Handbooks like Jackson's include chapters on corpus lexicography and e-lexicography, subjects Tollenaere and others wisely predicted, around the time *PiL* was published, would soon figure prominently in dictionary making and dictionary research. Attention would turn from the preoccupations of the Bloomington conference to other, rising subjects in the field, and having initiated academic study of lexicography and watched it emerge as an international profession, Householder and Saporta and all of the conference's participants surely wouldn't have it any other way. *PiL* continues resilient as the profession develops beyond all it proposed six decades ago. It is a book of its time, but also worth reading today.

Among other things, *PiL* offers our time a glimpse into what was at stake in lexicography during the 1950s, 1960s, and 1970s, not just the topics that preoccupied lexicographers and linguists then but also the ideologies that formed those disciplines and drove the discourse. When Kenneth Pike (1999, 3) wrote that Mary Haas figured prominently in "the explosive age of descriptive linguistics," he was doubly ideological, not just an advocate of a descriptive turn in American linguistics but an advocate because that turn enabled the missionary work of the Summer Institute of Linguistics (see chap. 1 and note 7). Our own attitudes toward language, linguistics, and lexicography reflect development from and away from the commitments of earlier generations; that is, we can only fully understand what we're doing if we know its intellectual and ideological lineage. From the vantage of history, we can take reception of *PiL* as part of its story, as a sometimes sharper enactment of ideologies—language ideologies, lexicographical ideologies, professional ideologies—that pervade the book and its chapters largely unacknowledged.

4

TEXT

The textual history of *PiL* is relatively straightforward. It appeared in four imprints, sometimes implausibly called "editions" in library records and bibliographies, as follows:

- It was first published in April 1962 as a freestanding supplement to the *International Journal of American Linguistics* (vol. 28, no. 2; henceforth, *IJAL*), in the journal's cream paper covers. The front cover reads,

PART IV

International Journal of American Linguistics

Volume 28 Number 2

APRIL 1962

Publication Twenty-one
of the

INDIANA UNIVERSITY RESARCH CENTER

in

ANTHROPOLOGY, FOLKLORE, AND LINGUISTICS
PROBLEMS IN LEXICOGRAPHY

Edited by Fred W. Householder
and Sol Saporta.

Individuals and libraries subscribing to *IJAL* received the supplement as a matter of course.

- *PiL* was also published as a book beyond the purview of *IJAL* in 1962, "Publication Twenty-one" in a series sponsored by the Indiana University Research Center in Anthropology, Folklore, and Linguistics edited by C. F. Voegelin, with Thomas A. Sebeok as Director of Publications for the center. *IJAL* was also a product of Indiana University, at the time also edited by Voegelin. The title page of this impression originally read:

PROBLEMS IN LEXICOGRAPHY

Report of the Conference on Lexicography

Held at Indiana University
November 11–12, 1960

Edited by
Fred W. Householder
and
Sol Saporta

Bloomington 1962

just as it had in the *IJAL* supplement. My copy of this imprint tells an interesting story, however. The brown, linen-finished paper covers identify Mouton & Co. as the publisher, but either Mouton wasn't always the publisher or wasn't the only publisher. A label reading "Mouton & Co." has been pasted over "Bloomington 1962" on the title page—one can read the original designation backwards, through the copyright page. The brown covers, in other words, may have been unique to the Mouton impression; the Indiana University Research Center in Anthropology, Folklore, and Linguistics series publication may have had different covers. It appears that, after the book had been published in the series, it was copublished and distributed by Mouton. Those who bought it as a volume separate from the journal paid $6.00.
- The book was published again, with changes and corrections, in 1967. The copyright page claims that it was a "[Second Edition with Additions and Corrections]." Whereas copies of the non-*IJAL* 1962 imprint are relatively rare, copies of the 1967 printing abound in libraries, personal and institutional. Its paper covers are light grey with dark grey bands toward the top and bottom on the front, but not across the spine and onto the back cover. In white lettering on

the top band we read "Fred W. Householder and Sol Saporta"; on the bottom band, also in white letters, "INDIANA UNIVERSITY, BLOOMINGTON / Mouton & Co., The Hague, The Netherlands," with Mouton clearly secondary on the marquee, but not as an afterthought this time. "**PROBLEMS IN LEXICOGRAPHY**" appears in red ink in the center of the cover. The title page of this imprint was revised and reformatted from that of 1962:

PROBLEMS IN LEXICOGRAPHY

Edited by FRED W. HOUSEHOLDER
and SOL SAPORTA

Published by

INDIANA UNIVERSITY, BLOOMINGTON

Mouton & Co., The Hague, The Netherlands

The overseas price is not recorded, but in the United States, by 1967, the book's price had increased to $7.00.

- The book was republished again, with a few superficial changes, in 1975. The front matter was once again revised and reformatted, although the text itself is otherwise exactly that of the 1967 impression. The copyright page records this imprint as the "Third edition," but the changes incorporated are so slight that they do not warrant the designation. The title page reads:

PROBLEMS IN LEXICOGRAPHY

Edited by
FRED W. HOUSEHOLDER
and
SOL SAPORTA

Published by

INDIANA UNIVERISITY, BLOOMINGTON

and there is no mention of Mouton & Co. The cover format replicates that of 1967, but with glossy paper of dusty pink, with brick-red bands to replace the grey ones of the preceding imprint. In this case, the bands do cross the spine and across the back cover. Mouton &

Co. is missing from the bottom band, of course. Both sides of the back cover list publications in the University Research Center in Anthropology, Folklore, and Linguistics and other related series, as did that of the 1967 imprint, although the lists are different.

Except for the reformatted frontmatter, the changes—outlined below—and the covers, the text is identical from imprint to imprint, generated from the original camera-ready copy, with changes in 1967 inserted into that copy. Regardless of copublishing arrangements, indicated variously on the covers and title pages, Indiana University retained sole copyright over all four impressions. The four editions are also paged identically, viii–286.

In 1962, the *IJAL* per se (Part I) ran to 303 pages over four numbers and was accompanied by seven supplements, somewhat confusingly attached to the journal's four regular issues: *Materials and Techniques for the Language Laboratory*, edited by Edward W. Najam (Part II, vol. 28, no. 1, January 1962); *The Grammatical Structure of Oaxaca Chontal*, by Viola Waterhouse (Part II, vol. 28, no. 2, April 1962); *In Feudal Africa*, by Edwin M. Loeb (Part II, vol. 28, no. 3, July 1962); *Verb Morphology of Modern Greek*, by Andreas Koutsoudas (Part II, vol. 28, no. 4, October 1962); *The Vowels and Tones of Standard Thai: Acoustical Measurements and Experiments*, by Arthur S. Abrahamson (Part III, vol. 28, no. 2, April 1962); *PiL*, edited by Fred W. Householder and Sol Saporta (Part IV, vol. 28, no. 2, April 1962); and *The Five Clocks*, by Martin Joos (Part V, V,vol. 28, no. 2, April 1962). Besides *PiL*, the works by Najam, Waterhouse, Koutsoudas, Abrahamson, and Joos, were also published in the University Research Center series—April 1962 was a busy month. Though a classic, *PiL* did not achieve cult status, like *The Five Clocks*.

When *PiL* was reissued in 1967, Voegelin was still editor of the University Research Center in Anthropology, Folklore, and Linguistics series, but Sebeok had been promoted to chairman of the Research Center, replaced by Andrew Vazsonyi as Director of Publications. Reprinting itself indicates the unexpected success of the original imprint, due partly to the international distribution that association with Mouton guaranteed. The so-called second edition, also published with Mouton, was successful enough, in turn, to prompt the further corrected reprint of 1975. The last imprint, however, which was not published by Mouton, seems to have met with less success. Currently, only one library worldwide holds a copy of it, which suggests that earlier imprints had saturated the library market.

The additions and corrections to the second impression, as Félicien de Tollenaere (1969, 253) noted in his review, were "neither numerous . . .

nor important, apart from postscripts and new references." He "found 10 specimens," but, in fact, there are a few more than that. Changes are easily located, because they mostly appear in lighter type, though not, I think, in a different font, as Tollenaere suggests. Changes were made on sheets of the first edition, which were then rephotographed—production in both cases was camera-ready. No change forced repagination. Although not especially important, some changes were relatively expansive and are not easily represented in a list, though I have no choice but to do so here, as follows:

    p. v   1967 (now of the University of Washington). ~ 1962 (now of the University of Concepcion, Chile).

    p. 43   1967 "On the Semantic Structure of Language," in *Universals of Language* (ed. J. H. Greenburg), 2nd ed., Cambridge, Mass., 1966, pp. 142–216 [corrected and reformatted, this edition] ~ 1962 "Semantic Universals," to appear in *Universals in Language* (ed. Joseph H. Greenberg) in 1962.

    pp. 43–44   1967 POSTSCRIPT added

    p. 45   1967 The ideal bilingual dictionary would anticipate every conceivable need of the prospective user. ~ 1962 Ideally speaking, the bilingual dictionary would anticipate every conceivable need of the prospective user.

    p. 48   1967 It is *not* true, however, that he derives any benefit from wasting even as much as five minutes finding out what geese means if he has not yet learned that particular irregular plural. [reformatted this edition] ~ 1962 It is *not* true, however, that he derives any benefit from wasting even as much as five minutes finding out what geese means if, by chance, he has not yet learned that particular irregular plural.

    p. 50   1967 note 1 added

    p. 50   1967 note 2 added

    p. 50   1967 Among monolingual dictionaries, however, Random House's *ACD* contains more of these features than any other dictionary I know. ~ 1962 In the realm of monolingual dictionaries, however, Random House's *ACD* contains more of these features than any other dictionary I know. [reformatted this edition]

    p. 50   1967 For some time past Danish-English dictionaries printed in Denmark have been almost unique in using English "four-letter" words to translate their Danish counterparts. In 1966 it is possible to state that recent trends in the United States are towards greater liberalization in these matters. Webster's *Third International*, a leading monolingual dictionary, has largely eliminated the omission of such words and bilingual dictionaries will probably follow suit. However, greater liberalization entails greater attention to item (4) and we find that Webster's *Third* carefully labels these words as "usu. considered vulgar" or "usu. considered obscene." [reformatted this edition] ~ 1962 Danish-English dictionaries printed in Denmark are the only dictionaries I know which use English "four-letter words" to translate their Danish counterparts. The result is not obscene—it is simply straightforward and accurate translation.

p. 50   1967 Since Random House's monolingual *ACD* provides exactly what is recommended here, it hardly seems necessary to point out that the information would be even more useful in a bilingual dictionary. [reformatted this edition] ~ 1962 In the realm of monolingual dictionaries, on the other hand, we again find that Random House's *ACD* provides exactly what is here recommended. If it has proven desirable to provide this information even for the native speaker, think how much more useful it would be in a bilingual dictionary.

p. 75   1967 I am not convinced that any one method is sufficient; perhaps there cannot be any one approach for some obscure theoretical reason. ~ 1962 At the moment I am not convinced that any one method is sufficient; perhaps there cannot be any one approach for some obscure theoretical reason.

p. 76   1967 Such *indices a tergo* are now available for Latin, ancient Greek, Italian, Biblical Hebrew, and Russian. For other languages the best that compilers have been able to produce are the deficient rhyming dictionaries. [reformatted this edition] ~ 1962 Such *indices a tergo* are now available for Latin, ancient Greek, Biblical Hebrew, and Russian. For other languages the best that compilers have been able to produce are the deficient rhyming dictionaries.

p. 102   1967 POSTSCRIPT added
p. 119   1967 Yale University ~ 1962 Columbia University
p. 123   This procedure clearly marks *1*, *2*, and *3* semantically exocentric, unitary lexemes; *4* as a composite lexeme; and *5* and *6* as non-lexemic, semantically endocentric constructions the initial lexeme of which is superordinately related to *4*. [reformatted this edition] ~ 1962 This procedure clearly marks *1*, *2*, and *3* semantically exocentric, unitary lexemes; *4* as a complex lexeme; and *5* and *6* as non-lexemic, semantically endocentric constructions the initial lexeme of which is superordinately related to *4*.

p. 137   1967 [Published in *Proceedings, Ninth Pacific Science Congress, 1957,* 4: 299–301, Bangkok, 1962.] [reformatted this edition]
p. 150   1967 NOTE added

Some of the additions, one suspects, capture elements of the lively discussion that surrounded the conference papers but were otherwise unrecorded for posterity. For instance, Mary Haas's treatment of the *American College Dictionary*, represented at the conference by its editor, Clarence L. Barnhart, in endnotes to her contribution (p. 50) may respond to Barnhart's on-site comments.

Changes to the 1975 imprint were yet more limited, as summarized in a memo from Nancy Quinn to Nancy Diamond, both the Linguistics program's secretary and the secretary supporting the Indiana University Research Center in Anthropology, Folklore, and Linguistics series: "Dr. Householder would like to make the following corrections: In the Foreword: line 9– . . . the late Austin E. Fife [/] add late [/] lines 9, 12 & 14—delete 'now' when used" (C450, Box 9, Publications, Miscellaneous). In fact, the 1975 text correctly inserts "the late" before Fife's name, rather than precisely what had been ordered. The text presented here incorporates these few changes and also corrects the errors introduced in 1967 while otherwise maintaining the 1967 text.

The three "editions" vary little from one another, but the articles within *PiL* vary considerably in the ways they cite sources, deploy punctuation, and so forth, and the whole book falls short of the sort of editorial regularity we've come to expect from university press published books. The present text thus updates the former ones in a wide array of publishers' conventions and attempts to bring the book to a pitch of formal consistency, without altering the substance much. I have supplied a references section that covers the introduction and the text, as well as an index, both conspicuously absent from the original publications.

Within the articles I have imposed a different kind of order, because they were not carefully edited in 1962 and remained unchanged in subsequent printings, except in the instances itemized above. Many such changes are trivial enough, which, one supposes, explains why the editors didn't bother to make them. For instance, Malkiel's punctuation appears outside of quotation marks—"human element".—while most of the other authors place the punctuation inside. Some apply the convention inconsistently within their chapters. Other changes reflect the history of academic publishing and printing and the difference between camera-ready copy generated on typewriters and conventional printing. Perhaps the most obvious of such adjustments is the use of italics rather than underlining for lexical items and book titles. Conklin included references at the end of his contribution and used parenthetical citations within it. Others, like Burrill and Bonsack, provided references in endnotes. Still others referred to works without providing bibliographical information at all, even resorting on occasion to short titles. That casual approach to sources also reflects the historical development of linguistics and lexicography. In 1962, both were relatively new academic subjects, and those practicing either knew the still spare professional literature well enough to drop titles among colleagues without further ado. Nowadays, many of these works are less familiar, so the current edition inserts parenthetical citations consistently throughout, keyed to the references section, in all but a few cases, where the books in question are so rare that I couldn't find the works or construct full references for them.

All sorts of irregularities within chapters have been regularized throughout the book in this edition. Gleason's article serves as a handy example for what I mean. Gleason capitalized elements of his section headings, as in "1. Scope of the Paper" and "2. Attitudes toward Grammar and Lexicon," that is, until he didn't, as in "3. The Bloomfield tradition" and "4. Current neglect of lexicon and dictionaries." He did not close those headings with periods—most would agree with that decision, I suspect—except when he did, just once, in "9. Class versus member." Again, striving for consistency in such matters of style is assumed in twenty-first century university press publishing and probably uncontroversial, even when republishing less consistent works of the past.

Only in a few instances have I intruded stylistically into authors' voices, imposed words on them, or omitted words they wrote. In the first instance, I have tried to set a consistent pattern of comma use. The authors varied widely in their use of commas, and, of course, we don't all agree on when and why they are necessary or appropriate anyway. Most readers and copy editors agree that I use more commas than they prefer, but at least they are deployed much more consistently in the text revised here than in the original. In the second instance, some authors using numbered sections followed the numbers with section headings and some did not (Haas, for instance). If headings serve readers in some cases, they probably do so in all cases, so I wrote headings for some of Weinreich's unlabeled sections; then, I omitted the numbers in Haas's and Read's contributions because none of their sections had headings. In the third instance, I omitted and replaced a few words (pronominal sentence heads, for instance) or borrowed them from the first sentence of a section into the section heading.

As an editor of journals and books, I have required such changes and many others besides. Had I edited *PiL* in the first place, the style throughout would be cleaner, some potentially confusing sections rewritten, the evidence more plentiful or robust, and so on. I would have intruded editorially in ways Householder and Saporta did not. But I haven't imposed broad revisions on *PiL* after the historical fact. We need to assess the book as it was and is, not as we might wish it to be.

5

CONTRIBUTORS AND CONTRIBUTIONS

Besides lacking references and an index, *PiL* also lacked notes on its contributors, though affiliations are indicated under the author's name under the title of each chapter. Today, one might find notes that outline a contributor's career and credentials, but often one finds a table of contributors with affiliations, no more informative an approach than that Householder and Saporta took. Some contributors to *PiL* are still well known to practitioners but not universally and not necessarily across generations—no one fresh out of graduate school today will meet any of the contributors at conferences but will know them only from their major works. Given the historical aspect of this new edition, it seems more than fitting to include substantial notes about them. Of course, the length and density of each note depends on the amount of information available on the contributor and his or her works, including the contribution to *PiL*.

Here, I provide a note, arranged in three sections, for each contributor. Section A is a short biography of the contributor; section B explains how the contribution to *PiL* extended the author's previous work and informed later projects; section C encapsulates the contribution's influence in linguistics, lexicography, anthropology, onomastics, and so forth, through the decades since *PiL* was first published. Section C is not a register of citations but merely illustrates the contribution's influence in lines of research pursued by scholars other than the author(s).

Clarence L. Barnhart

A. Barnhart (1900–1993) was born near Plattsburgh, Missouri, and took his undergraduate degree from the University of Chicago in 1930 (McMullen 1994). He completed three years of graduate work, where he had his first taste of lexicography, in courses taught by Sir William A. Craigie, one of the *OED*'s principal editors (Gilliver 2016, 444). He supported himself while in school by working first in the shipping department but later as an editor at the Chicago publisher, Scott Foresman. There, he supervised publication of the Columbia University psychologist Edward L. Thorndike's school dictionaries, based on lists Thorndike had compiled of the most frequent words read at various levels in school, including the *Thorndike-Century Junior Dictionary* (Thorndike and Barnhart 1935) and the *Thorndike-Century Senior Dictionary* (Thorndike and Barnhart 1941), revised editions of which, in the 1980s, were renamed "Thorndike-Barnhart" dictionaries. While serving during World War II, Barnhart supervised compilation of the *Dictionary of United States Army Terms* (Barnhart et al. 1944). After the war, he published *The American College Dictionary* (Barnhart et al. 1947), out of which grew the *Random House Dictionary of the English Language* (1966), edited by Jess Stein. Other significant works include *The New Century Cyclopedia of Names* (Barnhart and Halsey 1956), *The World Book Dictionary* (1963), and *The Barnhart Dictionary of New Words since 1963* (C. Barnhart, Stein, and R. Barnhart 1973), the first in a series edited with Stein and Barnhart's son, Robert. He collaborated with his other lexicographer son, David, in the *Barnhart Dictionary Companion: A Quarterly of New Words*, from 1982 until his death a decade later. In his obituary of Barnhart, Allen Walker Read (1994, 216) declared, "The death of Clarence Barnhart has taken away America's preeminent lexicographer. This is so generally acknowledged that I need not dwell on it."

B. Barnhart wrote several important articles on lexicography, despite the demands of commercial dictionary making, among them "Establishing and Maintaining Standard Patterns of Speech" (1957); "Plan for a Central Archive for Lexicography in English" (1973); and overviews of "General Dictionaries" (1969) and "American Lexicography, 1945–1973" (1978). The articles tend to focus on practical dictionary concerns, but in historically and linguistically well-informed ways—Barnhart "effectively juggled commercial demands against the requirements of sound scholarship" (Read 1994, 219). Two of them, at least, might be called classics, as they were prominently reprinted: Barnhart (1957) in Harold B. Allen's anthology, *Readings in Applied English Linguistics* (Allen 1958), and his contribution to *PiL* in both Allen (1964) and R. R. K. Hartmann's (2003) *Lexicography: Critical Concepts*.

C. Barnhart's contribution to *PiL* quickly entered the literature (see, for instance Quirk 1973), and many who write about practical problems of lexicography have turned to it (for instance, De Schryver and Prinsloo 2013). It also appears in articles focused on college dictionaries, which, given Barnhart's triumphant *American College Dictionary*, comes as no surprise (see, for instance, Arnold 1980–1981, via Allen 1964; Siegel 2007). Most important, however, as Robert Lew (2015b) writes, "Until fairly recently, dictionary users were not usually of central concern in the process of dictionary making, however strange it may sound today. Instead, the emphasis was largely on dictionary content and often on how to pack a lot into manageable physical space. The impulse for change is generally identified to have been Barnhart (1962), with attention to dictionary users." Thus, the practical, commercially minded Barnhart became the progenitor of metalexicography that privileges user perspectives, which is why works on the subject so often cite his *PiL* paper (see, for instance, Hartmann 1987a, 1987b, and 1998; Battenburg 1991; Lan 1998; Stark 1999; Dolezal and McCreary 1999; and Lew 2015a), and handbooks like those by Svensén (1993 and 2009) position it as such. One should note that Haas makes a case for user-friendliness in her contribution, too, and the subject rises often enough throughout *PiL* that Householder's concluding report identifies user perspectives as one of the conference's central themes.

Edwin Bonsack Jr.

A. Bonsack (1918–2005) began and finished his career as a scholar of Germanic languages, having taken BA and MA degrees from the University of Pennsylvania, where he taught German from 1946–1951, before taking a job with the Department of the Interior as a scientific linguist in the Office of Geography, where he worked under his coauthor, Meredith F. Burrill. In 1967, he took the position of cataloger of Scandinavian materials at the Library of Congress (information drawn freely from Anonymous 1972, 438). Besides a few articles on Scandinavian subjects, he is best known for a book about Dvalinn (1983), a dwarf who frequently appears in Old Norse literature.

B. His contribution with Burrill stems, not from his earlier teaching or scholarship, but from their professional proximity in 1960. He left toponyms behind when he left the Office of Geography and returned to matters Scandinavian.

C. Lexicographers and linguists did not make up the article's audience, and onomasticians seem to have overlooked it, probably because it appeared in a book with the wrong sort of title to attract their attention, and despite Burrill's reputation among them. The few citations come early, both in lexicography (Al-Kasimi 1977) and onomastics (Brown 1964; Grant 1966), with Wiegand (1995) the most recent citation I have located.

Meredith F. Burrill

A. Burrill (1902–1997) grew up in Maine, attended Bates College, did his graduate work at Clark University, taught at Oklahoma A & M University—where he overlapped with Sherman M. Kuhn, eventually chief editor of the *Middle English Dictionary* (Reidy 1984, ix)—and ended up, from 1943 to 1973, executive secretary of the US Board on Geographic Names (Thomas 1997; I draw freely on this obituary here). For decades, he advocated toponymic standardization at the United Nations and was a leader in the naming of Antarctica (see, for instance, Burrill, Bertrand, and Alberts 1956; Burrill 1957; Thomas 1997, D19/b). He was president of the American Name Society in 1955, and of the American Association of Geographers in 1965. His work on geographic names was collected and published posthumously (Burrill 2004), and the American Association of Geographers presents an annual award named after him, which suggests his professional standing. If you ever visit Antarctica, look out for Mount Burrill. He was "a toponymist's toponymist who made a name for himself as the world's foremost authority on what people variously—and sometimes perversely—call the earth's lakes, rivers, mountains, seas, cities, towns and other physical features and political subdivisions" (Thomas 1997, D19/a).

B. Burrill and Bonsack's contribution to *PiL* reflected Burrill's ongoing concerns, rather than Bonsack's. Burrill had written a fair amount about generic terms in toponyms before the Bloomington conference (1956a, 1956b, and 1956c, for example), and very early in his career wrote about problems of language planning and policy in naming places (1949). As with Conklin, language was only one of Burrill's professional subjects, but within toponymy he was especially famous for a lifetime interest in the generic names on which his article with Bonsack focuses (Thomas 1997, D19/b).

C. See the parallel section in the note on Bonsack.

O. L. Chavarría-Aguilar

A. Chavarría-Aguilar (1922–2005), a native of Costa Rica, took his PhD at the University of Pennsylvania in 1952, with a dissertation titled "A Grammar of Pashto." After a stint in India, where he published *Lectures in Linguistics*

(1954), he spent a decade at the University of Michigan (1957–1967), concurrently with Penzl, his *PiL* co-author, interrupted with a further sojourn in India, this time under the aegis of USAID, to organize an English department at the Indian Institute of Technology (O'Brien 2005, on which I draw freely here). While at Michigan, he published a book on the Pashto writing system (1962b)—orthography was an abiding interest (see, for instance, 1988)—a Pashto textbook (1962a), as well as one in Hindi (Chavarría-Aguilar and Pray 1961). None of these was a mainstream publication, which, I suspect, explains why Chavarría-Aguilar has left a smaller footprint in his chosen disciplines than other contributors to *PiL* have in theirs. His academic career may also have interfered with the sort of scholarly prominence achieved by many other contributors, too. He left Michigan to serve as chair of the Department of Linguistics at the University of Rochester, then moved to the City College of New York as dean of the College of Arts and Sciences, a position sure to short-circuit a scholarly career. Finally, he returned to Costa Rica to teach at the Universidad Nacional in Heredia, where, in retirement, he wrote two cookbooks (1994 and 2001) and, apparently, a lot of poetry.

B. Chavarría-Aguilar never wrote about dictionaries directly, except in *PiL*.

C. Al-Kasimi (1977) is the only work I have found that cites Chavarría-Aguilar and Penzl.

Harold C. Conklin

A. Conklin (1926–2016) is an extraordinarily interesting person. Apparently genial, he was also clearly a genius, with a happy tendency to encounter and the will to seize opportunities. While growing up in Patchogue, Long Island, he visited the 1933 Chicago World's Fair, where he was "invited to join a performance by a group of Plains Indians" (Dove and Kirch 2018, 2). Six years later, he was adopted by the Akwesasne Mohawk, and he worked as the only non-Native American "Indian lore" counselor at various First Nations summer camps. At the same time, he "was given a part-time volunteer position (1941–1943) in anthropology at the American Museum of Natural History" (Conklin 1998, xv; I draw freely on this source, as well as Dove and Kirch 2018). While at the University of California at Berkeley, he worked at the Berkeley Cyclotron and as a "hasher" at the Gamma Phi Beta sorority house, where he met a young Javanese cook from whom he learned Malay. He served in the United States Army from 1944 to 1945, and was stationed in the Philippines, the accident on which his career as an anthropologist of Philippine indigenous peoples, especially the Hanunóo and Ifugao, was founded, and which culminated in his *Ethnographic Atlas of Ifugao: A Study of Environment, Culture, and Society in Northern Luzon* (1980). After taking his PhD at Yale in 1954, he taught for eight years at Columbia University, then returned to Yale, where he eventually became the Franklin Muzzy Crosby Professor of Anthropology and curator of the Peabody Museum of Natural History. He was elected to the National Academy of Sciences and the American Academy of Arts and Sciences (both in 1976). Conklin (1998, xxvii) described himself reflected in other people: "In the field I have been inspired repeatedly by the intelligence, patience, and enduring friendship of many neighbors and friends, from small children to toothless elders. They have all served not just as respondents but as close coinvestigators of other cultural worlds. Often accompanied by zest, humor, and wit, their conduct, words, and shared understandings of ecological and cultural relations have made ethnographic field work a challenging and intellectually exciting enterprise." This captures the essence of the man, which explains why everyone he encountered, from the Plains Indians to his coinvestigators, wanted to adopt him as one of their own.

B. Of all the items in *PiL*, Conklin's has proven most influential—its audience has continually widened. Besides *PiL*, it appeared in Joshua Fishman's (1968) much-reprinted *Readings in the Sociology of Language*, as well as Steven A. Tyler's (1969) anthology, *Cognitive Anthropology*. In the meantime, what appealed to linguists and lexicographers turned to face sociolinguists and sociologists, too, while Conklin's natural disciplinary audience, the anthropologists, received his hundreds of offprints (see chap. 1) and referred to either of the nonanthropological texts when necessary, over a generation. The chapter was printed again in a collection of Conklin's (2007) most important articles in anthropology, extending its influence well into the twenty-first century. Language and lexicography were but a fraction of his interests. His *Hanunóo–English Vocabulary* (1953) was published before he completed his PhD. His contribution to *PiL*, an extension and perfection of Conklin (1957), stemmed from that work but also his dissertation, "The Relation of Hanunóo Culture to the Plant World" (1954), and led, not to more lexicography, but to *Folk Classification: A Topically Arranged Bibliography of Contemporary and Background References through 1971* (1972). He was an "outside consultant" on Austronesian etymologies and definitions for *Webster's Third* (1961) and, significantly, reviewed Zgusta's *Manual of Lexicography* (Conklin 1975).

C. As Weinreich worked over the semantic theory he presented at the Bloomington conference, he incorporated Conklin's paper (Weinreich 1968 and 1972), but others also cited it early on, not all of them uncritically (see Burling 1964). It has worn well in the literature of semantics, still cited in the twenty-first century (see, for example, Geeraerts 2010). Berlin, Breedlove, and Raven (1973, 214) identify the beginnings of classification in folk biology as "about 1954," essentially with Conklin's (1954) dissertation (though see Mayr, Linsley, and Usinger 1953), and explain (Berlin et al. 1973, 240n4) that their approach to Tzeltal plant taxonomy "derives in large part from Harold Conklin's important paper on the nature of folk taxonomies (Conklin 1962)." That annotation is typical as the article's influence extended from biological taxonomies in various cultures to law (Black and Metzger 1965) and other subjects, like translation (see, for example, Nida 2001). The published paper was thus a point of reticulation for many a discipline. The cognitive element of Conklin's argument has not been overlooked, either in semantics or in anthropology, and has influenced the development of folk biology more generally: "Cognitive anthropology is responsible for initially mapping out folk-biology as a field of study (Conklin 1962)" (Coley et al. 1999, 205). Conklin's article is present in Zgusta (1971)—well below the rates of Malkiel, Gleason, Weinreich, Swanson, Martin, and others—but its influence is not primarily lexicographical. When it reappears in dictionary discourse it is, unsurprisingly, in the cognitive semantic arena (see, for example, Wierzbicka 1985, 156 and 200).

William S. Cornyn

A. Cornyn (1906–1971) took his undergraduate degree from UCLA and his graduate degrees from Yale University, where he studied with Leonard Bloomfield and subsequently taught, serving for a considerable time as chair of the Department of Slavic Languages and Literatures (Schenker 1971, 718; I draw freely on this obituary here). He wrote the pioneering textbook *Beginning Russian* (1950) but also wrote and compiled many works for the study of Burmese, including *Spoken Burmese* (1945–46)—in the same ACLS series as works by Haas, the Kahanes, and Penzl—an anthology of texts (1957), a glossary (Cornyn and Musgrave 1958), and *Beginning Burmese* (Cornyn and Roop 1968). Much of his career focused on language pedagogy, in which he followed Bloomfield's "behavioristic approach," whereby "the student recreates, as it were, the process of acquisition of his first language" (Schenker 1971, 718–19). He toiled away on a Burmese-English dictionary, "emphasizing modern colloquial speech, and having a scope of from 30 to 40 thousand words . . . Work on this dictionary was begun by Dr. Cornyn under a grant from the American Council of Learned Societies. A final manuscript is to be completed in 1961. The dictionary will be published by Yale University Press" (US Office of Education 1960, 22/b). But it wasn't, nor ever, finished, though clearly Cornyn (1967, 778) expected to complete it well after this announced deadline.

B. Cornyn's role in the conference and *PiL* less reflects the success of his Burmese glossary than the promise of his never-completed bilingual dictionary, into which, unfortunately, it provides little insight, although he compares languages from the Burmese family with Greek and Turkish, as presented in the session for which he was responsible, by the Kahanes and Tietze, respectively.

C. Sections titled "Comments" are rarely cited, and, except for the general works discussed earlier in this introduction, Cornyn's comments have drawn little scholarly notice.

William Gedney

A. Gedney (1915–1999) grew up in Washington State, attended Whitman College there, and proceeded to Yale University, where he studied Sanskrit. During World War II, he worked in the Army Language Unit on the *Dictionary of United States Army Terms* (Barnhart et al. 1944), and thereafter as an associate editor on the *American College Dictionary* (Barnhart et al. 1947) while he finished his graduate work (Harris and Chamberlain 1975, vii–ix; I draw freely from this account). From 1960 on, he taught at the University of Michigan, serving as interim chair and then chair of the Department of Linguistics (1970–75). He was "instrumental in developing language programs for the earliest Peace Corps training programs" (Hudak 2000, 223; I draw freely on this obituary, as well), and wrote *English for Speakers of Thai* (Gedney 1956), so he very much attended to bilingual matters and language pedagogy. He donated his collection of Thai books and materials—over 14,000 items—to Michigan in 1975 (Hudak 2000, 223). Gedney's students and colleagues in the United States, Thailand, and around the world honored him with no less than five festschrifts (Gething 1975; Harris and Chamberlain 1975; Gething and Liên 1979; Bickner, Hudak, and Peyasanitwong 1986; and Compton and Hartmann 1992).

B. At first glance, Gedney seems not to have done any lexicography after the 1940s, but, in fact, he was a continual but unpublished lexicographer. For decades, while conducting "strenuous fieldwork" (Hudak 2000, 223), he collected material on some twenty-two Thai languages and dialects, including lexical material, which he compiled into glossaries. The results of that fieldwork remained unpublished until Thomas J. Hudak organized them into a series of books (for example, Gedney 1991 and 1993), including a Saek-English, English-Saek dictionary (Gedney and Hudak 2010). His "Comments" in *PiL* are simply ancillary to all that work.

C. Sections titled "Comments" are rarely cited, and, except for the general works discussed earlier in this introduction, Gedney's comments have drawn little scholarly notice.

H. A. Gleason, Jr.

A. Gleason (1917–2007) graduated with a degree in botany from Cornell University and was long associated with the Hartford Seminary Foundation, from which he took his PhD in 1946 (Apgar and Moulton 1956, 476) and at which he taught until relocating to the University of Toronto, in 1967, for the rest of his academic career (Forrest 2007). He wrote two unusually influential books, *Introduction to Descriptive Linguistics* (1955) and *Linguistics and English Grammar* (1965). In their review of the former, Apgar and Moulton (1956, 469–70) wondered at Gleason's boldness at writing such a book after Bloomfield's *Language* (1933)—"Who would dare to rewrite the Bible, even though more and more parts of it should be declared apocryphal?" Though they had plenty of criticisms and were sure that "better books than Gleason's will be written," they also agreed that "until they are, our growing science can use his with profound gratitude" (Apgar and Moulton 1956, 477). The latter, too, has had considerable continual influence since its publication, despite a lengthy, largely negative review by Sledd (1966). Gleason figured prominently in twentieth-century American linguistics. Writing about its history, Koerner (2002) refers to Haas, Hoenigswald, Householder, Malkiel, and especially Weinreich, among those contributing to *PiL*, as well as Sebeok and Voegelin, and Gleason, too, but not the others. Enthusiastic about more or less all the contents of *PiL* and their contributors, Zgusta (1971, 15) singled out Gleason in his *Manual* as "a scholar of our epoch." Himself a missionary and pastor (see Gleason 1962), Gleason influenced the practice of linguists in the Summer Institute of Linguistics, though he did not participate in the organization (Rensch 1977, 95). A festschrift (Avery et al. 1983) celebrated his career.

B. Gleason's interest in the intersection of language structure and meaning leads into *Linguistics and English Grammar*, but that's a much larger work, and the contribution to *PiL* merely a premonition. Gleason's lexicographical commitments were few. He had been an "outside consultant" on language names for *Webster's Third*. And he planned a dictionary of linguistic terminology (Gates 1979, 115)—"We linguists are inordinately proud of our jargon," he wrote, explaining how he resisted too much of it in *An Introduction to Descriptive Linguistics* (Gleason 1974, 17)—and it's clear that he made some progress, since a manual of procedures had been drawn up finally enough to be cited (Roberts, Yoder, and Valdman 1980–81, 144), but the work was never completed. In view of that project, he wrote about collecting a corpus to support a technical dictionary (Gleason 1961) and also contributed a paper on "grammatical prerequisites" to McDavid and Duckert (1973). Nevertheless, he was a long time member of the Dictionary Society of North America, probably introduced to the society by his former student and erstwhile colleague, J. Edward Gates (see Adams 2014, 17–18; Adams 2019, 23–24).

C. Gleason's contribution to *PiL* has maintained a role in the lexicographical literature for decades, cited, for instance, in Tollenaere (1973)—somewhat surprisingly, given his negative review of the book (see chap. 3)—McMillan (1978), Jackson (1985), Benson, Benson, and Ilson (1986), Nguyen (1986), Toury (1989), Béjoint (1994), Yong and Peng (2007), and Béjoint (2010). It raised questions that have proved important to computer applications in lexicography (see, for instance, Janssen 1971; Coward and Grimes 1995), but its influence has not extended into the era of e-lexicography. In linguistics more broadly, Lehrer (1969) identifies it as the first essay toward a structural semantics; see also Nida (1975).

Mary R. Haas

A. Haas (1910–1996) was a leading scholar of Amerindian languages and reconstruction of their protolanguages (see Golla and Matisoff 1997, 828). She studied with Edward Sapir, first at the University of Chicago and then at Yale, where she earned her doctorate in 1935 and lit the fuse of "the explosive age of descriptive linguistics" (K. Pike 1999, 3; I draw freely on this account and that of Golla and Matisoff). She was elected to the American Academy of Arts and Sciences (1974) and the National Academy of Sciences (1978) and received honorary degrees from Northwestern University (1975), University of Chicago (1976), Ohio State University (1980), and her alma mater, Earlham College (1980). She was president of the Linguistic Society of America in 1963. For most of her career, she taught at the University of California at Berkeley, where she cofounded the Department of Linguistics, in 1953 (Matisoff 1997, 594). Haas's bibliography in Amerindian studies exceeds summary here—it would have justified the careers of several linguists (see Turner 1997). In the run-up to World War II, under the aegis of the American Council of Learned Societies and the Army Specialized Training Program, Haas was assigned to work on Thai and learned it from scratch at the University of Michigan. "The Thai thing," as Haas put it later (Haas and Murray 1977, 703), got her to Berkeley, and she published an introductory Thai textbook (1942), a Thai reader (1945a and 1954), a manual of Thai conversation (1945b), a treatment of Thai vocabulary (1955), a structural description (1956a), a description of the writing system (1956b), and, with Heng R. Subhanka, *Spoken Thai* (1945–48). For an assessment of her work on the language, see Matisoff (1997); for a comprehensive and varied account of her career and influence as a linguist and teacher, see the special issue of *Anthropological Linguistics* devoted to her (Parks 1997).

B. Haas's substantial work on Thai was, in a sense, accidental and not her professional focus—"I committed myself a little too long to Thai," she would later remark (Haas and Murray 1997, 710)—but it was mostly in Thai that she worked as a lexicographer. Along with her other war work, she produced a Thai phrase book (1945c), a large Thai dictionary (1945d), and, later, published a *Thai-English Student's Dictionary* (1964). She also compiled a dictionary of Tunica (1953a) and edited Sapir and Swadesh's *Yana Dictionary* (1960), so lexicography figured in her Amerindian research, as well. The specific contribution to *PiL* does not obviously develop into other items in Haas's bibliography, although she did write about bilingualism and language learning (see 1943, 1953b, 1953c, and 1960). After 1964, she eschewed further lexicography.

C. Haas's contribution has never been overlooked (see, for instance, Al-Kasimi 1977; Nguyen 1980, 1980–81, and 1986), but bilingual lexicographers and those who study bilingual dictionaries have "rediscovered" it for the twenty-first century—it currently has a robust presence in the literature. While it appears in articles addressing languages around the world, African lexicographers and metalexicographers seem to cite it at an especially high rate (see, for instance, Kosch 2013; Prinsloo 2016 and 2020). It does appear in some of the standard works of lexicography, including Béjoint (1994), Landau (2001), Swanepoel (2003), and, perhaps surprisingly, twice in chapters of Pedro A. Fuertes-Olivera and Henning Bergenholtz's *e-Lexicography* (Bothma 2011; Verlinde 2011), making it one of the few contributions in *PiL* to find a place in the most contemporary of contemporary discourses within lexicography. Haas may owe some of this late attention to R. R. K. Hartmann's (2007, 7) remark that his "favourite piece" about dictionary structure "is the classic paper presented by Mary Haas at the famous Conference on *Problems in Lexicography* at Bloomington, back in 1960," noting that her list of desiderata is "ambitious and tongue-in-cheek" (176), an astute reading.

Richard S. Harrell

A. Harrell (1928–1964), according to his colleague, Wallace M. Erwin, "was in every sense a brilliant man. Although his life was barely half the usual span, his accomplishments are equalled [*sic*] by few who live to twice the age" (quoted in Stuart 1967, xi; I draw freely from this account here but depart from the appended bibliography of Harrell's works, which isn't entirely reliable). Indeed, he died unexpectedly while on sabbatical in Cairo, just shy of his thirty-sixth birthday. A Texan, Harrell studied English and French at Texas Christian University, German over a summer at the University of Texas, took an MA in French from Harvard University, where he also earned a PhD, with a dissertation titled *The Phonology of Colloquial Arabic*, subsequently published (1957) in the same series as Haas (1956b) and Penzl (1973). He established the Arabic Research Program at Georgetown University, under the aegis of the National Defense Education Act, publishing, among other things, a grammar of Moroccan Arabic (1963), a colloquial Egyptian Arabic textbook (Harrell, Selim, and Tewfik 1963), and the English–Moroccan component of a dictionary of Moroccan Arabic (Sobelman and Harrell 1963). The reverse component appeared posthumously (Harrell et al. 1966), as did his Moroccan Arabic textbook (1965). Harrell did not live nearly as long as many contributors to *PiL*, so did not publish as much as they or receive recognition and awards, but he probably would have. Harrell was so admired at the age of thirty-five that the series of Arabic publications he founded was named for him; a portrait was painted posthumously, in 1966, by Alexander Yaron, and colleagues organized a memorial volume (Stuart 1967a).

B. I assume with Harrell's admiring contemporaries that had he lived longer this section would be correspondingly dense. Clearly, his perspective at the conference and in the ensuing book grew out of his own lexicography (Sobelman and Harrell 1963; Harrell 1966). One suspects that he'd have continued to produce bilingual dictionaries of English and varieties of Arabic other than Moroccan, and that as bilingual lexicography entrenched itself in the American academy, he'd have been called upon to speak and write more about it.

C. Harrell's contribution was cited quickly after publication, by none other than Einar Haugen, who barely mentions Harrell in his review of *PiL* (1963a) but rehearses Harrell's most memorable argument without attribution (Haugen 1963b, 755). The article appears in classic works on bilingual dictionaries (Al-Kasimi 1977, for instance) and is cited as taking a "user's perspective" approach (Tono 1998). Most often, however, others cite Harrell on one important point: that bilingual dictionaries cannot satisfy the needs of both X-speakers and Y-speakers equally (see, for example, Nielsen 1994; Yong and Peng 2007; and Bergh and Ohlander 2012).

Henry Hoenigswald

A. Hoenigswald (1915–2003), like the Kahanes and Malkiel, fled Europe on the cusp of World War II. Born in the formerly German city of Breslau (now Wrocław, Poland), he studied in the universities of Munich, Zurich, Padua, and Florence, taking his doctorate at the last. An Indo-Europeanist and theoretical linguist (also a civil rights activist), he finally established himself at the University of Pennsylvania, in 1948—"at this point, nine years after he had reached the US, he could feel that the horrors were over" (Davies 2008, 861)—but before and even once embedded there lived "a life of scholarly peregrination" (Cardona 2006, 6; henceforth, I draw freely on this memoir and Davies's; see also Hoenigswald 1980), initially landing at Yale, whence he moved to the Hartford Seminary Foundation (overlapping with Gleason), Hunter College, the University of Texas at Austin, and the Foreign Service Institute, then later visiting at the University of Michigan, Georgetown, Yale, Princeton, the Catholic University in Leuven, St. John's College, Oxford, the University of Kiel, and Deccan College in what was then Poona, India. He was a member of the American Philosophical Society (1971), the American Academy of Arts and Sciences (1974), and the National Academy of Sciences (1988), as well as a corresponding fellow of the British Academy (1986). Intellectually formidable, "he also showed extraordinary warmth and lack of pretense" (Cardona 2006, 13). Soon after he arrived in the United States, he contributed a basic course in spoken Hindustani to the American war effort (1945) and later wrote the classic *Language Change and Linguistic Reconstruction* (1960), which Householder (1962) reviewed approvingly in the *International Journal of American Linguistics*, as well as *Studies in Formal Historical Linguistics* (1973). He edited an important historical work, *The European Background of American Linguistics* (1979).

B. Hoenigswald's contribution to *PiL* is unusual, the only article he published of a specifically lexicographical nature. Given the examples therein, the article does extend from some of his earliest scholarly interests, such as Greek word formation, the subject of his doctoral thesis, and his earliest publications, for example, Hoenigswald (1940) (Davies 2008, 860–61). He seems never to have cited the article in his later work, but his publications are various and sometimes appear in less accessible journals, so I have not been able to check every item. He was, however, an "outside consultant" on Greek and Latin etymologies for *Webster's Third* (1961).

C. Hoenigswald's is among the least influential articles in *PiL*, though it occasionally appears in dictionary research, with regard to lexicographical description (Benson, Benson, and Ilson 1986), lexicology (McMillan 1978), pedagogical lexicography (Diab 1990), historical lexicography (Adams 2006), and grammatical information in learners' dictionaries (Nguyen 1986).

Fred W. Householder Jr.

A. Householder (1913–1994) had moved from Texas to Rhode Island, and from there to Maryland and Massachusetts before his family settled in Vermont. After years mixed with labor and higher education, his father joined the mathematics faculty at the University of Vermont, from which Householder took his A.B. in 1932 (Bender 1997, 560–61; I draw freely on this memorial article here). While working on his PhD in classics at Columbia, completed in 1941, he took seminars with Roman Jakobson and participated in meetings of the Linguistic Circle of New York. During World War II, he worked in the Army Language Unit at 165 Broadway (1980, 197–98; I draw freely on this memoir, too) and afterward taught at Allegheny College in Pennsylvania, finally arriving at Indiana University in 1948. He was a full professor by 1956. He helped to organize first the interdisciplinary graduate program in linguistics and then the Department of Linguistics in 1964, which he chaired from 1974 to 1980, having already served as acting chair in the 1960s. Remarkably, he directed or codirected over ninety dissertations, including those of some of the next generation's leading linguists (see

Al-Ani 1984, 11–17 for a complete list). He was a remarkably agile scholar and linguist. He published his dissertation on Lucian (1941) and remained a classicist throughout his career, producing an edition of Apollonius Dyscolus's ancient Greek syntax exactly forty years later (1981). In 1952, Thomas A. Sebeok invited him to teach Turkish and Azerbaijani at Indiana University, for the United States Air Force, and from that experience he produced a foundational textbook on the latter (Householder and Lofti 1965). He also produced one on Demotic Greek (Householder, Kazakis, and Koutsoudas 1964), and one can see how this work of the 1950s informed his choice of topics and personnel for the conference's fourth session. He edited or coedited two widely used anthologies (1972; Hamp, Householder, Austerlitz, and Joos 1966). His masterpiece is surely *Linguistic Speculations* (1971), an unapologetically idiosyncratic survey of the discipline—Householder followed no school of thought. Chomksy and Halle (1965) disputed his article, "On Some Recent Claims in Phonological Theory" (1965), and so, Bender (1997, 564) writes, "All too many younger linguists remember him simply as the 'heavy' in this particular exchange, and as waging some sort of structuralist rearguard action to the paradigm shift that was then taking place, while nothing could have been further from the truth." Dwight Bolinger (1991, 23) complained, "Householder I think is the best critic our field has, and a highly original thinker besides, and it annoys me that he has not received the recognition he deserves." He did, however, become president of the Linguistic Society of America (1981) and was elected to the American Academy of Arts and Sciences (1977).

  B. Despite his lifelong love of them (1980, 193, and 1971, 1) and his wartime work on them (see chap. 1), dictionaries never figured as a subject of Householder's scholarship, either before or after the 1960 conference, except in a miscellaneous piece he cowrote on their treatment of the term *linguistician* (Householder and Sebeok 1951).

  C. Householder's "Summary Report" has been cited regularly if not copiously over the decades since publication of *PiL*, including in classics like Al-Kasimi (1977) and McMillan (1978), and in preeminent works of the present day, for instance, Tarp (2008), Bergenholtz and Tarp (2010), and Béjoint (2010). It has proven a slight but durable summary of the features that marked the conference and its proceedings as so important from the outset. Otherwise, of course, all the citations of all the contributions to *PiL* and the book's reception (see chap. 3) testify to Householder's success as lead editor of the whole work.

James E. Iannucci

A. Iannucci (1914–1991), after taking his PhD from the University of Pennsylvania, taught at St. Joseph's College (now St. Joseph's University) in Philadelphia for decades, where he was a professor of linguistics specializing in Spanish, on which his scholarly profile was founded (see Iannucci 1952).

B. Among the conferees, Iannucci was likely the one with the heaviest teaching load—he wasn't on the faculty at a "Research I" university, let alone at an Ivy League school or something comparable. His research record is thus correspondingly thin. His paper at the conference was preceded by a similar treatment of the subject (1957) and by another brief but internationally prominent article (1959), and he later published on bilingual dictionaries occasionally (1985, 1986a, 1986b). I assume he supplied the contributor's note to his 1986 article, which suggests a great deal more involvement with bilingual lexicography than the published record illustrates: "He has served as a consultant in the preparation of several bilingual dictionaries and is currently engaged as a consultant in a major project to produce a Chinese–English dictionary" (1986b, 328). He was a charter member of the Dictionary Society of North America (Adams 2019a, 54).

C. Iannucci's contribution to *PiL* is marked as a classic by its inclusion in Hartmann (2003), and it is cited in many staples of the literature of bilingual and pedagogical lexicography (see, for instance, Al-Kasimi 1977; Nguyen 1986; Dolezal and McCreary 1999; Hartmann 2007; Yong and Peng 2007; Franjié 2009). Nevertheless, the substance of the article is often cited from Iannucci (1957), instead (see for instance, Ilson 2016). As with Conklin's and Weinreich's contributions, earlier and later iterations compete with Iannucci's contribution to *PiL*.

Henry and Renée Kahane

A. Henry (1902–1992) and Renée (1907–2002) collaborated throughout their careers, only occasionally publishing individually or with others. They met while doctoral students at the University of Berlin and taught at the University of Florence during the middle 1930s. After Mussolini briefly imprisoned Henry as a Jewish hostage while Hitler visited Florence in 1938, the Kahanes fled to Cephalonia, one of the Ionian islands, Renée's childhood home, until they could attain safe passage to the United States (Kahane 1991, 192–93 and 196–97). After a brief stay in Los Angeles, Henry was hired by the University of Illinois, in Urbana, where they lived for the rest of their lives. Despite these early disruptions, they published some seventy-five items between 1940 and 1962, including six books (Pietrangeli 1962), with half their careers still ahead of them. Early on they contributed to the American war effort by writing a textbook on a critical language, in their case Modern Greek (Kahane, Kahane, and Ward 1945–46). Mostly, they wrote articles about Mediterranean languages and literatures, many of them later collected (Kahane and Kahane 1979, 1983, 1986), although Henry also published in Spanish linguistics (Kahane and Pietrangeli 1954, 1959), and they wrote about a number of other Romance languages occasionally. At Illinois, Henry invented and led the Program in Linguistics (1960–1962) and "ultimately succeeded in creating the Department of Linguistics" (Kachru 2005, 241; see also Zgusta 1993, 47–48). Henry was elected to the American Academy of Arts and Sciences (1989) and served as president of the Linguistic Society of America (1984); he also received several honorary degrees, including one from the University of Illinois (1968), and the Silver Award of the Academy of Athens (1973), both explicitly shared with Renée (Kachru 2005, 242; Malkiel and De Marco 1993, 301). They were also cohonored with a festschrift (Kachru et al. 1973), but renown was unfairly distributed between them. In Henry's obituary, Kachru (2005, 237) writes, "The lives of Henry and Renée were a unique blend of harmony, mutual dedication, and utter devotion—they were an inseparable academic pair." As Malkiel and De Marco (1993, 299) note, in many ways, despite his intellectual heritage, "Kahane [Henry, that is] adopted the American approach to linguistics, with its emphasis on structuralism; Renée Kahane, however, continued to bring to bear on dialectology the classic methods of research which she had absorbed in Europe." The two methodologies might have competed; for the Kahanes, they proved complementary.

B. The Kahanes practiced lexicography of a kind from their earliest years (Kahane and Kahane 1940), nearer the Bloomington conference (Kahane, Kahane, and Tietze 1958), and subsequently (Kahane, Kahane, and Bremner 1968), but they focused on how language contact, diffusion, bilingualism, and borrowing produced lexica in history, rather than on bilingual dictionaries, for which their text on spoken Greek served as prolegomenon and qualified them to serve as advisors on Georgacas's dictionary of Modern Greek (see chap. 1). After *PiL*, they never wrote about bilingual lexicography again, but they did write an idiosyncratic piece on dictionaries and ideology (Kahane and Kahane 1992), and Henry joined with Kachru to edit a festschrift for Zgusta (Kachru and Kahane 1995), which was, unfortunately, Henry's final, posthumous publication. Henry also served on the committee that organized a joint meeting of the Dictionary Society of North America, the Linguistic Society of America's Summer Linguistics Institute, and the Division of Applied Linguistics at the University of Illinois (Zgusta 1980, v).

C. Cited a handful of times, the Kahanes' contribution to *PiL* has unfortunately left barely the trace of a footprint on dictionary research, metalexicography, or even the lexicography of Greek.

Yakov Malkiel

A. Malkiel (1914–1998) begins his "Autobiographic Sketch: Early Years in America" with a sentence relevant to his paper for the Bloomington conference: "It has been partly my fortune and partly my misfortune to have lived practically five different lives—successively rather than concurrently, I hasten to add. Five is, incidentally, the minimum that I have arrived at in my gropings for the most cogent segmentations; a division into six or even seven stretches of time, very loosely connected with one another, could, I suppose, be defended with equal cogency" (1980b, 79). Groping for groupings and segmentations, rearranging them, and considering their cogency—these were temperamental tendencies reflected not only in his contribution to *PiL* but much of his other scholarly work. *Tentative* was one of his favorite words.

He taught for decades at the University of California at Berkeley, by way of Kiev, his birthplace, through Poland and Berlin, Rotterdam and New York—"I escaped the Holocaust," he wrote, "by a hair's breadth" (1980b, 81)—and then on to Laramie, Wyoming, on the way to the West Coast (see Dworkin 2004, on which I draw freely here). Malkiel founded the journal *Romance Philology*—a journal not incidental to the fortunes of *PiL* (see Uitti 1963)—and published about 850 books, articles, chapters, reviews, and so forth, in his long career—Dwight Bolinger (1991, 22) would remark that Malkiel logged "more mileage as a writer of linguistics than anyone else in the field"—most of it accounted for in *A Tentative Autobibliography: Yakov Malkiel* (1988), with impressive self-appreciation (see also Fulk 1996, 173). Lexicography and typologies were only two among many scholarly interests. He was, to say the least, a memorable character, with an identifiable idiom captured by "Jan Cosinka"—actually, Ian Jackson—in *Teach Yourself Malkielese in 90 Minutes* (2006), a typology of Malkielese in a word book, a cleverer than usual attempt to celebrate someone of Malkiel's complexity.

B. *Etymological Dictionaries: A Tentative Typology* (1976) followed on a series of preparatory articles (1957, 1959, 1960), the latter two of which were significantly more detailed than his contribution to *PiL*. He was well aware that linguistics and literary studies were elbowing etymology to the disciplinary margins but optimistically declared that it had "lost a battle but not the war, provided some of its devotees are willing to take the risk of seeing its challenges, assets, and liabilities in a new perspective" (1976, vii). He was similarly, incredibly, optimistic in *Etymology* (1993), in which, like some of his favorite etymologists, he "attempts to break out of the confines of etymological dictionaries and squibs" (Fulk 1996, 173). Indeed, he had left them behind, as far as I can determine, after 1978, when he presented a paper on "The Lexicographer as a Mediator between Linguistics and Society" (1980a).

C. The effect of Malkiel's paper at the 1960 conference was nearly immediate, though unacknowledged. Sebeok (1962) wrote about his recently completed (1961) thesaurus and concordance of literary Cheremis (a Finno-Ugric language) in terms of dictionary typology. We have good reason to think (see chap. 1) that he reviewed the manuscript of *PiL* before it was published in 1962. Sebeok wrote the article in question "during [his] residence, in 1960–61, as a Fellow of the Center for Advanced Study of Behavioral Sciences, in Stanford, California" (1962, 372), which explains why he missed the Bloomington conference on lexicography, but not why he seems unaware of Malkiel's contribution. Indeed, he almost surely was. He probably also knew Lev Shcherba's earlier typological proposals, published in Russian in 1940, summarized by Paul Garvin (1947), but available in full English translation much later (see Farina 1995). From that point forward, dictionary typology became a regular subject of discussion within lexicographical circles and is represented in all major handbooks on the subject. Malkiel's article motivates many treatments of the subject in general works. See, for example, Zgusta (1971); Svensén (1993); Béjoint (1994); Svensén (2009); Landau (2001); the section of Hartmann (2003) that reprints Malkiel's article among seven others; and Béjoint (2010); as well as the many chapters on dictionary types in Hausmann, Reichmann, Wiegand, and Zgusta (1990).

Kemp Malone

A. Malone (1889–1971) was the oldest of speakers on the Bloomington program and perhaps the most distinguished. He hailed from Mississippi, graduated from Emory College (now University) at the age of eighteen

(Pyles 1972, 499; I draw freely on this account here), and took his PhD from the University of Chicago, with the formidable John Matthews Manly as his director. He arrived at Johns Hopkins University in 1924 and, though he retired from teaching in 1956, worked there until he died, primarily on older Germanic languages and literatures. He wrote such works as *The Literary History of Hamlet* (1923a) and *The Phonology of Modern Icelandic* (1923b) and managed to publish over five hundred works by 1959 (Eliason 1969, 163; I draw freely on this source, too). He was a founding co-editor of the then monthly journal, *American Speech*, in which role he served for seven years. He was a foundation member of the Linguistic Society of America and served as its president (1944) and was also president of the American Dialect Society (1944–46), the American Name Society (1956), and the Modern Language Association (1962), a unique array of presidencies, though, on all but the last, other contributors to *PiL* filled the same offices. He received honorary doctorates from Emory University, the University of Chicago, Yale University, the University of North Carolina, Johns Hopkins University, and Kenyon College. As if these honors weren't enough, he also received the King Christian X Liberty Medal—as did, among about three hundred others, Winston Churchill and King Haakon VII of Norway—and was a knight both of the Danish Order of the Dannebrog and the Icelandic Order of the Falcon. He was twice honored with a festschrift (Kirby and Woolf 1949; Einarsson and Eliason 1959). Others of the Bloomington conferees would end up as distinguished, perhaps, but none was nearly as distinguished as Malone at the time of the conference.

 B. Malone was a philologist, so etymology was one of his stocks in trade, and he wrote many articles on individual words throughout his career, my favorite of which, by way of example, concerns *runt* (1944). His skill in such matters led to his serving as chief etymologist of the *American College Dictionary* (1947) and subsequently on the massive dictionary built from it, the *Random House Dictionary of the English Language* (1966)—though not a conventional lexicographer, he nonetheless contributed significantly to leading commercial dictionaries. His interests extended beyond etymology, however, and his contribution to *PiL* derives as much from his work on defining, an example of which is his classic article on *mahogany* (1940).

 C. At first, it's difficult to see why the most distinguished scholar's contribution to the conference would end up one of the least cited. The answer lies, I think, in Malone's rhetorical and substantive approach: he misconceived his audience and delivered something too basic. The structuralism on which he relied lost its theoretical sure-footing in linguistics soon after. If it was too basic for the 1960 audience, it might seem not only too basic but theoretically naive today (see chap. 2). Still, metalexicographers and those interested in practical bilingual lexicography have turned to the piece on occasion. The references tend to appear in dissertations or the usual suspects (for instance, Nguyen 1986; Béjoint 2010), but the article continues to draw attention from others (for example, Tono 1998).

Samuel E. Martin

A. Martin (1924–2009) left his hometown of Emporia, Kansas, for the University of California at Berkeley, where he earned his BA and began graduate study. He completed his PhD at Yale in Japanese linguistics in 1950, under Bernard Bloch, and taught there from that year until he retired in 1994. He did not serve in the Army Language Section, but, like Conklin, discovered his passion for a language and culture while serving overseas, in his case, in Japan, as a graduate of the Navy Language School (Ramsey 2004a, 260; I draw freely on this account here). Martin made foundational contributions to Chinese, Japanese, and Korean phonemics and morphophonemics, as well as their orthographies. Indeed, he developed a transliteration system for Korean known as Yale Romanization, which quickly became the preferred method. Dozens of articles on these subjects led to magisterial works late in his career, including *A Reference Grammar of Japanese* (1975), *The Japanese Language through Time* (1987), and *A Reference Grammar of Korean* (1992). He also worked on Dagur Mongolian (1961), protolinguistics of the Altaic family (1996a), and pragmatics (for example, in 1952 and 1996b). Colleagues celebrated his career with a special issue of *Japanese Language and Literature* (Ramsey 2004b), which includes a bibliography of his work to that date. His contributions to the study and state of Korean language were so profound that the Republic of Korea presented him with its Presidential Medal of Honor in 1994.

B. Like some of the other conferees, Martin had notable experience in lexicography by the time of the conference. He had compiled an English–Japanese/Japanese–English conversation dictionary (1957), his work on Dagur Mongolian (1961) included not only a grammar and texts but a lexicon, and he was already at work on a massive Korean–English dictionary (Martin, Lee, and Chang 1968), so his views were far from merely theoretical. Though he did not write about dictionary-making after 1962, he continued practicing lexicography, with "pocket" (1990) and "concise" (1994) dictionaries of Japanese—at 724 pages, the former required a big pocket. He was engaged in a dictionary of Middle Korean at the time of his death, never completed.

C. Martin's contribution to *PiL* has made a good showing in the relevant lexicographical literature (for instance, in Al-Kasimi 1977; Nguyen 1980 and 1986; Snell-Hornby 1984; Benson, Benson, and Ilson 1986; Béjoint 1998; Yong and Peng 2007; Franjié 2009) and attracts scholars even today (for example, Trklja 2016). Dolezal and McCreary (1999) include few items from *PiL* in their critical bibliography of pedagogical lexicography, but Martin's is one of three.

Herbert Penzl

A. Penzl (1910–1995) grew up in Vienna, attended university there, and took his doctorate from the University of Vienna in 1935, with a dissertation on Middle English *a* in New England speech, an unlikely topic on which he settled while serving as a research assistant to Hans Kurath on what would be published as the *Linguistic Atlas of New England* (Kurath et al. 1939–43; henceforth, *LANE*). He emigrated to the United States in 1936, first teaching at Rockford College but proceeding to the University of Illinois in 1938, the University of Michigan in 1950, and ultimately to the University of California at Berkeley in 1963, where he taught until he retired in 1979 (Kyes 1995; I draw freely on this obituary here). During World War II, he worked in the Army Language Section, primarily on a dictionary of Norwegian. Like many other contributors to *PiL*, Penzl was a versatile linguist who published widely on Germanic languages—see, for example, work on Gothic (1950), Old High German (1949 and 1961a), Middle High German (1989a), Modern German (1975), Old English (1944 and 1947), Middle English (1937), Early Modern English (1994), American English (1934 and 1993)—he continued on the staff of *LANE* while at Illinois (see Kurath et al. 1939, v) and on the Linguistic Atlas advisory board long after that (see Kretzschmar et al. 1994, xii)—and even Pennsylvania German (1938). He could also claim authority over Pashto (1955, 1961b, 1962), the subject of his contribution with Chavarría-Aguilar to *PiL*, and linguistic theory (1974, 1989b). He was elected to the Austrian Academy of Sciences and celebrated in a festschrift (Rauch and Carr 1979).

B. Dictionaries and the practice of lexicography were not Penzl's regular research topics, though early in his career he brought dictionaries into his discussion of New England vowels (1940), and, much later, he addressed

Noah Webster's sense of American English (1990). He served as an "outside consultant" on Iranian etymology for *Webster's Third*, so had some minimal contact with the commercial dictionary world. He was, for a few years, a member of the Dictionary Society of North America, presumably from when he published the 1990 article, since he does not appear in previous membership lists, and membership was required for publication in *Dictionaries* at the time.

C. See the parallel section in the note on Chavarría-Aguilar.

Allen Walker Read

A. Read (1906–2002) was, like Malkiel and Malone, unbelievably prolific, as one can see from a recently published bibliography of his work (Adams and Bailey 2017). He was born in Iowa and educated there, in Missouri, and at the University of Oxford, from which he took a BLitt in 1933, with a thesis on Johnson's dictionary. He never earned an American PhD, but Oxford awarded him an honorary doctorate in 1988, and he received others from Indiana State University (1984), Iowa State University (1985), and the University of North Carolina at Chapel Hill (1990). In the mid-1930s, he was an assistant editor on the *Dictionary of American English* until he won a Guggenheim fellowship to compile a dictionary of Briticisms—he never finished it. Overtaken by the war, he worked under Barnhart on the *Dictionary of United States Army Terms* (Barnhart et al. 1944), after which he taught at Columbia University. He was a charter member of the Dictionary Society of North America and its president (1981–1983), as well as a fellow of DSNA, its highest honor. He was also president of the American Dialect Society, the American Name Society, the Semiotic Society of America, the International Linguistic Association, and the American Society of Geolinguistics (Levitt 2004). His intense research into words like *blizzard*, *fuck*, and *O.K.* led to celebrity; he is one of the few lexicographers or historians of English to be profiled in the *New Yorker* (Stacey 1989). His colleagues celebrated his work, too (see, for instance, Bailey 2003), collected it (Read 2001, 2002), and honored him with festschrifts (for example, Seits 1988), and he also profiled himself informatively (Read 1991), at the same time shedding light on many of his contemporaries, some of them present at the Bloomington conference.

B. Much of Read's early work on dictionaries remains unpublished (see Adams 2018a), and much of the later work was told at conferences (Adams and Bailey 2017), but Read wrote several important lexicographical pieces, some scholarly and some public-facing. In the latter category, we might include his entry for "Dictionary" in the *Encyclopedia Britannica* (Read 1974) and articles about dictionaries for *Consumer Reports* (Read 1963a, 1963b, 1964). Of the scholarly ones, those leading out from his contribution to *PiL* include his paper in McDavid and Duckert (1973) and another developed in several iterations over decades and published posthumously (Read 2003). Sebeok may have invited Read's "Approaches to Lexicography and Semantics" (1973) for one of his innumerable collections partly from awareness of the article in *PiL*.

C. Read's work figures in important general works on lexicography (for instance, Hartmann and James 1998; Béjoint 2010), but the article in *PiL* was barely noticed.

Sol Saporta

A. Saporta (1925–2008) graduated from Brooklyn College and earned his PhD from the University of Illinois in 1955. He immediately moved to Indiana University, which he left for the University of Washington before the Conference on Lexicography in 1960, where he taught until his retirement in 1990. He was chair of the Department of Linguistics there from 1962 to 1977 (Al-Madani 2006, xiii). His major works, besides *PiL*, include a foundational anthology on psycholinguistics (1961), a Spanish grammar (Saporta and Contreras 1962)—a work that competed for his attention on *PiL*—and a book directed at a general audience, *Society, Language, and the University* (1994). Late in life, he self-published an edition of his letters to various editors on various subjects, which he prefaced thus: "Sometime in the late 1970s I concluded that traditional linguistic scholarship was no longer very gratifying. I thought that most of what I had written was either derivative or mistaken" (2006, xi). He was honored with a festschrift (Brame, Contreras, and Newmeyer 1986).

B. Saporta seems to have had little interest in lexicography or dictionaries. One suspects that editing *PiL* was opportunistic.

C. Unlike Householder, Saporta did not contribute an article to *PiL*. One might be inclined to credit him with the volume's success, though I have argued in chapter 1 that he contributed next to nothing as co-editor.

James Sledd

A. Sledd (1914–2003) was a leading Chaucerian early in his career (1947, 1953), became a notable linguist (1956—see Stockwell 1998, 236–37; and 1959—see

Gunter 1960), and ended up a controversialist of the first order. To grasp this latter point, one must attend to his article titles: "On Not Teaching English Usage" (1965); "Bi-dialectalism: The Linguistics of White Supremacy" (1969); "Doublespeak: Dialectology in the Service of Big Brother" (1972); the slightly scatological "Or Get Off the Pot: Notes toward the Restoration of Moderate Honesty even in English Departments" (1977); and "Grammar for Social Awareness in Time of Class Warfare" (1996). Such articles often drew fire, in others titled "Reflections on How Much We Don't Need Wild Men, even Make-Believe Wild Men Who Are Really Professors: Reply to James Sledd" (Eskey 1975), for instance, which would in turn prompt rejoinders, sometimes specific, sometimes general, like "Linguistics, Obeah, Acupuncture, and the Teaching of Composition by That Bastard Sledd" (1982), which pithily concludes of prescriptive teaching attitudes and practices, "The basics to which we are exhorted to go back are often no more than the linguistic prejudices, reasonable and unreasonable, of WASPs like me" (152). "The ultimate insider," Beth Daniell (2003, 218) would write memorially, "Sledd positioned himself on the margins, speaking against the status quo in ways that some found hurtful but others found precisely on target." Later in his career, he continually "spoke out against injustice wherever he saw it, weaving into his criticisms of the profession his keen insights into American society and politics" (218). The title of some of his collected work, *Eloquent Dissent* (1996), characterizes his contentions, and he was, by nature, a contentious character (see note 4). As Stockwell (1998, 238n2) puts it of a specific instance, "Sledd, as usual, was just skeptical about everything, even if eloquently so."

B. The polemics might obscure Sledd's abiding interest in dictionaries and lexicography. His dissertation was about John Baret's *Alvearie* (1947), and he published derivative and related articles (such as 1954). Then, he cowrote the paradigm-shifting book about Samuel Johnson's dictionary (Sledd and Kolb 1955), just before his contribution to *PiL*, which was just before publication of *Webster's Third*, which prompted his co-edited casebook about the controversy surrounding it (Sledd and Ebbit 1962). Later, he contributed to two significant collections, *New Aspects of Lexicography* (1972) and *Lexicography in English* (1973). He also assisted Mitford M. Mathews in preparation of an abridged version (1966) of *A Dictionary of Americanisms* (1951). Despite his interest in and love of dictionaries, in his controversialist phase, he saw them as class-promoting and norm-enforcing works. Thus, he didn't write about them specifically after 1973. Nevertheless, several of his students wrote important works in lexicography, for instance, M. Sue Hetherington and Jeffrey Huntsman, both charter members of the Dictionary Society of North America (Adams 2019a, 5–6, 54).

C. Sections titled "Comments" are rarely cited, and, except for the general works discussed earlier in this introduction, Sledd's comments have drawn little scholarly notice.

Donald C. Swanson

A. Swanson (1914–1976), a native Minnesotan, took his undergraduate degree from the University of Minnesota, did his graduate work at Princeton, under Harold Bender—notable, perhaps, because Bender worked as chief etymologist on *Webster's New International Dictionary of the English Language* (1934)—served in the Armed Forces Language Unit (see McDavid 1980, 20), and arrived at the University of Minnesota again in 1946, where he taught to the end of his career. He was an outstanding classicist and practicing lexicographer.

B. By the Bloomington conference, Swanson had published a well-regarded bilingual dictionary of modern spoken Greek (1959), which marked him as one of the principal authorities on the conference's topic. His contribution to *PiL* thus distills considerable relevant experience. Later, he published a very different dictionary, one of all the names in Latin poetry (1967), a quixotic project beautifully executed. He gathered so much material on the semantic, etymological, phonological, morphological, and stylistic complications of those names that he published a book of all he couldn't include in the dictionary's introduction (1970, v).

C. Swanson's contribution has made only a slight impression on the literature of lexicography, present in classics of bilingual lexicography (Al-Kasimi 1977; Nguyen 1986), as well as more recent works (such as Tarp 2008; Franjié 2009), that is, not often cited, but not forgotten, either.

Andreas Tietze

A. Tietze (1914–2003), like so many of the Bloomington conference's speakers, fled Europe in advance of World War II, but not toward America; instead, already enamored of Turkey, he left his native Vienna for a position at the University of Istanbul (Griswold 2004, 142; I draw freely on this account here), where he taught German and English language, although his dissertation had analyzed the agricultural theories of early modern Italian economists. He joined the Kahanes at the University of Illinois in 1952 but left in 1957 for UCLA, the same year in which Worth joined the faculty there. In 1974, he returned to Vienna to direct the University of Vienna's Oriental Institute, where he also edited the journal *Wiener Zeitschrift für die Kunde des Morgenlandes*. Tietze specialized as much in Turkish folklore as in lexicography, especially in shadow plays and riddles (for the latter, see especially 1966; Basgöz and Tietze 1973). He wrote, over decades, what one might consider a series of articles on loanwords from other languages into Turkish (including, for instance, 1955 and Tietze and Lazard 1967), which is obviously closely allied to his dictionary work. He was a charismatic teacher and speaker—while at UCLA, he received its Distinguished Teaching Award—and was honored with at least one festschrift (Lowry and Quataert 1993). The University of Vienna commemorates him in the annual Andreas Tietze Memorial Fellowship in Turkish Studies.

B. Tietze arrived in Bloomington a well-credentialed lexicographer. While teaching in Istanbul, he had led the team that revised the 1890 edition of Sir James Redhouse's English and Turkish Dictionary, a bidirectional bilingual dictionary, as the *New Redhouse Turkish–English Dictionary* (1968). He had also collaborated with the Kahanes (1958) on an etymological dictionary of Turkish nautical terms that was astonishingly well and widely reviewed internationally (see Pietrangeli 1962, 210). His most important lexicographical work was a historical and etymological dictionary of Turkish (Tietze et al. 2002–2016), of which he had finished only the first volume before he died. He did not write much about the history or practice of lexicography beyond his contribution to *PiL*, with the notable exception of his article on Ottoman Turkish dictionaries in the international encyclopedia of lexicography edited by Hausmann, Reichmann, Wiegand, and Zgusta (1991).

C. Tietze's contribution to *PiL* has proved most influential in the study of Turkish lexicography, less in general works, although he is cited in Al-Kasimi (1977). More typical references to it include Yüksekkaya (1998), Boz, Bozkurt, and Doğru (2018), and Święcicka (2020). The last two demonstrate that, while the work's influence may be narrow, it is nonetheless durable. Because Tietze chose to discuss the cultural sources of lexicographical problems, rather than the problems themselves, his contribution has proved less resilient among dictionary makers. Perhaps, in the long run, metalexicographers will seize upon the ideological implications of the piece.

Uriel Weinreich

A. Weinreich (1926–1967) was to the manor born, the son of renowned Yiddish linguist Max Weinreich, who popularized the saying, *A shprakh iz a dialect mit an armey un flot* (A language is a dialect with an army and a navy). The Weinreichs arrived in the United States when Uriel was fourteen years old, yet another refugee who participated in the 1960 conference (Malkiel and Herzog 1967; Malkiel 1968b; I draw freely from both sources here). He studied at Columbia, under Roman Jakobson and André Martinet, with the latter of whom he was co-editor of *Word* (1953–60) and co-originator of *Linguistics Today*, in 1954. Before he published an elegant version of his hefty dissertation as *Languages in Contact* (1953), he had already published *College Yiddish: An Introduction to the Yiddish Language and to Jewish Life and Culture* (1949). He would later edit/co-edit three volumes of *The Field of Yiddish: Studies in Language, Folklore, and Literature* (1954, 1965, and Herzog, Ravid, and Weinreich 1969), and, with Beatrice Weinreich, compile *Yiddish Language and Folklore: A Selective Bibliography for Research* (1959). Among sociolinguists, he is famous for his collaboration with William Labov and Marvin I. Herzog titled "Empirical Foundations for a Theory of Language Change" (1966). He was just forty years old when he died, which prompted Malkiel to write, "It was unquestionably in the concluding five years of his life—and therein lies the full measure of our loss—that Weinreich's research reached that degree of originality, forcefulness, and maturity which stamped his as a first-rate theorist and a fine practitioner" (Malkiel and Herzog 1967, 606), a span that included his contribution to *PiL*.

B. Weinreich further developed the argument of his *PiL* chapter prominently over the ensuing years, in Greenberg (1963, 1966a), Sebeok (1966), and, posthumously, in Weinreich (1972), but also obliquely in Weinreich (1964). Worth predicted this serial development: "One anticipates with interest Mr. Weinreich's further studies in this timely and fascinating area" (206). On the practical side of things, one counts his posthumously published English–Yiddish/Yiddish–English dictionary (1968), in which, Edward Stankiewicz (1969, 369/a) would write, Weinreich achieved "a work of permanent scholarly value, an excellent tool for the mastery of Yiddish, a mirror of its riches and lexical possibilities, and a model of scholarly precision."

C. While his contribution to *PiL* is not the most cited item in the book, his influence in semantics on the edge of lexicography has been profound, fully justifying Malkiel's prediction of his significance. The effect of his contribution was all but immediate (Aitken 1973), reaches into major textbooks, handbooks, monographs, and proceedings (Benson, Benson, and Ilson 1986; Stock 1988; Battenberg 1991; Béjoint 2016), receives consideration by metalexicographers (Reichmann 1976; Wiegand 1992), and has especially influenced Anna Wierzbicka (1972, 1985, 2001; and Wierzbicka and Goddard 2017, for example). One may consider it a foundational contribution to late twentieth-century semantics, cited, for instance, by Kempson (1977). Lyons (1977), though present at the Bloomington conference, has preferred to cite the later, more fully developed iterations of Weinreich's theory.

Dean Stoddard Worth

A. Worth (1927–2016), after an undergraduate degree at Dartmouth and post-graduate work at the École nationale des langues vivantes and the Sorbonne, proceeded to Harvard, where Roman Jakobson directed his dissertation (Anderson 2016, 269; I draw freely on this account). Within a year, in 1957, he had settled at UCLA, where he taught until his retirement in 1994. Over a long career, during which he had published 171 items by 2000 (see Dingley and Ferder 2000, 263–75), he traversed many Slavic languages and literatures—he was more philologist than linguist—with emphases on Russian and Western Kamchadal, or Itelmen, the last surviving Kamchatkan language. He served as chair of the Department of Slavic, Eastern European, and Eurasian Languages and Cultures at UCLA several times, and he was honored by colleagues and students with two festschrifts (Birnbaum and Flier 1995; Dingley and Ferder 2000). He edited the *International Journal of Slavic Linguistics and Poetics* from 1959 to 2006.

B. Lexicography played a significant role early in Worth's career. He published *Kamchadal Texts Collected by W. Jochelson* (1961) and later would publish a Western Kamchadal dictionary (1969) that drew primarily but not exclusively on that corpus. Robert Austerlitz (1971, 907/a) criticized it as "less rewarding from a grammatical point of view," which is perhaps interesting given the number of papers at the Bloomington conference devoted to the lexical/grammatical interface, but also proclaimed that "The material is so clearly presented that even the least enterprising reader will find scanning the pages of this dictionary rewarding," suggesting careful attention to the user's perspective, another topic central to the conference and *PiL*. A Russian derivational dictionary followed quickly (Worth, Kozak, and Johnson

1970), and Worth continued to work on the subject (see, principally, 1977). His "Comments" in *PiL* mark the beginning of his lexicographical work—they were only his sixteenth publication.

C. Sections titled "Comments" are rarely cited, and, except for the general works discussed earlier in this introduction, Worth's comments have drawn little scholarly notice.

NOTES

1. Householder recounted his love of dictionaries on different but complementary terms in *Linguistic Speculations* (1971, 1) with this memory: "When I was in high school, our house burned down with all its furnishings and books; one of the new things we acquired as a result was a Webster's Unabridged Dictionary with an introduction and list of Indo-European roots; this fascinated me, and I resolved to study as many languages as I could. I took a series of degrees in Greek (and Latin), as the most relevant field available. By chance there was a war, and by chance I heard of an Army establishment concerned with grammars and dictionaries. I decided to apply for a job, in the hope of maybe being assigned there later if drafted. By chance I got the job. The place was, of course, full of young linguists." By chance, as I'll go on to demonstrate, he met many of those who participated in the 1960 conference on lexicography during the war years. Householder and Thomas Sebeok (1951) had taken lexicographers to task for their treatment of the term *linguistician* many years in advance of the conference, perhaps emblematic of the uneasy relationship between the two disciplines until the Bloomington conference brought them together.

2. Smith and 165 Broadway come up several times in the linguistic memoirs collected in the three *First Person Singular* volumes, including those by Householder, Raven McDavid (1980, 4 and 8), Stanley S. Newman (1991, 218–19), Herbert Penzl (1991, 247), Allan Walker Read (1991, 281–83), and Ernst Pulgram (1998, 179); further, contemporaries of those in the Army Language Section served under Mortimer Graves, executive secretary of the American Council of Learned Societies (ACLS), in the Intensive Language Program sponsored by ACLS, including William G. Moulton (1961; 1980, 61), Charles F. Hockett (1980, 103), J Milton Cowan (1991, 71–78), Robert A. Hall (1991, 177), and Newman again (1991, 217). These and many others formed a dense network of wartime linguists who became a somewhat more diffuse network as they spread through the American university system once the war was won. Cowan reports (1991, 77–78) that several participants in the Bloomington conference worked for Graves on a series of language guides, including Cornyn (*Spoken Burmese*; Cornyn 1945–46), the Kahanes (*Spoken Greek*; Kahane, Kahane, and Ward 1945–46), Hoenigswald (*Spoken Hindustani*; Hoenigswald 1945), and Mary Haas (*Spoken Thai*; Haas and Subhanka 1945–48). Sebeok contributed guides to Spoken Finnish and Spoken Hungarian. Einar Haugen, who would later review *PiL*, wrote the guide for spoken Norwegian.

3. The bilingual dictionaries Householder has in mind are restricted phrase books of the Technical Manual (TM) 30–600 series, which were underway at the US Army Forces Institute and American University in Washington, DC, in 1942, but became the province of 165 Broadway in June 1943 (Hall 1991, 155–56). Those in the Intensive Language Program (see note 2) compiled language guides in the TM 30–300 series. Over the years, I've collected some of these ephemeral but historically significant booklets—each of them 5 ½ by 4 ¼ inches—including those for Spanish (TM 30–300), Portuguese as spoken in Brazil (TM 30–301), Swedish (TM 30–312), North African Arabic (TM 30–321), Thai (TM 30–331), Chinese (TM 30–333), Cantonese (TM 30–334), Malay (TM 30–339), and Japanese

(TM 30–341), as well as the phrase books for Turkish (TM 30–618), Chinese (TM 30–633), and Greek (TM 30–650). It surprises me that I've held on to these pamphlets for decades, but Householder (1971, 1) understood that research often enough involves "a succession of coincidences and marginal motivations." Pamphlets in the 600 series included sections on emergency expressions, general expressions, personal needs, location and terrain, roads and transportation, communications, reconnaissance, landing a plane, numbers, size, time, letters, etc., additional terms, important signs, international road signs, and an alphabetical word list. What constituted sample sentences within these pamphlets is unclear—what's printed does not quite align with Householder's description of the process of writing one. Or, perhaps 165 Broadway produced other artifacts I have not yet seen.

4. Edwin Bonsack Jr., also served during World War II, from September 1942 to January 1946, in the US Army Air Force (Library of Congress 1972, 438/a), but he was not associated with the 165 Broadway linguists. Neither were Chavarría-Aguilar, who served in the US Army on the Aleutian Islands (O'Brien 2005), Conklin, who was stationed in the Philippines (Conklin 1998, xviii–xx), and Martin in Japan for the US Navy (Ramsey 2004a, 260). Cornyn, Haas, and the Kahanes participated in an American Council of Learned Societies collaboration with the Army Specialized Training Program, producing language-learning materials—textbooks, dictionaries, etc.—for critical languages (see note 2 and References). In postwar America, they shared the important credential of wartime service, uniformed or not.

5. If we examine the participants in the spirit of Householder's comment, we find further micronetworks multiplying and intensifying. For instance, the Kahanes and Malkiel were intimate colleagues, despite half a continent's distance between them (Kahane 1991, 200). The Kahanes were in place at Illinois when Tietze taught there, and later, when Saporta did his doctoral work there. (Years of service underlying these relationships appear in the notes on contributors in Chapter 5 and in the memorial articles cited there.) Tietze and Worth arrived at UCLA in the same year. Haas and Penzl taught concurrently at Berkeley, after Penzl had overlapped with Gedney at Michigan for three years. Conklin first encountered Gleason at monthly Yale Linguistic Club meetings (Conklin 1998, xxiv), and he met Martin while at Yale, too, in the early 1950s (1998, xxv). Later that decade, Conklin, Weinreich, and Read were all at Columbia together. One must remember that, in the early 1950s, universities were smaller than they are today, and linguists were dispersed among departments. Throughout the 1950s and 1960s, Read regularly spoke at meetings of the Linguistic Circle of Columbia University and the Linguistic Circle of New York (later, the International Linguistic Association), the organization that sponsored Martinet and Weinreich's journal *Word* (Adams and Bailey 2017, 388–94). So, though one might not think of Weinreich, Conklin, and Read as natural associates, they surely knew one another (see Conklin 1998, xxvi, for Weinreich), and, despite his very different scholarly preoccupations and commitments, Read may have influenced them as he did Weinreich's close associate, William Labov (see Labov 2005). Along another thread of affiliation, Read had contributed to Malone's festschrift (Kirby and Woolf 1949) as an author and editor of *American Speech*, the ties that bound them together. At Yale, with Cornyn already teaching there, Haas and Hoenigswald barely overlapped in the late 1930s; Gedney (PhD 1947) and Martin (PhD 1950) overlapped there too. Hoenigswald arrived at Penn in 1948, while Iannucci and Chavarría-Aguilar worked on the degrees they took there in 1952. Bonsack taught German at Penn for several years until 1951. Davies (2008, 869) writes of Hoenigswald, "in what for a long time was a very small department he had acted as a linking factor. George Cardona (200[6]:13) remembers that in

1965 the department 'was a small close-knit group of scholars who not only regularly met to exchange ideas but frequently also attended one another's seminars. Henry was central to this group,'" as he may well have been a decade or so earlier. In other words, taking these academic connections and the refugee, wartime, and Linguistic Society networks altogether, pretty much everyone on the conference program knew, if not quite everyone else, a rather large proportion of those speaking. How these relationships may have informed Householder's choice of participants is, alas, unknown and perhaps unknowable, but that they had some effect seems likely.

6. Sledd had been publicly critical of George L. Trager and Henry Lee Smith's *An Outline of English Structure* (1951) before he published *A Short Introduction to English Grammar* (1959), but trenchantly in that book too. D. F. Theall (1960, 62) noted in a review that Sledd's book "probably demonstrates more pointedly than any previous work the problems of an age of transition in grammatical studies." For, alongside Sledd and Trager and Smith, Chomsky had simultaneously redirected linguistics, first in his book *Syntactic Structures* (1957) and then in his infamous review (1959) of B. F. Skinner's *Verbal Behavior* (1957). Sledd appreciated Chomsky (Theall 1960, 66) and was always interested in his work (Daniell 2003, 219), but never became a Chomskyan—Sledd never followed anyone. Still, in his iconoclastic way, he moved linguistics forward. As Theall (1960, 60) would write, "In a recent review in *Language*, Fred Householder criticized the conservatism of Hockett's *Course in Modern Linguistics*. Anyone with such inclinations would be totally alarmed at Sledd's *Short Introduction*." Sledd's appeal to Householder was complicated. Sledd's manner provoked as much controversy as his linguistics—he had long been "the chief gadfly on the body of American linguistics" (Gunter 1960, 125). Robert P. Stockwell—Bolinger (1991, 22) would write that Stockwell was "the true no-nonsense linguist" whose "fairness [was] impeccable"—admitted that "Sledd was, and is, intimidating, at least to me. Dwight Bolinger described himself as 'a kind of sorcerer's apprentice of the counterexample' . . . but Sledd was more so. And he did it with more glee" (Stockwell 1998, 236). One hears the gadfly buzzing, perhaps with glee, in Sledd's response to the conference session/book section on "Structural Linguistics and the Preparation of Dictionaries."

7. Many SIL missionary-linguists operated according to tagmemics, a theory of language in human behavior proposed and developed by Kenneth L. Pike, of the University of Michigan and longtime president of SIL International. As Richard W. Bailey explained (K. Pike 1981, viii), "Pike rejected the organization of linguistic study from smaller units to larger ones that was a hallmark of so-called post-Bloomfieldian linguistics: if the next level of linguistic structure could not be described until the level below had been perfectly analyzed—as the tenets of Bloomfieldian orthodoxy claimed—then how could the practical work of Bible translation go forward?" Pike answered by flipping the hierarchy, by starting with cultural meaning rather than phonology. For more on tagmemics, see Kenneth Pike (1981) and Waterhouse (1974). Given SIL's emphases, its missionaries were naturally interested in taxonomies, semantic theory and lexicography, and the relations between semantics and syntax so well represented at the Bloomington conference.

8. A brief comment here may serve better than citations in the cases of Moyne and Irving, as I've mapped their careers in biographical notes in their books, affiliations in journal article by-lines, etc. The list of sources is too long and their yields individually too little to give them space in this edition.

9. One of Balint's publications on pidgins and creoles counts as a curiosity, despite its real scholarship. The *English–Pidgin and French Dictionary of Sports and Phrase Book* (1969),

printed on glossy paper by *The South Pacific Post* of Port Moresby, the capitol of Papua New Guinea, is eighty-nine pages of handy phrases (1–46)—topically similar to those produced at 165 Broadway and in the Intensive Language Program (see note 3)—and a rather more serious lexicographical treatment of sports terms understood trilingually (49–89). Perhaps the most interesting feature of the book, due to its publication by a newspaper, is the fourteen pages of adds following the glossary text, but the book was a guide to the area in several ways, as a special publication to support the third South Pacific Games of 1969, held in Port Moresby—a seal announcing the affiliation appears on the cover in the same ink as the book's title. Besides this little dictionary, he had lexicography on his mind, publishing "Towards an Encyclopedic Dictionary of Nuginian (Melanesian Pidgin)" (1973), though no such dictionary appeared.

10. By an odd coincidence, Joseph K. Yamagiwa, though a Japanese linguist by the time he wrote the review in question, was also an experienced lexicographer. He had started his academic career in English and, after taking his MA at the University of Michigan in 1930, worked as a subeditor for several years on the *Early Modern English Dictionary* project—for more on which, see Richard W. Bailey (1980 and 1985), and Adams (2009 and 2010)—under the direction of Charles C. Fries. He had also served as a language specialist in World War II, as director of the Army Military Intelligence Japanese Language School and supervisor of the Japanese Translation Program, but he was stationed in Ann Arbor, Michigan ("Memorial" 1968), so outside of the New York/Philadelphia/Washington, DC, axis that defined Householder's wartime network.

11. Another Indiana University conference, "Style in Language," organized by Sebeok and held in 1958, involved precirculation of papers: "A year beforehand, selected scholars wrote papers, copies of which were sent to all participants" (Messing 1961, 257), which, within a shorter time frame, seems to have been the procedure for the 1960 conference, as well. See also note 20.

12. The Kahanes proposed that Georgacas might follow the example of some etymological dictionaries by organizing all related terms under the etymon, but they thus also seem to endorse the *stammwortprinzip*, which used the same organizational scheme in more general dictionaries, as early as Robert Estienne in the *Latinae Linguae Thesaurus* (1543), Henri Estienne in the *Thesaurus Graecae Linguae* (1572), and Jean Nicot (1530–1600) in *Thresor de la Langue Françoise* (1606) and subsequently codified in German philology (see Béjoint 2010, 21; Boulanger 2003, 423; Reichmann 2012, 176; and Considine 2014, 75–6 and 134–5). The most visible English dictionary compiled by this method is Charles Richardson's *New Dictionary of the English Language* (1836) (see Adams 2019). The problem did not rise high enough among topics of the conference to appear even briefly in Householder's "Summary Report" (383–86).

13. Some years ago, Connie Eble sent me a collection of offprints Norman Eliason had received over the decades. Eliason taught at the University of North Carolina, specializing in Old and Middle English language and literature, the history of the English language, and American speech. He was not notably interested in dictionaries, not in a *PiL* way. When he retired, he donated the offprints to Eble, his student and successor, who kept an eye on them until she, too, thought of retiring, at which point she started to empty her office of unnecessary things, like the offprints. I gladly added them to my collection. Eliason might have met any or all of the participants in the Bloomington conference at one or another institute, meeting, or event, but he had longstanding professional relationships with Read and Malone. We know this in part because he had several Malone offprints in his files—

he was one of Malone's students. One suspects Malone, reciprocally, had several of his. Unsurprisingly, then, one discovers offprints of Malone's and Read's contributions to *PiL* among all the others. Though he ordered enough offprints to supply many a linguist he didn't yet know, Conklin's offprint is absent from Eliason's files.

14. Aside from the *OED*, little is written about major historical dictionaries. Gilliver (2016) includes useful information about the other dictionaries mentioned in this paragraph. For the *Century*, see a special section devoted to its centenary in *Dictionaries* (1996), comprising articles by Bailey, Metcalf, Liberman, Gilman, Lance, Hancher, and Barnhart. Dareau (2012) epitomizes the complex history of *The Dictionary of the Older Scottish Tongue*, while Bailey (1980 and 1985) and Adams (2009 and 2010) account for the *Early Modern English Dictionary* project. The *Middle English Dictionary* is well represented by Lewis, Williams, and Miller (2007) and Adams (2009). The *Dictionary of American Regional English* has been written about piecemeal, but Adams (2011 and 2013a) are good overviews, and Adams (2013b) provides a bibliography of relevant works about *DARE* to that date. General accounts of the *Dictionary of American English* and the *Dictionary of Americanisms* have yet to be written, though see Adams (1998 and 2020).

15. Bogaards's way of titling the conference reminds me, just as an historical matter, to clarify what people called it at the time, simply "Conference on Lexicography" (see Kahane and Kahane, page 353). It's only natural for later commentators to assume that the conference was called "Problems in Lexicography," as Hartmann (2007, 7) and Franjié (2009, 34) assume, but for our purposes, it's important to note that *Problems in Lexicography* is the not especially inspired title at which Householder and Saporta arrived when required to title their book, in this sense distinct from their conference.

16. Here follows an accounting of whom Zgusta cited from *PiL* and how often: Malkiel (23), Weinreich (19), Martin (13), Swanson (11), Harrell (10), Gleason (9), Householder (9), the Kahanes (7), Gedney (6), Iannucci (5), Hoenigswald (4), Malone (4), Sledd (4), Barnhart (3), Cornyn (3), Conklin (2) Haas (2), Chavarría-Aguilar and Penzl (1). Note the ways in which this adjusts the book's influence: one way in 1971 when focused on lexicography, another way across disciplines in the decades to follow. Here, Martin, Swanson, and Harrell are much more important than they would prove to be over time, while, for lexicographical theory, Barnhart and Conklin barely register, though their contributions would figure importantly in later work. Malkiel knew what he was doing—all metalexicography has to account for the different types of dictionaries—and his contribution thus became indispensable to the lexicographical literature. Of course, Zgusta refers to many other works, some cited in the original *PiL* and in the introduction to this edition, including reviews of *PiL*, specifically those by Uitti and Urdang, and other works by contributors to *PiL*—that is, Read appears in the *Manual*, just not in his *PiL* guise.

17. These estimates of significance depend partly on accurate chronology, and I wonder whether sometimes, in the profession's memory, the sequence of events isn't a bit confused. For instance, Gouws (2011, 20) writes, "the introduction of mainstream lexicography has been as a subsection of linguistics. Some of the early publications in this regard were Chapman (1948), Doroszewski (1954), Garvin (1955), Országh (1962), and the significant Householder & Saporta (1967), a book in which the majority of contributions focused on problems of a linguistic nature." Put aside, for the moment, that the volume inaugurates the "user's perspective," a nonlinguistic issue (see chaps. 2 and 5). It makes a difference that *PiL* was published concurrently with Országh, not subsequently, and that it's a decade older than Zgusta's *Manual* (1971). I'm not complaining about Gouws's reference to the "second

edition" of *PiL*. Indeed, I've made the same mistake (see Adams 2014, 14). In fact, I think our confusion is helpfully suggestive. Many cite *PiL* from 1967 rather 1962, which suggests that the 1962 versions made an impression in North America, but that it took the 1967 version to extend the book's influence further (for more on different textual states of the book, see chap. 4). Tollenaere's (1969) late review suggests the same, although Országh, among Europeans, reviewed the earlier version. The current edition justifies itself partly on clarifying the historical and textual record, lost in the ferment of an emerging profession.

18. Among these, Franklin was the least generally prominent, though he figured significantly in the Summer Institute of Linguistics, as the world's leading linguist of Kewa, a language of New Guinea (see Waterhouse 1974, *passim*; and Rensch 1977, 92–93, 99, 117). He was also more closely affiliated with lexicography than other SIS linguists, becoming a charter member of the Dictionary Society of North America in 1977. Tollenaere, at the time of his review, had recently written an important book on lexicology (Tollenaere 1963) and published a revision of Jan de Vries' *Nederlands Etymologisch Woordenboek* (De Vries and Tollenaere 1965); one may read of his exploits, lexicographic and otherwise, in Heestermans (2012). Jablonski (2003) provides an interesting account of Oszágh's life and work. Urdang received considerable memorial attention, from Zimmer (2008), Weber (2008), and *The Times of London* ("Laurence Urdang" 2008). Dembowski (2000) epitomizes Uitti's prolific career in a festschrift that goes some way to explaining both his students' affection for him and his most careful attention to *PiL*—you would have wanted him to direct your dissertation. Haugen's significance as a scholar of language contact and bilingualism is well attested in obituaries by Clyne (1994), Meyers-Scotten (1995), and, most extensively, Fishman (1995), but he also told his own story (Haugen 1980) alongside Hoenigswald (1980), Householder (1980), and Malkiel (1980).

19. Interestingly, this isn't the first time the blind men and elephant fable appeared as criticism of an Indiana University linguistics conference; see Messing (1961, 256) and notes 11 and 20.

20. The contrast between the receptions of *Style in Language* and *PiL* could not be starker. The latter came in for criticism, some of it grumpy if legitimate, but the former was thoroughly castigated. In his review, Gordon Messing (1961, 256–57) announced, "I can say flatly that I regard both the conference and its printed record as largely a waste of time and money." He was unimpressed with the transcript of postpaper discussion: "Again, I am not at all happy at Sebeok's decision to 'preserve a flavor of spontaneity' (4) by including the ipsissima verba of the participants. Spontaneity, a dubious virtue in this context, might have better yielded place to coherence and clarity" (257). In his review, Malkiel (1962, 269/a) called Messing's "an especially acrimonious review" and recommended "for a better balanced, though by no means uncritical, appraisal," a review by, of all people, Karl Uitti (1962, 425), who explained, "the ultimate failure of *Style in Language* is to provide a clear statement of the problems suggested by its title." Comparing Uitti's reviews of *Style in Language* and *PiL* suggests the relative merits of the two conferences and the proceedings that followed them. Malkiel (1962, 271/b), always the gentleman, tempered his dismay with sentences like, "Another source of the book's imbalance is the bizarre distribution of brainpower by ages or generations." I think we'd find this less bizarre today, but it's worth noting that Sol Saporta, barely out of graduate school, was on the program with René Wellek, I. A. Richards, John Hollander, W. K. Wimsatt, Jr., Monroe Beardsley, and Roman Jakobson, not all of whom linguists will know, but who figured among the great literary theorists and aestheticians of the day. I'm less concerned with the imbalance of experience, prestige, and putative

"brainpower" than I am with the fact that Saporta witnessed the mayhem firsthand—so did Householder—and whatever criticism I have of the Conference on Lexicography's organization (see chap. 1), their ringside view may have influenced many of the parameters they set and some of the conference mechanisms they eschewed, like recording the discussions. The reviews of *Style in Language* itemized here all appeared after the dictionary conference, so did not influence planning directly, but such reactions may well have been in the air—Haugen, for instance, may have breathed it—ambient elements of the professional niche the dictionary conference and *PiL* also inhabited.

21. Although I allow for more computer awareness at the 1960 conference than Tollenaere, one cannot but agree with him that, by 1969, *PiL* was outdated when it came to automation. Introducing his book, *Computing in the Humanities*, Richard W. Bailey (1982, 1) nodded to Tollenaere (1963), but also observed that, in North America, at least, the humanities and computing didn't really connect until September 1964, when IBM sponsored its Literary Data Processing Conference. Participants in the 1960 conference who already had significant experience in computing were very much in the vanguard of what we now take for granted. It's worth noting, I think, that Tollenaere (1953) and Bailey (1982) were both published by North-Holland Publishing, and that Bailey, who had written a fair amount about computer applications in lexicography by then—see, for instance, Robinson and Bailey (1973), in the same section of a book about the computer and literary studies as Tollenaere (1973)—contributed a paper on the *Early Modern English Dictionary* project to Pijnenburg and Tollenaere's collection on problems of historical lexicography (Bailey 1980), in the meantime.

PART TWO:
PROBLEMS IN LEXICOGRAPHY

Edited by

FRED W. HOUSEHOLDER

and SOL SAPORTA

FOREWORD

On the eleventh and twelfth of November 1960, a small group of linguists and lexicographers met at Indiana University to discuss a variety of problems related to the making of dictionaries. The conference was organized at the contractual instigation (Contract no. SAE 8965) of the US Office of Education, as a possible help to the various teams of scholars then (and now) at work on bilingual dictionaries under contract with them (in accordance with Title VI, Section 602 of the National Defense Education Act). The moving spirit at NDEA headquarters was the late Austin E. Fife, of Utah State University, who was unfortunately not able to attend the conference himself. The task of organizing the conference was undertaken by Sol Saporta (of the University of Washington) and Fred W. Householder, ably assisted before, during and after the sessions by Dr. Heles Contreras (of the University of Washington).

The present volume, supported in part by Indiana University through the Research Center in Anthropology, Folklore, and Linguistics, contains the papers read and discussed at that conference, with (in most cases) only a minimum of revision by the authors or interference by the editors. Though the proceedings were recorded on tape, it has not proved possible to incorporate any of the lively discussion of the meetings in this volume; the comments of the four official "discussants" are, however, included, as is the summary report prepared by Householder for the Office of Education. It is hoped that the present publication may prove stimulating and helpful to other scholars who face similar problems of dictionary-making, as well as those who are interested in theoretical problems of lexicon and semantics.

FRED W. HOUSEHOLDER
INDIANA UNIVERSITY

[The editor of this monograph series approved with pleasure the publication of the Lexicography Symposium in RC-PAFL, as edited by Professors Saporta and Householder; but the pleasure was tinged with regret.

[The Conference papers are now published in the order in which they were planned, before the Conference, regrettably without benefit of discussant emphasis which remains unpublished and largely unreflected in this volume, though all authors had opportunity to reorganize their papers in the light of the discussion, and some took advantage of this opportunity. The planners and the authors of the Conference deserve congratulations on summing up the end of an epoch in lexicography, now that we are on the eve of another epoch which will give more emphasis to typology and include the use of computers in lexical work. That the discussants of the Conference papers which follow were not insensitive to this transition of epochs in dictionary making is stated in detail in the context of my review of several dictionaries in a series begun by the Summer Institute of Linguistics (*American Anthropologist* 63:876–78). C. F. Voegelin]

I

THE PREPARATION OF DICTIONARIES I: THEORETICAL CONSIDERATIONS

A TYPOLOGICAL CLASSIFICATION OF DICTIONARIES ON THE BASIS OF DISTINCTIVE FEATURES

Yakov Malkiel
University of California, Berkeley

1. Background

This paper embodies a report on an experiment undertaken some two years ago. The results of this specific experiment may or may not lend themselves to generalization. From the mid-1940s, I had engaged for fifteen years in various studies of Romance etymology and derivation with a clearly discernible emphasis on Hispanic material. These researches were based in part on the perusal of original texts, but inescapably, a wide range of dictionaries had been tapped for miscellaneous bits of information. There exists a tradition among lexicologists to offer to their fellow-workers, besides the genuine fruits of their researches, also an inventory of the tools employed. Thus, W. von Wartburg's monumental *Französisches Etymologisches Wörterbuch* (1922–2002), slanted in the direction of dialectology, was accompanied by a bibliography of patois vocabularies. Instead of preparing, along traditional lines, a similar Hispanic bibliography containing items either arranged in a straight alphabetical sequence or subdivided into several regional groups— say, Asturian, Andalusian, Mexican—I began asking myself whether a pervasive classification by lexicographic genres was at all feasible. A rough break-down of this kind was, of course, nothing new, since numerous research-library catalogues make it a point to distinguish between mono-, bi-, trilingual, and polyglot dictionaries and likewise set apart encyclopedic, historical, comparative, and etymological reference works, and surely many other sharply delineated varieties, especially those appealing to a specific kind of reader. As is frequently the case with classification, the core of the difficulty seemed to lie in the overlapping of the categories hastily established on the basis of first impressions. To adduce but one example: aside from straight etymological dictionaries, geared to the one purpose of supplying information on word origins (on various levels of scholarly sophistication), there exist all-purpose monolingual dictionaries and, far less commonly, bilingual dictionaries which, in response to the layman's curiosity, also carry stray bits of etymological information, representing, in a way, mixed genres of lexicography. In simplified listing, should such transitional types be altogether disregarded, and the pure types alone be placed in the focus of attention? Such an arbitrary decision would tend to curtail unduly the available material. The alternative would be to do justice to as many titles as possible, on condition that either the number of categories be radically increased or that each item, i.e., each lexicographic venture, instead of being treated as an inseparable unit, be decomposed into a number of salient features allowing of a large number of combinations. The obvious model that I had in mind was the separation of a speech sound into a number of distinctive features, an analysis originally practiced with particular skill by the school of European phonologists but at present widely adopted on both sides of the Atlantic. Was it legitimate to regard a reference book as a bundle of characteristic features which could be reassembled in some kind of arrangement that might be expressed in a simple formula? The article in question stopped short of this last step of providing actual formulas but was designed to lead the reader to the precise point from which such a succinct formulaic labeling could be freely envisaged.[1]

For this particular experiment, limited to a single language and involving, all told, not much more than five hundred items, the distinctive features were chosen so as to satisfy two fundamental requirements: range and neatness of contour. First, the greatest possible number of the vocabularies and glossaries collected at random were to lend themselves to this type of composite characterization. Second, any degree of redundancy in the delimitation of distinctive features was to be scrupulously avoided, each being selected on the basis of its discreteness, i.e., independence of the others. The existence of tendential convergences and affinities was, from the outset, taken for granted, but every feature, to qualify for inclusion, was to preserve under any circumstances its unmistakable identity.

2. A Set of Broad Classificatory Criteria

These aims, it seems, call for the establishment of the following three classificatory criteria, each subject to further subdivision:

1. Classification by *range*;
2. Classification by *perspective*;
3. Classification by *presentation*.

2.1. **Range.** The volume and spread of the material assembled represents, from the layman's and the specialist's viewpoint alike, the most obvious criterion; it is also the most objective, involving by definition tangibles alone. Further subdivision is possible, according as to whether attention is focused on (a) density of entries, (b) number of languages covered or resorted to, (c) degree of concentration on strictly lexical data (at the expense of *realia*, proper names, and the like).

2.2. **Perspective.** Under this label it is advantageous to subsume several broad directions in which bundles of lexical facts are apt to be projected irrespective of the scope of each vocabulary and of the favored style of presentation. Perspective essentially involves the deliberate or semi-naïve attitude of the collector toward the chosen slice of material, i.e., the type of curiosity that drives him in the first place to delimit and launch his project. The specific attitude is best determined if one selects the proper components of the ensemble from a number of oppositions, binary or triadic: (a) with regard to the time axis, the outlook may be historical (dynamic) or synchronic (static); (b) with regard to the basic arrangement, the sequence may be conventional (alphabetic), semantic (ordering by "parts of speech" or provinces of life), or entirely arbitrary (chaotic); (c) with regard to avowed purpose, the prevalent tone may be objective, preceptive (also, viewed from the opposite pole, prohibitive), or jocular. In theory, any vocabulary may be scrutinized from all three angles, and the combination of the three separate analyses determines the composite perspective. On a higher plane of abstraction, one may attempt to establish certain steady or tendential relationships between subclasses within the three categories of temporal projection, sequence of items, and purpose of enterprise.

2.3. **Presentation.** If operating with "perspectives" helped us account for the broad policies, "presentation" serves as a convenient term for subsuming narrower preferences, such as typographic style, use of special symbols and abbreviations, inclusion of incidental grammatical remarks, latitude of definition, volume of verbal documentation and of graphic illustration (if any), and many similar externals. In other words, perspective concerns the lexicographer's logistics and strategy, while presentation involves his tactics. To achieve simplification, analysis may be reduced to the discussion of four salient points: (a) definition; (b) exemplification; (c) graphic illustrations (including maps); and (d) special features (localization in territorial terms, on the social scale, or along the axis of "affectivity"; marking of pronunciation).

Ideally, a formal bibliography or a research-library catalogue may well be based on this (or any improved) set of classificatory principles. While conventional bibliographies and catalogues adequately describe the externals of a publication (format, number of pages, place and date of appearance, etc.), a typological repertory may effectively convey an analytical bird's-eye view of the inner configuration of each item (short of value judgments): its spatial and temporal range, its degree of selectivity, the interplay of its three basic perspectives (distance from the historical axis, schema of arrangement, and level of discourse), plus its editorial and typographic techniques of presentation.

3. Some Special Conditions

Last year's original monograph underlying the present paper (Malkiel 1959) supplied only a few particularly representative instances of a given variety or subvariety, sometimes out of more than twenty available illustrations. As long as the classificatory schema is valid, expanding such a skeletal documentation to one of fuller size or of relative completeness remains a matter of space budgeting. Little more than a vague hint of the preliminary bibliographic spadework can be provided in the present epitome.

What marks an item for inclusion in a typological survey is less the intrinsic quality of craftsmanship than the novelty of the architectural design. In extreme cases, an elaborate work structured along conventional lines may fall short of acceptance if it enriches the existing models by no truly original device or daring combination of familiar devices. Conversely, a departure from earlier practice—even if deemed by hindsight a failure or at best a controversial accomplishment—deserves consideration as an attempt at innovation. At its most austere, a typological classification should steer clear of value judgments; in practice, succinct appraisals amounting to merely parenthetic remarks may be condoned as long as they do not interfere with actual analytical operations.

Aside from its intrinsic significance and charm, the typological approach may produce a wholesome controlling effect: it is apt to disclose noteworthy gaps, identifying combinations of features not yet tried out and may thus open up avenues of approach, not only to all sorts of impracticable oddities, but also to rewarding possibilities so far overlooked. In chosen instances, one can point out how similar lacunae have been successfully filled by fellow-workers concerned with other languages.

Typological sketches are not meant to replace the time-honored genre of formal bibliographies, which are, by and large, more circumstantial, and which silhouette with equal sharpness each work captured by the observer's lens, lending themselves smoothly to evaluative comments. Typology, being the more abstract mode of classification, simply acts as a corrective of straight bibliographic records, breaking loose of anecdotal detail and of the all too often obtrusive "human element." Jointly, bibliography and typology reflect the dual focus of linguistics on individual facts of language, viewed in their undistorted richness and uniqueness and on the underlying broader patterns.

4. Classification by Range

This approach, we recall, allows of further subdivision, according to the variable emphasis on (1) density of entries, (2) number of languages, and (3) extent of concentration on purely lexical data.

4.1. **Measurement of density**. Though ideally a dictionary's relative density, being a quantitative feature, should be subject to precise measurement, there exist in practice almost insurmountable obstacles to a neat statistical tabulation. It is, of course, possible to compute the actual number of entries, and some publishers flaunt it in a subtitle or in commercial advertisement (others claim credit not for the total coverage, but for specific accretions, choosing some earlier authority as an appropriate frame of reference). The figures thus obtained, though accurate in isolation, lend themselves to no meaningful comparison in the absence of generally accepted norms for the selection and grouping of entries. Thus, a few reputable lexicographers, for the sake of maximum compactness, consolidate homophones, subsuming under a single entry two or more words treated separately by such (more conservative) authors as prefer to heed semantic or etymological considerations.

In the case of a living and dynamically changing language, the primary hindrances to a valid comparison of coverage are: (a) the essential instability of its lexicon, a condition precluding the establishment of any definitive repository based on exhaustive excerpts from a finite corpus of texts; (b) the, strictly speaking, incompatible scopes of even the best lexicographic projects so far launched, as a result of sharply divergent objectives and techniques. Among the compilers of dictionaries few have bothered to lay down binding norms or to abide by any. Numerous dictionaries allow the inclusion of archaisms, whether or not marked as such; only a few workers resolutely attempt to weed out obsolete terms by starting from entirely fresh collections of raw data or settle on a compromise by making carefully pre-established concessions to the dominant preference (e.g., by respecting the usage of a few classics, explicitly identified). As regards coverage in breadth, it seems inadmissible, then, to maintain that a given dictionary contains, say, 80% of the total lexicon, as long as that total remains undefined; and it is hazardous to assert that one dictionary is more comprehensive than another, unless they are modeled on exactly the same pattern. To compound the difficulty, lexical range is concomitantly determined by coverage in depth, i.e., by the wealth of recorded meanings (including, rightly or wrongly, contextual connotations) and congealed sequences (idioms). Since an objective, absolute classification of meaning has so far remained an unattainable goal, much depends on the intended degree of elaborateness and, in a bilingual venture, also on the distance between the two languages at issue: for practical purposes, a Spanish–Portuguese dictionary need not be as detailed on the phraseological side as, say, its Spanish–Aztec counterpart. Under these circumstances, it may often be wiser to dispense altogether with statistics and to rely on rough impressionistic appraisals for their provisional usefulness. One paradoxical comment on monumentality in this field: frequently, the most voluminous collections must receive a conspicuously low rating on grounds other than that of sheer size.

At the opposite extreme of the continuum, one encounters exceedingly brief and casual word-lists: collections of medieval glosses (some of them very meager and not even organized as miniature vocabularies), miscellaneous records of dialect forms, countless short arrays of words pertaining to ultramodern slang or to certain professional jargons of striking, sometimes perverse, appeal to readers at large. Most of these lists, scattered over obscure or ephemeral periodicals, are doomed to remain practically unavailable for ordinary research purposes [but see Liberman 2010]. Other short word-lists difficult of access to the uninitiated include the vocabularies—some of them gems of neat workmanship—appended to collegiate editions of literary masterpieces in classical and modern foreign languages and, on the trade book market, glossaries accompanying contemporary novels and short stories written in a national language, but, for the ordinary reader's comfort at least, excessively spiced with regional flavor. To these nuggets of knowledge, one may add those extra-brief word lists (sometimes reduced to a single page) that form part of the typical "academic" editions of classical and medieval texts. There exist trustworthy catalogues of such editions, both mono- and bilingual, but very few and at that fragmentary master-lists of the items actually contained in these minimum lists.

We have so far worked on the assumption that dictionaries represent variously scaled abridgments of an ideally complete lexicographic record. This premise requires a corrective: not a few compilations include words that have never existed in the reality of living speech or of written usage. This excess baggage embraces, first of all, isolated "ghost words"—old misprints or spurious readings inadvertently carried over from one dictionary into another. Such blemishes modern workers, at the cost of hard labor, endeavor to ferret out one by one. Far more numerous and, worse, more insidious are the "latent words" smuggled in deliberately. In languages possessing an arsenal of productive suffixes (such as Slavic or Romance) a lexicographer can quite unobtrusively manufacture, by the hundreds and thousands, derivatives of his own making. These formations are readily understandable and give the appearance of authenticity; the truth is that speakers, for some reason or other, have not bothered to activate on the same scale all these grammatical potentialities. It is difficult to detect such camouflaged illicit entries, especially in view of legitimate borderline cases (nonces); an unduly geometric design of representative word families, a dictionary's too heavy saturation with certain recurrent derivational schemes at once arouses the suspicion of an experienced reader.

The average dictionary not only tends to overlook differences in chronological levels but as a rule represents a medley of diverse social and regional dialects. Full-scale lexical treatment of a strictly defined social dialect has so far been relatively infrequent; concomitantly, however, the social category of speakers may be implied in the researcher's choice of a regional sector (rural versus urban speech). In inquiries concerned with peculiar linguistic milieus (immigrants, "bohemians," and the like), the threads of regional and of social dialects are inextricably interwoven. At this point, the original monograph examines in considerable detail the patterns of dialect vocabularies and those of philological glossaries.

The unadorned dialect vocabulary must be distinguished from monographs balancing lexicography with grammar and with specimens of texts, also from word indexes attached to or implied in grammatical analyses. The dialect area selected as a unit may vary from a hamlet to a continent, the controlling factors being the diversification of speech, the configuration of the terrain, the pattern of political allegiances, and the availability of field workers and informants. As research grows more and more specialized, master dictionaries for dialect groups become an urgent *desideratum*, and the scope of a regional vocabulary based on field work will depend on the number of interviewers and interviewees. Most regional vocabularies, instead of affording a total view of the chosen lexicon, are satisfied with recording deviations from standard usage, like so many tidbits; a few subdivide them further into archaisms, broad and narrow localisms, foreignisms, etc. A special, neatly detachable strain in a given regional variety may be the object of a separate vocabulary. This is true in particular of those monographs which concern themselves with autochthonous Indian [i.e., Native American] words absorbed by a national variety of American Spanish, e.g., the Araukan components of Chilean.

The range of a philological vocabulary may be delimited by the distance between points selected along the time axis. The historical dictionary of the future may dissolve into a series of chronologically bounded vocabularies reflecting a roughly fixed number of superimposed layers. One finds a variety of narrower scopes in exegetic vocabularies, assembled around the usages of individual authors, texts, or genres—some of them aiming at exhaustiveness (concordances), while others are overtly and explicitly, or tacitly and loosely, selective. The compiler's readiness to do full or partial justice to the manuscript tradition and the inclusion of supporting evidence, in varying dosages, from miscellaneous collateral sources, yield two further yardsticks for the measurement of lexicographic scope. Though dialectology stresses space, while philological analysis entails movements along the time axis, the two approaches are not mutually exclusive, since artistic works may display adequate and not infrequently unique specimens of speech dialectally tinged—inviting glossaries straddling the two disciplines.

The density of a vocabulary may be determined by the degree of commonness (in statistical terms, frequency) of the words to be included—a distinctly modern criterion. In certain lines of practical work (preparation of graded elementary textbooks, dilution of fine literature for classroom use) the need has arisen for precisely circumscribed core vocabularies. Some workers distinguish between the coordinates of "range" and "frequency," for which one may substitute breadth and depth of penetration. Aside from statistically slanted word lists there exist at present comparable tabulations of phrases (idioms) and syntactical constructions; from all such storehouses of data one may extract direct or, at least, indirect information on this particular aspect of the lexicon. Printed sources may be freely supplemented or even replaced by samples of spontaneous or controlled speech. One may subdivide the body of the vocabulary into several layers, on the basis of increasingly higher frequency; one worker (Eaton 1940) discriminates between four such groups, recording them both separately and in a master list in which raised numerals act as classifiers, and noteworthy transparent derivatives not caught in the meshes of the statistical network are added as a bonus.

The various formats that have become the stock-in-trade of the publishing business specializing in dictionaries frequently offer excellent outlets for the varying patterns of amplitude selected by the lexicographers—or by the masterminds in charge of their projects.

4.2. Number of languages involved. A second way of classifying dictionaries by range is to rate them by the number of languages covered or resorted to. Does the use of a second language entail no more than a special type of definitions, namely translations, and does the contrast between mono- and bilingual works consequently involve a matter of presentation rather than of scope? The answer to this question is in the negative; not only is the argument hardly applicable to plurilingual dictionaries, which patently mark an increase in coverage, not a refinement in explanatory technique, but worse, it discounts the fact that numerous bilingual dictionaries are bipartite, hence geared to serving two separate needs measurable in terms of sheer volume.

The monolingual dictionary constitutes a fairly recent genre: even the earliest editions of many tone-setting Academy dictionaries, which one inclines to regard as monolingual almost by definition, made it a point to translate all entries into Latin. In a conservative country like Spain, the unadulterated monolingual dictionary is a creation of the nineteenth century. By modern standards, the only admissible residue of Latin in any such reference work would be the identification of vernacular names of, say, plants and animals by the tags assigned to them in international scientific nomenclature.

The bilingual dictionary (or, if it happens to be short, glossary) is the vocabulary *par excellence*, associated from time immemorial with casual exposure to, or systematic training in, foreign languages, dead or living. In Western civilization, which is not the sole inventor of this genre, rudimentary glossaries (Greek–Latin, Latin–Germanic, Latin–Romance) are traceable to late Antiquity and the early Middle Ages; throughout, the preponderance of Latin, either as the tool language providing the "glosses," or as the language requiring itself a measure of exegesis, is quite evident. It took the tremendous shifts of the sixteenth century to create a large-scale demand for bilingual reference works involving either two modern western languages (say, Spanish and Italian, or Spanish and English), or one western and one "exotic" language, the latter typically one of special concern to colonizers and missionaries (e.g., Granadine Arabic, Aztec, Maya). The only recent additions to this stock of patterns are dictionaries prepared in the "western" style but serving to contrast two "exotic" languages—of which one, for instance, may very well be Japanese; and a sprinkling of dictionaries pairing off a major "natural" with some "artificial" or "auxiliary" language, e.g., Esperanto, Ido (or Reformed Esperanto), and Volapük.

Many, if not most, bilingual dictionaries are bipartite, irrespective of size and quality. Occasionally (as in the case of Slabý-Grossmann's [1932] German–Spanish venture), the two parts were produced by different compilers, each starting with a clean slate, and as a result, show unintentional discrepancies in bulk and craftsmanship. Then again, in some instances the two sections deliberately have not been planned on the same footing, the need for translations from the foreign into the native language being apparently deemed far more urgent than translation in the reverse direction. This consideration favors the coupling of a full-sized "dictionary" and a meager "vocabulary" typically one fourth or one fifth its size, which in reality is little more than a makeshift index. This asymmetric architectural design would be inappropriate where the two languages are equal partners, as regards social prestige and actual use (say, English and Russian); it is marginally acceptable if some kind of hierarchy has crystallized, the dead language normally surpassing in importance its living counterpart as an object of lexicographic curiosity, since few persons would care to translate modern texts *into* Latin or Old Norse, while dialect speech and cant, for similar reasons, carry greater weight as exhibits than the corresponding literary tongues, used preeminently as tool languages.

At least two categories of bilingual dictionaries are seldom bipartite. Temporarily, this restriction applied to those compiled by proselytizing clergymen for overseas use. Then again, dialect vocabularies and glossaries of medieval words—if at all classifiable as bilingual—almost never contain so much as an index of meanings cast in the modern language chosen as the frame of reference, let alone a full counterview of lexical relationships, to the lasting detriment of advanced research.

A trilingual dictionary may be the outgrowth of a bilingual prototype, whether the author (or a reviser) himself arranges for the expansion or a plagiarist enlarges upon a chosen model. Frequently a preexistent cultural or political climate favors such a necessarily high-aiming venture. Thus, the dual foundation of classical learning accounts for such dictionaries as involve Greek, Latin, and a modern vernacular. Since the interest of Spaniards, Frenchmen, and the Dutch-speaking natives for a while converged on Flanders, it is small wonder that, in response to this demand, a trilingual dictionary should have been engineered at the critical point (Oudin 1639–40). Two important French–Spanish–Basque dictionaries, M. de Larramendi's (1745) and R. M. de Azkue's (1905–06), have their roots in the geographic position of the Euskarian territory, astride the Pyrenees. In another context, one may find a trilingual dictionary at the intersection of two or three cultural traditions; cf. the obvious historical pattern underlying F. Cañes' voluminous *Diccionario Español–Latino–Arábigo* (1787). As a rule, trilingual dictionaries, chiefly for reasons of economy, are unidirectional, i.e., each offers maximum usefulness only to that segment of consulters which has mastered the privileged among the three languages (e.g., Spanish in the case of Cañes). Where differently architected works of this type bear on the same subject, the expert is best served by combining imaginatively these sources of information.

Theoretically, the quadrilingual dictionary leaves room for a vastly increased variety of sequences and combinations, but in practice few of these mathematical possibilities have been exploited on account of the comparative rarity of the genre. The kernel of Howell's genteel *Lexicon tetraglotton* (1660) is a unidirectional dictionary providing for the translation of each English entry into French, Italian, and Spanish. Terreros y Pando's life-work contains three volumes of consecutive Spanish entries translated into French, Spanish, and Italian, and, in a fourth volume, three alphabetic indexes in the reverse direction, each with separate paging.

In contrast to the polyglot Bible, a milestone in the growth of Humanism, the multilingual dictionary, as a scholarly institution, has failed to exert any lasting influence on European (still less on American) intellectual life. Compilations of this kind have usually been manufactured either as saving devices (to economize time, effort, production costs, shelving space) or as veritable *tours de force*, for the sake of the bizarre effects. Of late, the best-known among them have tended to involve from five to ten languages; the arrangement offers almost limitless possibilities.

On the whole, dictionaries contrasting more than two languages have failed to maintain the position of eminence which the intellectual élite assigned to them in the 17th and 18th centuries, as works of scholarship and even of art. In the contemporary world, they have been relegated to the unattractive role of tools in strictly commercial and industrial relations, quite unexciting on the linguistic side. The need for these glossaries of technical terms may soon altogether recede as a result of the invention of electronic translating devices. In a way, the steady decline of the polyglot dictionary has been, paradoxically, a direct consequence of increased lexicographic sophistication: if the semantic, syntactic, and phraseological details which a fastidious reader nowadays demands of his mono- or bilingual dictionary were furnished on this grandiose scale, the resulting increase in bulk would at once defeat the chief purpose of lexical telescoping.

4.3. Extent of concentration on lexical data. Much as biographical dictionary and straight bibliography for centuries tended to represent a single undifferentiated genre, so dictionary and encyclopedia were not always recognized as guides to discrete provinces of knowledge. The infiltration of any encyclopedia-style data is recognizable (a) by the inclusion of proper names, sometimes accompanied by biographic vignettes and profuse geographic descriptions; (b) by a prodigality of comments on ordinary words that seems far in excess of the need for sober definition.

Encyclopedic entries may be relegated to a supplement or a string of supplements (gazetteer, etc.), as has become the dominant fashion in recent decades. Also, they may be intercalated so as to form part of the same unique alphabetical succession of items as the ordinary words. Finally, the trained observer may be in a position to grasp them obliquely, through internal analysis of the definitions. In the first eventuality, there subsists a clear boundary between purely lexical and other bits of information; in the second, the frontier-line is less sharply perceptible; in the third, these extraneous, non-lexical ingredients are submerged beneath the unruffled surface of a deceptively balanced and unified dictionary.

Where the publisher furnishes supplements, by way of bonuses to prospective buyers, one finds a motley array filling needs at present preferably met by separate books (rosters of proper names, guides to pronunciation, grammar, and conversation, collections of proverbs, miniature rhyming dictionaries, lists of synonyms, corrections of misprints, and the like). It has likewise become increasingly customary to provide a separate list of toponyms and anthroponyms in glossaries to medieval texts.

The larding of dictionaries with non-lexical elements, presented as matters of sober fact or in a genial vein, became fashionable toward 1700. In some of its key points (Paris, Barcelona) the book trade, for two long centuries, continued stuffing dictionaries with shreds of information which no discriminating linguist would, but the less knowledgeable public at large frequently does, expect a lexicon to provide into the bargain, as it were—through interfiling, in the compiler's workshop, of authentic word cards and brief excerpts from encyclopedias. This hybrid genre has been mostly known under the name of "encyclopedic dictionary." The same publishing centers have tolerated multi-volume encyclopedias shot through, in defiance of common sense, with genuinely lexical entries.

The least easily detectable dilution of a bi- or trilingual dictionary is achieved by the inclusion of such parenthetic information as is linguistically immaterial. The ideally tight dictionary adds comments to translations only under three conditions: (a) where ambiguity might result from maximum concision, as in the case of homonyms; (b) where circumlocution is inherently in order, on account of a physically, socially, or linguistically conditioned lack of nearly perfect lexical equivalents; (c) where foreseeable grammatical complications may arise. Any other remarks should be rated as redundant. At certain periods, this ideal of stringency was not yet—or no longer—appreciated. Thus, in the Renaissance dictionary, the two halves of each succinct correspondence were of approximately equal length, except where a lexicographer bothered to adduce "authorities" in support of the posited equations. Two centuries later, at the height of the "encyclopedic vogue," the entries as a rule remained brief, but the glosses tended to become more and more inflated.

5. Classification by Perspective

The three basic perspectives, as defined at the outset, involve (1) the fundamental dimension (diachronism versus synchronism), (2) the basic arrangement of entries (conventional, semantic, or arbitrary), (3) the level of tone. Accordingly, the typologist must arrange for three separate analyses.

5.1. The fundamental dimension. The ideal synchronic dictionary would be one least contaminated by acknowledged or, worse, unacknowledged archaisms (many of them—this is the root of the difficulty—firmly engraved, at the very least, in the passive memory of the average literate speaker). The logical avenue of approach to the unadulterated diachronic view is the historical dictionary, provided its materials are so ordered as to bring out plastically the dynamics of lexical development, with heightened attention to the succession and mutual compatibility of meanings. For not a few languages, even those subject to philological inspection, no dictionary aiming uncompromisingly at this particular goal exists or is clearly in sight at present. In the existing historical dictionaries, all too frequently the meaning listed first is not the oldest on record, nor indeed the oldest by the standards of reconstruction, but the one most familiar to moderns or held "fittest" to have acted as a semantic fountainhead.

Over against the historical ordering of linguistic facts, one may place etymological studies, i.e., conjectural research in the *prehistory* of the lexicon. These inquiries fall into several categories, the simplest criterion of classification being that of scope. Even the full-sized etymological dictionaries are diversified, some being ostensibly confined to a single language—Kluge (1883), Skeat (1910), Wartburg (1922–2002)—while others are avowedly comparative—Diez (1869–70), Meyer-Lübke (1930–35), and Pokorny (1957–1969). In practice, one can hardly draw a sharp line of demarcation between isolationists and comparatists; and titles are scarcely reliable guides to treasuries of etymological hypotheses and material. Conceivably, the clearest separation lies between those dictionaries which start from the base, real or assumed, and lead the reader to the product(s), and those that invite one to follow the opposite course. At least one recent venture, V. Garcia de Diego's (1954), is bipartite and tries, between two covers, to afford both views in close succession (unfortunately, with less than satisfactory results).

Aside from fully integrated etymological dictionaries one encounters loosely strung miscellanies of etymological notes, of varying length; "gleanings" for the most part provided by gaps and deficiencies in recently published book-length reference works; and all sorts of concomitant references to etymological clues, usually of scant value to the expert—in glossaries attached to anthologies and chrestomathies, in old-fashioned dialect word-lists, and the like. There exist further etymological vocabularies devoted to specific lexical strains—say, Arabisms, Gallicisms, Italianisms, and Lusisms in Spanish; that is to say, closely coherent groups of borrowings.

5.2. **Three contrasting patterns of arrangement**. The basic arrangement of dictionary items may be alphabetic, semantic, or casual. Each of these categories lends itself to further subdivision; a loose combination of the first two patterns is likewise conceivable.

The alphabetic arrangement, though strictly conventional, is so overwhelmingly dominant that the ordinary person associates with this familiar sequence the very genre of the dictionary, on a par with a catalogue, a directory, or a mailing list. Even where an ancient text has been edited with every conceivable paleographic nicety, the accompanying glossary, as a rule, parades the words in normal script, following the alphabetic order. Such occasional deviations and complications as do come to mind represent frills; thus, as regards Old and even Classical Spanish, there exist conflicting traditions for placing words beginning with c, ch, h, i, j, k, y, z, to say nothing of l, n, r vis-à-vis ll, nn (ñ), rr (R). In dialect works, the use of phonetic (less so of phonemic) transcription imposes an aberrant sequence of letters on account of special characters and unfamiliar diacritic marks. A few lexicographers assemble in alphabetic order, not all words, but only the heads or reputed heads of families. A final formidable obstacle to quick, smooth consultation has been in some countries the inflationary spiral of supplements and even supplements to supplements, a veritable cancergrowth, especially where the accretion amounts to a mere handful of last-minute gleanings.

Remotely akin to the alphabetic dictionary is the rhyming dictionary, which ideally absorbs the totality of a lexicon, distributing the items on the basis of form rather than of meaning. What sets it apart is not only the choice of the stressed vowel rather than of the initial letter as the classificatory norm, but also the departure from the straight linear sequence in favor of sundry groups of varying size. Students of suffixes have derived considerable benefit from rhyming dictionaries and from their close congeners, the "reverse" (*rückläufig*) dictionaries, of which there exist specimens, e.g., for classical Greek, Latin, and modern Russian.

The semantic (analogical, ideological) dictionary unites words by bonds of meaning. Its roots are old; thus, Isidore of Seville's *Etymologiae* subdivide the entire material into certain provinces of cosmic structure and human endeavor. Within each group and subgroup so circumscribed, one may, but need not, maintain the alphabetical order. The result of such a compromise is a mixed classification. Consistently semantic ramification is difficult to achieve, because only relatively few and isolated semantic "fields" (e.g., anatomical, color, and kinship terms) fall into a neatly delineated schema. Another prototype of the semantic dictionary is the book-length list of synonyms, actually near-synonyms. The project of such a book, typically—but not exclusively—monolingual, may materialize in different ways (clusters of synonyms supported by well-chosen quotations from authors; "ideological index" to a standard dictionary; array of regional or temporal counterparts of each basic entry—an arrangement sometimes called "onomasiologic" in the Central European tradition of modern language scholarship).

Concerning recent experiments with the fragmentation of the "world of words" into discrete semantic provinces, one may safely affirm that, where short texts are involved, such an approach has turned out to be unpromising. However, the method, duly refined, may someday yield satisfactory results when extended to distinctly bulkier objects—say, the complete works of a prolific writer noted for his abundant and delicately nuanced lexicon. The worthwhileness of semantic classification, in other words, seems to increase proportionately with the absolute size and the relative density of the network. Meanwhile, Roget's *Thesaurus*, Boissière's *Dictionnaire analogique*, and Casares' *Diccionario ideológico* remain interesting testing grounds.

If it is true that the time-honored "parts of speech" (as against the modern descriptivist's form classes) were semantically rather than behaviorally defined, then some older dictionaries resorting to them (e.g., P. de Alcalá's *Vocabulista arábigo*, which, under each letter, subdivides the entries into verbs, nouns, and adverbs, then reserves a concluding cross-alphabetic section for numerals) show close affinity to the semantic ordering.

It is unusual for any book-length dictionary to present its entries in completely haphazard fashion, yet a few books, not only by amateurs, illustrate just this bent for eccentricity, which, the sober-minded may argue, squarely defeats the very purpose of a reference work. A grammar, whether historical or descriptive, even though not primarily planned as a lexicographic guide, may incidentally be so used, in default of a more appropriate source, if equipped with a handy index. Without this device the lexically oriented scholar may find its consultation forbiddingly time-consuming— just how prohibitive depends not only on the neatness and transparency of organization, but also on the reader's skill, knack for hunches, and sheer luck. In the case of a loose collection of notes, with etymological, phraseological, or puristic overtones, the alphabetic order is common and desirable, but far from obligatory, especially in periodicals. One also comes across miscellanies displaying a fundamentally free sequence with intermittent stretches of alphabetic ordering.

5.3. **Three contrasting levels of tone**. The tone of a dictionary may be detached, preceptive, or facetious. Only the first possibility insures a rigorously erudite approach; what complicates matters is that some normative and jocose dictionaries, though plainly falling short of the minimum standard for scholarly performance, nevertheless may contain slivers of information which, after proper filtering, are apt to be of real help to the serene researcher.

The category of dictionaries designed to report facts objectively includes the great majority of mono- and bilingual reference works and practically all historically slanted glossaries. Among regional word lists, however, the consensus of taste is less in evidence. Many of these vocabularies are intended to be descriptive, with a light undercurrent of innocuous pride in local traditions. Ordinarily enlightened amateurs are at their best when native dialect speech represents to them neither a matter of painful "guilt or inferiority complex," nor the pretext for some morbidly passionate commitment, still less a source of cheap entertainment, but a quietly treasured possession, a kind of revered family piece surrounded by affectionate curiosity.

Over against this gratifying attitude, one finds all too frequently the purist's preceptive (normative, didactic) approach. Regionalisms are collected for the purpose of warning the group of speakers concerned *against* their use. Outside the domain of dialectology, there also exist all sorts of corrective and remedial dictionaries exposing impropriety of speech and writing—among the semiliterate, certain peculiar population groups (e.g., immigrants), snobs succumbing willingly to the influence of foreign usage, white-collar workers endangered by professional hazards (translators, journalists), and the like. Though the analyst may find himself in basic disagreement with the bulk of this output, he can, with a measure of skill, extract useful information from such lists of "dos" and "don'ts," provided they are not entirely arbitrary.

A playful, teasing attitude toward language may be part of a general cultural pattern and heritage. Inevitably, a sophisticated worker's initial reaction to the brochures and pamphlets, mostly by unknowns or incompetents, containing all sorts of lexical scraps and tidbits is violently unfavorable; but, after calming down, he may discover that these humorously tuned collections are not necessarily worthless, if seen and assessed in the proper perspective, after very careful sifting.

Can any sets of relationship be established between these three major patterns of arrangement? A historical dictionary may correspond to alphabetic, infrequently to semantic, seldom (if ever) to casual ordering, and its tone is likely to be matter of fact rather than admonitory or exhilarating; a synchronic dictionary, unless scientifically designed, need not be hemmed in by comparable restrictions. Alphabetic arrangement goes well with a descriptive, preceptive (curative), or entertaining purpose and matches equally the diachronic and the synchronic perspectives, while casual arrangement and amusement are at all times easily reconcilable. These few examples show the tendential rather than obligatory character of all conjunctures.

6. Classification by Presentation

The four salient points to which we agreed to reduce the aggregate of narrower preferences were definition, verbal documentation, graphic illustration, and the presence of special features (e.g., localization or phonetic transcription).

The degree of specificity and of fullness in a lexical definition (gloss) represents some kind of continuum, ranging from extreme parsimony to profusion of technical detail. However desirable the goal of maximum information, one is led to posit, in two directions, a saturation point beyond which further accumulation of details threatens to detract from the architectonic value of a tightly built dictionary. One such menace is the infiltration of historical or naturalistic excursuses, in most instances, mere bric-à-brac; even those minute descriptions of household utensils and trade tools that so conspicuously benefit the *Wörter-und-Sachen* school of etymology belong, strictly speaking, in a portfolio or a manual of material civilization. The other kind of otiose superabundance stems from the indiscriminate recording of contextual shades of meaning: the harmoniously structured dictionary must remain a compact depository of steady designations.

In appraising documentation, it is advantageous to separate the literary language (past and/or present) from, on the one hand, living dialect speech, unsupported by texts, and, on the other, such samples of regional speech as are reflected in locally colored literature.

Where literary usage alone is at issue, the specificity of documentation may oscillate between (a) a generously carved-out passage, (b) a shorter segment of that passage, (c) a bare reference to line, quatrain, folio, page, or chapter, and (d) a simple computation of frequency—range plus incidence—at best interspersed with occasional quotations of characteristic words in their immediate environments (e.g., qualifiers). A few dictionaries, gambling on the layman's indifference, identify the author cited, but neither the particular work nor the specific locus, thus obviating all possibility of effective control.

In the rare dialect glossaries displaying the chosen words in any kind of meaningful context, the compiler faces the dilemma between coining suitable model sentences of his own (if he happens to be an uninhibited speaker of that dialect) and citing such utterances of his informants as he has unobtrusively overheard or—a quicker but less felicitous alternative technique—deliberately elicited. Some such glossaries have a comparativist superstructure.

If the tradition of a national literature has favored the production of texts entirely or partially dialectal (an example of the latter would be the dialogues, as against the narrative sections, of a novel or short story), it is possible to manufacture a regional vocabulary based in its entirety on excerpts from written and, as a rule, published sources, or to combine field notes and aural impressions with the testimony of *belles-lettres*. At this juncture, the support of folklore plays a signal part: proverbs, riddles, nursery rhymes, puns, and idiomatic sayings may be either appended as a separate exhibit or absorbed as an essential ingredient, sometimes specifically announced in title or subtitle.

Though stylized adornments embellished a few of the older vocabularies, the inclusion of functional pictorial material became standard practice only after 1800. For the purposes of a lexicographic rather than typographic or bibliophilic survey one may distinguish between drawings, sketches, and photographs, on the one hand, and charts and maps, on the other.

The drawing or sketch in a dictionary adds that dosage of concreteness which quickens the lay reader's grasp of a scientific definition or an abstract description. The photograph contributes the dual touch of authenticity and plastic suggestiveness. The option between drawing and photograph dwindles frequently to a matter of printing costs and available space;

where the budget allows for separate plates, these may be inserted between pages, assembled at the end of the volume, or segregated in an accompanying portfolio. An independent volume containing drawings or photographs of objects rich in lexicographic implications or else an imaginative combination of both media is equally conceivable. Pictures pertinent to linguistic inquiries are normally in black and white, the chromatic scale being regarded more as a potential amenity than as an actual asset; nevertheless, multicolored plates, the trademark of leading encyclopedias, might be useful, especially to the sensorially perceptive etymologist, as a frame of reference for the vernacular nomenclature of minerals, flowers, birds, and garments. A different use of photographic plates may be visualized in connection with painstaking editions of medieval glosses and glossaries.

While iconography, as a rule, plays a subordinate role in lexical undertakings, it may in exceptional cases assume a commanding position. The German "Duden" method embodies a miniature pictorial encyclopedia: in imitation of the "direct" approach, it bluntly juxtaposes label and image, rather than entry and gloss, in a preeminently semantic ordering of the lexicon, thus short-circuiting wearisome definitions. There exist well-established adaptations in numerous other countries. The affinity of the underlying principle and practice to recent trends of language instruction and to current auditive experiments centered around wire and tape recorders is unquestionable. What ties these endeavors together, harmonizing them with broader cultural trends the world over, is their strong sensory, anti-conceptual proclivity.

Regional dictionaries and monographs accompanied by folding maps or smaller charts are no longer uncommon. The inclusion, in studies of this scope, of a small-scale linguistic atlas remains a desideratum, for the most part unfulfilled; and even where one has been provided, as in Navarro (1948) on Puerto Rican, complete integration of the lexical and the cartographic sections proves difficult of achievement.

Special features worthy of mention include: the use of abbreviations or peculiar ideogrammatic classifiers to mark for a given word its grammatical or semantic category, social plane or emotional slant, or else territorial limitation; the extra measure of attention accorded to pronunciation, conducive to the parenthetic use of phonetic transcription or, at least, to the consistent marking of stress (a sideline leads from here to the orthological dictionary as an autonomous genre); the narrow specification of locale, unless implied in the announced scope of the project: a message conveyed in a variety of ways, e.g., by substituting arbitrary numerical symbols for recurrent reference to townships and villages and, where generations are contrasted, even to informants.

7. Special Dictionaries

The classificatory schema here advocated is so flexible as to be readily adaptable to all but an inconsequential percentage of lexical compilations. Any vocabulary offering a fair cross-section of a lexical system, however selective or arbitrarily arranged that cross-section may be, should, at least in theory, be analyzable in terms of distinctive features. A few residual groups of vocabularies, however, which cannot be credited with presenting such a cross-section, must be segregated from the common flock.

The words *vocabulary* and, especially, *dictionary* upon occasion apply quite loosely to any reference work arranged by words or names (collection, index, checklist, catalogue, set of paradigmatic tables, gazetteer, etc.); in most instances, the confusion may initially have been caused by the alphabetic order as the common trait. As a result, the visitor to a library finds on dictionary shelves collections of idioms, literary clichés, proverbs, family and given names, toponyms, fictional personages, topics and topoi, and the like.

The second exceptional group comprises highly specialized vocabularies of trades, crafts, arts, and sciences unrepresentative of the core of the common lexicon. Among these, lists of navigational terms, including terms of shipbuilding, have been in special demand since the 16th century. Agriculture has been another longstanding purveyor of specialized dictionaries. A matter of heightened concern to our own guild is the dictionary of linguistic or grammatical terms. The problem lies in drawing a cogent borderline between straight vocabularies of this kind and, among the older vintage of scientific treatises, a few so clearly patterned and, terminologically, so comprehensive as to provide, at a glance, the needed lexicographic information without, in the process, acquiring the status of a formal dictionary, not even one of the "semantic" variety.

8. Interaction of Distinctive Features

Systematic inquiry into the interaction of the features here isolated—aside from the three "perspectives" already viewed from this angle—would in itself require a study of monographic proportions, but a few random examples of seemingly admissible and inadmissible (or, at least, common and uncommon) constellations of such traits are easily supplied. Customarily, there prevails a definite relation between size and tone: dictionaries written in an entertaining vein tend to be slender. Again, historical slant and profusion of pictorial illustrations do not go together: maps, sketches, drawings, and photographs befit the synchronic dictionary, geographically oriented. Graphic documentation and a tone either morosely preceptive or irrepressibly jocose are, for all practical purposes, mutually exclusive. Bi- and plurilingual dictionaries are very seldom diachronic, overwhelmingly favor alphabetic arrangement, increasingly shy away from pedantry and jokes; also, they display the barest minimum of graphic illustrations, since the cumulative effect of a gloss (i.e., definition) and a drawing would tend to be tautological.

NOTES

1. A condensation, with modifications, of Yakov Malkiel (1959).

2. This paper, as well as its companion piece (Malkiel 1960), are to be included in a miscellany of the author's shorter writings, entitled *Essays on Linguistic Themes* (Malkiel 1968a).

LEXICOGRAPHIC DEFINITION IN DESCRIPTIVE SEMANTICS

Uriel Weinreich
Columbia University

1. Semantic Description and Lexicography

1.1. **Semantics and intuition**. The speakers of a language intuitively feel a relationship between certain pairs or sets of words which is not accounted for by any overt phonological or grammatical similarity. As speakers of English, we can state with little hesitation that in each of the following triplets two words belong more closely together than a third: *up, high, small; open, eat, close; end, after, grass*. We could probably obtain a consensus on the way to complete a proportion like *son : daughter :: brother* : _____. We would also presumably agree about the ambiguity of such expressions as *She couldn't bear children* or (*Was the weather good or bad?*) *It was fair*. To give an explicit account of such intuitions is a good way of beginning descriptive semantics.

1.2. **Semantic interaction**. The semantic description of a language consists of a formulation, in appropriate terms, of the meanings which the forms of that language have, to the extent that these meanings are interpersonal (cf. section 3). The forms whose meanings must be described are of many kinds: usually morphemes, often sets of morphemes in construction, and occasionally submorphemic components; but also prosodic contours, morpheme classes, construction classes, and grammatical processes, to the extent that their selection is not automatic.

When forms of a language are grammatically combined, their meanings, as is well known, interact. To a large degree the forms of such semantic interaction seem to be universal; but if there should be some that are specific to a particular language (e.g., some that depend on grammatically differentiated forms of predication), they too must be included in the semantic description of that language.

1.3. **Adequate description**. There is no known discovery procedure for correct semantic descriptions. The best we can hope for is an adequacy test which will enable us to decide between alternative descriptions. Ideally a description is adequate if it supplies us with overt means for approximating the intuitions of native speakers about the semantic relationships of words in their language. That is to say, we require that the overtly formulated meanings of such terms as *open*, *eat*, *close*—and not our intuition as speakers of English—permit us to say that *close* is more similar to *open* than to *eat* and to perform similar metalinguistic operations. Furthermore, semantic descriptions should be as complete as possible; they should be consistent; they should perhaps also be simple and elegant, although the criteria of simplicity are (as in other fields) obscure, and one should certainly beware of sacrificing consistency to elegance—a sacrifice which is the curse of many existing dictionaries.

1.4. **Integrative approaches**. The semantic description of individual terms (in such contexts as may be appropriate) is the customary province of lexicography. The study of recurrent patterns of semantic relationship, and of any formal (phonological and grammatical) devices by which they may be rendered, is sometimes called "lexicology." In addition to descriptive problems, lexicology may treat of historical and comparative questions.

The product of lexicographic work appears in many variants: unilingual and plurilingual dictionaries, synonym dictionaries, thesauruses, encyclopedic dictionaries, word-field studies, and the like. There are also other approaches to semantic description—association tests, semantic-differential tests, frequency counts—in which experimental and quantitative methods play a major role. A complete design for semantic description should provide for the integration of these approaches. This paper, however, restricts itself to the lexicographic approach, except that section 3 discusses a fuller use of experimental procedures even in lexicography proper.

1.5. **Missing methodology**. We have spoken of the lexicographic "approach" rather than "method," because lexicography itself uses many methods, none of which has been fully explained. The indifference which lexicography displays toward its own methodology is astonishing. Perhaps lexicographers are complacent because their product "works." But it is legitimate to ask in what way it works except that dictionaries sell. The fact that in our peculiar culture there is great demand for unilingual defining dictionaries, which include definitions of words so common that no one would conceivably want to look them up, is itself an interesting ethnographic datum. (Where else do high school teachers of the native language work to instill in their pupils "the dictionary habit"?) But this fact is no substitute for methodological investigation. The existing literature is far from satisfactory. The present paper is concerned with some of the methodological issues in lexicography about which lexicographers have been surprisingly silent.

1.6.1. **Semantic structure v. lexicographic convention**. Purely theoretical reflections on semantic description should be supplemented by comparative analysis of existing dictionaries. The English field is especially attractive since there are so many competing unilingual dictionaries to compare. But it should be borne in mind that even competing dictionaries copy from each other. For theoretical considerations it is unfortunate that we are restricted to evidence mostly from a single lexicographic tradition, not only in English-speaking countries, but throughout the western world. This makes it difficult to distinguish similarities of semantic structure in two languages from similarities in lexicographic convention. How refreshing it would be to have as evidence the products of a folk lexicography in an unwesternized society!

1.6.2. **Lexical hypertrophy**. Not only is the sample of lexicographic traditions small, but the major European languages, like their dictionaries, are probably quite atypical. The explosive growth of the quasi-international specialized language of science; the prestige and diffusion of scientific knowledge throughout society; and the maintenance of access to earlier periods of the language through the cultivation of literature, have not only made the dictionaries of the major western languages bigger, but these languages themselves, as objects of semantic description, are also, in a way, bigger.

The hypertrophy of a language like English can be characterized in various ways. One of them is the sheer size of its dictionaries, or the fact that its dictionaries are cluttered by words labeled *Arch.*, *Obs.*, *Rare*, *Zoöl.*, *Astron.*, and so on. A less obvious way is illustrated by the following experiment. A group of graduate students was presented with this set of 8 synonyms: *crabby, gloomy, glum, morose, saturnine, sulky, sullen, surly*. All said they "knew" the words, and all claimed that no two were perfectly identical in meaning. The students were then presented with the corresponding definitions from *Webster's New Collegiate Dictionary* (1953) and were asked to match the terms with their definitions. The results were poor.

1.6.3. Obstacles to reform. We may arrive at some commendable suggestions for reforming lexicography, but the task of describing a language like English all over again on the scale of Merriam-Webster's unabridged *Second New International Dictionary* (1934) would be so staggering as to discourage any radical departure. Yet perhaps it is justified to think of that portion of English (or French, or Russian, etc.) vocabulary which lies in the highest frequency ranges (e.g., the 5,000 or 10,000 most frequent words) as being analogous to the total vocabulary of a lexically less hypertrophied language. Under such a reduction, the semantic description of English would be more similar to the comparable task for most languages of the world (see also section 2.6.)

1.7. Theories of meaning. Unilingual lexicography, like any other approach to semantic description, presupposes a specific theory of meaning. Of the several varieties of semantic theory, defining dictionaries appear to be based on a model which assumes a distinction between meaning proper ("signification," "comprehension," "intension," in various terminologies) and the things meant by any sign ("denotation," "reference," "extension," etc.). This dichotomy, which is at least of medieval origin, was discussed in 19th-century linguistics under the heading of "inner form," and in (post-)Saussurean linguistics in connection with content substance vs. content form (*valeur*, etc.); it appears in modern philosophy in many guises, e.g., in the works of J. S. Mill, Frege, Peirce, Morris, as well as in those of Carnap and Quine, who have studied the possibility of eliminating the distinction. Several alternative semantic theories, on the other hand, seem to be excluded as bases of lexicography, for instance:

> a. The "linguistic meaning" of a term is the probability that it will occur, calculated from the context of other forms in the same discourse.

Conventional lexicography is not interested in any "linguistic meaning" separate from "cultural meaning." From the point of view of a dictionary, the probability of a term's occurrence, if at all calculable, measures only its banality or meaninglessness. It would not suffice to analyze speech as alternating pulses of banality.

b. Meanings as psychic states are inaccessible to observation, and descriptive semantics must wait until further progress in neurology will make them accessible.

This messianic "reductionism" characteristic, for example, of Bloomfield is theoretically alien to lexicographic description. For even if we had neurological specifications of, say, the emotions, the semantic description of emotion terms could be continued independently, just as the semantic description of color terms can be highly independent of the already known psychophysics of vision.

c. The meaning of a term is its use in the language.

This slogan of British linguistic philosophy may offer an escape from certain lexicographic impasses in connection with polysemy, but as a general theory it would require us to renounce dictionaries and to be satisfied, at most, with concordances.

A fourth theory of meaning needs to be mentioned which is complementary to that of conventional lexicography (at least when it appears in its less aggressive forms). This is the theory of the emotive power of words, particularly of the capability of a term to "evoke" other terms by an associative leap across their inner semantic structures. Some dictionaries informally acknowledge this possibility when they label words as "Contemptuous," "Endearing," etc., but their use of it is casual. Since psychologists have demonstrated the existence of impressive interpersonal norms for the emotive force of many words, these findings may deserve systematic inclusion in full-fledged semantic descriptions of languages.

1.8. **The intent of the following discussion** is twofold: to explain and to criticize what lexicographers do when they define words.

We proceed to a critical analysis of lexicographic definition as a device in the arsenal of descriptive semantics.

2. Definition

2.1. **Structure of definitions**. In order to give a rational reconstruction of what a dictionary does, it is useful to conceive of the meaning of a term as the set of conditions which must be fulfilled if the term is to denote. On this view, a formulation of the meaning amounts to a list of these conditions for denotation.

An obvious objection to dictionaries is that the conditions in such a "set" are not necessarily discrete, and that any analysis is therefore largely artificial. It is the classical gestalt problem. A natural language, being articulated, is not an adequate metalanguage for the analysis of its semantic *gestalten*, and no more suitable metalanguage has been devised. (Compare our efficiency in recognizing faces with our helplessness in describing them in words.) But we need not restrict lexicography by requiring that a definition be a *perfect* rendition of a meaning, or that the *definiendum* be recognizable from the *definiens* by mere inspection. Much less can we claim for natural-language lexicography that the *definiens* should be literally substitutable for the *definiendum* in normal discourse. What we are, perhaps, entitled to require from a rationalized lexicography is that the coding of the meaning gestalt into the discontinuous code of the defining metalanguage be performed under certain restrictions of form, and that the resulting definition be acceptable to representative lay speakers of the language who understand the formal restrictions which govern it.

The consistency of lexicography could be improved if dictionary makers were held to the assumption that the terms of a language are on the whole complementary (see also section 2.5). This assumption implies that the most important case to deal with in semantic description is one in which, where the signification of one term ends, that of another begins. On the whole, a semantic description should aim not at "absolute" definitions, but at definitions which delimit the meaning of a term from that of terms with similar meanings (synonyms). The circularity which results should be frankly admitted, not as a vice but as a guiding principle of lexicography.

The grouping of synonyms along a continuum yields a thesaurus, like Roget's. No doubt significant aspects of vocabulary structure can be studied on the basis of a thesaurus alone, just as features of a geographic area can be studied even from an unoriented map. For example, the list of words in a thesaurus can be interpreted as a series of one-dimensional projections (mappings) of the multidimensional semantic structure of the vocabulary. The dimensions of the vocabulary might then be studied in terms of the intersections of synonym lines (= cross-references between paragraphs of the thesaurus). But this perfectly "formal" lexicology would probably be as unsatisfying as a completely formal phonology, which makes no reference to the phonic substance. In contrast to a normal map, which is a two-dimensional projection of a three-dimensional space, the thesaurus as a semantic description maps a space of a great many dimensions (in fact, an unknown number). In the case of ordinary maps, we understand their semiotic mechanism perfectly and can make them as precise and univocal as we like. In the case of language as a map, we have no a priori knowledge of the object space, of the elastic "scale" of the map, or of certain other properties of the representation. It is therefore important, if we are to get far, to "orient" the description against its semantic substance. Otherwise, we may learn that *green* is between *blue* and *yellow,* as *vermilion* is between *red* and *blue,* without knowing whether *green* and *vermilion* cover equal or unequal segments of the spectrum. To determine that, we would have to orient the linguistic line of synonyms against the physical spectrum.

Orienting a map corresponds in semantic description to the demonstration of some denotata. This is also known as "ostensive definition." To be effective, ostensive definition must produce not only positive instances of denotata of a term, but also negative counter-instances (= positive instances of denotata of a synonymous term). Thus, a single swatch of red does not yield a sufficient ostensive definition of *red;* the limits of the meaning must be established by showing various kinds of red and also samples of what is similar to red but not red (e.g., orange, pink, reddish black). Denotata may be presented physically, or by being named; thus, a series of colored swatches, or the terms *red, blue, yellow,* etc., constitute two varieties of ostensive definition of *color.*

On the basis of the above analysis, we may construct a canonical form of lexicographic definition. Let X be the term of a language whose meaning is to be described, and let X', X", etc., be synonyms of X (i.e., terms similar, but not necessarily identical, in meaning); let c_1, c_2, etc., be conditions which must be fulfilled if X is to denotes, and let d_1, d_2, etc., be sample denotata. A lexicographic definition then has the following form:

X denotes if c_1 and c_2 and... c_n; for example, d_1 or d_2 or ... d_n.
X' denotes if c'_1 and c_2 and... c_n; for example, d'_1 or d'_2 or ... d'_n.

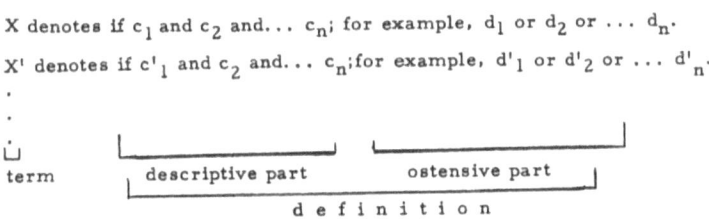

The classical form of definition *per genus et differentiam* can be transformed into canonical form; see section 2.6.4.

We may now consider a number of properties of lexicographic definitions (sections 2. 2–2.4 and 2.7) and of systems of definitions (sections 2.5–2.6).

2.2. Specificity of definitions. Of two definitions, that one is more specific which has a greater number of conditions. Consider the following schematic pair:

X denotes if c_1 and c_2
X denotes if c_1 and c_2 and c_3

We may say that the latter definition is more specific. But it makes sense to compare the specificity of definitions only if they share some conditions as the above pair shares c_1 and c_2. Another definition, e.g.,

Y denotes if c_4 and c_5 and c_6 and c_7

is not comparable with the previous pair as to specificity.

Modern dictionaries seem, on the whole, to be careful to make their definitions adequately specific. Definitions of the type exemplified by

VERST 'a Russian measure of length'

are avoided as insufficiently specific, since they do not differentiate VERST from other Russian measures of length.[1] On the other hand, a definition like

TRIANGLE 'a figure that has three sides and three angles, the sum of which is 180°'

is avoided as over specific, since TRIANGLE is sufficiently defined by the number of sides. Excessively specific definitions may be called encyclopedic.

An examination of the Merriam-Webster dictionaries shows that considerable care has been exercised to control the specificity of definitions, but specialized scientific definitions (preceded by such labels as *Bot.*, *Zoöl.*, etc.) are often encyclopedic. With reference to the names of plants and animals, encyclopedic definitions even occur without any label, e.g.,

CARROT 'a biennial plant (*Daucus carota sativa*) with a usually orange-colored, spindle-shaped edible root . . .'

Here "biennial" may well be over specific for lay (non-botanists') usage of English.

If two terms have definitions of adequate but different, and yet comparable, specificity, the meanings of the terms may be said to be of different specificity.

2.3. Criteriality of conditions. A condition for denotation may be considered criterial if, were it unfulfilled, our informants would refuse to apply the term in question. Thus, if an alleged chair showed evidence of not having been made to sit on (e.g., only two legs, or cardboard legs), informants might decline to call it *chair*, and we would conclude that 'having been made to sit on' is a criterial condition for this term. In natural languages, meanings often include conditions which are not so definitely criterial.

Dictionaries have an informal way of indicating doubtful criteriality by special markers. The word "especially" preceding the statement of a condition indicates that what follows is less criterial than the rest; "usually" seems to indicate a still lower degree of criteriality. Some dictionaries use "loosely" to set apart non-criterial parts of ostensive definitions, e.g.,

> COLOUR '... a particular hue ... including loosely black, white ...' (*Concise Oxford Dictionary* [1951])

But such markers occur not only in the lexicographer's jargon. Ordinary languages seem to contain terms for related purposes, e.g., English *true* as in a *true patriot* (= 'take the conditions of patriotism criterially').

In practice lexicographers determine degree of criteriality by individual introspection or "collective introspection" (the editor checks the staff worker's draft definitions); in the case of scientific terms, they even ask the experts. But if lexicography is to be truly descriptive, all interesting doubtful cases of criteriality should be verified by polling a sample of users of the language (cf. section 3).

2.4. Nature of conditions. Meanings differ as to the nature of the "operations" required to ascertain whether the conditions for denotation are fulfilled. Unfortunately, lexicography seems bent on suppressing this fact by the easy elegance and spurious uniformity of its definition style.

The "operations" range from immediate inspection by one's sense organs to more complex experimental or deductive procedures. Assuming that *carrot* is adequately defined as 'edible, tapering, orange-colored root,' its tapering form and orange coloring are immediately apparent to the sense of sight; whether it is edible might require more complex operations (with certain risks to one's teeth and stomach, which would make it preferable to dismiss edibility as non-criterial in this case). Meanings may be classified according to the sense appealed to in their several conditions, but there are certainly meanings which resort to no sensory evidence, or to sensory evidence mixed with other kinds, e.g., *early* or *wonder* ('... to query in the mind...').

To classify a vocabulary on a phenomenological basis is an intriguing task and a feasible one, provided that one has a corpus of adequate definitions. The first step in such an investigation would be to distill a corpus of adequate definitions from a conventional dictionary in which interesting and significant "cracks" between portions of the vocabulary are stuffed with elegant verbiage.

Many dictionaries prefer to formulate conditions in the form of physicists' experiments, at least as a parallel to a layman's operations. But few are consistent. Thus, the *Concise Oxford* (1951) defines *blue* ostensively only, while *color* is defined by psychophysical procedures. It is worth pondering whether the speakers of a language should not be allowed themselves to suggest the proper type of conditions for the meanings of the various terms of their language. Admittedly, in our society the conditions suggested by laymen would not infrequently resemble physical experiments, as in the case of *edible* or *out-of-order*, which might involve as a condition 'not doing what it should do when plugged into an electric circuit and switched on'. But there would be hope of avoiding the obvious irrelevance of specialized information from optics in defining, let us say, *blue*.

2.5. **Continuity of the definition system**. The semantic coverage of the world by a language would be strictly continuous if, for every term X defined as 'c_1 and c_2 and ... c_n,' there were in this language a synonym X' adequately defined as 'c_1 and c_2 and ... c_n'' (i.e., by changing one of the conditions).[2] It is, however, a matter of fact that a language is not semantically continuous through the full range of its vocabulary. For example, even though the tapered shape of a carrot seems to be a criterial condition in the definition of English *carrot*, there appears to be no English word designating a vegetable similar to a carrot in all ways except that it is spherical in shape.

There is hardly a more crucial topic in lexicology than the comparison of semantic continuities and discontinuities of languages. For while some discontinuities, as between the terms for discrete biological species, appear to be (largely, not wholly) determined by nature, many others are specific to a language and culture.

A discontinuity has been described as a case in which, if we alter a definition by changing some c_i to c_i', there is no term in the language defined by the altered definition. This places importance on the detailed way in which the conditions are formulated. Consider the following definition: X 'c_1 and c_2 and c_3 and c_4'. Suppose that changing c_1 to c_1' yields no definable term in the language but changing c_1 to c_1' and at the same time changing c_2 to c_2' does yield a definition of an existing term, X'. In such a case, overschematized though it may be, ad hoc intralinguistic considerations suggest that 'c_1 and c_2' should have been considered a single condition. For example, assuming that *beet* is like *carrot* except that it is red (not orange) and ▽-shaped (not tapered), and, assuming that there are no "intermediate" edible roots, should not color-and-shape be considered a single condition? In this easy example, the objection may be refuted by the argument that there is not only extralinguistic reason for treating color and shape separately but also good linguistic reason, given the separate English vocabularies for shape and color. But in other cases, especially where the appeal of the conditions is not to the senses, their discreteness may be problematic and may have to be resolved with an eye on pattern congruity (a problem not unfamiliar to linguists from phonology and grammar).

A corollary question concerns the choice of a defining metalanguage. The most ambitious defining dictionaries have probably been unilingual, i.e., the metalanguage in which the conditions for denotation are formulated (and, if appropriate, in which instances are named) has been the same as the object language described. The situation would not be very different in a bilingual defining dictionary in which both languages belonged to the same major culture and stood at approximately the same level of lexical development (cf. section 1.6.2)—e.g., object language English, metalanguage French. But consider a pair of languages like German and Romansch, of which the latter is less developed (i.e., roughly, it has fewer words): the problems of formulating conditions are very different for the *Dicziunari Rumantsch Grischun* (Societad 1938–2000)—object language Romansch, metalanguage German—from what they would be for an imaginary reverse dictionary. It is worth exploring to what extent the absolute degree of lexical development of a language, and in bilingual defining dictionaries also the degree of development of one language relative to the other, affects the efficiency of the language as a medium of formulating definitions. A lower degree of development probably helps avoid unjustified splittings of some conditions, but it also encumbers certain required splits.

166 | *Problems in Lexicography*

Finally, the concept of semantic continuity and discontinuity may provide a framework for studying unequal density of vocabulary within a language or between languages. This notion has come up in connection with narrow and wide semantic "spectra," for example, when languages were found to be lexically rich in domains associated with cultural "themes" (Arabic camels, Eskimo snow, medieval German chivalry, Yiddish poverty). Richness could be defined as a high degree of semantic continuity in sequences of definitions of relatively high specificity (cf. section 2.2).

2.6. Lexical structure and economy

2.6.1. Synonym sets and metalanguage. In section 2.1 we presented the notions of synonym and condition as interdependent, since a synonym of X was called a term definable when one of the conditions for X was altered. In section 2.5 we showed, speaking of semantic discontinuities, that synonymy and condition, though generally interrelated, are not necessarily completely dependent on each other in each individual case. This more subtle view may now be pursued further.

Let us define a synonym set of first degree as a set of those synonyms which differ by only one condition. A pair of antonyms would be a two-member synonym set of first degree. Synonym sets of higher degree could be described accordingly. We could also chart the various complicated intersections between synonym sets. For example, given the following terms:

$$X \; \text{'}c_1 \text{ and } c_2 \text{ and } c_3\text{'}$$
$$X' \; \text{'}c_1' \text{ and } c_2 \text{ and } c_3\text{'}$$
$$X'' \; \text{'}c_1'' \text{ and } c_2 \text{ and } c_3\text{'}$$
$$Y \; \text{'}c_1 \text{ and } c_2' \text{ and } c_3\text{'}$$
$$Z \; \text{'}c_1 \text{ and } c_2' \text{ and } c_3'\text{'}$$
$$Z' \; \text{'}c_1 \text{ and } c_2' \text{ and } c_3''\text{'}$$

We can formulate the intersection of the sets in three dimensions:

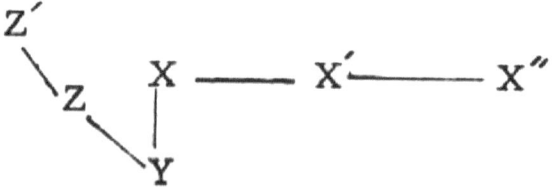

But it is useful to stress that the explication of lexicography in this manner can be profitable only if dictionary makers apply the most austere standards of verbal economy in the formulation of definitions. The proliferation of defining vocabulary characteristic of many dictionaries makes them unsuitable sources of material for critical lexicographic research. Thus, if we examine the *Webster's New Collegiate* (1953) definition of *end*: 'a limit or boundary; esp., a limiting region or part ... The extremity or conclusion of any event or series of events ... The extreme or last purpose ...' there is little hope of detecting the first-degree synonymy with *beginning* ('the commencement; the start ... a point in space or time at which a thing begins ...'), or the synonymy of first, or slightly higher, degree between *end* and *after*, *end* and *(not) more*, etc.

Conventional lexicography apparently believes that the defining metalanguage should contain at least the entire object language. This belief may be unwarranted. Ideally, we might wish for an "absolute" metalanguage which is entirely independent of the object language, or of any natural language. But since this ideal in semantics is illusory (in contrast to phonetics), we should seek ways to make the metalanguage less rich, rather than as rich as, or richer than, the object language.

One way of progressively reducing the defining metalanguage in richness would be to require that the definition of a term X be formulated only in words of frequency greater than that of X. Another, less rigorous but perhaps more workable limitation, would be to see, by trial and error, how extensively the metalanguage can be economized by agreeing to use as few different words in definitions as possible but to use each as often as possible. The reduction is similar to that which was aimed at in the construction of Basic English, although that purely pragmatic enterprise has produced little theory on the side. There is no reason to suppose that the 800 or so words of Basic represent the minimum metalanguage for defining English; one could probably reduce it beyond the limits of Basic by such formulations, for example, as (y is the) *end* (of x) 'there is no x after y'; (z) *help* (s x to do y) 'x cannot do y alone, x can do y with z'; (x is) *full* 'something is in x, nothing else can be in x'; etc.

It may well be that the more the defining metalanguage is reduced, the more frequent and more complex becomes the need to resort to ostensive definition. But these relations have not been investigated, so the question of optimization cannot seriously be formulated.

2.6.2. **Strata of vocabulary.** If a controlled reduction of the metalanguage should be feasible along the suggested lines, the vocabulary of a language might be viewed as consisting of strata, as follows:

Stratum 0: terms definable only circularly and by ostensive definition
Stratum 1: terms whose definitions contain only stratum-0 terms, but without circularity

Stratum 2: terms whose definitions contain only stratum-0 and stratum-1 terms, without circularity

Stratum n: terms whose definitions contain only terms of strata 0, 1, 2, ... n-1.

The defining language, thus stratified, could then be said to include the entire object language except the vocabulary of the outermost stratum, n.

This scheme is probably idealized, since there is little ground for supposing that a vocabulary of a natural language will yield discrete strata—in particular, whether circularity can be excluded from all but the 0-stratum. But the scheme does have some intuitive appeal and might help to reconstruct the organization of a thesaurus like Roget's. It also suggests a way for distinguishing between more and less "basic" elements of a vocabulary.

2.6.3. Strata and defining. Several alternative ways of slicing up a vocabulary have been suggested. One would apply to natural language the logician's distinction between (descriptive) terms and (logical) operators. Indeed, an austere defining procedure could reduce some of the conjunctions of English to more primitive terms (*unless*, *if*, perhaps even *and* to 'not,' 'or'). But some English terms would contain, in their definitions, a mixture of operators and descriptors (e.g., *negative* 'resulting from the *no*-operation'), and the 0-stratum as defined above would surely contain descriptive as well as logical terms. Another dichotomy is that between symbols and indexes (deictic elements, "shifters," "egocentric particulars"). These two types of terms indeed display different semiotic mechanisms, but again their separation is not always neat (thus, the adverbs *home* or *along* contain an element of back-reference to the subject of the sentence, which may be 'I'), and again it would be difficult to conceive of a core stratum consisting only of the basic indexical words of a language and no others.

2.6.4. Genera and differentiae. At this point it is convenient to consider genus-and-differentia definitions. One way of transforming a definition of the classical type into canonical form would be to consider the name of the genus as c_1, e.g., *bench* 'a seat which is long ...' as equivalent to

BENCH denotes if (c_1) it is a seat, (c_2) it is long ...

In this case 'seat' adds criterial information and, what is more, *seat* could in turn be defined without 'bench' as a sample denotatum. On the other hand, if we define *azure* as 'sky blue', we are using a genus name, 'blue,' which is itself defined ostensively in *blue* 'the color of the sky, deep sea, etc. . . .' In other words, some genus names are of much less help as conditions than others. Expressions like 'a thing which . . .,' 'one who . . .,' etc., are of so little help that in transforming definitions which contain them into canonical form, it might be best to drop them.

It is likely that different languages differ as to the "depth" at which hierarchies of genera could be constructed. In English, the economy of definition is different from that of a language which has no term corresponding to *quality*, and in which *color* could not be defined as 'a quality which . . .'

2.7. **Syntax of the defining metalanguage.** In addition to the problem of metalinguistic vocabulary, we may consider the syntax of the metalanguage. Conventional lexicography observes certain rules in this domain. For examples, dictionaries are bound by the restriction that the definition must be an endocentric phrase, subject to the rules of ordinary object-language syntax, a phrase functionally equivalent to the defined terms. Thus: *flow* n. 'act of flowing,' (to) *flow* v. 'to move or circulate, as a liquid . . .,' etc. This convention, though conducive to elegance, seems due to a claim of interchangeability between the term and its definition, which is preposterous for natural languages.

And yet, despite the unnecessary pretense of interchangeability, dictionaries quite unexpectedly lapse into a different metalanguage, e.g., *not* 'an adverbial particle expressing negation' (*Webster's New Collegiate* 1953) or *good* 'a term of general or indefinite commendation' (*Concise Oxford* 1951). A critical approach to lexicography requires that we determine whether, and on what occasions, such switches of metalanguage are legitimate.

One undesirable consequence of the syntactic limitations which lexicographers place on their metalanguage is that relational terms are treated as if they were absolute; in logical wording, predicates requiring more than one variable are treated as one-place predicates. Thus, *Webster's New Collegiate* (1953) definition of *between* gives no hint that this term requires an object of the form x *and* y, or at least a plural noun; nor is this evident from the wording of the definition: 'in the space or interval which separates.' ("Separates" can have a single object.) In the definition of *end* referred to at the end of section 2.6.1, there is no indication of the relational nature of the term (*end of* . . .). Some of the economies urged in this paper could be achieved if dictionaries were granted greater freedom to display the relational nature of many terms of a language, e.g., by using algebraic variables (x, y, . . .) in the term and again in the definition, as illustrated for e*nd, help,* and *full* in section 2.6.1.

2.8. A classification of definitions. One of the fullest discussions of definition in non-technical form is contained in a monograph by Richard Robinson (1954). It may be useful to conclude the present analysis by comparing its results with Robinson's. Let us consider the seven methods of "word-thing" definition which Robinson has delineated, placing them in the framework of our model.

(a) The Method of Synonyms. It consists in saying "that the defined word means the same as some other word." But perfect synonyms are rare in natural languages, especially in the non-hypertrophied majority, and they are an inefficient and undependable means of description. On the other hand, the linear listing of *non-*perfect synonyms of a term does not effectively narrow down its meaning. Therefore method (a), though common in elegant dictionaries, should be discarded.

(b) The Method of Analysis and (c) The Method of Synthesis. This distinction is not clear enough to be applicable to natural languages; even in his own presentation Robinson feels it necessary to refute a related but separate view (Lewis 1943) of the same dichotomy. According to the theory of lexicographic definition which we have outlined, the distinction between analytic and synthetic is, at best, a matter of degree, being a function of the kind, or perhaps of the difficulty, of the operations needed to ascertain whether the conditions for denotation are fulfilled (see section 2.4). Perhaps only terms which are commonly known to be non-denoting (e.g., *centaur*) would be completely analytic, although even *centaur* might (truly) denote a pictured animal of the intended kind.

(d) The Denotative Method and (e) The Ostensive Method. They are one and the same, except that (d) presents sample denotata by describing them in words, whereas (e) produces physical instances.

(f) The Implicative (or Contextual) Method. Here the term and the definition are fused; no equivalence or interchangeability is claimed; the term is exhibited in use, in a context where only this term can occur (for example, *diagonal* is "defined" by the sentence: 'A square has two *diagonal*s, and each of them divides the square into two right-angled isosceles triangles'). But it would seem this category is based only on a superficial syntactic peculiarity, since implicative definitions can be transformed into canonical form: *diagonal* 'that which a square has two of . . . etc.'.

(g) The Rule-Giving Method. Example: "The rule for the word 'I' is that it is to be used by each utterer to indicate himself." But all definitions are semantic rules; it is a question only of defining style. In our discussion we have subdued the rule character of definitions by omitting the phrase "denotes if." It can be reinstated at will, in many variants. Thus, the definition of *blue* may be given the explicit form of a rule if we say: *blue* 'an adjective applied to colors such that . . .' (or, '. . . such as . . .'). It is doubtful whether (g) is a useful subclass of definition.

3. Empirical Validation of Semantic Descriptions

It was stated in section 1.3 that there is no discovery procedure for *correct* semantic descriptions. This is not to say, however, that there are no stateable ways of obtaining *tentative* descriptions, from among which the most adequate might be selected or synthesized.

One family of procedures may be characterized as "extensional." Some writers believe that in an extensional procedure, the describer is restricted to an observer role: he watches the "co-occurrences" of certain terms with certain features of the non-linguistic context. But obviously this can do justice only to a fragment of a language; for example, the situation co-occurring with *Napoleon* would generally be that of a classroom and not the distinctive situation of France around 1800. An extensional procedure involving the describer in a more active role would have him present the informant with tentative sample denotata, and from his assents and dissents an ostensive definition would be culled. Perhaps this is the way in which a pseudo-behavioristic model involving "dispositions to respond" (e.g., Quine 1960, 28; Morris 1946, 19) could be translated into behavioral tests. A further modification of the procedure would have the describer not only present physical instances of denotata, but also describe imaginary instances to the informant. Carnap (1947, 48–59) believes that this is an intensional rather than an extensional investigation, but according to our theory it still deals with ostensive definitions.

For those who cannot be satisfied with ostensive definitions—and they are insufficient, according to the theory developed here—there remains the problem of deriving descriptive ("intensional") definitions from the ostensive ones. It is apparently a biological fact that human beings *are* capable of deriving intensional definitions from instances ("perceiving universals"): not only lexicographers, but all children do it, and they do it well. It therefore seems wasteful to put the whole burden on the lexicographer, or any other lone semantic descriptivist. Why not enlist the help of a sample of speakers of the language?

We would like to assume that the metalinguistic operation of defining is a cultural universal. That is to say, all languages furnish a way of asking "What's an X?" and in all cultures at least children make use of this device. By using it they obtain meaningful answers, some of which are quite satisfactory. We therefore believe that it is possible to obtain tentative definitions from naive speakers of any language.

But we would like to make a much stronger assumption still: the definitions elicitable from informants by asking them, in their language, "What's an X?" (i.e., obtaining their responses to the stimulus, "What's an X?") are not completely random; on the contrary, they will show a certain recurrent pattern for any X, and it is this pattern which constitutes the culturally shared structure of the meaning of X. The replication of this pattern may be one of the tasks of the semantic describer, although it should be determined how the aim of such replication can be accommodated with other criteria for the adequacy of semantic descriptions (cf. section 1.3).

The philosophy of language keeps running into the crude fact of structured meaning. Frege and Peirce faced it in connection with modal logic problems, and it keeps cropping up in more recent literature under the headings of indirect quotation, "oblique discourse," "opacity of description" (Quine 1960, 144–51), "intensional structure" and "intensional isomorphism" (Carnap 1947, 56). Psychologists have demonstrated the existence of norms by non-lexicographic methods of semantic description (associations, semantic differential). We would like to assume that "folk definition" would manifest cultural norms as well, and they would be of particular interest to a lexicographer concerned with the empirical foundations of his science.

In this light, the lexicographer's definition may be viewed as one man's, or a committee's, hypothesis, which must be validated by showing that it is acceptable to the speakers of the language, or to a representative sample of the speakers. Language description is sometimes concerned with idiolects, but, on the whole, it aims higher—at the features common to many idiolects. Lexicography as a descriptive (rather than a normative) discipline must also take the criterion of interpersonality seriously. Every aspect of the lexicographer's product can and should be subjected to interpersonality tests: the choice of terms to be defined (which would rule out, or at least set apart, rare and therefore largely meaningless words); the specificity of definitions (section 2.2) and the criteriality (section 2.3) and nature (section 2.4) of conditions for denotation. Possibly even the structure of definition *systems* (as discussed in sections 2.5–2.6) can in part be tested for acceptability.

It would not be difficult to outline a practical interdisciplinary research program to test the above suggestions for making lexicography more scientific than it has been so far.[3]

NOTES

1. Hereafter we symbolize the term by capital letters and the definition by enclosing single quotation marks and omit the words "denotes if."
2. For X' we must rule out a compound phrase like "X EXCEPT THAT NOT c BUT c'" which can always be formed ad hoc. It is the possibility of forming such phrases which makes of languages the semantically flexible instruments they are.
3. A number of ideas contained in this paper are developed further in Weinreich (1966a).

POSTSCRIPT

Since the original publication of the preceding article, I have continued to elaborate my ideas on lexicographic definition. Of particular relevance to this subject are Weinreich (1964) and Weinreich (1966b). In the latter article, I explore the possibility of bridging the discontinuity between the object language and the defining metalanguage which modern linguistics had borrowed, perhaps without sufficient warrant, from symbolic logic.

On the matter of empirically validating descriptive statements in semantics, I wish to refer now to two studies that deal, in part, with this topic, Zimmer (1964) and Bendix (1966).

URIEL WEINREICH
JANUARY 1967

WHAT BELONGS IN A BILINGUAL DICTIONARY?

Mary R. Haas
University of California, Berkeley

THE IDEAL BILINGUAL DICTIONARY WOULD ANTICIPATE EVERY conceivable need of the prospective user. (1) It would provide for each word or expression in the source language (SL) just the right translation in the target language (TL) including, most importantly, the one needed for the passage in hand. (2) It would contain all the words, locutions, circumlocutions, and idioms that any user might ever want to look up. (3) It would contain all the inflectional, derivational, syntactic, and semantic information that any user might ever need. (4) It would contain information on all levels of usage, including special warnings about words not to be used in the presence of ladies, in the presence of children, or to or in the presence of one's superiors. (5) It would contain all personal names, names of personages past and present, place names, names of famous books and plays, names of characters therein, and any other names that any user might want to look up. (6) It would contain all the specialized vocabulary items of all the sciences, professions, manufacturing industries, and trades, each carefully and appropriately labelled as to its field. (7) It would contain all necessary information about correct spellings, as well as information on alternate or commonly encountered incorrect spellings.[1] (8) It would include all the information needed to instruct the user in the proper way to pronounce each word so as to be indetectable from the pronunciation of a native speaker.

But this is not all. In order to be truly ideal, the bilingual dictionary would have to meet not less than three other tests. (9) It ought to be equally oriented to speakers of both languages. (10) It ought to be as well-adapted to purposes of machine translation as it is to human translation.[2] (11) Above all, it should be compact—at the most no bigger than Random House's

American College Dictionary (Barnhart et al. 1947) or *Webster's New Collegiate* (1953).

A final desideratum, (12), not on a par with the others, would be the inclusion of illustrations to picture items unfamiliar to speakers of the target language.

The desiderata listed as items (1) to (8) above are important, I think, for all bilingual dictionaries. If all these were properly executed, virtual completeness would be assured, but in most cases several volumes would be needed to accommodate the results. It is for this reason that item (11), pointing out the value of compactness, is necessary. In order to achieve this compactness certain limitations have to be introduced. The nature and extent of these limitations should, however, be independently determined for each pair of languages. In general, the compactness should be achieved by the omission of entries rather than by the neglect of any of our first eight desiderata.

To the best of my knowledge, no existing bilingual dictionary contains all of these features.[3] Most dictionaries are quite lackadaisical about (4), information on levels of usage. Really troublesome words are omitted altogether.[4] Many otherwise excellent bilingual dictionaries omit item (5), names, or relegate it to a separate section of the dictionary, or, more commonly, to several separate sections, viz., personal names, place names, etc. This is not only wasteful of the time and energy of the user; it sometimes occasions strange-looking gaps in the main part of the dictionary. Thus, *The Concise Oxford French Dictionary* (Chevalley and Chevalley 1935, 877) contains in its French–English part the following entries:

voltaire, fauteuil-voltaire (vɔltɛr, fotoej-vɔltɛr),
    s.m. [f. prop. n. *Voltaire*] *Voltaire* (armchair).
voltairianisme (vɔltɛrjanism), s.m. [f. *Voltaire*]
    Voltairianism, Voltairism.
voltairien, -ne (vɔltɛrjɛ̃), adj. *Voltairian.*

The proper name *Voltaire*, however, from which all these are derived, is nowhere to be found; it is not even given separately in the "List of Names."

So far, we have considered only items (1) to (8) and have concluded that they are all useful, provided they are tempered with item (11), the ideal of compactness. What about items (9) and (10)? Are they also necessary and useful? Or can one or the other or both be dispensed with?

At the present time, I am not prepared to discuss item (10), usefulness for machine translation. The demands made by machine translation may differ too much from those required for human translation. I suspect, however, that dictionaries prepared for machine translation will eventually lead to ways of improving dictionaries intended primarily for human use.

This leaves item (9), which states that the ideal bilingual dictionary should serve the needs of the speakers of both languages with equal felicity. This is the only one, I think, which must be dispensed with, at least as long as we must continue to use our present types of book format. (The reason is largely that it cannot be accomplished without introducing cumbersomeness—pronunciation, for example, would have to be shown for both languages in every entry.) Having to give up this ideal is unfortunate, though, because this one, more than any other, is tacitly assumed by the public to be the one above all others which is fulfilled. Worse yet, there is rarely, if ever, any specific warning to the potential user that such, indeed, is not actually the case. If a given French–English dictionary is useful to an American who wishes to translate spoken or written French into English, how can it be that this same book is not equally useful to the Frenchman who has the same goal in mind? The answer is that there are innumerable covert facts about English which are known to the native speaker thereof, but which are not at all clear or obvious to the native speaker of French. Book publishers can scarcely be expected to take kindly to the thought, but it is nevertheless true that bilingual dictionaries should be titled in such a way that the language of the intended user is made clear, e.g., *French–English Dictionary for Americans* as against *French–English Dictionary for Frenchmen*. What is even more deplorable, however, is the fact that often the compilers are not aware of the problems involved. Thinking they are preparing a dictionary for speakers of both languages, they may easily end up producing a dictionary which is not as useful as it should be to speakers of either language.

A couple of examples taken from Thai–English and English–Thai dictionaries will help show why such a separation of goals is necessary. In Manich's *English–Thai and Thai–English Dictionary* (1952), a handy volume which has seen many editions, the word /róɔŋ /, which means "to cry" in the sense "utter its characteristic cry," is elaborated by two pages of material designed solely to show that in English one uses a large number of different verbs to translate /róɔŋ/ depending on the bird or animal being described, e.g., the cow *lows*, the crow *caws*, the cat *mews*, the horse *neighs*, the lion *roars*, the elephant *trumpets*, etc. Now this kind of information is no doubt useful to the Thai speaker who wishes to find the proper English word to express his thought, but to the native speaker of English such a listing is nothing short of tiresome. And worse yet, from the standpoint of the speaker of English, nothing is included to warn him that in spite of its broad coverage the Thai word cannot be used in place of English *cry* (in the sense "weep")—for this meaning the term /róɔŋhâj/ must be used.

In Prachāchāng's *Siamese–English Dictionary* (1948), we find again that the orientation is toward the speaker of Thai, not of English. The English pronoun *me*, for example, is glossed /chǎn/, /phǒm/, /khâaphacâw/, etc., with no hint to the unwary that /chǎn/ is used in speaking to inferiors and intimates, /phǒm/ is used only by men, and /khâaphacâw/ is most commonly used in speeches and editorials. And, of course, only the native speaker of Thai would have any idea of what is included under "etc."

Since both of these dictionaries are actually intended for native speakers of Thai, not of English, no criticism is intended in these examples. They are cited to show why dictionaries intended for native speakers of one language are likely to be inadequate for speakers of another language.

There is another desideratum for a good dictionary, monolingual or bilingual, which can be stated very simply. A good dictionary is one in which you can find the information you are looking for—preferably in the very first place you look. Nothing could be sillier than the tacit assumption, far too commonly encountered, that it is somehow good for the soul of the user if he has to work hard to find what he is looking for. This means that everything will have to be in strict alphabetical order. It is "no fair" to list some words in alphabetical order while others are to be found only in groups or sets. Followed out to its logical conclusion, this means that in an English–X dictionary, *geese* will be separately listed from *goose* (though cross-referenced), *sang* will be separately listed from *sing*, etc.[5] It is perfectly true, of course, that a foreign student studying English will have to learn our irregular plurals and past tenses. It is *not* true, however, that he derives any benefit from wasting even as much as five minutes finding out what *geese* means if he has not yet learned that particular irregular plural.

Experience has shown me, however, that the definition of a good dictionary as stated above (one in which you can find what you are looking for—preferably on the first try) is one which is extremely difficult to adhere to at all times. This is not necessarily because of any intrinsic difficulty but rather because limitations of space sooner or later make themselves strongly felt even in the most ambitious project. Furthermore, each different language tends to have its own brand of difficulties, and in some instances the difficulties even seem to be intrinsic. I should like to give a couple of examples of some kinds of difficulties that may be encountered.

In the compilation of the Thai–English dictionaries I have attempted to adhere to this dictum. This means that everything in the files has been completely cross-referenced. But when the files are used as the basis for the actual dictionaries, we find that there would be a great many instances of multiple listing if the dictum were always carried out to its strict logical conclusion. Thai is a language which is rich in composite expressions of all sorts. It is not at all uncommon for such expressions to contain a sequence of four or more morphemes which must be translated as a unit into English, e.g.,

/chɛ̌ŋ chág hàgkradùug/ "to curse roundly," composed of /chɛ̌ŋ/ "to curse, revile," /chág/ "to pull," /hàg/ "to break," /kradùug/ "bones."

Since Thai is conventionally written without any spaces between words, the English-speaking student has no clue as to which elements form a semantic unit and which do not. Following our dictum that it should be possible to find what one is looking for in the first place one looks, the above Thai expression would have to be placed under all four of its constituent parts. But when this instance is multiplied by hundreds of other instances, we find that a staggering amount of space is required. Still, how are we going to decide which composites should be given the preferential (multiple listing) treatment and which should not?

There is, however, an even more intractable type of language, so far as our dictum is concerned. This is the type of language which has a multiplicity of prefixes and infixes, such as Tagalog or other Malayo-Polynesian language. It is customary to make dictionaries of such languages in terms of stems only. Expansions containing prefixes and/or infixes must be searched for under the appropriate stem. But this requires considerably more grammatical sophistication on the part of the user than is ever required, for example, on the part of the user of the ordinary English or French dictionary. Words found in actual texts would have to be analyzed before they could be looked up. The human dictionary-user might proceed by trial and error, but how could a machine be programmed to cope with this kind of dictionary? On the other hand, if we try to follow our dictum and list everything in strict alphabetical order, the number of entries becomes enormous. It would almost seem to be necessary to make a separate dictionary for every text.

In spite of special types of difficulties that may be encountered from time to time, and from language to language, the dictum remains a highly useful one which can profitably be much more widely followed to improve the quality of bilingual dictionaries in general.

NOTES

1. This is more important for some languages than for others. It is particularly important for a language which has recently introduced spelling reforms.

2. This is no longer considered a meaningful test. On the other hand, if a computerized dictionary (with access by individual console) could be implemented, each of the nine preceding tests could be adequately met and (11) would be rendered unnecessary.

3. Among monolingual dictionaries, however, Random House's *American College Dictionary* (Barnhart et al. 1947) contains more of these features than any other dictionary I know.

4. For some time past, Danish–English dictionaries printed in Denmark have been almost unique in using English "four-letter" words to translate their Danish counterparts. In 1966, it is possible to state that recent trends in the United States are towards greater liberalization in these matters. *Webster's Third New International Dictionary* (1961), a leading monolingual dictionary, has largely eliminated the omission of such words and bilingual dictionaries will probably follow suit. However, greater liberalization entails greater attention to item (4) and we find that Webster's *Third* carefully labels these words as "usu. considered vulgar" or "usu. considered obscene."

5. Since Random House's monolingual *American College Dictionary* (Barnhart et al. 1947) provides exactly what is recommended here, it hardly seems necessary to point out that the information would be even more useful in a bilingual dictionary.

SOME NOTES ON BILINGUAL LEXICOGRAPHY

Richard S. Harrell
Georgetown University

With an Appendix by Ann M. Driscoll

A MEETING SUCH AS OURS IS NOT THE place for a detailed technical discussion either of general lexicographical methodology or of the specific details involved in the construction of a bilingual dictionary for any given pair of languages. Witness the fact that time taken up with external consultants and with staff meetings to iron out the details of our Arabic lexicographical problems at Georgetown University has already exceeded the time allotted to this conference. Our colleagues working in the fields of Greek and Pashto lexicography surely have a similar story to tell.

It seemed more profitable, and more likely to be of interest to this group, to fasten upon a few specific problems of general lexicographical interest and then to show, *grosso modo*, how these problems were met in the Arabic lexicographical work now in progress at Georgetown. The points offered for consideration are: For speakers of what language is the bilingual dictionary intended? Is the bilingual dictionary to concern itself primarily with written or with spoken material? Is the bilingual dictionary primarily to serve as an aid to comprehension or to expression? Finally, an appendix is added outlining the organizational routine of the lexicographical work in progress at Georgetown.

1. Three General Problems

A primary problem in the composition of a bilingual dictionary is to decide whether the work is intended principally for the speakers of X-language or the speakers of Y-language. It is clearly impossible to pay equal attention to both X-speakers and Y-speakers in one and the same work.

Points of conflict already arise at the preliminary point of deciding what items are to be entered in the dictionary. Suppose that X is English and that our dictionary is intended primarily for English speakers. Given this, there is no good reason why such an English word as *circumnavigate* should be included. The English speaker already knows what *circumnavigate* means, and, to learn how to express its meaning in Y-language, he can look up such periphrases as *to sail around* or *to go around*. If, however, our dictionary is intended primarily for Y-speakers, there is no guarantee that the Y-speaker will not somewhere or other encounter *circumnavigate*, and he would need to be able to look it up.

Fortunately, this is one point on which some double service is possible: theoretically, it does not *hurt* the English speaker to have *circumnavigate* included in the alphabetical English word list. Practically, however, there actually is some disadvantage to the English speaker in having *circumnavigate* included in the dictionary. In the real world, no dictionary is ever written without some a priori limitation on size and cost. With a limitation on size, the need of Y-speakers to have such an entry as *circumnavigate* in an English–Y dictionary can only be given limited attention, and then only after the contrary needs of the English speaker have been given fullest consideration.

On the other hand, if the compilers of an English–Y dictionary have primarily in mind the needs of Y-speakers, entirely other considerations will prevail. Since no countries other than the United States and Canada indulge in football, an English–Y bilingual dictionary oriented solely to the needs of English speakers would be wasting space to include the word *tackle* in its sporting sense (with the possible exception of Canadian French). But, for the Y-speaker who is to have any broader cultural contact with the American scene, *tackle* would be an appropriate dictionary entry. The same is true of numerous cultural words which a Y-speaker would encounter on the scene of the English-speaking world but for which an English speaker would not expect to find equivalents in Y-language. One has only to think of such items as *forty-niner, mugwump,* and *chile con carne* to perceive the extent of the problem. The item *chile con carne* (usually just *chile*) can serve to illustrate the pitfalls involved. There is no Spanish equivalent for this item. The food preparation referred to was invented in Texas and is unknown in Mexico. The etymologically equivalent Spanish words *chile con carne* have only the literal meaning 'red pepper with meat,' and the average monolingual waiter in a Mexican restaurant would probably be greatly puzzled to hear a customer request such a thing.

The above considerations are all stated in the context of an alphabetical English word list with Y-equivalents. Exactly the same considerations apply, *mutatis mutandis*, to an alphabetical list in Y-language with English equivalents.

Beyond the level of vocabulary selection there are two further main points where a decision must be made as to whether the dictionary is designed for primary utility to X-speakers or Y-speakers. In what language are general directions to be given, not merely in the introduction but in individual entries, and in what way are multiple meaning equivalents to be handled? In neither case is a really fruitful compromise possible, at least not in the real world.

A bilingual introduction to a dictionary is easy enough to arrange but to have such indices as "irregular plural," "imperative," "noun," etc. given bilingually in every entry is beyond the pale of practical manageability. There is no middle ground on this issue. Either X-speaker or Y-speaker must be discriminated against at the expense of the other. The most nearly successful attempt that I have seen at favoring speakers of both languages in a bilingual dictionary is in the *German–English, English–German Dictionary of Everyday Usage* (Pfeffer 1951) In cases where an entry has multiple glosses, an illustrative sentence, in both English and German, is given for each gloss. Such an ideally helpful approach, however, is likely to be possible only in the case of dictionaries of relatively modest scope—each section of Pfeffer (1951), for instance, contains fewer than 10,000 headwords. A dictionary aiming at a broader lexical coverage would be made too expensive and too bulky by such an approach.

The problem of indicating multiple meanings is a manifestation at the semantic level of the familiar phenomenon that different languages are self-contained systems exhibiting only limited isomorphism with one another. What does the lexicographer do when confronted with one X-word for which there are two or three or perhaps five or six Y-equivalents, each one with its own unique shade of meaning and not interchangeable with the others? An example may be taken from a readily available contemporary Spanish–English, English–Spanish dictionary (Castillo and Bond 1948). The Spanish word *pera* is glossed "pear; goatee; sinecure, easy job . . .," and the English word *hot* is glossed "caliente; caluroso; cálido; picante (como el pimentón chile, aji, etc.); furioso; fresco, reciente . . ."

These two items were taken at random and are excellent illustrations of the point at issue. It is obvious that the gloss of *pera* is entirely in favor of the English speaker. A Spanish speaker seized by an urge to know the English equivalent of *pera* would receive only limited help from this gloss. He will certainly know that *pear, goatee,* and *sinecure* are each the equivalent of some shade of meaning of *pera*, but he has no way of telling which of the three English glosses refers to a fruit, to chin whiskers, or to bogus employment. Presumably, with an exercise of ingenuity and considerable cross-referencing, the Spanish speaker could solve this problem, but the dictionary does not immediately do it for him.

The English word list, on the other hand, is slanted in favor of the Spanish speaker. A Mexican looking up *hot* would receive rather comprehensive information about its Spanish equivalents, but the American who simply wished to know how to say *hot* in some given context is confronted by a bewildering string of equivalents. He presumes they are not mutually interchangeable, but he is given no clue as to what the semantic range of each is.

The Castillo and Bond dictionary thus arranges its English–Spanish section for maximum utility to Spanish speakers while arranging the Spanish–English section for maximum utility to English speakers. It would have been equally possible to favor either the Spanish speaker or the English speaker in both parts. A bilingual dictionary which goes both ways, as the Castillo and Bond dictionary does, is in a sense two works in one; and the solution they have adopted is a common one, that is, to arrange the glosses of the alphabetical word list for the benefit of the foreign rather than the native speaker.

The implied assumption of the approach illustrated by the Castillo and Bond dictionary is that the English speaker will mostly look up Spanish words and that the Spanish speaker will mostly look up English words, and scarcely at all vice versa. The generalization of the assumption is that the user of a bilingual dictionary is primarily concerned with *understanding* a foreign language and scarcely at all with *expressing* himself in a foreign language.

And what is this assumption but a disguised reassertion of our traditional academic approach to foreign languages, an approach which emphasizes reading for comprehension and which scarcely conceives of any other possible goals in foreign language education? The needs of contemporary foreign language education are more involved, both in the United States and in the rest.of the world. More and more people have an active need to express themselves in foreign languages, both in writing and in speaking. What of the American in Japan, who, although expecting a monolingual

Japanese friend, has to go out unexpectedly? He might like to do such a human thing as tack a note on his door. And what of the American working in an Egyptian village who needs to talk about things for which he does not know the Arabic equivalents? In the past the American would either have had no monolingual Japanese friends or he would have had an interpreter-translator to help him along. Likewise, there would have been little chance, in the past, of finding an American in an Egyptian village. In the world of today more and more Americans are abroad, and they are having to do both their own talking and their own writing. Fortunately, a fair number of them show signs of actually wanting to do it in addition to merely having to do it. The traditional bilingual dictionary is poorly adapted to their needs.

The "For-speakers-of-what-language?" problem of the bilingual dictionary is doubled in cases where there is a serious gap between spoken and written forms of a language. The question faced is "For speech or for writing?" The problem is doubled again if the dictionary maker is faced with the practical limitations of being able to do either an X–Y or a Y–X dictionary but not both. The question then faced is, "Which is to be stressed, comprehension or expression?" By now it is clear that to speak of composing a bilingual dictionary of X language and Y language is a misapprehension. There are various possible varieties of bilingual dictionaries of X and Y languages.

2. Arabic Lexicographical Problems

The Georgetown Arabic Research Program had to contend with all three issues discussed above. The decision was to compose primarily with the needs of the English speaker in mind, to favor speech over writing, and to favor expression over comprehension. The Georgetown schedule accordingly calls for the preparation of an English–Arabic dictionary in each of three modern Arabic dialects, Moroccan, Syrian, and Iraqi. The allotted work period is two years, from June 1960 to June 1962, and the goal is medium sized dictionaries of maximum everyday utility for the educated layman. At present there are no English–Arabic dictionaries at all in these dialects, not even poor ones.

Many of the problems peculiar to Arabic lexicography have their roots in the tangled socio-linguistic phenomena of the well-known dichotomy between Classical Arabic and the various colloquial dialects. Briefly put, the sociolinguistic situation of the Arab world is today roughly parallel to that of the Latinized provinces of the Roman empire just before the emergence of the modern romance languages as publicly accepted media of written communication and serious intellectual culture.

There are several immediate consequences of this diglossia for the maker of a colloquial Arabic dictionary (cf. Ferguson 1959). To begin with he must work almost solely with oral material. Such usual sources of lexicographical raw materials as magazines, novels, etc. are not available for him. And how is his material to be transcribed? There is no conventionalized spelling to be followed. The lexicographer must invent his own.

Inventing a spelling for an Arabic dialect is not a trivially simple task. What is to be done about a host of foreign loan words which are often only imperfectly assimilated to Arabic phonology? And in the case of many loan words which are perfectly assimilated at an unsophisticated level, educated Arabs use the pronunciation of the source language and consider the assimilated pronunciation vulgar. Furthermore, Arabic morphophonology is intricate, and a strictly phonemic transcription of any Arabic dialect is never satisfactory. A separate decision as to whether and how much a morphemic as opposed to a strictly phonemic transcription should be used must be made on each of a large number of separate points, and no two people ever quite agree on every one of them.

But even before he can permit himself the luxury of any of the above considerations, the lexicographer of colloquial Arabic has to decide exactly whose speech he is writing a dictionary of. There is a gross reality to such terms as "Moroccan Arabic" and "Iraqi Arabic," just as there is in such terms as "British English" and "American English," but there are many internal differences within each of these macro-varieties. In Egypt, despite great local diversity, the dialect of Cairo is a fairly normalized educated standard, spoken and understood everywhere within the country. The three "macro-dialects" which are the subject of the Georgetown dictionary project—Moroccan, Syrian, and Iraqi—present far more painful problems. For Iraqi the educated speech of Baghdad has been taken as the base for work, and for Moroccan the educated speech of Casablanca/Rabat. But in neither Morocco nor Iraq is there an exclusively accepted colloquial standard throughout the entire country.

"Syrian Arabic" is an even more complex matter. The spoken Arabic of historical geographical greater Syria (i.e., the area now divided among the political units of Syria, Lebanon, Israel, and Jordan) is a palpable linguistic unity, but village dialects aside, there is no metropolitan educated standard for the entire area. Of the three metropolitan centers of Damascus, Beirut, and Jerusalem, there is no compelling sociological or linguistic reason for choosing one over the others. The Georgetown solution was to make the English–Syrian dictionary basically an English–Damascene dictionary and to include Beirut and Jerusalem forms wherever these differ from Damascene usage. It would have been equally possible to use either the speech of Jerusalem or Beirut as a base. Our decision to use Damascene as our point of departure was determined by the simple non-linguistic fact that our Syrian staff is most directly familiar with it.

APPENDIX

On August 29–30, 1960, Miss Ann M. Driscoll of the G. and C. Merriam Company and Professor W. Freeman Twaddell of Brown University visited the Georgetown University Arabic Research Program as consultants. The following outline on methodology was prepared for Georgetown by Miss Driscoll, and its suggestions have been adopted. The references to "Pfeffer" in the outline refer to the *German–English, English–German Dictionary of Everyday Usage* (Pfeffer 1951), the alphabetical English word list of which was adopted as a point of departure for the English–Arabic dictionaries being compiled at Georgetown.

Methodology for Arabic Dictionaries Project

Ann M. Driscoll
G. and C. Merriam Company

Submitted: August 30, 1960

I. Keep everything relating to all three dictionaries on colored 3 x 5 slips, giving the following significance to each color:
   1. green—definitions from Pfeffer and others
   2. pink—manuscript for Iraqi
   3. blue—manuscript for Moroccan
   4. yellow—manuscript for Syrian

Some Notes on Bilingual Lexicography | 187

    5. white—comment slips, query slips, supplementary slips, AA slips

II. To prevent any confusion of colors, give the supply of slips for his color to each editor and let no one else have access to them.

III. Cut and paste Pfeffer on the green slips, starting ahead of the place where editors are now working.
  1. Paste an entire entry in sequence, continuing on a second slip, if necessary.
  2. Paste each phrase on a *separate* slip, with the entry word written at the top of the slip, keeping the phrases in alphabetical order under the entry word, thus: *get, get around*. . . .
  3. Paste as close to the top left-hand corner of the slip as possible and leave about 1/2 inch at the bottom of each slip.
  4. Write *cont* at the bottom of every continued slip and *entry word—cont* at the top of the next slip. Use 1, 2, etc. after *cont* at the top of the next slip if there is more than one continued slip.

IV. Set these green slips up in a filing cabinet with removable drawers as the beginning of a file into which every scrap of material used for or in all three dictionaries will be filed. In each drawer leave room for expansion.

V. In the file keep the slips in this order:
  1. definitions from Pfeffer and other dictionaries (green)
  2. Iraqi manuscript (pink)
  3. Moroccan manuscript (blue)
  4. Syrian manuscript (yellow)
  5. comment slips, etc. (white)

VI. As soon as enough material has been gathered in three drawers to warrant it, assign a drawer to each of the three editors. Each will then edit the drawer by writing his entries on slips of the color assigned to him and inserting them in the file. The entry should be handled as follows:
  1. a single sense to each slip, with all of the "heading" material (as entry word, inflected forms, feminine form) either on the same slip with sense 1 or on a separate slip depending on its length.
  2. *cont* at the bottom of each continued slip.
  3. the entry and *cont* (with 1, 2, etc. following when necessary) and 1, 2, etc. (sense numbers) preceding when necessary.
  4. These slips should be prepared with the idea that they will be used as copy for the printer, which means that all typography and

punctuation should be clearly indicated. Typography is indicated by underscoring as follows:

roman—	no underscoring
boldface—	～～～～～
italic—	————
small caps—	════

5. Perhaps no systematic proofreading need be done until the galley stage.
6. Every slip handled by an editor should be stamped with his name and the date. This may be done by the editor himself as he goes along or by a clerk boy as the editors finish with them.
7. The Pfeffer and similar green slips are to be used as guides only, not a copy.
8. At the end of the editing, slips of each color will be extracted from the file and taped to 8 1/2 by 11 sheets for the printer.

VII. As an editor thinks of a comment he wishes to make about a word anywhere ahead of the edited part of the alphabet, he makes out a white slip and puts the word in the upper left corner, the comment, his name and the date in the lower right corner and drops the slip in an "out" box on his desk. Such slips will be picked up periodically and filed at their own alphabetical places in the main file.

VIII. When an editor wishes to put a comment slip in the section of the alphabet on which he is working, he merely inserts it unless it is a question to someone else. If it is a question to someone else that he needs answered immediately, he writes in the upper right of the slip the name of the person to whom it is addressed and drops the slip in the "out" box. It is then delivered, answered directly on the slip or on an attached slip, dropped in the "out" box of the answerer, and thus returned to the questioner. The questioner then writes "closed" across the top of the slip and sees that it gets filed in its proper alphabetical place as "backing." If it is something he wishes to call to the attention of an editor who will be working on the drawer after, he leaves the slip in its alphabetical place in the drawer.

IX. When an editor comments on a term that has already been edited, the comment is to be *filed in a supplementary file*, which will not be reviewed until A- Z has been edited. It is the responsibility of the file clerks to see that *nothing new* is added to a section that has already been edited.

X. When an editor needs a policy decision, he writes the general heading (as Plurals) in the upper left and AA in the upper right. These slips should then be delivered to Mr. Harrell who either writes the answer immediately or has the slip filed for the staff meeting. Whether answered immediately or in a meeting, every policy decision would be recorded on 3x5 white slips in copies enough for each editor to have one at his desk.

XI. If an editor wishes to omit a word or a sense included in Pfeffer or another source, he does not mark the green slip but makes out a slip of his color with the headword and, if it seems desirable, a brief identification, marks an o in the upper left corner, and stamps his name and the date in the lower right.

XII. As a drawer is finished by one editor, it is passed on to the next, until all three editors have inserted their entries in it. The order in which this is done seems immaterial.

XIII. The green slip should always indicate "potential dictionary entry for us." Thus, if anyone sees an entry in a dictionary other than the Pfeffer one that he considers a worthy candidate, he should have it either cut and pasted or typed on green for insertion in the file. If such a word merely occurs to him, he should write it on green for insertion.

XIV. Omission of a headword or of a name and date stamp from *any* slip (including those for AA) should be considered high treason.

XV. Misalphabetizing should be judged even more fiendishly. Once a slip gets in the wrong place it is virtually lost.

XVI. The main file should be kept in one place and a record kept of everything taken from it. If an editor wishes to see the material for a word in a section not at his desk at the moment, he should drop into his "out" box a request slip with Miss Za'arur's name in the upper right. When she removes the material for him, she will insert a slip in the file recording that this has been done. The editor may return the material via his out box, at which time the record slip in the file will be torn up.

XVII. Work done to date can be transferred to slips of appropriate color by typists and filed. After editors have completed the rest of the alphabet, they can return to these sections to style them according to the latest style decisions and to correct typists' errors.
XVIII. Someone should perhaps collate a few pages of Pfeffer (1949) with a few pages of *Webster's New Collegiate* (1953) to see if such collation would yield some of the terms essential to an Arabic dictionary although not to a German. If any such terms are found, they should be marked with a marginal X in the *Collegiate*. If there are many of them, they can be cut and pasted; if not, they can be typed. In either case, they should be on green.

RECOMMENDATIONS ON THE SELECTION OF ENTRIES FOR A BILINGUAL DICTIONARY

Donald C. Swanson
University of Minnesota

1. Assumptions

A bilingual dictionary can be useful and desirable to several kinds of people: students, travelers, translators, and linguists. The last group is and will be, in the foreseeable future, the smallest, and we may as well face the fact that only a small percentage of potential users of bilingual dictionaries (at least of those of major languages) will be linguistically alert.

There can be two principal purposes of a bilingual dictionary: the customary one of reference for the student (of either language); the other that of a ready guide for the linguist who is not a specialist, and to whom each half of the dictionary serves as an index for the other.

In this paper, remarks will be based chiefly on the Indo-European (IE) languages. A bilingual dictionary composed between almost any two of these will be easy to set up because of similarity of the major grammatical and syntactic categories, but of course caution is needed even here, since translation or equivalence is not a clue to classification, and more especially because of the frequent contrastive overlappings like English *this, that* with Latin *hic, iste, ille*. A bilingual dictionary can retain, for the sake of the general public, much of the traditional approach, but the more firmly established techniques of recent linguistics must be unobtrusively adopted.

The number of entries necessary for usefulness in a general bilingual dictionary is anybody's guess. I suggest for English and many other IE languages 5000 main entries as a bare minimum and perhaps 10,000 as a working solution. Above this figure there is a drop-off in utility, and the extra entries tend to pad the work with mere word-lists.[1] A presentation of word-formational principles (see below, section 2.3) in IE and certain other language families can serve to compensate for many absent entries.

According to my records on bilingual dictionaries of IE dialects, English and German have developed the most productive traditions in dictionary making, followed at a distance by French, Russian, and Italian, in that order.[2] Since the number of English speakers (and of those to whom English is a well-understood second language) is very large, the tradition of English lexicography is likely to continue and even expand. Because of recent improvements in our understanding of English structure and the possibility of still further analysis of English for the purpose of squeezing out all its translation powers, we can now make this language as useful as it can be as a translating and indexing medium, in other words not just a tool for English speakers but a kind of international language for general lexicography. English is not (as of course no natural language is) suited for facile interpretations of all kinds of structures, is loosely Germanic in structure, and partly bound to one environment. But, by exhausting all its native possibilities, then by utilizing the tradition of "translation English" (long in use to handle Greek and Latin), and finally adding scientific vocabulary (based on neo-Latin) and international loanwords, we may arrive at a reasonable ideal. This international English will have to be defined as a combination of American and British, the main varieties,[3] for in practice Americans have used American words and usage in lexicography and the English have used British, each without a thought for the other.

2. Selection of Entries

Entries will be, as conventionally, primarily words. Current linguistic analysis provides us with more precise (though not yet definitive) criteria for "words." For IE languages in general, there is no important problem either in the nature of the word or of its categories. In a language like English, phonetic criteria may determine the words (usually but not always coinciding with spelled words);[4] for "archaic" IE languages morphology will have to suffice as our clue.[5] A typical archaic feature is the group of four enclitics (a variety of quasi-word) in Latin, namely *-que*, *-ve*, *-dum*, *-ne*. These have no stress and may not stand alone; but they are not suffixes and they may in part be substituted by free forms (*et*, *vel*, *nonne*, or *num*). They will not satisfy Francis's (1958, 204) definition (based undoubtedly on English): "a linguistic form consisting of a base and a superfix." Hockett's definition

(1958, 167), although also not considering this particular problem, could conceivably subsume the group: "any segment . . . bounded by a succession of points at which pausing is possible." (We may invent a distinction between full pauses and half pauses.)

Nida (1960, 138) reminds us of words based on phrases whose second constituent has become atonic; *kind-of, sort-of, used-to* illustrate the type, and these words should be entered, if only to call attention to their real existence.

Another type of main entry to be considered (on the English side of our dictionary) consists of a group of nominal compounds or phrases (the phrase being composed of adjective plus noun, or adjunct noun plus noun): *adhesive tape, hiding place, carbon paper*. Such words (or phrases) need not be sub-entered under their constituents, especially if the first constituent is unimportant statistically or otherwise. A word like *no one* is often missing as a lexical main entry (and even as a subentry) because the orthographic space between constituents gives the whole word the appearance of a phrase.

Assuming the impossibility of a complete bilingual dictionary, I give a list of criteria to use in realistic selection of entries, based on the four properties of form, syntax, meaning, and relative frequency. To this list will be added two incidental bilingual by-products: feedback and cultural items.

2.1. **Relative frequency**. We may judge the most frequent words (and morphemes) the most complicated in form or meaning and therefore the most in need of elaborate treatment in a bilingual dictionary. Only a few languages have been provided with frequency lists, namely American English, Classical Latin, Greek (Homeric and New Testament), Arabic, German, French, Spanish, Brazilian Portuguese, and Swedish.[6] We need such tallies for all languages. There also exist *indices verborum* for a variety of texts in some other languages, but these have only substitute value. Several of the older frequency lists were of word-forms (that is, inflected words); furthermore, certain naïve practices have spoiled the usefulness of some lists,[7] such as failure to include sandhi variants under the full forms. In the Thorndike-Lorge list of 1000 most frequent "words" occur 63 forms which can be deleted as grammatical variants: 4 plurals (*feet*, etc.), 3 gerunds, 2 comparatives, one sandhi variant (a) 5 phrases (*don't*, etc.), and 48 preterites (including *fell*, but *fall* is not in the list). In their original 1000 (Thorndike and Lorge 1944, 270–274) occur 104 words not found in the later list.[8] One may (pending the compilation of a scientific list) use these cast-offs to replace the 63 false inclusions; this gives us a net total of 1041 most frequent American English words (including some which are unfortunately homonym-clusters) based on a count of written documents.

2.2. Function words. The particles (traditional prepositions, conjunctions, and adverbs) which constitute the syntactic cement of discourse must be completely entered and given full treatment, even to the extent of making this lexical group an index of particle syntax. The two recent works of Nida and of Francis,[9] despite their different approaches to the subject, give us handy classifications and lists of this lexical area for English. It may be noted that Nida's treatment of adverbs is fuller than Francis's.

2.3. Word-formation. In a bilingual dictionary there should be a fairly detailed essay (either in the preface or as an appendix) on word-formational habits of the target language (and presumably most languages have devices for forming derived words from morphemes or prime words). This essay is also ideally present in a grammar of a language, of course, but in practice many grammars (even recent ones) ignore or minimize word-formation.[10] Such a guide will cut down the need for extensive lists whose synchronic etymology (derivability) is obvious and simple, as, e.g., English *goodness*, *wholesomeness*, and the like. Some obvious items in a derivational paradigm may be listed for other reasons, of course. A preliminary study of derivation will have yielded the processes by which "new" words are made. Generalizing only for the IE type, I may name the following four major categories:

a. compounding (composition): occurs in either prefixal or "covalent" types and will be found in most word-classes.[13]
b. suffixation: found in most word-classes but showing extreme variation in the noun and adjective.
c. zero-change (Bloch and Trager 1942, 59 and 63–64): new formation by shift of a word from one class to another, with or without other changes including ablaut, but not including formative suffixation or compounding. Denominative verbs and deverbative nouns are typical cases.
d. reduplication: rare (lexically) in archaic IE, mildly productive in some recent IE languages.

One will be on guard in equating English with foreign word-formational devices. For example, English *-ish* (as in *reddish*) comes out as a prefix in

Latin *sub-* (in *subrufus*). Formative affixes of these types are easily included as main entries.

It appears that, in general, prime words have a higher frequency in actual discourse than derived words. For instance, in the Thorndike-Lorge list, of the first 500 words only 19 (3. 8%) are derived (e.g., *any/thing*); but in the second 500 words 35 (or 7%) are derived from primes. Obviously as the relative frequency goes down the percentage of derived words rises.[12]

In our foreign language, we must look for various kinds of formatives, but we must not be surprised to find gaps of one kind or another. For example, although a vast majority of IE languages show "diminutive" suffixes, there appear to be none in Modern Indic;[13] and compounds (covalent type) occur almost universally in IE, but Pashto seems to show few or none.[14] Relative frequency of derivational type is also unpredictable: modern English has but few dvandvas outside of scientific terms, but modern Greek and Hindustani have many examples of this compound type.

While word-formational patterns will give us rules and obviate the necessity of including vast numbers of rare or easily derived words, we must watch for those which have to be included because of morphophonemic peculiarities or unexpected meanings (e.g., shifted or metaphorical: German *Hochzeit*, Latin *comprehendo*, English *buttercup, heavy-weight*).[15]

I may summarize at this point an unpublished study intended to show what the examination of word-formation in one text of a language may reveal when one has in mind the morphological structure of its vocabulary.[16] Lucretius, the Epicurean poet of the first century B. C., has a total of 4293 different words, excluding sandhi and grammatical variants. Of the total, 1456 are prime words, and 2837 are derived words (ratio 1:2); in his text of 7415 lines of dactylic verse (about 240 printed pages) two of every three different words are derivable from primes by compounding, suffixation or zero-change. The breakdown (by processes) of the derived words in Lucretius is: suffixed 1064 items, compounded 1088, zero-change 683; in addition there are two cases only of reduplication (*quisquis; quantus ... quantus*, a phrase). Since the number of root-words (primes) in any IE language is finite, we may tentatively conclude that for any text of a language, the greater the bulk the lower the ratio of primes to derived forms.

2.4. **Semantic criteria**. Bloomfield (1933, 40) has caused undue pessimism among many students of language. In daily practice we deal with meanings, and especially in translating or working with a dictionary.[17] I suggest two alternative techniques for handling many words.[18] Assume that we have first isolated and classified words on a morphological basis. We can then attempt:

   a. a classification by contrasts ("What is the antonymous expression of . . .?")
light rain (snow, dumbbell) : heavy rain (snow, dumbbell)
light complexion (color, red) : dark complexion (color, red) deep blue (etc)

or
wide door (board) : narrow door (board)
wide array : small array
wide difference (of opinion) : slight difference

or
dry towel (street) : wet towel (street)
dry wine (martini) : sweet wine (—)
dry skin : oily skin

   b. a classification by substitution: If we are confronted by an isolated utterance, "He walked up to the bar," we can determine from this sentence (the "inner context") only that *bar* is a noun. If we consult the "outer context" (the paragraph or the situation), we determine that *bar* is, by substitution, either a "counter (for serving drinks)"; or "a barbell," or a "sandbar," etc.

The number of possible contrasts and substitutions gives us a rough notion of the number of meanings in the same form. We may, of course, choose to consider some of the possible meanings as impractical for our dictionary on the grounds that they are vestigially archaic, slangy, or otherwise of little use. Homonyms should usually be distinguished, especially if they show differences in morphology or syntax (congruence or word-order). Thus, Latin *multa* "many things" and *multa* "fine" coincide phonologically only at one point.

Although the procedure may be difficult to justify, we should set up semantic categories as a guide to selecting useful entries (useful despite the relative infrequency of some members of such categories). Compilers such as Roget (1852), Soule (1871), and C. D. Buck (1949) have given us convenient lists to work from. But all three have started from English only or primarily and some adjustments would be necessary to allow a more universal approach.[19] A potentially helpful guide in this instance, although intended for cultural anthropologists, is Murdock (1945).

In the special area of plants and animals a general bilingual dictionary cannot attempt to give the complete rundown one would expect in a technical botanical/zoological lexicon. The well-known varieties and local items (farmers and rural dwellers will have a greater knowledge than city-folk) can probably be limited to a total of 100 or 200. Folk-terms and scientific terms for plants and animals are often at variance (sometimes by choice, as a result of language migration). Thus, the American *robin* (actually, a thrush) resembled the English *robin* to early settlers, and our *buffalo* (really bison) resembled an animal of the Eastern Hemisphere.

Favorite expressions may sometimes be cast in patterns and make us seek other, comparable patterns. An English pattern which comes to mind is the substitution in a half-dozen or more phrases or compounds of a metaphor for the qualifier *very*. Thus, instead of *very high* we may prefer *sky-high* and, for *very deaf, stone-deaf*.[20] A too mechanical approach to lexicography may cause us to overlook legitimate data, and this is one area where we can encourage our informants (of the foreign language) to produce semantic paradigms when we suspect that they exist. And in like fashion it does not seem to be a dangerous practice to inquire about metaphorical meanings in those words whose primary meanings are animal names, body parts, and color terms.[21]

2.5. Feedback from the foreign-to-English part. Assuming that we begin work on a bilingual dictionary by eliciting foreign equivalents of English sentences, phrases and words (in a variety of simple contexts), we will occasionally encounter foreign items not anticipated in the English part. Thus, if we get only Spanish *remoto* as an equivalent to English *remote*, we may get, in another context, Spanish *rincón* 'inner angle,' but also 'remote locality,' 'out-of-the-way place.' The English entries hence become an index to unexpected foreign items or ones not easily discoverable.

By paying continuous attention to morphemic analysis, we may get another kind of feedback. Many German–English dictionaries translate *Wirt* by "landlord; owner; host." If we notice in other contexts (or from our own lexical data), such compounds as *Gastwirt, Landwirt*, we are justified (although this morpheme is rare finally) in adding the meaning 'keeper, tiller,' In this connection it is important to have at hand a *reverse index* of the foreign language to check the relative distribution of final compositional or suffixal morphemes.[22] With English *instead* of (archaic *in (my) stead*) may be associated, by some cross reference, a final element *-stead* in *bedstead, roadstead,* and *homestead.*

2.6. Cultural items. A culture (defined here as a more-or-less unified linguistic area) is not aware that its facets are different, peculiar, or even characteristic, unless so informed by an outsider or unless confronted suddenly by another culture. A part of the business of a bilingual dictionary is to recognize lexical items reflecting these differences and to treat them accordingly, that is, not to minimize them by seeking an exact (often artificial) equivalent in the other language. Thus, *king* will translate ancient Greek *basileús* only if accompanied by a cultural note explaining the differences in connotation.

The dictionary must be careful to include older items in a continuing culture even where, as in many parts of the USA, technology has replaced many traditional things and concepts. The old may not only be encountered in literature (history, novels, ballads) but it may yet live on residually in the most advanced societies or be present among out of the way members of the culture. The most obvious lexical area here is the realm of handicrafts and home manufacture, such as weaving, pottery, working with leather, metals, wood. We can neglect neither the "latest terms" of science nor the older terms for an older technology. But there are other lexical items, more or less unpredictable, and the following lists indicate the better-known examples, and ones which will be suggestive of still other items. The terms (and the things or concepts) may not be structurally significant in the culture,[23] but they may be contrastively interesting and important as regards their treatment in a bilingual dictionary:

>American English: *attic, blizzard, ice cream, cocktail, bathroom, date* (v), *the West, coffee break, drugstore, boyfriend, hitchhike, weekend, teamster.*
>Latin: *ars, imperium, pius, auctoritas, virtus, officium, religio, fas, cliens, rex, patria.*
>Ancient Greek: *hybris, atĕ, logos, kosmos, nemesis, daimōn, polis, paideia, aretĕ, gnosis, sophrosynĕ, xenos.*
>Modern Greek: *onoma'sia, papa'dja, 'glendi, fi'lotimo, 'kalanda* (pl), *kafe'nio, kombo'loi, ta'verna.*
>Sanskrit: *dhárma, ártha, kárman, kāma, brahmán, ṛṣi.*
>Old Italian: *gentile, donna, cetera, innamorato, corteggiano, piazza, uomo-di-corte.*

3. A Proposal

Everyone who has worked with informants has grown impatient with the time-waste involved in writing English equivalents. An official or semi-official alphabetized checklist of English entries and sub-entries could be easily prepared by an ad hoc committee of the Linguistic Society of America (LSA), perhaps in conjunction with a British committee. A preliminary compilation could then be mailed out to volunteer members of the LSA, the Modern Language Association, and the American Anthropological Association for criticism and addenda; by this means accidental oversights and regional variants could be gathered in by the committee for consideration.[24] The final publication, mimeographed or multilithed, would provide a definitive workbook for all lexical purposes. If each page is doubled, the carbon copy would easily be used for reversing the entries. An appendix of semantic categories would relieve the strain on the memory of both the interviewer and the informant.[25]

NOTES

1. Technical vocabularies like the medical/biological had best be handled in separate works. There is a well-established tradition for this. But the ordinary bilingual work will include a sampling of better-known terms.

2. Of 84 extinct and extant IE languages there are 62 English bilingual dictionaries, good, bad, or indifferent; for the same group there are 46 German dictionaries, 23 French, 15 Russian and 10 Italian. (The records are probably incomplete but also probably representative of the real ratios.) Among the 22 languages for which there are no English dictionaries the minor Germanic, Slavic, and Romance dialects constitute a majority. Many of the English–IE dialect dictionaries are poor or out-of-date and need re-doing. Furthermore, there is no reason why regional dictionaries could not be made of, e.g., English–Andalusian, English–Sardinian, English–Pomeranian, English–Frisian, this to avoid the taken-for-granted omissions in a Castilian–Andalusian, Italian–Sardinian, or Polish–Pomeranian dictionary.

3. A master-list of English entries could accommodate varieties of both regions by simple abbreviation marks (A, B). The researches of A. W. Read would be extremely valuable for the British part of our entries. Examples of lexical deviation: *thumb tack* : *drawing pin*, *trunk* (of auto) : *boot*, *garter* : *suspender*. The main stumbling block that I can foresee is the large number of these variants.

4. Including the (sometimes sole) criterion of open juncture which is the same as unfilled phonetic space.

5. "Archaic" here refers to the type of grammatical (esp. inflectional) format associated with Greek, Latin, and Sanskrit, and usually labeled synthetic. "Recent" refers to the other end of the (historical/typological) pole and includes a variety of disparate items usually

labelled analytic. Archaic-type languages are mostly extinct, but archaic features remain in some extant languages in varying proportions.

6. The Swedish list, by Allwood and Wilhelmsen (1947), is not based on a count of Swedish texts but is a translation of Helen S. Eaton's (1940) conflated list. The fact is that few of the frequency lists are satisfactory. Attention should be called, finally, to West (1953), dealing with semantic frequencies in British usage.

7. For example, in Diederich (1939), ill-advised short-cuts or misapprehensions have caused the following pairs of words to be counted together: *qui* and *quis*, *hie* (pron.) and *hie* (adv.), *cum* (prep) and *cum* (conj.), but *nec* and *neque* (mere sandhi variants) are counted separately.

8. For the record, these additional 104 items in Thorndike and Lorge (1944) are:

apple	chose	flow	nest	shake
attend	Christmas	former	noise	sheep
asleep	clock	fourth	noon	shine
band	cloth	gentle	oak	shut
basket	clothe(-ing)	gift	path	silk
beast	coast	grace	pen	slow
bee	corn	grain	perfect	sometime
bell	cow	grave	proper	strike
bless	crown	hide	proud	tail
blind	delight	hunt	pure	teacher
bone	divide	journey	quick	thick
bottom	dust	jump	quiet	throw
bow	entire	lesson	rapid	tongue
brave	equal	ion	roof	unite
breakfast	extend	list	row	wash
bread	fancy	load	sad	waste
brook	fat	loud	sand	weak
butter	feed	mail	seed	wheat
cake	fence	mill	seize	wheel
cap	firm	moon	(self)	yesterday
careful	fix	narrow	separate	

9. Nida (1960) lists and discusses limiting substitutes (52), clause markers (54), coordinators (59), antecedents (93f), and conjunctive markers (190f). Francis (1958) gives prepositions and prepositional phrases, a total of 76 (306–308); 16 adjective qualifiers (278), to which add the colloquial *real*; coordinators, such as *and*, *or* (279); and includers, about 46 in number, e.g., *after*, *as . . . as*, and *till* (390).

10. Francis (1958) is interested primarily in analysis; one must consult his scattered paragraphs (e.g., 208, 240, and 260) for word-formation. For better sustained treatment,

see Marchand (1960). Of four US Army dictionaries produced at the end of the war, the Russian–English and the Spanish–English (as technical manuals; see Introduction, pages 4–5 and note, pages 118–19), despite otherwise elaborate grammatical treatments of their specific languages, omit word-formation; the German one devotes about seven pages to the subject; and the Chinese nothing, though one would not expect much. Word-formation is the one subject I expect to see in both grammar and dictionary.

11. "Prefixal" is self-explanatory; "covalent" is used here (instead of non-prefixal) to refer to all other types collectively, since many of them contain noun + noun, adjective + adjective, etc. The classification is based primarily on archaic IE languages, and the two types seem to be equal in bulk.

12. In Diederich (1939, note 9), the first hundred Latin words include 15 derived words, the second hundred 17, the third hundred 37 derived words.

13. I have been unable to elicit any from speakers of Sindhi, Hindi, Oriya, or Maithili, except the cases of diminution by shift of gender, e.g., Sindhi / ši'šo/ (masc., "bottle") : /ši'ši/ (fem., "small bottle").

14. This, according to Penzl (1955, 68). The absence of compounds in Pashto is a major deviation from IE structure. Kurdish, on the other hand (McCarus 1958, 83–87) has the "normal" types of compounds.

15. Formations like *baker, carver, starter*, and numerous other agents/instruments in *-er* need not be fully listed, but morphophonemic exceptions like *lawyer* (and *sawyer*?) should be entered. Important suffixes can be entered with suitable statistical and semantic information. For example, the English suffix *-age* (about 85 formations in current American English) shows three main semantic groups:

    a. quantity/bulk: *acreage, dosage, silage*
    b. residence: *hermitage, orphanage, parsonage*
    c. status (rare): *marriage, parentage*

16. Lexical structure can be determined only in part from a dictionary (itself a secondary source of information), but it can be determined fairly precisely from a sampling of texts, and the resulting information is useful in compiling a dictionary. For such a sampling of ancient Greek, see Clay 1958, 1960). (This may be the answer to Worth's [1960, 277f] query: "the basic and still unsolved problem is to discover the systematic framework in terms of which the lexicon can be described.") The ratio of derived to underived words in Greek tragedy is about 4 : 1; Euripides, whose bulk is about 3 times that of Sophocles, shows, of the total vocabulary, 77% derivatives; Sophocles shows 75%.

17. Bloomfield (1933, 140) lists four types of definitions, one of which, demonstration, is, or can be, non-linguistic. Types one and three ("in terms of another science" and "circumlocution") are in reality the same. Type four (translation) takes the problem out of the language concerned. Another type, not mentioned by Bloomfield, is one which could be called "bracketing"; it is well illustrated by Aristotle in his definitions of philosophical terms, especially in his *Ethics*. His technique is related to his theory of the "mean" and also to the current doctrine of semantic spectra.

18. I do not pretend that these two devices will handle the whole vocabulary, nor even representatively all word classes. Nor do they necessarily exclude other devices such as the type of lexical hierarchy described so ably in Mr. Conklin's paper at this meeting, or Mr. Gleason's semantic spectra. I am not convinced that any one method is sufficient; perhaps there cannot be any one approach for some obscure theoretical reason.

19. The synonymies prepared for an assortment of languages, while they may suffer from a variety of malpractices, can be of some use.

20. Others in daily use by myself are *ice-cold, red-hot, snow-white, pitch-black, bone-dry, brand-new, dog-tired*. A related type, not substituting for *very*, but based on simple similes, is found in *sky-blue, knee-deep, shoulder-high* (or *waist-*), etc.

21. My wife reminds me of a *locus classicus* in (pseudo-) Demetrius's *On Style* (1902, 109), where we read "Not all metaphors can . . . be used convertibly . . . Homer could call the lower slope of Ida its 'foot,' but he could never have called a man's foot his 'slope.'" *Tiger* seems to have no metaphorical meaning in English, but the Sindhi word for 'tiger' (*či'to*) means also 'bully.'

22. Such *indices a tergo* are now available for Latin, ancient Greek, Italian, Biblical Hebrew, and Russian. For other languages the best that compilers have been able to produce are the deficient "rhyming" dictionaries. Rhyming indices for specific verse texts (based on actual rhymes and not on eye-rhymes or misleading spellings) are better, but they do not represent colloquial or prosaic language.

23. This fact should not worry anybody, since, if a lexicographer is justified in atomizing normal speech flow into the convenient units of words, he may do the same with the cultural complex underlying the lexical symbols. Furthermore, he may use the same judgment in inclusion or exclusion of cultural items as he does for word entries.

24. The *Linguistic Atlas* worksheets are geared primarily to the rural vocabulary. Since, in this country at least, the urbanites and suburbanites have become a sizeable percentage of the population, non-rural variants can be given more attention in our check-list, for instance ordinary but easily overlooked equivalents like *rubber-band*: *rubber-binder*; *stuffing* (in a turkey): *dressing*; *dish-rag*: *dish-cloth*; etc. But some judgment must be exercised to avoid annoying batches like *couch, sofa, davenport, divan, lounge, settee, chesterfield* (see also note 3).

25. Some major semantic regroupings are listed here, in no particular order. There should be two separate lists for flora/fauna, namely an Arctic/Temperate list, and a Tropical/Subtropical list; then food and drink, food-preparations, tools and weapons, natural phenomena, topography and geography, body parts (and those of animals), kinship, social status and occupation, colors, size shape direction and position, clothes and ornament, religion, metals and natural substances, excretions, time (and its parts), amusements (sports, games), buildings, the house and its parts, furnishings and furniture, folklore and folk literature, manufactures and products, political and administrative terms, business and trade, ailments, cures and physical conditions, military and naval, fishing and the sea, the farm and farming. It should be clearly understood that these lists constitute only a mnemonic aid and not a means to force a foreign equivalent for every English meaning or vice-versa

COMMENTS

Dean Stoddard Worth
University of California, Los Angeles

THIS MORNING'S PAPERS HAVE COVERED QUITE A RANGE of topics including what ought to be in a dictionary (Miss Haas, Mr. Harrell, Mr. Swanson), what actually is in dictionaries (Mr. Malkiel), and what lexicology is or should be about (Mr. Weinreich). The following discussion can of course only skip about among the many points of practical and theoretical interest which have been raised.

Mr. Malkiel's "Typological Classification of Dictionaries on the Basis of Distinctive Features" has the merit of being based not entirely on theoretical constructs but also on the detailed examination of hundreds of actual works. One wonders, however, whether such a typology might not prove more valuable in the library cataloguing room than in the office of the lexicographer, at least until the analogy with phonology has been worked out more thoroughly. What are the lexicographic phonemes (i.e., the dictionaries) consisting of these distinctive features? If such a feature analysis does not result in a set of discrete, mutually opposed dictionary types, and if almost all features (except jocularity, which can perhaps be omitted as irrelevant to a serious discussion) can co-occur freely in all dictionaries, then there seems to be little that is distinctive in the features themselves. A few other points seem to call for comment: (1) the inaccurate Saussurian equation of historic = dynamic and synchronic = static has long since been rejected by modern structural linguistics; (2) there seems to be no reason to restrict etymology to the pre-history of the vocabulary, to the exclusion of loanwords and loan translations; (3) forms which are "firmly engraved, at the least, in the passive memory of the average literate speaker" can hardly be considered "unacknowledged archaisms," unless the vocabulary of a language is to be restricted to items used actively by the average speaker—a restriction which is surely too severe for languages with a long written literary tradition. In general, however, one must agree that the suggestion that scholarly works may themselves be amenable to a typological classification is an interesting one and deserving of further study.

Miss Haas, in answer to her own query, "What Belongs in a Bilingual Dictionary?" provides a list of desiderata which add up to a fairly exhaustive compendium of human knowledge, preferably with pictures, and above all in a handy, compact form. One's first reaction, that such wishes are a trifle unrealistic, may be unfair both to the speaker and to the future of lexicography. Noticeably absent from Miss Haas's list was any stipulation that the finished product produce a profit on the open market, so let us consider what could be done without worrying about the cost. Suppose we wish to construct a super-dictionary that will tell us all about the Russian language, history, geography, economics, authors, missile bases, epic poems, etc. etc. Let us begin by translating and cross-indexing several of the best Russian dictionaries, encyclopaedias, gazeteers, grammars, and what not. Then let us put all this information on the memories of an electronic computer, so programmed as to let us seek out various classes of material and various depths of detail, as desired. Then let us wire this colossus up to highspeed teleprinters in the offices of all those who wish to use the dictionary (or—who knows?—let us use video tapes and TV screens). Later on, when better techniques have been developed, we will of course feed the memories with information from more and more publications, all of which will have been mechanically read, mechanically translated, and mechanically indexed. Such an arrangement would overcome the presently vexed problem of combining an adequate amount of information in a form small enough to be manageable—in short, there may very well be no other way of providing ad hoc supplies of information from particular fields, for particular purposes, in a particular degree of detail. Of course, such an electronic monster may be only an impractical dream; on the other hand, much good has come from those dreams which, like human flight, were so wildly impractical that they required a radical change in theory as well as technique.

Mr. Swanson's "Recommendations on the Selection of Entries for a Bilingual Dictionary" are based more on morphological, especially derivational criteria than on semantic classes. One wonders whether the Indo-European languages really have such "similar grammatical and syntactic categories and word-classes" that a "bilingual dictionary between any two of them will be easy to set up"; it is not at all easy, for example, to state precise English equivalents for the witnessed vs. non-witnessed past of Balkan

Slavic, or for that matter to equate the Slavic aspects in general with the tense and aspect markers of English, French, or German. If frequency is to be a criterion for the selection of entries, which of the two languages will be chosen as base? Among Mr. Swanson's derivation types, one wonders why prefixing and compounding are grouped together, and opposed to suffixing; surely a more accurate division is into affixing (pre- or suf-) vs. compounding, particularly for the "archaic" languages with their emphatic dichotomy of grammatical and lexical elements. Among the semantic criteria, one must note that classification by contrast (*light, heavy*) will be useful only for a fraction (mostly adjectival) of the vocabulary, and that classification by substitution is in danger of becoming only an elaborately circular justification of *a priori* definitions, since the procedure implies the referential identity of substituted forms (*bar* = 'counter for serving drinks,' etc.); a real substitution test, if I understand it, would list the tokens which can fill the slot in, say, "He *walked* up to *the* . . .," thus producing the semantic (and in this case banal) category of "things which can be walked up to." In general, however, one must agree with Mr. Swanson that dictionary-writing would probably be improved by the unobtrusive adoption of "the more firmly established techniques of recent linguistics."

Mr. Harrell's "Notes on Bilingual Lexicography" not only emphasize the need to define scope and purpose precisely before beginning any lexical venture, but also touch on certain problems of theoretical interest. One wonders whether the problem of indicating multiple meaning is not secondary to that of defining it: what are the differences among (1) the nuances of meaning of a single word, (2) different meanings of one and the same word, and (3) meanings of two or more homographic or homophonic words? Once identified, multiple meanings can be specified by co-occurrent forms (although probably not always), e.g., "*hot (pepper, mustard)* = *picante* . . ." In other words, it is one thing to segment a semantic continuum in language X, and another to define the correspondences between the already determined segments of language X and those of language Y. Behind the decision to enter, or not to enter, such a form as *circumnavigate* lies a theoretical problem of some importance: should the head words in a dictionary isolate their referents as precisely as possible, or should they relate these referents within broader semantic classes (say, *motion, sailing*)? The decision is easier in the case of such heavy Latinisms as *circumnavigate* vs. *sail around*, but must one omit *enter* in favor of *go in, come in,* or *leave* because we already have *go away, go out, go off*? The less precise the semantic pinpointing, the larger will be the entries, and the closer the dictionary will come to a description of semantic fields. This all means, of course, that lexicography is dependent on, but by no means the same as, lexicology, and that the writer of dictionaries, as Mr. Harrell so clearly points out, would do well to separate the practical from the theoretical.

Mr. Weinreich's stimulating discussion of "Lexicographic Definition in Descriptive Semantics" raises a whole series of theoretical issues too thorny to be seized very firmly here. The conception of "the meaning of a term as the set of conditions which must be fulfilled if the term is to denote" is suggestive but imprecise (what sort of "conditions" are these?), and might well have been explained in more detail, or perhaps illustrated by more actual words and fewer algebraic symbols. This conception seems to imply the existence of a discrete set of semantic features, the presence or absence of which serves to distinguish among synonyms. One wonders if it would not be useful to insist more firmly on the differential nature of these features, or (as is probably still necessary) to find out which features are differential. One might then arrive at semantic analogs of the distinctive features familiar on the phonological level. Any given word would be semantically characterized by the marking or non-marking of such broad semantic categories as space (is the word meaningful only if one assumes three-, two- or one-dimensional space), time (is a temporal axis assumed), degree (various kinds of intensity markers and quantifiers), sensory perception (does the word imply taste, touch, hearing, etc.), relation to speech situation (deictics, emotives, etc.). When words have been classified on such a basis, it should be simpler to arrange them into associative clusters based on opposition (Weinreich's *open*, *close*) and implication (his *end*, *after*). Furthermore, a descriptive semantics based on the differential principle would be flexible enough to permit semantic overlapping (the layman's "synonyms"), a phenomenon so frequent it must be accounted for; rather than insist that the entire semantic continuum be divisible into mutually exclusive segments, one might suppose that the "allo-meanings" of two distinct words could coincide in some, although never in all, environments. However, to pursue this idea would take us too far afield. One anticipates with interest Mr. Weinreich's further studies in this timely and fascinating area.

ize II

STRUCTURAL LINGUISTICS
AND THE PREPARATION OF
DICTIONARIES

THE RELATION OF LEXICON AND GRAMMAR

H. A. Gleason, Jr.
Hartford Seminary Foundation

1. Scope of the Paper

In this paper, I am charged with discussing the relation between lexicon and grammar. This might be interpreted as meaning either of two similar but not identical problems: the relation of grammar (a portion of language structure) with lexicon (another portion of the total language structure), or the relation of a grammatical statement to a dictionary (both documents of some sort). In the former case, the question is one of language theory; in the latter, one of practical descriptive technique. I shall not choose between these but rather say something about each. However, I believe that it is important to keep the two clearly distinct. This I will try to do by being careful with the terminology, even if this forces me to a somewhat awkward phraseology. I shall use the terms as I just have: *grammar* and *lexicon* will be sectors of language structure, *grammatical statement* and *dictionary* will be descriptive instruments or products of linguistic research. This is, of course, a restriction of the use of both *grammar* and *lexicon*, since these are commonly used of linguists' output, as well as of their subject matter. I shall try to make the distinction because I feel that the terminological confusion here has been at the root of some of our difficulties in thinking on these matters.

2. Attitudes toward Grammar and Lexicon

For the American descriptive linguist there is a very sharp contrast in attitudes toward the two members of either of the relationships. Grammar and grammatical statements are for him, respectively, a central portion of his subject matter and his basic product. If he gives much thought to theoretical matters—and many linguists do, of course—a great deal of that thought is devoted to the nature and internal structure of grammar. Much of his practical work is that of producing grammatical statements or portions thereof, of investigating techniques for finding or organizing such statements, or in appraising and perhaps restating the grammatical statements of others. He is always interested in new fragments of theory, new twists in organization, a new device for analysis, a new notation.

Not so, however, with either lexicon or dictionaries. Very little thought is given to *lexicon*, and few have any clear idea what they mean when they say the word. Commonly, it is treated as essentially equivalent to *vocabulary*, perhaps only a slightly more elegant synonym. Certainly, we descriptive linguists tend to be contemptuous of vocabulary. It is almost a dogma among us that vocabulary is the least significant part of language (save for a group among us who even doubt that vocabulary is really a part of language after all). Clearly this is, in part at least, a reaction to the equally naive popular tendency to identify language and vocabulary. But we can hardly excuse ourselves from so thoroughly degrading vocabulary by the fact that it has been by others so unduly exalted.

3. The Bloomfield Tradition

There is certainly more that figures in this attitude than just the reaction to popular pseudo-linguistics. We stand in the Bloomfield tradition, and our thinking is rooted rather deeply in his *Language* (1933), whether we get it direct or second-hand. In the first place, Bloomfield also was infected by the confusion of lexicon and dictionary. He gives at least two definitions of lexicon: "The total stock of morphemes in a language is its *lexicon*" (162) and "The lexicon [dictionary] is really an appendix of the grammar, a list of basic irregularities" (274). But Bloomfield (in contrast with some other linguists) does not seem to use *lexicon* and *grammar* as easy transitions to carry his argument from language to description and back again; he had too strictly logical a habit of thinking and writing for that.

Apart from the failure to distinguish language and description, these two definitions are not in conflict. Of the two, it is the second that reveals the more. Bloomfield is defining *lexicon* in terms of "basic irregularities." He goes on to point out that both meaning and class membership are irregularities and so assigned to the lexicon.

Nothing might be better calculated to divert the interest of the typical American descriptive linguist from the lexicon. He is primarily—often almost solely—interested in the regularities. Indeed, "irregular" is almost a tabooed word for many of us. We dislike such statements as that *man* has an irregular plural, euphemistically preferring to rephrase it in terms of a "small class." We have also an underlying dislike for the irregularity itself and we spend a great deal of our time seeking a statement that will reduce the number of irregularities (or small classes) by finding common features (regularities) which run through them. Sometimes, we resort to some rather remarkable gymnastics to bring such irregularities in line, e.g., the "replacive" which quite artificially makes an affix out of a process. Or we look for excuses to shove these irregularities outside our jurisdiction—is not linguistics basically the study of the regularities in language behavior? To a very real extent, we have made the dictionary exactly what Bloomfield suggests—a list of irregularities, the refuse of grammatical description, the repository of things put aside because they did not give a clear and incisive picture of an all-pervading *structure* (for some of us, nothing more than a fancy synonym for *regularity*) which the descriptive linguist finds aesthetically pleasing.

4. Current Neglect of Lexicon and Dictionaries

We don't talk much about either lexicon or dictionaries. My own *Introduction to Descriptive Linguistics* (1953) will serve as an example. Neither word appears in the index, though I have a little statement of what might be considered as a minimally adequate description of a language including "a summary of the phonology and morphology; a vocabulary of, say, several thousand words" (347). Lower on the same page, I say "incredibly few languages have, for example, an adequate dictionary, that is, one in which the vocabulary entries run to tens of thousands and in which the definitions are not merely one-word translations but include citations of usages and discussion of the range of meanings. Many more such dictionaries are needed." That's pretty sparse treatment!

Hockett's *A Course in Modern Linguistics* (1958) does little better. He has two entries under "dictionaries" in his index. They lead to the following statements. "Bilingual dictionaries and easy word-by-word translations are inevitably misleading; the shortcut of asking what a form means must ultimately be supplemented by active participation in the life of the community that speaks the language" (141), and "In theory, and largely in practice, idioms are the stuff of which dictionaries are made. The reason is obvious: a dictionary-maker need not include a non-idiomatic nonce-form, since a speaker of the language would never look up such a form. He would look up the component parts, if he needed to, and automatically know the meaning of the whole. In practice, of course, no dictionary is ever complete. There are far too many idioms in any language, and more come into existence every day" (173). Not really a very good showing either! And in some other good or widely used books in general linguistics, I could find nothing at all.

Nor do descriptive linguists do much with the production of dictionaries. In at least one of the recent conferences on language materials for the National Defense Education Act (1958), there was a definite and completely general reluctance to undertake dictionary preparation. This was in sharp contrast to the almost universal eagerness to take on certain other tasks. Dictionary making is tedious in the extreme. It is exacting. It is an incredibly large job. As now practiced, its operations are quite different from those in which the descriptive linguist feels thoroughly at home.

Descriptive linguists have been immensely critical of dictionaries and dictionary makers. Commonly, the principles on which they have based their criticism have been of very little relevance to dictionaries. It seems to me that we commonly make quite unreasonable demands and show little if any understanding of the limitations within which a dictionary maker must operate. And I think it is on the whole fair to say that some of the most vociferous critics have been those with the least actual experience in dictionary making.

Not only so, but I think it can be shown that relatively few of the dictionaries produced by American descriptive linguists have actually conformed to the standards that we have talked of. The dictionaries with good and copious citations of usages and a conscientious effort to explore areas of meaning have been mostly produced by people outside the fraternity— non-American linguists or people laying no claim at all to the title of linguist. Those American descriptive linguists who have produced dictionaries are often known for their other work much more than for their lexical contributions.

5. The Total Descriptive Task

Bloomfield (1933, 138) says, "The description of a language, then, begins with phonology, . . . When the phonology of a language has been established, there remains the task of telling what meanings are attached to the several phonetic forms. This phase of the description is *semantics*. It is ordinarily divided into two parts, *grammar* and *lexicon*." Apart from the use of *meaning* and *semantics* in ways that are not now current, I consider that this is an important emphasis in Bloomfield that has, unfortunately, not been strongly maintained. It would mean, I believe, that an adequate description at our present state of development would necessarily include not only a grammatical statement but also a dictionary. But it is clear that not many descriptive linguists have felt any strong sense of responsibility beyond the production of the grammatical statement.

There must, of course, be some outer bound to the responsibility of a linguist to a language—he is not called on to describe the total speech behavior of a person or a community. It can be debated where this bound should be set. It seems to me that the most logical bound would be such as to include within the linguist's domain at least a considerable part of the material ordinarily relegated to the dictionary. I consider that there are two compelling reasons why this should be so.

First, it seems well-nigh impossible to carry on a reasonable grammatical analysis without at the same time building some sort of a lexical file. Nor is it possible to do anything particularly useful with a grammatical statement in the absence of any lexical information. Both of these would suggest that the grammatical statement and the dictionary are interdependent in some important way.

Second, I feel that it will only be by wrestling seriously with the problem of compiling a dictionary that we can overcome our habit of excluding from the grammatical statement certain inconvenient details on what is really no other ground than merely that they are inconvenient. Whether we like it or not, every grammatical statement implies some delimitation of scope as between itself and the dictionary. But we have examined and defined that limit from one side only. There ought to be positive reasons for assigning a feature to the dictionary rather than simply negative reasons for banishing it from the grammatical statement. Or putting it another way, the best way to cure ourselves of sweeping things under the rug is to accept the responsibility for cleaning the whole floor.

We may follow Bloomfield in considering the descriptive task as divided between the grammatical statement and the dictionary. (And, of course, the phonological statement, but we will not mention this explicitly every time.) On what basis is this division to be made? This is not a matter which is commonly defined or even discussed. The current practice is largely a result of slowly accreting tradition. There is little reason to expect that it can be precisely formulated, or even that the division is very effective. There is overlapping of function, and probably parts of the task that are left in no-man's-land. Our notions of what a grammatical statement should do have grown up without much reference to the functions of dictionaries, and conversely. Nevertheless, there are several possible bases that have been suggested, assumed, or merely accepted in default of any formulation of principles. All of them have important points of contact with Bloomfield's definition of lexicon in terms of "basic irregularities."

6. Form versus Meaning

One very common implication is that the grammatical statement deals with form, the dictionary with meaning. This is seldom if ever advanced as a definition since, as soon as it is, its difficulties become clear. Yet it does seem to have had some influence in determining practice. Traditionally, the dictionary is a list of words (here meaning, properly, paradigms, as exemplified by some single form or selection of forms). As such it can handle only those meanings which inhere in words. Meanings of constructional patterns, inflectional affixes, and often also derivational morphemes are necessarily entered, if at all, in the grammatical statement. For some grammarians the giving of such meanings is an important function of the grammatical statement itself, perhaps even its main function. For others, including most American descriptivists, the meanings in a grammatical statement are quite incidental, and from a rigorous point of view out of place. To prevent the grammatical statement resting in any way on meanings, they are so inserted as to make them totally independent of the structure of the statement, so that they might be expunged from it without destroying the integrity of the whole. Perhaps it is this reluctance to view meanings as any other than improper intruders in a grammatical statement that has led many descriptive linguists to minimize this by removing much of it to the dictionary. They tend to make the dictionary not so much a list of words as of morphemes. However, even when inflectional morphemes are all listed in the dictionary, and their meanings given there, it is in general still necessary to refer to the grammatical statement to get the maximum amount of information on their meaning. This is simply because it is only in the grammatical statement that the contrasts, collocations, and other pertinent elements of the meanings of inflectional morphemes are ordinarily given. Their meaning inheres, in part, in their place within a system and cannot easily be made clear when they are treated outside that system.

Conversely, of course, the dictionary always carries a considerable mass of formal information, even if this is nothing more than the assignment of words to "parts of speech." But ordinarily this is not all. Hidden away in our advocacy of copious citations of usages may indeed be a demand for additional formal information—in this case largely the collocational possibilities of the forms. With function words, of course, the dictionary definitions, generally thought of as statements about meaning, are actually largely statements about use, as may be seen in any good English dictionary in the articles for *the, not*, etc.

7. Tight Structure versus Loose Structure

Linguistic structure is normally considered by linguists as quite tight and hence properly amenable to the yes-or-no type of description which is traditional in descriptive linguistics. However, occasionally, sets of language phenomena are observed which, though apparently structured, seem not to be so rigorously structured as this. There seems to be a feeling that such items are more appropriately assigned to the dictionary than to the grammatical statement. However, such a formulation raises more questions than it answers. In the first place, many might raise doubts as to the validity of the conception on which it is based. Past experience has shown that many of these loosely structured subsystems are such simply because they have not yet been properly analyzed. Every field linguist has had the experience of finding such a bundle of refractory material which later turns out to be as regular and systematic as any other part of its structure. It would be most unfortunate if the distinction between the grammatical statement and the dictionary were to rest so directly on our analytic shortcomings.

If the grammar of a language consists of a tightly integrated core surrounded by a penumbra of less tightly structured material gradually fading out into nothing, then grammar itself becomes an undelimitable concept. There must either be some reasonably clear bounds to grammar or, if there should be any such loosely integrated structures, there must be some further principle of internal organization of grammar which gives some real basis for cohesion. This is most probably provided by the idea of degrees of grammaticalness. It may then be that part of what is meant by this criterion of tight structure versus loose structure is merely that the grammar should attempt to cover only down to some definable degree of grammaticalness, leaving tag ends beyond to the dictionary. If this is what is meant by the suggestion, then it deserves a restatement in these terms.

There are other possibilities of interpreting what is meant by loose structure as against tight structure. In some cases, no kind of analysis or reanalysis can force the material into the sort of model that descriptive linguistics finds appropriate to grammatical statements. In such an instance the issue may not be the degree of structuring so much as the kind. It would be most strange if only one kind of structuring should actually apply to any set of patterns as complex as speech behavior. No linguist can defend the proposition that his discipline can properly handle all that is worth description in speech. Crossing grammatical structure in various ways are certainly other types of structurings, some of them, at least, so different in form as to be unrecognizable as structure by the methods of descriptive linguistics. Others are parallel enough that the linguist inevitably finds part of the patterning in the course of seeking out the grammar. Some of these loosely structured systems (from this grammar-oriented point of view) may be merely the imperfect projection onto a grammatical plane of structures which are more appropriately studied on some other plane by some other method.

That which would be most likely to obtrude on the attention of a linguist doing grammatical analysis would be any system of structure which had numerous contacts with grammar, and which so paralleled grammar in structure that very similar methods of analysis might appropriately be applied. I believe that there is such, and that its contacts with and general structural similarities to grammar are so strong that it belongs within linguistics rather than just outside linguistics. It is this that I mean by content.

8. Widespread versus Isolated

Another possible basis for defining the scope of grammatical statement and dictionary is in the breadth of relevance of patterns. All matters that apply to a considerable number of items would belong to the grammatical statement; those which apply to a single item to the dictionary. Thus, the fact that a considerable number of English words occur in pairs, one singular and one plural, justifies inclusion of this phenomenon in the grammatical statement. The fact that the plural formation in *men* is isolated would suggest that it should be treated in the dictionary.

While such a discrimination may be broadly workable, it is not easily applied in some cases. At a low level of grammaticalness, it presents little trouble. Groups of items may be sorted out and assigned labels, among them determiners and nouns, and each of these groups has several members.

But a grammatical statement at this level of grammaticalness has rather little value. If, however, the statement is based on a much deeper level of grammaticalness, the situation is much different. Most of the small closed classes (like "determiner") must be considerably subdivided. The result is that there are now a considerable number of unique items. But it will not do merely to exile these to the dictionary. Consider a single example: among the nouns is a considerable subclass including *United States*, *Thames*, *Battery* (New York), *Hague* (city), *Hartford* (an insurance company). These are all alike in that they are always preceded by *the*, except in noun-adjunct position. At this level, *the* is isolated, among other things by the fact of this special relationship to the subclass of nouns just mentioned. We have here a grammatical fact that connects a class of items with an isolated item. Is the rule to be assigned to the grammatical statement on the basis that it applies to a plurality of items, or to the dictionary on the basis that it applies to a single item?

If this criterion were to be followed quite literally, I believe that it would destroy any useful conception of grammar and render grammatical statements largely worthless. It would have the peculiar property of assigning a larger proportion of the material to the dictionary at every successive degree of grammaticalness, perhaps even to the extent that the total bulk would shrink as it gets more detailed. Certainly, it would have the effect of destroying the cohesiveness which we normally take to justify a grammatical statement. Indeed, if we speak not of words, but of morphemes, the structure is shipwrecked to begin with, since most of our English inflectional morphemes are unique on even the grossest level.

9. Class versus Member

There is an obvious way around the difficulty of the last proposal. An item like *the* must be in the grammatical statement, isolated or not. The best way to accomplish this is to set up a class or subclass to include it, with no concern as to whether there are other items to be included with it. At the first sight, it would seem that we are accepting two different criteria for classes. One is based on groups of items sharing a significant distribution and justifies classes such as that mentioned above, including *United States*, etc. The other causes us to set up single member classes for every instance where exclusion from the grammatical statement will render the latter fatuous (e.g., by reason of excluding from the grammatical statement the only relationship which makes it worthwhile to define the subclass of nouns including *United States*). Actually, it is much better to bypass any such definitions and merely consider that the classes are set up in the process of analysis simply because they seem to be needed in the analysis; they are not found in the corpus but created as the analysis is created.

The grammatical statement then takes care of all relationships between classes. It says nothing at all about words, morphemes, or any other items, only about classes which bear a very special kind of relationship with the items. We ordinarily call the latter "members" of the classes, but we must be clear that this means nothing like being part of the classes. The class is given a very different status than was suggested in the last section. But a discussion of this point would take us too far into grammatical theory for the present context.

The dictionary will be left with the responsibility for those matters which pertain to the members of classes. Among other things, this would leave the dictionary to identify the class (and subclasses) to which an item is related.

10. Functions of a Dictionary

This proposal does not, of course, answer the question, "What is the function of a dictionary under this plan?" There are several possibilities; probably more than one of these functions could be discharged in combination.

10.1. **Index to the grammar.** The dictionary might be an index to the grammar. Thus, for each item it would state to what class and subclass it is related. Class-cleavage, in some languages an extremely important phenomenon, would be shown in the dictionary by the mention of two classes at one entry.

10.2. **Amendment to the grammar.** The dictionary might serve as amendment to the grammar. Assume that there are two or more forms whose distribution is not absolutely parallel on a grammatical plane. Those might nevertheless be assigned to the same class or subclass. If this were done, the grammatical statement would either state the common distribution of the two or their total distribution, or some compromise. Then the dictionary might correct the statement by making clear the departures of each from the idealized distribution ascribed to the class. We descriptive linguists don't like to contemplate the notion that our grammatical statements may not actually fit the structure of the language precisely. Perhaps we are right in this; either they fit absolutely, or we have not formulated them correctly. But perhaps we are merely presumptuous in assuming this sort of a fit between statement and grammar. It may be that language description is a bit like chain and compass traverse. The surveyor fits a sequence of straight lines and measured angles to a winding road. A skillful surveyor comes out with a pretty fair approximation. But he also brings back a set of field notes which state the places and extent of departures from his traverse. The draftsman takes both to construct the map. Is a grammatical statement analogous to the rectilinear traverse, the dictionary to the field notes, and both therefore necessary to give a true picture of the sometimes imprecise meanderings of language?

Perhaps this truth has been pretty well hidden from us by a variety of things. Among the more important, we have tended to concentrate on structural sketches dealing only with reasonably high levels of grammaticalness. I would venture the guess that as we reach deeper into a language structure the precision of language structure blurs. If this is so, the ultimate limit of grammar in this direction is at the place where our traditional yes-or-no grammatical statements cease to be useful descriptively, i.e., at that place where the basic statement is so poorly fitted to the structure that the amendments and reservations which must be registered in the dictionary overwhelm it and make it useless. Or otherwise, the place where it is better to merely describe ad hoc rather than attempt to formalize and systematize.

10.3. **Beyond the grammar**. Not so different from the final outcome of the last suggestion is the suggestion that the dictionary might be assigned the task of carrying the description beyond the bound in grammaticalness set for the grammar. That is, the grammatical statement might be required to state the structure down to level n, but the dictionary to give, so far as it can be given, the structures at levels $n + 1$. . . . This limitation might be imposed by incompleteness of the analysis—there is no real object in presenting another level of grammaticalness in the grammatical statement if it has not been sufficiently well worked out that its cohesiveness is demonstrable—by convenience—for some purposes a very highly explicit grammatical statement may be inconvenient to use, particularly at the deeper levels of grammaticalness—or by the fact that we have approached the limit of grammar.

10.4. **System of cross-reference**. The dictionary might serve as a system of cross-reference and correlation of entries within the grammatical statement. Highly explicit types of grammatical statements—and the trend of development is in this direction—are quite rigidly ordered by their own requirements of explicitness and simplicity. It may be that there are reasons to bring together statements which are widely separated in the grammatical statement. When, as often, these involve small classes or subclasses, the dictionary might well serve this function. It would, in effect, assemble the various rules bearing on a particular vocabulary item and thus circumvent, for certain purposes, the rigor of the statement itself.

10.5. **Correlation among structural systems**. The dictionary might serve as a device to correlate the several structural systems, grammar being one of them, which bear on the usage of individual items. It would do this by indexing the several systematic statements in which these structural systems are described.

10.6. **Referential meaning**. The dictionary would define referential meaning.

11. Grammar and Lexicon

None of these suggestions for the division of the descriptive task between the grammatical statement and the dictionary seems to provide any very adequate basis for a parallel distinction between grammar and lexicon. That is, none seems to correlate in any very satisfying way with a possible view of language structure that would seem theoretically adequate. The great problem is that most seem to point very strongly toward viewing grammar as an integrated system and lexicon as a miscellaneous remainder. If lexicon can be given no better basis than this, it is clearly not to be considered as a basic segment of language structure in the way that the grammar and the phonology are to be considered. In short, rather than ask, "What is the relation between grammar and lexicon?" it may be more meaningful to ask whether lexicon is properly to be considered as a portion of language structure at all. The answer to this question is certainly no, if lexicon is not in some way structured, and, indeed, structured in some characteristic way.

Now, there is certainly some structure in the material generally excluded from the grammatical statement and thus relegated to the dictionary. The literature has frequently noted the structural nature of certain segments of "meaning," particularly within the system of basic color terms. In any one language, however, systems of this sort are not generally considered to be numerous or, within the framework of the total vocabulary, important.

The structuring of color terms is commonly considered exceptional. But, of course, it may well be that this is because we have not yet developed adequate methods of finding those structures which actually exist. Perhaps the structuring of the color vocabulary is atypical only in that it is so obtrusive as to require no very sophisticated techniques for its discovery. And again, it may be, like the phonology and grammar, that the structuring is very much more apparent against a background of the total system than it will be if individual segments are viewed separately. Perhaps what we have blithely called "lexicon" is after all a residuum of unanalyzed material out of which there remains to be sorted a system, or even a number of systems of diverse types. This latter I would consider the most likely situation.

If so, my difficulty in finding much concrete to say about the relation of grammar to lexicon is precisely because of the non-homogeneous nature of what we have been treating as lexicon. The question must remain cloudy until we are able to delimit one or more of these systems. What is required at this stage is not so much a discussion of the relation of grammar and lexicon, as an effort to bring some order into the chaos we have been calling "lexicon."

12. The Content System

The most accessible (at least to linguists) of the possible systems confused within the lexicon is the content, as I have used the term in the *Introduction to Descriptive Linguistics* (1955, 12–13). This is certainly not identical with Hjelmslev's (1953, 30–35) use, or any of the common understandings of his use, and was not intended to be. It may, indeed, be radically different, in which case I ought not to have even considered the term *content* for it. But what suitable alternative is there? Perhaps it might be referred to as "semantic structure." But I dislike the term, since *semantic* and its congeners have been almost completely emptied of meaning by extremely loose and often contradictory usages.

By content here I mean a systematic structure which relates items—some kind of -eme (again, no satisfactory term is at hand, though *sememe* has been used; see, for instance, Bazell 1954, and Trager 1956)—in a variety of ways. The structure as a whole is related at many points with the grammar but it is not isomorphic. The relationships which are pertinent are a different set of relationships and sometimes cut across those which are grammatically pertinent. They must be analyzed by a different set of comparisons, and the results must be analyzed in a different way. But it seems to me that the differences in analytic method and structure of the resulting statement are not more different from those of grammatical analysis than are those of phonological analysis. That is to say, content stands with phonology and morphology in contrast with certain other much more different structurings which apply to speech behavior and are perhaps better considered as outside linguistics proper.

The content structure seems to involve at least three types of interrelations. And it is these three with which content analysis must operate. These are the following:

12.1. Paradigmatic relationships between contrasting entities. The type case here is the familiar description of the primary color term system. The basic color terms of English are a closed class of eleven terms. Typically, they are all designated by adjectives, but the primary color terms are not a grammatically definable subclass of adjectives, at least, not at any fairly reasonable depth of grammaticalness. Not only do the basic colors contrast with one another; they contrast in a quite definite way. The whole set is ordered into a network—*green* contrasts in a special way with *blue* and *yellow*, which is quite different from the way in which it contrasts with *purple*. Grammatically, there is no discernable difference between the contrasts *green* : *blue* and *green* : *purple*.

12.2. Alternative structures. There are many other color terms in English. They all relate to this basic system, but through a different type of structure. Among the others are such terms as *vermilion, scarlet, emerald,* and *cyanic.* The first three can be substituted for by *red, red,* and *green,* respectively, in a very large number of contexts with minimum alteration of semantic appropriateness of the sentences. But all other substitutions have a quite different effect. These substitution relationships order these terms into a kind of hierarchy, making each of the larger set dependent in some definable way on one member of the basic colors. *Vermilion* and *scarlet,* both subsumed under *red,* contrast directly with each other; their contrast with *emerald* is in some way tied up with the contrast of *red* and *green. Cyanic* stands in a third level in the hierarchy; substitution relations of this type exist with *blue, purple,* and *red.* Moreover, it contrasts only with one term, *xanthic.*

12.3. Interrelated structures. The third kind of content structure is that of collocations. *Cyanic* and *xanthic* are shown to be very specialized by the fact that they occur only in contexts dealing with flowers. The others are mostly more general. The basic color terms are most general, much the commonest, and incidentally the best defined. Some of the lower level of the hierarchy are quite specialized. *Buff* occurs most commonly in contexts with *paper*, *card*, and similar items, and *goldenrod* (an adjectival) only in such contexts.

We noted that the basic color terms could not be defined as a class grammatically. That is, there are no grammatical properties which they do not share with other adjectives which from the point of view of content structure are unrelated. However, that content structure and grammatical structure are closely interrelated is shown by the fact that within the total class of color terms, the three levels in the hierarchy are grammatically distinct. The eleven basic color terms all occur with the suffixes *-er* and *-est*. The secondary color terms seem to include none which are so used, though all can occur with *more* and *most*. (Color terms are often homonymous with nouns, but they are never nouns in noun-adjunct position.) Finally, *cyanic* and *xanthic* do not seem to occur in either construction, though that they are adjectival is demonstrable from their behavior in certain transformations.

The set of color terms is of particular value also in that it shows quite clearly another special characteristic of content structure. It consists in the grouping of non-linguistic variations on the basis of a linguistically controlled system. It is thus comparable with the phonology which groups acoustic phenomena into linguistically significant units. The color system apportions all possible physical stimuli in its domain among its members in a way that is essentially exhaustive and mutually exclusive. It gives, therefore, a systematic basis within which to describe the referential meaning ranges of the items concerned. The same is true, with interesting variations, in a number of other content sub-systems which similarly apportion "reality." Another example is the system of shapes. Continual variation is possible from the geometrically perfect circle to the geometrically perfect square and from each of those and all the intermediates to a variety of other shapes. There is thus a multidimensional shape-space. The English language cuts a great portion of this into blocks to which are attached terms. These terms contrast in a set of ordered interrelationships, much like what was observed in the case of colors. This system differs from the color system in a number of respects, but most importantly in that it does not exhaustively cover its domain. There are vast number of shapes for which no simple term is available. This is very probably associated with the very much greater complexity of the shape-space than of the color-space. We do not in English have a very well-ordered hierarchy of more and less inclusive shape terms, but other languages do. In German for some speakers, *Viereck* includes *Rechteck*, and this, in turn, *Quadrat*.

13. The Content System in Lexical Definition

I would like to suggest that the task of giving adequate definitions to such words as *red*, *vermilion*, and *cyanic* would be greatly facilitated and the definitions greatly improved, by defining in relation to the total system of color terms. But only as a temporary expedient is it feasible to do this within the framework of a dictionary. It is obviously inefficient to describe the whole structure at each article. Yet the whole structure is in some way pertinent. It would be possible, and it might be very advantageous, to state the most relevant parts of the system in an individual dictionary article, much as the two very special relationships of synonymy and antonymy have long been singled out.

But the ultimate solution does not rest here anymore than the ultimate solution for grammatical description rests in giving the relevant grammatical information at each dictionary entry, and for the same reasons. Grammar and content are both networks of interrelationships, and they cannot be done justice to proceeding from individual nodes in the networks. Just as we find it desirable to have a systematic grammatical statement to which the dictionary refers, so we would find it useful to have a systematic content description to which the dictionary might refer. Structure is always best presented systematically. Or if a structure is presented in fragments for reasons of convenience, it is essential that this be done against the background of a systematic statement, preferably one which is available to the user of the dictionary. A complete language description would require a grammatical statement, a content description, and a dictionary.

14. The Function of the Dictionary Again

If the proper description of a language contains, not only a grammatical statement, but also a content description, what is the function of a dictionary? I suggest that it is basically that which was listed above as number 5, to correlate the several structural systems, in combination with that listed as number 6, to define referential meaning. In a sense these are quite similar. Referential meaning is presumably a vast assortment of structures, mostly outside and indeed far removed from linguistics. The dictionary is then the meeting place of all the systems, linguistic and non-linguistic, which bear relevantly on speech behavior. It is this nature of the dictionary that demands that it be arranged in some non-systematic way. (In the sense that, say, alphabetic order has no real linguistic significance.) It can only be a series of loosely articulated articles each bringing together elements from several disparate structural systems. This is true whether those structure systems are structurally understood or not. From the linguist's point of view, it is essential that for every morpheme or word (or whatever sort of items are to be included) the dictionary give its relations to the grammar in terms of the classes and sub-classes to which it is related, its relations to the content structure in terms of the classes, hierarchies, and collocational restrictions to which it is related, and of course its phonemic and/or morphophonemic shape.

A dictionary ought also to relate the vocabulary of the language to certain extra-linguistic systems. The referential meaning is the most obvious. Along with this, however, is required some relation to the culture in the form of statements about the cultural implications of items, their appropriateness in various culturally definable situations, and the like.

15. A Few Suggestions for Lexicographical Practice

What I have said above is of little immediate relevance for dictionary making, though it does suggest certain lines for basic research which may ultimately be of significance to lexicography. However, there are a few suggestions which arise out of these remarks that may be of some more immediate significance.

15.1. **Unified language description**. Dictionaries and grammatical statements can profitably be designed as parts of a unified program of language description. The objective of such a program should be the adequate description of all language phenomena within its terms of reference. This can be most efficiently fulfilled when the several descriptive instruments are closely keyed to each other.

15.2. **Grammatical index**. The dictionary should give for each item all pertinent grammatical identification. It is inadequate, particularly in a bilingual dictionary, merely to label items as noun or verb if it is known that there are significant subclasses within such classes. The dictionary should indeed index the grammatical statement.

15.3. **Adequate definition**. Conversely, the grammatical statement should be organized in such a way as to facilitate the use of the dictionary and give adequate definition of the grammatical identifications which are there given.

15.4. **Class-cleavage**. The dictionary should give particular attention to class-cleavage, as this is an important factor in understanding the grammatical structure of a language which can seldom be adequately treated in a grammatical statement.

15.5. **Evidence of order**. Pending the day when we may have content analyses which are systematic and reasonably complete, we ought to make maximum use of the available scraps of information about ordered contrast, hierarchical substitution relations, and patterned collocations. In particular, the latter notion should give some guidance in the selection of illustrative citations.

POSTSCRIPT

The rapid development of transformational-generative grammar since 1960 has put the relation of lexicon and grammar in a new light but does not seem really to have contributed much to a solution of the problem. A few possibly useful ideas have been suggested and a number of new dead ends have been explored, both by transformational-generativists and others. Section 12 of the paper sets forth a primitive form of stratificationalism. Today I would add here a much clearer insistence that the *content system* (I now prefer the term *semology*) must have a full tactic system as well as an organized inventory. I would make no claim that stratificational theory has already provided any well worked out solution, nor that it is likely soon to do so, but I would claim that it provides the framework within which such a solution is most worth pursuing. I would assert much more strongly that we linguists have a responsibility to lexicography that we have continued to shirk, and that neither the practical nor the theoretical questions posed by the relation of lexicon to grammar will be clarified until we have done a great deal more thorough, imaginative, and well-considered lexicographic work and have seen this work as within our central concern as linguists.

H. A. GLEASON, JR.
JANUARY 1967

LEXICOGRAPHY AND GRAMMAR

Henry M. Hoenigswald
University of Pennsylvania

FEW DIVISIONS APPEAR TO BE MORE FUNDAMENTAL THAN that between grammar and lexicon. It is firmly rooted in convention and, at the same time, it is accepted as a safe and reliable theoretical dichotomy. This dichotomy is sometimes seen as holding the center of language structure, with phonology and semantics (or semantics plus stylistics) at the flanks. One of the great neogrammarians once said of dictionaries, "what were they, in effect, but indexes to grammars?" What he had in mind were in fact etymological dictionaries and historical grammars—two types of work in which we are not especially interested at this moment. The aphorism strikes us perhaps as amusing and narrow-minded; it is worlds removed, say, from Ernout and Meillet's (1939) ideal of the etymological dictionary as an "histoire des mots." But as it was made, and as it was intended, it holds good for descriptive, synchronic work as well. It is, in fact, a rather neat and pointed formulation of the theoretical dichotomy. One fundamental aspect of dictionaries is surely the fact that they are *lists*—lists of "items" above all, although perhaps also lists of "arrangements" (the boundary is notoriously difficult to draw). On the other hand, neither grammars nor semantic treatises, whatever they may be, are essentially examples of listing per se.

If this is true, it is also true that the dichotomy has been very rarely pushed to its extreme. Lexicographical practice has allowed for a generous admixture of elements other than mere enumeration, and it is our purpose to look at some instances of such admixture more closely. Some works, like Dornseiff's monstrous *Wortschatz* (1933–40) or other thesauri of synonymies, are arranged according to semantic areas ("nature," "man," "relationships," and what not). Others contain pictures, or verbal comment (definitions, descriptions), or—as in the most familiar case—translations. These we like to lump together under the heading "meaning." But we are also used to the idea of going to the dictionary for grammatical information in the strict sense. We can never be sure just how much we will find; but there is probably no Latin dictionary worth the name that doesn't contain the principal parts of the verbs, or that fails to tell us that *urbs* is feminine or that *ūtor* 'I use' governs the ablative case. In other words, it is either their grouping or some added matter which—implicitly or explicitly—gives us added information, going beyond the "index" principle. It is as though we had here either an attempt to provide separate indexes to separate portions of the "book" (namely, of the grammar or the semantic treatise, as the case may be); or else an attempt at not merely *referring* to page and line, chapter and verse, but proceeding to *quote* and *excerpt* from the "book" right then and there.

To find our bearings, we may ask just what absolute lexical purity would have to imply; and, in order to answer that question, it may be useful to pursue the obvious theoretical parallel—if it does not quite fit, we shall find out soon enough. The parallel which I have in mind belongs, of course, to phonology: as lexicon stands to grammar (and semantics), so does the phoneme inventory stand to the phonemic system. In a familiar view (which is neither the only one defensible nor even one that is any too widely carried out in actual practice), the inventory is a list, while the system is, if you will, a grammar. The inventory is essentially unordered: nothing would be lost if the listing were random, so long as it contained a reference to a place in the phonemic system. At least for pedagogical reasons, we maintain frequently, however, that phonemes can be first discovered, and *labeled*, by observing the physical properties of short segments, where the segmentation is not necessarily unique. Thus, if the arrangement of the inventory is not random, its principle can be derived only from the presumably "lower" level of mere phonetic shape—or else the inventory will not be independent from the system. In this view—whether it is completely fruitful or not we shall not decide—the inventory is arranged by phones, while the system is arranged by co-occurrence classes. The inventory might be called a phonetic index to the phonemic system, inasmuch as it answers such question as: "how does the clustering of the voiceless dental stop (in English) differ from the clustering of the voiceless labial stop?" This may be the theory. In our practice, we are no more consistent than we are on the side of lexicography: we are apt to mix inventory and system, first, by using co-occurrence factors while pretending that we are only listing, and, second, by employing phonetic language when we are already setting up co-occurrence classes. Just because of that, the parallel is valid. A "Simon Pure" lexical listing ought to presuppose a morphic segmentation (not necessarily unique); the items in the lists should be minimal, that is, they should be single morphemes; their arrangement might be random, although there can be no objection to an arrangement by morphs, that is, by the phonemic shape of the allomorph or allomorphs making up the morpheme; and finally, the "reference" should be to the appropriate paragraph in the morphology and syntax, or in some imaginary, comprehensive treatment of meanings and meaning differences in the guise of a repertory of semantic fields. At this point, the views would begin to diverge widely. I myself am inclined to liken the step from grammar to semantics to that from the setting up of such classifications as syllabic vs. non-syllabic, on one hand, to the study of the overlapping among the ranges of individual phonemes, on the other. Luckily this is another question which we need not decide here. Perhaps we can agree that the privileges of occurrence for morphemes are of interest both to the grammarian and to the lexicographer. We shall have occasion to come back to this point.

Of course, we are familiar enough with the principle of listing morphemes by grammatically irrelevant arrangement. Before the invention of alphabetization (partial or total) something like random listing was actually practiced in the western world. In logographic scripts arrangement can be based on the shape of the character, that is, on an essentially non-linguistic criterion. Otherwise, we alphabetize morphemes by the phonemic shape of their morphs, according to the way in which the conventional writing represents it. It is odd that the only mere listings that are familiar to us in any practical sense seem to be certain secondary rearrangements of existing dictionaries like the reverse indexes found in some Indic *kośas* or, for that matter, in modern works such as Gradenwitz's Latin reverse index, *Laterculi vocum Latinarum* (1904), and its followers.

Even in such an ideal, lean, and somewhat sterile list, where the items are morphemes, in a morph-based order three kinds of analytical results are already implicit: first, phonemicization (which is irrelevant); second, the establishment of morph boundaries (which need not be uniquely established); and third, morphophonemics. In everyday western practice, the phonemes are more or less consistently represented in alphabetic script. The morph boundaries are much less consistently handled; our dictionaries list words, including compounds and sometimes other close-knit constructs. One almost has to go to Pāṇini's *Dhātupāṭha* to find roots, that is, minimal morphemes of a certain, especially important, and well-set-off co-occurrence class; but in any event, at least *some* morph boundaries, setting off *certain types* of morph sequence—even if they are not minimal ones!—are always recognized. And as for morphophonemics, it is fair to say that it represents the area of grammar (if we wish to include it there) which is most fully and most anciently treated in our dictionaries. To be sure, the way in which this treatment is executed varies greatly with various language structures and various strains of tradition. So-called automatic alternation need not, of course, be treated at all. Other alternations may require cross-reference from allomorph to allomorph, or reference from each allomorph directly to the grammar. The current dictionaries of the classical languages (which I would like to use here as examples) exemplify this. Insofar as their lemmata—their entry-heads—refer to a specific morpheme in the word, the irregular allomorphs are frequently assembled in one place, while reference is made to that place from other entries involving the allomorphs. Thus, in Greek under *horá-ō* 'see,' we find a synoptic paradigm in which figures a suppletive future, *óp-somai*; there is further a cross-entry to *horá-ō* precisely under *óp(-somai)*. This is not the place to describe the peculiar conventions which govern the system of cross-referencing in detail; but we should not forget that our peculiar "word-and-paradigm" tradition is apt to play us a few tricks: while inflectional morphophonemics may be fairly well taken care of, derivational processes are not. The alternants in derivatives are, as a rule, nowhere assembled; only one-sided reference is made, quite unsystematically, under a heading which deserves the deepest possible distrust, even in otherwise reliable dictionaries, namely, that of etymology. Nor does implicit or explicit reference to existing grammar help in this case. However, we should mention, in passing, a small bit of salutary inconsistency, on the part of our Greek dictionaries, in the application of the word-and-paradigm habit. The so-called contract verbs are listed in the "open," uncontracted, and strictly speaking non-existent name form of the type *timáō* 'honor'/*philéō* 'love'/*doulóō* 'enslave': the only forms that occur in the kind of Greek which the dictionaries are primarily designed to represent are *timô*/*philô*/*doulô*. The reason is obvious: the uncontracted forms are base forms that permit the application of more regular morphophonemic rules.

Even if we could agree that minimal, one-morpheme length is ideal for dictionary lemmata, there is still the question of completeness, and one particular aspect of it which impinges on grammar. There are, in the view of many linguists, morphemes and morpheme-like entities with so-called grammatical meanings. Is it reasonable, for instance, to consider the sentence intonations of English on a par with the segmental morphemes? Many of us would answer in the affirmative and would relegate the problem of whether or not to include them in a dictionary to the realm of mere expediency—and probably leave it there until we know more about the facts. What about constructions? Where would it lead us if we were to consider constructions, in the abstract, as "items" to be classified in grammar but listed in the lexicon? The least difficult side of this question arises where segmental morphs form morphemes with grammatical meanings. In fact, both the theory pertaining to such forms and their actual lexical treatment are enlightening. As for the theory, it is surely true that the discovery of their special nature is part of the co-occurrence study to which all morphemes may be subjected. There is, therefore, no reason not to list them, along with the other morphemes in the dictionary. Our practice is, first of all, vitiated by a coincidence: in languages like Greek and Latin, many of the morphemes in question have morphs that are affixes and are therefore by custom excluded from separate listing. But not all are affixes; some are what has been called function-words. Take the Greek particles. What is the meaning of *án*? Go to some dictionaries and you may find translations such as 'perhaps.' These translations are offered with evident diffidence; obviously, they will do no one any good. The dictionary maker, with a sigh of relief almost, proceeds then to quote sample sentences or actually to state—and that means to quote from the grammar—the environments for *án*: it occurs with secondary tenses if an *if*-clause nearby also shows a secondary tense and so forth. The "use," as it is called, seems to be identical with the "meaning" of these words—there are few things which could more forcefully illustrate the gradual rather than absolute nature of the difference between grammar and meaning, and hence at least in the popular sense between grammar and lexicon of which we have spoken before.

    Here we have been anticipating our final question: how do dictionaries in the popular sense (and perhaps in any sense that is useful) modify the ideal of listing-plus-indexing? What information on grammar or on co-occurrence in general is excerpted and transferred to the list; how is it done; what are the advantages and the disadvantages of the system? How can the disadvantages be remedied?

    First, as indicated already, such information can be implicit in the very selection of the entry. Especially if the lemma goes beyond minimum length, if it consists of a construct (a complex form, a compound, an "idiom"), co-occurrence data are included at the start. Depending on the language structure, this may further imply syntactic information. All Greek entries ending in *-omai* are safely characterized as verbs and would need no further labeling to that effect although they usually get it. Of course, this type of redundancy may in principle attach to a minimal form—in a language where, say, "nouns" have canonic phonemic shapes.

Second, there are the part-of-speech labels to which we have just alluded; in other words, our verb in *-omai* will be labeled "v." This, of course, has the force of an outright reference to the grammar. Somewhat the same is true of the equally familiar references to noun gender. Often these labels do not stand by themselves but are combined with indications that are really morphophonemic or that apply to the selection of allomorphs in the context. This is what is involved in such labels as "third declension nouns" and the like.

Third, there is translation, definition, or description, as the case may be. This would seem to benefit semantics and be relatively far removed from grammar if it were not for two factors: (a) the function words and the lesson which they teach us with regard to the connections between lexical and grammatical structure, and (b) the danger of glottocentrism, on which I shall have to say a word in a moment.

Fourth, if semantics deals with the mutual co-occurrence of one type of morphemes (noun stems, verb stems, certain adverbs of Latin or Greek)—the lexical type—and grammar deals with the various relationships in which morphemes of other types (affixes, function words; also perhaps constructions as such) are involved, there is quite naturally one field of grammar in which dictionaries are particularly strong. That is the field of government, roughly the co-occurrence of lexical-type morphemes with such entities as affixes and constructions outside the domain of inflection and derivation. Thus, we have the case-government of prepositions and of verbs, or the facts concerning dependent clauses: *ūtor* occurs with the ablative, *iubeō* 'bid' takes the infinitive of "indirect discourse"; *imperō* 'bid' takes the conjunction *ut*. If I may digress for a moment, here is an untapped source of historical and comparative research problems which, to be sure, cannot be attacked with the help of the existing dictionaries alone. It is known that the Indo-European languages sometimes agree on highly specialized unexpected quirks of selection from verb root or verb stem to dependent case, etc.

In conclusion, it may be said that our dictionaries—those of the classical languages among them—carry a great deal of grammatical information, and that we have every reason to be thankful for this mixed tradition. One's complaint is certainly not that they have compromised a rigid ideal demanding an abstract dichotomy; this is an ideal which it would be preposterous to uphold anyway. But there have been some very specific weaknesses of omission which should be named.

As regards the morphology of the paradigm: paradigms are represented by way of noting deviations and irregularities, with a so-called regular paradigm in the background. Sometimes, this is a type with a minimum of morphophonemic trouble; on other occasions, it is simply a statistically prevalent type. So long as no information on forms is supplied, it is implicit (in many dictionaries) that there is a full paradigm of so-called regular forms. This is not so, but the dictionaries do not as a rule enlighten us on those gaps (even though there is eminently respectable precedent: an Alexandrian grammarian wrote a treatise entitled "on the fact that not all verbs have all tenses"), and not even the practice of writing (Greek and) Latin composition gave rise to any change. It is an old complaint; but nothing much is ever done—nor is it limited to Greek and Latin. There may be German dictionaries in which it is said in so many words that *Morgen* 'morning' has no plural; but I haven't seen them. The ordinary coverage of *singularia tantum* is mostly limited to mass nouns.

Some confusion exists in the field of case government. For example, transitive verbs are usually defined as such, and instances of cases "accompanying" verbs are mentioned with fair fullness. But we are rarely enlightened on whether, say, a prepositional phrase is required or optional. I can put the car in the garage and I can wash the car in the garage. I can also wash it, but I cannot put it. It is of course understandable that when it comes to features of this sort the dictionaries cannot possibly be better than the grammars; but here is perhaps the greatest opportunity for improvement in the future.

Finally, the bilingualism of dictionaries is a dangerous source of unsystematic omission. Translation is a guiding principle, not only for the more narrowly lexical aspect of meaning, but also in questions of compounding, construction in general, and particularly, again, government. If a transitive Latin verb is given an English translation which is also "transitive," it is assumed that the parallelism is somehow simple and complete, and that no more need be said about it. The fact that *pōnō* 'I put' is accompanied by *in* with the ablative is neatly stated in the dictionaries (and in the grammars), because in some of the European languages into which Latin gets translated

(German), the translation required is a goal construction (rather than a locative construction), the same goal construction which ordinarily translates *in* with the accusative. In some cases, the abuse was checked because the writing of Latin composition required greater explicitness; but even this did not help where there seemed to be no special translation problem in *either* of the two directions.

I would like to close on a note of applause and admiration for a development which has gained in strength, and which emphasizes the complementary nature of grammar and the lexicon. This is the grammatical companion sketch which goes with the dictionary. It has had its humble beginnings in the synopses often carried by practical dictionaries: paradigms, lists of irregularities, etc. But these beginnings are hard to recognize in some of its latest specimens.

STRUCTURAL LINGUISTICS AND BILINGUAL DICTIONARIES

Kemp Malone
Johns Hopkins University

THE USUAL BILINGUAL DICTIONARY IS MADE UP OF two vocabularies, one for each language, and its primary purpose is to help the user in his task of translating from one of the languages to the other. If you want to say something in a foreign tongue and cannot think of some word or phrase you need to express your thought in that tongue, you turn to a bilingual dictionary, look up the word or phrase that would express your meaning in your native tongue, and hope that the dictionary will give you the corresponding word or phrase in the other tongue. If you find what you are looking for, you will have done a bit of translating from native to foreign speech. Or you may be reading a text in the foreign tongue and come upon an expression that you do not understand. In this case, you look up the expression in the bilingual dictionary in the hope that you will find it duly interpreted in your native tongue. Here again, we have translation, but it goes the other way, from foreign to native speech. A bilingual dictionary, then, may be called a two-way translation aid.

Bilingual dictionaries have other functions besides, functions definitely subordinated to their main one of translating but important, nevertheless. I will mention first their function as a guide to pronunciation. Information on this subject appears, as a rule, both in the front matter and in the individual entries in the body of the book. The entries give the phonetic or phonemic composition of the entry words as said in isolation and with full stress, though sometimes weak as well as strong variants are entered. In an English–French/French–English dictionary, the words entered are commonly respelled to indicate their pronunciation. In an English–Italian/Italian–English dictionary, only the English entry words would be respelled in this way; for the Italian words, it is thought to be enough to mark the stressed syllable of words not stressed on the penult; to distinguish between close and open stressed vowels where these are represented by the same symbol; and to indicate the surd or vibrant value of ambiguous consonantal signs. In the front matter, it is customary to outline the spelling systems of the two languages, that is, the relation between the written and spoken units. If there is a one-to-one correspondence, only this fact needs to be pointed out, but often—if not usually—a much more complex system of correspondences exists and must be made clear. In any case, the sounds of the languages are commonly presented in terms of the conventional spelling, together with some description of how the sounds are made and some comparison of the two sound-systems, each in terms of the other.

Again, bilingual dictionaries usually give a certain amount of information about affixation, inflection, and classification. In the entries, the part of speech of the entry words is commonly marked, and the gender of words that have it may also be marked. If the entry word is subject to inflection, some clue to this is usually added, as principal parts of verbs and the name or number of the declension that a noun belongs to. Irregular and anomalous forms are often entered for themselves, with cross-reference to the appropriate head-form. In the front matter, one may find a list of the commoner suffixes (less often, of prefixes, too) and an outline of the inflectional system of each language dealt with in the dictionary. In a good many bilingual dictionaries, much is made of irregular verbs, sometimes as part of the front matter, sometimes in a special appendix. Here such verbs are listed in full, and the irregular forms of each verb are entered against the head-form.

Finally, a bilingual dictionary may include historical information, such as the etymology of entry words, words marked obsolete, etc.; dialectal information, as words marked local or regional or otherwise restricted in currency; and stylistic information, as distinctions in levels of usage.

What have the structural linguists to say about the bilingual dictionaries as I have described them? In this paper, I speak only for myself. Others in attendance will doubtless be able to add to my observations; they may even be able to subtract from them. I will begin with the body of the dictionary, the entries themselves. In the conventional bilingual dictionary, the entries are devoted to words and phrases, chiefly individual words but with some attention to phrases as well. If the dictionary were remodeled to conform to structural principles, the entries would be devoted to morphemes and morphemic sequences and taken together would constitute what it is now fashionable to call an "inventory," or rather two inventories, one for each language.

A morpheme, or minimal unit of meaning, may be a whole word or part of one. If it is a word, it is called a "free" form; if part of a word, a "bound" form. Thus, in *asparagus*, the boundaries of word and morpheme coincide, giving a free form, but, in *likemindedness*, we have a word made up of four morphemes, and each of these is a bound form. Some morphemes never occur except as bound forms: e.g., the last two morphemes of *likemindedness*. Others may occur bound or free, as the first two morphemes of *likemindedness*. Still others occur only as free forms, that is, as monomorphemic words. In English, the definite article is an example of a morpheme that is always a free form, but in the Scandinavian languages the article may be a bound form. This difference raises a number of questions: Are proclitics and enclitics free or bound? Is the English article a proclitic? In classifying morphemes as free or bound, are we to go by the conventional writing and spacing of words in the two languages with which our bilingual dictionary is concerned? I will not try to answer these questions but I submit them to you for your consideration. In general, a morpheme that occurs only as a word not subject to inflection, affixation, or composition is always a free form. On the face of it, the English definite article conforms to this description. What about *asparagus*? In theory, it would be possible to inflect this word, but in practice, the word is not inflected, and our dictionary would have to classify it accordingly. We cannot be so sure about composition. Let us consider the case of *asparagus soup*. In English, this morphemic sequence is written as two words, and *asparagus* here, as elsewhere, is a free form. Not so German *Spargel* in the corresponding sequence *Spargelsuppe*, which is written as one word. Parallel cases are to be found by the thousand. Is this difference between English and German a mere matter of orthography or does it go deeper? Another question that I will not try to answer.

Luckily, we do not have to solve such problems in order to make a bilingual dictionary that conforms reasonably well to structural linguistic principles. The main thing is to make the morpheme, not the word, our unit in determining what items to include in the inventory. This means that we should have entries for the morphemes that occur only as bound forms, as well as for those that occur as free forms. Phrases, and words made up of two or more morphemes, would both come under the head of morphemic sequences and would be entered much as they are now. The main difference, then, would be that inflectional endings and affixes would be systematically entered in the body of the book. The problem children would be morphemes like English *stand/stood* and *self/selv-*, where unwelcome complications arise. Let us look at these for a moment.

    The verb *stand*, preterite and past participle *stood*, has two built-in markers which, for the moment, we may call infixes. One infix, *-an-*, marks presentness; the other, *-oo-*, pastness. But these infixes are more than markers of time; they also make part of the morphemes *stand* and *stood*, respectively. Without them, these morphemes become meaningless and thus, by definition, are no longer morphemes at all. We cannot describe *stand* as a word made up of two morphemes, the verb *st . . d* and the present-marking grammatical infix *-an-*. The word *stand* is monomorphemic, even though the *-an-* part of it does double duty by having a present-marking function besides. This *-an-*, then, is not a true infix but an integral part of the morpheme *stand*. That is to say, it cannot be abstracted from *stand* without destroying the morpheme of which it makes part. Here, it differs fundamentally from true grammatical morphemes like the final *-s* of *stands*. It will not do, therefore, to set up a present-marking morpheme *-an-* and a past-marking one *-oo-*. These markers of time are not morphemes but morphemic parts, and we can only say that each has a special function within the morpheme to which it belongs, besides making part of that morpheme. To put the matter a bit differently, our verb consists of two morphemes, *stand* and *stood*, each of which is temporally marked, and one of these morphemes, *stand*, by virtue of its present-time marking, is subject to combination with the grammatical morphemes *-s* and *-ing*. In our dictionary, both *stand* and *stood* should be entered, but the entry *stood* may reasonably be reduced to a mere cross-reference, and all the inflectional forms may properly be given in the entry *stand*. The morphemes *-s* and *-ing*, which combine not only with *stand* but also with a multitude of other verbs, rate entries of their own in which their function is explained.

    The case of *self/selv-* is somewhat different. *Self* may be bound or free, whereas *selv-* is always bound, occurring only before the plural-marking morpheme *-es*, a position in which *self* never occurs. We may say (1) that *self* and *selv-* are two closely related morphemes, the one being a singular, the other a plural, but the plurality of *selv-* is dependent on the plural-marking morpheme *-es* with which it always combines. Or we may say (2) that *self* and *selv-* are allomorphs of a morpheme that ends in /v/ before the plural-marking morpheme *-es* but in /f/ elsewhere. The second way of looking at the matter is simpler and, I think, more satisfactory. If the two forms are only allomorphs of one morpheme, they should be treated in a single entry and the entry-form should be *self/selv-* (not simply *self*), But in a bilingual dictionary it might be well to have an entry for *selves,* explained as the plural of *self,* in addition to the entry *self/selv-,* as a concession to human weakness. Allomorphs distinguished in speech but not in conventional writing (e.g., the various spoken forms of *either*) may be taken up in one entry, as scientific rigor prescribes, without sacrifice of the practical convenience of the user of the book. Such an entry, of course, would include transcriptions of the allomorphs and would specify the distribution of each.

This brings us to the sounds of the languages, and, at once, the question arises, how these sounds are to be described and represented. In structural linguistics, of course, the phoneme is the thing, and to any structuralist the necessity of working out and presenting the system of phonemes characteristic of a language goes without saying. I must confess that my own chief interest lies here. But phonemics must be built on phonetics, and in learning a language the phonetic nuances make the great difference between the pronunciation of the beginner and that of the master. That is to say, phonetics is essential, both in theory and in practice, if you are to know your language properly. Not only the phonemic but also the phonetic side of pronunciation, then, must be dealt with in our bilingual dictionary. If this be granted, how should we proceed? The two sides are best combined, I think, by bringing in phonetics in allophonic terms. The front matter should include a systematic presentation of the phonemes of each language, and under each phoneme its chief allophonic types should be described with phonetic precision.

The spelling system of many languages is phonemic in principle, though nearly always faulty from the start and made worse in the course of time by traditional spellings that reflect etymological learning true and false, past rather than current speech, and the like. It is a matter of practical importance in a bilingual dictionary to bring out the correspondences between the spelling system and the system of phonemes, and such correspondences have scientific interest besides. Certainly, I for one am far from objecting to an analysis of conventional spelling and a comparison of it with phonemic transcription as part of the front matter of a bilingual dictionary. I reckon it important, however, that the user of such a dictionary be encouraged to learn the phonemic approach, and it does not make for his linguistic enlightenment to have the material presented as it is in too many dictionaries, where he is simply told what the values of the letters are in the conventional spelling. A bilingual dictionary should give its users at least a glimpse of linguistic science, and this can best be done by ordering and presenting the material in a scientific way, however modest the undertaking.

Instead of beginning with *a*, therefore, and going on to *b, c, d*, etc., one ought to begin by explaining what phonemes are and making clear the standard method of isolating them, the setting up of minimal pairs. Next allophones should be explained, and after them the syllable. This would lead naturally into a grouping of phonemes in terms of their function as members of syllables. From this one could go on to groupings of other kinds: vibrants vs. surds (or, if you will, voiced sounds vs. voiceless sounds), stops vs. patents, etc. You would now be ready to take up the individual phonemes: first, the stops, including affricates (i.e. phasal stops) and trills (i.e., intermittent stops); then the lateral and nasal patent; and, finally, the medial patents. These last fall into two main classes, straits and broads. The straits may be rough (close fricatives) or smooth (open fricatives and semivowels); the broads include vowels, glides, and breathings. The so-called primary phonemes are now behind you, and it is time to take up such matters as length, stress, pitch, and boundary phenomena, brought out in conventional writing, if at all, by a variety of marks: macron, accents, hyphen, comma, period, interrogation point, and exclamation point.

In the foregoing I have said nothing about the notation to be used. The alphabet of the International Phonetic Association (IPA) is basic for phonetic transcription but it is commonly modified more or less from language to language to make it fit better the needs or wishes of the various transcribers. I have myself worked out a system of phonemic transcription for English which I think well of, but I will not present it here. For a full discussion of it, see Malone (1959, 226–67). The conventional orthography of languages that have a good spelling system (as Italian, Spanish, and Turkish) can be used as a basis in phonemic writing; with a little modification it serves admirably. In general, it is unwise to impose any preexisting system of phonemic or phonetic transcription on your bilingual dictionary. The needs of such a book are best determined after a thorough study of the two languages with which it deals.

Both phonemic and phonetic transcriptions must be used, of course, in the combined phonemic and phonetic analysis that makes part of the front matter in the bilingual dictionary. But what of the body of the book? Should the entry forms be systematically transcribed and, if so, should the transcriptions be phonetic or phonemic? In my opinion, practical considerations should govern here. I will mention two cases and I welcome discussion of them: (1) the so-called hollow [l] of English, and (2) the quantity of /i/ in word-pairs like English *beat* /bit/ vs. *bead* / bid/. Should the hollowness of the *ll* in *hill* and the greater length of the *ea* in words like *bead* (as compared with *beat*) be brought out in the transcription? These features are allophonic, not phonemic, and they are easy to note in phonetic transcription but cannot be noted in a transcription that is phonemic. The student should of course be told about such allophonic features in the discussion given in the front matter. Is that enough, or should he be reminded of these allophones in the transcription of the individual entry-forms in the body of the book? This is an important practical question, and it should be answered in the light of the experience that teachers and students have had in using bilingual dictionaries. A good general principle to follow might be this: make the transcription phonemic for all entries except those where the user of the book may be expected to go seriously wrong unless he is given phonetic rather than merely phonemic guidance. And naturally the two systems should be sharply distinguished in the usual way, phonetic transcriptions being set off by square brackets, phonemic ones by diagonal lines.

We come now to morphology, or the analysis of utterances into their minimal units of meaning. In the entries of the dictionary devoted to single morphemes, the entry-form itself represents such an analysis, of course, but all morphemic sequences (i.e., phrases and pleiomorphemic words) that are entered need to be analyzed into their constituent morphemes. This is done by marking the morphemic boundaries, so far as they are not already shown in the conventional writing by spacing or hyphenation. The hyphen is the obvious mark to use for this purpose. Morphological analysis enables one to determine the systems of inflection, derivation, and composition characteristic of the vocabulary of the language in question. Limitations of space make it impossible to present these systems at length and in full in a bilingual dictionary, but an outline that brings out the main features of each system would be a valuable addition to the front matter of the book.

Vocabulary entries are commonly classified in inflectional terms, if possible. And since an inflection has the function of indicating the relation of the inflected item to another (or others) in connected speech, classification by inflection takes us into syntax. Dictionaries, in the nature of the case, deal little with syntax, but it is customary to include in the entries a classification of the entry-forms by parts of speech, and here structural linguistics can have something to say. To the extent that the classification rests on inflectional distinctions, it is structurally valid. Thus, in English, nouns and verbs have distinctive inflections and can therefore be set up as separate form-classes or parts of speech, and, if we reckon the comparison of adjectives and adverbs as a kind of inflection, we can set up a third class based on this feature. In some languages, adjectives are sharply distinguished from the adverbs by the fact that they are declined as well as compared, whereas adverbs are only compared. This was once true of English, too, but is no longer so. Pronouns are another form-class that can be set up by virtue of distinctive inflectional features, though in English this holds to a limited extent only. Words not marked as nouns, verbs, adjectives, or pronouns by inflection but behaving like members of these form-classes in connected speech are commonly classified accordingly. Thus, *asparagus* is classified in English as a noun despite its want of inflection, because in syntactical structures it behaves like a noun. Uninflected words that do not go into any of these classes by virtue of their behavior are lumped as particles. The subclasses of particles can be distinguished only in terms of their syntactical functions. Another formal device for marking the form-class to which a word belongs is the suffix. Thus, *-ness* is a noun-marking, *-ize* a verb-marking suffix in English. Many English adverbs are marked as such by adding the suffix *-ly* to the corresponding adjective, but this marker is not too dependable, since a word so marked may be an adjective. Thus, both *sick* and *sickly* are adjectives in English.

In nearly everything that I have said in this paper, I have had inflected languages in mind. I am not competent to deal with languages that have no inflections, let alone those that have no words. In the discussion of our theme, to which you are now invited to contribute, I hope that much will be brought out that I have only touched upon or neglected altogether. Our time is limited, but our topic is as wide as the world.

LEXICOGRAPHICAL TREATMENT OF FOLK TAXONOMIES[1]

Harold C. Conklin
Yale University

1. Introduction

Many lexical problems are of considerable importance to linguists and ethnographers. With the interests of both groups in mind, I would like to discuss certain aspects of folk classification which I feel deserve more rigorous lexicographic attention than they have typically received.

An adequate ethnographic description of the culture of a particular society (Goodenough 1957) presupposes a detailed analysis of the communications system and of the culturally defined situations in which all relevant distinctions in that system occur. In this regard, accurate knowledge of both the grammar and lexicon of the local spoken language constitutes a minimum requirement. When the ethnographer works in an area for which adequate statements about the local language are unavailable in published sources, his first and often continuing task is the construction of a set of valid rules for the interpretation of the local language. In his phonological and grammatical analysis of new speech forms, he may find many helpful models in the descriptive linguistic literature. In attempting, however, to account for the obligatory semantic relations inherent in his lexical corpus, he may not be so fortunate. While extant dictionaries and vocabularies do provide glosses and definitional information, many of the nontrivial, and often essential, semantic and contextual relationships obtaining among lexical items are often either neglected or handled in an imprecise and unsystematic manner (cf. Newman 1954, 86).

For formal linguistic analysis, it is necessary that utterances be acceptable and interpretable grammatically. For ethnographic (including lexicographic) analysis, utterances must also be acceptable and interpretable semantically. While an "appeal" to meaning does not improve grammatical analysis, neither does an intuitive appeal to morphosyntactic form yield the most appropriate analysis of meaning and reference (see 2.5. below). In fact, an adequate grammar may generate semantically unacceptable propositions (Chomsky 1955, 149; Chomsky 1957, 103–4; cf. Landar 1960, 352; Frake 1961, 113). Results of some recent attempts to develop non-intuitive procedures for the evaluation of the grammaticalness and meaningfulness of sentences (e.g., Maclay and Sleator 1960; cf. Joos 1958) indicate that this difference is of considerable importance. The distinction between these two aspects of the analysis of speech is apparent even in the treatment of isolated forms.

In the course of several years of linguistic and ethnographic field work among the Hanunóo in the Philippines, it became abundantly evident that providing such segments as *sah, tabākuq, samparansisku-qalistun,* and *lāda. balaynun. tagnānam. qiruŋ-pādiq* each with the same gloss '(distinct) kind of plant' was—while adequate for certain syntactic purposes—most unsatisfactory for the task of semantic analysis. Had I not modified this procedure, I would have ended up with more than 2000 lexical items (including several hundred referential synonyms) each labeled identically. While employing glosses like 'tea' and 'tobacco' (in the first two cases above) proved useful in labeling familiar objects, the majority of these culturally significant Hanunóo designations referred to entities which to me were quite unfamiliar. In this type of ethnographic context, one finds many instances where the problems faced traditionally by the compilers of bilingual dictionaries are considerably magnified (Nida 1958). For the ethnographer, the semantic structure of such folk classification is of paramount significance. Upon his analysis of it depends the accuracy of many crucial statements about the culture being described. Problems of analyzing and presenting such structures in a succinct fashion may be of interest even to lexicographers who work only in relatively familiar cultural surroundings.

2. Folk Classification

In the lexicographic treatment of folk classification, we are concerned primarily with (1) the identification of relevant syntactic segments, (2) the identification of fundamental semantic units in specific contexts, (3) the delineation of significant sets of semantic units in particular domains, and (4) the translation (and marking) of these units so that important semantic relationships will not be obscured. In discussing different systems of classifying segments of the natural and social environment, the neutral term *segregate* (Conklin 1954) serves as a label for any terminologically distinguished (i.e., conventionally named) grouping of objects.

2.1. Linguistic structure. The shape and combinatorial structure of the linguistic forms which designate folk segregates are irrelevant, in a strict sense, to the analysis of the system of classification itself, i.e., to the semantic structure (Conklin 1957). Labels and categories can change independently and therefore must be analyzed separately. On the other hand, a knowledge of the linguistic structure involved is essential for understanding the principles of folk *nomenclature*; and in working out this structure, clues for isolating folk segregate labels and for eliciting information about such segregates may be found.

2.2. Lexical units and contexts. A full lexical statement (i.e., an adequate dictionary) should provide semantic explanation, as well as phonological and grammatical identification, for every meaningful form whose signification cannot be inferred from a knowledge of anything else in the language. It is convenient to refer to these elementary lexical units as *lexemes* (cf. Swadesh 1946; Newman 1954; Jorden 1955; Goodenough 1956), although other terms have been suggested (e.g., *idiom* [Hockett 1956; cf. Householder 1959, 508–24; Weinreich 1960, 337]). So far as lexemic status is concerned, the morphosyntactic or assumed etymological relations of a particular linguistic form are incidental; what is essential is that its meaning cannot be deduced from its grammatical structure. Single morphemes are necessarily lexemes, but for polymorphemic constructions the decision depends on meaning and use (implying an analysis of the constraints imposed by the semantic structure, and the specification of relevant immediate contexts).

Formal segments such as *black bird* (vs. *blackbird*) or *in the old house* (vs. *in the doghouse*) can be excluded from the lexical statement because they are predictable, meaningfully, in that they can be considered *semantically endocentric* (Nida 1951, 12–13; Nida 1958, 286; cf. Chao 1953, 385). Put another way, those constructions which are never *semantically exocentric* may be classed as *nonlexemic* forms (e.g., *sunburned face, long pink strand*). Problems do arise, however, in degrees of lexemic *exocentricity* (Nida 1958, 286) and, again, if caution is not exercised in distinguishing clearly between grammatical and semantic criteria. The compounds *firewater* and *silverfish*, for example, are endocentric morphosyntactically, either on an attribute-plus-head basis or on the perhaps stronger grounds of formal selection rules (Lees 1960, 128 and 158), but semantically they are as exocentric as *vodka* and *moth*.

In the study of segregate labels in folk classification, and despite some of the difficulties of technical definition noted, I find it useful to distinguish by explicit semantic criteria two kinds of lexemic units: *unitary lexemes* (no segments of which may designate categories which are identical with, or superordinate to, those designated by the forms in question) and *composite lexemes* (one or more segments of which, under specified conditions, may [a] designate the same categories as those designated by the forms in question [abbreviation], or [b] designate categories superordinate to those designated by the forms in question [generalization]; see 3–3.2.) Unitary lexemes may be either *simple* (unsegmentable) or *complex* (segmentable). These distinctions are exemplified below:

Lexemes

Unitary simple	Unitary complex	Composite
oak	poison oak	white oak
pine	pineapple	pitch pine
son	grandson	son-in-law
dart (an artifact)	darts (a game)	Baldwin apple
jack	jack-in-the-pulpit	Port Orford cedar
dandelion	black-eyed Susan	black-crowned night heron
caterpillar (larva)	cat's-eye	caterpillar tractor

For contrast, consider a few similar but *nonlexemic* forms: *cheap pine*, *pine and oak*, *black-eyed Joe*, *darts* (plural of *dart*; see Hockett 1956, 229). For a native speaker, such distinctions cause little concern, but in new linguistic and cultural environs difficulties may arise.

For example, on first inspection, the following partially identical Hanunóo forms (Conklin 1954) might appear to belong to a simple paradigm (they could all be recorded during a conversation about rice cultivation and weeding problems):

1   *paray : paray*   'cattail'
2   *pāray : māyah*   'immature wild pādaŋ) (plant)'
3   *pāray : qiŋkantuh*   'kind of wild sedge'

4	pāray : bīhud	'kind of rice'
5	pāray : tāwuh	'some one (else)'s rice'
6	pāray : tīdah	'that rice'

The glosses, however, indicate that several types of lexical units may be involved. Are there any formal linguistic clues?

Each of the six forms is easily segmented into two morphs, as I have indicated by the use of dots. Loose-joining, phonemically, is represented by a single raised period. Except for the closely joined doubling in item number 1, the forms in this set provide no obligatory intonational or junctural contrasts. Furthermore, each form occurs in many identical frames such as *tūhay ŋāni ti* _____ ' _____ is (are) certainly different.' Thus, for most of the semantically distinct types of joining suggested by the glosses, there are no phonological clues and few, if any, immediate, formal indications. (A full syntactic statement covering the structure of compounds would separate out some of these forms on grammatical grounds; cf. Lees 1960.) Given the necessary semantic information, however, these distinctions can be noted easily for lexicographical purposes by rewriting the forms as follows:

1   pārayparay
2   pāray-māyah
3   pāray- qiŋkantuh
4   pāray. bīhud
5   pāray tāwuh
      (5a)   (5b)
6   pāray tidah
      (6a)   (6b)

This procedure clearly marks 1, 2, and 3 as semantically exocentric, unitary lexemes; 4 as a composite lexeme; and 5 and 6 as nonlexemic, semantically endocentric constructions the initial lexeme of which is superordinately related to 4. Minimally, forms 1, 2, 3, 4, 5a, and 6a could be labeled 'kind of plant,' but, by not attending to essential semantic distinctions, this type of short cut would obscure such important contrastive relations as the mutual exclusion of coordinate categories (1 : [*pādaŋ*, implied—but not covered—by the specific growth stage term number 2] : 3 : 5a or 6a), and the possible total inclusion of subordinate categories (4 by 5a/6a; but *not* 1, 2, or 3 by 5a/6a). Statements about such relations, hinted at in some glosses and definitions, may be demonstrated only by systematic pairing in minimal, and relatively controlled, linguistic and semantic contexts.

2.3. **Lexical sets and domains**. In many ways it can be said that the more discrete the phenomena referred to, the simpler the task of treating the associated terminology in a lexicographically adequate manner (cf. Wallace and Atkins 1960). If this is true for particular lexical items, it is equally true for the semantically structured sets which such items may comprise (Frake 1961). Minimally, a *lexical set* consists of all semantically contrastive lexemes which, in a given culturally relevant context, share exclusively at least one defining feature (Lounsbury 1956, 61–62). The semantic range of all such lexemes defines the *domain* of the lexical set. The initial establishment of domain boundaries, while widely recognized as an ideal goal, is often a very difficult task (cf. Voegelin and Voegelin 1957). Effective eliciting frames and procedural tests used to determine such boundaries, and convincing demonstrations of their intracultural reality, are subjects not often discussed in the linguistic or ethnological literature. Some of the essential factors involved in this type of analysis are treated briefly below under "levels" (section 3) and "dimensions" (section 4) of contrast. In general, the number and complexity of boundary problems increases as one moves from the investigation of lexical domains within a particular language to an attempt to "match" the domains of different languages (Öhman 1953; cf. Quine 1960, 26–79). This does not, however, preclude rigorous contrastive analysis.

2.4. **Translation and semantic structure**. With few exceptions, the lexical items employed in systems of folk classification always comprise a segment of the everyday vocabulary of the particular language (Conklin 1957). The rules governing the obligatory semantic relations among the categories in such lexical sets are thus to be determined, evaluated, and described for each language. Such rules cannot be prescribed merely on the basis of familiarity *in another system* with the "concrete" denotata of the sets involved. In the case of folk botany, for example, this means that a local system of plant classification cannot be described accurately by attempting to obtain only vernacular "equivalents" for botanically recognized species. Translation labels (glosses) are frequently necessary, but they should be considered neither as definitions nor as exact equivalents (Lounsbury 1956, 163; for an attempt to use acronyms as a partial mnemonic solution to such translation problems, see Landar, Ervin, and Horowitz 1960, 371). This well established and perhaps obvious semantic principle is sometimes forgotten, where the assumed absolute nature (in a cross-linguistic sense) of "scientific" names or of other long-established traditional distinctions in certain Western languages is involved (Öhman 1953; cf. Simpson 1961, 11).

2.5. **Syntactic vs. semantic structure**. Implicit in the preceding remarks is the assumption that the relation between formal linguistic (syntactic, in the general, semiotic sense; see Morris 1946) structure and semantic structure need not be isomorphic (Lounsbury 1956, 189). If this assumption is taken seriously, a full dictionary should state explicitly the necessary and sufficient conditions for the unambiguous structural interpretation of each included lexeme in the context of the total lexicon as well as in that of the grammar. While such coverage has rarely been achieved, even for relatively small lexical domains, I feel that recognition of this goal has considerable relevance for this discussion. A brief illustration may help to indicate the kind of crucial lexical data that are often ignored, especially where meanings are either assumed on the basis of semantic patterning in a more familiar language, or where they are treated only partially (as in the derivation of definitional statements from translational labels).

Consider the following situation (which, with minor differences, I have encountered on a number of occasions): a woman, whose brother (x) and husband (y) are both named Juan, has a son, also named Juan (z), and a daughter who in turn has a son named Pedro (P). The genealogical situation is diagrammed in Fig. 1 (we can ignore the broken lines for a moment). Two fluent speakers of English, F, a Filipino whose first language was Tagalog, and A, a native speaker of a dialect of American English, both know Pedro and the specified members of his family. The fact that one of the Juans (x, y, or z) has died is known only to A (or F) who in turn wishes to relate this circumstance to his friend F (or A). A straightforward statement completing the sentence *P's _____ Juan died* would seem to do the trick; and, depending on the circumstances, one of two unitary lexemes (*grandfather, uncle*) might be used to fill the blank:

1. *Pedro's Grandfather Juan died.*
2. *Pedro's Uncle Juan died.*

However, if A uses *Grandfather*, F may ask, *Which grandfather?*; if F uses *Uncle*, A may ask, *Which uncle?* indicating a kind of two-way ambiguity

250 | Problems in Lexicography

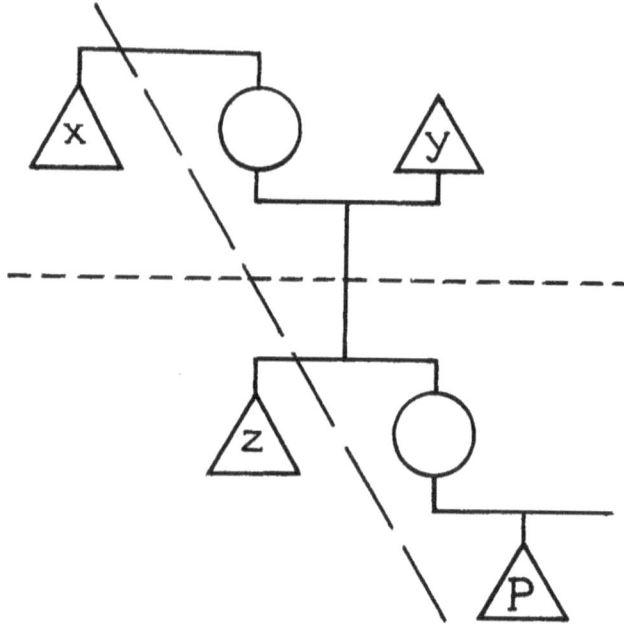

Figure 1. A genealogical illustration of contrasting systems of kinship classification.

which can only be resolved by recognizing that despite their unquestionable grammatically and morphosyntactic identity, A's sentences 1 and 2 and F's sentences 1 and 2 differ semantically:

Sentence	Kin term used	Kin type(s) included	(Pr = parent's)
A1	Grandfather	Y	(PrFa)
F1	"	x and y	(PrFa, PrPrBr)
A2	Uncle	x and z	(PrBr, PrPrBr)
F2	"	z	(PrBr)

This, of course, reflects only a small part of a very fundamental structural difference in Central Philippine and North American systems of kinship classification: universal terminological recognition of generation in the former vs. universal terminological recognition of degree of collaterality in the latter (these two "limits" to the lexical extension of kin class membership are indicated on the kinship diagram in Fig. 1 by the horizontal and diagonal broken lines, respectively). Although any careful investigator might learn this systematic distinction after a few days of field work, the principle goes unaccounted for in the relevant and extant bilingual dictionaries. The restrictions involved in this illustration are just as obligatory and inescapable within the respective semantic systems represented as is the distinction of singular vs. plural in English grammar.

3. Levels of Contrast

Folk categories within the same domain may be related in two fundamentally different ways: by *inclusion*, which implies separate levels of contrast, and by *exclusion*, which here applies only within single-level contrastive sets. There may also be subcategoric, or componential, *intersection* (see section 4, below). In studying semantic relationships, as among folk categories, it has often been demonstrated that likeness logically and significantly implies difference (Kelly 1955, 303–5). It is also pertinent, however, to note that total contrast (complete complementary exclusion)—which logically relates such segregates as *ant* and *ship* or *cough* and *pebble*—is less important than restricted contrast within the range of a particular semantic subset (compare the relations within and between the partial sets *robin – wren – sparrow*; *spaniel – terrier – poodle*; and *bird – dog*). When we speak of the category *dime* being included in the category COIN, we imply that every dime is also a (kind of) coin—but not necessarily the reverse. Furthermore, when we state (a) that the category *dime* contrasts with that of *quarter* and (b) that the category *coin* contrasts with that of *bill* we are speaking of two instances of relevant mutual exclusion at two different levels of contrast (Conklin 1955; Conklin 1957; Frake 1961). Such alignments of folk categories are common to all languages, though systematic indications of these relationships are rare, even in the more detailed monolingual dictionaries.

3.1. **Hierarchic structure**. Where the articulation between successive levels, each consisting of a set of contrastive lexical units, is ordered vertically by inclusion, such that each monolexemic category at one level is totally included in only one category at the next higher level, we can speak of a lexical hierarchy. The two axes of such a structure involve the horizontal *differentiation* of contrastive but coordinate categories and the vertical increase of *generalization* or *specification* resulting from ascent to superordinate (including) or descent to subordinate (included) levels, respectively (Gregg 1954; Conklin 1957; Beckner 1959, 55–80; Frake 1961, 117). These axes are fixed and cannot be merged or interchanged, nor can the succession of levels be modified. *Dime* is not contrasted with COIN, but at the same level with *nickel, quarter, penny*, etc. Subhierarchies of varying "depths" are often discernible within larger hierarchic structures. The depth (in levels) of the subhierarchy including the categories HAWK, PIGEON, and STARLING is less than that of the subhierarchy including HAWK, HORSE, and CROCODILE; i.e., the first three segregates are included in a superordinate category at a lower level than that of the segregate ultimately including HAWK, HORSE, and CROCODILE. The embedding of shallow subhierarchies within increasingly deeper ones is characteristic of many systems of folk classification.

3.2. **Folk taxonomy.** A system of monolexemically labeled folk segregates related by hierarchic inclusion is a *folk taxonomy*; segregates included in such a classification are known as *folk taxa* (Conklin 1957; cf. Lawrence 1951, 53; Simpson 1961, 19). Some of the additional requirements of "model" or "regular" taxonomic systems (Woodger 1952, 201ff.; Gregg 1954; Beckner 1959, 55–58; Simpson 1961) are: (1) at the highest level, there is only one maximal (largest, unique) taxon which includes all other taxa in the system; (2) the number of levels is finite and uniform throughout the system; (3) each taxon belongs to only one level; (4) there is no overlap (i.e., taxa at the same level are always mutually exclusive). Folk systems vary widely with respect to these more specific "requirements," but the presence of hierarchically arranged though less "regular" folk taxonomies is probably universal. Most of the examples given here are taken from folk botany, but similar illustrations could be taken from other domains (Thomas 1957; Frake 1961).

Several important differences distinguish folk taxa from the taxonomic groups of biological systematics (Conklin 1957; Simpson 1961). The former usually relate only to locally relevant or directly observable phenomena. They are defined by criteria which may differ greatly from culture to culture. The number and position of levels of contrast may change from one sector of a folk system to another. There are no formal rules for the nomenclatural recognition or rejection of taxa (cf. Lawrence 1951, 213–15), though new groupings may be added productively with considerable ease. In respect to any particular local biota, there is no reason to expect the folk taxa to match those of systematic biology—either in number or in range. The Hanunóo classify their local plant world, at the lowest (terminal) level of contrast, into more than 1800 mutually exclusive folk taxa, while botanists divide the same flora—in terms of species—into less than 1300 scientific taxa.

3.3. **Special problems**. Although they cannot be discussed here at length, a number of lexicographically important problems encountered in the analysis of folk taxonomies include:

(1) Multiple and interlocking hierarchies. Unlike scientific taxa, folk segregates may belong simultaneously to several distinct hierarchic structures. The same segregates maybe classed as terminal categories in a taxonomy based on form and appearance and also as terminal or nonterminal categories in another taxonomy based on cultural treatment (e.g., morphologically distinguished kinds of floral segregates vs. functional categories of plants as food cultigens, medicines, ornamentals, etc.) (Conklin 1954). Subhierarchies may be interarticulated in numerous ways (e.g., Joos 1956, 296–97) and there is always the potentiality of partial inclusion or domain overlap.

(2) Extrahierarchic relations. Not all folk categories are directly related by class inclusion or contrast within the range of a particular superordinate category. For example, numerous difficulties may arise if lexemes designating separate ontogenetic stages or parts of members of particular segregates (see section 2.2, above) are not distinguished from hierarchically arranged folk taxa (Chao 1953, 387–89; Conklin 1954; Conklin 1957; Frake 1961). *Part-of* (part-whole) relations are often complicated by ambiguities (Nagel 1961, 381–83) not encountered in the analysis of *kind-of* (class inclusion) relations (e.g., the segregates *plant, stem, sap* are not related taxonomically like *plant, tree, elm*).

(3) Synonymy and homonymy. When, within the context of a particular folk taxonomy, a single taxon may be labeled by phonemically distinct forms, as in the case of minor dialect variants or abbreviated terms (see section 1.2), we may speak of referential synonyms (or synonymous lexemes); e.g., *fin, finnif, five, fiver, five-spot, five-dollar bill*. In many such cases, it may be difficult to demonstrate taxonomic identity and the absence of categoric overlap. Alternative substructuring of the subhierarchy may be involved. Phonemically identical (homonymous) lexemes may designate separate taxa of different ranges of generalization at successive levels. Such situations (e.g., *animal* and *man* in the following partial contrastive sets: *animal^1* vs. *plant, animal^2* vs. *man^1, man^2* vs. *woman*; cf. Frake 1961, 117–19) are not uncommon but they require careful contrastive pairing and testing for inclusion at each level involved. Similar steps must also be taken in working out problems concerned with distinguishing polysemy from homonymy (Wells 1958, 662–63; cf. Chomsky 1957, 95; Garvin 1960,147).

(4) Types of contrast. Paired folk taxa of some lexical subsets are related by simple, binary, segregate opposition. Many larger sets and some dyadic ones involve important types of semantic contrast other than antonymy (cf. Lyons 1960, 622). Structurally, for example, taxa may be contrasted in serial, complementary, or discontinuous arrays. (For subcategoric attribute relations, see section 4, below.)

3.4. **Folk vs. botanical taxonomy.** Ideally, in the study of interrelated lexical sets in folk taxonomies, priority and preference should be given to unanimously agreed upon, obligatory distinctions in specified contexts. When tested by means of what are essentially crucial experiments—by pairing and contrasting negatively and positively—one should be able to construct a model (i.e., a theoretical statement) of the hierarchic structure such that assertions of membership and inclusion in any of the implied taxa are unanimously and unambiguously denied whenever such assertions are incongruent (i.e., meaningless within the system) (cf. Joos 1958, 65). The assertion "Poodles, dogs, and animals are kinds of snails" would thus be rejected by speakers of my dialect of English—and on very easily specified semantic grounds. Within a particular universe of discourse (a taxonomic domain), how can one construct a nontrivial model by means of which only semantically acceptable, congruent propositions may be generated? An example from Hanunóo folk botany may serve as a partial answer.

In a situation where one Hanunóo farmer wishes to draw another's attention to a particular individual pepper bush Q, he may, of course, attempt to describe some of Q's unique attributes without naming the plant. Much more often, however, even in the course of a "unique" description, he will resort to the use of one or more of at least eight lexical units each of which might complete the frame *māluq, qinda pag* _____ 'Hey, take a look at this _____,' but at different levels of contrast (allowing for different degrees of desired or required specificity):

I.	*kuwaq*	'entity' (i.e., something that can be named)
II.	*bāgay*	'thing' (not a person, animal, etc.)
III.	*kāyuh*	'plant' (not a rock, etc.)
IV.	*qilamnun*	'herbaceous plant' (not a woody plant, etc.)
V.	*lādaq*	'pepper (plant)' (not a rice plant, etc.)
VI.	*lāda.balaynun*	'house yard pepper (plant)' (not a wild pepper plant)
VII.	*lāda.balaynun. mahārat*	'house yard chili pepper (plant)' (not a house yard green pepper plant)
VIII.	*lāda.balaynun. mahārat. qūtin-kutiq*	'"cat-penis" house yard chili pepper (plant)' (not a member of any of five other terminal house yard chili pepper taxa such as *lāda. balaynun. mahārat. tāhud-manuk*, the "cock's-spur" variety).

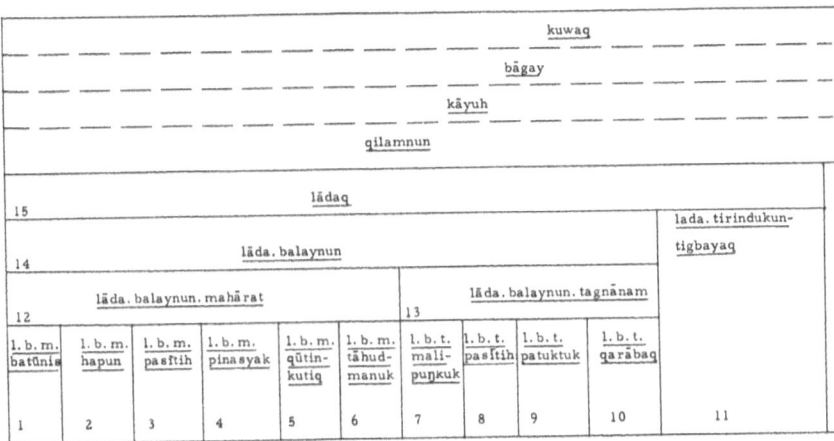

Figure 2. A segment of Hanunóo plant taxonomy. All folk taxa included in the taxon *lādaq* are indicated.

Within the domain of Hanunóo plant taxonomy, from level III down, and specifically within the range of *lādaq*, from level V down, conversations recorded during many similar situations would ultimately provide the lexicographer with fifteen unitary and composite lexemes (including a terminal set of eleven 'pepper plant' names) arranged at four levels in the form of a discrete subhierarchy (Fig. 2). Specification below the level of the terminal taxa noted in the diagram (Fig. 2:1–11), and hence outside this system of classification, may be provided only by semantically endocentric constructions describing individual plant variations, on which unanimous accord is rare and unpredictable. In this particular case, folk taxa 15, 14, and 11 happen to correspond rather closely with the scientific taxa *Capsicum*, *C. annuum* L., and *C. frutescens* L., respectively; but the twelve remaining folk taxa involve distinctions not recognized as significant botanical subspecies by taxonomic botanists who have classified the same flora. Structurally speaking, however, some of the most important patterns of semantic contrast involve not only the hierarchic separation of these varied, lower-level, folk taxa, but also a large number of nonhierarchic relations governed by sublexemic class intersection (see section 4.2). Although such relations cannot be diagrammed with the taxonomic implications of Fig. 2, nor can they be treated effectively at all in terms of our hierarchic model, they should nevertheless be of considerable interest to linguists and others concerned with systems of folk classification.

4. Dimensions of Contrast

At any given level within a well-defined folk-taxonomic subhierarchy, the relations obtaining among three or more coordinate taxa may involve varying dimensions, or kinds of subcategory contrast. The conjunction of these dimensions, or more precisely, of the values (or specific attributes; cf. Bruner, Goodnow, and Austin 1956, 26–30) along the several dimensions, define the categories involved within an essentially paradigmatic (i.e., nonhierarchic) subsystem (Lounsbury 1956; Lounsbury 1960, 27–28; for a discussion of the structurally similar though more typologically oriented procedures of attribute space substruction and reduction, see Greenberg 1957 and Lazarsfeld 1961).

4.1. **Nonhierarchic structure**. Such multidimensional contrasts do not imply, and indeed do not allow, the ordering of the resultant categories by hierarchic inclusion. These features of nonhierarchic semantic structures, while not always sharply distinguished from the principles inherent in hierarchic systems, have been recognized and carefully analyzed in a number of domains, notably in kinship (Goodenough 1951, 92–110; Goodenough 1956; Lounsbury 1956; Frake 1960; Wallace and Atkins 1960), color (Conklin 1955; cf. Lenneberg and Roberts 1956; Landar, Ervin, and Horowitz 1960), orientation (Haugen 1957), disease (Frake 1961), and, beginning with Jakobson's pioneering efforts, in such partly modulational (Joos 1958, 70) paradigms as case and pronoun systems (Jakobson 1936; Sebeok 1946; Harris 1948; Lotz 1949; Wonderly 1952; Austerlitz 1959). The following example of multidimensional contrast in a regular paradigmatic structure will illustrate some of these points.

4.2. **Significant classification vs. cataloguing**. If, omitting the high-level, wide-ranging *kuwaq* (see section 3.4), we list all the Hanunóo personal name substitutes occurring in various frames such as *māluq, qinda pag binwat ni* _____ 'Hey, take a look at what _____ did (here),' we will invariably end up with an exhaustive and mutually exclusive lexical set consisting of just eight units (in each case representing a single morpheme). Arranged in the least meaningful type of catalogue, an alphabetical *index* (as in a dictionary), these lexical units are:

dah   'they'
kuh   'I'
mih   'we'

muh	'you'
tah	'we two'
tam	'we all'
yah	'he, she'
yuh	'you all'

The shapes provide little that is structurally suggestive, but the glosses do indicate that an ordering in terms of eight "traditional" distinctions along three quasi-semantic dimensions

(1) first person : second person : third person
(2) singular   : dual   : plural
(3) exclusive   : inclusive   :

might be attempted. But the resulting applied structure is hardly elegant, economical, or convincing:

kuh 1s	*tah* 1d	*mih* 1pe
---	---	*tam* 1pi
muh 2s	---	*yuh* 2p
yah 3s	---	*dah* 3p

If a close examination is made of the distinctive contrasts involved, not in terms of labels but in terms of actual, minimal, obligatory differences, a more satisfactory, economical, and semantically verifiable solution is reached. The necessary and sufficient conditions for defining each of the eight categories depend on the regular intersection of six components which comprise three simple oppositions:

minimal membership : nonminimal membership (M : $\overline{M}$)
inclusion of speaker : exclusion of speaker (S : $\overline{S}$)
inclusion of hearer : exclusion of hearer (H : $\overline{H}$)

These relations can be represented in list or diagrammatic form (Fig. 3). Even without further elaboration, the basic semantic structure of this lexical set should now be clear. (In passing, it may be noted that pronoun systems in Tagalog, Ilocano [Thomas 1955], Maranao [McKaughan 1959], and some other Philippine languages exhibit very similar, if not identical, obligatory semantic relationships.)

d a h	M̄ S̄ H̄
y u h	M̄ S H̄
m i h	M̄ S H̄
t am	M̄ S H
y a h	M S̄ H̄
mu h	M S̄ H
k u h	M S H̄
t a h	M S H

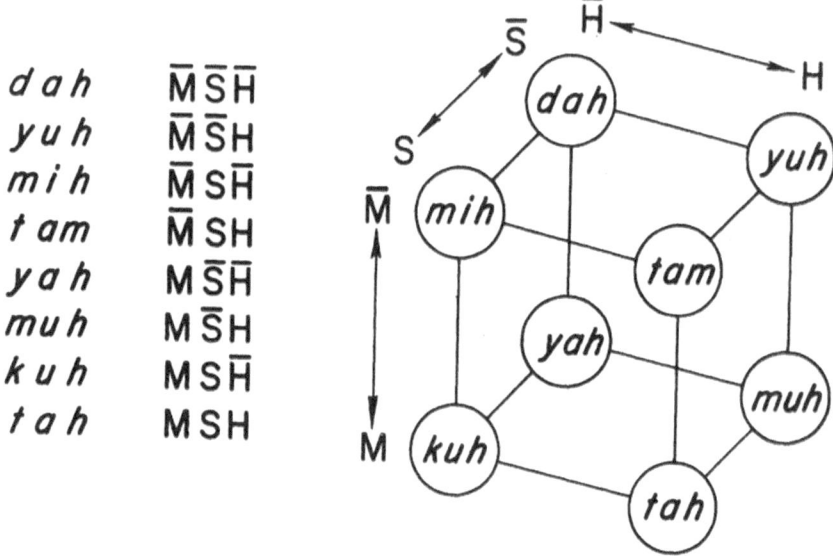

Figure 3. Paradigmatic structure of a Hanunóo pronominal set.

This example also illustrates a very important, though perhaps less obvious, characteristic of paradigmatic relations at one level in a taxonomic subhierarchy in contrast to the noncommutative relations of class inclusion governing the larger taxonomic system. Within such a contrastive lexical set (as in Fig. 3), ordered by class intersection, the constituent categories cannot be arranged in a taxonomic hierarchy. Any arrangement (e.g., a circular, block, or branching diagram) superficially appearing to contradict this statement will prove on closer inspection either (a) to constitute what the biologists call a *key* (Mayr, Linsley, and Usinger 1953, 162–68; Simpson 1961,13–16), essentially another kind of catalogue or finding list ordered by successive—but not necessarily taxonomically significant—dichotomous exclusion, or (b) to be based on some other artificially imposed, and hence semantically nonsignificant, classification.

5. Lexicographic Treatment

The ways in which the problems mentioned in this paper may be treated in bilingual dictionaries, especially ethnographic dictionaries, are practically unlimited. That very few of the possibilities have been explored to date is disappointing, but not discouraging. There have been a number of new attempts at expanding the analytic procedures of descriptive linguistics to include a more rigorous, thorough, and theoretically rewarding analysis of semantic structure (e.g., Goodenough 1956; Lounsbury 1956; Nida 1958; Frake 1961). Despite these more encouraging signs, I realize that most dictionaries will continue to be organized primarily as alphabetical indices. Suggestions regarding the ways in which structural semantic information (especially with reference to folk taxonomies) might be more adequately covered in such dictionaries would include, wherever possible: (1) consistent marking of each entry as to its status as a lexical unit and taxon, its immediately subordinate taxa and super ordinate taxon, and all coordinate taxa included with it in this next higher taxon (simple diacritics and abbreviations can be devised for systematic use in compilation and checking); (2) differential marking of translation labels and of definitions; (3) concise indication of distinctive attributes which define categories belonging to analyzed lexical sets; (4) systematic cross-referencing to maximal taxa in all major subhierarchies, to referential synonyms, and to all units involved in categoric overlap; and (5) frequent use of structural charts and diagrams. Where only limited opportunities are available for accomplishing such tasks, priority might be given to those parts of the lexicon which, on the basis of nonintuitive and intracultural criteria, appear to involve semantic relations of an everyday, obligatory nature. In number of segregates, paradigmatic complexity, and hierarchic depth, certain lexical domains are likely to be more highly structured than others (Brown 1956, 307; Nida 1958, 283–84; Worth 1960, 277; Frake 1961, 121–22). For the student of folk taxonomy, focusing attention on these domains should lead not only to more interesting analytic problems but also to results of greater lexicographical and general cultural relevance.

NOTES

1. The work on which most of this paper is based has been supported by the National Science Foundation. A number of students and other friends have offered constructive criticism of an earlier draft of this statement. For especially helpful and more detailed comments I am particularly indebted to Y. R. Chao, David Crabb, Arthur Danto, C. O. Frake, Paul Friedrich, W. H. Goodenough, J. H. Greenberg, Einar Haugen, P. F. Lazarsfeld, F. G. Lounsbury, and Volney Stefflre.

COMMENTS

James Sledd
Northwestern University

SINCE I CAN CONTRIBUTE NOTHING ORIGINAL TO THIS discussion, and since you hardly need summaries of papers which are already in your hands, I can define my function only as provocative misunderstanding; and even that definition may be optimistic: *provoking* might be a better word.

As a pedagogue attempting to teach both the English language and English literature, I consider bewilderment my natural state. Anything can happen today in an English department, and departments of linguistics are in the midst of one of their recurrent revolutions. Young men who assured me, eight or ten years ago, that Trager and Smith (1951) had produced a paperback *summa linguistica* assure me now, with equal confidence, that taxonomic linguistics was relatively sterile; Joos's *Readings* (1952) announced the consolidation of the old regime when the palace guard had already gone over to the rebels. Though I hope and believe that the change is for the better, the distinctive feature of the present moment is confusion—grave, acute, and stridently voiced confusion. The innocent bystander, still puzzled by glossematics, glottochronology, and prosodic analysis, must now acquaint himself with yet another theory and must assess its possible usefulness in his own teaching. I am still trying to catch up on all this homework.

My distinguished colleagues are naturally less overawed by the transformationists than I am, and though I detect some echoes of Chomsky, Halle, and Lees in their remarks, I believe I also detect some disagreements. To begin with the echoes, Mr. Gleason's *grammaticalness*, with its degrees and levels, suggests Chomsky's *grammaticality*; but since we are rightly forbidden to ask for the definition of a term which a whole grammar will ultimately explain, I will make no inquiries but will content myself with saying that I have all the familiar troubles with the concept of grammaticality. (1) Are my grammatical intuitions those of an unspoiled native speaker, or are they dim memories of what Miss Ruby Crawford taught me in high-school English? (2) Are figures of speech ungrammatical? It might seem so, since Lees stars the sentence *Cadillacs admire him*, though it might very well occur in a child's story where automobiles are personified. Do we need another set of rules for figurative use? (3) Grammaticality cannot be identified with actual occurrence—for example, Chomsky's formula for the English verb-phrase will correctly produce monsters like *will have been being built*, which one can scarcely find in millions of words of text. Is it the grammarian, then, or someone else who must record the extent to which Mr. Hoenigswald's paradigms are filled? (4) In this situation, how seriously should we take behavioral tests for grammaticality? As Chomsky says, the tests themselves must be tested by our intuitions; and my informants stubbornly refuse to behave as I am told they should. Without a stammer, my literary students will recite, "Furiously sleep ideas—green, colorless." (5) I myself am perfectly happy with many sentences which Chomsky and Lees have exiled from English: to rule out a phrase like *ancient babies* or a sentence like *Bob is tall in America* simply because the contexts where they would occur are a little odd is to define grammaticality in terms of meaning (mummies may be ancient babies). If I may be allowed to mention discovery procedures, surely one excellent procedure, in these difficult circumstances, is to consult the big dictionaries; for the native speaker cannot determine, by hasty and unaided introspection, what sentences are grammatical and what are not, and initial misjudgments of grammaticality will defeat the grammarian's effort to generate all and only the grammatical sentences of his language. We must at least account for all *observed* sentences.

The meaning of meaning troubles me quite as much as the concept of grammaticality. Everybody seems agreed that meaning cannot be used in the investigation of grammatical form and that dictionaries must deal with meaning, whatever grammars do; yet the transformationists have rehabilitated techniques which once were stigmatized as semantic, and since transformations often keep meaning essentially unchanged, they sometimes may not be very different from a definition like that of a dog-catcher as a man who catches dogs. When are we talking about meaning, and when are we talking about form? Lees gives some long lists which he says show "differences in grammatical form." They include pairs like these:

puppydog—'dog which is a puppy'
watchdog—'dog which watches something'

police dog—'dog used by the police'
sheep dog—'dog which herds sheep'
prairie dog—'dog which inhabits the prairie'

If these are differences in form, what would be a difference in meaning? The question is immediately relevant to Mr. Conklin's list of six Hanunóo forms in section 2.2, where he asks if there are any formal linguistic clues to the semantically distinct types of joining. Knowing nothing whatever of Mr. Conklin's material, I would still guess that it might yield to transformational analysis, and that he has perhaps drawn the line between form and meaning as the lexicographer draws it when the lexicographer "defines" a dogcart as a cart drawn by a dog or a dogfight as a fight between dogs. The transformationists might draw the line very differently. As Chomsky says, if we use the term *meaning* as a cover term for everything that we do not understand about language, in the course of their development other studies (including grammar) must constantly encroach upon the area of semantics.

But to return to our speakers' echoes of the transformationists. "No transformational sophistication is required," Mr. Hoenigswald rightly tells us, to see that in Latin dictionaries, and hence in English ones, the classifications of the verbs are weak. To his suggestion that the transformationists are greatly extending these classifications, Mr. Hoenigswald might have added that not all English dictionaries are equally weak in this respect: for example, an elaborate classification into numbered classes is made and used in the *Advanced Learner's Dictionary* (1952), which A. S. Hornby and others edited some years ago. Applied linguistics has its own contributions to make to the development of linguistics as a science.

That trivious remark is certainly no echo of the transformationists, who have little interest in pedagogic problems; and I shall say nothing more of transformational echoes in our four papers, where indeed the disagreements with transformational theory seem to me more notable. Does Mr. Gleason announce one disagreement in his first paragraph, when he contrasts the relation of grammar with lexicon, as a theoretical question, to the relation of a grammatical statement with a dictionary, as a question of "practical descriptive technique?" *Theoretical* and *practical*, like *pure* and *applied*, are tricky terms. In Chomsky's view, "the basic notion to be defined in linguistic theory . . . is 'grammar of L,' for arbitrary language L," and an adequate generative grammar "is essentially a theory of" the sentences of a language." What is theoretical for Chomsky is practical for Mr. Gleason.

Mr. Hoenigswald, in turn, seems both to begin and end on a note of disagreement with the transformationists. Contrasting grammars with dictionaries in his first paragraph, he says that "dictionaries are essentially lists;" and, in his conclusion, he characterizes grammar and lexicon as "complementary ways of organizing the corpus," the text which is more basic than either. For transformationists, however, a taxonomic grammar is itself "a set of lists," lists of "phonemes, morphophonemes, morpheme classes, and morpheme class sequences;" and "organizing the corpus" is simply a way of re-arranging the data, which tells us nothing new, leads to no "deep generalizations," and finds no explanations for the listed facts.

Mr. Malone, again, seems to make a number of assumptions which the transformationists would reject. For example, if one does not insist that all the phonemes in a form be assigned to morphemes, *stood* represents two morphemes, *stand* plus past, but one does not need to ask what physical part of the word belongs to one morpheme and what part to the other; similarly, marking morpheme boundaries in a phonemic transcription would often be quite impossible. Chomsky would be even more disturbed by Mr. Malone's statement that classification into parts of speech "is structurally valid" only "to the extent that the classification rests on inflectional distinctions." Though I would never set myself up as a judge in such matters, these instances (and several others which I have not cited) make it quite clear that our four speakers are not whole-hearted transformationists. Perhaps it might be useful if they would say something more on this subject in the context of our meetings.

To do so might further clarify the relation of grammar to lexicon, which I should think (abandoning Mr. Gleason's distinctions) might shift quite strikingly from one linguistic theory to another. Thus, Chomsky's grammar would include a lexicon within itself. As Lees (1960, 20) describes the plan, at the end of the constituent-structure grammar "all the individual morphemes" would be listed and assigned to the grammatical categories of lowest level which had been "developed in the constituent-structure strings." Halle's (1959, 27) comments in *The Sound Pattern of Russian* seem to be somewhat different—for example, he notes that a distinction seems to be necessary between grammatical and lexical morpheme classes, "and that lexical morphemes must be introduced into the representation before grammatical morphemes"; but he too provides that the rules which "comprise the *dictionary* of the language" (Halle 1959, 26) be incorporated within the grammar. Since the grammar will also include "all or most of the selectional restrictions on choice of elements" (Chomsky 1961, 16), and since the transformations which produce compounds like *dog-catcher* and *water-spot* will resemble a kind of verbal definition, I am quite uncertain what part of the total description of a language, according to transformational theory, would *not* be grammatical. Thinking along these lines, I should want to ask a man for his theory of grammar if I were going to study his theory of meaning. What, for example, does Mr. Conklin understand by linguistic form when he says, "that the relation between formal linguistic (syntactic) structure and semantic structure need not be isomorphic?" The application of that proposition would be more restricted for a man who finds a formal distinction between *prairie-dog* and *puppy-dog* than for a man who finds no such distinction.

Other theories than Chomsky's can, of course, be baffling, too. I have to confess almost complete failure to understand Mr. Gleason. I do not understand what he means by tight structure and loose structure, by the "very special kind of relationship" between classes and items, or by content; and I cannot see why color terms should be chosen to provide the "three types of interrelations . . . with which content analysis must operate." I am not persuaded that such ideas and methods will take us far toward theories of meaning which might allow the integration of grammars and dictionaries in full-scale descriptions of languages; but in these deep speculations I have no competence. My homework keeps me busy, and my maximum contribution to the theory of lexicography would be to persuade dictionary-makers to abandon the metaphor of *levels of usage*, with its implied false judgment of value. Of higher integrations, such as Professor Jakobson promises for contemporary Russian, I can only vaguely dream; and since structural linguistics, after thirty years, has produced neither a single big structural grammar of English, nor a single small structural history, nor a good English dictionary, my dreams are not too bright.

The pedagogue, I am afraid, like the lexicographer, must humbly muddle through to his own solutions of his own problems. Of course, he cannot be indifferent to theory. At the present time, indeed, he is called upon to compare basically different theories and to choose between them. But he cannot shift with every wind that flutters the leaves of *Word*. He has a responsibility to tradition, which he will not discharge if he allows himself to be lightly persuaded either that a whole generation of structural linguists have wasted their lives or that outspoken young men have nothing to say simply because they are young and outspoken. The pedagogue's best protection against unwisdom may be the practical demands of his teaching: he cannot teach what he does not understand, and there are no significant applications for nonsense.

I should like to conclude, in this rather dull and moderate spirit, with a few limited comments and questions which I hope are somehow relevant to our four papers. One question has to do with the definition of grammatical terms like *noun, verb, compound*. I can understand Mr. Malone's definitions; I have spent some time in making others like them. But the transformationists tell me that I wasted my efforts. In their grammar, if I understand it, many of the terms of conventional analysis are just not needed; for there seems to be no obvious reason to label constructions like subject and object or even to introduce the term *construction* itself, if the purpose of one's grammar is to generate sentences, and though the transformationist will need a very elaborate set of parts of speech, he will not need terms or definitions for such of their characteristics as gender, number, or case. For him, nouns are the forms which are listed as nouns at the end of the phrase-structure rules, and the characteristics of nouns appear from the positions of the symbol N in the phrase-structure rules and the rules for transformations.

What then is a dictionary-maker to say when he comes to the word *noun*, and what am I to say in my classroom? It is a practical problem. I admit that my definitions are theoretically questionable and that perhaps I accepted a theoretical wooden nickel from the people who taught me how to make them; yet they do allow me and my students to use words like *noun*, when we talk about our language and the surface of its literature, with fairly precise reference. In optimistic moments, I suppose the answer to my question is that substantial fragments of a transformational grammar, when they have been constructed, will provide me with even more extensive and satisfactory clues for identification, as well as a theoretically defensible though not yet realized ideal of definition. In pessimistic moments, I am inclined to believe that there will never be anything *more* than fragments of the theoretically possible grammar which would generate all and only the grammatical sentences of English, and that, for my purposes, my definitions or others like them will be a permanent temporary expedient. I leave the dictionary-maker to decide for himself how to tell compounds from phrases and which compounds to enter in his dictionary. He can take what comfort he can from Lees' (1960, xxiv) statement that "... there simply *is* no neat physical or semantic criterion for compounds,... there need not be any such, and ... the point of linguistic research is to find grammatical descriptions, not to classify physical or semantic 'objects.'"

A second question is that of phonetic or phonemic transcriptions or representations. "The phoneme is the thing," Mr. Malone tells us, and a bilingual dictionary "should include a systematic presentation of the phonemes of each language," with the "chief allophonic types" of each phoneme "described with phonetic precision." Perhaps, but whose phonemics, whose phonetics, and whose pronunciation? The Trager-Smith notation has never been popular outside this country; it has been severely criticized even here; and Chomsky and Halle, in their forthcoming monograph on the English sound pattern, not only blast the iniquitous semivowel /h/ once more but make out a strong argument that phonemics since Bloomfield has developed a suspicious resemblance to the bogy of pre-Bloomfieldian phonetics. In their own analysis, they happily "mix levels" so as to embed the description of the sound system in the full description of the language, and one result is that their morphophonemic transcriptions from even the most divergent dialects are virtually identical; the differences between the dialects can be stated in terms of a small number of "marginal ... phonetic rules." I am impressed by their work, which makes hash of some of mine; but I am certainly not ready to use it in my classes, and still-unpublished studies are of no immediate value to the practicing lexicographer. In this country, the commercial lexicographer today must choose, I should think, between something like a Kenyon–Knott phonetic transcription and one of the familiar textbook systems of re-spelling; and the choice can only be made on practical grounds. There is much to be said for the textbook respelling.

My last question is for information only. Mr. Gleason suggests that "the dictionary might serve as amendment to the grammar." I suppose he speaks from the experience which everyone has had, that a good dictionary, like a good big old-fashioned grammar, supplies us with a mass of information which we do not get in structural sketches. The information may not be well arranged, but it is there, and analyzed at least so far as to be accessible and useful to the average student. I grow uneasy, however, when Mr. Gleason speaks of "the sometimes imprecise meanderings of language" and of the point in description where it is better merely to "describe ad hoc" than to continue the effort at systematic treatment. If we are thinking in distributional terms, can we really say that the "meanderings" of language are ever "imprecise" or that its classes are fuzzy round their edges? Are we not then saying that given forms both occur and do not occur in certain positions? And if a theory of grammar leads us to points where we must make ad hoc decisions, is that not a condemnation of the theory? Maybe no good grammars exist, just as there are no ethnographic descriptions which would be adequate by Mr. Conklin's standards; but it also may be that it is the grammarian who is imprecise and not the language. In Mr. Conklin's table in section 4.2, the language seems to meander because the choice of the wrong coordinates leaves "holes in the pattern;" the proper coordinates, in figure 3, show the language marching like a veteran. Would not real imprecision be really indescribable in either grammar or dictionary? Yet when a good linguist speaks of imprecise meanderings, he goes on to tell us, when we press him, precisely what they are.

NOTE

This paper was written several years ago when the writer knew even less than he does now. As contemporary grammarians say of their last week's lectures, it is now of purely historical interest. Recent research, done when I went to the library on Thursday between 1:15 and 3:00, has conclusively proved, etc., etc.

III

THE PREPARATION OF DICTIONARIES II: PRACTICAL CONSIDERATIONS

SELECTION AND PRESENTATION OF READY EQUIVALENTS IN A TRANSLATION DICTIONARY

Samuel E. Martin
Yale University

MAKING A BILINGUAL DICTIONARY INVOLVES FRUSTRATION AND compromise. You set out with the cheerful view that you can produce a work that will be all things to all men—and perhaps to all machines; you end up with a feeling that you are failing one and all. You want to make a dictionary that will be concise but exhaustive; exact while not exacting; linguistically adequate for *both* languages yet uncluttered with trivial details. Sooner or later, you have to concentrate on certain goals and forget others. Each dictionary represents some unique compromise, useful—we hope—for some purposes and frustrating for others.

Dictionaries are usually made by scholars, and many, as a result, are made *for* scholars. Perhaps we can define a scholar as a man of insatiable curiosity for whom, wisely or unwisely, time is infinitely expendable. A student, on the other hand, can be defined as a person who enjoys a curiosity that is specific and limited, and who must husband his time well if he is to survive. A machine can then be defined as a very fast but dumb student, with a literal mind and a nagging insistence on explicit directions and forced choices.

We are now in a period that requires bilingual dictionaries both for the student and for the computer. I think of each sort of dictionary as a "direct-access translation dictionary," a kind of machine that has built into it much of the information that a scholar's dictionary might take for granted. For translation by a computer, it is desirable that *all* grammatical information somehow be incorporated into the dictionary entry, so that the dictionary itself—with proper programming—can function as a kind of sentence generator. In a sense, the beginning student needs something very similar: a machine that will do the work for him automatically; a dictionary that will produce an adequate, if uninspired, translation with a minimum of human cogitation and with little or nothing in the way of other reference works.

Now, it is too much to expect such a dictionary to work both ways at once. A dictionary that turns out intelligible English (or near-English) sentences for an American who looks up the words in a Japanese sentence will be put together in a different way from one that does the opposite. We must make an early decision: *who* will use the dictionary? If it is a Japanese person, he will want much more information included in the English representations (information on the pronunciation, the syntactic class, the inflection, etc.) than he will need on the Japanese side; if he is an American, he will want more than just the graphic representation of the Japanese. The native speaker of a language is in a position to supply much information that must be made explicit for either the foreigner or the computer.

Despite bulk and good intentions, existing dictionaries lack sufficient information, apparently, to keep a Professor of English in Seoul University from writing "these two vocabularies," when he means "these two vocabulary items" (or, actually, "the two words"), or to discourage him from saying "I have to mail one letter," when he means "I have a letter to mail." They do not keep a Yale professor of Japanese from translating 'they sell cars' as *zidoosya ourimasu*, when the Japanese say . . . *utte imasu*, nor warn the student that while *hasitte imasu* is equivalent to 'is running,' *itte imasu* may not be equivalent to 'is going' but rather to 'is gone.' Neither our dictionaries nor our grammars prepare the American student for his surprise in finding that the Japanese expression *matte imasu* commonly translates as '*will* be waiting' rather than (what he expects) '*is* waiting.' And what dictionary shares the student's eventual discovery that Japanese *yori* translates not only 'than' but sometimes 'other than' and sometimes 'rather than'?

For the translating *machine*, a dictionary must contain a great deal more information about both languages than is currently available; the translating *student* can get by with a good deal less information, but—directly or indirectly—he too will have to have available much of the same sort of unusually detailed data. The area of greatest weakness in current dictionaries is that of the tough hard problems of syntax in each language, problems thrown into focus by the skewness found in drawing up rules of translation into another language. These are the problems with which we must come to grips in creating new dictionaries, whether we approach them in terms of a generative grammar or a distributional description.

While we are gathering the sort of information on which dictionaries of the future will thrive, there are certain kinds of small improvements we can make on dictionaries that are in being or in prospect. It is in this area that I would like to bring up for discussion a number of thoughts that have occurred to me in working on the problem of translation dictionaries for students.

1. We want to put in *what* the student is likely to look for *where* he is likely to look for it. Our dictionaries of Japanese or Korean, for example, should be expanded to include the shorter inflected forms of common verbs, especially where these involve convergence of different stems and/or homonymy with uninflected forms:

Korean *kanun*, ignored by dictionaries, can be 'X that is going,' the processive modifier from *ka*; 'X that (someone) is grinding,' the processive modifier from *kal-*; or 'X that is slender,' the plain modifier from *kanul-*. In normal Korean orthography, the same sequence can also represent *kan un* (any of several nouns *ka* + the topic particle); and in speech (or misspelling), it can additionally represent *kan un* (any of several nouns *kan* + the topic particle).

Japanese *itte* can be the gerund of *iku* 'goes,' of *iu/yuu* 'says,' or of *iru* 'be needed' or 'enter,' etc.

Japanese dictionaries will tell you that *sita* means 'under' or 'tongue'—they neglect to tell you that it also means 'did' (past of *suru*). They will tell you that *kita* means 'north,' but forget to mention that it also means 'came' (past of *kuru*) and 'put on (clothing for the torso)' (past of *kiru*).

In a somewhat hit-or-miss fashion, our selection of dictionary entries is based on frequency, whether sampled or intuited. Beyond a certain point, each new noun we add has a decreasing usefulness. On the other hand, the inflected forms of common stems, the particles and particle sequences—these words not only have a high frequency but are a recurrent stumbling block to the student. Such forms must be included in our dictionary; we cannot expect the foreign student to have the native speaker's mastery of the grammar.

2. Some bad pennies of everyday conversation are shunned by dictionaries and grammars alike, despite their frequency: connective phrases (*The thing is . . .*), non-fluencies (*uh . . .*), greetings (*Hi there!*), interjections (*uh-huh*, and surprisingly *oh-oh*, despite the fact that *oho!*, beloved of poets, often makes the grade). When you start working in this area, you find some delightful things about your own language: How do you call a dog? My

informants use a bilabial click—which I spell *pskl* —often followed by *here boy!* How do you spell the gasp of sudden fright commonly heard in America (but not in Japan)? My most helpful informant suggested "Novelists use the device *Oh my goodness*" but admitted its inadequacy.

3. We want to boil our material down to essentials. In the interest of conciseness, we should aim at a single translational equivalent whenever possible. If several equivalents are presented, some indication should be given of the context (or kind of context) that would provoke the less expected versions. Our choice of *the* equivalent (or the first equivalent) will be determined primarily by the decision which one is most broadly applicable; it should be the particular equivalent that the student is most likely to need. There are, apparently, two purposes behind the common technique of piling up a group of synonyms in the target language: (1) to suggest to the translator a range of choices; (2) to give a clearer picture of the semantic spectrum of the entry item. But unless you give explicit directions for choosing among the synonyms, the list will be confusing to machine and student alike. And sometimes the uncritical heaping up of near-synonyms is simply an evasion of responsibility on the part of the dictionary maker: unable (or too little informed) to make up his own mind, he shifts the burden of choice to the user of the dictionary. When different translations are provided in order to show clear divergences in meaning, cross references to the appropriate synonyms in the source language are helpful both to the native speaker and to the foreign learner.

4. One indication of context that proves of value for the preceding purpose (showing divergences of meaning), as well as for other less obvious purposes, is to state the specific objects or kinds of objects that a particular transitive verb can take as its goal. This can be done unobtrusively by citing typical objects in parenthesis (in either the source language or the target language) before or after the appropriate translation. It is also desirable to indicate the specific words (or kinds of words) that a modifying word—adjective, adverb, etc.—can modify. This is especially important for intensifiers: the many translations of *very* in another language can be tricky, indeed.

5. Examples of usage are helpful but only when they are *critical*. A single short example made up by a well-trained native speaker to illustrate a specific point is usually far superior to the motley collection of lengthy sentences culled in rote fashion by underpaid "researchers" out of novels and magazines. The purpose of an example is to show you something you would not have realized (or been sure about) from reading the suggested

equivalent. Often the example serves to provide grammatical information in a less explicit (and perhaps more palatable) form than that demanded by, say, a translation machine.

6. Whenever possible, grammatical categories should be equated between the two languages, and each category (or translational device) should be used consistently. In other words, there ought to be an accepted (and expected) translation of major form classes. The reader has a right to expect, for example, that if Japanese verbs are usually translated as English verbs, an adjective will not turn up without some compelling reason. If *kurai*, a Japanese adjective, is translated as 'is dark,' it will be misleading to translate *kumoru*, a Japanese verb, as 'is cloudy'; the appropriate translation is 'gets (becomes) cloudy.'

7. One of the traditions of Western lexicography is to use the so-called "infinitive" form for both the entry heading and the translation of verbs. In English, this produces ungainly phrases of *to* + the unmarked form of the verb. In many parts of the world, verbs are usually entered under the plain present (or non-past) form, and it is misleading to translate such headings with English *to* + constructions. Japanese *suru* does not mean 'to do'; it means '(someone) does' or 'will do.' The one advantage of the *to* + translation is that it clearly marks the word as a verb, and in English many verb forms are homonymous with nouns; simply dropping the *to* (as many dictionaries and word lists do) often adds to the student's immediate confusion when he locates an equivalent. By using the third person singular (the marked form of the present), we do not avoid noun homonymy entirely; *forms* could be the plural of *a form*. But if you expect the translation of nouns and verbs alike to be singular whenever possible, there is seldom much danger of confusion. And there is an advantage to a translation like 'does' rather than 'to do': the verb is all ready to go into a sentence and do much the same work that the Japanese verb does. This is why we like to translate the adjectives of Japanese and Korean, and those of Chinese, not by the bare English adjective ('good,' 'tall,' 'red') but by *is* + the adjective ('is good,' 'is tall,' 'is red').

8. The little word *it* is very handy in English equivalents. When the source language has two verbs, transitive and intransitive, that correspond to a single English form, we can show the difference most effectively (both for ready intake and for permanent memory) by something like this:

    aku   'it opens'
    akeru 'opens it'

We need not mark *all* transitive and intransitive verbs in this way, only those pairs that cause confusion in the translation.

By translating the so-called copula of languages like Japanese (*da/desu*, etc.), Korean (*ita*), and Chinese (*shyh*) as 'it is,' rather than just 'is,' we prepare the student for sentences like *Watasi wa Maru-biru desu* which does not translate 'I am the Marunouchi Building!' (The closest equivalent is 'As for me, it is the M. B.' Note that *Are wa Maru-biru desu* 'As for it/him/her, it is the M. B.' in the 'it' sense can mean either 'It is the M. B.' or 'It is in the M. B.')

9. To show translational syntax complications in an unobtrusive fashion, we can either use real, but succinct, examples or resort to a form of light-weight algebra (A *shows* X to B), rather than clutter up space with clumsy frames like *somebody shows something to somebody else* or the eyesore *sbd shows sthg. to sbd.*

10. Required prepositions (or postpositions) should be clearly marked. If the foreign verb corresponds to English verb + preposition, the English phrase should be given as a unit:

sagasu   'looks for'

But we will want some way to distinguish English verb transitive + adverb from verb + preposition (+ prepositional object), e.g.:

ireru   'puts (in); inserts'
haku   'puts (footwear, trousers) on'

11. Whenever possible, it should be clear from the translation what the subjects and objects of the entry verb might be. If there is a problem of literal versus free translation, I favor giving the literal translation first, so that the student gets the proper syntactic orientation immediately:

iru   'is needed': *A ni/wa X ga* . . . 'A needs X.'

12. It is useful to include notes on "zero" elements in the translation situation—those (1) required, (2) preferred, and (3) optional:

(E-J) *the* USUALLY UNTRANSLATED; SOMETIMES = 'that'
a USUALLY UNTRANSLATED; SOMETIMES = 'one'
(J-E) *san* 'Mr' . . . (= *si*), 'Miss' . . . (= *san no ozyoosan*;
= *zyosj*), 'Mrs' . . . (= *san no okusan*);

'the person from' (AFTER PLACE NAME);
BETTER NOT TRANSLATED (AFTER
GIVEN NAME OR JOB NAME).

Sometimes, it is convenient to set up conventional translation devices; instead of marking some words Honorific and others Humble, you may want to make a practice of translating the Honorific nouns '(your) esteemed ...' and the Humble nouns '(my) humble ...,' thus preserving the full flavor of the original at the expense of an exaggerated English.

13. Should we include an article with each English noun? From the point of view of the English speaker, the article is useful only when it tells something about the foreign word (e.g., whether it is a count-noun or mass-noun when these are homophones in English). Some European dictionaries put in the definite article for all nouns indiscriminately, influenced by German and French dictionaries (where the article is a concise way of noting gender). It seems clumsy and even ludicrous to see every noun in an English version of a German picture dictionary marked 'the boot,' 'the stirrup,' 'the harness,' 'the bit,' etc., with the heavy foot everywhere in evidence.

14. We ought to include information on the appropriate classifier for nouns in languages with classificatory genders. But in modern Chinese, Korean, and Japanese (in contrast with Vietnamese and Thai), it is possible to ignore the vast majority of the count-nouns, since specific classifiers are used for only a small minority of them. Then the dictionary user must be sure that he is to be alerted whenever a specific classifier is preferred, optional, or obligatory.

PROBLEMS IN EDITING COMMERCIAL MONOLINGUAL DICTIONARIES

C. L. Barnhart
Reference Books

THIS PAPER DEALS WITH SOME OF THE EDITORIAL problems in the production of commercial monolingual English dictionaries. Such dictionaries, out of necessity, are of a popular nature because they must depend for their existence upon widespread acceptance by the general public. The publisher usually determines the audience for which he wishes to make a book. His determination of the market he would like to reach depends upon the type of his previous publications. His salesmen are probably trained to reach only one type of market, and ability to sell in that particular market conditions to a great extent the type of dictionary to be made. A publisher of schoolbooks will probably start with a school dictionary, a publisher of trade books with a college dictionary.

It is the function of a popular dictionary to answer the questions that the user of the dictionary asks, and dictionaries on the commercial market will be successful in proportion to the extent to which they answer these questions of the buyer. This is the basis on which the editor must determine the type of information to include. The editor's very first concern, therefore, must be to determine the probable buyer of a particular book. The amount of information that the editor can give is limited by the price that the buyer will pay for a dictionary in a particular market; his editorial judgment is always limited by the space available. All of these factors must be considered in order for the commercial editor to produce a single dictionary or a series of dictionaries that will enable him to stay in business.

To what extent, then, can the editor answer the questions of any buyer about any word of the English language? This depends to some extent upon the number of words in actual use in the literature (reading matter) of today and in the literature of the past that is widely read and studied today. For the popular dictionary tends to be a dictionary of the standard language and is concerned with slang and various specialized vocabularies only so far as they may appear in current newspapers, magazines, and books.

Some years ago, Professor Robert L. Ramsay, of the University of Missouri, estimated the size of the working vocabulary of the English language—the words which any literate person may encounter and about which he may have questions dealing with spelling, pronunciation, meaning, idiomatic use, synonyms, levels of usage, and origin—to be around 250,000 active words.

The usual desk dictionary of educated people in the United States is a college dictionary containing 120,000 to 150,000 of these words. Unabridged dictionaries may contain as many as 500,000 words and one-volume or two-volume dictionaries may contain 200,000 or 250,000 words but they are priced so high that there is little bookstore market for them. The ordinary college dictionary will contain somewhere between 14,000,000 and 17,000,000 characters. Since there are five-and-a-half characters to the average word, a college dictionary will contain some three million running words. If the editor attempted to include the complete active vocabulary, he would have to use 500,000 or more words simply to list the entries and the pronunciations. He would have only ten words to define the entry, provide illustrative sentences and phrases, give the etymology, and list synonyms and antonyms. Since there are approximately twice as many meanings as entries put in college dictionaries, this would reduce the amount of space for each definition to about four words a definition and leave only two words for illustrative phrases, etymologies, synonym studies, and so forth. This is obviously an impossible situation. The editors of all college dictionaries are forced, then, to make a selection of the terms which they put in their dictionaries.

Which 125,000–150,000 words should be entered, and how should they be treated? This selection of material to be included depends upon the judgment of the editor as to the type of user of his book and the kind and level of information that the user will want. One important market for the college dictionary is the freshman composition market. In 1955, I circulated 108 questionnaires in 99 colleges in 27 states (5 eastern, 8 southern, and 14 western) reporting on the use of the dictionary by some 56,000 students. The teachers were asked to rate six types of information commonly given in college dictionaries according to their importance to the college freshman. Their replies indicate that the college freshman uses his dictionary most frequently for meaning and almost as frequently for spelling. Pronunciation is third with synonym studies and lists, usage notes, and etymologies far behind.

The selection of the 125,000–150,000 terms to be included depends to some extent upon the importance the editor assigns to the six types of information given. An editor of a college dictionary who emphasizes the importance of meaning may consider the omission of all or part of the meanings of such "easy" words as *good* or *bad* or *with*. An editor interested in spelling may give more irregular inflected forms. One interested in usage may omit spellings of irregular inflected forms and undefined run-on entries such as *absolutely* or *badness*. A college dictionary editor interested in pronunciation may give more variant pronunciations than one primarily interested in meaning. The selection of material to be included should depend upon the interests and needs of the buyer and not upon the specialized interest of the editor. For example, it is possibly an editorial mistake to include rare Scotticisms, as William Allen Neilson did in the last *Webster's Second New International Dictionary* (1934), for they take up at least some of the space of the 70,000 compounds Tom Knott crossed out.

If the interest of the buyer is a primary consideration, certainly spelling would require major consideration, for spelling is one of the principal problems of the users of dictionaries and one of the principal reasons for buying dictionaries. What are the spelling difficulties that most people encounter? Where the difficulty in spelling is in the middle or end of a root word, it is easy to verify the spelling in almost any dictionary. The distinction in spelling between *capital* and *Capitol* or between *principal* and *principle* is easy to find. Treatment of inflected forms (*antagonize, antagonized, antagonizing; travel, traveled,* or *travelled,* and *traveling* or *travelling*) in which the inflected form is not a simple root + a suffix is handled differently by different dictionaries. If the editor feels that the average buyer of the dictionary knows the rules for dropping *e* or doubling of the consonant when *-ed* and *-ing* is added, he will not list these inflected forms.

One of the principal spelling difficulties with derivative or run-on entries is the recognition of the root form. Derivative words in which the root form is clearly recognized (such as *absolutely* or *resolutely*) might well be run-ons unless there is a meaning or pronunciation problem as there is for *absolutely*. Of the four major college dictionaries on the market, one omits the entry entirely, two others enter it as a run-on with pronunciation, and the fourth enters, pronounces, and defines it. *Resolutely* is not entered in one, is spelled out in full as a run-on after *resolute* in two and is entered as a *-ly* run-on in the fourth. Those derivative entries that have some change in the root (e.g., *arbitrarily, atomization, archaistic*)—often throwing them out of alphabetical order or making it hard to recognize the root—must either be put in the alphabetical list in the proper place or run-on. To do this, however, takes a certain amount of space that cannot be used in defining some rare and difficult word. In this conflict between the user of the dictionary for spelling and the one who uses it for the meaning of hard words, the editor must make a choice unless he has enough space to include both types of information. His first problem, then, is to choose whether he will give more importance to information about spelling or about meaning. Since meaning difficulty outranks all other uses of the dictionary in importance so far as college freshmen are concerned, the editor usually compromises and enters derivatives without meaning difficulty but with simple spelling or pronunciation difficulty as run-ons instead of as main entries. *Arbitrarily* is a main entry in one of the four college dictionaries and a run-on in the other three; *atomization* is omitted in two of the college dictionaries and given as a run-on in the other two; *archaistic* is run-on in two of the college dictionaries and defined in the other two. If you are making a dictionary for college freshmen or for secretaries, the dictionary that enters most forms in their proper alphabetical place would be most useful to the buyer.

Having made a fundamental decision whether to define all entries or to have run-ons, the editor is in a position to select the 125,000–150,000 entries to be included in his dictionary. Nearly all college dictionaries agree close to 90 percent of the time upon the choice of words to be entered and differ largely in the number of abbreviations, geographical names, and biographical names to be included. All include all types of entries but differ markedly in the treatment of the basic vocabulary, the inclusion of idioms, the fullness of the definitions of scientific and technical terms, the illustrative sentences, phrases, and quotations used, the type of etymology given, and so forth. In spite of the fact that the real difference of most dictionaries lies in the description of the words entered, there are a few important differences that each editor must face in the selection of entries.

The agreement among the editors of college dictionaries on a basic, common vocabulary of 100,000 terms is due to the fact that we have such a rich storehouse of material from which to choose. The history of English words and meanings is probably fuller than that in any other language. The commercial dictionary editor can turn to the big *Oxford English Dictionary*

(1933; henceforth *OED*), to the ten-volume *Century Dictionary* (1895), to the *Dictionary of American English* (1938–44), and to the *Dictionary of Americanisms* (1951) for scholarly information. Quotations for each important sense are abundantly supplied in these dictionaries. When I was corresponding with the compiler of the Hungarian–English dictionary (Országh 1953), Professor Ladislas Országh, he stated that they had nothing comparable to the *OED* on which to draw. He had to collect quotations in order to proceed with his book; there was no historical dictionary of the Hungarian language. All dictionary makers owe a great debt to the *OED* and they owe a similar debt to the big ten-volume *Century* prepared by one of the great linguists of the nineteenth century, William Dwight Whitney, who produced a superb descriptive dictionary of the English language and was the first to give adequate treatment to scientific terminology.

Probably no proper survey of the thousands of pages in the *OED* and the *Century* (there are over 8,000 pages in three columns in this book alone) has ever been made. These mines of information can be read and studied again and again. On my first high-school dictionary, a staff of ten editors spent over five years combing the *OED*. Out of this mass of material, we selected the meanings that were to be included in our high-school dictionary. We were aided in this task with a semantic count which Dr. E. L. Thorndike had made of current standard literature that assigned meanings to some 5,000,000 words in running context. In this fashion, we could determine the order in which the meanings of words were used in the current English language in material ranging from children's books to the *Britannica* and through technical literature. This count was of enormous importance in verifying editorial judgment in collecting definitions. In Table I, I have given the semantic count for the word *create* as a sample of the usefulness of this count. Many semantic counts should be made, but evidence, such as a typical quotation for each meaning, should also be provided. Counts are one criterion for selecting meanings (and entries), but more data is needed.

Commercial dictionary editing, however, that depends only upon scholarly dictionaries is out-of-date because the language recorded is out-of-date. The record of English from 1900 to the present should be sampled. In Table II is a sample of the books in a long-time reading project of standard literature to remedy this lack of a modern record. In order to meet the needs of modern users of the college dictionary, it is necessary to sample the reading of the public to which you address your book. If a word or meaning occurs in several different sources over a wide range of magazines and books during a considerable period of time, such a word or meaning may be worth considering for inclusion in a current, college dictionary. Obviously, we must get a wide enough sampling to help the editor decide which words and meanings are important enough to include in a college dictionary. In reading for this purpose, we read for words and meanings normally in an unabridged dictionary but not in current college dictionaries, as well as for new words and meanings making their way into the language. Our selection of new words and meanings depends upon the extent and accuracy of our sampling. Too large a sampling is expensive and serves no purpose if it duplicates information already existing in the *OED*, the *Century*, the *Dictionary of Americanisms*, and the *Dictionary of American English*. Our problem is to add to that material which has been compiled before us. With the commercial resources that we have at hand we need to sample newspapers, popular magazines, literary magazines, and technical magazines, and to keep at this sampling systematically over a period of years. This is expensive. Every quotation that reaches my files costs approximately 30 cents. When one considers the vast amount of printed matter, probably no sampling would be adequate with fewer than 50,000 quotations a year; 100,000 quotations would be a more adequate sampling. Perhaps reading of such scientific magazines as *Scientific American*, *Science News-Letter*, and *New Scientist*, and such newspapers as the *Wall Street Journal*, the *Manchester Guardian*, and the *New York Times*, and such general magazines as *Harper's*, the *Atlantic Monthly*, the *Saturday Review*, and the *Listener* will give a fairly good picture of the magazine and newspaper reading of educated people. Reading various annuals and yearbooks, as well as a number of important current novels and books, will give an adequate basis for the selection of new definitions and entries. In all reading, it is important to sample both British and American usage. See Table II for a partial sample of the standard literature that could be read to bring the record of standard English up to date.

Adequate sampling, then, is one of the editor's major considerations, and he can accomplish this with a continuing group of readers who are aware of what is already in the file. A balanced quotation file of perhaps half a million modern quotations that supplements the file of the *OED*, the *Century*, and the *Dictionary of Americanisms* would be adequate to give authority to the selection of new material. See Table III for a sampling of new words and meanings which results from such a reading.

Table 1

CREATE	524/29	
create, ppl. a.		
	1. ppl. a. *created*. no occ.	
008/2	2. as adj. *arch*.	
	1477 Norton *Ord. Alch.* v. in Ashm. (1652) 62: A create perfection.	
create, v.		
055/11	3. *trans.* Said of the divine agent: To bring into being, etc.	
006/3	3b. with complemental extension.	
574/24	4a. *gen.* To make, form, constitute, or bring into legal existence, etc.	
011/4	4b. *absol.* 1775 Sheridan *Rivals* Pref.: The imagination . . . becomes suspicious of its offspring, etc.	
004/2	4c. Of an actor: To be the first to represent (a part or role), etc.	
078/6	5. To constitute (a personage of rank or dignity), etc.	
256/24	6. To cause, occasion, produce, give rise to (a condition or set of circumstances).	
created, ppl. a.		
002/1	7. Brought into being by an agent or cause, esp. a. Made or formed by the divine power.	
	7b. Constituted of a certain dignity or rank.	
creating, vbl. sb.		
002/1	8. The action of the verb, *create*.	
creating, ppl. a.		
002/1	9. That creates.	

The count is to be read as follows: *create* occurred 524 times in 29 different types of reading. Eight thousandths of these occurrences in two different types of material were for the second meaning of *create*, ppl. a; fifty-five thousandths in eleven different types of material were for the third meaning of *create*, v. Ability to select important meanings as indicated by a semantic count makes it possible for a commercial publisher to use the *OED* in making a dictionary.

To select 125,000–150,000 terms to include in a college dictionary means combing the standard scholarly sources such as the *OED*, *Century*, and the two American dictionaries, the using of the counts, and accumulating a modern quotation file which will supplement and amplify the information

Table 2

	Author	Title	Date	Type	Nation
54.	Edman, Irwin	*Philosopher's Holiday***	1938	Essay	Amer.
55.	Eliot, T. S.	*For Lancelot Andrewes****	1928	Essay	Amer.
		*The Sacred Wood****	1920	Essay	Amer.
56.	Faulkner, Wm.	*The Hamlet****	1940	Novel	Amer.
		*Sanctuary***	1931	Novel	Amer.
57.	Fisher, Vardis	*No Villain Need Be**	1936	Novel	Amer.
58.	Fitzgerald, F. S. K.	*Tender Is the Night***	1934	Novel	Amer.
		*The Crack-up***	1945	Novel	Amer.
59.	Ford Madox Ford	*No More Parades***	1925	Novel	Brit.
60.	Forster, E. M.	*Howard's End****	1910	Novel	Brit.
		*Abinger Harvest***	1936	Essay	Brit.
61.	Waldo, Frank	*City Block**	1922	Novel	Amer.
62.	Galsworthy, J.	*The Man of Property**	1906	Novel	Brit.
63.	Garland, Hamlin	*A Son of the Middle Border***	1917	Novel	Amer.
64.	Gerould, Katherine F.	*Conquistador***	1923	Novel	Amer.
65.	Glasgow, Ellen	*They Stooped to Folly*	1929	Novel	Amer.
66.	Greene, Graham	*The Labarynthine Ways***	1940	Novel	Brit.
		*The Heart of the Matter****	1948	Novel	Brit.
67.	Hammett, Dashiell	*The Maltese Falcon**	1930	Novel	Amer.
68.	Hand, Learned	*The Spirit of Liberty***	- - - -	Essay	Amer.
69.	Hemingway, Ernest	*Green Hills of Africa***	1935	Essay	Amer.
		*Death in the Afternoon***	1932	Essay	Amer.

Code : Essential***
Desirable**
Possible*

that has been collected in the past. This work can only be done by a well-trained staff over a period of years.

However, an editor with this trained staff, a modern quotation file, and the backing of a publisher who seeks a particular market must make numerous policy decisions involving a great many areas of linguistic knowledge. No single editor can have the necessary knowledge to formulate the policy in matters of pronunciation, etymology, definition, and levels of usage, but one way of acquiring trustworthy advice is to form an editorial advisory

Table 3

	New Word or New Meaning	No. of Quotes
Not added WU o	**abbatoir**, *n.*	
	2. (figuratively) a place of physical punishment, as of a boxing or wrestling ring, bull-fighting arena, etc.: *two heavyweights in an abattoir.*	2
WU o	**abc** or **ABC weapons**,	
	atomic, bacteriological, or chemical devices or substances, as instruments of war.	3
Not added WU o	**abegging**, *adv.*	
	in an unwanted or overlooked condition: *Used books often go abegging.*	1
Not added WU o	**Abell/comet**,	
	a new comet sighted (1953) in the range of the pole star (named after its discoverer, George Abell).	1
Not added WU o	**Abenlens**, *n.*	
	a race of Pygmies of the Philippines.	2
WU +	**ablare**, *adj.*	
	noisy; raucus.—*adv.* full of noise.	0
WU o	**ablative**, *adj.*	
	2. *Especially British.* of, having to do with, or designating a material that will accomplish or permit ablation.	1
WU o	**ablation**, *n.*	
	3. *Aerospace. a.* the removal or carrying away of heat by melting or vaporization.	3
	b. the removal of the nose cone of a ballistic missile by burning and falling away when the missile reenters the atmosphere.	
WU o	**ab/natura**,	
	Latin. unnatural.	1
WU o	**aboard**, *adj.*	
	5. *Baseball.* on base: *to hit a double with three runners aboard.*	2

	New Word or New Meaning	No. of Quotes
WU o	**A-boiler**, *n.*	
	a boiler for which the heat is generated by an atomic reactor.	1
WU o	**about-towner**, *n.*	
	a man or woman who frequents the fashionable night clubs, the theaters, etc., of the city.	1
WU +	**accession/number**,	
	the number given to a book, periodical, etc., when it is entered in an accession book.	0
WU o	**access/time**	
	The time required for an electronic computer to respond to a request for stored data.	5
Not added WU +	**accidental**, *n.*	
	2. the accidental, that which occurs by accident or is developed without plan or design: *The freedom of science is so important . . . because it allows the accidental to occur* (Bulletin of the Atomic Scientists, 1955).	1
Not added WU o	**accident-tout**, *n.*	
	British Slang. . . . *an ambulance-chaser is an accident-tout* (*London Journal*, 1952).	1
WU o	**accordionize**, *v.t.*	
	U.S. Informal. To compress; condense.	2
WU o	**ace**, *n.*	
	7. aces (or **aces-high**) **with**, *U. S. Slang.* highly regarded by: *He's aces with me.*	1
WU o	**aces**, *v.t.*	
	U.S. **2.** *Informal.* to achieve a high mark in: *He aced the examination.*	1
Not added WU o	**Achhut**, *n.*	
	(in India) an untouchable.	1

Table 3 (Cont).

	New Word or New Meaning	No. of Quotes
WU +	**achy**, *adj.*	
	Informal. full of aches.	1
WU +	**acneform**, *adj.*	
	resembling acne.	0
WU o	**acrylic/fiber,**	
	any of various synthetic textile fibers produced from acrylonitrile,	8
	as Acrilan, Dynel, and Orlon.	
WU o	**act**, *n.*	
	get into the act, *Informal.* to do what is currently fashionable, expedient, etc., to do.	3
WU o	**actual**, *n.*	
	a motion picture, radio, or television program based upon real events;	2
	documentary.	
WU o	**add-on**, *n., adj.*	
	n. an added sum, quantity, item, etc.	1
	adj. that may be added, accessory.	1
WU o	**adless**, *adj.*	
	U.S. Informal. without advertising.	2
WU +	**adolesce**, *v.i.*	
	1. to be or become adolescent. 2. to behave like an adolescent.	1
WU +	**adoral**, *adj., n.*	
WU adj. 2 o	*Anatomy.*—1. near or adjacent to the mouth: *adoral cilia.*	1
	2. having a mouth: *an adoral organ.*—*n.* an adoral part or function.	
WU o	**adultly**, *adv.*	
	in the manner of an adult; maturely: . . . *two small, adultly dressed boys* . . . (*New Yorker*, 1957).	1
WU +	**advisee**, *n.*	
	1. a person who is advised. 2. *Education*, especially *U.S.* a student assigned to an adviser.	1

	New Word or New Meaning	No. of Quotes
WU o	**adwoman**, *n.*	
	U.S. Informal. a woman engaged in the business of advertising.	2
WU o	**aelurophile**, *n.*	
	a person who likes cats.	1
WU +	**aelurophobia**, *n.*	
	a morbid fear or hatred of cats.	1
WU o	**aerobee**, *n.*	
	any of several rockets used for exploring the upper atmosphere, of which an advanced version is able to attain an altitude of 300 miles.	11
WU +	**aerophilately**, *n.*	
Run-on WU +	the branch of philately that specializes in air-mail stamps.	1
	aerophilatelist, *n.*	1 (run-on)
WU o	**affinal**, *adj., n.*	
	1. having a common origin or source.	1 *adj.*
	2. related by marriage.—*n.* a relative by marriage; kinsman.	1 *n.*
WU +	**affronted**, *adj.*	
	offended; slighted; insulted.	1
WU o	**Afrika/Korps**,	
	a specially trained and equipped unit of the German army in World War II that served in northern Africa under Field Marshal Erwin Rommel.	4
WU o	**à/froid**,	
	French. without prejudice or passion; calmly and coldly: . . . examined *à froid, the thing appears to make a lot of sense* (*New Yorker*, 1955).	1
WU o	**afterhours**, *adj.*	
	that takes place or is in effect after the usual time: *afterhours conferences, afterhours recreation.*—*adv.* after the appointed time: *we do not serve afterhours.*	21 *adj.*
		3 *adv.*

committee. The function of a committee is to supplement the experience, training, and information of the editor; it does not do the work of special editors or supervise or direct the work that is done. Such a committee should have members who represent various points of view, and more than one scholar should represent any particular field such as etymology, pronunciation, or usage. Curiously enough, specialists in one particular field often give very useful suggestions in nonrelated fields. A large committee, representing many points of view, is one of the most useful adjuncts to an editor in framing policies. Otherwise, policies are very likely to be decided in the seeming commercial interest of the publisher or limited by the narrowness of the editor. Such a committee, however, cannot function by majority vote. To vote democratically about matters of information is not the way to settle an intellectual problem. Some one person, in this case, the editor, must have the power of final decision and this power of final decision should be made on the side of the agreed-upon knowledge of the experts. The function of a general reference book is to make available to the general public in understandable language the knowledge upon which scholars and specialists are agreed. It is the function of the editorial advisory committee to remind the editor of this agreed-upon knowledge. The editor must be able to evaluate his committee and to know when to take the advice of a particular scholar and when not to. The editorial advisory committee makes it possible for the editor to set policies which are in accordance with the advances in knowledge of the day.

What are some of the important policies that an editorial advisory committee, the editor, and his staff must consider? One of the most pressing of these and one that occupies a great deal of time and attention is pronunciation. Opinions on pronunciations are likely to vary violently according to the experience and background of the person who holds them. Two great scholars, Leonard Bloomfield and Harry Morgan Ayres, said that the pronunciation key was of no importance whatsoever; they felt that any key that used symbols consistently was adequate. Other scholars, such as the late Miles Hanley, feel that the only key to be used is the International Phonetic Alphabet or some adaptation of it. Others now hold out for a Trager–Smith key as the only defensible key from a theoretical point of view. Is there one key suitable for all types of transcription—for the scholar, for the worker on a linguistic atlas, for the teacher of speech, for the student of linguistics, for a newspaper reader, for the high-school graduate, for the fourth grade child? There are four possible keys—a textbook key using diacritics on letters of the alphabet, the IPA key using few diacritics and based on continental speech habits, a Smith–Trager key that analyzes the make-up of sounds, and a newspaper key that uses familiar letters of the alphabet to respell a word. See Table IV below for the equivalent symbols for the vowels in these keys. Which of these different kinds of keys are suitable for a college dictionary? This central problem of a key must be faced; and it is more difficult when there is a series of dictionaries involved than when there is only one dictionary.

By what standards should we select a key? Should it fit the speech habits of the largest body of users of the dictionary? Must the symbols be easily written and easily read? Should there be only one symbol for each sound? Since the letters of the alphabet are directions to say sounds, which of various letters of the alphabet can be used, and which should be modified either by substituting some other letter from some other alphabet or by using some kind of diacritic or special symbol? If some form of IPA is to be used, what form—that by Daniel Jones (1917) or that used by Kenyon and Knott (1944)? Is the key to be phonetic or phonemic? The choice of a pronunciation key is of no great importance in a scholarly dictionary, since scholars are trained to read many keys, but a commercial man bets his economic life on ideas that are advanced by linguists. The editor has to have some assurance that the principles on which he bases his key are going to stay alive. The editor must further believe that the pronunciation key chosen permits an accurate statement of the pronunciations given and is, once learned, simple to use.

Another important problem the editorial committee must consider is the order of definitions. Should the historical order be followed, or should the dictionary be a descriptive dictionary of the current English language and start with the central or core meaning today? If we decide upon the historical method, how are we going to determine the dates of each meaning? Must we rely upon the *OED* and the *Dictionary of American English* or do we have additional information that we can turn to in our own files to verify dates? What attempt will be made to change the order of the definitions as dates in the *OED* and the *Dictionary of American English* are corrected by new information? If we have the central or core meaning as the basis of organization, how are we to determine the central or core meaning? Are there any semantic counts that would show what is commonest today? (See Table I showing the frequency of the meanings of *create*.) Would the frequency of the modern quotations give some clue?

Are the definitions to be written on the same level, or is the editor to make some effort to determine what type of person will look up a particular word or meaning and then frame definitions in language suitable for the person looking them up?

What is to be done with scientific entries, particularly the names of plants and animals? Is the technical name to be given or is it to be excluded as useless and the space devoted to other more important matters? What is to be the differentiation in the treatment of words like *get*, *with*, and so forth, as over against a word like *aristocracy*? When are illustrative sentences to be used? To what degree are idioms to be covered? See Table V showing the distribution of 30 possible idioms in three college-level dictionaries priced at five dollars and four desk-level dictionaries priced around three dollars. Should illustrative sentences be made up, should they be from modern sources, or should they always be quotations of some author? If the latter is given, should chapter and verse be cited in a book for general reference? How much space should be devoted to illustrative sentences? College dictionaries have devoted from 54 to 61 per cent of their space to definitions and from .7 to 1.3 per cent to illustrative sentences and phrases. Should more space be devoted to illustrative sentences and less to definitions?

How are various levels of usage to be labeled? Should the spoken vocabulary be labeled *Colloq.*? Should the formal vocabulary be labeled *Literary*? How can the uniqueness of a spoken word and a formal written word be established? How should we distinguish between informal spoken and informal written? Or should the distinction be between formal and informal?

Should the current dialects of English be recorded and to what extent? Should we include only those dialectal words that occur in newspapers, magazines, and novels? To what extent should we include South African, Anglo-Indian, and Australian words? What words in different parts of the United States should be included? What about Briticisms? Is *Briticism* a good restrictive label or should we say, *in England*? So, also, should we use *in India* instead of *Anglo-Indian*?

When is a word or meaning archaic and when is it obsolete? Is a word archaic when it is used only to give an old-fashioned flavor to writing? Can we define *obsolete* as a word that is not used at all? What happens if an obsolete word is revived, say, by Spenser, Scott, or Robert Graves, and becomes current for a while among literary people? Is it then an obsolete word or an

Table 4

Example Word	Textbook Key	A "K + K" System	A "S-T" System	Newspaper Key
hat	(a)	[æ]	/æ/	a
age	(ā)	[e]	/ey/	ay as in *day*; aCe as in *date*
care	(âr)	[ɛr]	/ehr/	are as in *care*; air as in *air, fair*
father	(ä)	[ɑ]	/ah/	ah as in *calm*
let	(e)	[ɛ]	/e/	e
equal	(ē)	[i]	/iy/	ee as in *bee, meet*
term (stressed)	(ėr)	[3´]	/ər/	ur as in *fur*
other (unstressed) (ər)	[ə]	/ər/	er	
it	(i)	[I]	/i/	i
ice	(ī)	[aI]	/ay/	igh as in *sigh, sight*; ie as in *tie*; iCe as in *mine*; y as in *my*; ye as in *dye*
hot	(o)	[ɑ]	/a/	o
open	(ō)	[o]	/ow/	o as in *go*; oe as in *toe*; oh as in *oh*; oCe as in *poke*; oa as in *boat*
order	(ô)	[ɔ]	/oh/	o as in *for*; aw as in *law*
oil	(oi)	[ɔI]	/oy/	oi
house	(ou)	[au]	/aw/	ou as in *out*; ow as in *now*
cup	(u)	[ʌ]	/ə/	u
full	(u̇)	[ʊ]	/u/	oo as in *book*
rule	(ü)	[u]	/uw/	oo as in *food*
use	(ū)	[ju]	/yuw/	ew as in *few, pew, mew*
about	(ə)	[ə]	/ə/ or /i/	u in unstressed closed syllables
taken (unstressed) open pencil lemon circus				uh in unstressed syllables

archaic word? The same problem, incidentally, arises in dialect words. Of what value is the label *poetic*? Does a poetic language exist?

Below are 30 idiomatic expressions (e.g., *taken aback, abide by*, etc.) in a combined list from seven different dictionaries ranging from college dictionaries at $5 or $6 to desk dictionaries. These idiomatic expressions are phrases or expressions that cannot be understood from the meanings of the words which combine to form them; they deserve special attention in a dictionary.

I have listed some of the policy problems of pronunciation, meaning, and levels of usage so that you may have some idea of the problems that could be submitted to an advisory committee. The process of submitting problems to the committee is illustrated by a questionnaire on derogatory words. Several questions are asked about a list of words which are often used to convey an unfriendly attitude toward or opinion of some person, class, or group of persons. The words included are *Canuck, Chinaman, Chink, dago, frog, greaser, guinea, hunky, Jap, kike, limey, mammy, mick, nigger, polack, Shylock, spik, wop*, and *yid*. The advisors are first asked to indicate their judgment on the present status of the words under one of three headings: "Always unfriendly, a 'fighting' word"; "Likely to be unfriendly"; or "Relatively innocuous."

The second question concerns the exclusion of derogatory words ("Always unfriendly") and words which may be derogatory ("Likely to be unfriendly") from school dictionaries at different levels, i.e., whether they should be excluded from all school dictionaries, or whether they should be excluded only from those used up to the sixth grade, in junior high school, or in high school. Those advisors who suggest exclusion of any words at the school level are asked to check the words they would exclude from college-level dictionaries.

For terms which they think should be included, the advisors are asked to suggest a qualifying or restrictive label. A list of typical restrictions used in dictionaries is attached to the questionnaire for help in framing the labels:

> Linguistic labels: (1) *Pop.* (= popular usage); (2) *Colloq.*; (3) *Slang*; (4) *Loosely*; (5) *Local*; (6) *In the S United States*; (7) *Americanism, Southern*; (8) *Esp. in Southern States.*
> Social labels: (1) *Unfriendly use*; (2) *Used in an unfriendly way*; (3) *In discourteous use*; (4) *An objectionable usage*; (5) *Offensive*; (7) *Originally a corrupted form of speech; now generally coarse, always offensive*; (8) *Opprobrious use*; (9) *A derogatory term*; (10) *Derogatory*; (11) *Derogatory use*; (12) *Usually*

Table 5

		Coll. 1	Coll. 2	Coll. 3	Desk 1	Desk 2	Desk 3	Desk 4
1.	from A to Z	+	−	−	−	−		−
2.	taken aback	+	+	+	+	+	+	+
3.	in abeyance	+	+	−	+	−	+	−
4.	abide by	+	+	+	+	+	+	−
5.	all aboard	−	−	−	+	−	−	−
6.	abreast of or with	+	−	−	+	−	+	−
7.	in the abstract	+	+	+	+	−	−	−
8.	accessible to	+	+	+	+	−	−	−
9.	of one's own accord	+	+	+	+	+	+	−
10.	with one accord	−	−	−	+	−	−	−
11.	according to	+	+	+	+	+	+	+
12.	according as	+	+	+	+	+	+	−
13.	call to account	−	−	−	+	−	−	−
14.	on account	−	−	−	+	−	−	−
15.	on account of	+	+	−	+	+	−	−
16.	take account of	−	−	−	+	−	−	−
17.	take into account	+	−	−	+	−	−	−
18.	turn to account	−	−	−	−	−	+	−
19.	account for	+	+	+	+	+	−	−
20.	accredit with	+	−	−	+	+	−	−
21.	within an ace	+	−	+	−	+	+	−
22.	be acquainted with	+	+	−	+	+	−	−
23.	acquit oneself	+	+	+	+	+	+	−
24.	come across	+	−	+	+	−	−	−
25.	act on or upon	+	+	−	+	−	−	−
26.	act as	−	+	−	+	−	−	−
27.	act for	+	−	−	+	+	+	−
28.	act up	−	−	−	+	−	−	−
29.	take action	+	−	−	+	−	−	−
30.	in addition to	+	−	−	+	−	+	−
	TOTALS	22	14	11	27	12	12	2

derogatory; (13) *Used chiefly in contempt*; (14) *Often used familiarly, now chiefly contemptuous*; (15) *Hostile and contemptuous term*; (16) *A hostile and contemptuous term*; (17) *A shortened form often expressing contempt, hostility, etc.*; (18) *A term of contempt or derision*; (19) *Vulgar term of prejudice and contempt*; (20) *Now a vulgar usage*; (21) *A vulgar, offensive term of contempt, as used by Negrophobes*; (22) *Vulgar term indicating a contemptuous or patronizing attitude*; (23).*Vulgar, offensive term of hostility and contempt, as used by anti-Semites.*

When the questionnaires are returned, the opinions are collected, sifted, analyzed, collated, and often returned to the members of the committee to be reviewed a second time. Finally, a decision is made by the editor.

Once the editor and his committee have settled on the policies for the dictionary, the editor then has the problem of combing the vast amounts of information available to him, selecting it, arranging it, and preparing it for publication. Usually, an office staff prepares the copy for the dictionary, in order that everything included may be adjusted to the space that we have and a proper balance between the various types of information presented may be maintained. This involves people who are highly skilled in the art of abstracting, careful and judicious in their judgments, and capable of writing good clear English. Even etymologies and pronunciations are best prepared by a staff.

Assuming that the staff has looked carefully through secondary sources and followed the policies of the editorial advisory committee as set by the editor, there is the problem of checking the accuracy of the facts given in the dictionary. No dictionary should be content to merely abstract secondary sources. There are a great many fields of knowledge. It is very hard to conceive of a dictionary for general use being prepared by a staff inside an office without any special checks of accuracy made by an outside staff. Nowhere is this principle of outside checking more important than in the handling of scientific material. The names of plants and animals, the terms in chemistry, physics, aeronautics, electronics, and so forth should be checked by at least one specialist in each field. Is one specialist enough? Is it better to have both a British and an American critic, if we are to have a representative dictionary of the English language?

I have gone into some of the various editorial problems from the standpoint of a statement of policies, the work of the staff, and the work of the special editors. The work of all editors must be coordinated by the general editor and put into a book which the publisher promotes on the general market. The editor has combined the thinking of all of these people and balanced one interest against the other, in order to furnish a book which will be acceptable to all the parties concerned, as well as to the general public. He is the interpreter of the linguist to the publisher, the publisher to the linguist, the definer or staff member to the etymologist in the conflicts for space. The editor has given from 54 to 61 per cent of space to definitions, .7 to 1.3 per cent to illustrative phrases, from 5 to 8.5 per cent to etymologies, from 2.1 to 4.4 per cent to synonym studies and lists, and around 28 per cent to entries, pronunciations, parts of speech, inflected forms, usage notes, and other material.

I hope from these general observations and from the specific problems that I have listed that you will get at least some idea of the special editorial problems that the editor of a commercial dictionary has. Many of these problems are the same as those of the scholarly dictionary. For any dictionary—commercial or scholarly—is more valuable when it gives the agreed-upon knowledge of the experts, carefully labels opinions as such, and balances the types of information given to meet the needs of its public.

USE AND PREPARATION OF SPECIALIZED GLOSSARIES

Meredith F. Burrill and Edwin Bonsack, Jr.
Office of Geography, Department of the Interior

THE PURPOSE OF THIS PAPER IS TO RAISE some questions, to suggest some possible answers, to open some lines of inquiry, and to describe some resources, procedures, and observations, all stemming from practical experience with or related to glossaries in a specialized activity—geographic name standardization.

In the performance of staff work leading to the standardization of geographic names, the Office of Geography both uses and produces specialized glossaries. The standardized names are published by the Board on Geographic Names in gazetteers produced from punched cards at the rate of a quarter to a third of a million names per year, covering all foreign areas of the world. About fifty are now available in inexpensive editions for sale by the Government Printing Office. This activity has offered an opportunity to view in some detail lexical problems presented by a large volume of toponyms in all kinds of areas, and to observe some phenomena of toponymy and geographic terminology that are very widespread.

Since the number of names and named entities is too large to be observed by any one person, we have begun experimenting with procedures for developing and testing generalizations (about names or terms and the entities to which they apply) from the individual observations of 40 staff members. Experience so far suggests that the experiment will have useful results. It appears that some patterns of thought and terminology approach universality, which suggests that we are dealing with general principles. We find this a stimulating thought.

The gazetteers list the standardized names and variant names of the geographic entities in the country under consideration, in alphabetical order of the specific element. The elements of geographic names that indicate the class of the entity, e.g., in *Red Hill*, a name referring to a hill, or *Lake Erie*, the name of a lake, *Hill* and *Lake*, are the generic elements (or "generics"). The elements that identify the particular entity, in the above instances *Red* and *Erie*, are called the specific elements (or "specifics"). In our gazetteer entries, the specific element is always given first, so that the name of the above lake would read **Erie, Lake**. Each name is followed by a coded four-letter "designation" word characterizing the entity, the geographic coordinates, a number identifying the overlying administrative division, and a coded reference to a map that shows it. A foreword carries an alphabetical list of the code words and the designations so coded, and a glossary of foreign generic terms found in the names that are listed.

In preparing the gazetteers, a card is made up for each geographic entity, recording the name(s) and the nature of the entity as interpreted from current maps officially recognized for the area in question, official listings, and other authoritative text materials. The cards are then reviewed individually by senior geographers who verify, often with the help of further reference works, the designations and coordinates entered, and by linguists who verify the choice of the name of the entity as being in the most appropriate and correct form. The names, with the exception of a few so-called "conventional" names for major features, retain as closely as possible the form they had in the source-language. Geographers and linguists have worked together closely in this process since early in 1943, providing a rare instance of large-scale, long-continued combination of the knowledge and skills of these two disciplines.

Production of a large volume of standardized names requires the application of routine procedures, which means that the great bulk of the names can be processed without unusual individual attention, which is also true. However, the exceptions that present some kind of special challenge seem to have a significance out of proportion to their numbers.

Curiosity about some "unusual" terms encountered in names led by a series of steps some years ago to a full-scale study of the occurrence, connotation, and distribution of all the generic terms used in all the geographic names on all of the topographic maps and nautical charts of the United States (Burrill 1956b and 1956c). The findings were astounding and started off a whole series of other inquiries and attempts to frame new generalizations.

Early in the course of that study, it was discovered that the words *hope* and *folly*, encountered in some names, have a topographic meaning and are used as generics in England. *Hope* is used as a common noun, *folly* is not, in this connection. This led to suspicion about other words and frequent recourse to dictionaries and glossaries, with such interesting results that all the terms encountered were checked in about a hundred monolingual and bilingual dictionaries, glossaries and word lists. All pertinent definitions found were compiled for each term, along with a record that a given source included the word but no pertinent definition. A sample compilation is appended. In addition to its usefulness as an office tool, this has given us some better understanding of the sources and work of the lexicographers.

These studies have opened a number of doors. Each new concept has posed a number of fundamental questions that still await satisfactory answers but, at the same time, has modified the intellectual climate. We can now entertain some ideas that earlier we would have rejected and can focus on the problems some facts the relevance of which we would previously not have admitted.

The step in the process of geographic name standardization in which the glossaries are most used is "the identification of the kind of entity to which the name applies and the selection of the 'designation' to convey that identification." Since the geographers who prepare the name cards are not required to know the language of the areas on which they work, it is necessary to provide lexical aids. As one such aid, the linguists have recently begun to compile preliminary glossaries defining the various generic terms found in an inspection of the names that are to be standardized or in glossaries of map terms. Such lists are not foolproof, as will readily be seen from what follows, but they do contain a large part of the words that will be encountered and they are easy to use, and as the work progresses the gaps in the lexical information are filled in.

The final glossaries in the gazetteer forewords include the non-English generic terms encountered in the geographic names listed, with their dictionary definitions and other definitions derived from the name sources consulted. This is a fairly simple process for most terms, but there always remains a residue of words of questionable validity as generic terms, as indicators of the nature of the features in the names in which they play a part. The linguists scrutinize these closely to see whether they should be included in the final glossaries.

The process of selection of the four-letter code for designations has helped to isolate some problems. It was agreed early that all populated places, regardless of size and function would be coded POPL, and all running water bodies STRM. This has made it possible to avoid much argument over what kind of populated place or water body a given one was. It also has avoided the changing of code references when changes occur in the entities themselves, as when towns become cities.

For reasons that need not be enumerated, people do apply names to *parts* of populated places or to *parts* of watercourses. These were first designated "section of a city" (or town) and "section of a stream" and coded SECP, SECS. As designations came to hand for parts of still other entities, it was decided that the code reference might more usefully identify the kind of entry at the beginning and the modification next. POPL and STRM were therefore shortened to PPL and STM, and X as a fourth letter was picked to mean 'section of,' as in PPLX and STMX. Other four-letter codes are being reduced to three letters when it appears that grouping by three letters and subgrouping by a fourth will be helpful.

The staff discussions of coding questions, involving more people at the same time and all the designations in a gazetteer, have helped to focus and test some developing ideas, particularly about the geographic entities that people do or do not distinguish and the relation of this to terminology.

It is well known that different generics are commonly used for similar, even adjacent, entities. A new idea is that in some cases the generic refers to a complex entity that we have not consciously distinguished and named as such, and having elements or attributes usually referred to by "distinctive" terms. Reference to it has perforce been in terms of one or another of its elements that we do consciously recognize and for which we do have a term.

Many of the "swamps" along the middle Atlantic seaboard offer good examples that contributed to formulation of the concept of the TOPOCOMPLEX, as we have called this combination of geographic and linguistic phenomena. The "swamps" referred to combine the following elements: low-gradient stream flowing sluggishly in a shallow, narrow valley with a flood plain normally flooded shallowly and supporting an association of hygrophilous vegetation including trees and a tangle of lesser plants. The generic in the names of such complexes is not always *swamp*; it may be *branch*, *creek*, or some other term (McJimsey 1940, s.v. **branch** and **swamp**). The important point is that the name refers to the complex, not merely to the single element usually connoted by the generic.

A logical next question was, "Do other sorts of entities having geographic names provide examples of such complexes?" They do, and in a variety that challenges the ingenuity of the would-be categorizer. A *rambla* in Spain is a complex of a bare gravel stream bed and, seasonally, swiftly flowing water (Bennett 1960). The bed, at the bottom of a V-shaped valley, has a moderate gradient and a flat transverse profile. Most watercourses are topocomplexes. The names of land masses projecting either upward (mountains) or outward (points) commonly refer both to the whole mass and to the extremity. A *ranch* is a complex, a functional entity including land, structures, people and the things being produced. The ranch name may, in a different context, refer to the whole complex or to a single element (*Dictionary of American English* 1936–1944, s.v. **ranch**). The word *Alpe* is found on German maps in names so placed that they have been interpreted as applying either to the structures or to the mountain grassland pastures that are associated. It is now thought that the name usually applies to both, as a topocomplex.

Selecting a designation looks easy but in practice has often presented difficulties. Staff members have frequently differed as to the proper one to select. If, as often happens, there is some logical basis for each alternative and no way to establish positively the concept that the name itself was intended to convey, subjective administrative decision has resolved the questions. The fact that for years such questions came up and required prompt answers one by one or in small groups, made it difficult to draw any general conclusions. It is still difficult, but we have made some progress.

Part of the progress has come from attention to our own mental processes as a basis for hypotheses. In our staff discussions of glossary words, terms, and designations, it has repeatedly come out that the members of the staff not only have different ideas about the meaning of a given geographic term but also experience difficulty in conveying to one another what they think the meaning is, partly because there is no more agreement on words used in the attempted definition than on the word being defined. Sometimes colleagues have rejected each other's suggestions without being able to say why. Rejection has sometimes been accompanied by a feeling of irritation, sometimes not. It is interesting to compare the fact that a given individual may be irritated by some mispronunciations but not by others and cannot explain why.

One of the results of the US generics study was the recognition, in ourselves and others, of a "mental set" with reference to meanings of terms, more or less comparable to the mental set reflected in reluctance to attempt foreign language speech sounds. As in the case of sounds, recognition of the mental set has reduced its restricting influence. It has also alerted us to look for it and for its significance in other aspects of our own thinking, as well as in the material that comes under our scrutiny.

Although the anthropologists had made us aware that each culture group analyzes nature and experience in its own way, we were not at first prepared to accept the fact that individuals also differ significantly in this respect, even within our own culture groups, even within our own office. We knew, of course, that different words are used regionally for geographic entities considered essentially similar, e.g., *run* and *branch* for minor tributaries, but we did not anticipate that the US generics study would show that practically all the terms for wetland are also used as generics in the names of standing water bodies, or that half or more of the US generics would be new to all of the staff. Nor, until we began to ask the right questions, did we discover that several of us had used relatively common geographic terms in communication as colleagues for more than a decade without realizing how often the words did not evoke the same image for all. Sometimes, the differences were in the primary meaning of the term, sometimes in the periphery of its applicability.

Attention to peripheries and to differing ideas as to the variation from "normal" meaning allowable in a given term called for a way of referring to extent, field, or range of meaning. The German expression *bedeutungsfeld* was suggested and, though it has received a mixed reception, has been used to some extent in communications to the staff and professional groups. Exploration of the concept led quickly to the following hypothesis:

> Individuals entertain in the *bedeutungsfeld* of any geographic term both a primary connotation and a general one. The primary connotation is based on personal experience with entities known by the term or on visualization in the absence of observation. Once such a connotation based on an archetype is mentally set, it is thought of as "precise" and is rarely displaced as the primary meaning. The general connotation includes additional entities considered to be in the same class of feature as the archetype but with critical attribute(s) modified or missing, or with attributes that the archetype does not have, up to the point where the differences make the features more like another feature that the individual distinguishes.

Since individuals are not familiar with all the generics or with the generic connotation of terms also used for other things, and since there are no accepted rules to determine when the metaphorical use of a term like *arm* or *sugarloaf* has actually become "generic," there is room for differences of opinion. Among the names encountered in any gazetteer file there are always some containing elements that may or may not be properly considered as generics. Decision on this point will govern whether they are included in the glossary and whether they will be transposed in the listing. Let us examine some of the problem types.

1. **Vestiges of elements from substratum languages which were originally generic terms.** Words which had the force of generic terms in substratum languages may not be understood as generic terms by the present-day populace, even local residents. An example would be the *Unstrut*, a river name in Germany concealing in the syllable *strut* an ancient Celtic word meaning 'river.' An example requiring less philological delving would be any of a number of river-names in Japan which end in *-betsu*, which ordinarily means 'separate' but is used as a phoneticization of the Ainu word *pet* 'river' (Haguenauer 1952, 479–80). In areas from which Ainu has long since disappeared, it is probable that the word element no longer conveys any more to anybody than the *-ec* in *Kennebec River*. In such instances, the Japanese, similarly, add their own river term, *kawa*. However, it is possible that some present-day speakers of Japanese know that *-betsu* in geographic names means 'river,' in which case we would consider including the term in the gazetteer glossary.

2. **Archaic and dialectal generic terms.** Similarly, archaic and obsolete words or generic connotations in the mother tongue may not be understood generally, or even by local residents of an area. If they are understood locally, they may be regarded as dialect words. Often it is impossible to distinguish between archaic and dialect forms without inquiring of a native of the area. For example, Turks have been asked if they knew the word *öz* which, though not entered in the dictionaries consulted, is found in an apparently generic connotation in many river-names and occurs in Old Turkish (Uigur) with the meaning 'valley,' and presumably 'river-valley' and 'river,' as well (von Gabain 1950, 324). Those asked said that they did not know the word in the sense of 'river' or in any similar sense. The question is, do the people living along such a river know *öz* to mean 'river' or 'valley'? Field work is called for here, such as we are seldom in a position to undertake.

3. **Uncommon metaphorical usages as generic terms.** A large share of the major generic terms encountered the world over are obvious metaphorical extensions of meaning, such as the English *head* meaning 'point' or 'cape' or the Russian *nos* and the Japanese *hana* 'nose' in the same sense. Parts of

the human body are favorite sources of this type of generic term in many languages, and there is often remarkable agreement from language to language between the geographic object and the part of the body chosen to describe it. Familiar metaphors cause little difficulty, but when a term with whose metaphorical generic use one is familiar is found applied also by metaphor but to a feature that one does not even include in the same category, communication is interrupted. *Head*, applied to low, flat, forested wetland (USGS 1946) or to a short, steep, tributary stream (USGS 1938), *reef* applied to an upstanding layer of hard rock far inland (e.g., Capitol Reef, in Capitol Reef National Monument, Utah), or *glade* for a gently flowing stream (USGS 1954) will at least surprise one unfamiliar with these regional usages in the United States. Some may even entertain doubt that they are really generics in these cases, or that they actually apply to the features to which they seem to refer, particularly if few examples of the usage come to hand. Bilingual glossaries from English to another language will not provide these meanings. Neither do foreign language to English glossaries provide much help for us in similar cases in other countries, nor are native speakers of the foreign language of much assistance either, unless they happen to know the feature in question.

Even if the usage is repeated several times in an area there may be doubt or disagreement as to whether a term qualifies as a generic, e.g., *kala* 'castle' in Albania, as in *Kala e Skënderbeut* 'Skanderbeg's Castle,' the name of a peak. The fact that one can find a half-dozen other peaks with names containing *kala* suggests that the word can mean 'hill resembling a castle' to an Albanian, and the commonness of this metaphor in other languages points in the same direction, but this is not conclusive evidence.

4. Non-metaphorical elements in a name which appear to function as generics, for which the fact cannot be established. It often occurs that the specific part of a name will contain an element which resembles a generic term, as the element *water* in *Whitewater Lake* (in Manitoba, Canada). In this case, *water* is clearly a part of the specific not the generic term. Now it is true that in English most lake names contain a generic, *lake*, *pond*, or some other term. Hence, it is clear that *water*, as in in *Whitewater Lake*, is not a generic, even though it sometimes occurs as a generic in lake names, e.g., *Derwent Water* in the English Lake District. The significance of *water* in river names is less clear, since in English the generic term *river* is sometimes not expressed but is implied.

Is *water* in the stream name *Maidenwater*, in Utah (USGS 1952), a generic term, or not? Assuming that we have decided that it is not a generic term—and that the "full name" of the river might be the *Maidenwater River*—would not the occurrence of the name *Big Running Water*, a river in Arkansas (Army Map Service 1935), perhaps cause us to reconsider?

This problem occurs in other languages, e.g., *Gök Su* 'Blue Water,' in Turkey, and in names for other kinds of features, e.g., *Gur' i Zi* 'the Black Rock,' a mountain in Albania.

5. **Generic terms which carry a meaning apparently not in harmony with the character of the feature.** In many cases where generic terms seem inappropriate to the entities named, it is difficult to establish which of the possible explanations is correct. Is it a misnomer, has the geographic character of the entity changed since it was named, has there been an unusual or unrecorded semantic development in the word, or is there reflected a difference in concepts or categories of entities?

In almost every quarter of the globe, one finds peninsulas bearing in their names a generic meaning 'island.' This may have resulted from a connection with the mainland having come about after naming, either by deposition or by coastal emergence. On the other hand, it may be that in a particular region a distinction between island and peninsula is not made at all or is not considered important, even if the distinction is ordinarily made in the language. It may also be that the feature is an island at high tide and a peninsula at low tide, which the map may not show.

Dual aspect features are not uncommon. Chinese *shan* 'mountain' is used as a generic in names of islands that are also mountains, and most dictionaries give 'island' as one definition of *shan*, though glossaries may not (Mathews 1943, 774). In this case, combining the two ideas in a two-word designation on the work card encounters the fact that neither 'island mountain' nor 'mountain(ous) island' conveys quite the right picture. The solution will be to designate 'island' and to clarify in the glossary the nature of the *shan*s that are islands. This fits the language/nature categorization pattern of the gazetteer users and does not conceal the Chinese concept.

Where the generic in names on maps seems to have a meaning quite contrary to that implied by its dictionary definition, some of the cases appear to result from semantic shift. Albanian *qafë* 'neck, pass' occurs on the maps in the meaning of 'mountain peak' as well as 'pass.' Serbo-Croatian *uvala*, given in the dictionaries to signify 'ridge' or 'valley'—already here the meanings contrast sharply enough—occurs on maps in the names of coves and inlets. These seem to be omissions in the dictionaries—the rare geographical meaning has been slighted. Many Spanish dictionaries fail to give the meaning 'pass' for *collado* 'hill,' and many Romanian dictionaries give simply 'valley' for *vale*, while others include the definition 'stream' (Macrea 1958, 916).

Some other cases involving duality are thought by some of the staff to be topocomplexes, by others not. Examples are forested mountains with names using a generic meaning 'forest'—German *Wald*, Turkish *orman*, Japanese *mori*, and others, that apply to forests in general.

6. **Generic terms which classify the feature adequately for members of another culture group, but not for speakers of English.** Just as many languages do not, on the everyday level, make use of the concept PENINSULA, even though English may, just so English is often lacking in terms for geographic entities as conceived by other peoples. Such a type of generic term is the Arabic *sayhad*, applied to hills as well as to desert areas—an apparent discrepancy (Hava 1951, 408). But when one considers that *sayhad* implies something like a 'scorched place,' it appears that the Arab must, in designating a feature quite outside the everyday experience of the English speaker, use a generic term which has no exact counterpart in English. The English speaker, in designating that feature, will tend to use a generic term already familiar to him, and, noting the discrepancy in meaning between the English and the Arabic word, will hesitate to regard the latter as a *bona fide* generic term. Nevertheless, the Arabic word is just that, and is capable of application both to hills and desert areas.

The examples given above by no means exhaust the types of generic term problems. We have only scratched the surface. The problems arising for northeastern Asia, most of Africa, the islands of the Pacific, and much of North and South America—areas for which suitable linguistic material is lacking, or available and usable only with the greatest difficulty, will undoubtedly give us both new troubles and new understanding.

Enough has been learned to give us an appreciation of both the help and the frustration that we can get from glossaries and dictionaries. The help will be obvious. The frustration stems partly from the fact that, by selecting the more common words and meanings, the lexicographers have left out the ones on which we need help most. We are aware of their selection problem and take no issue with their solutions but wish the results were better adapted to our purpose. Frustration also stems in part from our doubts about the meaning of the lexicographers' defining words. Unless we are told, we can only guess at which of alternative meanings of, for instance, *meadow*, the lexicographer had in mind when he equated a word in another language to it. In fact, we do not even know, unless it is made clear, whether the lexicographer was any better versed in the variation of *meadow* than we were some years ago.

The problems and examples that have been discussed have indicated that our work with glossaries and maps is closely interconnected. When the glossary and dictionary definitions obviously do not fit an entity named on a map, one looks to the map itself, or other maps, for an additional connotation of the term. Sometimes this readily produces a satisfactory answer, sometimes not. The symbols used on maps are conventions and, therefore, comprehensible only by parties to the agreement on the convention and are almost inevitably inadequate for certain kinds of entities.

It is possible to symbolize on a map almost any phenomenon or attribute, but since the inclusion of many different symbols on a single map tends to obscure relationships, it is customary to use relatively few symbols, to combine things that could be distinguished, and to omit things considered dispensable. It is also a cartographic necessity in maps of smaller than large scale to generalize features that can be shown in more detail on the large-scale maps. Contours or form lines that are used to show relief features are drawn much straighter on the small-scale and medium-scale maps than they would be shown on the large-scale maps. Small projections from a relief feature may either not be shown at all or be indicated only by so few contour or form lines that distinguishing characteristics are omitted.

Features such as vegetation that grade from one association into another with no sharp boundary pose a special problem for the cartographer in applying symbols. This is notably true in the case of wetlands or the unsharp boundaries that one often finds between water and land, or between forest and grassland. Sometimes zones of different characteristics or with elements in changing ratio are so narrow that either one cannot put in all the necessary boundary lines or cannot include enough of a particular symbol to show the difference in zones, even if one can readily determine exactly where on the map the zone boundary lines should go.

Where several things have been combined in a single symbol, there is usually no explicit statement of what has been combined. Lacking such a statement, the absence of distinctions in a key to the symbols does not necessarily mean that no distinction was made; it could reflect the absence of entities to be distinguished or combined. If an element or attribute which is critical to the choice of designation is unsymbolized, the map leaves one in doubt as to which to use and almost enforces the use of a term that generalizes rather than distinguishes. This might, for instance, be true in the case of a named area of wetland. The cartographer may use the word *swamp* to identify the symbol in the key on the map, probably without being explicit as to whether he is generalizing and meaning any kind of wetland or referring to a wetland with specific attributes that is the only kind of wetland occurring in the map area. If, in turn, we include *swamp* as a designation for this name in the gazetteer, we would be unable to say, unless other sources of information make it clear, whether this is a generalization or in this instance a distinction from other kinds of wetland. It might be possible by examination of photographs to deduce what the cartographer did. This, however, would certainly be laborious and time consuming, and in some cases where we have made some search, the necessary precisely located pictures were not available.

The maps of Antarctica are now made for the most part from aerial photographs, of which there are already many thousands. These we have used by necessity in giving or approving names. Here one can usually see what the cartographers have done, or even ask the cartographer. This is not feasible for the world as a whole now, but it offers interesting possibilities for the future, particularly if map publishers will keep records of what the cartographer had in mind when the symbol was put down and the key prepared.

A further problem in the symbolization of phenomena on maps arises if the map maker is not familiar with the culture of the country or region being mapped. As is well known, each culture group analyzes nature in its own particular way and may have concepts of entities that can be named, and located on maps, that people in other culture groups do not have. If an incomprehensible name or term is encountered by the cartographer, he may either not symbolize it at all or equate it to a concept that he considers most nearly parallel to it for symbolization. If the name appears on the map without a symbol, there is no clue to the concept. If the symbol is for an "equated" entity, the existence of a different original concept may not be suspected by the map user, who will tend to attach his own concept to the feature that is symbolized.

When a name is recorded and standardized, the entity has to be called something. An inordinate amount of time can be spent either in detective work trying to discover what the entity really is, or in inconclusive argument based on different guesses as to significance of things around it. The results are likely to be far from the truth and three or four such names can use up more time than would have been required to process 300 or 400 names in a routine fashion. In an operation where volume of production is a consideration, there is good reason to throw such names out of the file and not spend the time that would be required to solve the problems. Omission of a few such names does not affect materially the value of a gazetteer, but ducking the problems precludes a full understanding of the nomenclature of the particular area and perhaps of some fundamental principles that would be widely applicable.

We have been assisted in our work at almost every turn by the work of the lexicographers. Independently, we have made occasional discoveries which may be of use to them, and occasional "rediscoveries" which bear out their conclusions, arrived at possibly by other channels. Our work has led to what we believe are new insights into the terminology of one specialized field, which suggests that joint study of the vocabulary of other fields by subject-matter specialists and linguists working closely together might be fruitful. The work along these lines must be exhaustive if it is to yield a corpus which will serve the person consulting it. Without this exhaustive work, many of the less common but possibly more revealing items will be missing.

The unanswered problems set forth in this paper are offered as a challenge and an invitation to the lexicographers, in the belief that joint research in this field would be mutually profitable.

Appendix: Definitions of *glade*

Webster's New International Dictionary (1934)
glade. 1. An open passage through a wood; a grassy open or cleared space in a forest. 3. *Local, U.S.* b. An everglade.

Dictionary of American English (1938–44)
*glade. *1. A natural or artificial opening or clearing in a forest, b. A particular area of this kind. 3. A tract of low swampy land, sometimes inundated and often overgrown with grass; an everglade. +b. Used also as the name of a particular area of this sort. +4. A tract devastated by hail.

Oxford English Dictionary (1933)
Glade sb. . . . 1. A clear open space or passage in a wood or forest, whether natural or produced by the cutting down of trees. The

Use and Preparation of Specialized Glossaries | 311

                earlier examples often explain the word as meaning a light or sunny place. From the latter part of the 17th c., when the word had perh. become merely literary, many writers have associated it with shade, b. An opening in a wood, etc., utilized for snaring birds. 2. *U.S.* a. ... 1796 Morse *Amer. Geogr.* 1. 649 Interspersed through the other parts, are glades of rich swamp. 1859 Bartlett *Dict. Amer., Glades,* everglades; tracts of land at the South covered with water and grass. So called in Maryland, where they are divided into wet and dry glades. 6.... 1828–32 Webster. *Glade.* 2. In *New England,* an opening in the ice of rivers or lakes, or a place left unfrozen. *Ibid., Glade,* smooth ice. (New England). [In recent American Diets, stated to be *Local, U.S.*]

Townshend (1890)   glades. Old English, *glade,* "shining," "bright." Tracts of land in the Southern States covered with water. In Maryland and Virginia they are divided into wet and dry glades. In Kentucky *glady ground* is used to designate a district where the surface is diversified by alternate forests and openings. (See Everglades.)

Navigation Dictionary (1956)
                glade. Polynya.

Mathews (1951)   *glade. 1. A marshy tract of low ground covered with grass, b. Used as the name of a particular area of this sort. 3. (See quots.) ... The Glades are the mountain meadows, a region on the high table land at the summit of the Alleghany mountains.

Clapin (1902?)   Glade. (Old Eng. primarily, a bright open spot in a wood). (1) In New England, a tract of smooth ice. (2) In the Southern States, a tract of land covered with water and grass. Evidently here a curtailment of everglade.

McJimsey (1940)   glade. Primarily a marshy tract of low ground covered with grass. Sometimes extended to poorly drained forested and upland areas and to streams.

McMullen (1953)   glade. (1) A natural opening or clearing in a forest. DAE. (2a) A tract of low, swampy land, sometimes inundated and often over-grown with grass; an everglade. DAE. Poss. Southern. Spec., a wet down; a savanna or wet glade, (b) The name of a particular area of this sort. DAE.

New Comprehensive "Standard" Dictionary (1944)
                glade 1. A clearing or open space in a wood. 2. [*Local, U.S.*] A smooth tract of uncovered ice, or an unfrozen space surrounded by ice. 3. An everglade; by apheresis.

Whitney (1888)   A glade is ... an "opening" or "clearing" in the forest, either ... a space naturally destitute of trees, or ... where they have been removed by... man. "Glade" is defined by Skeat as "an open space in a wood." Wedgwood says: "a light passage made through a wood, also a beam or breaking in of the light" ... of Scandinavian origin; the original sense being an opening for light, a bright track, hence an open track in a wood ... in Kentucky "glady ground" ... [refers to a] surface ... diversified by alternate forests and openings. "Glade" is a favorite word with the poets, especially ... Scott ... In the works of American authors it is much less frequently found. There is a certain vagueness of meaning in the word "glade" which makes it very convenient for poetical use.

Glossary of Names (n.d.)
Glade. A grassy opening or natural meadow in the woods; a small park. Applied in western Maryland to a brushy, grassy, or swampy opening in the woods.

Hale (1932)
Glade.... may be heard anywhere in the West, but not often as a familiar term in ordinary speech. In some places *opening* is used, in some *prairie*, in some, *park*.

Wilson (1890)
GLADE: A grassy opening or natural meadow in the woods; a small park. In western Maryland, applied to a brushy, grassy, or swampy opening in the woods.

Bartlett (1896)
GLADE. In New England, smooth ice.

GLADES.
Everglades; tracts of land at the south covered with water and grass. So called in Maryland, where they are divided into wet and dry *glades*.

MEANING DISCRIMINATION IN
BILINGUAL DICTIONARIES

James E. Iannucci
Saint Joseph's College

VARIOUS KINDS OF SEMANTIC PARTICULARIZATION, REFINEMENT OR discrimination may be required and sometimes found in bilingual dictionaries. This paper deals with the kind of semantic discrimination most frequently sought and also most frequently found in bilingual dictionaries, namely, discrimination of the meanings of a polysemous entry word.[1] An examination of 32 bilingual dictionaries revealed a variety of procedures for dealing with this problem. The dictionaries examined are all bilingual dictionaries in which one language is English and the other is another Indo-European language. They include some of the largest dictionaries in each field.

Even in the best bilingual dictionaries, we find many entries, sometimes very long ones, with no discrimination at all. This type of entry is illustrated in specimens 1 to 7. In specimen 2, for example, the French word *tour* is given 27 translations with nothing to indicate which meaning of *tour* each of the English words translates. A kind of negative discrimination is provided by punctuation: the commas separating synonyms or near synonyms and the semicolons separating words of more or less different meanings. The English-speaking user of an entry like this will probably find it adequate enough. He has found the word *tour* in a French context and wants to know what it means. As a native speaker of English, he is likely to know the meanings of the English words and should therefore be able to find the appropriate meaning for his context. If he is translating into English, he should be able to choose the appropriate word or perhaps even to supply a word which is more appropriate than any of those listed in the entry. The French-speaking user, however, would refer to this entry in order to express himself in English. He has a particular meaning of *tour* in mind and wants to find the appropriate English word for that meaning. Since English is a foreign language to him, he is much less likely to know the meanings of the English words in the entry, and he therefore needs information on how these English words differ in meaning. If he is translating a French text into English, he still needs this information.

Bilingual dictionaries attempt to provide this information in various ways. Some dictionaries, particularly the older ones, give long formal definitions of the type found in monolingual dictionaries. This sort of treatment is illustrated in specimens 71 to 74. In specimen 72, for example, one of the translations of English *spring* is Spanish *primavera*, and this is accompanied by the definition, "*estación del año en la cual comienzan las plantas á brotar y crecer*." Such definitions are unnecessarily long for a bilingual dictionary and extremely wasteful of space. The same meaning of *spring* is discriminated much more briefly in specimen 70 by "*estación del año*." As a matter of fact, this could be cut down to simply '*estación*' without any loss of information, since all that is needed is enough information to distinguish one meaning of *spring* from any of its other meanings.

For the most part, such discriminations are kept fairly brief in most bilingual dictionaries. Sometimes they are in the form of synonyms as, for example, in specimen 59. Here the German word *nett* is given 16 English translations with 11 German synonyms to discriminate the different meanings of the entry word. Often the discrimination is in the form of a context word or phrase. The subject or type of subject may discriminate the meaning of a verb as, for example, in specimen 32 where different French translations of the verb *sway* are given, depending upon whether the swaying is done by a drunkard, by a tree, or by a balance. The object or type of object may also discriminate the meaning of a verb as, for example, in specimen 42 where different Spanish translations of the verb *sink* are given depending upon whether the object is a well or a post. It is easy to fall into ambiguity here, since in some cases the discriminating noun could be understood as a subject or as an object. In specimen 48, for example, the discriminating noun *fish* after the verb *nibble* is intended as a subject, but it could also be understood as an object. The meaning of an adjective is sometimes determined by the noun or type of noun to which it is applied as, for example, in specimen 41, where the adjective *dull* has different German translations depending upon whether the quality is applied to eyes, fire, colors, metals, the weather, etc. In specimen 11, subject labels serve to discriminate two meanings of the English noun *band* in music and in architecture. (See also specimens 8 to 13.) In specimen 15, the usage label *colloquial* might serve to discriminate one of the meanings of Spanish *chispa* (see also specimens 14 to 17). Sometimes, meaning discrimination is effected by the designation of the part of speech of the entry word and, in verbs, by the designations *transitive* or *intransitive* (see specimens 18 to 21). Illustrative sentences or phrases are also used for meaning discrimination. We see this device illustrated in specimens 26 to 30. This device takes up a great deal of space, and it is not always used very effectively. In specimen 30, for example, it is difficult to see what purpose the illustrative sentence serves.

Important as it is to provide meaning discriminations which are brief and clear, the choice of the language in which these discriminations should be given is even more important. Many bilingual dictionaries give meaning discriminations in the target language in both sides of the dictionary. The *Appleton's Revised English–Spanish and Spanish–English Dictionary* (Cuyás 1953) uses this procedure. In the English–Spanish side, meaning discriminations are in Spanish, and in the Spanish–English side, they are in English. Other dictionaries give meaning discriminations in the source language in both sides. The *Muret-Sanders Encyclopaedic English–German and German–English Dictionary* (1944) also follows this procedure. The discriminations are in English in the English–German side and in German in the German–English side. Still other dictionaries use the same language for meaning discrimination in both sides. This means that in one side the source language is used and in the other the target language. This is the procedure followed by *McKay's Modern Spanish–English, English–Spanish Dictionary* (Raventós 1953) in which discriminations are in English in both sides. Only one of the dictionaries examined here, *Heath's French and English Dictionary* (Mansion 1939), gives discriminations consistently in both languages in both sides of the dictionary. Specimens 52 and 75 are typical examples. These represent four consistent approaches to the problem: 1) target language in both sides, 2) source language in both sides, 3) the same language in both sides, 4) both languages in both sides.[2] Not all dictionaries are so consistent. In some dictionaries we find now one language, now the other used for discriminating meanings in the same side of the dictionary.

Which of these procedures makes for the greatest efficiency in a bilingual dictionary? To answer this question, we must determine what kind of use requires meaning discrimination. Any entry in a bilingual dictionary may serve two purposes. It may serve the target-language speaker for comprehension of a foreign-language text or for translating into his own language. This is the foreign-to-native use. The same entry may also serve the source-language speaker for expressing himself in the foreign language or for translating into the foreign language. This is the native-to-foreign use. In the discussion of specimen 2, the French entry *tour*, we noted that the French-speaking user required meaning discriminations while the English-speaking user did not, that is, the native-to-foreign use required discriminations, while the foreign- to-native use did not. Since discriminations are required by the native-to-foreign use, they should be in the native language of the user, that is, in the source language. (Specimens 31 to 35 and 55 to 66 show discriminations in the source language. Specimens 36 to 39, 42 to 50 and 62 to 74 show discriminations in the target language.)

It also seems to be better lexicographical procedure to place the discrimination before the target word, as in specimen 35, rather than after the target word, as in specimen 41, since explanatory matter in dictionaries conventionally refers to what precedes, and these discriminations refer to different meanings of the entry word, rather than to different meanings of the target word.

The best way to handle meaning discrimination in any given dictionary should be determined by the kind of use each side of the dictionary is intended for. A bilingual dictionary can have four possible uses: native-to-foreign and foreign-to-native in each side. For example, if an English and French dictionary is designed to serve all four uses, it should have meaning discriminations in the source language in both sides, in English in the English–French side and in French in the French–English side. If it is intended for both native-to-foreign and foreign-to-native use, but only for English-speaking users, the native-to-foreign use would be removed from the French–English side making it unnecessary to include discriminations in this side. Various arrangements are possible, the determining factors being for whom the dictionary is intended and for what use or uses it is intended. In any case, the meaning discriminations would be in the source language. I can see no kind of use which would be served more efficiently by having the discriminations in the target language. In an entry like specimen 47, for example, in order to justify the use of discriminations in French (the target language), we must assume that they are intended for the French-speaking user in translating from English to French, and that he needs to be told which of the four French words is the appropriate one for any particular context. We must further assume that the English-speaking user, translating from English to French, does not need this information, or that if he needs it, it should be given to him in French.

In view of these considerations, it is surprising that so many bilingual dictionaries give meaning discriminations in the target language in both sides. The English and Spanish field is particularly bad in this respect. Six large English and Spanish dictionaries of over 100,000 entries—Martinez Amador (1953), *Cassell's* (Peers et al. 1959), Cuyás (1953), Neuman and Baretti (1854), Velázquez (1953), and Williams (1955)—all have discriminations in the target language in both sides. Two of these are new dictionaries, published within the last five years, and most of the others have had recent revisions. The smaller Raventós (1953) and MacDonald (1946) have discriminations in English in both sides, that is, in the source language in the English–Spanish side and in the target language in the Spanish–English side.[3]

Ideally, a bilingual dictionary designed for native-to-foreign use would have a discrimination for every translation of an entry word which has several meanings. Our present dictionaries fall far short of this ideal. Specimen 70 is typical, or perhaps even better than typical. In this entry, the noun *spring* has 21 Spanish translations with only three discriminations, two in the form of subject labels and one in the form of an abbreviated definition. If one wants to say in Spanish, "This board has a spring in it," there is no way of finding the Spanish word for *spring* in this sense, even though it is included in the entry. Or, if one wants to talk about the spring of an arch, there is no way of knowing that the Spanish translation for this sense of *spring* is not included in the entry. This incompleteness is no doubt dictated by considerations of economy of space. To provide a discrimination for every target word would increase the size of a dictionary considerably and would also make the longer entries more unwieldy.

This problem could perhaps be solved by coordinating the bilingual dictionary with a monolingual dictionary by a system of number references, thus making the definitions in the monolingual dictionary serve as meaning discriminations for the bilingual dictionary. This is illustrated in the examples following specimen 75. While such a system would make full discrimination available for the native-to-foreign use of the bilingual dictionary, it does present a number of practical problems. One would be bound by the semantic breakdown in the monolingual dictionary. The discrimination there may be too fine at some point and not fine enough at some other point. Where it is too fine, more than one number could be assigned to a given translation, but where it is not fine enough, one would have to discriminate further by conventional means. Also, senses that you want to include may be omitted in the monolingual dictionary, and senses that you don't want may be included. Editorial work would be complicated by the fact that one book could not be revised independently of the other. If two publishers are involved, the difficulty is increased. Last, but not least, is the objection to using two books for one purpose, or two parts of one book, if they are bound together. Although these are difficult problems to solve, I think the gain in economy and efficiency would be well worth the trouble. Meanwhile, the efficiency of the present type of bilingual dictionary would be greatly increased by having meaning discriminations in the source language instead of in the target language.

APPENDIX: SPECIMEN ENTRIES FROM BILINGUAL DICTIONARIES

1. **rubber** ... *s.* caucho; hule; fregador; goma de borrar; estropajo; paño de cocina; lima de mano; jugada que desempata; partida de juego; piedra de afilar ... (Martinez Amador 1953)
2. **tour** ... *n. m.* Turn, round, twining, winding; revolution, circumference, circuit, compass; twist, strain; tour, trip; trick, dodge, wile; feat; office, service, vein, manner, style; place, order; lathe; turning-box; wheel; mould ... (Baker 1932)
3. **pârlì** ... *v. a.* to brown; to roast brown; to dupe, cheat; to steal; pilfer, draw away ... (Axelrad 1942)
4. **balance**, *subst.*, Waage, Bilanz, *f.*, Saldo Ruckstand; Transport, *m.*; Restbetrag, *m.*; Gleichgewicht ... (Bithell 1954)
5. **rough** ... *a.* áspero; tosco; fragoso, escabroso; erizado; peludo, encrespado; duro, bronco, desapa cible; bruto; tosco, cerril; rudo, inculto; grosero, brusco; tempestuoso, borrascoso, agitado; chapucero, mal acabado; approximativo, general; preliminar, preparativo. (Cuyás 1953)
6. **subtil** ... *adj.* ... Subtle, subtile, evasive; tenuous, fine; nice, refined; acute, subtle, keen, crafty, smart ... (Chevalley and Chevalley 1935)
7. **fair** ... *adj.* justo, recto, honrado; imparcial; equitativo, regular, mediano; rubio, blondo; bello; despejado, claro ... (Castillo and Bond 1948)
8. **dowel** *s.* (Ing.) espiga; **bed dowel**, (Alban.) roza de sujeción; **peg-and-cup dowels**, (Mold.) pasadores de unión. (Chambers 1952)

9. **bay** ... *s.* Bahía; cala, rada, ensenada; (bot.) laurel; ladrido, aullido; acorralamiento; pajar; (arq.) intercolumnio; crujía; nave; compuerta de dique; caballo bavo ... (Martinez Amador 1953)
10. **spore**, (bot.) espora, (zool.) germen, *m.* (Raventós 1953)
11. **band** ... *s.* faja, fleje, venda, tira, lista, vencejo, cordon, correa, cinta, franja, precinta; abracadera, zuncho; lazo, enlace, unión, conexión, coyunda, cuadrilla, gavilla, partida, bandería; (mus.) banda, charanga, música; murga; (arq.) filete, listón. (Cuyás 1953)
12. **oxeye** ... *n.* (Bot.) Grande marguerite, *f.*; (Ornith.) mésangère, *f.* ... (Baker 1951)
13. **demoiselle** ... *s.* damisela; (orn.) antropoide, grulla de numidia; (ent.) caballito del diablo. (Williams 1955)
14. **ratón** ... *n. m.* Little rat; racoon; (fig.) little pet, darling. (Baker 1932)
15. **chispa**, *f.* Spark, ember; sparkle; flake; very small diamond; ace, bit, small particle of anything; penetration, acumen, brightness; mother wit; fire; scale; (coll.) tipsiness, jag ... (Martinez Amador 1953)
16. **sport** ... *s.* deporte; juego, diversion, entretenimiento, pasatiempo; deportista; caballero, hidalgo, persona campechana o noble; burla, broma; hazmerreír; (biol.) individuo anormal; monstruo; (fam.) tahúr ... (Cuyás 1953)
17. **gadoue** ... *n. f.* Night-soil, sewage used as manure; dirt, slush; (slang) trollop. (Baker 1951)
18. **in** ... *prep.* em, por, a, de, durante ... *a.* interno ... *adv.* dentro, em casa ... *s.* canto; partido politico que está no poder ... (Ferreira 1939)
19. **after** *adv.* depois, em seguida; *conj.* depois que; *prep*, depois, após; conforme; segundo ... (Richardson, Sá Pereira, and Sá Pereira 1944)
20. **falsear**, *v. tr.* To falsify, counterfeit, forge; distort, pervert; to pierce, to penetrate an armour; (carp.) to bevel ... *v. intr.* To slack(en); (mus.) to be false (a string) ... *v. r.* to warp. (Martinez Amador 1953)
21. **sport** ... *v. i.* jugar; recrearse, divertirse. *v. t.* llevar; ostentar, lucir ... (Raventós 1953)
22. **Wunderbaum** (nu): locust-tree (*Robinia pseudacacia*); castor-oil plant (*Ricinus communis*) (Webel 1952)
23. **palmarosa**, *f.* palmarosa (*Cymbopogon martini*), ginger grass (*Cymbopogon flexuosus*). (DeVries 1951)
24. **perce-pierre**, *f.* parsley piert (*Aphanes arvensis*), saxifrage (*Saxifraga*). (DeVries 1951)

25. **grosbeak** ... *s.* (orn.) pico duro (*Pinieola enucleator*); (orn.) degollado; (orn.) cardenal de Virginia. (Williams 1955)
26. **spring up**, *v. i.* I (a) Sauter en l'air ... 2. (a) (of plants, etc.) Pousser, croitre. *The wheat is beginning to s. up* le blé commence a pousser; le blé sort de terre. *As soon as the corn sprang up* ... des qu'on vit poindre le blé ... (b) *A breeze sprang up*, une brise se leva. *A belief has sprung up that* ... la croyance s'est formée, a pris naissance, que ... *An intimacy* sprang up between them, l'intimité s'établit entre eux. *A doubt sprang up in his mind*, un doute germa dans esprit. (Mansion 1939)
27. **stamp**, stampa *f.*, imprónta *f.*, ségno *m.*, marchio *m.*; stampo carattere *m.*, maglio *m.*, mazzuolo *m.*; punzone *m.*, frantóio *m*. *This law carried with it the divine —*, questa legge portava la sanzione divina ... (Hoare 1925)
28. **spring** ... *s.* I (a) Source *f.* (d'eau) ... (b) Source, origine *f. The custom had its s. in another country* cet usage a eu son origine dans un autre pays, est originaire d'un autre pays ... 2. Printemps *m. The glory of an English s.*, la splendeur du printemps en Angleterre ... *A lovely s. evening*, une belle soirée de printemps. *Spring is in the air*, on respire le printemps dans l'air ... (Mansion 1939)
29. **poste**, *s. m.* I. Post, station, (a) Mil. *La sentinelle était a son p.*, the sentry was at his post ... (Mansion 1940)
30. **exhibition** ... *s.* esposizione *f.*, mostra *f.* ... *Everyone admired the wonderful Turin exhibition,* tutti ammirarono la splendida esposizione di Torino ... (Lysle and Gualtieri 1957)
31. **recede**, zuriicktreten; (prices) weichen, sinken, abschlagen ... (Bithell 1954)
32. **sway** ... *v. i.* (a) balancer; osciller; ballotter; (of drunkard) vaciller; (of trees) *To s. in the wind*, se balancer au vent ... (c) (of balance, etc.) pencher; incliner ... (Mansion 1939)
33. **realize**: verwirrklichen; (a profit) aufbringen ... (Bithell 1954)
34. **nest** ... 1. nest, nidus; (eines Eichhornchens) dray; (eines Tieres) lie, lair; (eines Vogels am Boden) ground-nest ... (*Muret-Sanders* 1901)
35. **dim** ... *a.* ... (of light) Faible, pale; (of colour) efface; (of sight) faible; (of memory) incertain, vague ... (Mansion 1940)
36. **éclater** ... 2. *v. i.* (Of boiler, shell, gun) To burst, explode; (of mine) to blow up; (of tyre) to burst; (of glass) to fly (into pieces); (of mast) to split, splinter ... (Mansion 1939)

37. **jadish** ... *adj.* Rendido; (yegua) viciosa; (mujer) impudica. (Martinez Amador 1953)
38. **sonner** ... I. *v. i.* To sound; (of clock) to strike; (of bell) to ring, to toll ... (Mansion 1940)
39. **rare** ... *adj.* ... 5. (of plants) *thin*; 6. (Med.) of the pulse) *very slow* ... (Spiers and Quackenbos 1889)
40. **rare** ... a. Rare; clairsemé; fameux; à moitié cru (of meat) ... (Baker 1932)
41. **dull**, I *adj.* ... matt (*as eyes*); schwach (*as the fire*); matt (*as colors or metals*); trübe (*as weather*); dumpf (*of sounds*); fau, still, stockend (*as trade*) ... (Breul 1939)
42. **sink** ... *va* hundir, sumergir; echar a pique; abrir, cavar (*un pozo*); enter rar (*un poste*) ... (Williams 1955)
43. **brocher** ... *v. a.* to stitch (a book); to figure (stuffs) to emboss (linen); to strike (a nail into a horse's foot) ... (Baker 1951)
44. **dünn**, *adj.* thin, fine; slender, slim; slight (silk); weak, diluted (fluids); carce; rare (air) ... (Breul 1939)
45. **prime** ... *v.* preparar, informar, instruir de antemano; cebar (un carburador, bomba o arma de fuego). (Castillo and Bond 1949)
46. **bar** ... *s.* I. (a) Barre *f.* (defer, de bois, de chocolat, etc.); barre, brique *f.* (de savon); lingot *m.* (d'or); lame *f.* (de commutateur, etc.) ... (Mansion 1939)
47. **return** ... *v. tr.* I. (a) Rendre (un livre emprunté); restituer (un object vole); renvoyer (un cadeau); rembourser (un emprunt) ... (Mansion 1940)
48. **picar**, *v. t.* to prick; sting; peck; chop fine; mince; nibble (fish); irritate (skin); (sew.) pink; burn (the tongue); eat (grapes); goad; spur; stipple (walls) ... (Raventós 1953)
49. **spread** ... *v. tr.* ... (Ex) tender, desarrollar; de(spa)-rramar, esparcir, propalar, propagar; untar con; exhibir; poner (la mesa); apartar ... (Martinez Amador 1953)
50. **gettare**, to throw, cast (bronzes), waste ... (Hoare 1947)
51. **sprinkle**. I. *v. tr.* ... (b) Asperger, arroser, bassiner (*with water*, d'eau); saupoudrer (*with salt*, de sel) ... (Mansion 1939)
52. **s'abattre**, *v. r.*, to fall, tumble down; to stoop; to abate ... to break down (of horses—*des chevaux*); to burst (of a storm—*d'un orage*) ... (De Lolme, Wallace, and Bridgeman 1903)

53. **ouverture** (d'un objectif) (*n. f.*), aperture (of a lens) . . .
ouverture (d'une caverne) (*n. f.*), mouth (of a cave) . . .
ouverture (d'un pont, d'une voûte) (*n. f.*), span (of a bridge, of an arch) . . .
ouverture (d'un palmer) (*n. f.*), capacity (of a micrometer) . . . (Kettridge 1949)
54. **ball**, *s.* . . . (of the thumb) yema (del pulgar), *f*.; (of the foot) planta (del pie) . . . (Raventós 1953)
55. **lapse** . . . *s.* I. (a) (Mistake) Erreur *f*.; faute *f*. . . . (b) (Moral fault) chute *f*., faute, défaillance; faux pas . . . (Mansion 1939)
56. **ball**, *s.* globo, *m.*, esfera, *f*.; (plaything) pelota . . . (shot) bala, *f*. . . . (dance) baile, *m.* . . . (Raventós 1953)
57. **fare**, *n.*, precio, precio de transporte; pasaje, viaje; (food) comida; (passenger) viajero; tarifa . . . (MacDonald 1946)
58. **inkling** . . . *s.* das unbestimmte Gerücht, Gemunkel; (hint) die Andeutung, der Wink; (slight foreknowledge) eine Ahnung, leise Idee . . . (Breul 1939)
59. **nett** . . . 1. (zierlich) elegant, (sauber) neat, tidy, (hübsch) pretty, good-looking, (schmuck, geputzt) smart, trim, spruce, (niedlich) nice, delicate, (allerliebst) charming, (gemütlich) jolly, (freundlich) pleasant, (liebenswürdig) amiable, lovable, (gütig) kind . . . (*Muret-Sanders* 1901)
60. **plain**, I. *adj.* 1, = smooth, *aequus, planus* . . . 2, = manifest, *clarus, planus, apertus, perspicuus, evidens, manifestus* . . . = unadorned, *simplex, inornatus* . . . (*Cassell's* 1955)
61. **sport** (*s*): giuoco (*m.*) divertimento (*m.*), passatempo (*m.*); (plaything) giuocattolo (*m.*); (jesting) burla (*f.*) . . . (exercise) esercizio . . . (Spinelli 1937)
62. **overwrought**, *adj.* or part, nimis elaboratus (= wrought too highly), laboribus confectus (= worn down by labours) . . . (*Cassell's* 1959)
63. **rag** . . . *n.* Chiffon (piece of cloth torn off); haillon, *m.*, guenille, loque (tatter), *f.* . . . (Baker 1932)
64. **spread**, I. *v. tr.* (ex)pandere (= to lay open), explicare (= to unfold), extendere (= to stretch out), sternere (= to lay out or flat), spargere (= to scatter) . . . (*Cassell's* 1955)
65. **fedele** (*m.*) true believer (vero credente), trusty follower (seguace meritevole di fiducia), loyal subject (suddito leale) (Spinelli 1937)

66. **perduto** ... lost; not visible, invisible (non visible); sunk (affondato); destroyed (distrutto); wasted, squandered (sciupato); not gained (non guadagnato); ruined (rovinato) (Lysle and Gualtieri 1957)
67. **heat** ... s. calor; ardor; vehemencia; celo (ardor sexual de la hembra); calefacción (para las habitaciones); corrida, carrera (de prueba) ... (Castillo and Bond 1948)
68. **rapport** ... *n. m.* 1. ... bearing (yielding produce) ... 3. ... produce (that which a th. yields) ... 7. ... report (official statement of facts) ... (Spinelli 1937)
69. **ginebra**, *f.* gin (drink); confusion; babble, din. (Raventós 1953)
70. **spring** ... (mec.) muelle, resorte; (carr.) ballesta; elasticidad, fuerza elástica; blandura o suavidad elástica; salto, brinco, corcovo, bote; vuelta a su posición anterior; motivo, móvil; primavera (estación del año); fuente, *f.*, manantial; origen, nacimiento; surtidor; alabeo, combadura. (Cuyás 1953)
71. **hoja**, *s. f.* 1. Leaf, the green deciduous part of trees, plants and flowers. 2. Leaf, anything foliated or thinly beaten; scales of metal. 3. Leaf, one side of a double door, shutter, etc. ... (Neuman and Baretti 1862)
72. **spring**, *s.* 1. Resorte, elasticidad, fuerza elástica; muelle, resorte; cualquier cuerpo elástico que vuelve á su forma normal cuando cesa de estar comprimido ... 4. Primavera, estación del año en la cual comienzan las plantas á brotar y crecer. ... (Velázquez de la Cadena 1953)
73. **diversion**, *s.* 1. Desvío, el acto de desviar alguna cosa ó quitarle la dirección que llevaba. 2. Diversión, entretenimiento, pasatiempo. 3. (Mil.) Diversión, el ataque que se hace al enemigo por diversas partes para obligarle a separar sus fuerzas. (Neuman and Baretti 1862)
74. **book** ... 1. livre *m.* a) assemblage de feuilles de papier écrites ou imprimées ensemble; b) ouvrage d' esprit d'assez grande étendue pour former un volume; c) division d'un ouvrage d'esprit, chant d'un poeme. (Clifton and Grimaux 1923)
75. **nice** ... *adj.* ... (delightful—charmant) joli; (delicate—delicat) délicat, fin; (exact—correct) exact, juste; (scrupulous—scrupuleux) (fastidious—difficile) difficile, severe, rigide, prude; (refined—raffiné) recherche, subtil ... (De Lolme, Wallace, and Bridgeman 1903)
    country ... *n.* ... **1**, a tract of land; a district; a region; **2**, rural parts, as opposed to cities or towns; usually with *the* **3**; one's native land; the land of one's citizenship; **4**, the territory of a nation that has a distinct

existence as to name, language, customs, government, and the like; also the people of such a nation; **5**, the people of a region or nation as a whole; the public; as, the *country* is opposed to war. . . . (Brown, Canby, and Lewis 1946)

English–French: **country** *n* **1** region, contree **2** campagne **3** patrie **4**, **5** pays, nation

English–German: **country** *n* **1** Gegend **2** Land **3** Heimat, Vaterland **4** Land, Nation **5** Volk, Nation

English–Italian: **country** *n* **1** regione, contrada **2** campagna **3** madrepatria, patria **4**, **5** paese, nazione

dull . . . *adj*. . . . **1**. Stupid; doltish. **2**. Slow in perception or sensibility; hence, unfeeling, insensible; as the *dull* clods. **3**. Slow in action or motion; hence listless; inert. **4**. Without zest; depressed. **5**. Not keen or sharp; blunt. **6**. *a*. Lacking brilliance of light; dim; as a *dull* fire, *b*. Lacking luster; as, a *dull* mirror. *c*. Of low saturation and low brilliance; as a *dull* green, *d*. Not clear and ringing;—of sound. **7**. Tedious; melancholy; as, a *dull* story. **8**. cloudy; overcast; as, a *dull* day. **9**. Sluggish—of trade. (Webster's 1953)

English–Spanish: **dull** *adj* **1** tonto, bobalicón **2** insensible, torpe **3** flojo, perezoso **4** desanimado, desalentado **5** romo **6** (a) poco claro (b) deslustrado (c) apagado (d) sordo **7** aburrido, tedioso **8** nublado, encapotado **9** inactivo, muerto

English–Italian: **dull** *adj* **1** stupido, balordo **2** insensibile, scipito **3** lento, inerte **4** abbattuto **5** smussato **6** (a) oscuro, scialbo (b) appannato (c) oscuro (d) sorbo **7** noioso **8** nuvoloso **9** calmo, morto

rather . . . *adv*. . . . **1**. (Obs. or British Dial.), more quickly; sooner; hence, **2**. more willingly; preferably: as, he would *rather* go than stay. **3**. with more justice, logic, reason, etc.: as, I, *rather* than you, should take the risk. **4**. more accurately; more precisely: as, it was in the morning, or *rather*, the early afternoon. **5**. on the contrary; quite conversely: as, we have not lost; *rather*, we have won. **6**. somewhat; to some degree: as, I *rather* enjoy singing. **7**. (Chiefly British Colloq.) certainly; assuredly: used as an answer. (Guralnik and Friend 1953)

English–Italian: **rather** *adv* **1** presto, più subito **2** piuttosto **3** piuttosto, anzi **4** per meglio dire **5** al contrario **6** abbastanza, un po **7** s'intende!

English–German: **rather** *adv* **1** schneller, früher **2** lieber, eher **3** vielmehr, eher **4** besser gesagt, vielmehr **5** im Gegenteil, eigentlich **6** etwas, einigermassen **7** gewiss!

NOTES

1. For other discussions of this problem see Iannucci (1957), Hietsch (1958), Williams (1959), and Williams (1960).

2. Recourse to a third language is seen in the occasional use in bilingual dictionaries of Latin scientific names for flora and fauna. See specimens 22 to 25.

3. In general meaning discrimination seems to be handled much more effectively in dictionaries designed exclusively for the speakers of one of the languages. In Latin and English dictionaries, for example, discriminations for the entry word are given in English in the English-Latin side while the Latin-English side contains little or no discrimination.

THE LABELING OF NATIONAL AND REGIONAL VARIATION IN POPULAR DICTIONARIES

Allen Walker Read
Columbia University

WHEN A LANGUAGE COMES TO BE SPOKEN OVER a wide area, divergences arise that cause problems for the recording lexicographer. A dictionary with the utmost rigor would of course be a word index of a single idiolect; but apart from scientific purposes this would not be useful generally. Any dictionary that has aspirations to general usefulness must take into account the regional variations throughout the area in which the language is spoken.

In the English language, world-wide though it is, the primary split is between the English of England and that of America. The attempt to discriminate between what originated in one country or the other lies in the field of cultural history and illustrates how interdisciplinary the field of lexicography is. The identifying of the word-stock that originated in America has been a continuing pursuit of scholars since the Rev. Jonathan Boucher in 1774 and culminated in Sir William Craigie's *Dictionary of American English* (1938–44; henceforth, *DAE*). It was based on a massive collection of illustrative examples, and I feel that the central practical procedure of lexicography will always be the gathering of documented evidence on all aspects of usage. This is laborious work, perhaps "donkey work," and can be mechanized, I think, only partially. Nevertheless, I will welcome the time when we can give the order, "Switch on the lexicography machine."

Sir William Craigie's plan called for marking a plus sign (+) before words or meanings that originated in the area that is now the United States. Baffling problems often arose over this plussing, for the evidence was frequently not definitive and judgments might differ. When M. M. Mathews worked over the material again for his *Dictionary of Americanisms* (1951), he altered many of the decisions that had been made earlier. I find, in turn, that I am in disagreement with a number of his decisions. The weighting of evidence and the turning up of new evidence will, it is to be hoped, gradually clarify the problems.

A typical example is provided by the word *spittoon*. Thornton (1912) found an American example of 1840, and this was in time to be used as the first in the *Oxford English Dictionary* (1933; henceforth, *OED*), along with an English example of 1841. The *DAE* carried the word back to 1823 with a quotation by an English traveler noting the absence of a spittoon at a certain American hotel. The *DAE* did not label it an Americanism, but Mathews, on the same body of evidence, did. The object referred to seems to have originated in England but was at first called a *spitting dish* or *porringer*.[1] Now the bit of new evidence that I can present is from a recently printed letter by Charles Dickens (1938, 1.395). In the course of his American tour, he wrote on March 6, 1842: "The jury are accommodated at the rate of three men to a spittoon (or spit-box as they call it here)." He is contrasting the term that is natural to him, *spittoon*, with the new *spit-box*. I lay much stress on Dickens's feeling for the word in that early period. Inasmuch as the first quotation of 1823 is by an Englishman, I think that the weight of evidence is in favor of *spittoon* as a Briticism rather than an Americanism. Other evidence could change the picture. Since about 1900, Englishmen have enthusiastically claimed *spittoon* as their own word, in contrast to the mealy-mouthed American euphemism *cuspidor*. When I investigate a single word in this way, I realize that I lay myself open to the accusation of being a mere antiquarian. But a sound labeling is dependent upon specialist studies of this type; and if one sees one's research in the larger pattern of working out social history, one can defend oneself against the charge of antiquarianism.

But decisions on origin, fascinating as they are, do not seem to me as important in lexicography as the building up of bodies of typical usage. I regard it as unwise and unfortunate that both Sir William Craigie and M. M. Mathews chose place of origin as their criterion for an Americanism rather than currency in usage. Thus, they have ignored one of the most important of the types of Americanism—that caused by survival in America with obsolescence in England. Questions of degree of currency are much more difficult to work with, since usage is fluid and the lines of distinction between England and America are often blurred. I have collected numerous bold statements that *railroad* is the American term and *railway* the British term, and yet in actuality usage is divided, with a certain preponderance in one country or the other. Since English capital was often invested in the early American railroads, the English lawyers drew up the papers and put the word *railway* into the official name of many lines. It is of interest that when Noah Webster first met these synonyms, his reaction was to establish an arbitrary distinction between them. In a letter of June 21, 1830, he wrote as follows to the English editor who was bringing out an English edition of his dictionary:

> I believe *rail-road* & *rail way* are now used as synonymous—but it might be well to suggest under these words, that a useful difference might be made—*Railroad* might be the name of the highway in which a railway is laid, but the *rail way* to be limited to the rails & appendages which support the vehicle. But this distinction will depend on circumstances, for I suppose the railway will often be made where there is no high way.[2]

Sometimes a usage pattern will fall in a way that is surprising to the investigator. When the first two parts of the *DAE* had appeared, Miles L. Hanley (1937, 590) reviewed them with sharp criticism, in particular because they included the terms *auger* and *auger-hole*. I replied to the review (1938) and met nearly all the criticisms, except that I was willing to concede that *auger-hole* could well have been omitted. To my surprise, Sir William Craigie (1938, 643) was not willing to admit even this, and in an addendum to my review he wrote:

> As the use of the simple word [*auger*] is chiefly technical (the usual implement being the smaller *gimlet*) ordinary occasions for using it [in England] are not frequent. There is every probability that the different conditions in the two countries helped to maintain both *auger* and *auger-hole* in more general use in the United States than in England.

In the more than twenty years that have elapsed since then, I have watched the words *auger* and *gimlet* carefully and I have found to my amazement that Americans really do have a predilection for *auger* and the English for *gimlet*. I have found, for instance, this direct statement by an English observer on the Indiana frontier in 1855: "In Europe four tools would have been required for this—a gimlet, a hammer, a plane, and a pair of pincers: here one sufficed. He [the American] never thought of using a gimlet" (Beste 1855, 1.278–79). One of my students, in a linguistic autobiography, utterly without coaching from me, wrote as follows: "The effect of these [British children's] books . . . was to give me an English vocabulary. I used such words as *gimlet*, *skirting-board*, *pipkin*, and such expressions as 'the chimney wants sweeping'" (Cleland 1949). The English have developed figurative uses of *gimlet* that are not known in America,³ and a literary critic has noted Hardy's use of it.⁴ The cocktail known as the gimlet originated in England,⁵ and the derivatives *gimlet-eyed*⁶ and *gimlety*⁷ can be found there. The derivative *auger-eyed* is not listed in any dictionary that I have consulted but nevertheless it was picked up by Vance Randolph (1927, 472; 1953, 225) as current in the Ozarks in 1927. I had supposed that the auger and the gimlet would be used in either country simply as those different instruments were needed; but the perceptive and acute observation of Sir William Craigie in 1938 seems to be substantiated by the pattern of the evidence. This is on the level of scholarly interest, however, and no regional labeling of either word would be expected in a popular dictionary.

The identifying of a body of Briticisms is more difficult than identifying a body of Americanisms because Americans have not held back from adopting anything that came their way. It is difficult to prove a negative, to show that certain expressions known to be current in England are absent in America. A device that I have found to be helpful is to search the writings of travelers who comment on words that are unfamiliar to them, especially of Americans in England. Their surprise at a term is circumstantial evidence that it does not have currency in America. Let me present three illustrations, one from the eighteenth century, one from the nineteenth, and one from the twentieth. In 1759, Jared Ingersoll, a Connecticut farmer, went to England to see if there had been any improvements in agricultural methods that Americans might adopt. He came across a topographical term that is still a Briticism—*downs*. In a letter of December 22, 1759 (qtd. in Beardsley 1876, 21), he reported: "The high smooth hills, as in Sussex, having neither tree, stone, nor fence,—[are] called Downs, that yield a fine dry grass, improved for feeding thousands of sheep." From the nineteenth century comes documentation for the equation of American *mucilage* with English *gum*. An American in London made the following report (J. W. F 1878, 1/h):*

> To-day I wanted a bottle of mucilage. I went into a shop on the Strand, and had this experience with the young lady in charge: "Have you any mucilage?" "Sir?" with a puzzled expression. "Mucilage; paste, . . . something which will stick some pieces of paper on other pieces. In this happy town of London is there such an article?" I have an idea the girl got a little mad here, for she said

---

* The work cited here refers to an item originally published in *The Baltimore Gazette*. It antedates Read's citation from *American Bicycling News* by several months and because it appears in early February, the original may have been published in the preceding year.

sharply: "We've gang, if that's what you want." "What do you call it?" "Gang!" earnestly and very loud. I am sure she said "gang." "Well, that may be it; never heard of it before, but I'll try it." She gave me a parcel. She was so angry that I was afraid to examine it at the store. When I reached my room I discovered it had "Gum" blown on the bottle, yet that English girl called it "Gang" as plainly as could be.

From the present century comes a traveler's report of the *geezer* (*geyser*), the English contraption for heating water in a bathroom. As the actress Louise Hale (1920, 109) described it,

The aristocratic landlady was telling me of the advantages of her own particular geezer. . . . I moved closer to descry the lettering on the cylinder, and lo! it was a geyser. I suppose the word is universally mispronounced over here because they have not been brought up in a geyser country. They probably pin their faith to the man who invented the first copper cylinder for heating water, he himself having picked the fanciful name out of the dictionary as a novelist picks heroines from a telephone-book.

From such sources and others, I have built up a body of nearly 10,000 entries, consisting of terms that could be labeled, if they were transferred to popular dictionaries, *British* or *Chiefly British*. The conspicuous Briticisms are for the most part labeled in American dictionaries of college size, although a reviewer (Traister 1949, 19/c) of the current edition of the *Webster's New Collegiate Dictionary* (1953) was able to point out shortcomings in this regard. As he accurately said: "Yet in words like 'draper,' 'greengrocer,' 'pram,' 'spanner' and 'trifle' there is no hint anywhere that each of these is chiefly British in use. Try asking your garage mechanic to lend you a spanner for a moment, or your waitress to bring you a trifle with your coffee."

So far, I have dealt with examples of divergences between Great Britain and the United States, and the political loyalties involved sometimes set the linguistic attitudes askew. The long history of Anglo-American bickering over language is a subject in itself, but these disputes make labeling a touchy matter. The average Englishman, accustomed to the labels *Americanism, Scotticism, provincialism*, etc., for designating locutions to be avoided, is unwilling to concede that his own speech may contain something called a Briticism. He has not caught up with the notion that the English language now has many co-ordinate branches, and that American English has historical sources that are just as direct as those of British English. The glimmering of a change can be observed in a statement of a British scholar (McDonald 1954, 96): "Americans are beginning to feel that they do not have to look to England for guidance in correct usage." That, mind you, in 1954! I have even found an instance in which an Englishman expressed his certainty that Jesus would use British English rather than American English. An English traveler in the Bahamas (Montague 1958, 14) heard a Negro preacher say that "Nassau was a wicked city." This followed the American custom of using *city* in a wide sense, in place of *village*, but the Englishman commented, "I thought that no doubt Jesus would call Nassau a village rather than a city."

Other nationalities within the English-speaking world give rise to the need for other labels. One of the most frequently overlooked of these is *Canadian*. The study of Canada's English has not had the attention it deserves, because it has lain in the shadow of the English of the United States and to a large extent has been part of an American complex. One of the few words labeled *Canadian* in the *OED* is the slang word *muffin*, illustrated from 1856, referring to a girlfriend or "steady." It was easy for this to deteriorate from its innocent sense, and by the 1870s no girl would admit to being a muffin (see Russell 1865, 149; Fitzgerald 1873, 118–20). A surge of interest has taken place in recent years, fostered by the new Canadian Linguistic Association, and the gaps in our knowledge may one of these days be filled. There has been perennial interest in Australianisms, and rich collections have been made, but the best-known collector of them (Baker 1945, 15n28) has complained that only about a dozen have been included in the *Concise Oxford Dictionary*. Other parts of the world have branches of the English language with characteristic developments—New Zealand, the Philippines, India, South Africa, Ghana, the Caribbean, etc.—and each offers a challenge for the lexicologist to assemble the material that can be drawn upon by the general lexicographer.

The problems of labeling are still with us even within a single country when that country is as varied as the United States. The label *Dial.*, for "dialect" leaves much to be desired. As used by the general public, the word *dialect* is accompanied by so many folkloristic misconceptions that it is hardly a useful term. The man-in-the-street will still tell you that dialect is a degraded, corrupted form of the standard language. Among American scholars, the term can be used without invidious effect, but still it has its dangers. I have been astonished to find that a scholar like André Martinet, of world-wide fame, has presented views that I regard as altogether wrongheaded. In a paper given at Harvard University on March 12, 1953, since published,[8] he wrote as follows (Martinet 1954, 3):

> "Language" and "dialect" form a fairly clear opposition. . . . Linguistically and sociologically, it makes a great difference whether a "dialect" is one of several

> equally legitimate forms of a given language or whether it is felt to deviate from an accepted standard.... Thus we distinguish between dialects that are, so to speak, fully legitimate representatives of the language and opposed to it only as parts to a whole, and others that are, in a way, marginal and opposed to the language as something at least partially different. In this country [the U.S.], no one can help speaking a "dialect," because there is no form of speech which is not a dialect; in Europe generally, there is in every country a segment of the population which does not speak any "dialect," but the "language."

I regard this as very bad doctrine indeed, representing a capitulation to the biases and prejudices of contemporary French culture. Although he uses the expression "legitimate form of a given language," he does not explain what makes a form "legitimate" and what "illegitimate." From an objective point of view, a so-called "standard language" is a form that has been accorded special prestige. The continued cultivation of it may make it seem truly superior, but to the linguist it remains a dialect that arouses a certain attitude in the participant of the culture. I believe that the members of the *Académie française* speak a dialect, albeit a prestige dialect. Martinet's use of the terms involves the incorporation of evaluations into our very terminology.

I can imagine that Martinet might answer that it is the American point of view that does not face the realities. He regards the regional state of affairs in the United States as exceptional, calling it "probably unique on so large a scale" (Martinet 1954, 3). But in cultural history can be found the explanations why no one regional speech has achieved overwhelming prestige. Other cultural explanations can be sought to explain balances of prestige in French. He notes that in Great Britain, "linguistically, a cultured speaker from the Midlands does not rank with comparable southerners" Martinet 1954, 3). But in England there is strong resentment against the self-assumed superiority of Southern English, and champions can readily be found for Midland and Northern forms. The least that linguistic science can do is not to take sides, in its very terminology, either for or against the "Establishment."

Equally shocking to me is Martinet's suggestion that *patois* should be adopted as a regular descriptive technical term (Martinet 1954, 9). The built-in prejudice of this term, in the culture of all countries where it is known, makes it decidedly undesirable. Nor will the term *vernacular* do, as it implies the contrast of a learned language like an active Latin. I do not mean to minimize the necessity of a copious terminology to describe the complications in the layering of Romance dialectization, of which Martinet is an outstanding master, but the suggestions of his that I have attacked seem to me most reprehensible.

The labels for American dialects that were in vogue a generation ago have been considerably modified in recent years. It had long been known that *Southern* was a catch-all term for many sub-dialects that appeared in various parts of the South. The findings of the *Linguistic Atlas of the United States and Canada*, in the perspicacious interpretations of its director, Hans Kurath, showed that the term *Northern* also had to be broken up. His postulation of a Midland type, moving westward from a Philadelphia matrix, is being tested in the continued investigations in the Middle West.

A term that is frequently met with, but suspect among scholars, is *general American*. The *Linguistic Atlas* materials, with their emphasis on origins and early divergences, would lead to a discarding of the term. Furthermore, it gives unfair advantage to the speakers of whatever it may be. The chief criticism, it seems to me, is that *general American* is misleading as applied to any dialect of the past. It can, however, reasonably refer to a pattern of speech that is now forming, largely a mixture of Northern and Midland as those two rub against each other in the Middle West.[9] I have a terminological suggestion to make about this emergent pattern, As it is the result of a process now taking place, I suggest that it should be called "generalized American." The new words in *-ize* are much criticized (*finalize, funeralize*), but the word *generalized* is very apt here in showing that a process is going on. As one listens to American speech, on the radio, in the academic classroom, and in casual conversation, one cannot help realizing that a leveling off of regional characteristics is taking place, an increasing substitution of schwa, the falling together of certain vowels. If a name is to be applied to this speech of the future, it might well be "generalized American." The term is much superior to "standard American," which we are otherwise likely to fall into.

Whether a compromise English may be reached for the English-speaking world as a whole remains to be seen. One sometimes hears references now to a "mid-Atlantic accent" that has been achieved by actors or by public figures. As long ago as 1917, the classicist Paul Elmer More envisaged this future, and, on the base of *Hellenistic*, he coined the word *Englistic* to describe the tendencies he observed.[10] The popular dictionaries would primarily have to record this *koiné* or "Englistic," and the labelings would be reserved for disappearing forms from the old national and regional reservoirs. The working lexicographer will keep his eyes open for such developments.

NOTES

1. The first reference to such an object that I have found is by Browne (1736, 21): "Let all be plac'd in Manner due,/A Pot, wherein to spit, or spue." Cf. also Clarke (1798, iv): "One thing I find I have great cause of rejoicing in. The Sp-t-g Dishes are vanishing, from the whole circle of my acquaintance."

2. In a letter to E. H. Barker, in MS Bodl. 1003, leaf 113, recto and verso.

3. See, for example, Raven-Hart (1938, 84), concerning mosquitoes: "I felt a need to examine the boat closely for leaks from their gimlets." See also Lewis (1943, 97): "Her gimlet eyes ... bored into you when she asked you 'personal' questions"; and Evans (1946, 14/d): "Crowthers was older than Ianto had expected; a little gimlet of a man with glasses."

4. See Gardiner (1932, 168): "An instance recently quoted from Thomas Hardy is *In the waves they bore their gimlets of light*, said of lamps on a sea-wall; this use of the word *gimlet* appears to be quite unprecedented, nor is it likely to be repeated."

5. An American traveler in England (Wesson 1928, 73) was constrained to explain it: "'The Gimlet' ... proved to be the well and flavorably known ricky, but described as 'gin, a spot of lime, and soda.'" It was remarked on in the Baltimore *Sun* ("'Arf" 1933 [November 9], 22/c; courtesy of Atcheson L. Hench): "The chiefs and petty officers [on a British ship] ... have their 'whisky and soda' and 'gin gimlet.'" Only in the past year or two, an American sales company has been advertising a "Gimlet Mix" in newspapers and magazines.

6. See, for example, Grantley (1946, 12/a): "Think of a high police executive and you conjure up a picture of a gimlet-eyed, trim, super-efficient man." See also Pendennis (1954, 9/g): "A sandy, gimlet-eyed, normally taciturn little man of fifty-six, he was born in Boldon in Durham"; and Tynan (1956, 15/b): "'All for Love, or the World Ill Lost' is the message that issues from Shakespeare's gimlet-eyed indictment of Helen and Cressida."

7. See Carew (1955, 44/b): "Corporal of Horse Pomfret ... subjected us to a dispassionate scrutiny. His gimlety eye fell on me."

8. In a widely circulated advertisement for the periodical, probably written by Dr. Yakov Malkiel, Martinet's contribution was described as "a brilliantly phrased, programmatic article."

9. The best map that I know of to show this is that given by George R. Stewart, with the advice of David W. Reed (1954, 30). As Stewart (1954, 31) says: "It also shows the breakdown of colonial regionalism, and the mingling of the colonial stocks in the West, together with a growing domination of the speech of the middle colonies."

10. See More (1917, 5): "Has English entered upon a stage corresponding in any way to that of Hellenistic Greek? ... Now 'hellenistic' is defined in the dictionary as 'resembling or partaking of a Hellenic character, but not truly Hellenic,' and as 'combining Greek and foreign characteristics or elements;' and by such a definition I am bound to say that much of the spoken and written language of this country at least is not properly English, but, if by analogy I may coin a barbarous word, 'Englistic.'"

COMMENTS

William Gedney
University of Michigan

I FEEL THAT I AM IN THE FORTUNATE position of having been given the most attractive assignment on the entire program. The general topic for this morning—practical considerations in the preparation of dictionaries—is one that requires a discussant to cope with neither the abstrusities of theoretical controversy as was the case yesterday afternoon, nor the technicalities of particular lesser-known languages as will be the case this afternoon. I count my blessings.

Mr. Martin's various suggestions based on his experience seem to me sound and sensible. Virtually all of his recommendations seem to me to be the sort of thing that any of us engaged in the preparation of a bilingual dictionary ought to adopt.

I am a little dubious only about his "bad pennies" in section 2. I'm in favor of including such things, if possible, in a colloquial dictionary, or indeed in any dictionary, because they are certainly part of the lexicon and are often of high frequency, but, in many cases of this sort, the practical question arises as to how one is to spell the entry, since these "bad pennies" tend to be peculiar precisely in the fact that they consist of or contain sounds that are outside the phonemic inventory of the language.

I should like to put in a special plea for Martin's recommendation (also made by others yesterday), in section 1, that inflectional and derivative forms be entered in their proper alphabetical sequence, if only with a cross-reference to the form treated as basic. All who have studied Sanskrit know how many weary hours one wastes because, for example, some forms of certain verbs begin with other sounds than the base form. Makers of Sanskrit dictionaries, however, have tended to assume that students know their grammar and so will seek such forms under the base form. The fact is that students in the elementary stage usually don't know their grammar that well, and if they do then they don't need to open the dictionary at all. We have learned that in elementary language instruction, it is more effective to avoid writing lessons in the form of puzzles to be deciphered. It is high time now that our bilingual dictionaries should begin to lean over backwards in the direction of giving quick and easy access to the desired information, instead of posing time-wasting puzzles to be solved. At best, any interruption that requires opening a dictionary is already a misfortune.

Martin raises another problem that was also mentioned yesterday, namely the importance of deciding for whom the dictionary is intended. Avoiding for a moment the jargon of *source language*, *target language*, and the like, and using the simplest terms, it seems to me there are four main aims open to a bilingual dictionary: (1) to tell a speaker of English the meaning of an expression that he hears or reads in the other language; (2) to tell a speaker of English how to say something English in the other language; (3) to tell a speaker of the other language the meaning of an expression that he hears or reads in English; (4) to tell a speaker of the other language how to say something from that language in English.

In the comments, not only by Martin, but also by others yesterday, there was a commendable tendency to advise us to decide in the beginning on our audience and our aim. I should like to suggest that, in some cases, this sort of limitation may be unfortunate. In the case of Western European languages, we may properly limit ourselves to a particular audience and aim, for example, to tell a speaker of English how to say something in French. In the case of such languages, there is an abundance of other dictionaries, no doubt inferior to ours, to which readers outside our chosen audience may turn if they find we have omitted the information they want. But for many languages on which people here are working, other dictionaries are non-existent or unusable. For example, I have every reason to believe that Professor Haas' Thai dictionary is going to be the first really good dictionary of that language. If she limits her audience and aim, though she will produce a better book, the job of preparing Thai dictionaries to meet the other three aims will remain to be done and will now perhaps become less attractive, precisely because she has done one-fourth of the job so definitively. It is certainly true, as Gleason and others said yesterday, that each of these is actually a separate job and a separate book, but it seems probable that in actual practice there would be sufficient duplication of effort that it might be better to seek ways and means, when one has finished one of these dictionaries, to go on and do the other parts.

There is one last point related to the above, and this has to do again with the scope of bilingual dictionaries in the less well-known languages. One may decide to include a limited general vocabulary with a sprinkling of special terms, personal names, geographical names, and what not. Again, for a language in which many other dictionaries are available, such a delimitation of scope may be the wisest solution, but for languages where previous dictionaries are poor or inadequate or non-existent, would it perhaps not make sense to go counter to that principle and aim for a dictionary that will try to be fairly exhaustive in the areas it chooses to handle? One might, for example, undertake to cover the vocabulary of speech. Necessary curtailments could be effected by specifically omitting certain easily defined categories—say personal names, geographical names, plant and animal names, and the like. What I have in mind is the difficulty we create for aftercomers, if we try to handle a part of every sector of the vocabulary. There is a danger that, in later years, those who might wish to expand or extend our work might have to undertake to redo all our work from scratch, since we have left no easily perceived boundary that would allow them to go on where we left off. Confronted with this problem, aftercomers are likely to decide to do nothing, so that there is the danger that, in doing a part of the job, we have spoiled it for those who might want to do other parts. We might avoid this result by making our exclusions specific, so that aftercomers may tackle special categories and prepare special glossaries.

Probably these arguments are of no validity because they run counter to the practical aims that most of us are forced to use as a basis for our selection of entry.

Mr. Barnhart has given us a privileged inside view of how commercial dictionaries are produced. One feels that like politics, commercial lexicography is the art of the possible. No doubt the other gentlemen representing publishers of commercial dictionaries could give us similar accounts. One feels, after reading his paper, that Barnhart has given away all his professional secrets, but I suppose he knows that few readers, after learning something of the problems, are likely to want to follow his detailed directions and set themselves up in competition.

Many of us here are engaged in the preparation of subsidized dictionaries with a captive audience and market, so that much of Barnhart's advice may seem irrelevant, but even such fortunate dictionaries, although they may not be forced to sink or swim in a competitive commercial market, still have time and space limitations. We might well, therefore, study Barnhart's paper in detail for lessons in how to make our compromises systematically, consistently, and purposefully.

I described Barnhart's work as the art of the possible. I have the impression that Burrill and Bonsack are trying to do the impossible. I was overwhelmed with pity and horror after studying their paper, for it seems to me that they have the awful job of trying to make impossible decisions for which they don't have the data, although I realize after hearing their oral presentation that their work in the main is interesting and useful and sensibly conducted; it is clear that, in their written paper, they overemphasized the difficulties.

An example of what I mean by a horrifying impossibility is the Turkish element found in river names (problem-type 2) on which neither dictionaries nor available informants could give information. Obviously, if proper detailed dictionaries of older Turkish and of Turkish dialects existed, or if the investigator could take a month off and make a trip to the region, the problem could be solved. One admires the courage and fortitude of scholars compelled to cope constantly with the frustrations caused by not being able to lay hands on information that surely exists and ought to be accessible.

With no reflection on the authors or their paper, one might point out that this kind of activity is typical of an increasing American tendency toward organized large-scale research enterprises based sometimes on inadequate data, and I wonder if perhaps these authors might not be strong advocates for much, much more old-style long-term intensive narrow-range research in order to strengthen the factual basis for such large-scale crash programs. I should think one might also find among those of us assigned to big dictionary projects due to be completed in short periods a similar feeling of growing danger in our modern American tendency toward large-scale organized research programs as contrasted with old-fashioned intensive studies that set out to do things right, even if it took a lifetime.

I am afraid my reaction to the two parts of Mr. Iannucci's paper was extreme in opposite directions.

The first part of his paper, in which he studied analytically the organization and arrangement of definitions in a large number of dictionaries, is a priceless piece of work which each of us ought to study and restudy and keep handy for later reference. It seems to me to be one of the most valuable pieces of paper I shall carry away from this conference.

I am sorry to say, however, that the recommendation which Iannucci proposes as a result of this fine analysis seems to me unworkable.

Three reasons for this opinion strike me:

First, though the proposal to utilize the organization of definitions in existing monolingual dictionaries as a basis for the organization of definitions in a bilingual dictionary would have great advantages, as pointed out by the author, there would be formidable problems in the choice of the monolingual dictionary to be followed. And what about copyright?

Second, if the foreign material were printed in the same volume with the monolingual English dictionary, the result would be a big expensive book for French, another for German, another for Russian, and so on. If, on the other hand, the foreign material were printed separately with keyed references to an existing monolingual dictionary, a student might have to buy a Merriam-Webster to use with his French–English dictionary, an *American College Dictionary* (Barnhart et al. 1947) to use with his German–English dictionary, and so on.

Third, though Iannucci is able to find a Spanish monolingual dictionary good enough to use as a model for the organization of definitions on his Spanish–English side (and incidentally, this means another book to be purchased by the student for use as a key to the Spanish–English side), there are many languages for which no such satisfactory monolingual dictionary exists.

I suspect that there is a further doubtful consideration which I have not really studied. I wonder if the best organization and arrangement of definitions in a monolingual English dictionary would always turn out to be the best arrangement for speakers of another language, or even perhaps for English speakers studying another language.

But, finally, I want to reiterate my abounding admiration and gratitude for Iannucci's laborious but clear analysis of definition arrangements in existing dictionaries.

Mr. Read's paper, for my money, is a good choice, though perhaps accidental, to close this session, because it reinforces so cogently the point I raised earlier as to the eternal need for long-range intensive research in depth as a sound basis for the large-scale quickly organized research projects so popular nowadays. My only quarrel with Read would be for his hint that he may be accused of antiquarianism. I urge him to take a less apologetic posture, since it is clear that no decent lexicographical work can be accomplished without this sort of research in depth. Our speakers on geographical names, for example, would have no problem if an Allen Walker Read had collected Turkish dialect forms.

Yesterday before Read arrived, Professor Haas made an appeal for a short American–British glossary for ready reference. I should like to steal her thunder now and ask Read if he would consider taking a month out to compile such a glossary. [Read's reply was that, in his experience, a month taken out for such work usually developed into a much longer period.]

IV

LEXICOGRAPHICAL PROBLEMS IN SPECIFIC LANGUAGES

LEXICOGRAPHICAL PROBLEMS IN PASHTO*

O. L. Chavarría-Aguilar and Herbert Penzl
University of Michigan

1. Introduction

1.1. **Statistics.** Pashto is, along with Persian, Kurdish, Balochi, and Ossetic, a member of the Iranian branch of the Indo-European languages and is spoken in Eastern and Southern Afghanistan and in Northwestern Pakistan and the tribal areas between these two countries. The number of speakers can be estimated at close to ten million, divided about equally between the two countries. Some of the published estimates as to numbers of speakers of Pashto, e.g., 4,000,000 in Meillet and Cohen (1952) and elsewhere, are much too low; the census of Pakistan of 1951 lists about 5,000,000 in that country and the border areas nominally under its control who use Pashto as their mother tongue. On the other hand, some of the estimates coming from official and semi-official sources in Afghanistan may be considerably too high: 60% of an estimated total population of thirteen million, i.e., 7,800,000, have been estimated to be speakers of Pashto just in Afghanistan (Pazhwak 1952, 122ff.). In D. N. Wilber's *Afghanistan* (1956), in the Country Survey Series, the number of Afghan "Pushtu" speakers is given as 4,500,000, and the total number of Pashto speakers in the world as 10,000,000; this would seem to us to be a fairly reasonable figure. Incidentally, the great variety of spellings for the language—Pashto, Pakhtō, Pushto, Pushtu, Pukkhto, etc.—is partly due to dialectal variation in the treatment of the second consonant (always written ښ), and partly to difficulties and differing conventions in transliteration (see Penzl 1955, § 1.1 note). The first is the one preferred here.

---

* I have been unable to confirm several incomplete citations in this chapter, so they do not appear as entries in the references section. In some cases, names and titles of works have been modernized.

1.2. **Pashto in Afghanistan.** That Pashto in Afghanistan has, in the past three or four decades, begun to experience a remarkable renaissance is due in some measure to the steps taken by former King Amanullah to raise Pashto to the status of the official language of the country and to the determined efforts of a relatively small number of dedicated Pashtun leaders and writers. But Persian, with its greater literary prestige, is beside Pashto still the official language of Afghanistan now. Persian is the language of the Royal Afghan Court. It is also the language of the capital of the kingdom, Kabul, where all the ministries and the only university—as well as the four or five most important secondary schools and special schools—are located. Before 1920, only Persian was used in Afghan schools; now Pashto is the medium of instruction in those primary and secondary schools situated in areas where it is the language of the majority of the population. In predominantly Persian-speaking areas, it is taught as a foreign language from the third grade on up. Pashto is used in the press and on the radio—both government-controlled—and there is a Pashto Academy in Kabul, also government-sponsored, which is concerned with publications and research in Pashto. Traffic- and street-signs in Persian-speaking Kabul are in Pashto now (see Penzl 1955, § 5.3).

1.3. **Pashto in Pakistan.** The position of Pashto in the new "one-unit" province of West Pakistan is none too secure, although it is the native language of the President of the Republic, Field Marshal Ayub Khan. Pashto is taught in the elementary schools of West Pakistan's Pashto-speaking areas and as an elective subject in its secondary schools, for example, at Islamia College in Peshawar, where Urdu and English are compulsory subjects, and where the medium of instruction, barring a few subjects taught in Urdu, is English. While Urdu has been pushed practically since independence as the sole medium of instruction in the elementary and secondary schools throughout West Pakistan, there has been increasing pressure for the use of Pashto in the former Northwest Frontier Province (henceforth, NWFP), and there are signs that, as texts and teachers become available, Pashto will replace Urdu as the medium of instruction in the Pashto-speaking areas. Only this year, the University of Peshawar instituted an M.A. program in Pashto. A city of the size and importance of Peshawar, the cultural center of the Pashto-speaking area and the former capital of the NWFP, has no daily newspaper entirely in Pashto. The number of publications by Pashto writers (prose fiction, poetry, magazines), however, has considerably increased since the beginning of the "Pashtunistan" conflict between Pakistan and Afghanistan about ten years ago.

2. Written Corpus and Lexical Studies

2.1. The written corpus of Pashto. The earliest Pashto manuscript dates from the seventeenth century. Its text and other texts with an allegedly even earlier date of composition do not give any evidence for morphological or phonological stages of Pashto earlier than those attested by the modern language. Thorough lexicographical investigation of these texts has yet to be performed (but see Dorn 1847, 387–618); only then will it become clear how their lexicon differs from that of the modern Pashto dialects. The lack of variety in the character of the literary monuments preserved to us, and the relative meagerness of the textual tradition, handicap any systematic historical investigation of the Pashto lexicon. There is, however, still a considerable corpus of unedited (and largely ignored) manuscript material in the India Office Library in London and a more modest collection at the Pashto Academy in Peshawar.

While a listing of the total annual literary production in Pashto from both sides of the Khyber Pass still would not offer a seriously taxing problem to bibliographers, the modern written corpus of Pashto is actually of considerable magnitude, for newspapers and magazines have appeared for decades in the cities of Afghanistan.

2.2. Lexicographical studies in Pashto. The lexicographical work done in Pashto consists of the following: (1) two dictionaries, Raverty (1867) and Bellew (1901), now out of print, both of which, as well as grammars, textbooks, and text editions, resulted from the efforts of the British administration to encourage proficiency in the native languages of British India. Assistant Surgeon Bellew (1901, xi) added also a "reversed part," English–Pashto, but the Pashto–English part, "aided" by Raverty's work, is his main contribution, mostly derived from his reading of "Pukkhtūn authors"; (2) Gilbertson (1932) contains a collection of Pashto sentences and their translations alphabetically arranged under one English key word or idiomatic phrase that has an equivalent in the Pashto sentences. They must have been collected from the three assistants (Árif Ullah, Yúsufzai; Alí Makhmúd, Afrídí; Alí Akbar Khán, Qandahárí) mentioned on the title page. A comprehensive *New English Pakkhto Conversational Dictionary* announced by the author in the foreword (1932, ix) apparently never appeared in print; (3) a Pashto–Russian and Russian–Pashto dictionary (Zudin 1950), containing 12,000 words and appended brief notes on Pashto by E. A. Bertels, as well as another by Zudin (1955), containing about 21,000 words and a brief grammatical sketch by D. A. Shafeev (Zudin 1955, 1035 ff.); (4) a variety of dictionary compilations published in Kabul, of which the older ones are no longer available, even in the libraries of Kabul, e.g., *De Pakhtu Sind* (Pashto–Persian; 1316 A. H.; 1937), by Mohammad Gul Khan Mohmand; by the Lexicography Branch of the Pashto Academy (Pashto–Persian; 1330–1333 A. H.; 1951–54); and Nawīs (1957), in which Persian entries are followed by Persian glosses and Pashto equivalents. A list of Pashto idiomatic expressions with Persian translations and commentary is contained in Nawri (1320 A. H.; 1941). The Pashto Academy at the University of Peshawar is engaged in a monumental Pashto–Urdu–English historical and dialectal lexicon project. At this writing they were halfway through the "Alif," the first character of the Perso-Arabic script which Pashto employs. Sayyid Rahatullah Rahat Zekheli published a Pashto–Urdu dictionary, *Lughāt Afghanī* (Peshawar, n.d.), with almost 10,000 entries; and (5) the etymologies of Pashto words were treated in Morgenstierne (1927).

3. Pashto Dialects in Field and Texts

3.1. **Dialectal variations in Pashto**. Pashto shows a great variety of dialectal subtypes. Pashto specimens in the *Linguistic Survey of India* (Grierson 1898–1928, 10.25–111) provide only a very inadequate sampling of the dialectal distinctions. They are phonemic and phonetic, morphological, and lexical. All dialects of Pashto seem to show the same syntactic structure and certainly the same grammatical categories. Needless to say, only extensive and systematic field work will reveal in detail the exact distribution of the dialects of Pashto, a task to date quite neglected. For our purposes it will be sufficient here to illustrate the three types of dialectal distinctions. The phonemic differences are the most striking. They involve differences in the phonemic pattern; the presence or absence of certain allophones; and the distribution of the phonemes and their frequencies. In the dialect of Kandahar—which agrees more than any other dialect with the generally accepted orthography for Pashto—retroflexed shibilants, both voiced and voiceless, appear medially, e.g., in *kēžī* 'becomes' and *paštō* 'Pashto,' respectively; there occur likewise a voiced alveolar affricate and a voiceless alveolar affricate, e.g., in *dzem* 'I go' and in *tsōk* 'who,' respectively. The dialect of Wardak, south of Kabul, has the same number of phonemic contrasts, but instead of the retroflexed shibilants, a contrasting pair of voiced and voiceless medio-palatal fricatives occur, e.g., *kēgī* and *paçtō*. Most dialects of the province of Kabul retain the medio-palatal voiceless fricative in *patō*, but the medial consonant in *kēžī* has coalesced with the voiced velar stop /g/: *kēgī*. In the dialect of the Peshawar area, as well as in some of the Eastern dialects, not one of the four phonemes mentioned above for the Kandahar dialect occurs; they have coalesced, the voiced retroflexed shibilant with the voiced velar stop, as in *kēgī*; the voiceless retroflexed shibilant with the voiceless velar fricative, as in *paxtō*; the affricates have been simplified and have coalesced with /z/ and /s/, as in *zem* and *sōk*. Worthy of note among the characteristic allophones of some of the dialects are the high allophones of the two mid vowels /ē/ and /ō/ before a following vowel of high tongue position; it is often difficult to distinguish clearly between /ē/ and /ī/ and between /ō/ and /ū/: e.g., /ē/ in *kēzī*, /ō/ in *gōrū* 'we see.'

Distributional differences of phonemes concern particularly the sibilants, where the dialects show varying distribution of /s/ and /š/ and also of /z/, /ž/ and /ĵ/ in some words of high frequency. In many dialects of the province of Kabul and Paktia, in Ghazni, Kandahar, and Herat in Afghanistan and Dera Ismail Khan in Pakistan, *sta* 'there is' and *səm* 'I can' are regularly heard instead of *šta* and *šəm*. For *žaba* 'language, tongue,' some central dialects have *žaba*, and some Eastern dialects in the Kunar Valley have *ĵeba*.

Morphological distinctions between the dialects concern, e.g., some substantive and verbal endings: *kōrō* (obl. p.) in Kandahar for *kōrúnō* 'houses'; *-āst* for *-əy* as the second person plural ending of the past tense and some present forms in Kandahar, Farah, Herat, and Dera Ismail Khan, e.g., *yāst* 'you are.' The third person singular masculine of the past of the verb can be -o ('zero'), *-ə*, *-ō,-əy*, e.g., *wəlid, wəlidə, wəlidō* (Peshawar), *wəlidəy* (Kandahar) 'seen.' It is interesting to note that, with few minor exceptions, Afghan grammarians, in their textbooks, describe as models for instruction the forms of their own dialects (see Penzl 1951 and 1952).

Lexical distinctions reveal dialect differences of considerable extent, e.g., such items as *dōbay* and *ōray* 'summer,' *lōy* and *star* 'great, big,' *tsōrmunay* and *psarlay* (also *sparlay*) 'spring,' *lmar* and *stərga* (*də lmar stərga*) 'sun.'

3.2. The dialect and the dictionary. One problem for the lexicographer is to what extent dialectal variation should be included in his lexicon and how it is to be treated. For Pashto, this is no great problem. There is a more or less standard orthography accepted throughout the Pashto-speaking world, an orthography which represents, for the consonants at any rate, the maximum phonemic distinctions as found in the dialect of Kandahar. Thus, phonemic variation can to a large extent be ignored. The one complicating factor—and it is not too serious as yet—is that a tendency seems to be arising among some writers to model the orthography in some respects after their spoken dialect (see MacKenzie 1959, 231ff.). Only a glossary based on one or a few specific texts can, however, include such variations, e.g., *xəza* for *sədza* 'woman' and hyperforms such as *dzmā* for *zmā* 'my,' even though their general textual frequency may be fairly high. Dialect dictionaries and glossaries, of course, would have to render the specific phonemic forms in question as do, e.g., Lorimer's (1902) Waziri study, and the Afridi word lists in *The Modern Pushtu Instructor* (Khan 1938–43, volume 2).

The morphological variants such as those mentioned above present no problems, since they are not the concern of the dictionary, but rather that of the descriptive and reference grammars of the language. The lexical variants which represent dialectal differences will have to be included if they occur in texts, their inclusion to be determined primarily by their textual rather than by their field frequency. This is true of such items as *stər* besides *lōy*, two morphemically entirely different lexical items, as well as of morphemic variants (which may really in some cases represent phonemically different dialectal types), such as *lyār* beside *lār* 'road,' *tund* beside *lund* 'wet,' *rwadz* beside *wradz* 'day,' *mzəka* beside *zməka* 'earth.' In morphology and lexicon there is very little difference between written and spoken Pashto within a single dialect or group of dialects. There is certainly nothing comparable to the "diglossia," to use Ferguson's term, that is prevalent in Afghan Persian, where a tremendous gulf separates the literary Persian of Afghan publication from the spoken "Kabuli" of daily discourse.

The Pashto Academy in Kabul has attempted in writers' conferences sponsored by it to establish morphological and sometimes morpho-lexical standards for writers on both sides of the Pakistan–Afghan border (see Käker 1958). It has upheld the standard orthography. Phonetic spellings such as *zəba* ض or *jəba* ݘ for *žəba* and the frequent Peshawar ح (ē, actually /ɛ/ contrasting with /ē/) for /ay/ in *kawəlay* were rejected. The zero ending for the 3rd asc. sing, preterite form, e.g., *wəlid* 'seen,' which is quite rare in the dialects, was recommended instead of -ə, -ō, -əy; the Kandahar -āst beside -əy for the 2nd pers. pl. of the verb was approved.

3.3. Textual and field frequencies.

We mentioned earlier that there is no great difference between spoken and written Pashto. A writer will therefore, while making concessions as to phonemic shape by adopting the "standard" shape as against that of his own dialect, otherwise feel free to make use of most of the lexicon of his own dialect in writing. This seems to imply for the lexicographer that the Pashto lexicon can be gotten either by means of a quasi-philological analysis of texts or through fieldwork with informants. The character of the available written corpus of Pashto is redundant to a considerable extent, thus limited in its total range. Some items will have a very low (or even zero) textual frequency, where the field frequency can be shown to be quite high.

The conclusion to be drawn would seem to be that, in the case of Pashto, a combination of textual analysis and fieldwork will yield the lexicon essential for a dictionary that is to contain all items of high textual and field frequencies.

4. Foreign Loanwords in Pashto

A special lexicographical problem arises from the presence in Pashto of many Persian, Arabic, Indic (Urdu) and western terms. Bellew (1891, vii) has already stated in his preface: "I have experienced considerable difficulty in deciding upon the words of foreign origin—principally Arabic and Persian, but still of common use in the Pukkhto—that should find a place in these pages."

The number of foreign words will differ in texts from different areas. Words with high textual and field frequencies have to be included. In Afghanistan a number of words that are puristic or artificial creations, sometimes intended to replace established Arabic–Persian terms, may have a higher text than field frequency; e.g., *šōwundzay* versus *maktab* 'school.' No term with a relatively high textual frequency can be excluded.

Some western terms show a morphemic variation that is not always represented by the Perso-Arabic orthography; e.g., *gēr* and *gīr* 'gear,' *klīnar* and *kilīnar* 'driver's assistant.' Lexical listing in such cases will have to include both possibilities. The reason for this morphemic variation is the increasing adaptation to native speech patterns by some, and the puristic attempts at remodeling by other speakers familiar with the languages from which the borrowings came. Western loans are found in the fields of politics, science, western culture, technology, motor transport, etc. (Penzl

1961b, 43ff.). Speakers familiar with especially English, French, and German have brought these words into the language. Sometimes the contact with specific languages will determine the particular shape of the loans; e.g., *sāyins* is competing with *siyāns*, English and French 'science,' *āstriā* with *ōtriš* 'Austria.' The role that English is playing in secondary education favors the spread of loanwords with an English base. The textual frequencies of some of these words is low, but their field frequencies high: e.g., *tšēn* 'chain (in motor-car),' *sīt* 'seat' (of bus or car), *bōlt* 'bolt,' etc. The dictionary will have to include all Arabic, Persian, western, and other terms whose frequencies justify it.

5. Nonlexical Problems in Pashto

5.1. **Transliteration and/or transcription**. The items collected from texts will, of course, be given in the standard Arabic orthography. As stated above, deviant phonetic spellings employed by writers of a dialect with a phonemic system different from that of the "standard" language as represented by the generally accepted orthography can only be included in special glossaries for specific texts or dialects. The same is probably true for occasional spellings that offer colloquially general or at least very widespread replacements, e.g., *p* for *f, k* for *q*, etc., in Arabic and Persian loans. If, however, their textual frequency in some lexical items should prove to be sufficiently high, they may have to be included as morphemic variants (of the type *wradz* and *rwadz* as mentioned in section 3.2).

On the Pashto–English side of the dictionary, every entry in the Arabic alphabet must be followed by an indication of its standard phonemic shape by means of a Roman alphabet notation. This is very necessary because Arabic orthography does not indicate the short vowels /ā/, /ə/, /i/, and /u/ nor does it make any distinction between /ō/, /ū/, /w/, /wa/, /aw/, /wə/, and /əw/, which are all written as *wāw* (,) (see Penzl 1954). The practices of the extant Pashto dictionaries (see 2.2 above) show some difference in the Romanized writing of Arabic (and Persian) loanwords. The entries in the dictionaries by Raverty (1867), Bellew (1901), and Gilbertson (1932) transliterate the Pashto letters not only by such symbols as *f* (ﻑ), *q* (ﻕ), ' (ﻉ), *h* (with a diacritic) for ﺡ, but distinguish ﺕ and ﻁ, ﺱ ﺹ ﻥ ﺯ ﻅ ﺽ by *t, s*, and *z* symbols with differentiating diacritics. This practice, incidentally, was continued in Penzl (1955; see §2.5), where diacritics are only used for optional transliteration, when their omission would not change the phonemic representation.

Bellew (1901) gave in the English–Pashto part of his dictionary only the Roman transliteration of the Pashto entries, which are however "reversible" into the Arabic orthography. In Zudin's dictionaries (1950, 1955), the Cyrillic transcription includes only f, but no special symbols for ق (written k), the glottal stop, and only one symbol each for /t/, /s/, and /z/.

In spoken Pashto in a varying degree (see Penzl 1955, §§ 37–40), the phonemes /f/ /q/ /ʕ/, and sometimes /h/—/h/ with pharyngeal friction—are used by literate speakers in a more formal style of speech. Should the dictionary indicate the formal pronunciation, which would agree with the Arabic spelling, should it substitute a colloquial transcription, or should it indicate both formal and colloquial pronunciation? Since the colloquial pronunciation can be derived from the formal and elegant one by some simple rules of transformation, but not vice versa, it will seem preferable to indicate consistently the formal pronunciation. However, with some lexical items of high field-frequency, a colloquial pronunciation may have to be added to the formal one.

Although there is no clearly defined standard of pronunciation for Pashto, the selection of a "standard" for the transcribed (or transliterated) entries will have to be determined by the phonemic distribution in the main dialectal types of Pashto, which, on the whole, agree quite well, at least in the case of the vowel phonemes. Zudin selected for his dictionaries a Kandahar pronunciation (see 2.2).

5.2. The grammatical identification of entries. A dictionary should include the grammatical information necessary to identify the word class and the essential morphological features of an entry. Text and field occurrences involve not just the "quotation" form. The Pashto word class will customarily be identified by the corresponding word class of the English gloss or definition. The morphemic subclasses can be indicated by either some additional forms, from which the remaining inflectional features can be derived, by suitable code symbols, if brevity is called for, or by a combination of both. In the glossary of Penzl (1955), for example, a combination of both practices was used to characterize the lexical items. For substantives, the gender and plural-formation, for adjectives the formation of their feminine, for verbs the formation of their past tenses (I and II) were considered the principal criteria for their subdivision into morphemic subclasses. Thus, substantives would be marked *m*(asculine) or *f*(eminine), and their plural and oblique forms indicated by a numeral: *m*1, *m*2, *m*3, *m*4, and *m*5; *f*1, *f*2, *f*3, *f*4, *f*5, and *f*6. For instance, *kōr* 'house' would be labeled *m*1, which implies a plural *kōruna* (also obl. II sing. *kōra*, obl. pl, *kōrō*); *špa* 'night' is *f*2, which indicates the plural *špe* (also obl. sing. *špe*, obl. pl. *špō*). The adjective *užd* is marked adj. II, which implies a feminine *uždá*, plus a whole set of other predictable endings. Five adjective classes are differentiated altogether.

The verbs were labeled Verb I, II, III, IV, IV-A: e.g., *tarəm* 'I bind' Verb I, which means a predictable formation of the past tenses with no change from the present stem; *rasēzəm* (past *rasēd-*) 'I arrive, reach,' Verb II, with the change in the past stem as indicated; the same way with *gōram* (past *kat-*), 'I look at,' Verb III, where present and past stems seem suppletive. Only seven verbs were marked "Verb IV," and the stems of present II, past I, and past II had to be indicated; e.g., *kawəm* (pres. II [wə] *kəm*, past I *kaw-*, past II [wə] *kr-*) 'make, do,' Verb IV. Verbs of the class IV-A, e.g., *jōrēžəm* 'I become well,' *jōrawəm* 'I make well, build,' are really compounds of *kēžəm* and *kawəm* (both class IV verbs), and four forms have also to be indicated there.

The principle of indicating, if space permits, all morphological features of entries not predictable from the shape of the quotation form (with a minimum of grammatical knowledge) seems sound.

PROBLEMS IN MODERN GREEK LEXICOGRAPHY

Henry and Renée Kahane
University of Illinois

THE US OFFICE OF EDUCATION IS SPONSORING A *Modern Greek–English Dictionary*, to be published by the University of North Dakota under the direction of Professor Demetrius Georgacas. We are consultants for the project, and various questions that have to be answered or, at least, asked at the present initial stage are closely related to the problems dealt with at the Indiana Conference on Lexicography. Thus, we are presenting them (on our own, to be sure, and not as spokesmen of the team) from the standpoint of this particular project in progress. On the other hand, Modern Greek is an excellent basis for a theoretical discussion of lexicographical problems. In terms of morphemics, it allows us to verify hypotheses about the present with data of the past. In terms of levels, it still preserves conditions for actual observation which in the Romance West have been gone for a long time. In terms of the corpus, it stays in the middle between the well-described and the undescribed languages, and thus offers good material for the development of scientific lexicography.

In the following brief sketch, the problems will be discussed under two main headings: 1. Levels of speech; and 2. Levels of analysis.

1. Levels of Speech

1.1. **Demotic vs. puristic**. During the Middle Ages, a very marked linguistic dichotomy prevailed in the once Romanized areas of Western Europe: the vernaculars continuing the colloquial form of Latin were used for informal communication, whereas a form of Latin that was based on ancient and early Christian models served the needs of formal expression. Since the Renaissance, this contrast between levels has diminished considerably.

In the Greek East, however, a linguistic situation analogous to that of the medieval West still obtains, probably for a number of cultural reasons. A marked opposition prevails between the puristic and formal levels of speech, the katharevusa (a continuation of the classical, Christian, and Byzantine written tradition) and the colloquial level, the demotic (a development of the popular usage of antiquity). This linguistic situation is an essential feature of the social structure of Modern Greece. The two language levels have turned into symbols of political philosophies. Rightly or wrongly, the katharevusa has become the emotional bridge to the glorious past; and past is, in a school sense, antiquity, and in a national sense, Byzantium. Similarly, the demotic has become the democratic symbol. The more conservative people are, the more they adhere to the katharevusa; the more liberal, the more to the demotic. Communist propaganda uses the demotic, exploiting the fact that the demotic is the level of the masses. This is, incidentally, quite unlike the medieval ecclesiastic habit of both the Western and the Eastern Churches, which impressed the masses through the medium of the traditional level, often difficult to understand, of ecclesiastic Latin and ecclesiastic Greek, respectively.

The difference between the two levels of speech occurs on all levels of analysis. It is least marked on the phonemic level, most striking in vocabulary. It has, of course, dominated the development of Greek lexicography. In late antiquity and the Middle Ages, colloquial words were often listed in glossaries and scholia, with a prescriptive purpose, together with their respectable synonyms. A real thesaurus of the spoken language does not yet exist in completed form. Only the first letters of the alphabet of the magnificent *Historical Lexicon of Spoken Greek* (Papadopoulos 1933–46) in progress at the Academy of Athens, are available. It includes, however, dialect material and is intended for research purposes. The large modern dictionaries mix the two levels within one alphabetic arrangement. It is interesting to notice that the inclusion of demotic material starts with bilingual glossaries and vocabularies. Apparently, for the foreigner, puristic prescription is irrelevant, but a basis of communication is necessary. A typical early example is a Hebrew–Greek glossary of about the tenth century (von Günzburg and Markon 1908, 68–96). In more recent times, from about the seventeenth century on, the bilingual dictionaries are about the best collections of demotic material. Among them just a few may be mentioned: da Somavera (1709; Greek–Italian), Legrand (1882; Greek–French), Missir (1952; French–Greek) and, an interesting experiment based solely on field work, Swanson (1959; English–Greek and Greek–English).

But "katharevusa" is an ambiguous concept. So far it has been used here as the designation of a language level, used in scientific writing, in legal procedure, in political articles of the newspapers, and contrasting with the informal level of daily communication and of fiction. On the other hand, the term *katharevusa* refers to the form of a word, indicating that it shows certain phonemic or morphemic features, classic or Byzantine, which the words of the demotic do not preserve. These katharevusa words are comparable to what Romance etymologists call Latinisms, i.e., words not (or only partially) participating in the changes of the phonemic and morphemic systems, or newly coined, with slight demotic retouches, by means of such conservative morphemes. But the form of the word is not necessarily correlated with the level on which it is used. Just as in Romance many Latinisms are used in everyday speech, so words of the katharevusa form may be used on the demotic level. The very fact that they may partake on either level, katharevusa or demotic, makes a clear-cut division between the two levels difficult. A few examples, representing various patterns of katharevusa words in the demotic, may illustrate the predicament of the lexicographer who wants to compile the corpus of the present-day demotic.

In the nineteenth and well into the twentieth century, 'post office' was expressed in Greek by the Italianism *pósta*. This was superseded in the period of modern administration by the katharevusa term, based on ancient material, *taxudromeío* 'courier-office.' It is general and would have to appear in the demotic glossary. Second example: the refrigerator, an institution vital mostly to Americans living in Greece, is called *psugeío*, also a katharevusa term. Along with many other terms of American gracious living it is certainly not generally used in Greece. Nevertheless, Messing (1960, 144) suggests its inclusion in a demotic list. A third pattern is represented by numerous katharevusa morphemes which are, for a number of reasons (Caratzas 1958, 206), preferred to their demotic allomorphs: with the names of various professions, for example, the semipuristic plural in *-és* is used rather than the demotic plural in *-ádes* (*mathētés* 'students' instead of *mathētádes*). Should these katharevusa morphemes be used instead of or together with their demotic allomorphs or not at all? A fourth pattern is exemplified by two designations of 'house': in advertising and on signs, you read in many places the ancient *oikía*, but you pronounce it *spiti*, the common colloquial designation. Here, the contrast between the katharevusa and the demotic term is more or less equivalent to that between passive and active elements of the vocabulary. Should the passive elements of the language be included in or excluded from a demotic glossary?

1.2. Colloquial vs. literary. A second dichotomy of levels is that of colloquial vs. literary demotic. Fiction (as distinct from non-fiction) represents the written tradition of the demotic. On the one hand, it is a source for demotic material; on the other, it is written, not spoken. There have been groups of writers, once nicknamed "the long-haired," who introduced a certain radicalism into the demotic. Some of the vocabulary of literature is about as distant from actual use as that of the purists. Just as many puristic forms are used commonly in everyday speech, so, in reverse, many demotic forms may not be used at all. Some of the *galano-* 'blue' compounds, merely literary coinages, may serve as an illustration (Papadopoulos 1933–1946, s.vv.):

galanóbathos	'blue and deep'
galanólouloudo	'blue flower'
galanómauros	'dark blue'
galanóxanthos	'blue with a golden gleam'
galanóphrúdēs	'with blue eyes'
galanófteros	'with blue wings'
galanófullos	'with blue leaves'
galanófōtos	'radiating blue'
galanokhrusōménos	'goldenblue'

Here, then, without the regulating and authoritarian bodies as we know them from the Western Academies, we come again to the age-old question about the source material of lexicography. Can literature serve as a source at all; and if so, must a body of authorities be defined whose usage is to be recognized as standard? The answer of present-day applied linguistics is (at least theoretically) in the negative. But, on the other hand, in view of the limited lexicographical material available in modern Greece, Greek literature has to be used (in contrast to that of various other languages), not as a preceptor, but rather as an informant, who, to be sure, as far as frequency is concerned, is right only part of the time. Literature, in other words, may be used as a visual informant to be checked by means of an audible one.

The use of written material brings up the question of the usefulness of frequency lists and their, transfer to other languages. To work with frequency lists of thé language under discussion is at present out of the question, since there are none in existence and their production would require time, means, and effort often not available. The Thorndike list (Thorndike and Lorge 1944) is only of reduced value outside of English, not so much because of the difference in material culture which could easily be taken account of, but because it is, to a great extent, based on English literature, whereas our target is neither English nor literature. It cannot be more than a stimulus and a starting point for an intelligent transfer to be made by someone or some team familiar with both cultures and languages. As an illustration of cultural differences, we may note that in Greek the terminology of opinion, impression, and sensation, with numerous shades and synonyms, is of the greatest frequency, and a realistic dictionary would have to register it carefully.

Here, then, the following questions remain. Is fiction a realistic basis for a description of the frequent and typical patterns of the spoken language? If so, on what basis should the literary samples be selected? Is this a return to the seventeenth-century principle of the authorities? Is reading, in addition to speaking, an aim in itself to be included in the type of dictionary under discussion?

1.3. **Standard vs. dialect**. It is customary to consider the well-educated Athenian as the speaker of Standard Greek. This is, incidentally, not a tradition stemming from antiquity but a recent one. In antiquity, the dialect of Attica evolves as the basis of the Koine, i.e., Standard Hellenistic Greek; in recent modern history (and in the twentieth more than in the nineteenth century) the new capital of the young state, arbitrarily chosen and not more than an insignificant country town with a brilliant name as its main asset, attracted large masses of population, coming from all parts of the country, swelling the population of the city to a million inhabitants. The Peloponnesian dialect becomes, in certain ways, the nucleus of the new Athenian standard (Caratzas 1958, 201). To the lexicographer, this situation means various things.

It establishes an intersection of two dichotomies: the area of the standard form of speech (as distinct from non-standard) overlaps the area of urban vocabulary (as distinct from provincial). This leads to an interesting pattern of evaluation: since urban is equated with standard, non-urban or "dialect" is often equated with substandard. In a study dealing with the treatment of speech levels in a recently published Greek glossary, 131 forms are rejected for various reasons; thirteen (or a tenth) of them because they are considered both dialectal and substandard. How far can and how far should this kind of selection be carried? Of course, one of the reasons for the system of lexical evaluation lies in the fact that, in Greece, the development of mass communications has not been as extensive as it has been in some other cultures. Therefore, the cultural and with it the linguistic contrast between urban and provincial (i.e., both rural and small town) communities is still very strong. We wonder how relevant the rural terminology is for a dictionary of about forty thousand entries.

But "Standard" may also appear in a purely regional contrast. Lexical variants in the designation of one sememe which are found in the provinces may still be used on the same social and educational level as their Athenian equivalent and therefore belong in a glossary of standard Greek. It is the well-known phenomenon treated at length by Kretschmer (1918) in his *Wortgeographie der hochdeutschen Umgangssprache*. His informants shared social status but differed as to regional provenience. This is a very common phenomenon in Greek (as in many other languages); and it is, indeed, questionable whether the Athenian should be allowed (and if so to what extent) to outweigh the others. One possible lexicographical criterion in this context is that a term that is known to and used by all should in a limited dictionary have the preference over a synonym used only by part of the speakers.

Standardization may be achieved by accepting one dialect as the "correct" form to which all material is to be adapted. The Greek dialects of the North, with many speakers, have a certain system of unstressed vowels that (*grosso modo*) can be stated as follows: where the Southern dialects use *e* and *o*, the North uses *i* and *u*; and where the Southern dialects use *i* and *u*, the North uses zero. Assuming that the fieldworker hears in Macedonia or Thrace [pidhák] 'little child,' he will have to standardize it to *paidáki* [pedháki]. The following is a typically Greek phenomenon involving consonant clusters, which raises again the question of standardization through consistency. The cluster syllable-final-nasal-plus-a-following-stop appears in two variants: many speakers pronounce the nasal, and many others do not; e.g., one hears both pronunciations for 'man'—[ándras] and [ádras]. Since both pronunciations are common, the lexicographer has various courses: he can list what he has heard (Gilliéron's credo), or he can standardize in either of the two directions. A case in point is Swanson's rendering of the negative particle *mē* as [mi] or [min] in the same environment. He worked with informants and did not hesitate to register what he had heard. If the lexicographer is a fieldworker, consistency is not a necessary virtue; and realism stands higher than consistency. If the lexicographer is an editor, things may be the other way around. The weaker the tradition in the lexicography of a given language, the greater the problem of standardization and consistency.

1.4. **Traditionalism vs. fieldwork.** A team of scholars charged with the collection of the corpus for a *Modern Greek–English Dictionary* is in a middle position on the continuum between the two poles of traditionalism (in this context, defined as reliance on written material, mostly existing glossaries) and fieldwork (i.e., the gathering of the material directly from the speaker). But the half dozen or so large dictionaries that could well serve as a starting point would have to be shortened, modified, and enlarged. On the whole, the *Modern Greek–English Dictionary* requires a skillful combination of traditionalism and fieldwork (since it is to be completed in a reasonable amount of time and can therefore not be based on fieldwork exclusively). This kind of fieldwork based on existing materials will have to clear up the following points: (1) Which of the demotic words found in available dictionaries are actually used? (2) Which of the katharevusa words have become part of the demotic? (3) Which is the most common allomorph of a morpheme in use?

It may be necessary to work through a team rather than have things decided by one man. The elusiveness of the concept of commonness is demonstrated by the *Historical Lexicon* (Papadopoulos 1933–46) which distinguishes, on the basis of discussion and consultation, among such ill-defined distinctions as "used in many places," "usual," "common." Of course, the demotic lexicographers disagree among themselves about the commonness of a given word. Koukoules compiled a list of 56 words, common in his opinion, which had been omitted in a certain glossary; of these, Georgacas recognizes only 33 as common; and Papadopoulos listed some 150 words as missing in the same work, not all of which are admitted by Georgacas (1958a; see also Georgacas 1958b). The members of the team should at least represent the main dialect areas: Athens, the North, and the South. They would function at the same time as fieldworkers and informants. In cases of doubt, other informants should be used. These should be, unless certain special terminologies are asked for, well-educated; for well-educated informants are usually better informants than less-well-educated, particularly in a country such as Greece with its burdensome dichotomy between demotic and katharevusa. The speakers with only some passive or no knowledge of the katharevusa grow up with the oppressive knowledge that there is somewhere a "good" and "beautiful" language which is unreachable to them. This makes them unsure of their own level of speech and confuses them. Here is one obvious limit to the belief in the native speaker's correctness. But the main reason that makes a democratic team (as contrasted to an authoritarian organization) almost mandatory is not so much the equal representation of dialect areas as the mutual education to tolerance. The Linguistic Society of America's principle of respect (voluntary or enforced) for everybody's "dialect" is still not practiced in many parts of the world, particularly where speech forms have become a basis for class distinctions. Often, to be sure, this boils down to the simple fact that somebody else's way of saying something is considered a bad way of saying it, just because it is different from yours. One of us knows from his own background, as a native speaker of German, how easily irritated he became not only by vocabulary differences but also by differences in vowel quality used in the dialects of other speakers.

2. Levels of Analysis

2.1. **Phonemics**. It is a question whether the dictionary should use a broad or a narrow transcription. Although (according to a remark by Navarro Tomás) incorrect allophones of a foreign speaker irritate the native more than incorrect phonemes, there are still, in a glossary not intended for linguists exclusively, various factors which militate against an allophonic transcription.

There exists a considerable amount of allophonic variation, a complete marking of which would be cumbersome. A selection would be arbitrary. The following illustrations represent some of the possible patterns: (1) Before voiced consonants a sibilant is voiced: [kóstas] 'endearing for Constantinus' vs. [kózmos] 'world.' This can still safely be transcribed, since, in certain distributions, /s/ and /z/ are phonemes (e.g., *sónei* [sóni] 'it's enough' vs. *zóne* [zóni] 'belt'); (2) The voiceless fricative appears as palatal before front vowels (*ékhei* 'he has,' with *kh* = Ger. *ach* sound) but as velar before back vowels (*ékho* 'I have,' with *kh* = Ger. *ich* sound); (3) Many speakers in many areas in varying degrees palatalize such consonants as *n, l, k* before front vowels but pronounce the same phonemes before back vowels without palatalization ([ñífi] 'bride' vs. [náftis] 'sailor'); and (4) Vowel quantity is not phonemic in Modern Greek as it was in the ancient language; quantity in Modern Greek is allophonic, determined by the accentual environment: stress lengthens (Pernot 1908, 1.49).

And, perhaps, this: an allophonic transcription of the target language intended to be an aid for pronunciation tells you only half the story; it presents the do's, not the don'ts. An English native speaker studying Greek would consistently also have to be reminded that voiceless stops in certain distributions are not aspirated or long vowels not followed by some glide. Just as these non-distinctive features of the user's native language (the allophones to be gotten rid of) are not marked and still have to be remembered once and for all, so the learner will have to remember once and for all the non-distinctive features of the target language (the allophones to be acquired).

Closely related to the question of transcription is the problem of transliteration. Modern Greece still uses the ancient alphabet. This alphabet could be given up completely and replaced by transliteration. This is now the case in many (but by no means all) learned journals outside of Greece. It would be by far the most simple and most practical solution. But Greeks and Hellenists resist this. In Greece, the alphabet—in all its Alexandrinian splendor—has remained a national symbol for centuries. Even the accent system, now obviously obsolete, is kept. If the Greek alphabet is used, again various ways are open, which would also have to be considered if transliteration, as distinguished from transcription, is adopted. One can stick to the traditional system, still widely used; one can go to a radically reformed system; one can steer a middle course, which throws off the most cumbersome ballast, but keeps etymological spelling reflecting the ancient background. This last is like the one used and propagated by the late Manolis Triantaphyllidis, who has done more than anybody else for the instruction of Greek children in a modernized and reasonable way. How important these questions of spelling are in a culture in which the alphabet plays a highly symbolic role, is shown by the recent struggle of the accents in which the fighter against the accents, an internationally respected scholar [Ioannis Kakridis], found himself in the hottest possible water [see Mackridge 2009, 306–10].

2.2. **Morphemics**. Perhaps the morphemic arrangement can be simplified. Dictionaries often tear apart what should be kept together. In our alphabetized dictionaries all prefixed and many suffixed derivatives are separated from the entry of their stem, so that the user loses the chance to grasp with a quick glance, the combinatory potentialities of the given stem. The same is true of many allomorphs (think, e.g., of English *duke* and *duchess*). There are certain attempts to remedy this situation. Such etymological dictionaries as the ones by von Wartburg (1922–2002) and Corominas (1954) group together what belongs together. Although a few descriptive modern dictionaries list suffixal derivatives with the base form, the rigid method followed by the etymological dictionaries should be transferred (supplemented by an index of cross references) on a large scale to the descriptive ones. It is, of course, easier to suggest this than to do it.

The difficulty lies in the necessity to morphemicize the corpus before grouping it. The etymological dictionary proceeds here solely along historical lines and is non-sensitive to the fact that two words put together for historical reasons may descriptively be "felt" or "non-felt" as belonging together. Thus, you find in von Wartburg (1922–2002) under the same heading **pensare** (among many others) such congeners as *peser* 'to weigh,' *pesant* 'heavy,' *penser* 'to think,' *pensée* 'pansy,' and *panser* 'to groom a horse.' Although all of them contain historically the same morpheme, how many do so descriptively? A beginning in a limited way may prove helpful: to consider those words as congeners (i.e., as containing the same stem morpheme) where analyst and informant are unanimous. A veto will prevent the too-much-historicity of the analyst and the too-little-historicity of the informant. Let us, then, discuss one example, independent of the question whether or not all the congeners and derivatives mentioned would appear in the actual dictionary.

The morpheme to be analyzed is {mer} 'day.' It occurs in two allomorphs /mer/ and /imer/. The distribution of these allomorphs has to be described in terms of levels: /mer / is more demotic than /imer/, although /imer/ is also used in the demotic. But in all words which are, historically speaking, of katharevusa origin, although they are common in the demotic, only the allomorph /imer / is used: *mesēméri* 'noon,' *hēmerológio* 'calendar,' *kathēmerinós* 'daily.'

Next to the question of allomorphs is that of the range of the morpheme. Various patterns can be distinguished.

(a) Homonymous morphemes. In addition to the morpheme {mer} 'day' with the allomorphs /mer/ and /imer/, Modern Greek has a morpheme {mer} 'part' and a morpheme {imer} 'tame,' both used in numerous prefixal and suffixal environments. In a dictionary arranged according to morphemes, both will have to be separated from {mer} 'day.' The immediate environment is not necessarily a reason for separation since two different morphemes may share it. There is an actual case of *anémera* containing both the morpheme {mer} 'day' (and translatable as 'on the same day') and the morpheme {imer} 'tame' (and translatable as 'cruelly'). And there is the potential contrast between the existing *apómera* containing the morpheme {mer} 'part' (and translatable as 'at a distance') and the possible formation *apómera* containing the morpheme {mer} 'day' (and translatable as 'from dawn on'). But the broader environment admits of hardly any doubt to the native speaker as to whether he deals with {mer} 'day' or with {mer} 'part' or with {imer} 'tame.' The combination of the broad environment with historical grammar is a specific situation in Greek. Historical grammar may be considered here a check for the development of methods of descriptive analysis, which then can be more safely applied to languages of which only the present is known.

(b) Unrecognizability. The question arises whether a morpheme that only the etymologist recognizes should still be listed under the morpheme to which it belongs historically, or whether it should be separated from it. A set of derivatives of {mer} 'day' represents a point in case. The derivative *holēmerís* 'the whole day' is still analyzable as consisting of /ol/ 'whole' and /imera/ 'day,' followed by an ending. But the derivative *lemeri* 'den' (a noun based on the intervening verb *lēmeriázō*, which in turn is formed on /olimer/) is hardly recognizable anymore. The intervening use 'place where you hide yourself the whole day' is apparently lost. In other words, historically, *lēméri* contains the morpheme {mer} 'day,' but does it descriptively?

(c) The place of blendings. Andriotes (1951, 141) lists a term, *meromēnia* 'the first fifteen days of August,' which he derives from *nerá mēnia* 'angry waters.' The question: is *mero* (which has obviously blended with {mer} 'day') here still *neró* 'water,' i.e., an allomorph /mer/ of {ner} used in the environment of -*ménia*? Or has it undergone a morphemic change from {ner} 'water' to {mer} 'day'? Where, then, is the place in a morphemic dictionary of the many morphs which either belong to two morphemes or have undergone a change in form from one to the other?

(d) Distant cognates. Where is the borderline that divides morphemic kinfolk? In Modern Greek, the general term for 'today' is *sēmera*. It continues Ancient Greek *sēmeron*. In the ancient language, this was a compound containing *hēméra* 'day' preceded by some pronominal element. Question:

should the term be listed under the morpheme {mer}? The accent and the fact that it would create a morpheme {*s} occurring in unique distribution militate against an isolation of {mer}.

2.3. Syntax. The problem of the arrangement of the material within one lemma is an old and thorny question in lexicography. The semantic grouping, although still widely practiced, gives way slowly to other modes of classification. I should like to illustrate some of these briefly by examples taken from a large-scale publication in progress, the *Lexikon des Frühgriechischen Epos* (Snell, Mette et al. 1955–) undertaken in Germany by the *Thesaurus linguae graecae*. The *Lexikon*, interestingly enough, and in a most unAmerican way, allows each contributor to be his own editor. Thus, the section B of each lemma, devoted to an analysis of the Bedeutung, is handled in various ways by the various contributors.

(1) The semantic approach attempting to classify the material according to shades of meaning is exemplified by the adjective *ákritos* arranged in three groups:

    1. 'confused, thoughtless';
    2. 'unsolvable, endless';
    3. 'undecided.'

(2) The mixed approach of semantic shades connected with and, at least partly, derived from grammatical environment may be illustrated by the arrangement of the material of *álapazō*:

    1. a. 'to empty' (*títinos* 'something of something')
       b. same, with omission of both objects
    2. 'to depopulate (a city), to destroy'
    3. 'to expel' (*tie ék tinos* 'something from something')
    4. with personal object, 'to kill.'

(3) In certain contributions the *Lexikon* attempts a description of meaning essentially in terms of the immediate morphemic environment of the verb stem (i.e., the inflectional endings of tense, mood, finiteness/nonfiniteness, as well as prefixes). The relational environment is placed (if listed at all) at the bottom of the hierarchy of arrangement. A typical example is the analysis of *alámai* 'to wander, to roam', by Jean Irigoin. His scheme:

I.   middle voice
    1.   theme of the present

a. participle
   α. without complement
      αα. with a verb that has the same subject
      ββ. with a verb that has a different subject
   β. with complement
b. indicative
   α. present
   β. imperfect
c. imperative
2. future
3. aorist (intrans., with compl.)
   a. indicative
   b. subjunctive
   c. participle
4. perfect
   a. indicative
   b. imperative
   c. infinitive
   d. participle
II. with preverbs

(4) Finally, opposed to this system which describes meaning in terms of immediate environment, the *Lexikon* contains several stimulating analyses by Hansjakob Seiler, in which the use of a term is described essentially by recourse to its syntactical environment. Seiler states (s.v. *akoúō*), "The syntactical relations (particularly to the content, the thing heard) reflect the semantic shades of *akoúō*. They, therefore, determine the hierarchy of our arrangement. The forms of the verb are of significance only on a lower level." As a typical example we present Seiler's analysis of the (syntactical) meanings of the noun *álgos* 'pain.'

1. as subject
   a. not with action verbs
      α. in nominal clauses
      β. with verbs of status
   b. with action verbs
2. as accusative object
   a. not with action verbs
      α. *páskhō* 'I suffer'
         αα. aorist (and imperfect)

                    ββ. present
                        δδ. participle
                β. *mogeo* 'I suffer'
                δ. *ékhō* 'I have'
                        αα. participle
                        ββ. other moods
            γ. other non-action verbs
        b. with action verbs
            α. *do-* 'give'
            β. *the-* 'put'
            δ. other action verbs
    3. as dative object
        a. not with action verbs
            α. without preposition
            β. with preposition
        b. with action verbs
            α. without preposition
            β. with preposition

This interesting experiment in lexicography leads to the question as to whether and to what degree a descriptive bilingual dictionary of a modern language could be arranged in a similar way; how far, in other words, relational meaning should supplement or even replace semantic groupings and classifications based on the narrow morphemic environment. The system of syntactical relationships would have to be established in a consistent way for each of the morphemes or morpheme sequences listed. For a verb, the indications may refer to the absence or presence of an object or predicative or subject; to the ways in which the object and the other function classes appear with this verb; to the way in which certain adverbial expressions are formed with this particular verb (as distinct from those adverbs which may accompany any verb); to whether or not it is a function verb, i.e., combined with another verb by means of the connectives *pōs* or *na* (*pōs* roughly corresponding to Romance *que* plus indicative, and *na* to Romance *que* plus subjunctive). In other words, the syntax of the verb, concisely and completely presented, would be used to describe its identity.

2.4. **Résumé**. In this way, then, we would try to tie together the levels of analysis; list in phonemic transcriptions the morphemes of a language; list under each morpheme the allomorphs with a brief description of their distribution, and the morpheme sequences of which the morpheme under discussion is a significant constituent; list under each of these sequences (the "words") the distinctive features of relationship which are typical of them. This arrangement would reduce the number of the lemmata considerably and familiarize the non-native, through concentration and arrangement, with the essential morphemes of the target language, their narrow and their broad environments, and through this medium, their use and their meaning.

PROBLEMS OF TURKISH LEXICOGRAPHY

Andreas Tietze
University of California, Los Angeles

THE LEXICOGRAPHER OF ANY LANGUAGE, CONSTANTLY FORCED TO compromise between theoretical stipulations and practical considerations, will always have his problems. But there are languages where he has special problems, and one of them is Turkish. I shall summarize the problems of the Turkish lexicographer under two headings: (1) problems of the language itself; (2) problems arising in lexicography.

1. Problems of the Language Itself

Turkish is a language with problems. These problems are essentially of an extralinguistic origin: they have to do with historical, cultural, and social phenomena, by which one's concept of the Turkish language is shaped but they also affect the language itself deeply. Before the lexicographer can sit down to start his work, he has to make many preliminary decisions, and in these decisions, he will follow his own concept of the language he is going to treat. Thus, the problems of the language will become the problems of the lexicographer.

Turkish is the language of the Turks, in the narrower sense of the people of Turkey. This sounds much simpler than it is. Linguistically, Turkish belongs to the large group of Turkic languages, which is itself a branch of the Altaic branch of languages. Culturally, the Turks have been an integral part of the Islamic culture area for the last 1000 years, and only within the last century has their attitude toward this cultural affiliation become somewhat ambivalent. Socially, the Turkish of the last 500 years was, in the first place, the language of the Ottoman dynasty (therefore, called Ottoman), of the court, of the bureaucracy, of the capital. In harmony with the classic cultural tradition of Islam, the art of literary expression was cultivated from the beginning, and there was always a deep rift between the spoken language and the lofty style of writing, in which Persian and Arabic vocabulary became dominant (the borrowings of morphological and syntactical elements were less conspicuous). The extensive absorption of linguistically alien elements (Persian is an Indo-European, Arabic a Semitic language) led to structural changes in Turkish itself. Turkish became a language with two phonemic systems, one for words of Turkish origin, the other for loanwords.

With the political changes of the last 100 years, the concept of the language changed, also. First came the break with the tradition of the high literary style: with the development of journalism and the appearance of new political groups with an urge to spread their ideas to the masses, the old esoteric style of writing became outdated, and a kind of standard colloquial was more and more used in its stead. Since the beginning of this century, this development was already partly tinged with nationalistic objectives: the Ottoman language should be purged of the foreign elements and re-Turkicised. World War I and its consequence, the dismemberment of the Ottoman Empire, led to a revolution of the Turkish way of life. The Kemalists of the 1920s and 1930s vigorously rejected the past, the cultural tradition of Islam, the dominance of the capital, the highbrow esthetic concept. They rejected the old language, which was the result of all these objectionable factors. In 1928, by introducing a Latin alphabet and outlawing the Arabic alphabet, they forcibly and irrevocably cut off the old cultural tradition and all ties with the Islamic world. They also announced a radical reform of the language itself.

Since 1935, many long lists and entire books full of proposed new vocables for all the walks of life were published. In the late thirties, daily papers would publish their articles of comment on the political situation with the new vocabulary. The commentator would write his article in "conventional" language, then a clerk would process it, replacing all Arabic (and Persian) by their "Turkish" equivalents, proposed in the official lists. However, he would add most of the eliminated words in parentheses after the new word, or in footnotes. As many of the new words were completely incomprehensible without annotation, the reader of the article had to rely strongly on the notes, or on a copy of the official word list (this time the one from Turkish to Ottoman). Undergoing this exercise every day, he would eventually learn to achieve a part of this manipulation in his mind: his eyes would read one word, but, mechanically, his mind would register another word, a mental habit which might be termed "schizoglossia." In spite of the enormous energy that went into this matter and the powerful official backing, only a part of the proposed vocabulary actually caught on. The words that entered the general language were relatively few, the great bulk pertained to special terminologies, mainly the terminologies of public administration, of the army, and of the sciences taught in high schools and colleges. The scientific terminologies had been very artificial before, too, when their elements were mostly borrowed from Arabic.

Now, after the change of the alphabet and the new orientation of the whole system of education away from Arabic and Persian and toward the Western world, a continuation of the earlier systems of terminology had become impossible. The result was a complete rift between the older and the younger generations of doctors, lawyers, engineers, etc.; the younger colleague had no way of discussing his problems with the older colleague. The younger generation started as a minority, but now the rift is in the mid-forties, and they have already started to outnumber the older generation, who, after two more decades, will practically have died out. Thus, the Turkish language, as a system, as a set of rules for communication, and as a social institution, with the relative distribution of the areas of application of these rules, is, at present, in a stage of transition. However, this evolution is not so straight and steady as one might conclude. A continual tampering with the language, although it was a historical necessity, has created contrasting attitudes of reaction toward stability and change: on the one hand, receptiveness for new fashions, imaginative creativeness, a bold rejection of past achievements, especially along the line of esthetic refinement; on the other hand, a sneering rejection of everything that is new, an emphasis on classicism and traditionalism. The constant fluctuations also produced a feeling of instability, which, cut off from traditionalism, sought for compensations in the language of the people, in regional dialects, in slang, and, in the higher spheres of thought, heavily relied on French, German, or English. A certain degree of impoverishment and of *Vergröberung* had to be taken for granted by everyone.

This state of the language, with its conflicting concepts, creates serious problems for the lexicographer. Which of these concepts is he going to follow? Can he combine more than one concept or all concepts? Before he begins his work, he has to make a number of decisions concerning the delimitations of his task. In each of these decisions, the problems inherent in the present stage of language with its conflicting concepts will stand in his way.

1.1. **Name of the language**. The Turks call their language Turkish, but they speak of Ottoman when they specifically refer to the language of the older generation or to the older literature. An approximative borderline between the two might be the end of the Ottoman Empire and the foundation of the Republic of Turkey (1923) or the abolition of the Arabic and introduction of the Latin alphabet (1928). But the term Turkish, of course, was used long before the foundation of the Turkish Republic, even long before the foundation of the Ottoman Empire, for that matter. In fact, it was known in the West (in Byzantine chronicles) since the sixth century A.D. There is enough difference between the Turkish of the rock inscriptions of the eighth century A.D. and the language of Turkey of today to necessitate a distinction in terms. Even scholarly terminology is not precise in this respect: We use the somewhat artificial term Turkic when we refer to the entire group of languages, including, e.g., Tatar, Bashkir, Kirghiz, Yakut, Uigur, etc. But this term is hardly used outside of linguistics: the historian speaks of the Turkish empire of Central Asia, the anthropologist speaks of Turkish shamanistic beliefs, etc. Not even the linguist is consistent; quite often he calls the language of the eighth century inscriptions Old Turkish instead of Old Turkic. For the language of the Ottoman Empire and of Turkey, the scholars use various terms: Ottoman, Ottoman-Turkish, Osmanli, and even Osman, furthermore Turkish, Turkey-Turkish, Empire-Turkish (*Reichstürkisch*), and, in French, *le Turquien* (on the model of *le Parisién* or *l'Alsacien*). When a child has so many names, there must be something wrong with him. Moreover, the child himself does not accept any of these names, with the exception of the ambiguous Turkish and, perhaps Turkey-Turkish (or Turkish of Turkey), which is innocuous, if unwieldy as a term. As, from the linguistic point of view, there is no justification in using one term for the language up to 1923 or 1927 and another term for the current stage of the same language, the simplest and most convenient way would be to continue using the term Ottoman, but here the Turks, who have made the new concept of the language their own, balk. Thus, already in naming the language, the lexicographer has reached a deadlock and has to compromise.

1.2. **Delimitation vis-a-vis related languages**. For some of the lexicographers of the second half of the nineteenth century, who in a romantic way delighted in the sense of unity of all the Turkic languages, appealing vocables or expressions of Jagatai and other non-Ottoman Turkic languages had a right to enter the (otherwise Ottoman) dictionary, and this highly arbitrary selection of intruders was again and again taken over by later lexicographers. As dictionaries usually stand firmly on the shoulders of older dictionaries, it takes a good deal of effort to discard materials which are so well attested by all the earlier standard works. Today, nobody would think of including Jagatai or Tatar words in a Turkey-Turkish dictionary. Not even other languages of the Southern Turkic or Oghuz subgroup, as Azerbaijani or Turkmen, would be considered. The only point where delimitation on linguistic grounds is difficult is with the Gagauz dialect of northern Bulgaria, the Dobrugea, and Moldavia. But the practical importance of this problem is negligible.

1.3. **Delimitation vis-a-vis earlier historical phases**. How far back ought the lexicographer to go in covering the language? For Turkish, a range of widely discrepant answers can be given, depending on the concept of the language: on the one hand, a word used by the popular Anatolian folk poet Yunus Emre around 1300 A. D. can be regarded fit to enter; on the other hand, a word commonly used as recently as the 1930s, but stigmatized by the language reform movement, may be rejected as obsolete. The vocabulary used by Ataturk in his speeches is largely incomprehensible for the younger generation of today; a dictionary which contains it would already be regarded as a historical dictionary. The lexicographer who includes "old" material (from 1300 to 1935) will have to be very careful to provide each word with an appropriate label: *learned, obsolete, archaic, only known to the older generation*, etc.

1.4. **Delimitation toward new developments**. The problem of what to do with newly coined words or expressions will be equally difficult. Does everything proposed by anyone have to be listed? Or, if the criterion is the degree of reception and assimilation by the language, how can this be measured? How can the schizoglottical pitfall be avoided? It will be very difficult to set up guiding principles of an objective character, and here again the lexicographer will have to rely on his discretion. No wonder that the policy of recent Turkish dictionaries, in this respect, varies radically. Some exclude the new material altogether; others link it by cross references firmly to the now rejected equivalents, thus introducing the principle of schizoglossia into the dictionary; others, again, apply various principles of selection.

1.5. **Borrowings from other languages**. For many centuries, and to a large degree even today, Latin (and, to a lesser extent, Greek) has been the *Kultursprache* of the European languages, a lexical reserve arsenal from which anybody at any time could borrow the tools for expressing a new idea. For Turkish, both Arabic and to a lesser extent Persian have functioned as *Kultursprachen* for many centuries. An Ottoman writer or poet had the liberty to borrow from these languages any noun or adjective he needed (the borrowing of other word classes was more restricted). Consequently, if an Ottoman dictionary-maker wanted his dictionary to be adequate, he had to include, apart from the Turkish words and from the loanwords used in Turkish, all nouns and adjectives that he might find in an Arabic or Persian dictionary. This is the reason why Meninski called his Turkish dictionary *Thesaurus Linguarum Orientalium, Turcicae, Arabicae, Persicae* (1680) or Handjéri the *Dictionnaire Francais-Arabe-Persan et Turc* (1840–41). Even James Redhouse, in *A Turkish-English Lexicon* (1890), could enter the entire noun and adjective material of the Arabic *Kamus* and of the Persian *Burhan-i Kati* without having to bother to find out which of these words, or which of their various meanings, had ever actually been used in Turkish; he was justified in doing this because all this material was, potentially, at least, a part of the Ottoman language. Today, after the reorientation of Turkish culture, the potential aspect of this material has vanished, and the lexicographer has to approach it from a historical point of view: his guiding principle must be to find out what has actually been used and what not, and the latter part he must discard altogether. For this the first requirement is a comprehensive *Belegwörterbuch*. Unfortunately, no such thing exists. All the attempts made so far have been concentrated on the Turkish materials. There is no hope that we will have such a work for many years to come; therefore, in this field, again, the lexicographer will have to go by his more or less arbitrary second sense, and the outcome will be a reflection of conflicting concepts of the language.

With the reorientation of Turkish culture, Arabic and Persian disappeared as *Kultursprachen*, but, though in a lesser degree, the Western languages stepped in, primarily French, but partly also English, German, and Latin. Whenever a Turkish scholar or scientist, banker, businessman, engineer, or even sports expert, wants to make a very clear statement, he uses a French term (even if he does not know French and if his training has been in another language). With the instability and confusion of Turkish terminology in many fields, this will happen quite often. Thus, French is, to some extent, the *Kultursprache* of modern Turkish: its abstract nouns, at least, can be regarded as potential Turkish vocabulary. How much of this is to be taken into the dictionary? Some lexicographers exclude all "international" terms, presumably because they are understood anyhow. Is this a correct principle? Also, from a practical point of view, it can have bad consequences: think of an American traveling through Turkey with a car and a Turkish dictionary who has engine trouble; it will be little help to him to learn that all the terminology of the automobile is, anyhow, in French.

1.6. Delimitation vis-a-vis substandard forms, slang, and regional vernacular. As to substandard forms and slang, the problems of a Turkish lexicographer will be more or less the same as those of lexicographers of other languages. But in his attitude toward dialects, his conceptual conflict will, again, come strongly to the fore. One of the revolutionary changes in the concept of the Turkish language within the last fifty years is the rejection of the cultural (and linguistic) hegemony of the capital (Istanbul). For many centuries, Istanbul, as the city of the court and of the central bureaucracy, had dictated to the country its standard language. In the provinces, only the representatives of the capital administrators, army officers, teachers, doctors, etc., and their families spoke the standard language (and were called Ottomans, Osmanli, by the local population). Today, with compulsory education, compulsory military service, newspapers, radio, and, in general, more moving about, the dominance of the Istanbul standard language is more deeply entrenched than it ever was. But, on the other hand, the political dethronement of Istanbul, the rejection, on ideological grounds, of the grand tradition it stood for, and the much closer and more intensive contacts between the cities and the countryside, have resulted in a vigorous influx of regional vocabulary into the standard language, especially in literature. Today, it has become impossible to read a contemporary novel with the help of any of the existing dictionaries. Here, new tasks arise for the lexicographer, and, again, he is confronted with the problem of how far he should go in covering this new material of regional proveniency. An almost infinite number of attitudes are possible: he could go by the frequency of occurrence in literature, using some statistical yardstick; he could go by the meaning, e.g., only accepting terms for things or ideas of local character; or he could divide the material by categories, accepting, e.g., proverbs, sayings, idioms, etc., perhaps also terms, but rejecting merely phonetic variants, etc.

2. Problems Arising in Lexicography

As we have shown, the problems resulting from the specific situation in which the Turkish language finds itself today are at the same time problems of the lexicographer. But there are also problems more closely connected with lexicography itself. I shall list only a few of these.

2.1. **Problems of coverage**. Above, in listing the problems of a proper delimitation of the historiographer's task, we have already indirectly outlined the difficulties with which he has to cope. After having made his decisions as to how to delimit the area he wants to cover, he will have to bring the materials within this area together. As his policy will probably not coincide with that of any of his predecessors, he will have to be very careful when using older dictionaries. He will have to discard thousands of items, meanings and entire entries that have become obsolete, or which may actually never have existed at all in Turkish, including the "potential" material from the older *Kultursprachen*, as well as neologisms, proposed but soon forgotten. On the other hand, he will have to cover new territory, for which he cannot rely on previous dictionaries nor even sometimes on any preparatory study. He will find the newspaper, fiction, the talk of people in the street, songs, all kinds of folklore, etc., inexhaustible sources. The tradition of the Turkish dictionary is of the learned type; when it comes to the vocabulary of practical life, of the bazaars, of the various trades, sports, games, even of the machinery of public administration, little preliminary work has been done, and the lexicographer has to be himself an explorer.

2.2. **Problems of the script and spelling**. The change thirty-two years ago from the Arabic to the Latin characters is another source of problems for the lexicographer. It is difficult to discuss these problems without becoming too technical. May I only give a few hints? The new (Latin) alphabet is not just a transliteration of the old (Arabic) with differently shaped symbols. The relation is much more complicated. For instance, one letter of the Arabic alphabet may correspond to four letters of the Latin alphabet (as in the case of *k*, *g*, *n*, and *ğ*, the latter, itself, having two different pronunciations), but also one letter of the new alphabet (e.g., *z*) may correspond to as many as four letters in the old alphabet. Moreover, vowels were often not indicated at all in the Arabic characters. Consequently, it is not possible from the mere sight of a word in Arabic script to know what its spelling would be in the Latin characters, or vice versa. It is therefore practically impossible to use a dictionary in the modern Latin script for a text in Arabic script, and vice versa. The only possibility of producing a dictionary that could be used for both scripts is by giving two complete alphabets, one Arabic, one Latin, of which one could be used for the discussion of the entries and the other for cross references, the way it was done, e.g., in Bertels' (1954) Tajik–Russian dictionary or in Borovkov's (1959) Uzbek–Russian dictionary.

One other consequence of the change of the alphabet is the instability and fluctuation of spelling habits and spelling rules. Although these concern mostly points of minor importance, they are a serious problem for the dictionary-maker. Should he just stick to one set of rules which happens to be accepted by the majority at the time when he starts his work, and ignore all deviating variants, or should he list them, too, with cross references?

A special headache are foreign words and foreign names. The new Turkish alphabet, though based on Latin, has some extra letters (e.g., ş for /sh/, ç for /ch/) and does not permit combined letters for the representation of one sound (like /sh/, /gh/); it does not have the letters *x* and *w*, and occurs only as a consonant. For this reason, Turkish is not so conservative in the spelling of foreign words as English; like Italian and other languages, it tends rather to reproduce their sound picture (French *guichet* is spelled *gişe duy* is the French *douille*, etc.) Proper nouns have a difficult fight against this tendency (*Avusturya* for *Austria* is standard, but one sees *Şikago* besides *Chicago*, *Kan* besides *Cannes*). How are famous persons of European history to be called and to be spelled? Is it more correct to call the great emperor *Charles V* or *S'inci Şarl* or (as it is often done) *Şarlken*?

2.3. **Problems of definition and glossing**. A number of problems arise when the lexical elements of one language have to be defined in terms of another language of entirely different character, e.g., when the elements of Turkish, an Altaic language, have to be defined in English, an Indo-European language. Let me give a few examples. The Turkish noun has a marked form only for the plural; the singular is an unmarked form which can refer to a single thing, but in many cases also to a plurality. Thus, *adam* means both 'man' and 'men, people,' at the same time. Furthermore, there is no definite article; the noun has a marked form only for indefiniteness. Thus, *adam* means 'man' or 'the man' or even 'a man.' This shows that already, for syntactical reasons, Turkish *adam* (or any other noun) has no exact equivalent in English. The Turkish adjective has lost its special form for the comparative. Therefore, Turkish *cok* means 'many,' but at the same time also 'more,' and even 'too many.' Turkish, also, does not distinguish between adjectives and adverbs, thus *cok* can also mean 'much' and 'very.' Nor does Turkish distinguish between adjective and noun, so that *cok* is also 'the greater part, most.' Again, there can be no exact equivalent in English for any Turkish adjective. I could go on with the other word-classes, but these examples may suffice.

Turkish, as an agglutinative language, has at least one advantage over the Indo-European languages: it considerably facilitates the task of integrating the lexical dictionary into a dictionary of morphemes. If we disregard a negligible number of exceptional cases, it has no intramorphemic changes and inter morphemic juncture problems are minimal. Furthermore, morphemes have, in general, retained their free affixibility and not lost their meaning. The number of their possible combinations is very high. In a morpheme dictionary, even of limited volume, the student would find the tools with the help of which he could analyze the most complex derivative or grammatical form, and even, if he is lucky, derive for himself more or less correctly the word form he needs.

COMMENTS

William S. Cornyn
Yale University

THE THREE PAPERS OF THIS LAST SECTION HAVE suggested a number of problems. Most of these have been discussed in earlier reports, but there are some that have not been given adequate attention. Of these, two seem to me to be of the first importance: the background and the audience. These problems are, of course, related, and different for each language situation.

We have here three languages. Each of them is in a different relationship to the culture of which it is a part. Pashtu, the first of them, is a language dominated by its neighbors, Persian and Urdu. It has no literary tradition. Demotic Greek, the second of our examples, is a powerful force competing with its own classical form but possessing, in its own right, a literature and an impregnable position as the colloquial medium of the whole country. Turkish is absolute in its field, with a literature both modern and ancient, but with a tremendous amount of innovation, such that a native literate can understand more easily the language of a thirteenth century poem than some of the coinages of the twenties and thirties of this century. And these are only three of the kinds of language situation with which lexicographers have to deal. There are many more, of course, but we can profit by bringing into the discussion two more situations, using as our examples the less familiar Burmese and Jinghpaw. Neither of these is like any of the first three.

Burmese is the national language of a country of some 20 million. It is spoken as a first language by about 70 percent of the population and is used by a large part of the rest. It has a literature with a history of a thousand years in which the earliest texts are not especially difficult of interpretation on the basis of today's colloquial language; certainly, they are no more difficult than many modern writings.

Jinghpaw, on the other hand, is spoken by a few hundred thousand people living in an area that comprises parts of India and China as well as a large part of northern Burma. It has no written literature other than a few texts recorded in a writing system designed by missionaries only a few decades ago. It does have, however, a great oral tradition of the highest interest. In addition, and perhaps most importantly, it is in a position to answer key questions put by comparativists interested in the languages of Southeast Asia.

Now, it is quite obvious that the demands on the lexicographer in each of these situations are quite different, and it is necessary in each case to devise an approach and technique that will not misrepresent either the facts of the language or its setting. These are problems inherent in the status of the language: Pashtu opposed to Persian in Afghanistan and Urdu in Pakistan; Demotic Greek competing with a puristic tradition; Turkish accepted as the standard. The problems of historicity and historical depth are different in each case, with little difficulty in Pashtu, the formidable bridge to the golden past in Greek, and the complexity of the discontinuity in Turkish. Interestingly enough, there seems to be no particular difficulty with dialects in the languages described. This problem arises sharply in Jinghpaw, where the status of the language as a lingua franca for a very large area makes it almost if not quite impossible to sort out regionalisms and even borrowings.

The other set of problems concerns the method of dictionary construction. For whom is it made? There are, I suppose, three classes of dictionary users: the scholar, the student, and the man in the street. Each of these groups needs a different kind of dictionary, not that the groups are mutually exclusive. Certainly, there are three kinds of dictionary: encyclopedic (treating of all aspects of cultural contexts); usage (attempting to portray the morphological and syntactic features); and glossary (a list of forms with a minimum of information). Add to this the question raised earlier of the importance, this time to the user, of historical information.

It is in this connection that there seems not to have been enough attention paid to the problem of sources. In the kinds of dictionaries I am at present concerned with, there is a tremendous difference in source potentialities. In the two languages, Jinghpaw and Burmese, the range is almost literally from texts recorded by the lexicographer in Jinghpaw to a vast corpus of written and otherwise recorded texts from all periods in Burmese. It would have been useful to hear descriptions of actual techniques and solutions to problems.

Many other questions have occurred throughout the meeting which have not been answered and for which there is no time now. Most of these have to do with technical and mechanical matters and were excluded by the nature of this symposium. I should like to close these remarks with a description taken from Martin's paper that "a dictionary . . . should be concise but exhaustive; exact while not exacting; linguistically adequate for *both* languages yet uncluttered with trivial details."

V

APPENDICES

SUMMARY REPORT

F. W. Householder
Indiana University

I. There were several points on which the conferees expressed unanimity or very general agreement.
   (1) Dictionaries should be designed with a special set of users in mind and for their specific needs, e.g., an English–Arabic dictionary for American users for help in speaking Arabic, or a Thai–English dictionary for British and American users for help in reading Thai, etc. The point was also made that, for languages where no good dictionary of any kind is available, it might be better for the first dictionary produced to be as general-purpose as possible, usable by speakers of both languages for reading, writing, or speaking. But this was conceded to be a counsel of perfection.
   (2) All entries should be as accessible as possible; irregular forms should either have a full entry (if possible), or at least a cross-reference to the main article. Idioms should be listed under each of their constituents, if possible. It was generally agreed that however scientific it might be to group all etymologically related words together, students derive no commensurate benefit from the hours of time wasted in hunting down words not in their obvious alphabetical place. The one or two dissenters argued for the mnemonic value of associating related words in learning.
   (3) Essential syntactic information should be included with each item—facts about kinds of objects, prepositional phrases, subjects, concord, etc. If, as about half the conferees recommended, a brief grammatical sketch is included as part of the dictionary, it could be used to provide and explain convenient symbols for conveying syntactic information. In some cases, syntactic information

should also serve the secondary purpose of meaning discrimination. Similar semantic information could be conveyed through indications of typical or normal collocations—e.g., favorite objects, subjects, etc., even where not grammatically inevitable. Two conferees suggested the advisability of giving syntactic information in the gloss: 'opens it' for a transitive, 'it opens' for an intransitive verb, for instance, and two others recommended the use of capital letters or similar symbols in expressions like 'X gives Y to Z.'

(4) Where there are distinct levels of usage (polite, literary, colloquial, vulgar, not among women, etc.), these should be carefully labeled, if possible. This applies also to dialect variation, diglossia, and similar situations.

(5) Thorough investigation of semantic structure is desirable, and where we have already sufficient knowledge to indicate relationships of incompatibility, hyponymy, synonymy, etc., this should be done in the most economical way possible. But more research in this whole area is much needed. Weinreich argued for actual field work on semantics in the preparation of every dictionary.

II. The points upon which there appeared to be some clear disagreement were chiefly minor ones.

(1) The principle of form-class equivalence, that glosses should be perfect and complete translations in respect to grammatical class, though agreed to by most of the conferees, was considered unnecessary by Weinreich, if the correct form-class is indicated in some other way.

(2) Few of the conferees expressed a view on the proper size of a dictionary, but those who did varied between 10,000 entries (Harrell and Swanson) and 50,000 or more (Haas, Barnhart and Tietze). The smaller size is perhaps correlated with a special purpose (conversational expression); certainly, the larger size is necessary for reading.

(3) The question of the inclusion or omission of extremely common words in common senses elicited two divergent views: Barnhart favored omitting them, on the ground that anyone qualified to use the dictionary at all would know them, while Swanson argued for including them, on the ground that it is impossible to predict what a user may not know.

(4) The use of technical Latin nomenclature in defining plant-names and animal names was favored by Iannucci but opposed by Conklin and Weinreich, for different reasons: Conklin felt it was not sufficient, Weinreich that it was not necessary or true to the status of natural languages.

(5) Mary Haas argued for the inclusion of common and familiar proper names (historical, literary, geographical, etc.); Malkiel objected that this information belonged in an encyclopedia rather than a dictionary. The sentiment of the group seemed to favor Haas, so long as the number included did not become excessive.

(6) Several conferees favored the inclusion of illustrative sentences; others objected to them as (a) space-wasting, or (b) often irrelevant and unhelpful. The general view was that a small number of such sentences might be worthwhile, if (a) they were kept brief, (b) always had distinct value for meaning discrimination and syntax, (c) could not be adequately replaced by short phrases, and (d) always illustrated important and frequent meanings.

III. A number of interesting points came up only once, and no record of divergent or supporting opinions could be made.

(1) Martin argued against an accumulation of unhelpful glosses.

(2) Martin also noted that the dictionary should warn the student about words which should not be translated (semantic "zeros").

(3) Barnhart argued that no etymological information be included, unless it had some real practical value.

(4) Both Barnhart and Haas called attention to the importance of having all technical vocabulary checked by specialists.

(5) Iannucci stressed the importance of having meaning discriminations in the source language (not the target language) and pointed out that in the foreign–native part of a dictionary such discriminations are unnecessary, if the work is to be used only by native speakers.

(6) In arranging glosses, several people argued, the first one should be that which has the most general application and utility, regardless of historical primacy or the current frequency of a more specialized sense.

(7) Swanson suggested that no matter how sketchy the grammatical sketch accompanying the dictionary, it should at least include a thorough treatment of word-formation, since in this way the

student can discover the probable meaning of words of regular formation which are not common enough to list in the dictionary.
(8) Harrell and Malone recommended the use of a hyphen or other similar notation to mark morpheme boundaries.

III. In general, nearly all important topics were covered more or less thoroughly during the conference. A few were mentioned without adequate discussion. Perhaps the most important point here is Iannucci's topic of meaning discrimination. What are the most economical and most helpful ways of indicating which gloss a user is to choose? A second point not thoroughly covered has to do with the various tricks and devices by which a dictionary can be made more useful. Several interesting ones were mentioned, such as Tietze's listing across the bottom of each page (for Turkish) all entries on *other* pages some of whose inflected forms might be sought on *this* page, and Balint's use of brackets and word order to indicate syntactic differences (transitive vs. intransitive verbs); but no exhaustive study or discussion of these was made. It was suggested that future conferences on lexicography might be wise also to include specialists in machine translation and experts on Soviet lexicographical methods.

PROGRAM OF THE CONFERENCE

FRIDAY

Registration:	8:00–8:30	Distinguished Alumni Room
First Session:	9:00–12:00	The Preparation of Dictionaries I: Theoretical Considerations

Chairman: Kemp Malone
Yakov Malkiel, "A Typological Classification of Dictionaries on the Basis of Distinctive Features"
Uriel Weinreich, "Lexicographic Definition in Descriptive Semantics"
Mary Haas, "What Belongs in the Bilingual Dictionary"
Richard S. Harrell, "Some Notes on Bilingual Lexicography"
Donald C. Swanson, "Recommendations on the Selection of Entries for a Bilingual Dictionary"
Discussant: Dean Stoddard Worth

Group Lunch:	12:15–1:45	State Room West
Second Session:	2:00–4:00	Structural Linguistics and the Preparation of Dictionaries

Chairman: Samuel E. Martin
H. A. Gleason, "The Relation of Lexicon and Grammar"
Henry M. Hoenigswald, "Lexicography and Grammar"
Kemp Malone, "Structural Linguistics and Bilingual Dictionaries"
Harold C. Conklin, "Lexicographical Treatment of Folk Taxonomies"
Discussant: James Sledd

Reception:	5:00–6:00	Home of Vice-President John W. Ashton

SATURDAY

Third Session:	9:00–12:00	The Preparation of Dictionaries II: Practical

Considerations
Chairman: James Sledd
Samuel E. Martin, "Selection and Presentation of Ready Equivalents in a Translation Dictionary"
Clarence Barnhart, "Problems in Editing Commercial Monolingual Dictionaries"
Meredith Burrill and Edwin Bonsack, Jr., "Use and Preparation of Specialized Glossaries"
James E. Iannucci, "Meaning Discrimination in Bilingual Dictionaries"
Allen Walker Read, "The Labeling of National and Regional Variation in Popular Dictionaries"
Discussant: William Gedney

Group Lunch:	12:00–1:45	State Room West
Fourth Session:	2:00–4:00	Lexicographical Problems in Specific Languages

Chairman: Yakov Malkiel
Oscar Chavarría-Aguilar and Herbert Penzl, "Lexicographical Problems in Pashto"
Henry and Renée Kahane, "Problems in Modern Greek Lexicography"
Andreas Tietze, "Problems of Turkish Lexicography"
Discussant: William S. Cornyn
Fred W. Householder, "Summary Report"

PARTICIPANTS IN THE CONFERENCE

Ani Moukhtar	Georgetown University
Bailey, Don C.	University of Arizona
Balint, Andras	Columbia University
Barnhart, Clarence	Reference Books
Be, Kim	Indiana University
Bonsack, Edwin	Department of Interior
Bridgeman, Lorraine	Summer Institute of Linguistics
Brown, Carl	Indiana University
Burrill, Meredith	Department of Interior
Chavarría-Aguilar, Oscar	University of Michigan
Conklin, Harold C.	Columbia University
Contreras, Heles	Indiana University
Cornyn, William S.	Yale University
Cowell, M. W.	Georgetown University
Fraenkel, Gerd	Indiana University
Gaarder, Bruce	Office of Education
Gedney, William	University of Michigan
Gleason, H. A.	Hartford Seminary Foundation
Gove, Philip	Merriam-Webster Company
Haas, Mary	University of California
Harrell, Richard S.	Georgetown University
Hoenigswald, Henry M.	University of Pennsylvania
Householder, Fred W., Jr.	Indiana University
Iannucci, James E.	St. Joseph's College
Irving, T. B.	Georgetown University
Kahane, Renée	University of Illinois
Kahane, Henry R.	University of Illinois

Lyons, John	Indiana University
Lyra, F.	Indiana University
Malkiel, Yakov	University of California
Malone, Kemp	Johns Hopkins University
Martin, Samuel E.	Yale University
Mcaninch, Alan	Georgetown University
Moore, Bruce	Indiana University
Moyne, John	Georgetown University
Penzl, Herbert	University of Michigan
Petrov, Julia	Office of Education
Prator, Clifford H.	U. C. L. A
Read, Allen Walker	Columbia University
Roca, José	Indiana University
Rosenberg, Alexander	Library of Congress
Saporta, Sol	University of Washington
Sledd, James	Northwestern University
Swanson, Donald C.	University of Minnesota
Tietze, Andreas	U. C. L. A.
Urdang, Laurence	American College Dictionary
Valdman, Albert	Indiana University
Voegelin, C. F.	Indiana University
Voegelin, F. M.	Indiana University
Wang, Fred	Yale University
Waterhouse, Viola	Summer Institute of Linguistics
Weinreich, Uriel	Columbia University
Wolski, Edward D.	Library of Congress
Worth, Dean S.	U. C. L. A.

REFERENCES

Items with an asterisk appear in the original text but may also appear in the Introduction.

Adams, Michael. 1998. "Credit Where It's Due: Authority and Recognition at the *Dictionary of American English*." *Dictionaries* 19:1–20.
———. 2003. *Slayer Slang: A Buffy the Vampire Slayer Lexicon*. New York: Oxford University Press.
———. 2006. "Quotation Paragraphs in Specialized Glossaries on Historical Principles." *Dictionaries* 27:155–61.
———. 2009. "The Period Dictionaries." In *The Oxford History of English Lexicography*, edited by A. P. Cowie, 1:326–52. Oxford: Oxford University Press.
———. 2010. "Legacies of the *Early Modern English Dictionary*." In *Adventuring in Dictionaries: New Studies in the History of Lexicography*, edited by John Considine, 290–308. Newcastle: Cambridge Scholars Publishing.
———. 2011. "Words of America: A Field Guide." *Humanities* 32 (5): 14–19, 53.
———. 2013a. "The Lexical Ride of a Lifetime." *American Speech* 88:168–95.
———. 2013b. "*DARE*: A Provisional Bibliography." *American Speech* 88:367–73.
———. 2014. "The Dictionary Society of North America: A History of the Early Years (Part I)." *Dictionaries* 35:1–35.
———. 2017. "The Dictionary Society of North America: A History of the Early Years (Part II)." *Dictionaries* 38 (1): 1–46.
———. 2018a. "Allen Walker Read's Unfinished Histories of Early English Lexicography." *Notes and Queries* 65:417–20.
———. 2018b. "Periodization in Historical Lexicography Revisited." *Dictionaries* 39 (1): 75–103.
———. 2019a. "The Dictionary Society of North America: A History of the Early Years (Part III)." *Dictionaries* 40 (1): 1–54.
———. 2019b. "The Lexical Object: Richardson's *New Dictionary of the English Language* (1836–1837)." In *The Whole World in a Book: Dictionaries in the Nineteenth Century*, edited by Sarah Ogilvie and Gabriella Safran, 34–53. New York: Oxford University Press.
———. 2020. "A Fair Road for Stumps: Language Ideologies and the Making of the *Dictionary of American English* and the *Dictionary of Americanisms*." *Dictionaries* 41 (2): 25–59.
———. 2021a. "Scale and Mode in Histories of English." In *Studies in the History of the English Language VIII: Boundaries and Boundary-Crossings in the History of English*, edited by Peter J. Grund and Megan E. Hartman, 23–43. Topics in English Linguistics 108. Berlin: De Gruyter Mouton.
———. 2021b. "The Dictionary Society of North America: A History of the Early Years (Part IV)." *Dictionaries* 42 (1): 1–94.
Adams, Michael, and Richard W. Bailey. 2017. "A Bibliography of the 'Special Studies and Publications' of Allen Walker Read." *American Speech* 92:377–425.

Agard, Frederick B., and William G. Moulton. 1956. Review of *An Introduction to Descriptive Linguistics*, by H. A. Gleason. *Language* 32:469–77.
Al-Ani, Salman H. 1984. *Fred W. Householder Bibliography*. Bloomington, IN: Eurolingua.
Algeo, John. 1987. "A Dictionary of Briticisms." *Dictionaries* 9:164–78.
Al-Kasimi, Ali M. 1977. *Linguistics and Bilingual Dictionaries*. Leiden: E. J. Brill.
Allen, Harold B., ed. 1958. *Readings in Applied English Linguistics*. New York: Appleton-Century-Crofts.
———. 1964. *Readings in Applied English Linguistics*. 2nd ed. New York: Appleton-Century-Crofts.
Al-Madani, Mohammed I. 2006. Introduction to *A Life in Letters: The Personal, Professional, and Political*, by Sol Saporta, xiii–xiv. New York: iUniverse.
*Alwood, Martin, and Inge Wilhelmsen. 1947. *Basic Swedish Word List, with English Equivalents, Frequency Grading, and Statistical Analysis*. Rock Island, IL: Augustana Book Concern.
Anderson, Henning. 2016. "Dean S. Worth In Memoriam." *Journal of Slavic Linguistics* 24:269–71.
*Andriotis, Nikolaos P. 1951. *Ετυμολογικὸ Λεξικό της Κοινής Νεοελληνικής*. Athens: Institut français d'Athènes.
*"'Arf Pint of Grog Attracts but 'Arf of Norfolk's Crew." 1933. *The (Baltimore) Sun* (November 9, 1933): 22.
*Army Map Service. 1935. Quadrangle map. Walnut Ridge, AR.
Arnold, Donna I. 1980–1981. College-level Dictionaries and Freshman Composition." *Dictionaries* 3:69–79.
*Austerlitz, Robert. 1959. "Semantic Components of Pronoun Systems: *Gilyak*." *Word* 15:102–9.
———. 1971. Review of *Dictionary of Western Kamchadal*, by Dean S. Worth. *American Anthropologist* 73:907.
Avery, Peter, Karen Carlyle, Susan Ehrlich, Sheila Embleton, and Guy Ewing, eds. 1983. *Focus on Discourse: Papers in Honour of H. A. Gleason, Jr.* Toronto: University of Toronto Press.
"Award." 1972. *Library of Congress Information Bulletin* 31 (October 6, 1972): 438.
*Axelrad, Philip. 1942. *Complete Roumanian–English Dictionary*. Philadelphia: David McKay.
Bahr, Joachim. 1966. "Technische verfahren in der lexikographie." *Zeitschrift für Deutsche Sprache* 22:96–111.
Bailey, Don C. 1962. *A Glossary of Japanese Neologisms*. Tucson: University of Arizona Press.
Bailey, Richard W. 1980. "Progress toward a Dictionary of Early Modern English." In *Proceedings of the Second International Round Table Conference on Historical Lexicography*, edited by W. Pijnenburg and F. de Tollenaere, 199–226. Dordrecht: Foris.
———. 1982. "Computing in the Humanities." In *Computing in the Humanities*, edited by Richard W. Bailey, 1–6. Amsterdam: North-Holland Publishing.
———. 1985. "Charles C. Fries and the *Early Modern English Dictionary*." In *Toward an Understanding of Language*, edited by Peter Howard Fries, 171–204. Current Issues in Linguistic Theory 40. Amsterdam: John Benjamins.
———, ed. 1987. *Dictionaries of English: Prospects for the Record of Our Language*. Ann Arbor: University of Michigan Press.
———. 1996. "*The Century Dictionary*: Origins." *Dictionaries* 17:1–16.
———. 2000. "Appendix III: The *OED* and the Public." In *Lexicography and the* OED*: Pioneers in the Untrodden Forest*, edited by Lynda Mugglestone, 253–84. Oxford: Oxford University Press.

———. 2003. "A Life in Lexicography: Allen Walker Read." *Dictionaries* 24:179–86.
*Baker, Ernest A. 1932. *Heath's New French and English Dictionary*. Boston: D. C. Heath.
*———. 1951. *Cassell's French-English and English-French Dictionary*. 5th ed. New York: Funk & Wagnalls.
*Baker, Sidney J. 1945. *The Australian Language*. Sydney: Angus & Robertson.
Balint, Andras. 1967. "A Critique of English-Hungarian and Hungarian-English General Lexicography." Unpublished PhD diss., Columbia University.
———. 1969. *English-Pidgin and French Dictionary of Sports and Phrase Book*. Port Moresby, Papua New Guinea: South Pacific Post.
———. 1973. "Towards an Encyclopedic Dictionary of Nuginian (Melanesian Pidgin)." *Kivung* 6:1–31.
Barnhart, Clarence L. 1969. "General Dictionaries." *American Speech* 44:173–78.
——— 1978. "American Lexicography, 1945–1973." *American Speech* 53:83–140.
Barnhart, Clarence L. et al. 1944. *Dictionary of United States Army Terms*. War Department Technical Manual, TM 20–205. Washington, DC: Government Printing Office.
*———. 1947. *The American College Dictionary*. New York: Random House.
———. 1955. *The American College Dictionary*. New York: Random House.
———. 1963. *The World Book Dictionary*. 2 vols. Chicago: World Book.
Barnhart, Clarence L., and William D. Halsey. 1954. *The New Century Cyclopedia of Names*. 3 vols. New York: Appleton-Century-Crofts.
Barnhart, Clarence L., Sol Steinmetz, and Robert K. Barnhart. 1973. *The Barnhart Dictionary of New Words since 1963*. Bronxville: NY: Barnhart/Harper & Row.
Barnhart, Robert K. 1996. "*The Century Dictionary*: Aftermath." *Dictionaries* 17:116–25.
*Bartlett, John. 1896. *Dictionary of Americanisms*. 4th ed. Boston: Little, Brown.
Basgöz, Ilhan, and Andreas Tietze. 1973. *Bilmece: A Corpus of Turkish Riddles*. Berkeley: University of California Press.
Battenburg, John D. 1991. *English Monolingual Learners' Dictionaries*. Lexicographica Series Maior 39. Tübingen: Niemeyer.
*Bazell, C. E. 1954. "The Sememe." *Litera* 1 (2): 17–31. Reprinted in *Readings in Linguistics II*, edited by Eric Hamp, Fred W. Householder, Robert Austerlitz, and Martin Joos, 329–41. Chicago: University of Chicago Press.
*Beardsley, E. Edwards. 1876. *Life and Times of Samuel Johnson, L.L.D.* New York: Hurd & Houghton.
*Beckner, Morton. 1959. *The Biological Way of Thought*. New York: Columbia University Press.
Béjoint, Henri. 1994. *Tradition and Innovation in Modern English Dictionaries*. Oxford: Clarendon Press.
———. 2010. *The Lexicography of English*. Oxford: Oxford University Press.
*Bellew, Henry Walter. 1901. *A Dictionary of the Pukkhto or Pukshto Language*. 2nd ed. Lahore, Pakistan: Rai Sahib M. Gulab Singh & Sons.
Bender, Byron W. 1997. "Fred Walter Householder." *Language* 73:560–70.
*Bendix, Edward H. 1966. *Componential Analysis of General Vocabulary: The Semantic Structure of a Set of Verbs in English, Hindi, and Japanese*. Supplement to the *International Journal of American Linguistics* 32 (2).
*Bennett, Hugh H. 1960. "Soil Erosion in Spain." *Geographical Review* 50:59–72.
Benson, Morton, Evelyn Benson, and Robert F. Ilson. 1986. *Lexicographic Description of English*. Amsterdam: John Benjamins.

Bergenholtz, Henning, and Sven Tarp. 2010. "LSP Lexicography or Terminography? The Lexicographer's Point of View." In *Specialised Dictionaries for Learners*, edited by Pedro A. Fuertas-Olivera, 27–37. Lexicographica Series Maior 136. Berlin: De Gruyter.

Bergh, Gunnar, and Sölve Ohlander. 2012. "Free Kicks, Dribblers, and WAGs: Exploring the Language of 'The People's Game.'" *Moderna Språk* 106:11–46.

Berlin, Brent, Dennis E. Breedlove, and Peter H. Raven. 1973. "General Principles of Classification and Nomenclature in Folk Biology." *American Anthropologist* 75:214–42.

*Bertels, E. E. 1954. *Tadzhiksko-russkiĭ slovar'*. Moscow: GINS.

*Beste, J. Richard. 1855. *The Wabash; or, Adventures of an English Gentleman's Family in the Interior of America*. 2 vols. London: Hurst & Blackett.

Bickner, Robert J., Thomas J. Hudak, and Patcharin Peyasanitwong, eds. 1986. *Stress in Thai: Papers from a Conference on Thai Studies in Honor of William J. Gedney*. Michigan Papers on South and Southeast Asia, 25. Ann Arbor: Center for South and Southeast Asian Studies, The University of Michigan.

Birnbaum, Henrik, and Michael S. Flier, eds. 1995. *The Language and Verse of Russia: In Honor of Dean S. Worth on His Sixty-fifth Birthday*. Moscow: Izdatel'skaja Firma Vostočnaja Literatura RAN.

*Bithell, Jethro. 1954. *German–English and English–German Dictionary*. 4th ed. London: Pitman & Sons.

Black, Mary, and Duane Metzger. 1965. "Ethnographic Description and the Study of Law." *American Anthropologist* 67 (6), part 2: 141–65.

*Bloch, Bernard, and George L. Trager. 1942. *Outline of Linguistic Analysis*. Baltimore: Linguistic Society of America.

*Bloomfield, Leonard. 1984 [1933]. *Language*. Chicago: University of Chicago Press.

Boatner, Maxine T., and J. Edward Gates. 1966. *Dictionary of Idioms for the Deaf*. West Hartford, CT: American School for the Deaf.

Bogaards, Paul. 2013. "A History of Research in Lexicography." In *The Bloomsbury Companion to Lexicography*, edited by Howard Jackson, 19–31. London: Bloomsbury.

*Boissière, Prudence. 1900. *Dictionnaire Analogique de la Langue Française*. Paris: Larousse.

Bolinger, Dwight. 1991. "First Person, Not Singular." In *First Person Singular II: Autobiographies by North American Scholars in the Language Sciences*, edited by Konrad Koerner, 19–45. Studies in the History of the Language Sciences 61. Amsterdam: John Benjamins.

Bonsack, Edwin. 1983. *Dvalinn: The Relationship of Friedrich von Schwaben, Volundarkvða, and Sorla þáttr*. Wiesbaden: Franz Steiner Verlag.

*Borovkov, A. K. et al. 1959. *Uzbeksko-russkiĭ slovar'*. Moscow: GINS.

Bothma, Theo JD. 2011. "Filtering and Adapting Data and Information in an Online Environment in Response to User Needs." In *e-Lexicography: The Internet, Digital Initiatives and Lexicography*, edited by Pedro A. Fuertes-Olivera and Henning Bergenholtz, 71–102. London: Continuum.

Boulanger, Jean-Claude. 2003. *Les Inventeurs de Dictionnaires*. Ottawa: Les Presses de l'Université d'Ottawa.

Brame, Michael K., Helas Contreras, and Frederick J. Newmeyer, eds. 1986. *A Festschrift for Sol Saporta*. Seattle: Not Amrofer.

*Breul, Karl. 1939. *Cassell's New German and English Dictionary*. Rev. ed. New York: Funk & Wagnalls.

Bridgeman, Loraine I. 1961. "Kaiwa (Guarani) Phonology." *International Journal of American Linguistics* 27:329–34.

———. 1966. "Oral Paragraphs in Kaiwa (Guarani)." Unpublished PhD diss., Indiana University.
Brown, Alan K. 1964. "San Matteo County Place-naming." *Names* 12:154–84.
Brown, Oral Carl, Jr. 1972. "Haitian Voudou in Relation to Negritude and Christianity: A Study in Acculturation and Applied Anthropology." Unpublished PhD diss., Indiana University.
*Brown, Roger W. 1956. "Language and Categories." In *A Study of Thinking*, by Jerome S. Bruner, Jacqueline J. Goodnow, and George A. Austin, 247–312. New York: John Wiley and Sons.
*Brown, Thomas Kite, Henry Seidel Canby, and William Dodge Lewis. 1946. *The Winston Dictionary*. College ed. Philadelphia: John C. Winston.
*Browne, Isaac Hawkins. 1736. *A Pipe of Tobacco*. London: L. Gilliver.
*Bruner, Jerome S., Jacqueline J. Goodnow, and George A. Austin. 1956. *A Study of Thinking*. New York: John Wiley and Sons.
*Buck, C. D. 1949. *A Dictionary of Selected Synonyms in the Principal Indo-European Languages: A Contribution to the History of Ideas*. Chicago: University of Chicago Press.
Burling, Robbins. 1964. "Cognition and Componential Analysis: God's Truth or Hocus Pocus?" *American Anthropologist* 66:20–28.
Burrill, Meredith F. 1949. "Principles Underlying Domestic Place Name Decisions in the United States." *Revue Internationale d'Onomastique* 1–3:197–212.
———. 1956a. "Names for Wetlands in the United States." *Revista Geográfica* 19:11.
*———. 1956b. "Toponymic Generics I." *Names* 4:129–37.
*———. 1956c. "Toponymic Generics II." *Names* 4:226–40.
———. 1957. "Antarctic Geographic Names." *The Professional Geographer* 9 (6): 2–5.
———. 2004. *The Wonderful World of Geographic Names: The Writings of Meredith (Pete) F. Burrill (Toponymist Extraordinaire)*, edited by Randall A. Detro and Jesse Walker. Geoscience and Man 39. Baton Rouge: Geoscience Publications, Department of Geography and Anthropology, Louisiana State University.
Burrill, Meredith F., Kenneth J. Bertrand, and Fred G. Alberts. 1956. *Geographic Names of Antarctica*. Washington, DC: United States Government Printing Office.
*Cañes, Francisco. 1787. *Diccionario Español–Latino–Arábigo*. 3 vols. Madrid: Antonio Sancha.
Cannon, Angela. 2013. "Union Catalogs for Slavic Publications in American Libraries, 1931–1980." *Slavic and Eastern European Information Resources* 14:3–71.
*Caratzas, Stam. C. 1958. "Die entstehung der neugriechischen literatursprache." *Glotta* 36:194–208.
Cardona, George. 2006. *Henry M. Hoenigswald 1915–2003: A Biographical Memoir*. Washington, DC: National Academy of Sciences.
*Carew, Tim. 1955. "The Day I Joined the Guards." *The English Digest* 48 (4): 43–44.
*Carnap, Rudolf. 1947. *Meaning and Necessity: A Study in Semantics and Modal Logic*. Chicago: University of Chicago Press.
*Casares y Sanchez, Julio. 1942. *Diccionario Ideológico de la Lengua Española*. Barcelona: Editorial Gustavo Gili.
Cassell's Latin–English and English–Latin Dictionary. 1955. Rev. ed. New York: Funk & Wagnalls.
Cassell's Spanish Dictionary. 1959. Edited by Edgar A. Peers et al. New York: Funk & Wagnalls.

*Castillo, Carlos, and Otto F. Bond. 1948. *The University of Chicago Spanish–English, English–Spanish Dictionary*. Chicago: University of Chicago Press.

The Century Dictionary. 1889–91. 6 vols. Edited by William Dwight Whitney et al. New York: The Century Company.

**The Century Dictionary*. 1895. 10 vols. Edited by William Dwight Whitney et al. New York: The Century Company.

**Chambers Diccionario Tecnológico Español–Inglés: Inglés–Español*. 1952. Barcelona: Ediciones Omega, S. A.

*Chao, Yuen Ren. 1953. "Popular Chinese Plant Words: A Descriptive Lexico-grammatical Study." *Language* 29:379–414.

Chavarría-Aguilar, Oscar. 1952. "A Grammar of Pashto." Unpublished PhD diss., University of Pennsylvania.

———. 1954. *Lectures in Linguistics*. Poona: Deccan College Post-Graduate and Research Institute.

———. 1962a. *Pashto Basic Course*. Ann Arbor: University of Michigan, Department of Near Eastern Studies.

———. 1962b. *A Short Introduction to the Writing System of Pashto*. Ann Arbor: University of Michigan, Department of Near Eastern Studies.

———. 1988. *La Ortografía in Perspectiva*. Cartago, Costa Rica: Editorial Tecnológica de Costa Rica.

———. 1994. *A Bite of Costa Rica*. San José, Costa Rica: Gall Pinto Press.

———. 2001. *Cocina para Hombres*. Cartago, Costa Rica: El Castillo.

Chavarría-Aguilar, Oscar, and Bruce R. Pray. 1961. *A Basic Course in Hindi*. Np: Np.

*Chevalley, Abel, and Marguerite Chevalley. 1935. *The Concise Oxford French Dictionary*. London: Oxford University Press.

Chicago Assyrian Dictionary. 1956–2011. 21 vols. Edited by. I. J. Gelb, A. Leo Oppenheim, Erica Reiner et al. Chicago: University of Chicago, Oriental Institute.

*Chomsky, A. Noam. 1955. "Semantic Considerations in Grammar." *Georgetown University Monograph Series on Languages and Linguistics* 8:141–50.

*———. 1957. *Syntactic Structures*. Janua Linguarum Series Minor 4. The Hague: Mouton.

———. 1959. Review of *Verbal Behavior*, by B. F. Skinner. *Language* 35:2–57.

*———. 1961. "On the Notion 'Rule of Grammar.'" In *Structure of Language and Its Mathematical Aspects*, edited by Roman Jakobson, 6–24. American Mathematical Society Proceedings of Symposium in Applied Mathematics 12. Providence: American Mathematical Society.

Chomsky, Noam, and Morris Halle. 1965. "Some Controversial Questions in Phonological Theory." *Journal of Linguistics* 1:97–138.

*Clapin, Sylva. [1902?] *A New Dictionary of Americanisms*. New York: Funk & Wagnalls.

*Clarke, Adam. 1798. *A Dissertation on the Use and Abuse of Tobacco*. 2nd ed. London: G. Whitfield.

*Clay, Dorothy M. 1958–60. "A Formal Analysis of the Vocabularies of Aeschylus, Sophocles, and Euripides." 2 parts. Unpublished PhD diss., University of Minnesota.

*Cleland, Eunice E. 1949. Unpublished student paper submitted to Allen Walker Read.

*Clifton, C. Ebenezer, and Adrien Grimaux. 1923. *A New French and English Dictionary*. Paris: Garnier Frères.

Clyne, Michael. 1994. "Obituary for Einar Haugen." *Multilingua* 13:441–42.

Coley, John D. et al. 1999. "Inductive Reasoning in Folk Biological Thought." In *Folk Biology*, edited by Douglas L. Medin and Scott Atran, 205–32. Boston: MIT Press.

Compton, Carol, and John F. Hartmann, eds. 1992. *Papers in Tai Language, Linguistics, and Literatures in Honor of William J. Gedney on his 77th Birthday.* Occasional Papers 16. DeKalb: Center of Southeast Asian Studies, Northern Illinois University.

Concise Oxford Dictionary. 1951. Edited by H. W. Fowler, F. G. Fowler et al. 4th ed. Oxford: Clarendon Press.

Conklin, Harold C. 1953. *Hanunóo-English Vocabulary.* Berkeley: University of California Press.

*———. 1954. "The Relation of Hanunóo Culture to the Plant World." Unpublished PhD diss., Yale University.

*———. 1955. "Hanunóo Color Categories." *Southwestern Journal of Anthropology* 11:339–44.

*———. 1957. "Ethnobotanical Problems in the Comparative Study of Folk Taxonomy." Paper read at the Ninth Pacific Science Congress, 1957. Bangkok. Published in *Proceedings, Ninth Pacific Science Congress, 1957* 4:299–301, Bangkok, 1962.

———. 1968. "Lexicographical Treatment of Folk Taxonomies." In *Readings in the Sociology of Language*, edited by Joshua L. Fishman, 414–33. The Hague: Mouton.

———. 1969. "Lexicographical Treatment of Folk Taxonomies." In *Cognitive Anthropology*, edited by Steven A. Tyler, 41–59. New York: Holt, Rinehart, and Winston.

———. 1972. *Folk Classification: A Topically Arranged Bibliography of Contemporary and Background References through 1971.* New Haven, CT: Yale University Department of Anthropology.

———. 1975. Review of *Manual of Lexicography*, by Ladislav Zgusta. *Language in Society* 4:241–43.

———. 1980. *Ethnographic Atlas of Ifugao: A Study of Environment, Culture, and Society in Northern Luzon.* With the special assistance of Puggūwon Lupāih and Miklos Pinther. New Haven, CT: Yale University Press, with cooperation of the American Geographical Society of New York.

———. 1998. "Language, Culture, and Environment: My Early Years." *Annual Review of Anthropology* 27:xiii–xxx.

———. 2007. *Fine Description: Ethnographic and Linguistic Essays.* Edited by Joel C. Kuipers and Ray McDermott. Yale University Southeast Asian Studies 56. New Haven, CT: Yale University Southeast Asian Studies Program.

Considine. John. 2014. *Academy Dictionaries 1600–1800.* Cambridge, UK: Cambridge University Press.

Cornyn, William S. 1945–46. *Spoken Burmese.* 2 vols. United States War Department EM 541–54. Madison, WI: United States Armed Forces Institute, the Linguistic Society of America, and the American Council of Learned Societies.

———. 1950. *Beginning Russian.* New Haven, CT: Yale University Press.

———, ed. 1957. *Burmese Chrestomathy.* Publications in Oriental Languages, Series A: Texts. Washington, DC: American Council of Learned Societies.

———. 1967. "Burma." In *Current Trends in Linguistics: Linguistics in East Asia and Southeast Asia*, edited by Thomas A. Sebeok, 777–81. The Hague: Mouton.

Cornyn, William S., and John K. Musgrave. 1958. *Burmese Glossary.* Publications in Oriental Languages, Series A: Texts 5. New York: American Council of Learned Societies.

Cornyn, William S., and D. Haigh Roop. 1968. *Beginning Burmese.* New Haven, CT: Yale University Press.

*Corominas, Joan. 1954. *Diccionario Crítico Etymológico de la Lengua Castellana.* 4 vols. Bern: Editorial Francke.

Cosinka, Jan [Ian Jackson]. 2006. *Teach Yourself Malkielese in 90 Minutes*. Berkeley: Ian Jackson Books.
Cowan, J Milton. 1991. "American Linguistics in Peace and at War." In *First Person Singular II: Autobiographies by North American Scholars in the Language Sciences*, edited by Konrad Koerner, 67–82. Studies in the History of the Language Sciences 61. Amsterdam: John Benjamins.
Coward, David F., and Charles E. Grimes. 1995. *Making Dictionaries: A Guide to Lexicography and the Multi-Dictionary Formatter*. Waxhaw, NC: SIL International.
Cowell, Mark W. 1964. *A Reference Grammar of Syrian Arabic (Based on the Dialect of Damascus)*. Washington, DC: Georgetown University Press.
Cowie, A. P. 1999. *English Dictionaries for Foreign Learners: A History*. Oxford: Oxford University Press.
*Craigie, William A. 1938. "Auger-hole." *Dialect Notes* 6:643.
Crawford, James, ed. 1992. *Language Loyalties: A Source Book on the Official English Controversy*. Chicago: University of Chicago Press.
*Cuyás, Arturo. 1953. *Appleton's Revised English–Spanish and Spanish–English Dictionary*. 4th ed. New York: Appleton-Century-Crofts.
Daniell, Beth. 2003. "In Memoriam: James Sledd." *College Composition and Communication* 55:217–20.
Dareau, Margaret G. 2012. "Dictionary of the Older Scottish Tongue." In *Scotland in Definition: A History of Scottish Dictionaries*, edited by Iseabail Macleod and J. Derrick McClure, 116–43. Edinburgh: Birlinn.
*Da Somavera, Alessio. 1709. *Tesoro della Lingua Greca-volgare ed Italiano*. Paris: Guignard.
Davies, Anna Morpurgo. 2008. "Henry Max Hoenigswald." *Language* 84:856–73.
Davis, Boyd H., and Raymond O'Cain, eds. 1980. *First Person Singular: Papers from the Conference on an Oral Archive for the History of American Linguistics*. Studies in the History of the Language Sciences 21. Amsterdam: John Benjamins.
*De Alcala, Pedro. 1505. *Vocabulista Arauigo en Letra Castellana*. Granada: Juan Varela.
*De Askue, Resurección Maria. 1905–1906. *Diccionario Vasco–Español–Francés*. Bilbao, Spain: published by the author.
*De Larramendi, Manuel. 1745. *Diccionario Trilingüe del Castellano, Bascuence, Latin*. San Sebastián, Spain: Bartolomé Riesjo y Montero.
*De Lolme, Jean-Louis, Robert Wallace, and Henry Bridgeman. 1903. *Heath's French and English Dictionary*. Boston: D. C. Heath.
Dembowski, Peter F. 2000. "Karl David Uitti: A Biographical Sketch." In *Translatio Studii: Essays by His Students in Honor of Karl D. Uitti for His Sixty-First Birthday*, edited by Renate Blumenfeld-Kosinski et al., 23–26. Amsterdam: Rodopi.
*Demetrius. 1902. *On Style*. Edited by W. Rhys Roberts. Cambridge, UK: Cambridge University Press.
De Schryver, Gilles-Maurice, and D. J. Prinsloo. 2003. "Compiling a Lemma-sign List for a Specific Target User Group: *The Junior Dictionary* as a Case in Point." *Dictionaries* 24:28–58.
De Vries, Jan, and F. de Tollenaere. 1965. *Nederlands Etymologisch Woordenboek*. 2nd ed. Leiden: Brill.
*DeVries, Louis. 1951. *French–English Science Dictionary*. New York: McGraw-Hill.
Diab, Turki. 1990. *Pedagogical Lexicography: A Case Study of Arab Nurses as Dictionary Users*. Lexicographica Series Maior 31. Tübingen: Niemeyer.
*Dickens, Charles. 1938. *The Letters of Charles Dickens*. Edited by Walter Dexter. London: Nonesuch Press.

Dictionary of American English. 1936–1944. 4 vols. Edited by W. A. Craigie, J. R. Hulbert, et al. Chicago: University of Chicago Press.
Dictionary of American Regional English. 1985–2013. 6 vols. Edited by Frederic G. Cassidy, Joan Houston Hall, et al. Cambridge, MA: Belknap Press of Harvard University Press.
Dictionary of the Older Scottish Tongue. 1931–2002. 12 vols. Edited by William A. Craigie, A. J. Aitken, et al. Aberdeen: University of Aberdeen Press; and other presses.
Dictionnaire du Français Contemporain. 1967. Edited by Jean Dubois et al. Paris: Larousse.
*Diederich, Paul B. 1939. "Frequency of Latin Words." Unpublished PhD diss., University of Chicago.
*Diez, Friedrich. 1869–70. *Etymologisches Wörterbuch der Romanischen Sprachen*. 3rd ed. 2 vols. Bonn, Germany: Marcus.
Dingley, John, and Leon Ferder, eds. 2000. *In the Realm of Slavic Philology: To Honor the Teaching and Scholarship of Dean S. Worth from his UCLA Students*. Bloomington, IN: Slavica Publishers.
Dolezal, Fredric Thomas, and Don R. McCreary. 1999. *Pedagogical Lexicography Today: A Critical Bibliography on Learners' Dictionaries with Special Emphasis on Language Learners and Dictionary Users*. Lexicographica Series Maior 96. Tübingen, Germany: Niemeyer.
*Dorn, Bernhard. 1847. *A Chrestomathy of the Pushtū or Afghan Language to Which Is Subjoined a Glossary in Afghan and English*. St. Petersburg: Imperial Academy of Sciences.
*Dornseiff, Franz. 1959. *Der Deutsches Wortschatz nach Sachgruppen*. 5th ed. Berlin: De Gruyter.
Dove, Michael R., and Patrick V. Kirch. 2018. *Harold Conklin 1926–2016: A Biographical Memoir*. Washington, DC: National Academy of Sciences.
Dubois, Jean, and Claude Dubois. 1971. *Introduction à la Lexicographie: Le Dictionnaire*. Paris: Larousse.
Durkin, Philip, ed. 2016. *The Oxford Handbook of Lexicography*. Oxford: Oxford University Press.
Dworkin, Steven N. 2004. "Yakov Malkiel." *Language* 80:153–62.
Eaton, Helen S. 1940. *Semantic Frequency List for English, French, German, and Spanish: A Correlation of the First Six Thousand Words in Four Single-Language Frequency Lists*. Chicago: University of Chicago Press.
Einarsson, Stefán, and Norman E. Eliason, eds. 1959. *Studies in Heroic Legend and Current Speech*. Copenhagen: Rosenkilde & Bagger.
Eliason, Norman E. 1969. "Kemp Malone: 14 March 1889–13 October 1971." *American Speech* 44:163–65.
*Ernout, A., and A. Meillet. 1939. *Dictionnaire Étymologique de la Langue Latine*. 2nd ed. Paris: Klincksieck.
Eskey, David E. 1975. "Reflections on How Much We Don't Need Wild Men, Even Make-Believe Wild Men Who Are Really Professors: Reply to James Sledd." *College English* 36:703–6.
Estienne, Henri. 1572. *Thesaurus Graecae Linguae*. Geneva: Henricus Stephanus.
Estienne, Robert. 1543. *Dictionarium, seu Latinae Linguae Thesaurus*. Paris: Roberti Stephani.
*Evans, Clifford. 1946. "Where There's a Will." *John Bull* 79, no. 2803 (May 18, 1946): 13–14, 16.
Farina, Donna M. T. Cr., ed. and trans. 1995. "Towards a General Theory of Lexicography." *International Journal of Lexicography* 8:314–50. See also Shcherba, Lev (1940) and Garvin, Paul L. (1947).
*Ferguson, Charles A. 1959. "Diglossia." *Word* 15:325–40.

*Ferreira, P. Julio Albino. 1939. *Diccionario Inglez-Portuguez*. Porto, Portugal: Edição do Autor.
Fishman, Joshua A. 1968. *Readings in the Sociology of Language*. The Hague: Mouton.
———. 1995. "Einar Haugen." *Language* 71:558–64.
*Fitzgerald, Robert Allan. 1873. *Wickets in the West*. London: Tinsley Brothers.
Forrest, William. 2007. "Obituary: H. Allan Gleason, Jr. 1917–2007." *LINGUIST List* 18. 619. https://linguistlist.org/issues/18/18-619.html
*Frake, Charles O. 1960. "The Eastern Subanun of Mindanao." In *Social Structure in Southeast Asia*, edited by George Peter Murdock, 51–64. Chicago: Quadrangle Books.
*———. 1961. "The Diagnosis of Disease among the Subanun of Mindanao." *American Anthropologist* 63:113–132.
*Francis, W. Nelson. 1958. *The Structure of American English*. New York: Ronald Press.
Franjié, Lynne. 2009. *La Traduction dans les Dictionnaires Bilingues*. Paris: Editions le Manuscrit.
Franklin, Karl J. 1965. Review of *Problems in Lexicography*, by Fred W. Householder and Sol Saporta. *Linguistics: An International Review* 14:70–76.
Fromkin, Victoria A. 1984. "Fred W. Householder and the Linguistic Society of America." In *Fred W. Householder Bibliography*, compiled by Salman H. Al-Ani, 25–26. Bloomington, IN: Eurolingua.
Fulk, R. D. 1996. Review of *Etymology*, by Yakov Malkiel. *Speculum* 71:172–74.
Funk & Wagnalls Standard Dictionary of the English Language, International Edition. 1961. Edited by Charles Earle Funk et al. New York: Funk & Wagnalls.
*Garcia de Diego, Vincente. 1954. *Diccionario Etimológico Español e Hispánico*. Madrid: Editorial SAETA.
*Gardiner, Alan H. 1932. *The Theory of Speech and Language*. Oxford: Oxford University Press.
Garvin, Paul L. 1947. "Experience of the General Theory of Lexicography. Study 1. Types of Dictionaries." *Word* 3:129–30.
*———. 1960. "On Structuralist Method." *Georgetown University Monograph Series on Languages and Linguistics* 11:145–48.
———. 1991. "Six Decades of a Linguistic Audience." In *First Person Singular II: Autobiographies by North American Scholars in the Language Sciences*, edited by Konrad Koerner, 125–38. Studies in the History of the Language Sciences 61. Amsterdam: John Benjamins.
Gates, Edward. 1972. *An Analysis of the Lexicographic Resources Used by American Biblical Scholars Today*. Society of Biblical Literature Dissertation Series 8. Missoula: University of Montana for the Society of Biblical Literature.
———. 1973. "A Bibliography on General and English Lexicography." In *Lexicography in English*, edited by Raven I. McDavid and Audrey R. Duckert, 320–37. Annals of the New York Academy of Sciences 211. New York: New York Academy of Sciences.
———. 1977. Review of *Manual of Lexicography*, by Ladislav Zgusta. *Language Sciences* 46:27–33.
———. 1979. "A Survey of the Teaching of Lexicography." *Dictionaries* 1:113–31.
Gedney, William J. 1956. *English for Speakers of Thai*. Washington, DC: American Council of Learned Societies.
———. 1991. *William J. Gedney's the Yay Language: Glossary, Texts, and Translations*. Edited by Thomas J. Hudak. Ann Arbor: Center for Southeast Asian Studies, University of Michigan.

———. 1993. *William J. Gedney's the Saek Language: Glossary, Texts, and Translations*. Edited by Thomas J. Hudak. Ann Arbor: Center for Southeast Asian Studies, University of Michigan.
Gedney, William J., and Thomas J. Hudak. 2010. *William J. Gedney's Concise Saek-English, English-Saek Lexicon*. Oceanic Linguistics Special Publication 37. Honolulu: University of Hawaii.
Georgacas, Demetrius J. 1958a. "Remarks on Andriotis' Etymological Lexicon." *Byzantinische Zetischrift* 51:43–52.
———. 1958b. "A Contribution to Greek Word History, Derivation, and Etymology." *Glotta* 36 (3): 161–93.
———. 1976. "The Present State of Lexicography and Zgusta's *Manual of Lexicography*." *Orbis* 25:359–400.
Gething, Thomas W., ed. 1975. *A Tai Festschrift for William J. Gedney: On the Occasion of His Fifth Cycle of Life Birthday Anniversary, April 4, 1975*. Southeast Asian Studies Working Paper 8. Honolulu: University of Hawaii.
Gething, Thomas W., and Nguyen Dang Lien, eds. 1979. *Papers in Southeast Asian Linguistics No. 6: Tai Studies in Honor of William J. Gedney*. Pacific Linguistics Series A.52. Canberra: Department of Linguistics, Research School of Pacific Studies, Australian National University.
*Gilbertson, George Waters. 1932. *The Pakkhto Idiom: A Dictionary*. 2 vols. Hertford, UK: published by author.
Gilliver, Peter. 2016. *The Making of the* Oxford English Dictionary. Oxford: Oxford University Press.
Gilman, E. W. 1996. "*The Century Dictionary*: Definitions and Usage." *Dictionaries* 17:55–67.
Glanze, Walter D., ed. 1978. *Studies in Lexicography as a Science and as an Art*. New York: Bantam Books.
Gleason, H. A., Jr. 1955. *An Introduction to Descriptive Linguistics*. New York: Henry Holt.
———. 1961. "A File for a Technical Dictionary." In *Report of the Twelfth Annual Roundtable Meeting*, edited by Michael Zarechnak, 115–22. Monograph Series on Languages and Linguistics 14. Washington, DC: Georgetown University Press.
———. 1962. "Linguistics in Service of the Church." *Practical Anthropology* 9:205–19.
———. 1965. *Linguistics and English Grammar*. New York: Holt, Rinehart, & Winston.
———. 1973. "Grammatical Prerequisites." In *Lexicography in English*, edited by Raven I. McDavid and Audrey R. Duckert, 27–33. Annals of the New York Academy of Sciences 211. New York: New York Academy of Sciences.
———. 1974. "A Successful Textbook." In *Linguistics: Teaching and Interdisciplinary Relations*, edited by Francis P. Dinneen, 15–22. Georgetown University Roundtable on Language and Linguistics 1974. Washington, DC: Georgetown University Press.
*"Glossary of Names for Topographic Forms." 1928. In *Topographic Instructions of the United States Geological Survey*, edited by Clarence L. Birdseye, chapter 6A3. Washington, DC: USGPO.
Golla, Victor, and James A. Matisoff. 1997. "Mary R. Haas." *Language* 73:826–37.
*Goodenough, Ward H. 1951. *Property, Kin, and Community on Truk*. Yale University Publications in Anthropology 46. New Haven, CT: Yale University Press.
*———. 1956 "Componential Analysis and the Study of Meaning." *Language* 32:195–216.
*———. 1957. "Cultural Anthropology and Linguistics." *Georgetown University Monograph Series on Languages and Linguistics* 9:167–73.

Gouws, Rufus H. 2011. "Learning, Unlearning and Innovation in the Planning of Electronic Dictionaries." In *e-Lexicography: The Internet, Digital Initiatives, and Lexicography*, edited by Pedro A. Fuertes-Olivera and Henning Bergenholtz, 17–29. London: Continuum.

*Gradenwitz, Otto. 1904. *Laterculi Vocum Latinarum*. Leipzig: S. Hirzel.

Grant, A. J. 1966. "Cartography and Australian Place Names, Part 2." *Cartography* 6:24–30.

*Grantley, John. 1946. "'King Gong' of Scotland." *The New Outlook on Motoring* (October): 12–13.

*Greenberg, Joseph H. 1957. "The Nature and Uses of Linguistic Typologies." *International Journal of American Linguistics* 23 (2): 68–77.

*Gregg, John R. 1954. *The Language of Taxonomy: An Application of Symbolic Logic to the Study of Classificatory Systems*. New York: Columbia University Press.

*Grierson, George Abraham. 1898–1928. *The Linguistic Survey of India*. 11 vols. Calcutta: Government of India Central Publication Branch.

Griswold, William J. 2004. "In Memoriam: Andreas Tietze (1914–2003)." *MESA Bulletin* 38:142–44.

Gudschinsky, Sarah C. 1977. "Literacy." In *The Summer Institute of Linguistics: Its Works and Contributions*, edited by Ruth M. Brend and Kenneth L. Pike, 39–56. The Hague: Mouton.

Gunter, Richard. 1960. Review of *A Short Introduction to English Grammar*, by James Sledd. *Journal of Developmental Reading* 3 (2): 125–27.

Guralnik, David B. et al. 1953. *Webster's New World Dictionary*. College ed. Cleveland: World Publishing.

Haas, Mary R. 1942. *Beginning Thai: Introductory Lessons in the Pronunciation and Grammar of the Thai Language*. Washington, DC: American Council of Learned Societies.

———. 1943. "The Linguist as a Teacher of Languages." *Language* 19:203–8.

———. 1945a. *Thai Reader*. Berkeley: Army Specialized Training Program, University of California.

———. 1945b. *Manual of Thai Conversations*. Berkeley: Army Specialized Training Program, University of California.

———. 1945c. *Thai Phrases*. Berkeley: Army Specialized Training Program, University of California.

———. 1945d. *Special Dictionary of the Thai Language*. 2 vols. Berkeley: Army Specialized Training Program, University of California.

———. 1953a. *Tunica Dictionary*. Berkeley: University of California Press.

———. 1953b. "The Application of Linguistics to Language Teaching." In *Anthropology Today: An Encyclopedic Inventory*, edited by A. L. Kroeber, 807–18. Chicago: University of Chicago Press.

———. 1953c. "Bilingualism and Acculturation." In *Results of the Conference of Anthropologists and Linguists*, edited by Claude Lévi-Strauss et al., 42–43. Indiana University Publications in Anthropology and Linguistics 8. Bloomington: Indiana University.

———. 1954. *Thai Reader*. Washington, DC: American Council of Learned Societies.

———. 1955. *Thai Vocabulary*. Washington, DC: American Council of Learned Societies.

———. 1956a. *Brief Description of Thai, with Sample Texts: Outline for Tyles of Linguistic Structure*. Berkeley: University of California, Department of Linguistics.

———. 1956b. *The Thai System of Writing*. Washington, DC: American Council of Learned Societies.

———. 1960. "Differences among Languages and Problems of Language Learning." *California Schools* 31:35–37.
———. 1964. *Thai-English Student's Dictionary*. Palo Alto, CA: Stanford University Press.
Haas, Mary R., and Stephen O. Murray. 1997. "A 1978 Interview with Mary R. Haas." *Anthropological Linguistics* 39:695–722.
Haas, Mary R., and Heng R. Subhanka. 1945–48. *Spoken Thai*. 2 vols. New York: Henry Holt.
Haguenauer, Charles. 1952. "Les parlers Aïnous." In *Les langues du monde*, edited by A. Meillet and Marcel Cohen, 475–83. Rev. ed. Paris: Centre National de la Recherche Scientifique.
*Hale, E. E. 1932. "Geographical Terms in the Far West." *Dialect Notes* 6:217–34.
*Hale, Louise Closser. 1920. *An American's London*. New York: Harper & Brothers.
Hall, Robert A., Jr. 1991. "Layers of Linguistics." In *First Person Singular II: Autobiographies by North American Scholars in the Language Sciences*, edited by Konrad Koerner, 167–86. Studies in the History of the Language Sciences 61. Amsterdam: John Benjamins.
*Halle, Morris. 1959. *The Sound Pattern of Russian: A Linguistic and Acoustical Investigation*. The Hague: Mouton.
Hallig, Rudolf, and Walther von Wartburg, eds. 1952. *Begriffssystem als Grundlage für die Lexikographie*. Berlin: Akademie Verlag.
Hamp, Eric P., Fred W. Householder, Robert Austerlitz, and Martin Joos, eds. 1966. *Readings in Linguistics II*. Chicago: University of Chicago Press.
Hancher, Michael. 1996. "*The Century Dictionary*: Illustrations." *Dictionaries* 17:79–115.
*Handjéri, Alexander. 1840–41. *Dictionnaire Francais-Arabe-Persan et Turc*. Moscow: Imperial University.
Hanks, Patrick. 2013. *Lexical Analysis*. Cambridge, MA: MIT Press.
*Hanley, Miles L. 1937. Review of *A Dictionary of American English*. *Dialect Notes* 6:583–91.
Harrell, Richard S. 1957. *The Phonology of Colloquial Egyptian Arabic*. Program in Oriental Languages, Publication Series B, Aids 9. New York: American Council of Learned Societies.
———. 1962. *A Short Reference Grammar of Moroccan Arabic*. With Louis Brunot. Arabic Series 1. Washington, DC: Georgetown University Press.
Harrell, Richard S. et al. 1965. *A Basic Course in Moroccan Arabic*. Richard Slade Harrell Arabic Series 8. Washington, DC: Georgetown University Press.
———. 1966. *A Dictionary of Moroccan Arabic: Moroccan-English*. Richard Slade Harrell Arabic Series 9. Washington, DC: Georgetown University Press.
Harrell, Richard S., George D. Selim, and Laila Y. Tewfik. 1963. *Lessons in Colloquial Egyptian Arabic*. Rev. ed. Arabic Series 2. Washington, DC: Georgetown University Press.
Harris, Jimmy G., and James R. Chamberlain, eds. 1975. *Studies in Tai Linguistics in Honor of William J. Gedney*. Bangkok: Central Institute of English Language, Office of State Universities.
*Harris, Zellig. 1948. "Componential Analysis of a Hebrew Paradigm." *Language* 24:87–91.
Hartmann, R. R. K., ed. 1984. *LEXeter '83 Proceedings: Papers from the International Conference on Lexicography at Exeter, 9–12 September 1983*. Lexicographical Series Maior 1. Tübingen, Germany: Niemeyer.
———. 1987a. "Four Perspectives on Dictionary Use: A Critical Review of Research Methods." In *The Dictionary and the Language Learner: Papers from the EURALEX Seminar at the University of Leeds 1–3 April 1985*, edited by Anthony Cowie, 11–28. Lexicographica Series Maior 17. Tübingen, Germany: Niemeyer.

———. 1987b. "Dictionaries of English: The User's Perspective." In *Dictionaries of English: Prospects for the Record of Our Language*, edited by Richard W. Bailey, 121–35. Ann Arbor: University of Michigan Press.

———. 1998. "Contemporary Lexicography, with Particular Attention to the User's Perspective." *Lexicon* 28:141–47.

———, ed. 2003. *Lexicography: Critical Concepts*. 3 vols. London: Routledge.

———. 2007. *Interlingual Lexicography: Selected Essays on Translation Equivalence, Contrastive Linguistics, and the Bilingual Dictionary*. Lexicographica Series Maior 133. Tübingen, Germany: Niemeyer.

Hartmann, R. R. K., and Gregory James. 1998. *Dictionary of Lexicography*. London: Routledge.

*Haugen, Einar. 1957. "The Semantics of Icelandic Orientation." *Word* 13:447–59.

———. 1963a. Review of *Problems in Lexicography*, by Fred W. Householder and Sol Saporta. *American Anthropologist* n.s. 65 (3.1): 752–55.

———. 1963b. "Notes on a Dictionary: John Brynildsen's *Norsk-Engelsk Ordbok*." *Scandinavian Studies* 35:295–306.

———. 1965. *Norwegian-English Dictionary: A Pronouncing and Translating Dictionary of Modern Norwegian [Bokmål and Nynorsk]: with a Historical and Grammatical Introduction*. Madison: University of Wisconsin Press.

———. 1980. "On the Making of a Linguist." In *First Person Singular: Papers from the Conference on an Oral Archive for the History of American Linguistics*, edited by Boyd H. Davis and Raymond O'Cain, 133–43. Studies in the History of the Language Sciences 21. Amsterdam: John Benjamins.

Hausmann, Franz Josef, Oskar Reichmann, Herbert Ernst Wiegand, and Ladislav Zgusta, eds. 1990. *Wörterbücher/Dictionaries/Dictionnaires: Ein Internationales Handbuch zur Lexikographie/An International Encyclopedia of Lexicography/Encyclopédie Internationale de Lexicographie*. 3 vols. Handbooks of Linguistics and Communication Science 5.1-3. Berlin: Walter de Gruyter.

*Hava, J. G. 1951. *Arabic-English Dictionary*. Beirut: Catholic Press.

Havránek, Bohuslav et al., eds. 1953. *Lexicographfický Sborník*. Bratislava: Vydavateľstvo Slovenskej akadémie vied.

Heestermans, Hans. 2012. "Félicien de Tollenaere." *Jaarboek van de Maatschappij der Nederlandse Letterkunde*, 162–67.

Herzog, Marvin I., Wita Ravid, and Uriel Weinreich, eds. 1969. *The Field of Yiddish: Studies in Language, Folklore, and Literature, Third Collection*. The Hague: Mouton.

*Hietsch, Otto. 1958. "Meaning Discrimination in Modern Lexicography." *Modern Language Journal* 42:232–34.

*Hjelmslev, Louis. 1953. *Prolegomena to a Theory of Language*. Baltimore: Waverly Press.

*Hoare, Alfred. 1947. *A Short Italian Dictionary*. London: Cambridge University Press.

*Hockett, Charles F. 1956. "Idiom Formation." In *For Roman Jakobson*, edited by Morris Halle, 222–29. The Hague: Mouton.

*———. 1958. *A Course in Modern Linguistics*. New York: Macmillan.

———. 1980. "Preserving the Heritage." In *First Person Singular: Papers from the Conference on an Oral Archive for the History of American Linguistics*, edited by Boyd H. Davis and Raymond O'Cain, 99–107. Studies in the History of the Language Sciences 21. Amsterdam: John Benjamins.

Hoenigswald, Henry M. 1940. "Pan-compounds in Early Greek." *Language* 16:183–87.

———. 1945. *Spoken Hindustani: Basic Course*. 2 vols. New York: Henry Holt.
———. 1960. *Language Change and Linguistic Reconstruction*. Chicago: University of Chicago Press.
———. 1973. *Studies in Formal Historical Linguistics*. Dordrecht, The Netherlands: Reidel.
———, ed. 1979. *The European Background of American Linguistics*. Dordrecht, The Netherlands: Foris.
———. 1980. "A Reconstruction." In *First Person Singular: Papers from the Conference on an Oral Archive for the History of American Linguistics*, edited by Boyd H. Davis and Raymond O'Cain, 23–28. Studies in the History of the Language Sciences 21. Amsterdam: John Benjamins.
Hornby, A. S. 1948. *A Learner's Dictionary of Current English*. Oxford: Oxford University Press.
*———. 1952. *Advanced Learner's Dictionary of Current English*. Oxford: Oxford University Press.
Householder, Fred W., Jr. 1941. *Literary Quotation and Allusion in Lucian*. New York: Columbia University Press.
*———. 1959. Review of a *Course in Modern Linguistics*, by Charles F. Hockett. *Language* 35:503–27.
———. 1962. Review of *Language Change and Linguistic Reconstruction* by Henry M. Hoenigswald. *International Journal of American Linguistics* 28:69–79.
———. 1965. "On Some Recent Claims in Phonological Theory." *Journal of Linguistics* 1:13–34.
———. 1971. *Linguistic Speculations*. Cambridge: Cambridge University Press.
———, ed. 1972. *Syntactic Theory 1: Structuralist: Selected Readings*. Harmondsworth, UK: Penguin.
———. 1975. Review of *Lexicography in English*, edited by Raven I. McDavid and Audrey R. Duckert. *Language Sciences* 37:26–28.
———. 1980. "A Sketch of How I Came to Be Interested in Linguistics." In *First Person Singular: Papers from the Conference on an Oral Archive for the History of American Linguistics*, edited by Boyd H. Davis and Raymond O'Cain, 193–202. Studies in the History of the Language Sciences 21. Amsterdam: John Benjamins.
———, ed. 1981. *The Syntax of Apollonius Dyscolus*. Amsterdam: John Benjamins.
———. 1983. "Kyriolexia and Language Change." *Language* 59:1–19.
Householder, Fred W., Jr., et al. 1964. *Some Classes of Verb in English*. Bloomington: Indiana University Linguistics Club.
———. 1965. *More Classes of Verbs in English*. Bloomington: Indiana University Linguistics Club.
Householder, Fred W., Jr., Kostas Kazakis, and Andreas Koutsoudas. 1964. *Reference Grammar of Literary Dhimotiki*. Research Center in Anthropology, Folklore, and Linguistics Publication 31. Bloomington: Indiana University.
Householder, Fred W., Jr., and Mansour Lotfi. 1965. *Basic Course in Azerbaijaini*. Uralic and Altaic Series 45. Bloomington: Indiana University.
Householder, Fred W., Jr., and Thomas A. Sebeok. 1951. "Linguisticians and Lexicographers." *American Speech* 26:221–22.
*Howell, James. 1660. *Lexicon Tetraglotton*. London: Samuel Thomson.
Hudak, Thomas John. 2000. "William J. Gedney (1915–1999)." *The Journal of Asian Studies* 59:223.
Hulbert, J. R. 1955. *Dictionaries British and American*. New York: Philosophical Library.

Iannucci, James E. 1952. *Lexical Numbers in Spanish Nouns with Reference to Their English Equivalents*. Series in Romanic Languages and Literatures Extra Series 12. Philadelphia: University of Pennsylvania Press.

*———. 1957. "Meaning Discrimination in Bilingual Dictionaries: A New Lexicographical Technique." *Modern Language Journal* 41:272–81.

———. 1959. "Explanatory Matter in Bilingual Dictionaries." *Babel* 5:195–99.

———. 1985. "Sense Discriminations and Translation Complements in Bilingual Dictionaries." *Dictionaries* 7:57–65.

———. 1986a. "Ghost Adjectives in Dictionaries." *Dictionaries* 8:164–68.

———. 1986b. Contributor note. *Dictionaries* 8:328.

Ilson, Robert, ed. 1986. *Lexicography: An Emerging International Profession*. Manchester, UK: Manchester University Press.

———. 2016. "Why Dictionaries Are No Better Than They Are—and No Worse." In *Proceedings of the XVII EURALEX International Conference: Lexicography and Linguistic Diversity*, edited by Tinatin Margalitadze and George Meladze, 49–60. Tbilisi, Georgia: Ivane Javakhisvili Tbilisi State University.

Imbs, Paul, ed. 1961. *Lexicologie et Lexicographie Françaises et Romanes: Orientations et Exigences Actuelles*. Paris: Centre National de la Recherche Scientifique.

Indiana University. 2013. *University Graduate School Bulletin 2013-2014*. Bloomington: Trustees of Indiana University. https://bulletins.iu.edu/iu/gradschool/2013-2014/overview/history.shtml.

Institute of Languages and Linguistics, Edmund A. Walsh School of Foreign Service. 1958. *Bulletin*. Washington, DC: Georgetown University.

Jablonski, John. 2003. "Politics, English, and the Hungarian–English Dictionary: The Work of László Országh." *Dictionaries* 24:227–35.

Jackson, Howard. 1985. "Grammar in the Dictionary." In *Dictionaries, Lexicography, and Language Learning*, edited by Robert Ilson, 53–64. London: Pergamon.

———, ed. 2013. *Bloomsbury Companion to Lexicography*. London: Bloomsbury.

Jackson, Ian, see Cosinka, Jan

*Jakobson, Roman. 1936. "Beitrag zur allgemeinen Kasuslehre." *Travaux du Cercle Linguistique de Prague* 6:240–88.

Janssen, Maarten. 1971. *SIMuLLDA: A Multilingual Database Application Using a Structured Interlingua*. Unpublished PhD diss., University of Utrecht.

*Joos, Martin, ed. 1952. *Readings in Linguistics: The Development of Descriptive Linguistics in American since 1925*. Washington, DC: American Council of Learned Societies.

*———. 1956. Review of *Machine Translation of Languages: Fourteen Essays*, edited by William N. Locke and A. Donald Booth. *Language* 32:293–98.

*———. 1958. "Semology: A Linguistic Theory of Meaning." *Studies in Linguistics* 13 (3–4): 53–70.

———. 1986. *Notes on the Development of the Linguistic Society of America 1924 to 1950*. Washington, DC: Linguistic Society of America.

*Jorden, Eleanor Harz. 1955. "The Syntax of Modern Colloquial Japanese." *Language* 31 (1) (part 3).

*J. W. F. 1878. "English Pronunciation of English." *Portland Daily Press* (February 15, 1878): 1/h.

Kachru, Braj B. 2005. "Henry Kahane." *Language* 81:237–44.

Kachru, Braj B. et al., eds. 1973. *Issues in Linguistics*. Urbana: University of Illinois Press.

Kachru, Braj B., and Henry Kahane, eds. 1995. *Cultures, Ideologies, and the Dictionary: Studies in Honor of Ladislav Zgusta*. Lexicographica Series Maior 64. Tübingen, Germany: Niemeyer.

Kahane, Henry. 1991. "A Linguist's Vita as Historiography." In *First Person Singular II: Autobiographies by North American Scholars in the Language Sciences*, edited by Konrad Koerner, 189–204. Studies in the History of the Language Sciences 61. Amsterdam: John Benjamins.

Kahane, Henry, and Renée Kahane. 1940. *Italienische Ortsnamen in Griechenland*. Texte und Forschungen zur Byzantinisch-Neugrischischen Philologie 36. Athens: Verlag der Byzantinisch-neugriechischen Jahrbücher.

———. 1979. *Graeca et Romanica Scripta Selecta, Volume 1: Romance and Mediterranean Lexicology*. Amsterdam: Adolf M. Hakkert.

———. 1983. *Graeca et Romanica Scripta Selecta, Volume 2: Byzantium and the West; Hellenistic Heritage in the West: Structural Analysis, Literary History*. Amsterdam: Adolf M. Hakkert.

———. 1986. *Graeca et Romanica Scripta Selecta, Volume 3: Humanistic Linguistics: The Mediterranean, Lexis, Romance Linguistics in Review, East and West in Medieval Literature, Personal Memoir*. Amsterdam: Adolf M. Hakkert.

———. 1992. "The Dictionary as Ideology." In *History, Languages, and Lexicographers*, edited by Ladislav Zgusta, 19–76. Lexicographica Series Maior 41. Tübingen: Niemeyer.

Kahane, Henry, and Angelina R. Pietrangeli, eds. 1954. *Descriptive Studies in Spanish Grammar*. Illinois Studies in Language and Literature 38. Urbana: University of Illinois.

———, eds. 1959. *Structural Studies on Spanish Themes*. Urbana: University of Illinois Press.

Kahane, Henry, Renée Kahane, and Lucille Bremner. 1968. *Glossario degli Antichi Portolani Italiani*. Quaderni dell' Archivio Linguistico Veneto 4. Firenze: Leo S. Olschki.

Kahane, Henry, Renée Kahane, and Andreas Tietze. 1958. *The Lingua Franca in the Levant: Turkish Nautical Terms of Italian and Greek Origin*. Urbana: University of Illinois Press.

Kahane, Henry, Renée Kahane, and Ralph L. Ward. 1945–46. *Spoken Greek*. 2 vols. New York: Henry Holt.

*Kelly, George A. 1955. *The Psychology of Personal Constructs*. Vol. 1, *A Theory of Personality*. New York: W. W. Norton.

Kempson, Ruth M. 1977. *Semantic Theory*. Cambridge, UK: Cambridge University Press.

*Kettridge, Julius O. 1949. *French–English and English–French Dictionary of Technical Terms and Phrases*. London: Routledge & Kegan Paul.

*Khan, Qazi Rahimullah. 1938–43. *The Modern Pushtu Instructor*. 2 vols. Peshawar, Pakistan: London Book.

Kirby, Thomas A., and Henry Bosley Woolf, eds. 1949. *Philologica: The Malone Anniversary Studies*. Baltimore, MD: The Johns Hopkins Press.

*Kluge, Friedrich. 1883. *Etymologisches Wörterbuch der Deutschen Sprache*. Strasbourg: Trübner.

Knudsen, Trygve, and Alf Sommerfelt. 1958. "Principles of Unilingual Dictionary Definitions." In *Proceedings of the Eighth International Congress of Linguists*, 92–98. Oslo: Oslo University Press.

Koerner, Konrad, ed. 1991. *First Person Singular II: Autobiographies by North American Scholars in the Language Sciences*. Studies in the History of the Language Sciences 61. Amsterdam: John Benjamins.

———, ed. 1998. *First Person Singular III: Autobiographies by North American Scholars in the Language Sciences*. Studies in the History of the Language Sciences 88. Amsterdam: John Benjamins.

———. 2002. *Toward a History of American Linguistics*. Routledge Studies in the History of Linguistics 5. London: Routledge.

Kosch, Inge. 2013. "Expectation Levels in Dictionary Consultation and Compilation." *Lexikos* 23:201–8.

Kreidler, Paul, ed. 1965. *Report on the Sixteenth Annual Round Table Meeting on Linguistics and Language Studies*. Monograph Series on Languages and Linguistics 18. Washington, DC: Georgetown University.

*Kretschmer, Paul. 1918. *Wortgeographie der hochdeutschen Umgangssprache*. Göttingen, Germany: Vandenhoeck & Ruprecht.

Kretzschmar, William A., Jr. et al. 1994. *Handbook of the Linguistic Atlas of the Middle and South Atlantic States*. Chicago: University of Chicago Press.

Kurath, Hans et al. 1939. *Handbook of the Linguistic Geography of New England*. Providence, RI: Brown University.

———. 1939–43. *Linguistic Atlas of New England*. 3 vols. Providence, RI: Brown University.

Kyes, Robert L. 1995. "Herbert Penzl 1910–1995." *American Journal of Germanic Linguistics and Literatures* 7:247–49.

Labov, William. 2005. Introduction to "Words Crisscrossing the Sea," by Allen Walker Read. *American Speech*, 80:115–16.

Lan, Li. 1998. "Dictionaries and Their Users in Chinese Universities, with Special Reference to ESP Learners." In *Lexicography in Asia: Selected Papers from the Dictionaries in Asia Conference, and Other Papers*, edited by Tom McArthur and Ilan Kernerman, 61–79. Tel Aviv: Password Publishers.

Lance, Donald M. 1996. "The Century Dictionary: Pronunciation." *Dictionaries* 17:68–78.

*Landar, Herbert J. 1960. "A Note on Accepted and Rejected Arrangements of Navaho Words." *International Journal of American Linguistics* 26 (4): 351–54.

*Landar, Herbert J., Susan M. Ervin, and Arnold E. Horowitz. 1960. "Navaho Color Categories." *Language* 36:368–82.

Landau, Sidney I. 1984. *Dictionaries: The Art and Craft of Lexicography*. New York: Scribner.

———. 2001. *Dictionaries: The Art and Craft of Lexicography*. 2nd ed. New York: Cambridge University Press.

"Laurence Urdang: Lexicographer and Linguist." 2008. *Times of London* (September 6, 2008): Features 65.

*Lawrence, George H. M. 1951. *Taxonomy of Vascular Plants*. New York: Macmillan.

*Lazarsfeld, Paul F. 1961. "The Algebra of Dichotomous Systems." In *Studies in Item Analysis and Prediction*, edited by Herbert Solomon, 111–57. Stanford, CA: Stanford University Press.

Leavitt, Robert Keith. 1947. *Noah's Ark: New England Yankees and the Endless Quest*. Springfield, MA: G. & C. Merriam.

*Lees, Robert B. 1960. "The Grammar of English Nominalizations." *International Journal of American Linguistics* 26 (3) (part II). [Also, Indiana University Research Center in Anthropology, Folklore, and Linguistics 12.]

*Legrand, M. Emile. 1882. *Nouveau Dictionnaire Français-Grec Moderne*. Paris: Garnier.

Lehrer, Adrienne. 1969. "Semantic Cuisine." *Journal of Linguistics* 5:39–55.

*Lenneberg, Eric H., and John M. Roberts. 1956. "The Language of Experience, a Study in Methodology." *International Journal of American Linguistics*, Memoir No. 13.
Levitt, Jesse. 2004. "In Memoriam: Allen Walker Read (1906–2002)." *Etc.: A Review of General Semantics* 61:438–43.
Lew, Robert. 2015a. "Research into the Use of Online Dictionaries." *International Journal of Lexicography* 28:232–53.
———. 2015b. "Dictionaries and Their Users." In *International Handbook of Modern Lexis and Lexicography*, edited by Patrick Hanks and Gilles-Maurice De Schryver. Berlin: Springer. Accessed December 6, 2021. https://doi.org/10.1007/978-3-642-45369-4_11-1.
*Lewis, Alun. 1943. *The Last Inspection*. London: George Allen & Unwin.
*Lewis, C. I. 1943. "The Modes of Meaning." *Philosophy and Phenomenological Research* 4:236–49.
Lewis, Robert E., Mary Jane Williams, and Marilyn S. Miller. 2007. *Middle English Dictionary: Plan and Bibliography*. Second edition. Ann Arbor: University of Michigan Press.
*Lexicography Branch of the Pashto Academy. 1951–54. *Pashtō Qāmūs*. Kabul: Pashto Academy.
Lexis: Larousse de la Language Française. 1975. Edited by Jean Dubois et al. Paris: Larousse.
Liberman, Anatoly. 1996. "*The Century Dictionary*: Etymology." *Dictionaries* 17:29–54.
———. 2010. *A Bibliography of English Etymology*. Minneapolis: University of Minnesota Press.
Library of Congress. 1972. "Award." *Library of Congress Information Bulletin* 31, no. 40 (October 6): 438.
Littré, Émile. 1863–72. *Dictionnaire de la Langue Française*. 2 vols in 4 parts. Paris: Chez Hachette.
———. 1880. "Comment j'ai fait mon *Dictionnaire de la Langue Française*." In *Études et Glanures pour Faire Suite à l'Histoire de la Langue Française*, 390–442. Paris: Chez Didier.
López, Marina, and Mari Carmen Campoy. 2003. "User Guides in Computer-Mediated Dictionaries." In *Internet in Linguistics, Translation, and Literary Studies*, edited by Santiago Posteguillo, 439–52. Castellón de la Plana, Spain: Publicacions de la Universitat Jaume 1.
*Lorimer, J. G. 1902. *Grammar and Vocabulary of Waziri Pashto*. Calcutta: Office of the Superintendent of Government Printing.
*Lotz, John. 1949. "The Semantic Analysis of the Nominal Bases in Hungarian." *Travaux du Cercle Linguistique de Copenhague* 5:185–97.
*Lounsbury, Floyd G. 1956. "A Semantic Analysis of the Pawnee Kinship Usage." *Language* 32:158–94.
*———. 1960. "Similarity and Contiguity Relations in Language and Culture." *Georgetown University Monograph Series on Languages and Linguistics* 12:123–28.
Lowry, Heath W., and Donald Quataert, eds. 1993. *Humanist and Scholar: Essays in Honor of Andreas Tietze*. Istanbul: Isis Press.
*Lyons, John. 1960. Review of *Language Change and Linguistic Reconstruction*, by Henry M. Hoenigswald. *Bulletin of the School of Oriental and African Studies* 27:621–22.
———. 1977. *Semantics*. Cambridge, UK: Cambridge University Press.
*Lysle, Andrea de Roever, and Lora Lamia Gualtieri. 1957. *Nuovo Dizionario Moderno delle Lingue Italiana e Inglese*. Torino: F. Casanova.
*MacDonald, George R. 1946. *Spanish–English and English–Spanish Commercial Dictionary*. London: Isaac Pitman & Sons.

*MacKenzie, D. N. 1959. "A Standard Pashto." *Bulletin of the School of Oriental and African Studies* 22:231–35.

Mackridge, Peter. 2009. *Language and National Identity in Greece 1766–1976*. Oxford, UK: Oxford University Press.

*Maclay, Howard, and Mary D. Sleator. 1960. "Responses to Language: Judgments of Grammaticalness." *International Journal of American Linguistics* 26:275–82.

*Macrea, Dimitrie. 1958. *Dictionarul Limbii Romine Moderne*. Bucharest: Editura Academiei RPR.

*Malkiel, Yakov. 1957. "A Tentative Typology of Etymological Studies." *International Journal of American Linguistics* 23:1–17.

*———. 1959. "Distinctive Features in Lexicography: A Typological Approach to Dictionaries Exemplified with Spanish." *Romance Philology* 12:366–99 and 13:111–55.

———. 1960. "A Tentative Typology of Romance Historical Grammars." *Lingua* 9:321–416.

———. 1962. Review of *Style in Language*, by Thomas A. Sebeok. *International Journal of American Linguistics* 28:268–86.

*———. 1968a. *Essays on Linguistic Themes*. Oxford, UK: Blackwell.

———. 1968b. "Necrology—Uriel Weinreich, Jakob Jud's Last Student." *Romance Philology* 22:128–32.

———. 1975. Review of *Étude Linguistique et Sémiotique des Dictionnaires Français Contemporains*, by Josette Rey-Debove. *Language Sciences* 37:29–33.

———. 1976. *Etymological Dictionaries: A Tentative Typology*. Chicago: University of Chicago Press.

———. 1980a. "The Lexicographer as a Mediator between Linguistics and Society." In *Theory and Method in Lexicography: Western and Non-Western Perspectives*, edited by Ladislav Zgusta, 43–58. Columbia, SC: Hornbeam Press.

———. 1980b. "Autobiographic Sketch: Early Years in America." In *First Person Singular: Papers from the Conference on an Oral Archive for the History of American Linguistics*, edited by Boyd H. Davis and Raymond O'Cain, 79–95. Studies in the History of the Language Sciences 21. Amsterdam: John Benjamins.

———. 1988. "A Tentative Autobibliography: Yakov Malkiel." Special issue of *Romance Philology*, edited by Joseph J. Duggan and Charles B. Faulhaber, and introduced by Henry Kahane. Berkeley: University of California Press.

———. 1993. *Etymology*. Cambridge, UK: Cambridge University Press.

Malkiel, Yakov, and Barbara De Marco. 1993. "Necrology: Henry Kahane." *Romance Philology* 46:297–301.

Malkiel, Yakov, and Marvin I. Herzog. 1967. "Uriel Weinreich (1926–1967)." *Language* 43:605–10.

Malone, Kemp. 1923a. *The Literary History of Hamlet*. Heidelberg: Carl Winter.

———. 1923b. *The Phonology of Modern Icelandic*. Menasha, WI: George Banta Publishing.

———. 1940. "On Defining *mahogany*." *Language* 16:308–18.

———. 1944. "On the Etymology of *runt*." *Language* 20:87–88.

*Manich, Jumsai M. L. 1952. *English–Thai and Thai–English Dictionary*. 4th ed. London: Macmillan.

*Mansion, Jean Edmond. 1939. *Heath's Standard French and English Dictionary*. 2nd ed. Boston: D. C. Heath.

*———. 1940. *Mansion's Shorter French and English Dictionary*. Boston: D. C. Heath.

*Marchand, Hans. 1960. *Categories of Present-Day English Word-Formation*. Wiesbaden: Otto Harrassowitz.

Martin, Samuel E. 1961. D*agur Mongolian: Grammar, Texts, and Lexicon*. Indiana University Publications Uralic and Altaic Series 4. Bloomington: Indiana University.
———. 1975. *Reference Grammar of Japanese*. New Haven, CT: Yale University Press.
———. 1987. *Japanese Language through Time*. New Haven, CT: Yale University Press.
———. 1990. *Martin's Pocket Dictionary of Japanese*. Rutland, VT, and Tokyo: Charles E. Tuttle.
———. 1992. *Reference Grammar of Korean*. Rutland, VT, and Tokyo: Charles E. Tuttle.
———. 1994. *Martin's Concise Japanese Dictionary*. Rutland, VT, and Tokyo: Charles E. Tuttle.
———. 1996a. *Consonant Lenition in Korean and the Macro-Altaic Question*. Honolulu: University of Hawaii Press.
———. 1996b. "The Middle Korean Marker of Politeness -*ngi*." In *Essays in Honor of Ki-Moon Lee*, edited by Jae-Kee Shim et al., 1011–22. Seoul: Shin-gu Publishing Company.
Martin, Samuel E., and Elizabeth F. Gardner. 1952. *Honorific and Familiar Speech in Japanese*. New Haven, CT: Yale University, Institute of Far Eastern Languages.
Martin, Samuel E., Yang-Ha Lee, and Sung-Un Chung. 1968. *A Korean–English Dictionary*. New Haven, CT: Yale University Press.
*Martinet, André. 1954. "Dialect." *Romance Philology* 7:1–11.
*Martinez Amador, E. M. 1953. *Shorter Spanish–English and English–Spanish Dictionary*. Boston: D. C. Heath.
Mathews, Mitford M. 1933. *A Survey of English Dictionaries*. Oxford: Oxford University Press.
*———. 1951. *A Dictionary of Americanisms*. 2 vols. Chicago: University of Chicago Press.
———. 1956. "Of Matters Lexicographical." *American Speech* 31:122–27.
———. 1966. *Americanisms: A Dictionary of Selected Americanisms on Historical Principles*. Chicago: University of Chicago Press.
*Mathews, Robert H. 1943. *A Chinese–English Dictionary*. Rev. ed. Cambridge, MA: Harvard University Press.
Matisoff, James A. 1997. "Remembering Mary R. Haas's Work on Thai." *Anthropological Linguistics* 39:594–602.
*Mayr, Ernst, E. Gorton Linsley, and Robert L. Usinger. 1953. *Methods and Principles of Systematic Zoology*. New York: McGraw-Hill.
*McCarus, Ernest N. 1958. *Kurdish Grammar: Descriptive Analysis of the Kurdish of Sulaimaniya, Iraq*. American Council of Learned Societies Program in Oriental Languages, Series B, Aids 10. Washington, DC: American Council of Learned Societies.
McDavid, Raven I. 1973. Opening Remarks in *Lexicography in English*, edited by Raven I McDavid and Audrey R. Duckert, 5–7. Annals of the New York Academy of Sciences 211. New York: New York Academy of Sciences.
———. 1980. "Linguistics, through the Kitchen Door." In *First Person Singular: Papers from the Conference on an Oral Archive for the History of American Linguistics*, edited by Boyd H. Davis and Raymond O'Cain, 3–20. Studies in the History of the Language Sciences 21. Amsterdam: John Benjamins.
McDavid, Raven I., and Audrey R. Duckert, eds. 1973. *Lexicography in English*. Annals of the New York Academy of Sciences 211. New York: New York Academy of Sciences.
*McJimsey, C. D. 1940. *Topographic Terms in Virginia*. New York: Columbia University Press.
*McKaughan, Howard. 1959. "Semantic Components of Pronoun Systems: Maranao." *Word* 15:101–2.

McMillan, James B. 1978. "American Lexicology, 1942–1973." *American Speech* 53:141–63.
*McMullen, E. Wallace, Jr. 1953. *English Topographic Terms in Florida, 1563–1874*. Gainesville: University of Florida Press.
McMullen, Wallace. 1994. "In Memoriam: Clarence L. Barnhart, 1900–1993." *Names* 42:201–4.
"Memorial: Joseph K. Yamagiwa (1906–1968)." n.d. *Faculty History Project*. Ann Arbor, MI: University of Michigan. Accessed December 6, 2021. faculty-history.dc.umich.edu/faculty/joseph-k-yamagiwa/memorial.
Meninski, Franciszek à Mesgnien. 1680. *Thesaurus Linguarum Orientalium, Turcicae, Arabicae, Persicae*. 6 vols. Vienna: published by the author.
*Messing, Gordon M. 1960. Review of *Vocabulary of Modern Spoken Greek*, by Donald C. Swanson. *Language* 36:143–46.
———. 1961. Review of *Style in Language*, edited by Thomas A Sebeok. *Language* 37:256–66.
Metcalf, Allan. 1996. "*The Century Dictionary*: Typography." *Dictionaries* 17:17–28.
Meyer-Lübke, Wilhelm. 1930–35. *Romanisches Etymologisches Wörterbuch*. 2nd ed. 20 parts. Heidelberg: Carl Winter.
Middle English Dictionary. 1952–2001. 115 parts. Edited by Hans Kurath, Sherman M. Kuhn, Robert E. Lewis, et al. Ann Arbor: University of Michigan Press.
Missir, Émile. 1952. *Dictionnaire français-roméique*. 2 vols. Paris: C. Klincksieck.
Moore, Bruce R. 1961a. "A Statistical Morpho-Syntactic Study of Colorado (Chibcha)." Unpublished PhD diss., Indiana University.
———. 1961b. "A Statistical Morpho-Syntactic Typology Study of Colorado (Chibcha)." *International Journal of American Linguistics* 27: 298–307.
———. 1977. "Translation Theory." In *The Summer Institute of Linguistics: Its Works and Contributions*, edited by Ruth M. Brend and Kenneth L. Pike, 147–64. The Hague: Mouton.
*More, Paul Elmer. 1917. "English and Englistic." *Proceedings of the Special Meeting of the American Academy of Arts and Letters*, 3–11. New York: American Academy of Arts and Letters.
*Morgenstierne, Georg. 1927. *An Etymological Vocabulary of Pashto*. Oslo: J. Dybwad for the Norske videnskaps-akademi i Oslo.
*Morris, Charles W. 1946. *Signs, Language, and Behavior*. New York: Prentice-Hall.
Morton, Herbert C. 1994. *The Story of Webster's Third: Philip Gove's Controversial Dictionary and Its Critics*. New York: Cambridge University Press.
Moulton, William G. 1961. "Linguistics and Language Teaching in the United States 1940–1960." In *Trends in European and American Linguistics*, edited by Christine Mohrmann, Alf Sommerfelt, and Joshua Watmough, 82–109. Utrecht: Spectrum.
———. 1980. "On Becoming and Being a Linguist." In *First Person Singular: Papers from the Conference on an Oral Archive for the History of American Linguistics*, edited by Boyd H. Davis and Raymond O'Cain, 55–65. Studies in the History of the Language Sciences 21. Amsterdam: John Benjamins.
*Murdoch, George. 1945. *Outline of Cultural Materials*. 2nd ed. New Haven, CT: Yale University Press.
Muret-Sanders Encyclopaedic English–German and German–English Dictionary. 1901. 5th ed. Berlin: Langenscheidtsche Verlagsbuchhandlung.
Murray, James. A. H. 1993. "The Evolution of English Lexicography." Edited by R. W. Burchfield. *International Journal of Lexicography* 6 (2): 89–122.
Myers-Scotten, Carol. 1995. "Obituary: Einar Haugen." *Language in Society* 24:407–8.

*Nagel, Ernest. 1961. *The Structure of Science: Problems in the Logic of Scientific Explanation*. New York: Harcourt, Brace & World.
*Navarro, Tomás. 1948. *El Español en Puerto Rico: Contribucióna la Geografía Lingüística Hispano-Americana*. Río Piedras: Editorial de la Universidad de Puerto Rico.
Navigation Dictionary. 1956. United States Naval Oceanographic Office Publication No. 220. Washington, DC: USGPO.
*Nawīs, Abdullah Afghānī. 1957. *Fārsī pə Pashtō*. 3 vols. Kabul: Pashto Academy.
*Nawri, Muhammad Gul. 1941. *Də paštō istilāhāt aw muhāwərē*. Kabul: Pashto Academy.
*Neuman, Henry, and Giuseppi M. A. Baretti. 1862. *A Dictionary of the Spanish and English Languages*. 10th ed. Revised by Mateo Seoane. 2 vols. London: Longman & Co., Simpkin, Marshall, & Co., and others.
New Comprehensive "Standard" Dictionary of the English Language. 1944. Edited by Frank H. Vizetelly and Charles Earle Funk. New York: Funk & Wagnalls.
*Newman, Stanley. 1954. "Semantic Problems in Grammatical Systems and Lexemes: A Search for Method." In *Language in Culture*, edited by Harry Hoijer. 82–91. Chicago: University of Chicago Press.
———. 1991. "How I Discovered Linguistics." In *First Person Singular II: Autobiographies by North American Scholars in the Language Sciences*, edited by Konrad Koerner, 205–26. Studies in the History of the Language Sciences 61. Amsterdam: John Benjamins.
New Standard Dictionary of the English Language. 1913. Edited by Isaac K. Funk et al. New York: Funk & Wagnalls.
Nguyen, Dinh-Hoa. 1980. "Bicultural Information in a Bilingual Dictionary." In *Theory and Method in Lexicography: Western and Non-Western Perspectives*, edited by Ladislav Zgusta, 163–75. Columbia, SC: Hornbeam Press.
———. 1980–81. "Teaching Culture through Bilingual Dictionaries." *Dictionaries* 3:57–68.
———. 1986. "How to Present Grammatical Information in a Learner's Dictionary of English." *Lexicographica* 2:61–77.
Nicot, Jean. 1606. *Thresor de la Langue Francoyse, tant Ancienne que Moderne*. Paris: David Douceur.
*Nida, Eugene A. 1951. "A System for the Description of Semantic Elements." *Word* 7:1–14.
*———. 1958. "Analysis of Meaning and Dictionary Making." *International Journal of American Linguistics* 24 (4): 279–292.
*———. 1960. *Synopsis of English Syntax*. Edited by Benjamin Elson. Norman, OK: University of Oklahoma for the Summer Institute of Linguistics.
———. 1975. *Exploring Semantic Structures*. Internationale Bibliothek für Allgemeine Linguistik 11. Munich: Fink.
———. 2001. *Contexts in Translating*. Amsterdam: John Benjamins.
Nielsen, Sandro. 1994. *The Bilingual LSP Dictionary: Principles and Practices for Legal Language*. Tübingen: Gunter Narr Verlag.
Öhman, Suzanne. 1953. "Theories of the 'Linguistic Field.'" *Word* 9 (2): 123–34.
*Országh, L. 1953. *Magyar-Angol Szótár*. Budapest: Akadémiai Kiadó.
———. 1963. Review of *Problems in Lexicography*, by Fred W. Householder and Sol Saporta. *Acta Linguistica Academiae Scientierum Hungaricae* 13:399–401.
*Oudin, César. 1639–40. *Le Grand Dictionaire et Tresor de Trois Langues François, Flameng, & Espagnol*. Antwerp: Trognesius.
Oxford English Dictionary. 1933. 13 vols. Edited by J. A. H. Murray, H. Bradley, W. A. Craigie, C. T. Onions, et al. Oxford: Clarendon Press.

*Papadopoulos, Anthimos A. et al. 1933–46. *Historikon Lexicon tēs Neas Hellēnikēs tēs te Koinōs Homiloumenēs kai tōn Idiōmatōn*. 4 vols. Athens: Maïsner & Kargadourē.

Parks, Douglas R., ed. 1997. "Mary R. Haas: A Memorial Issue." Special issue of *Anthropological Linguistics* 39.

*Pazhwak, Abdul Rahman. 1952. *Afghanistan: Ancient Aryana*. London: Key Press.

*Pendennis. 1954. "Table Talk." *The Observer* (London), September 19, 1954, 9/g.

Penzl, Herbert. 1934. "New England Terms for *poached eggs*." *American Speech* 9:90–95.

———. 1937. "Der [r]-einschub nach ME *ă* in Neu-England." *Anglia* 61:81–92.

———. 1938. "Lehnwörter mit Mittelenglisch *ă* for *r* im Pennsylvanisch-Deutschen dialekt." *Journal of English and Germanic Philology* 37:396–402.

———. 1940. "The Vowel Phonemes in *father, man, dance* in Dictionaries, and in New England Speech." *Journal of English and Germanic Philology* 39:13–32.

———. 1944. "A Phonemic Change in Early Old English." *Language* 20:84–87.

———. 1947. "The Phonemic Split of Germanic *k* in Old English." *Language* 23:34–42.

———. 1949. "Umlaut and Secondary Umlaut in Old High German." *Language* 25:223–40.

———. 1950. "Orthography and Phonemes in Wulfila's Gothic." *Journal of English and Germanic Philology* 49:217–30.

*———. 1951. "Afghan Descriptions of the Afghan (Pashto) Verb." *Journal of the American Oriental Society* 71:97–111.

*———. 1952. "Die Substantive des Paschto nach afghanischen Grammatiken." *Zeitschriften der Deutschen Morgenländischen Gesellschaft* 102:52–61.

———. 1954. "Orthography and Phonemes in Pashto (Afghan)." *Journal of African and Oriental Studies* 74:74–81.

*———. 1955. *A Grammar of Pashto: A Descriptive Study of the Dialect of Kandahar, Afghanistan*. Washington, DC: American Council of Learned Societies.

———. 1961a. "Old High German [l] and Its Phonetic Identification." *Language* 37:488–96.

———. 1961b. "Western Loanwords in Modern Pashto." *Journal of African and Oriental Studies* 81:43–52.

———. 1962. *A Reader in Pashto*. Ann Arbor: University of Michigan Press.

———. 1974. *Methoden der Germanischen Linguistik*. Historische Sprachstrukturen 1. Tübingen: Niemeyer.

———. 1975. *Vom Urgermonischen zum Neuhochdeutschen: Eine Historische Phonologie*. Berlin: Erich Schmidt.

———. 1989a. *Mittelhochdeutsch*. Bern and Frankfurt am Main: Peter Lang.

———. 1989b. "Positivism and 'Hocus-Pocus' in Germanic and English Linguistics." *Journal of Germanic Linguistics* 1:1–16.

——— 1990. "18th Century American English According to Noah Webster." *Dictionaries* 12:15–24.

———. 1991. "Must Linguists also Be Philologists?" In *First Person Singular II: Autobiographies by North American Scholars in the Language Sciences*, edited by Konrad Koerner, 239–54. Studies in the History of the Language Sciences 61. Amsterdam: John Benjamins.

———. 1993. "Paul Laurence Dunbar's Literary Dialects." *PMLA* 108:155–56.

———. 1994. "Periodization in Language History: Early Modern English and the Other Periods." In *Studies in Early Modern English*, edited by Dieter Kastovsky, 261–68. Topics in English Linguistics 13. Berlin: De Gruyter.

*Pernot, Hubert Octave. 1907–46. *Études de Linguistique Néo-Hellénique*. 3 vols. Fontenay sous Bois: Chez l'Auteur.

*Pfeffer, J. Alan. 1951. *German-English, English-German Dictionary of Everyday Usage*. New York: Henry Holt.
Pidal, Ramon Menendez. 1953. *Vox Diccionario General Illustrado de la Lengua Española*. Barcelona: Publicaciones y Ediciones Spes, S. A.
Pietrangeli, Angelina R. 1962. "An Analytical Bibliography of the Writings of Henry and Renée Kahane." *Romance Philology* 15:207–20.
Pijnenburg, W., and F. de Tollenaere, eds. 1980. *Proceedings of the Second International Round Table Conference on Historical Lexicography*. Dordrecht: Foris.
Pike, Eunice V. 1977. "Historical Sketch." In *The Summer Institute of Linguistics: Its Works and Contributions*, edited by Ruth M. Brend and Kenneth L. Pike, 1–14. The Hague: Mouton.
Pike, Kenneth L. 1981. *Tagmemics, Discourse, and Verbal Art*. Edited by Richard W. Bailey. Michigan Studies in the Humanities 3. Ann Arbor: University of Michigan.
———. 1999. *Mary H. Haas 1910–1996*. Washington, DC: National Academies Press.
*Pokorny, Julius. 1957–69. *Indogermanisches Etymologisches Wörterbuch*. 2 vols. Tübingen: A. Francke.
Prinsloo, D. J. 2016. "A Critical Analysis of Multilingual Dictionaries." *Lexikos* 26:220–40.
———. 2020. "Detection and Lexicographic Treatment of Salient Features of E-dictionaries for African languages." *International Journal of Lexicography* 33:269–87.
Proceedings of the Board of Regents of the University of Michigan. 1960. Ann Arbor: University of Michigan.
Proceedings of the Eighth International Congress of Linguists. 1958. Edited by Eva Sivertsen. Oslo: Oslo University Press.
Pulgram, Ernst. 1998. "... quem legis vt noris." In *First Person Singular III: Autobiographies by North American Scholars in the Language Sciences*, edited by E. F. K. Koerner, 159–85. Studies in the History of the Language Sciences 88. Amsterdam: John Benjamins.
Pyles, Thomas. 1972. "Kemp Malone." *Language* 48:499–505.
*Quine, Willard Van Orman. 1960. *Word and Object*. Cambridge MA: MIT Press.
Quirk, Randolph. 1973. "The Social Impact of Dictionaries in the UK." In *Lexicography in English*, edited by Raven I. McDavid and Audrey R. Duckert, 76–88. Annals of the New York Academy of Sciences 211. New York: New York Academy of Sciences.
Ramsey, S. Robert. 2004a. Introductory remarks to *Japanese Language and Literature* 38:259–66.
———, ed. 2004b. "In Honor of Samuel Martin." Special issue of *Japanese Language and Literature* 38.
*Randolph, Vance. 1927. "More Words from the Ozarks." *Dialect Notes* 5:472–79.
*———. 1953. *Down in the Holler: A Gallery of Ozark Folk Speech*. Norman: University of Oklahoma Press.
Random House Dictionary of the English Language: The Unabridged Edition. 1966. Edited by Jess Stein, Laurence Urdang et al. New York: Random House.
Rasico, Philip D. 2000. "Josep Roca-Pons (1914–2000): A Remembrance." *Catalan Review* 14:9–16.
Rauch, Irmengard, and Gerald F. Carr, eds. 1979. *Linguistic Method: Essays in Honor of Herbert Penzl*. Janua Linguarum Series Maior 79. The Hague: Mouton.
*Raven-Hart, Rowland. 1938. *Down the Mississippi*. Boston: Houghton Mifflin.
*Raventós, Margaret H. 1953. *McKay's Modern Spanish-English and English-Spanish Dictionary*. New York: David McKay.
*Raverty, H. G. 1867. *Dictionary of the Puk'hto or Pus'hto, or Language of the Afghāns*. 2nd ed. London: Williams & Norgate.

Read, Allen Walker. 1938a. "The Policies of the *Dictionary of American English*." *Dialect Notes* 6:635–42.
———. 1938b. "Plans for 'A Historical Dictionary of Briticisms.'" *American Oxonian* 25:186–90; reprinted in *Quarterly Journal of Speech* 24 (1938): 499–502.
———. 1947. "British and American English." In *American College Dictionary*, edited by Clarence L. Barnhart et al., xxvi. New York: Random House.
———. 1949. "English Words with Constituent Elements Having Independent Semantic Value." In *Philologica: The Malone Anniversary Studies*, edited by Thomas A Kirby and Henry Bosley Woolf, 306–12. Baltimore, MD: The Johns Hopkins Press.
———. 1963a. "That Dictionary or the Dictionary: An Expert Looks at the Book, Its Origins, and the Roots of the Controversy about It." *Consumer Reports* 28:488–92.
———. 1963b. "Desk Dictionaries." *Consumer Reports* 28:547–50.
———. 1964. "The Smaller Dictionaries." *Consumer Reports* 29:97, 145–47.
———. 1974. "Dictionary." *The New Encyclopedia Britannica, Micropedia* 5:713–22.
———. 1987. "A Dictionary of the English of England: Problems and Findings." *Dictionaries* 9:149–63.
———. 1991. "A Personal Journey through Linguistics." In *First Person Singular II: Autobiographies by North American Scholars in the Language Sciences*, edited by Konrad Koerner, 273–88. Studies in the History of the Language Sciences 61. Amsterdam: John Benjamins.
———. 1994. "Clarence Lewis Barnhart, 1900–1993." *Dictionaries* 15:216–19.
———. 2001. *America: Naming the Country and Its People*. Edited by Leonard R. N. Ashley. Lewiston, NY: Edwin Mellen Press.
———. 2002. *Milestones of the History of English in America*. Edited by Richard W. Bailey. Publication of the American Dialect Society 86. Durham, NC: Duke University Press.
———. 2003. "The Beginnings of English Lexicography." Edited by Michael Adams. *Dictionaries* 24:vii–x, 187–226.
Redhouse, James. 1890. *A Turkish–English Lexicon*. 2 vols. Constantinople: A. H. Boyajian.
Reichmann, Oskar. 1976. *Germanistische Lexikologie*. Stuttgart: J. B Metzler.
———. 2012. *Historische Lexikographie*. Studia Linguistica Germanica 111. Berlin: De Gruyter.
Reidy, John. 1984. "Sherman McAllister Kuhn." In *Studies in the Language and Poetics of Anglo-Saxon England*, by Sherman M. Kuhn, ix–xi. Ann Arbor: Karoma Publishers.
Reiner, Erica. 2002. *An Adventure of Great Dimension: The Launching of the Chicago Assyrian Dictionary*. Transactions of the American Philosophical Society 92/3. Philadelphia: American Philosophical Society.
Rensch, Calvin R. 1977. "The Contributions of SIL in Linguistics." In *The Summer Institute of Linguistics: Its Works and Contributions*, edited by Ruth M. Brend and Kenneth L. Pike, 85–128. The Hague: Mouton.
Rey-Debove, Josette, ed. 1970. *La Lexicographie*. Langages 19. Paris: Didier.
———. 1971. *Étude Linguistique et Sémiotique des Dictionnaires Français Contemporains*. The Hague: Mouton.
Richardson, Elbert L., Maria de Lourdes Sá Pereira, and Milton Sá Pereira. 1944. *Modern Portuguese–English and English–Portuguese Dictionary*. London: G. G. Harrap.
Roberts, Craige, Sarah Yoder, and Albert Valdman. 1980–81. "The Indiana University Haitian Creole Dictionary: Problems in Bilingual Lexicography." *Dictionaries* 3:129–45.
Robinson, Jay L., and Richard W. Bailey. 1973. "Computer-Produced Microfilm in Lexicography: Toward a Dictionary of Early Modern English." In *The Computer and*

Literary Studies, edited by A. J. Aitken, R. W. Bailey, and N. Hamilton-Smith, 3–14. Edinburgh: Edinburgh University Press.
Robinson, Jennifer. 1983. "A Glossary of Contemporary English Lexicographical Terminology." *Dictionaries* 5:76–114.
*Robinson, Richard. 1954. *Definition*. Oxford: Clarendon Press.
Roediger, David. 1995. "Guineas, Wiggers, and the Dramas of Racialized Culture." *American Literary History* 7:654–68.
*Roget, Mark Peter. 1852. *Thesaurus of English Words and Phrases*. London: Longman, Brown, Green, and Longmans.
Rosenberg, Alexander. 1957. *Russian Abbreviations: A Selective List*. 2nd ed. Washington, DC: Reference Department, Library of Congress.
———. 1958. *Russian-English Glossary of Guided Missile, Rocket, and Satellite Terms*. Washington, DC: Reference Department, Library of Congress.
*Russell, William H. 1865. *Canada: Its Defences, Condition, and Resources*. London: Bradbury & Evans.
Sapir, Edward, and Morris Swadesh. 1960. *Yana Dictionary*. Edited by Mary R. Haas. University of California Publications in Linguistics 22. Berkeley: University of California Press.
Saporta, Sol, ed. 1961. *Psycholinguistics: A Book of Readings*. New York: Holt, Rinehart & Winston.
———. 1994. *Society, Language, and the University*. New York: Vantage.
———. 2006. *A Life in Letters: The Personal, Professional, and Political*. New York: iUniverse.
Saporta, Sol, and Helas Contreras. 1962. *A Phonological Grammar of Spanish*. Seattle: University of Washington Press.
Saunders, Gladys E. 1978. "Experimental Lexicography in France: Theoretical and Practical Considerations." In *Studies in Lexicography as a Science and as an Art*, edited by Walter D. Glanze, 1–17. New York: Bantam Books.
Scargill, M. H. 1967. Preface to *A Dictionary of Canadianisms*, edited by Walter S. Avis et al., vi–vii. Toronto: W. J. Gage.
Schenker, Alexander M. 1971. "William Stewart Cornyn, 1906–1971." *Slavic Review* 30:718–19.
*Sebeok, Thomas A. 1946. *Finnish and Hungarian Case Systems: Their Form and Function*. Acta Instituti Hungarici Universitatis Holmiensis Series B, Linguistica 3. Stockholm: Ungerska Institutet.
———, ed. 1960. *Style in Language*. Cambridge, MA: MIT Press.
———. 1962. "Materials for a Typology of Dictionaries." *Lingua* 11:363–74.
Seits, Laurence E., ed. 1988. *Festschrift in Honor of Allen Walker Read*. Publications of the North Central Name Society 2. DeKalb, IL: North Central Name Society.
Shcherba, Lev. 1940. "Opyt obshchei teorii leksikographii." *Isvestija Akademii Nauk SSSR* 3:89–117.
**Siamese-English Dictionary*. 1948. Bangkok: Prachachang.
Siegel, Muffy E. A. 2007. "What Do You Do with a Dictionary? A Study of Undergraduate Dictionary Use." *Dictionaries* 28:23–48.
*Simpson, George Gaylord. 1961. *Principles of Animal Taxonomy*. New York: Columbia University Press.
*Skeat, W. W. 1910. *An Etymological Dictionary of the English Language*. 4th ed. Oxford: Clarendon Press.
Skinner, B. F. 1957. *Verbal Behavior*. New York: Appleton-Century-Crofts.
Skinner, David. 2012. *The Story of Ain't: America, Its Language, and the Most Controversial Dictionary Ever Published*. New York: HarperCollins.

*Slabý, Rudolf J., and Grossman, Rudolf. 1932. *Diccionario de las Lenguas Española y Alemana*. Leipzig: Bernhard Tauchnitz.

Sledd, James. 1947a. "Dorigen's Complaint." *Modern Philology* 45:36–45.

———. 1947b. "John Baret's *Alvearie*." Unpublished PhD diss., University of Texas.

———. 1953. "The 'Clerk's Tale': The Monsters and the Critics." *Modern Philology* 51:73–82.

———. 1954. "Nowell's *Vocabularium Saxonicum* and the Elyot-Cooper Tradition." *Studies in Philology* 51:142–48.

———. 1956. "Superfixes and Intonation Patterns." *Litera* 3:35–41.

———. 1959. *A Short Introduction to English Grammar*. Chicago: Scott Foresman.

———. 1965. "On Not Teaching English Usage." *The English Journal* 54:698–703.

———. 1966. Review of *Linguistics and English Grammar*, by H. A. Gleason. *Language* 42:797–809.

———. 1969. "Bi-dialectalism: The Linguistics of White Supremacy." *The English Journal* 58:1307–15, 1329.

———. 1972a. "Dollars and Dictionaries: The Limits of Commercial Lexicography." In *New Aspects of Lexicography: Literary Criticism, Intellectual History, and Social Change*, edited by Howard D. Weinbrot, 119–51. Carbondale: Southern Illinois University Press.

———. 1972b. "Doublespeak: Dialectology in the Service of Big Brother." *College English* 53:439–56.

———. 1973. "Dictionary Treatment of Pronunciation: Regional." In *Lexicography in English*, edited by Raven I. McDavid and Audrey R. Duckert, 134–38. Annals of the New York Academy of Sciences 211. New York: New York Academy of Sciences.

———. 1977. "Or Get Off the Pot: Notes toward the Restoration of Moderate Honesty Even in English Departments." *ADE Bulletin* 52:1–7.

———. 1981. "Linguistics, Obeah, Acupuncture, and the Teaching of Composition by That Bastard Sledd." *Journal of Advanced Composition* 11:147–52.

———. 1996a. *Eloquent Dissent: The Writings of James Sledd*. Edited by Richard D. Freed. Portsmouth, NH: Boynton/Cook.

———. 1996b. "Grammar for Social Awareness in Time of Class Warfare." *The English Journal* 85:59–63.

Sledd, James, and Wilma R. Ebbitt. 1962. *Dictionaries and That Dictionary: A Casebook on the Aims of Lexicographers and the Targets of Reviewers*. Chicago: Scott Foresman.

Sledd, James H., and Gwin J. Kolb. 1955. *Dr. Johnson's Dictionary: Essays in the Biography of a Book*. Chicago: University of Chicago Press.

*Snell, Bruno, Hans Joachim Mette et al. 1955. *Lexikon de Frügriechischen Epos*. 25 vols. to date. Göttingen: Vandenhoek & Ruprecht.

Snell-Hornby, Mary. 1984. "The Bilingual Dictionary—Help or Hindrance?" In *LEXeter '83 Proceedings: Papers from the International Conference on Lexicography at Exeter, 9–12 September 1983*, edited by R. R. K. Hartmann, 274–81. Lexicographica Series Maior 1. Tübingen: Niemeyer.

Sobelman, Harry, and Richard S. Harrell. 1963. *A Dictionary of Moroccan Arabic: English-Moroccan*. Arabic Series 3. Washington, DC: Georgetown University Press.

Socha, Joanna, and Franciszek Lyra. 2019. "Franciszek Lyra—First Polish Fulbright Grantee." *Fulbright Poland*, March 25, 2019. https://en.fulbright.edu.pl/franciszek-lyra/.

*Societad Retorumantscha. 1938–2000. *Dicziunari Rumantsch Grischun*. 14 vols. Cuoira, Switzerland: Bischofberger.

*Soule, Richard. 1871. *A Dictionary of English Synonyms*. Boston: Little, Brown.

*Spiers, Alexander, and George P. Quackenbos. 1889. *Spiers and Surenne's French and English Pronouncing Dictionary*. New York: D. Appleton.
*Spinelli, Nicola. 1937. *Dizionario Scolastico Italiano–Inglese: Inglese–Italiano*. Torino: Società Edetrice Internazionale.
Stacey, Michelle. 1989. "At Play in the Language." *New Yorker*, September 4, 1989, 51–74.
Staley, Stacey. 2013. "Bruce R. Moore." *InkFreeNews*, June 3, 2013. http://www.inkfreenews.com/2013/06/03/bruce-r-moore/.
Standard Dictionary of the English Language. 1893–95. 2 vols. Edited by Isaac K. Funk et al. New York: Funk & Wagnalls.
Stankiewicz, Edward. 1969. Review of *Modern English–Yiddish, Yiddish–English Dictionary*, by Uriel Weinreich. *Judaism* 18:368–71.
Stark, Martin. 1999. *Encyclopedic Learners' Dictionaries: A Study of Their Design Features from the User Perspective*. Lexicographica Series Maior 92. Tübingen: Niemeyer.
*Starnes, De Witt, and Gertrude E. Noyes. 1946. *The English Dictionary from Cawdrey to Johnson 1604–1755*. Chapel Hill: University of North Carolina Press.
Stein, Gabriele. 2002. *Better Words: Evaluating EFL Dictionaries*. Exeter, UK: University of Exeter Press.
*Stewart, George R. 1954. *American Ways of Life*. Garden City, NY: Doubleday.
Stock, Penelope. 1988. "The Structure and Function of Definitions." In *ZüriLEX '86 Proceedings: Papers Read at the EURALEX International Congress, University of Zürich, 9–14 September 1986*, edited by Mary Snell-Hornby, 81–89. Tübingen: A. Francke Verlag.
Stockwell, Robert P. 1998. "From English Philology to Linguistics and Back Again." In *First Person Singular III: Autobiographies by North American Scholars in the Language Sciences*, edited by E. F. K. Koerner, 227–45. Studies in the History of the Language Sciences 88. Amsterdam: John Benjamins.
Stowasser, Karl, and Moukhtar Ani. 1964. *A Dictionary of Syrian Arabic (Dialect of Damascus): English–Arabic*. Washington, DC: Georgetown University Press.
Stuart, Don Graham, ed. 1967a. *Linguistic Studies in Memory of Richard Slade Harrell*. Washington, DC: Georgetown University Press.
———. 1967b. "Richard Slade Harrell/Published Works of Richard Slade Harrell." In *Linguistic Studies in Memory of Richard Slade Harrell*, edited by Don Graham Stuart, ix–xv. Washington, DC: Georgetown University Press.
Supplement to the Oxford English Dictionary. 1972–86. 4 vols. Edited by Robert W. Burchfield et al. Oxford: Oxford University Press.
Svensén, Bo. 1993. *Practical Lexicography: Principles and Methods of Dictionary-Making*. Oxford: Oxford University Press.
———. 2009. *A Handbook of Lexicography: The Theory and Practice of Dictionary-Making*. Cambridge: Cambridge University Press.
*Swadesh, Morris. 1946. "Chitimacha." In *Linguistic Structures of Native North America*, by Harry Hoijer et al., 312–36. New York: Viking Fund.
Swanepoel, Piet. 2003. "Dictionary Typologies: A Pragmatic Approach." In *A Practical Guide to Lexicography*, edited by P. G. J. van Sterkenberg, 44–69. Amsterdam: John Benjamins.
*Swanson, Donald C. 1959. *Vocabulary of Modern Spoken Greek: English–Greek and Greek–English*. Minneapolis; University of Minnesota Press.

———. 1967. *The Names in Roman Verse: A Lexicon and Reverse Index of All Proper Names of History, Mythology, and Geography Found in the Classical Roman Poets*. Madison: University of Wisconsin Press.

———. 1970. *A Characterization of the Roman Poetic Onomasticon*. University Park: Pennsylvania State University Press.

Święcicka, Elżbieta, ed. 2020. *Dictionary of Italian–Turkish Language (1641) by Giovanni Molino*. Studien zur Sprache Geschichte und Kultur der Turkvölker 23. Berlin: Walter De Gruyter.

Tarp, Sven. 2008a. "Kan brugerundersøgelser overhovedet afdække brugernes lexicografiske behov?" *LexicoNordica* 15:5–32.

———. 2008b. *Lexicography in the Borderland between Knowledge and Non-Knowledge: General Lexicographical Theory with Particular Focus on Learner's Lexicography*. Lexicographica Series Maior 134. Tübingen: Niemeyer.

*Terreros y Panda, Esteban. 1786–93. *Diccionario Castellano con las Voces de Ciencias y Artes y Sens Correspondientes en las Tres Lenguas Francesca, Latina, e Italiana*. 4 vols. Madrid: Ibarra & Hijos.

Theall, D. F. 1960. Review of *A Short Introduction to English Grammar*, by James Sledd. *Canadian Journal of Linguistics/Revue Canadienne de Linguistique* 6:60–67.

*Thomas, David. 1955. "Three Analyses of the Ilocano Pronoun System." *Word* 11:204–8.

*———. 1957. *An Introduction to Mansaka Lexicography*. Nasuli, Philippines: SIL. Typescript.

Thomas, Robert McG., Jr. 1997. "Meredith F. Burrill, 94, Expert on World Geographic Names." *New York Times*, October 10, 1997, D19.

Thorndike, Edward L., and Clarence L. Barnhart. 1935. *Thorndike-Century Junior Dictionary*. Chicago: Scott Foresman.

———. 1941. *Thorndike-Century Senior Dictionary*. Chicago: Scott Foresman.

*Thorndike, Edward, and Irving Lorge. 1944. *The Teacher's Word Book of Thirty Thousand Words*. New York: Teachers College Press.

Thornton, Richard. 1912. *An American Glossary*. 2 vols. Philadelphia: Lippincott.

Tietze, Andreas. 1955. "Griechische Lehnwörter im Anatolischen Türkische." *Oriens* 8:204–57.

———. 1966. *The Koman Riddles and Turkic Folklore*. Berkeley: University of California Press.

———. 1991. "Die lexikographie der Turksprachen I: Osmanisch–Türkisch." In *Wörterbücher/Dictionaries/Dictionnaires*, 3 vols., edited by Franz Josef Hausmann, Oskar Reichman, Herbert Ernst Wiegand, and Ladislav Zgusta, 3:2399–2407. Handbooks of Linguistics and Communication Science 5. 3 vols. Berlin: De Gruyter.

Tietze, Andreas, et al. 1968. *The New Redhouse Turkish–English Dictionary*. Istanbul: Redhouse Press.

———. 2002–2016. *Tarihi ve Etimolojik Türkiye Türkcesi Lugati*. 4 vols. Edited by S. Tezcan. Ankara: Türkiye Bilimleri Akademisi.

Tietze, Andreas, and Gilbert Lazard. 1967. "Persian Loanwords in Anatolian Turkish." *Oriens* 20:125–68.

Tollenaere, F. de. 1962. "La documentation lexicographique et ses propres besoins." *Cahiers de Lexicologie* 3:101–15.

———. 1963. *Nieuwe Wegen in de Lexicologie*. Amsterdam: North-Holland Publishing.

———. 1965. "Lexikographie mit hilfe des elektronischen informationswandlers." *Zeitschrift für Deutsche Sprache* 21:1–19.

———. 1969. Review of *Problems in Lexicography*, by Fred W. Householder and Sol Saporta. *Lingua* 22:253–57.

———. 1973a. "Lexicographie et linguistique: Le signification du mot." *Meta: Journal des Traducteurs* 18:139–44.
———. 1973b. "The Problem of the Context in Computer-Aided Lexicography." In *The Computer and Literary Studies*, edited by A. J. Aitken, R. W. Bailey, and N. Hamilton-Smith, 25–34. Edinburgh: Edinburgh University Press.
Tono, Yukio. 1998. "Interacting with the Users: Research Findings in EFL Dictionary User Studies." In *Lexicography in Asia: Selected Papers from the Dictionaries in Asia Conference, and Other Papers*, edited by Tom McArthur and Ilan Kernerman, 97–118. Tel Aviv: Password Publishers.
Toury, Gideon. 1989. "The Meaning of Translation-Specific Lexical Items and Its Representation in the Dictionary." In *Translation and Lexicography: Papers Read at the EURALEX Colloquium Held at Innsbruck 25 July 1987*, edited by Mary Snell-Hornby and Esther Pöhl, 45–53. Amsterdam: John Benjamins.
*Townshend, Malcolm. 1890. *Index to the U.S.A.* Boston: D. Lothrop.
*Trager, Edith Crowell. 1956. "Superfix and Sememe: English Verbal Compounds." *General Linguistics* 2:1–14.
*Trager, George L., and Henry Lee Smith. 1951. *An Outline of English Structure*. Norman, OK: Battenberg Press.
*Traister, Aaron. 1949. Review of *Webster's New Collegiate Dictionary*. *New York Times Book Review*, May 15, 1949, 19/c.
Trench, Richard Chenevix. 1860. *Some Deficiencies in Our English Dictionaries*. London: John W. Parker & Son.
Turner, Katherine. 1997. "Bibliography of Mary R. Haas." *Anthropological Linguistics* 39:508–21.
*Tynan, Kenneth. 1956. "Young Lions' Den." *Observer* (London), March 18, 1956, 15/b–c.
Uitti, Karl D. 1962. Review of *Style in Language*, by Thomas A. Sebeok. *Romance Philology* 15:424–38.
———. 1963. Review of *Problems in Lexicography*, by Fred W. Householder and Sol Saporta. *Romance Philology* 16:416–28.
*United States Geological Survey. 1938. De Funiak Springs, Florida, quadrangle map. Washington, DC: USGS.
*———. 1946. Wilma, Florida, quadrangle map. Washington, DC: USGS.
*———. 1952. Mt. Hillers, Utah, quadrangle map. Washington, DC: USGS.
*———. 1954. Fairmount, Delaware, quadrangle map. Washington, DC: USGS.
United States Office of Education. 1960. *National Defense Language Development Research and Studies*. Washington, DC: United States Government Printing Office.
Urdang, Laurence. 1963. Review of *Problems in Lexicography*, by Fred W. Householder and Sol Saporta. *Language* 39:586–94.
———. 1975. Review of *Manual of Lexicography*, by Ladislav Zgusta. *Language* 51:220–30.
———. 1984. "A Lexicographer's Adventures in Computing." *Dictionaries* 6:150–65.
Valdman, Albert. 2019. Personal communication with the author, February 7, 2019.
Valdman, Albert, et al. 1981. *Haitian Creole–English–French Dictionary*. 2 vols. Bloomington, IN: Creole Institute, Indiana University.
———. 1998. *Dictionary of Louisiana Creole*. Bloomington, IN: Indiana University Press.
———. In progress. "The Differential, Historical, and Etymological Dictionary of Louisiana French."
Valdman, Albert, Marvin D. Moody, and Thomas E. Davies. 2017. *English–Haitian Creole Bilingual Dictionary*. Bloomington, IN: iUniverse.

Valdman, Albert, Charles Pooser, and Rozevel Jean-Baptiste. 1996. *A Learner's Dictionary of Haitian Creole*. Bloomington: Creole Institute, Indiana University.

Valdman, Albert, Kevin J. Rottet, et al. 2009. *Dictionary of Louisiana French*. Jackson: University of Mississippi Press.

Vancil, David. 2010. "A Researcher's Guide to the Warren N. and Suzanne B. Cordell Collection of Dictionaries." In *Insights into English and Germanic Lexicology and Lexicography: Past and Present Perspectives*, edited by Laura Pinnavaia and Nicholas Brownlees, 231–49. Monza: Polimetrica.

*Velázquez de la Cadena, Mariano A. 1953. *New Pronouncing Dictionary of the Spanish and English Languages*. Chicago: Wilcox & Follett.

Verlinde, Sege. 2011. "Modelling Interactive Reading, Translation and Writing Assistants." In *e-Lexicography: The Internet, Digital Initiatives and Lexicography*, edited by Pedro A. Fuertes-Olivera and Henning Bergenholtz, 275–86. London: Continuum.

*Voegelin, C. F. 1961. Review of *Vocabulario Tarahumara*, by K. Simon Hilton et al.; *Vocabulario Cora*, by Ambrosio McMahon and Maria Aiton de McMahon; *Vocabulario Zapateco del Istmo*, by Velma Pickett et al.; and *Vocabulario Popoluca de Sayula*, by Lorenzo Clark and Nancy Davis de Clark. *American Anthropologist* 63:876–78.

*Voegelin, C. F., and F. M. Voegelin. 1957. "Hopi Domains, a Lexical Approach to the Problem of Selection." *International Journal of American Linguistics* Memoir No. 14.

*Von Gabain, Annemarie. 1950. *Alttürkische Grammatik*. 2nd ed. Wiesbaden: Harrassowitz.

*Von Günzburg, David, and Isaak D. Markon, eds. 1908. *Festschrift zu ehren des Dr. A. Harkavy*. Berlin: H. Itzkowski.

*Von Wartburg, Walther et al. 1922–2002. *Französisches Etymologisches Wörterbuch*. 25 vols. Bonn: F. Klopp.

*Wallace, Anthony F. C., and John Atkins. 1960. "The Meaning of Kinship Terms." *American Anthropologist* 62:58–80.

Waterhouse, Viola Grace. 1962. *The Grammatical Structure of Oaxaca Chontal*. Indiana University Research Center in Anthropology, Folklore and Linguistics 19. Bloomington: Indiana University; and *International Journal of American Linguistics* 28 (Part II).

———. 1974. *The History and Development of Tagmemics*. Janua Linguarum Series Critica 16. The Hague: Mouton

*Webel, A. 1952. *A German–English Dictionary of Technical, Scientific, and General Terms*. London: Routledge & Kegan Paul.

Weber, Bruce. 2008. "Laurence Urdang, Language Expert Who Edited Dictionaries, Dies at 81." *New York Times*, August 26, C10.

Webster's International Dictionary of the English Language. 1890. Edited by Noah Porter et al. Springfield, MA: G. & C. Merriam.

*Webster's New Collegiate Dictionary. 1953. 6th ed. Springfield, MA: G. & C. Merriam.

Webster's New International Dictionary of the English Language. 1909. Edited by William Torrey Harris, F. Sturges Allen, et al. Springfield, MA: G. & C. Merriam.

*Webster's New International Dictionary of the English Language. 1934. 2nd ed. Edited by W. A. Neilson, Thomas A. Knott, et al. Springfield, MA: G. & C. Merriam.

Webster's New World Dictionary of the English Language. 1951. 2 vols. Edited by David B. Guralnik, Joseph H. Friend, et al. Cleveland: World Publishing.

Webster's Seventh New Collegiate Dictionary. 1963. Edited by Philip Babcock Gove et al. Springfield, MA: G. & C. Merriam.

*Webster's Third New International Dictionary. 1961. Edited by Philip Babcock Gove et al. Springfield, MA: G. & C. Merriam.

Weinbrot, Howard D., ed. 1972. *New Aspects of Lexicography: Literary Criticism, Intellectual History, and Social Change.* Carbondale: Southern Illinois University Press.
Weinreich, Uriel. 1949. *College Yiddish: An Introduction to the Yiddish Language and to Jewish Life and Culture.* New York: YIVO.
———. 1953. *Languages in Contact: Findings and Problems.* New York: Linguistic Circle of New York.
———, ed. 1954. *The Field of Yiddish: Studies in Language, Folklore, and Literature.* New York: Linguistic Circle of New York.
*———. 1960. "Mid-century Linguistics: Attainments and Frustrations." *Romance Philology* 8:320–41.
*———. 1963. "On the Semantic Structure of Language." In *Universals of Language*, edited by Joseph H. Greenberg, 142–216. Boston: MIT Press.
*———. 1964. "Webster's Third: A Critique of Its Semantics." *International Journal of American Linguistics* 30:405–9.
———, ed. 1965. *The Field of Yiddish: Studies in Language, Folklore, and Literature: Second Collection.* The Hague: Mouton.
*———. 1966a. "On the Semantic Structure of Language." In *Universals of Language*, edited by Joseph Greenburg, 142–216. 2nd ed. Boston: MIT Press.
*———. 1966b. "Explorations in Semantic Theory." In *Current Trends in Linguistics III: Theoretical Foundations*, edited by Thomas A. Sebeok, 396–477. The Hague: Mouton.
———. 1968. *Modern English-Yiddish, Yiddish-English Dictionary.* New York: McGraw Hill for the YIVO Institute for Jewish Research.
———. 1972. *Explorations in Semantic Theory.* Preface by William Labov. The Hague: Mouton.
Weinreich, Uriel, William Labov, and Marvin I. Herzog. 1968. *Empirical Foundations for a Theory of Language Change.* Austin: University of Texas Press.
Weinreich, Uriel, and Beatrice Weinreich. 1959. *Yiddish Language and Folklore: A Selective Bibliography for Research.* The Hague: Mouton.
*Wells, Rulon. 1958. "Is a Structural Treatment of Meaning Possible?" *Proceedings of the Eighth International Congress of Linguists*, edited by Eva Sivertsen, 654–66. Oslo: Oslo University Press.
*Wesson, Douglas B. 1928. *I'll Never Be Cured and I Don't Much Care.* New York: J. H. Sears.
*West, Michael. 1953. *A General Service List of English Words.* London: Longman, Green.
White Christmas. 1954. Directed by Michael Curtiz. Written by Norman Krasna, Norman Panama, and Melvin Frank. Hollywood, CA: Paramount Pictures.
*Whitney, J. D. 1888. *Names and Places.* Cambridge: Cambridge University Press.
Wiegand, Herbert Ernst. 1992. "Elements of a Theory towards a So-Called Lexicographic Definition." *Lexicographica* 8:175–289.
———. 1995. "Zur einführung und bibliographischen orienteriung." *Lexicographica* 11:1–14.
*Wilber, Donald N. 1956. *Afghanistan.* New Haven, CT: Human Relations Area Files.
Wierzbicka, Anna. 1972. *Semantyka i Słownik: Praca Zbiorowa.* Wrocław: Zakład Narodowy im. Ossolińskich.
———. 1985. *Lexicography and Conceptual Analysis.* Ann Arbor: Karoma Press.
———. 2001. "Australian Culture and Australian English: A Response to William Ransom." *Australian Journal of Linguistics* 21:195–214.
Wierzbicka, Anna, and Cliff Goddard. 2017. "Talking about Our Bodies and Their Parts in Warlpiri." *Australian Journal of Linguistics* 38:31–62.
*Williams, Edwin B. 1955. *Spanish and English Dictionary.* New York: Henry Holt.

*———. 1959. "The Problems of Bilingual Lexicography Particularly as Applied to Spanish and English." *Hispanic Review* 27:246–53.
*———. 1960. "Analysis of the Problem of Meaning Discrimination in Spanish and English Bilingual Lexicography." *Babel: Revue Internationale de la Traduction* 6 (3): 121–25.
Williams, Krista M. 2016. "A New Typology of Color Term Defining Strategies." *Dictionaries* 37:1–35.
*Wilson, Herbert M. 1900. "A Dictionary of Topographic Forms." *Journal of the American Geographic Society of New York* 32:32–41.
*Wonderly, William L. 1952. "Semantic Components in Kechua Person Morphemes." *Language* 28:366–76.
*Woodger, J. H. 1952. *Biology and Language: An Introduction to the Methodology of the Biological Sciences Including Medicine*. Cambridge: Cambridge University Press.
Worth, Dean Stoddard. 1959. "'Linear Contexts,' Linguistics, and Machine Translation." *Word* 15:183–91.
*———. 1960. Review of *Leksikologija anglijskogo jazyka*, by A. I. Smirnickii. *Word* 16:277–84.
———, ed. 1961. *Kamchadal Texts Collected by W. Jochelson*. Janua Linguarum Series Maior 2. The Hague: Mouton.
———. 1969. *Dictionary of Western Kamchadal*. Berkeley: University of California Press.
———. 1977. *A Bibliography of Russian Word-Formation*. Columbus, OH: Slavica Publishers.
Worth, Dean S., Andrew S. Kozak, and Donald B. Johnson. 1970. *Russian Derivational Dictionary*. New York: Elsevier.
Yamagiwa, Joseph K. 1963. Review of *A Glossary of Japanese Neologisms*, by Don C. Bailey. *Journal of Asian Studies* 22:485–86.
Yong, Heming, and Jing Peng. 2007. *Bilingual Lexicography from a Communicative Perspective*. Amsterdam: John Benjamins.
Yüksekkaya, Hadi Yasar. 1998. *Die Deutsch–Turkische Lexikographie: Eine Metalexikographische Untersuchung der Allegemeinen Großen Wörterbücher*. Lexicographica Series Maior 85. Tübingen: Niemeyer.
Zgusta, Ladislav. 1971. *Manual of Lexicography*. Prague: Academia.
———, ed. 1980. *Theory and Method in Lexicography: Western and Non-Western Perspectives*. Columbia, SC: Hornbeam Press.
———. 1988. *Lexicography Today: An Annotated Bibliography of the Theory of Lexicography*. With the assistance of Donna M. T. Cr. Farina. Lexicographica Series Maior 18. Tübingen: Niemeyer.
———. 1990. "Demetrius J. Georgacas." *Dictionaries* 12:165–69.
———. 1993. "Henry Kahane, 1902–1992." *Names* 41:45–49.
———. 2006. *Lexicography Then and Now: Selected Essays*. Edited by Fredric S. F. Dolezal and Thomas B. I. Creamer. Lexicographica Series Maior 129. Tübingen: Niemeyer.
Zimmer, Ben. 2008. "RIP, Larry Urdang, Logophile." *Language Log*, August 26, 2008. https://languagelog.ldc.upenn.edu/nll/?p=535.
*Zimmer, Karl E. 1964. *Affixal Negation in English and Other Languages: An Investigation of Restricted Productivity*. Supplement to *Word* 20 (2).
*Zudin, P. B. 1950. *Kratkii Afgansko–Ruskii Slovar*. Moscow: GINS.
*———. 1955. *Russko–Afganskii Slovar*. Moscow: GINS.
Zúñiga, Alejandro. 2005. "Poet, Teacher, Linguistics Scholar Dies at 83." *The Tico Times* September 16, 2005. https://ticotimes.net/2005/09/16/poet-teacher-linguistics-scholar-dies-at-83.

INDEX

Note: Biographical notes on contributors and the pages of their contributions are indicated in boldface. Because references to dictionaries generally, bilingual dictionaries, and English are profuse throughout the text, those items are not indexed here.

Abrahamson, Arthur S., 82
Academie française, 332
Academy of Athens, 104, 354
Acta Linguistica Academiae Scientarum Hungaricae (journal), 66
Adams, Jennifer, xii
Afghanistan (Wilber), 343
Afrídí, 345, 348
Ainu, 304
Akwesasne Mohawk, 92
Albanian, 305–6
Alford, Emily, xi
Algeo, John, 69
Allegheny College, 101
Allen, Harold B., 40, 64, 89
allomorphic variation, 229–30, 232, 238–39, 355, 359, 362–63, 366,
allophonic variation, 50, 240–41, 346–47, 360–61
Altaic, 376
Amanullah (King of Afghanistan) 344
American Academy of Arts and Sciences, 8, 93, 97, 100, 103
America: Naming the Country and Its People (Read), 111
American Anthropologist (journal), 66
American Association of Geographers, 91
American Bicycling News (magazine), 329
American College Dictionary, 17, 29, 49, 69–70, 85, 89–90, 95, 107, 175, 179, 339, 390
American Council of Learned Societies, 8, 94–95, 98, 118–19, 121
American Dialect Society, 107, 110
American Glossary (Thornton), 327
Americanisms, 57, 326–34

Americanisms: A Dictionary of Selected Americanisms on Historical Principles (Mathews), 70, 112
"American Lexicography, 1945–1973" (Barnhart), 89
American Museum of Natural History, 92
American Name Society, 91, 107, 110
American Philosophical Society, 8, 100
American Society of Geolinguistics, 110
American Speech (journal), 31, 107, 119
American University, 118
Analysis of the Lexicographic Resources Used by American Biblical Scholars Today (Gates), 39
Andalusian, 199
Ani Moukhtar, 15, 389
Appleton's Revised English–Spanish and Spanish–English Dictionary (Cuyás), 315, 317–19, 323
"Approaches to Lexicography and Semantics" (Read), 111
Arabic, 46, 59, 99, 143, 147–48, 166, 181, 185, 193, 307, 349–51, 369–71, 373, 375, 383
Arabic, Classical, 184
Arabic, Egyptian, 184–85
Arabic, Granadine, 142
Arabic, Iraqi, 184–87
Arabic, Moroccan, 29, 99, 184–87
Arabic, North African, 118
Arabic, Syrian, 15, 184–87
Araukan, 140
Aristotle, 201
Ashton, John W., 19, 387
Atkins, B. T. S., 77
Atlantic Monthly (magazine), 283
Austerlitz, Robert, 116

Index

Austrian Academy of Sciences, 8, 109
"Autobiographic Sketch" (Malkiel), 105
Ayers, Harry Morgan, 290
Azerbaijani, 4, 13, 102, 372
Aztec, 138, 142

Bailey, Don C., 16, 389
Bailey, Richard W., xi, 28, 30, 64, 120, 124
Balint, Andras, 16, 120–21, 386, 389
Balochi, 343, 347
Baltimore Gazette (newspaper), 329
Baret, John, 112
Barker, E. E., 334
Barnhart, Clarence L., 6–7, 9, 17–18, 29, 34, 37–38, 40, 54–55, 57–59, 64–65, 69, 72, 76–77, 85, **88–90**, 110, 122, **278–97**, 337–38, 384–85, 388–89
Barnhart, David K., 89
Barnhart Dictionary Companion (journal), 89
Barnhart Dictionary of New Words since 1963 (Barnhart, Stein, Barnhart), 89
Barnhart, Robert K., 89
Bartlett, John, 312
Bashkir, 371
Basic Course in Azerbaijani (Householder and Lofti), 102
Basic Course in Hindi (Chavarría-Aguilar and Pray), 92
Basic Course in Moroccan Arabic (Harrell), 99
Basic English, 167
Basic Japanese Conversation Dictionary (Martin), 108
Basic Swedish Word List (Alwood and Wilhelmsen), 200
Basque, 143
Bates College, 91
Beardsley, Monroe, 123
Beginning Burmese (Cornyn and Roop) 94
Beginning Russian (Cornyn), 94
"Beginnings of English Lexicography" (Read), 111
Beginning Thai (Haas), 98
Begriffssystem als Grundlage für die Lexikographie (Hallig and von Wartburg), 32
Béjoint, Henri, 77–78

Bellew, Henry Walker, 345
Bender, Harold, 113
Berg, C. C., 32
Bergenholtz, Henning, 77
Bertels, E. E., 346, 376
"Bi-dialectalism" (Sledd), 112
Bilmece: A Corpus of Turkish Riddles (Basgöz and Tietze), 114
Bite of Costa Rica (Chavarría-Aguilar), 92
Bloomfield, Leonard, 7, 73, 94, 96, 120, 158, 195, 201, 210, 212–13, 266, 290
Bloomsbury Companion to Lexicography (Jackson), 77
Boatner, Maxine T., 38
Bogaards, Paul, 35, 77, 122
Boissière, Prudence, 148
Bolinger, Dwight, 105, 120
Bonsack, Edwin, 6, 18, 22, 40, 53, 55–56, 58, 65, 74, 86, **89–90**, 91, 119, **298–312**, 338, 388–89
Borovkov, A. K., 376
Boucher, Jonathan, 326
Bridgeman, Loraine I., 12–14, 389
Brief Description of Thai (Haas), 98
Briticisms, 57, 69, 110, 292, 326–34
British Academy, 8, 100
Brooklyn College, 111
Brown, Oral Carl, 13, 389
Brown University, 186
Buck, Carl Darling, 196
Buffalo University, 4
Burchfield, Robert W., 28
Burmese, 61, 70, 94–95, 378–79
Burmese Chrestomathy (Cornyn), 94
Burmese Glossary (Cornyn and Musgrave), 70, 94
Burrill, Meredith F., 6, 9, 18, 22, 40, 55–56, 58, 65, 74, 86, 90, **91**, **298–312**, 338, 388–89

Cahiers de lexicologie (journal), 35
Canadianisms, 58, 331
Canadian Linguistic Association, 29, 331
Cañes, Francisco
Cantonese, 118
Cardona, George, 119
Carnap, Rudolf, 158
Casares y Sanchez, Julio, 148

Cassell's French–English and English–French Dictionary (Baker), 319, 321
Cassell's Latin–English and English–Latin Dictionary, 322
Cassell's New German and English Dictionary (Breul), 321–22
Cassell's Spanish Dictionary, 317, 322
Cassidy, Frederic G., 28, 37, 39
Castilian, 199
Catalan, 14, 148
Catholic University, Leuven
Celtic, 304
Center for Advanced Study of Behavioral Sciences, 106
Center for Applied Linguistics, 36
Century Dictionary, 28, 282–84, 311
Chambers Diccionario Tecnológico Español–Inglés : Inglés–Español, 318
Chao, Y. R., 259
Characterization of the Roman Poetic Onomasticon (Swanson), 113
Chavarría-Aguilar, O. L., 6, 40, 59, **91–92**, 109, 119, 122, **343–52**, 388–89
Cheremis, 106
Chilean, 140
Chinese, 108, 118–19, 201, 275–77, 306
Chomsky, Noam, 52, 120, 260–64, 266
Churchill, Winston, 107
City University of New York, 10, 92
Clapin, Sylva, 311
Clark University, 91
"'Clerk's Tale': The Monsters and the Critics" (Sledd) 111
Cocina para Hombres (Chavarría-Aguilar), 92
Cognitive Anthropology (Conklin), 93
Collecting and Collections of Rare and Out of Print Dictionaries (conference), 39
College Yiddish (Weinreich) 115
Colloquium on Historical Research on English Dictionaries (conference), 39
Columbia University, 7, 11, 16, 89, 93, 101, 110, 115, 119, 155, 326, 389–90
Comment j'ai fait mon dictionnaire de la langue française (Littré), 30
Complete Roumanian-English Dictionary (Axelrad), 318

Concise Oxford Dictionary, Fourth Edition, 164, 169, 331
Concise Oxford French Dictionary (Chevalley and Chevalley), 175, 318
Conference on Style (Indiana University), 12, 121
Conference on the History and Making of Dictionaries, 40
Conklin, Harold C., 6, 8–9, 11, 14, 16, 20, 24–25, 27, 34, 40, 42–43, 50–51, 53, 56, 58, 60, 64, 69–70, 72, 85, **92–94**, 108, 119, 122, 201, **243–59**, 262, 264, 267, 385, 387, 389
Conseil International de la philosophie et des sciences humaine, 32–33
Considine, John, xii
Consumer Reports, 111
Contreras, Heles, 13, 22, 26, 127, 389
Cordell Collection, 39–40
Cordell, Warren N., 39
Cornell University, 12, 96
Cornyn, William, 6–7, 11, 40, 61, 65, 68, 70, **94–95**, 118–19, 122, **378–80**, 388
Corominas, Joan, 362
Cosinka, Jan. *See* Jackson, Ian
Course in Modern Linguistics (Hockett), 120, 211
Cowan, J Milton, 118
Cowell, Mark W., 15, 389
Cowie, A. P., 77
Crabb, David, 259
Craigie, William A., 28, 88, 326–27, 329
"Critique of English–Hungarian and Hungarian–English General Lexicography" (Balint), 16
Cultures, Ideologies, and the Dictionary (Kachru and Kahane) 105
Curtiz, Michael, 8

Dagur Mongolian (Martin), 108
Daniel, Beth, 112
Danto, Arthur, 259
Dartmouth College, 116
Da Somavera, Alessio, 354
Davies, Anna Morpurgo, 119
Davis, Phil, 8
De Alcala, Pedro, 148

428 | Index

De Azkue, Resurección Maria, 143
Deccan College, 100
Definition (Robinson), 41, 170–71
definition and defining, 18, 41–42, 44–45, 50, 54–57, 61, 72, 76, 94, 107, 135–36, 141, 144, 150–52, 154–73, 177, 186–87, 192, 201, 205–206, 210–11, 214–16, 218, 224–27, 232, 238, 246, 248, 257, 259–61, 264–65, 279, 281–83, 285, 291–92, 297, 300, 302, 306–8, 310–12, 314, 317, 334, 338–39, 351, 376, 385
De Gruyter (publisher), 21
De Larramendi, Manuel, 143
De Marco, Barbara, 104
Demetrius, 202
De Pakhtu Sind (Mohmand), 346
Də paštō istilāhāt aw muhāwərē (Nawri), 346
Der Deutsches Wortschatz nach Sachgruppen (Dornseiff), 227
"Der [r]-einschub nach ME *ă* in Neu-England" (Penzl), 109
Descriptive Studies in Spanish Grammar (Kahane and Pietrangeli), 104
"Desk Dictionaries" (Read), 110
Dhātupātha (Pānini), 229
dialect, 53, 55, 58–60, 69, 96, 115, 138–40, 142–43, 147, 149–51, 184–86, 192, 199, 236, 249, 253–54, 266, 292, 294, 304, 331–33, 338–39, 343, 345–51, 354, 357–60, 370, 372, 374, 379, 384
Diamond, Nancy, 85
Diccionario Critico Etymologica de la Lengue Catellana (Corominas), 362
Diccionario Español-Latino-Arábigo (Cañes), 143
Diccionario Etimológico Español e Hispánico (Garcia de Diego), 146
Diccionario Ideológico de la Lengua Española (Casares), 148
Diccionario Inlez-Portuguez (Ferreira), 319
Diccionario Trilingüe del Castellano (De Larramendi), 143
Diccionario Vasco-Español-Francés (De Askue), 143
Dickens, Charles, 327
Dictionaries (journal), 40, 110
Dictionaries and That Dictionary (Sledd and Ebbitt), 112
Dictionaries British and American (Hulbert), 30
Dictionaries of English (R. W. Bailey) 64
Dictionaries: The Art and Craft of Lexicography (Landau) 73, 76
"Dictionary" (Read), 110
"Dictionary as Ideology" (Kahane and Kahane), 104
Dictionary of American English, 28, 30, 69, 110, 122, 282–83, 291, 302, 326–28
Dictionary of Americanisms (Bartlett), 312
Dictionary of Americanisms, (Mathews) 28, 70, 112, 122, 282–83, 311, 327
Dictionary of American Regional English, 28, 122
Dictionary of Idioms for the Deaf (Boatner and Gates) 38
Dictionary of Moroccan Arabic: English-Moroccan (Harrell) 70, 99
Dictionary of Moroccan Arabic: Moroccan-English (Sobelman and Harrell), 99
Dictionary of Syrian Arabic: English-Arabic (Ani and Stowasser), 15
Dictionary of the Older Scottish Tongue, 28, 122
Dictionary of the Puk'hto or Pus'hto, or Language of the Afghans (Raverty), 345, 350
Dictionary of the Pukkhto or Pukshto Language (Bellew), 345, 350–51
Dictionary of the Spanish and English Languages (Neuman and Baretti), 317, 323
"Dictionary of Topographic Forms" (Wilson), 312
Dictionary of United States Army Terms, 70, 89, 95
Dictionary of Western Kamchadal (Worth), 70, 116
Dictionary Society of North America, ix, 35, 38–40, 64, 97, 103, 105, 110, 113, 123
Dictionnaire analogique de la langue française (Boissière), 148
Dictionnaire du français contemporain, 75
Dictionnaire Étymologique de la Langue Latine (Ernout and Meillet), 227
Dictionnaire Francais–Arabe–Persan et Turc (Handjéri), 373

Dictionnaire français-roméique (Missir), 354
Dicziunari Rumantsch Grischun, 165
"Die lexikographie der Turksprachen I: Osmanisch-Turkische" (Tietze), 114
diglossia, 185, 348, 384
Dizionario Scolastico Italiano-Inglese: Inglese-Italiano (Spinelli), 322–23
Dolezal, Fredric Thomas, 65
"Dorigen's Complaint" (Sledd) 111
Dornseiff, Franz, 227
Dosch, Elsie, 21
Driscoll, Ann M., 46, **186–90**
Dr. Johnson's Dictionary: Essays in the Biography of a Book (Sledd and Kolb), 31, 112
Dubois, Claude, 35
Dubois, Jean, 35
Duckert, Audrey R., 36, 64, 111
Dunham, Gary, xi
Durkin, Philip, 77
Dutch, 143

Earlham College, 98
Early Modern English Dictionary, 28, 121–22, 124
Eble, Connie, xi, 121
Eckert, Penelope, xi
École nationale des langues vivantes, 116
"18th Century American English According to Noah Webster" (Penzl), 109
Eighth International Congress of Linguists (Oslo), 72
Eliason, Norman, 121–22
Eliopoulos, Socrates, 4, 19
Eloquent Dissent (Sledd), 112
Emory University, 106–7
"Empirical Foundations for a Theory of Language Change" (Weinreich, Labov, and Herzog), 115
Emre, Yunus, 372
Encyclopedia Britannica, 111, 282
"English and Polish in Contact" (Lyra), 13
English Dictionary from Cawdrey to Johnson 1604-1755 (Starnes and Noyes), 31
English for Speakers of Thai (Gedney), 95
English-Pidgin and French Dictionary of Sports and Phrase Book (Balint), 120

English-Thai and Thai-English Dictionary (Manich), 176
English Topographic Terms in Florida (McMullen), 311
Ernout, Alfred, 227
Erwin, Wallace M., 99
Eskimo (i.e., Inuit or Yupik), 166
Esperanto, 142
Essays on Linguistic Themes (Malkiel), 154
"Establishing and Maintaining Standard Patterns of Speech" (Barnhart), 89
Estienne, Henri, 121
Estienne, Robert, 121
Ethnographic Atlas of Ifugao (Conklin), 93
Étude linguistique et sémiotique des dictionnaires français contemporains (Rey-Debove), 35
Etymological Dictionaries (Malkiel), 106
Etymology (Malkiel), 106
etymology, 19, 42, 54, 58, 70, 93, 101, 106–7, 110, 113–14, 121, 133–34, 137, 146–47, 149–50, 181, 194, 203, 227, 230, 236, 239, 245, 279–81, 285, 290, 296–97, 346, 361–62, 383, 385
EURALEX, 40
European Background of American Linguistics (Hoenigswald), 101
Evolution of English Lexicography (Murray), 30
"Experience of the General Theory of Lexicography" (Garvin), 106
"Explanatory Matter in Bilingual Dictionaries" (Iannucci), 103
Euripides, 201

Farahi, 347
Fārsī pə Pashtō (Nawīs), 346
Feely, Pete, xi
Ferguson, Charles, A., 348
Field of Yiddish (Weinreich), 115
Fife, Austin, 85, 127
"File for a Technical Dictionary" (Gleason), 97
Finegan, Edward, xii
First Person Singular (book series), 8, 118
Fishman, Joshua, 64, 93
Five Clocks (Joos), 82
Folk Classification (Conklin), 93

Fontenelle, Thierry, 77
Fraenkel, Gerd, 13, 389
Frake, Charles O., 259
Francis, W. Nelson, 192, 194, 200
Franjié, Lynne, 65
Franklin, Karl J., 66, 68, 73, 75, 123
Französisches Etymologisches Wörterbuch (von Wartburg), 133, 362
Frege, Gottlob, 158, 172
French, 143, 146, 158, 165, 175–76, 192–93, 199, 205, 235, 277, 313–14, 316–24, 332, 336, 339, 350, 354, 370, 373, 376
French-English and English-French Dictionary of Technical Terms and Phrases (Kettridge), 322
French-English Science Dictionary (De Vries), 319
Friedrich, Paul, 259,
Fries, Charles C., 28, 121
Frisian, 199
Fromkin, Victoria, 9
Funk & Wagnalls (publisher), 29
Funk & Wagnalls' New Standard Dictionary of the English Language, 29, 311
Funk & Wagnalls' Standard Dictionary, International Edition, 69
Funk & Wagnalls' Standard Dictionary of the English Language, 29

Gaarder, Bruce, 16, 20, 26, 389
Gagauz, 372
G. & C. Merriam Company, *See* Merriam-Webster
Garcia de Diego, Vincente, 146
Garvin, Paul L., 10, 106
Gates, J. Edward, 31–35, 38–40, 97
Gedney, William, 6–7, 9, 11, 18, 40, 55–56, 58, 65, 68, 70, **95–96**, 119, 122, **335–40**, 388–89
"General Dictionaries" (Barnhart), 89
General Service List of English Words (West), 200
"Geographical Terms in the Far West", 312
Georgacas, Demetrius J., 17–20, 33, 35, 104, 121, 353, 359
Georgetown Arabic Research Program, 15, 46, 99, 184, 186

Georgetown University, 10, 15, 100, 181, 389–90
German, 25, 142, 152, 165–66, 182, 192–93, 195, 197, 199, 205, 234, 237, 277, 303–4, 307, 314–15, 318–24, 339, 350, 360, 370, 373
German, Middle High, 109
German, Old High, 109
German, Pennsylvania, 109
German-English, English-German Dictionary of Everyday Usage (Pfeffer), 182, 186–90
German-English and English-German Dictionary (Bithell), 318, 320
German-English Dictionary of Technical, Scientific, and General Terms (Webel), 319
Germanic, 142, 192, 199
Ghazni, 347
"Ghost Adjectives in Dictionaries" (Iannucci) 103
Gilbertson, George Waters, 350
Gilliéron, Jules, 358
Gleason, H. A., xii, 6, 9, 11, 14, 37–43, 48–49, 51–52, 56, 58, 69–71, 86, 94, **96–97**, 119, 122, 201, **209–26**, 260, 262–64, 266, 336, 387, 389
Glossario degli Antichi Portolani Italiani (Kahane, Kahane, Bremner), 104
Glossary of Japanese Neologisms (D. Bailey), 16
"Glossary of Names for Topographic Forms", 312
Goodenough, W. H., 259
Google Scholar, 64
Gothic, 109
Gouws, Rufus, 122
Gove, Philip B., 17, 69, 389
Gradenwitz, Otto, 229
Graeca et Romanica Scripta Selecta (Kahane and Kahane), 104
"Grammar for Social Awareness in a Time of Class Warfare" (Sledd), 112
Grammar of Pashto (Penzl), 109, 350–51
"Grammatical Prerequisites" (Gleason), 97
Grammatical Structure of Oaxaca Chontal (Waterhouse), 82
Graves, Mortimer, 118

Greek, Ancient, 4, 7, 60, 142–43, 147, 192–93, 198–99, 201–2, 230–33, 334, 355, 357, 363, 372, 379
Greek, Demotic, 4, 19, 60, 354–56, 360, 362, 378–79
Greek, Modern, 4, 17–19, 59–60, 95, 104, 119, 195, 198, 353–67
Greenberg, Joseph H., 259
Grimes, Joseph E., 37
Gudenau, Allison, xi

Haakon VII, King of Norway, 107
Haas, Mary, 6, 8–10, 25, 29, 40, 42, 45–47, 50–53, 61–62, 64, 70, 74, 76, 78, 85–86, 89, 94, 96, **97–99**, 118–19, 122, **174–79**, 203–4, 336, 340, 384–85, 387, 389
Hackerd, Jeremy, xi
Haitian Creole-English-French Dictionary (Valdman et al.), 14
Haitian Voodoo, 13
Hale, E. E., 312
Hale, Louise, 330
Hall, Robert A., 118
Halle, Morris, 10, 260, 263, 266
Handbook of Lexicography (Svensén), 77
Handjéri, Alexander, 373
Hanks, Patrick, 41, 77
Hanley, Miles L., 290, 328
Hanunóo, 244, 246–47, 252, 254–58, 262
Hanunóo-English Vocabulary (Conklin), 70, 93
Hardy, Thomas, 334
Harper's (magazine) 283
Harrell, Richard S., 6, 9–10, 15, 40, 42, 45–46, 61, 70, 76, **99–100**, 122, **180–90**, 203, 205, 384, 386–87, 389
Harrison, Ed, 8
Hartford Seminary Foundation, 38, 96, 100, 209, 389
Hartmann, R. R. K., 40, 64–65, 77, 89, 99
Harvard University, 11, 99, 116, 331
HathiTrust, x
Haugen, Einar, 26, 46, 51, 55, 57, 61, 66–68, 72–74, 123–24, 259
Hausmann, F. J., 77, 114
Heath's French and English Dictionary (De Lolme, Wallace, and Bridgeman), 321, 323

Heath's French and English Dictionary (Mansion), 315, 320–22
Heath's New French and English Dictionary (Baker), 318–21
Hebrew 202, 354
Heid, Ulrich, 77
Hench, Atcheson L., 334
Herati, 347
Herbst, Thomas, 77
Herzog, Marvin I., 115
Hetherington, M. Sue, 113
Hindi, 195, 201
Historical Lexicon of Spoken Greek (Papadopoulos), 354, 359
Hitler, Adolf, 103
Hockett, Charles F., 118, 120, 192, 211
Hoenigswald, Henry, 6–10, 40, 49, 52, 69, 96, **100–101**, 118–20, 122–23, **227–34**, 261–63, 387, 389
Hollander, John, 123
Holt, Rinehart and Winston of Canada (publisher), 36
Hornby, A. S., 29, 262
Householder, Fred W., xi, 3–5, 7–14, 17, 19–28, 31, 37–38, 40–41, 47, 54, 61–62, 65, 67–68, 74–77, 79–82, 85, 87–89, 96, **101–2**, 111, 118–24, **127**, **383–86**, 388–89
Howell, James, 143
Hudak, Thomas J., 96
Hulbert, James R., 30
Hungarian, 16, 282
Hunter College, 100
Huntsman, Jeffrey, 113

Iannucci, James E., 6, 40, 56–57, 65, 69, **103**, 119, 122, **313–25**, 338, 385, 388–89
IBM, 124
Ido, 142
Ilocano, 257
Ilson, Robert, 40
Index to the U. S. A., (Townshend), 311
Indiana State University, 39, 110
Indian Institute of Technology, 92
Indic, 195, 229, 349
Indo-European, 191–92, 194–95, 199, 201, 313, 343, 369, 376
Indo-Iranian, 59, 343

In Feudal Africa (Loeb), 82
Ingersoll, Jared, 329
International Conference on English Lexicography, 36–37
International Journal of American Linguistics, 12, 20–21, 26–27, 38, 63, 79–80, 82, 79–82, 101
International Journal of Slavic Linguistics and Poetics (journal), 116
International Linguistic Association, 110, 119
International Phonetic Alphabet, 290–91
International Phonetic Association, 240
Introduction à la lexicographie (Dubois and Dubois), 35
Introduction to Descriptive Linguistics (Gleason), 96–97, 211, 221
Iowa State University, 110
Iranian, 110
Irving, T. B., 15–16, 120, 389
Islamia College 344
Italian, 142, 147, 192, 199, 202, 235, 320, 322, 354–55, 376
Italian, Old, 198
Italienische Ortsnamen in Griechenland (Kahane and Kahane), 104
Itelman. *See* Western Kamchadal

Jackson, Howard, 77
Jackson, Ian, 105
Jakobson, Roman, 10, 44, 101, 115–16, 123, 264
Japanese, 52, 108, 118, 121, 184, 272–73, 275–77, 304, 306
Japanese Language and Literature (journal) 108
Japanese Language through Time (Martin), 108
Jinghpaw, 61, 378–79
"John Baret's *Alvearie*" (Sledd), 112
John Benjamins (publisher), 21
Johns Hopkins University, 107, 235, 390
Johnson, Gary, xii
Johnson, Samuel, 31, 71, 110, 112
Jones, Daniel, 291
Joos, Martin, 7, 11, 82, 260

Kabuli, 347–48
Kachru, Braj, 104
Kahane, Henry, 6–10, 18–19, 40, 59–60, 70, 94–95, 100, **103–5**, 114, 118–19, 121–22, **353–67**, 388–89
Kahane, Renée, 6–10, 18–19, 40, 59–60, 70, 94–95, 100, **103–5**, 114, 118–19, 121–22, **353–67**, 388–89
Kakridis, Ioannis, 361
Kamchadal Texts Collected by W. Jochelson (Worth), 116
Kandahari, 346–48, 350–51
katharevusa, 354–55, 360, 362
Kenyon, John S., 291
Kenyon College, 107
Kewa, 123
Khán, Alí Akbar, 345
Khan, Ayub, 344
Kierstein, Paul, xii
Kim, Be, 13, 389
King Christian X Liberty Medal, 107
Kirghiz, 371
Kish, Kelly, xi
Knott, Thomas A., 266, 280, 291
Kolb, Gwin J., 31
Koman Riddles and Turkic Folklore (Tietze), 114
Korean, 52, 108, 273, 275–77
Korean-English Dictionary (Martin, Lee, and Chang), 70
Koutsoudas, Andreas, 82
Kratkii Afgansko-Ruskii Slovar (Zudin), 346, 350
Kretschmer, Paul, 358
Kuhn, Sherman M., 91
Kultursprache, 372–73, 375
Kunari, 347
Kurath, Hans, 28, 109, 333
Kurdish, 201, 343

labels and labeling, 49, 57–58, 84, 134, 157, 162, 179, 199, 216, 228, 232, 244–47, 248–49, 252–53, 257, 259, 292, 294, 297, 314, 317, 326–27, 329–33, 352, 384
Labov, William, 115, 119
Landau, Sidney I., 73, 76
Language (Bloomfield), 96, 210, 212–13
Language (journal), 66, 120

Language Change and Linguistic Reconstruction (Hoenigswald), 101
Languages in Contact (Weinreich), 10, 115
Laterculi vocum Latinarum (Gadenwitz), 229
Latin, 4, 7, 113, 142–43, 147, 191–93, 195–96, 198–99, 201–2, 205, 228–29, 231–32, 262, 322, 325, 353–55, 371–73, 375–76, 385
Latinae Linguae Thesaurus (R. Estienne), 121
Lazarfeld, Paul F., 259
Leavitt, Robert Keith, 30
Lectures in Linguistics (Chavarría-Aguilar), 92
Lees, Robert, 260–61, 263, 265
Legrand, M. Emile, 354
"Lehnwörter mit Mittelenglisch *ā* for *r* im Pennsylvanisch-Detuschen dialekt" (Penzl), 109
Lessons in Colloquial Egyptian Arabic (Harrell, Selim, and Tewfik), 99
Lew, Robert, 89
Lexical Analysis (Hanks), 41
Lexical Numbers in Spanish Nouns (Iannucci), 103
"Lexicographer as Mediator between Linguistics and Society" (Malkiel), 106
Lexicographica Series Maior, 21, 65
Lexicography: Critical Contexts (Hartmann), 89
Lexicography in English (McDavid and Duckert), 36, 39, 64, 112
Lexicography Today (Zgusta), 31
Lexicon tetraglotton (Howell), 143
Lexikografický sborník (Havránek), 32
Lexikon des Frühgriechischen Epos, 364
Lexis: Larousse de la langue française, 75
Library of Congress, 16, 90, 390
Life in Letters (Saporta), 111
Lingua (journal), 66
Lingua Franca in the Levant (Kahane, Kahane, and Tietze), 70, 104, 114
Linguistic Atlas of New England (Kurath et al.), 109, 202
Linguistic Atlas of the United States and Canada, 333
Linguistic Circle of Columbia University, 119
Linguistic Circle of New York, 10, 101

"Linguisticians and Lexicographers" (Housholder and Sebeok), 102, 118
Linguistics and English Grammar (Gleason), 96–97
Linguistics: An International Review (journal), 66
"Linguistics, Obeah, Acupuncture, and the Teaching of Composition by That Bastard Sledd" (Sledd), 112
Linguistic Society of America, 7–8, 10–12, 98, 103, 105, 107, 120, 360
Linguistic Speculations (Householder), 4, 102, 118
Linguistic Survey of India, 346
Linguistics Today, 115
Listener (magazine), 283
Literary History of Hamlet (Malone), 107
Literary Quotation and Allusion in Lucian (Householder), 101
Littré, Emile, 30
Loeb, Edwin M., 82
Longman Group (publisher), 36
Lounsbury, F. G., 259
Lucian, 4
Lucretius, 195
Lughāt Afghani (Zhekeli), 346
Lyons, John, 14, 74, 390
Lyra, Franciszek, 13, 390

Magyar-Angol Szótár (Országh), 282
Makhmúd, Alí, 345
Makkai, Adam 34
Malay, 93, 118
Malayo-Polynesian, 178
Malcolm-Clarke, Darja, xi
Malkiel, Yakov, 6–10, 24, 37–38, 40, 42–43, 45, 47, 56, 58, 64–65, 68, 73–74, 76–77, 85, 94, 96, 100, 104, **105–6**, 110, 115, 119, 122–23, **133–54**, 203, 334, 385, 387–88, 390
Malone, Kemp, 3, 6–9, 40, 49–52, 69, **106–8**, 110, 119, 121–22, **235–42**, 263, 265–66, 386–87, 390
Manchester Guardian (newspaper), 283
Manich, Jumsai M. L., 176
Manly, John Matthews, 107
Mansion's Shorter French and English Dictionary (Mansion), 320–21

Manual of Lexicography (Zgusta), 31, 33–37, 62, 65, 73, 76, 94, 96, 122
Manual of Thai Conversation (Haas), 98
Maranao, 257
Martin, Samuel E., 6, 9, 40, 42, 52–54, 65, 70, 72, 74, 76, 94, **108–9**, 119, 122, **271–77**, 335, 385, 387–88, 390
Martinet, André, 10, 58, 115, 119, 331–32, 334
Martin's Concise Japanese Dictionary (Martin) 108
Martin's Pocket Dictionary, Japanese-English (Martin), 108
Materials and Techniques for the Language Laboratory (Najam), 82
"Materials for a Typology of Dictionaries" (Sebeok), 1006
Mathews, Mitford M., 28, 30–31, 70, 112, 326–27
Mathili, 201
Maya, 142
McAninch, Alan W., 15, 390
McCreary, Don R., 65
McDavid, Raven I., 36, 39, 64, 111, 118
McJimsey, C. D., 311
McKay's Modern Spanish-English, English-Spanish Dictionary (Raventós), 315, 319, 321–23
McMullen, E. Wallace, 311
McRobbie, Michael, xi
meaning. *See* semantics
"Meaning Discrimination in Bilingual Dictionaries" (Iannucci), 103
Meillet, Antoine, 227
Mellon, Mary, xi
Meninski, Franciszek, 373
Merriam-Webster (publisher, imprint), 29, 36, 38, 46, 162, 186, 339, 389
Messing, Gordon, 123
Middle English Dictionary, 28, 91, 122
Milestones of the History of English in America (Read), 111
Mill, John Stuart, 158
Missir, Émile, 354
Mittelhochdeutsch (Penzl), 109
Modern English-Yiddish Yiddish-English Dictionary (Weinreich), 10, 70, 115
Modern Greek-English Dictionary (Georgacas), 17–19, 60, 104, 353, 359

Modern Language Association, 20, 107
Modern Philology (journal), 31
Modern Portuguese-English and English-Portuguese Dictionary (Richardson, Sá Perreira, and Sá Perreira), 319
Modern Pushtu Instructor (Khan), 348
Mohmand, Mohammed Gul Khan, 346
monolingual dictionaries, 51–57, 72, 83–84, 134, 141, 148, 177, 179, 251, 278–97, 300, 314, 317–18, 339
Moon, Rosamund, 77
Moore, Bruce R., 12–13, 390
More, Paul Elmer, 333
morphology, 49, 59–60, 82, 113, 155, 178, 192–98, 204, 210–11, 214, 217–18, 222, 225, 229–33, 236–39, 241, 245, 253, 256, 345–48, 351–52, 263, 355, 359, 362–64, 366–67, 369, 377, 379, 386
morphophonology, 49, 108, 195, 201, 225, 229–30, 232–33, 263, 266
morphosyntax, 244–45, 250
Morris, Charles W., 158
Moulton, William G., 118
Mouton & Co. (publisher), 26, 80–82
Moyne, John, 15, 74, 120, 390
Muret-Sanders Encyclopaedic English-German and German-English Dictionary, 315, 320, 322
Murray, James A. H., 30
Musgrave, John K., 70
Mussolini, Benito, 103

Najam, Edward W., 82
names, 45, 55–56, 89, 91, 97, 113, 135, 141, 144–45, 153, 162, 169, 174–75, 197, 249, 255, 281, 292, 296, 298–312, 325, 337–39, 355, 371, 376, 385
Names in Roman Verse (Swanson), 113
National Academy of Sciences, 8, 93, 97, 100
National Defense Education Act, 5, 15, 46, 48, 99, 127, 212
National Science Foundation, 259
Navarro Tomás, Tomás, 360
Navigation Dictionary, 311
Nāwis, Abdullah Afghānī, 346
Nawri, Muhannad Gul, 346
Nederlands Etymologisch Woordenboek (De Vries and Tollenaere), 123

Neilson, William Allen, 280
New Aspects of Lexicography (Weinbrot), 64, 112
New Century Cyclopedia of Names (Barnhart and Halsey), 89
New Dictionary of Americanisms (Clapin) 311
New Dictionary of the English Language (Richardson), 121
"New England Words for *poached eggs*" (Penzl) 109
New English Pakkhto Conversational Dictionary, 345
New French and English Dictionary (Clifton and Grimaux), 323
Newman, Stanley S., 118
New Pronouncing Dictionary of the Spanish and English Languages (Velázquez), 317, 323
New Redhouse Turkish-English Dictionary, 70, 114
New Scientist (magazine), 283
New York Academy of Sciences, 36–38
New York Times (newspaper), 283
Nicot, Jean, 121
Nida, Eugene A., 193–94, 200
Noah's Ark, New England Yankees, and the Endless Quest (Leavitt), 30
North-Holland Publishing, 124
Northwestern University, 97, 260, 390
Norwegian-English Dictionary (Haugen), 72
Nouveau Dictionnaire Français-Grec Moderne (Legrand), 354
Noyes, Gertrude E., 31
Nuovo Dizionario Moderno delle Lingue Italiana e Inglese (Lysle and Gualtieri), 320, 323

"Of Matters Lexicographical" (Mathews), 31
Ohio State University, 97
Oinas, Felix J., 20
Oklahoma A & M University, 91
"Old High German [l] and Its Phonetic Identification" (Penzl), 109
Old Norse, 142
"On Defining *mahogany*" (Malone), 107
165 Broadway. *See* United States Army
"On Not Teaching English Usage" (Sledd), 112

On Some Deficiencies in Our English Dictionaries (Trench), 30
"On Some Recent Claims in Phonological Theory" (Householder), 102
On Style (Demetrius), 202
"On the Etymology of *runt*" (Malone), 107
"Opyt obschei teorii leksikographii" (Shcherba), 106
Orbis (journal), 33
Order of the Dannebrog (Denmark), 107
Order of the Falcon (Iceland), 107
"Or Get Off the Pot" (Sledd), 112
Oriya, 201
Országh, László, 52, 66, 71–73, 122–23, 282
orthography, 92, 98, 108, 147, 229, 237, 240, 273, 346, 348–51, 375, 379
"Orthography and Phonemes in Wulfila's Gothic" (Penzl), 109
Ossetic, 343
Ottoman, 369, 371
Outline of Cultural Materials (Murdoch), 197
Outline of English Structure (Smith and Trager), 4, 120, 260, 266, 290–91
Oxford Advanced Learner's Dictionary, 29, 52, 262
Oxford English Dictionary, 28, 30, 122, 281–84, 291, 310, 327, 331
Oxford Handbook of Lexicography (Durkin), 77

Pakhto Idiom: A Dictionary (Gilbertson), 350
Pāṇini, 229
Papadopoulos, Anthimos A., 354, 359
Parker, William Riley, 20
Pashto, 59–60, 109, 195, 343–52, 378–79
Pashto Academy, 344, 346, 348
Pashto Basic Course (Chavarría-Aguilar), 92
"Paul Laurence Dunbar's Literary Dialects" (Penzl), 109
Peabody Museum of Natural History, 93
Peirce, Charles S., 158, 172
Penzl, Herbert, 6–10, 59, 69, 92, 94, 99, **109–10**, 118–19, 122, **343–52**, 388, 390
"Periodization in Language History: Early Modern English and the Other Periods" (Penzl), 109

Persian, 343–44, 346, 348–50, 369–70, 373, 378–79
"Persian Loanwords in Anatolian Turkish" (Tietze and Lazard), 114
"Personal Journey through Linguistics" (Read), 110
Peshawari, 344–48
Petrov, Julia, 390
Pfeffer, J. Alan, 25–26, 182
Philological Society of London, 28, 30
"Phonemic Change in Early Old English" (Penzl), 109
"Phonemic Split of Germanic *k* in Old English" (Penzl), 109
phonetics, 49–50, 147, 150, 152, 167, 192, 199, 212, 228, 235, 239–41, 266, 290–91, 304, 346, 348, 350, 374
Phonological Grammar of Spanish (Saporta and Contreras), 111
phonology, 48–50, 59–60, 99, 102, 107, 113, 120, 147, 155–56, 160, 165, 185, 196, 203, 206, 211–13, 220–23, 225, 227–29, 232, 235, 239–41, 243, 245, 247, 263, 266, 291, 335, 345–51, 354–55, 360–61, 366, 369
Phonology of Colloquial Egyptian Arabic (Harrell), 99
Phonology of Modern Icelandic (Malone), 107
Pijnenburg, W., 64, 124
Pike, Kenneth L., 13, 37, 78, 120
"Plan for a Central Archive for Lexicography in English" (Barnhart), 89
PMLA (journal), 20, 31
Polish, 199
Pomeranian, 199
Portuguese, 147, 319
Portuguese, Brazilian, 118, 138, 193
Prague School, 44
Prator, Clifford, 390
Present-Day English Section, Modern Language Association, 36–37
Presidential Medal of Honor (Republic of Korea), 108
Princeton University, 16, 100, 113
Proceedings of the Second International Round Table Conference on Historical Lexicography (Pijnenburg and Tollenaere) 64

pronunciation, 43, 45, 54, 136, 145, 152, 174, 176, 185, 235, 239, 266, 272, 279–81, 285, 290–91, 294, 296–97, 351, 358, 361, 375,
Psycholinguistics (Saporta), 111
Pulgram, Ernst, 118

Qandahárí, 345
Quine, W. V. O., 158
Quinn, Nancy, 85
quotations and sentences, illustrative 4, 31, 34, 119, 148, 151, 182, 211–12, 215, 226, 231, 279, 281–83, 291–92, 297, 315, 326, 385

Ramsay, Robert L., 279
RAND Corporation, 74
Randolph, Vance, 329
Random House (publisher), 29, 74
Random House Dictionary of the English Language, 17, 29, 69–70, 89, 107
Raverty, H. G., 345
Read, Allen Walker, 6–9, 24, 27, 31, 37, 40, 57–59, 65, 69, 72–74, 86, 89, **110–11**, 118–19, 121–22, 199, **326–34**, 339–40, 388, 390
Reader in Pashto (Penzl) 109
Readings in Applied English Linguistics (Allen), 89
Readings in Linguistics (Joos), 260
Readings in Linguistics II (Hamp, Householder, Austerlitz, and Joos), 102
Readings in the Sociology of Language (Fishman), 64, 93
Redhouse, James, 70, 114, 373
Reed, David W., 334
Reference Grammar of Japanese (Martin), 108
Reference Grammar of Korean (Martin) 108
Reference Grammar of Literary Dhimotiki (Householder, Kazakis, and Koutsoudas), 102
Reference Grammar of Syrian Arabic (Cowell), 15
"Reflections on How Much We Don't Need Wild Men Who Are Really Professors" (Eskey), 112
Reichman, Oskar, 114
"Relation of Hanunóo Culture to the Plant World" (Conklin), 93

Research Center in Anthropology, Folklore, and Linguistics, Indiana University, 20–21, 26, 63, 79–80, 82, 85, 79–82, 127, 129
Rey-Debove, Josette, 35, 37
Richards, I. A., 123
Richardson, Charles, 121
Riverside Conference on Lexicography, 64
Robinson, Jennifer, 65
Robinson, Richard, 41, 170–71
Roca-Pons, Josep, 14, 390
Rockford College, 109
Roget, Mark Peter, 148, 168, 196
Romance, 142, 199, 332, 353, 355, 366
Romance Philology (journal), 66, 105
Romanian, 307, 318
Romansch, 165
Rosenberg, Alexander, 16, 390
Rundell, Michael, 77
Russian, 16, 116, 142, 147, 158, 192, 199, 201–2, 204, 264, 304, 339, 346, 376
Russian Abbreviations: A Selective List (Rosenberg), 16
Russian Derivational Dictionary (Worth, Kozak, and Johnson), 70, 116
Russian-English Glossary of Guided Missile, Rocket, and Satellite Terms (Rosenberg), 16
Russko-Afganskii Slovar (Zudin), 346, 350

Sanskrit, 198–99, 335
Sapir, Edward, 9, 29, 98
Saporta, Sol, 5, 9–10, 14, 20–23, 25–26, 38, 40–41, 47, 54, 67–68, 75–77, 79–82, 87–88, **111–12**, 119, 122–23, 127, 390
Sardinian, 199
Saturday Review (magazine), 283
Saunders, Gladys E., 75
Saussure, Ferdinand de, 158
Scargill, M. H., 37
schizoglossia, 369
Science News-Letter (magazine), 283
Scientific American (magazine), 283
Scott, Foresman and Company (publisher), 36, 89
Scotticisms, 58, 280, 330
script. *See* orthography
Sebeok, Thomas, 7–8, 10, 20–22, 80, 82, 96, 106, 111, 118, 121, 123

Seiler, Hansjakob, 365
Semantic Frequency List for English, French, German, and Spanish (Eaton), 200
semantics, 5, 12, 14, 34, 41–42, 44, 48, 50–51, 56–57, 60–62, 66, 68–69, 73, 83–84, 94, 97, 111, 113, 115–16, 120, 127, 135, 137–38, 144, 146–48, 150, 152–53, 155–74, 177–78, 181–83, 193, 195–97, 199, 200–202, 204–6, 209–15, 221–29, 231–37, 241, 243–59, 261–62, 264–66, 274, 279–89, 291–92, 294, 299, 302–25, 336–37, 364–66, 374, 377, 384–85
Semiotic Society of America, 110
Semitic, 369
"Sense Discriminations and Translation Complements in Bilingual Dictionaries" (Iannucci), 103
Serbo-Croatian, 306
Shafeev, D. A., 346
Shcherba, Lev, 106
Shorter Spanish-English and English-Spanish Dictionary (Martinez Amador), 317–19, 321
Short Introduction to English Grammar (Sledd), 11, 120
Short Introduction to the Writing System of Pashto (Chavarría-Aguilar), 92
Short Italian Dictionary (Hoare), 320–21
Short Reference Grammar of Moroccan Arabic (Harrell), 99
Siamese-English Dictionary (Prachāchāng), 177
Sinclair, John, 77
Sindhi, 201
Skinner, B. F., 120
Slavic, 199, 205
Sledd, James, 6–7, 11, 18, 31, 36–37, 39–40, 52, 58, 65, 68, 70, 73, 96, **111–13**, 120, 122, **260–67**, 387–88, 390
"Smaller Dictionaries" (Read), 110
Smith, Henry Lee, 4, 118, 120, 260, 266, 290–91
Society, Language, and the University (Saporta), 111
Solic, Peggy, xi
Sophocles, 201
Sorbonne, 116
Soule, Richard, 196

Sound Pattern of Russian (Halle), 263
sources (of dictionary material), 34, 61,
   140–41, 143, 151, 166, 184, 243, 283–84, 292,
   296, 300, 305, 309, 330, 343, 375, 379,
Spanish, 104, 118, 142–43, 148, 197, 201, 205,
   307, 314–15, 317–24, 339
Spanish, American, 138, 140, 182–83
Spanish, Classical, 147
Spanish, Costa Rican, 152
Spanish, Old, 147
Spanish and English Dictionary (Williams),
   317, 319–21
*Spanish-English and English-Spanish
   Commercial Dictionary* (MacDonald),
   317, 322
Special Dictionary of the Thai Language
   (Haas), 70
spelling, 45, 54, 174, 179, 185, 202, 236, 239–40,
   266, 279–81, 343, 348, 350–51, 361, 375–76
Spoken Burmese (Cornyn), 94, 118
Spoken Greek (Kahane, Kahane, and Ward),
   104, 118
Spoken Thai (Haas and Subhanka), 98, 118
Stankiewicz, Edward, 115
Starnes, DeWitt, 31
Stefflre, Volney, 259
Stein, Jess, 89
Steiner, Roger, 34
Stewart, George R., 334
St. John's College, Oxford, 100
St. Joseph's College, 103, 313, 389
Stockwell, Robert, 112, 120
Stowasser, Karl, 15
structuralism, 104, 107. *See also* Bloomfield
Structural Studies on Spanish Themes
   (Kahane and Pietrangeli), 104
Studies in Formal Historical Linguistics
   (Hoenigswald), 101
*Studies in Lexicography as a Science and as
   an Art* (Glanze), 75
Style in Language (Sebeok), 68, 68, 123–24
Summer Institute of Linguistics, 12–14, 29,
   78, 96, 120, 123, 129, 389–90
Sun (Baltimore newspaper), 334
Supplement to the Oxford English Dictionary,
   28
Survey of English Dictionaries (Mathews), 30

Svensén, Bo, 77, 89
Swadesh, Morris, 98
Swanson, Donald C., 6–7, 21, 40, 42, 47, 61,
   70, 94, **113**, 122, **191–202**, 203–5, 355, 358,
   384–85, 387, 390
Swedish, 118, 193, 200
Syntactic Structures (Chomsky), 120
Syntactic Theory 1 (Householder), 102
syntax, 4–5, 47–48, 53, 59, 102, 120, 141, 144,
   169–70, 174, 191, 193–94, 196, 204, 229, 232,
   241–42, 244, 247, 249–51, 264, 272, 276,
   346, 364–66, 369, 376, 379, 383–86
Syntax of Apollonius Dyscolus
   (Householder), 4, 102

Tadzhiksko-ruskii slovar' (Bertels), 376
Tagalog, 178, 249, 257
Tajik, 376
Tarihi ve Etimolojik Türkije Türkcesi Lugati,
   114
Tatar, 371
taxonomy, 50, 94, 252–56, 259
*Teacher's Word Book of Thirty Thousand
   Words* (Thorndike and Lorge), 193–95,
   200, 357
Teach Yourself Malkielese (Jackson), 105
Tentative Autobibliography (Malkiel), 105
terminology, 43, 45, 65, 70, 97, 209, 248, 282,
   298, 301, 310, 332, 357–58, 370–71, 373–74,
*Tesoro della Lingua Greca-volgare ed
   Italiano*, (Da Somavera), 354
Texas Christian University, 99
Thai, 29, 70, 98, 118, 176–78, 277, 383
Thai-English Student's Dictionary (Haas), 9,
   70, 98, 336
Thai Phrases (Haas), 98
Thai Reader (Haas), 98
Thai System of Writing (Haas), 98
Thai Vocabulary (Haas), 70, 98
"That Dictionary or the Dictionary" (Read),
   110
Theall, D. F., 120
Thesaurus Graecae Linguae (H. Estienne), 121
*Thesaurus Linguarum Orientalium, Turcicae,
   Arabicae, Persicae* (Meninski), 373
Thesaurus of English Words and Phrases
   (Roget), 148, 168

Thorndike, Edward L., 89, 282
Thorndike-Century Junior Dictionary
   (Thorndike and Barnhart), 89
Thorndike-Century Senior Dictionary
   (Thorndike and Barnhart) 89
Thornton, Richard H., 327
Thresor de la Langue Françoise (Nicot), 121
Tietze, Andreas, 6, 9, 40, 60–61, 70, 95, **113–14**, 119, **368–80**, 384, 386, 388, 390
Tollenaere, F. de, 38, 64, 66–67, 71, 73–74, 77, 82, 123–24
topocomplex, 56, 58, 301–2, 307
Topographic Terms in Virginia (McJimsey), 311
"Towards an Encyclopedic Dictionary of Nuginian" (Balint), 121
Townshend, Malcom, 311
Trager, George L., 120, 260, 266, 290–91
Trench, Richard Chenevix, 30
Triantaphyllidis, Manolis, 361
Tsachi people, 13
Tunica Dictionary (Haas), 70, 98
Turkic, 371
Turkish, 59–60, 95, 114, 119, 306–7, 338–39, 368–80, 386
Turkish-English Lexicon (Redhouse), 373
Turkish, Old, 304, 371
Turkmen, 372
Turton, Stephen, xii
Twaddell, W. Freeman, 186
Tyler, Steven A., 93
typology, 41, 43, 64, 76, 105–6, 129, 133–54, 203, 256

Uigur, 304, 371
Uitti, Karl D., 38, 43, 45, 48–49, 51, 55, 66–67, 71, 74–75, 122–23
Ulla, Árif, 345
"Umlaut and Secondary Umlaut in Old High German" (Penzl), 109
UNESCO, 32–33
Union Académique Internationale, 32
United States Air Force, 5, 12, 74
United States Army, 119
United States Army, Information and Education Division, Language Section, 7–8, 10–11, 19, 26, 28, 95, 101, 108–109, 113, 118–19, 121

United States Army, Specialized Training Program, 98, 119
United States Army Air Force, 119
United States Army Forces Institute, 118
United States Board on Geographic Names, 91, 298
United States Defense Language Institute, 15
United States Department of the Interior, Office of Geography, 90, 298, 389
United States Department of State, Foreign Service Institute, 100
United States Department of State, School of Language and Linguistics, 4
United States Government Printing Office, 298
United States Navy, 119
United States Navy Language School, 108
United States Office of Education, 5–6, 16–20, 22, 28, 33, 45–46, 59, 73, 127, 353, 389–90
United States Peace Corps, 95
Universidad Nacional, Heredia, Costa Rica, 92
University of Arizona, 16, 389
University of Berlin, 103
University of California, Berkeley, 92, 98, 105, 108–9, 119, 133, 174, 389–90
University of California, Los Angeles, 11, 94, 103, 114, 116, 119, 203, 368, 390
University of Chicago, 28, 88, 97, 107
University of Chicago Spanish-English, English-Spanish Dictionary (Castillo and Bond), 182–83, 318, 321, 323
University of Delaware, 34
University of Exeter, 40
University of Florence, 100, 103
University of Illinois, Chicago, 34
University of Illinois, Urbana, 35, 103–4, 109, 111, 114, 119, 353, 389
University of Istanbul, 113
University of Kiel, 100
University of Michigan, 13, 16, 28, 92, 95, 98, 100, 109, 119–21, 335, 343, 389–90
University of Minnesota, 16, 113, 191, 390
University of Missouri, 279
University of Munich, 100
University of North Carolina, Chapel Hill, 107, 110, 121

University of North Dakota, 17, 33, 353
University of Oklahoma, 10
University of Padua, 100
University of Papua New Guinea, 16
University of Pennsylvania, 90–91, 100, 103, 119, 227, 389
University of Peshawar, 344
University of Rochester, 92
University of Texas, Austin, 99–100
University of Toronto, 96
University of Vermont, 101
University of Victoria, 37
University of Vienna, 109, 114
University of Washington, 13, 111, 390
University of Wisconsin, 28
University of Zurich, 100
Urdang, Laurence, 17, 33–34, 36–38, 40, 51–54, 57, 61, 66–67, 69–72, 74–76, 122–23, 390
Urdu, 344, 346, 349, 378
USAID, 92
users (of dictionaries), 43, 46, 49–50, 53–54, 56, 58–60, 83, 90, 100, 116, 122, 163, 174–78, 183, 191, 224, 235, 239–41, 274, 277–82, 291, 306, 313, 316, 361–62, 379, 383–84, 386
Utah State University, 127
Uzbek, 376
Uzbeksko-ruskiĭ slovar' (Borovkov), 376

Valdman, Albert, 14, 20, 390
Vazsonyi, Andrew, 82
Verbal Behavior (Skinner), 120
Verb Morphology of Modern Greek (Koutsoudas), 82
Vietnamese, 277
Vocabulary of Modern Spoken Greek (Swanson), 70, 113, 355, 358
Vocabulista Arauigo en Lettra Castellano (De Alcala), 148
Voegelin, C. F., 8–12, 14, 20–23, 40, 68, 74, 80, 96, **129**, 390
Voegelin, F. M., 390
Volapük, 142
Vom Urgermonischen um Neuhochdeutschen (Penzl), 109
Von Wartburg, Walther, 133, 362
Vowels and Tones of Standard Thai (Abrahamson), 82
Vries, Jan de, 123

Wallace, Bob, 8
Wall Street Journal (newspaper), 283
Wang, Fred, 390
Wardaki, 347
Waterhouse, Viola, 12, 82, 390
Waverly, Thomas F., 8
Waziri, 348
Webster, Noah, 110, 328
Webster's International Dictionary of the English Language, 29
Webster's New Collegiate Dictionary, Sixth Edition, 158, 167, 169, 175, 190, 324, 330
Webster's New International Dictionary of the English Language, 29
Webster's New World Dictionary of the English Language 29, 324
Webster's Second New International Dictionary, 29, 158, 280, 310
Webster's Seventh New Collegiate Dictionary, 38
Webster's Third New International Dictionary of the English Language, 17, 36, 38, 69, 94, 97, 101, 110, 112–13, 179
Weinbrot, Howard D., 64
Weinreich, Max, 10, 115
Weinreich, Uriel, 6, 9–11, 21, 25, 40–45, 48, 50–52, 56, 58, 64–65, 70–71, 77, 86, 94, 96, **115–16**, 119, 122, **155–73**, 203, 205, 384–85, 387, 390
Wellek, René, 123
Western Kamchadal, 116
"Western Loanwords in Modern Pashto" (Penzl), 109
Where Are You From? (radio show), 4
White Christmas (film), 8
Whitman College, 95
Whitney, William Dwight, 28, 282
Wiegand, Herbert Ernst, 77, 114
Wiener Zeitschrift für die Kunde des Morgenlandes (journal), 114
Wierzbicka, Anna, 116
Wilber, D. N., 343
William J. Gedney's Concise Saek-English, English-Saek Lexicon (Gedney and Hudak), 96
Williams, Krista, 41

Wilson, Herbert M., 312
Wimsatt, W. K., 123
Winston Dictionary (Brown, Canby, and Lewis), 323–24
Wm. Collins Sons & Company (publisher), 36
Wolfram, Walt, xi
Wolski, Edward, 16, 390
Word (journal), 10, 52, 58, 115, 119
World Book Dictionary, 89
WorldCat, 63
World Publishing, 29
Wortgeographie der hochdeutschen Umgangssprache (Kretschmer), 358
Worth, Dean Stoddard, 6, 9, 11, 40, 42, 47–48, 65, 68, 70, 74, 114–15, **116–17**, 119, **203–5**, 387, 390
writing system. *See* orthography

Yakut, 371
Yale Linguistic Club, 119
Yale Romanization, 108
Yale University, 28, 93–95, 100, 107–8, 119, 243, 271, 378, 389–90
Yale University Press, 95
Yamigawa, Joseph K., 121
Yana Dictionary (Sapir and Swadesh), 98
Yaron, Alexander, 99
Yiddish, 10, 29, 166
Yiddish Language and Folklore (Weinreich and Weinreich), 115
Yúsufzai, 345

Zekheli, Sayyid Rahatullah Rahat, 346
Zgusta, Ladislav, 31–35, 37, 62, 65, 73–74, 76–77, 94, 105, 114, 122
Zudin, P. B., 346